THE MODERN LIBRARY

OF THE WORLD'S BEST BOOKS

THE COMEDIES OF

SHAKESPEARE

*The publishers will be pleased to send, upon request, an
illustrated folder setting forth the purpose and scope of
THE MODERN LIBRARY, and listing each volume
in the series. Every reader of books will find titles he
has been looking for, handsomely printed, in definitive
editions, and at an unusually low price.*

The

Comedies

of

Shakespeare

VOLUME ONE

THE MODERN LIBRARY

NEW YORK

Random House IS THE PUBLISHER OF

THE MODERN LIBRARY

BENNETT A. CERF · DONALD S. KLOPFER · ROBERT K. HAAS

Manufactured in the United States of America

By H. Wolff

CONTENTS

THE TEMPEST
1

THE TWO GENTLEMEN OF VERONA
65

THE MERRY WIVES OF WINDSOR
129

MEASURE FOR MEASURE
203

THE COMEDY OF ERRORS
281

MUCH ADO ABOUT NOTHING
337

LOVE'S LABOUR'S LOST
409

A MIDSUMMER-NIGHT'S DREAM
485

THE TEMPEST

CAST OF CHARACTERS

ALONSO, *King of Naples*
SEBASTIAN, *his Brother*
PROSPERO, *the right Duke of Milan*
ANTONIO, *his brother, the usurping
    Duke of Milan*
FERDINAND, *Son to the King of Naples*
GONZALO, *an honest old Counsellor*

ADRIAN
FRANCISCO } *Lords*

CALIBAN, *a savage and deformed Slave*
TRINCULO, *a Jester*
STEPHANO, *a drunken Butler*
Master of a Ship
Boatswain
Mariners

MIRANDA, *Daughter to Prospero*

ARIEL, *an airy Spirit*

IRIS
CERES
JUNO } *presented by Spirits*
Nymphs
Reapers

Other Spirits attending on Prospero

SCENE

The Sea, with a Ship; afterwards an Island

THE TEMPEST

ACT ONE

SCENE ONE

*On a Ship at Sea. A tempestuous noise of thunder and
lightning heard.*

Enter a Shipmaster and a Boatswain severally

MASTER. Boatswain!

BOATSWAIN. Here, master: what cheer?

MASTER. Good, speak to the mariners: fall to 't yarely, or we
run ourselves aground: bestir, bestir.   *Exit*

Enter Mariners

BOATSWAIN. Heigh, my hearts! Cheerly, cheerly, my hearts!
Yare, yare! Take in the topsail. Tend to the master's
whistle! Blow, till thou burst thy wind, if room enough!

*Enter Alonso, Sebastian,
Antonio, Ferdinand, Gonzalo, and others*

ALONSO. Good boatswain, have care. Where 's the master?
Play the men.

BOATSWAIN. I pray now, keep below.

ANTONIO. Where is the master, bos'n?

BOATSWAIN. Do you not hear him? You mar our labour: keep
your cabins: you do assist the storm.

GONZALO. Nay, good, be patient.

BOATSWAIN. When the sea is. Hence! What cares these roar-
ers for the name of king? To cabin! silence! trouble us not.

GONZALO. Good, yet remember whom thou hast aboard.

BOATSWAIN. None that I more love than myself. You are a
counsellor: if you can command these elements to silence, and work the peace of the present, we will not
hand a rope more; use your authority: if you cannot,
give thanks you have lived so long, and make yourself

ready in your cabin for the mischance of the hour, if it
so hap.—Cheerly, good hearts!—Out of our way, I say.

Exit

GONZALO. I have great comfort from this fellow: methinks
he hath no drowning mark upon him; his complexion is
perfect gallows. Stand fast, good Fate, to his hanging!
Make the rope of his destiny our cable, for our own doth
little advantage! If he be not born to be hanged, our
case is miserable. *Exeunt*

Re-enter Boatswain

BOATSWAIN. Down with the topmast! Yare! Lower, lower!
Bring her to try with main-course. (*A cry within*) A
plague upon this howling! They are louder than the
weather, or our office.—

Re-enter Sebastian, Antonio, and Gonzalo

Yet again! What do you here? Shall we give o'er, and
drown? Have you a mind to sink?

SEBASTIAN. A pox o' your throat, you bawling, blasphe-
mous, incharitable dog!

BOATSWAIN. Work you, then.

ANTONIO. Hang, cur, hang! you whoreson, insolent noise-
maker, we are less afraid to be drowned than thou art.

GONZALO. I'll warrant him for drowning; though the ship
were no stronger than a nutshell, and as leaky as an un-
stanched wench.

BOATSWAIN. Lay her a-hold, a-hold! Set her two courses!
Off to sea again! Lay her off!

Enter Mariners, wet

MARINERS. All lost! To prayers, to prayers! All lost!

Exeunt

BOATSWAIN. What, must our mouths be cold?

GONZALO. The king and prince at prayers! Let us assist
them,

For our case is as theirs.

SEBASTIAN.   I am out of patience.

ANTONIO. We are merely cheated of our lives by drunk-
ards.—

This wide-chapp'd rascal,—would thou might'st lie
drowning,

The washing of ten tides!

GONZALO.   He'll be hang'd yet,

Though every drop of water swear against it,

And gape at wid'st to glut him.

(*A confused noise within*)　　　　　'Mercy on us!'—
'We split, we split!'—'Farewell, my wife and children!'—
'Farewell, brother!'—'We split, we split, we split!'—

ANTONIO. Let 's all sink wi' the king.　　　　　*Exit*

SEBASTIAN. Let 's take leave of him.　　　　　*Exit*

GONZALO. Now would I give a thousand furlongs of sea for
an acre of barren ground; long heath, brown furze, any
thing. The wills above be done! But I would fain die a
dry death.　　　　　*Exit*

SCENE TWO

The Island: before the Cell of Prospero.

Enter Prospero and Miranda

MIRANDA. If by your art, my dearest father, you have
Put the wild waters in this roar, allay them.
The sky, it seems, would pour down stinking pitch,
But that the sea, mounting to th' welkin's cheek,
Dashes the fire out. O! I have suffer'd
With those that I saw suffer: a brave vessel,
Who had, no doubt, some noble creatures in her,
Dash'd all to pieces. O! the cry did knock
Against my very heart. Poor souls, they perish'd.
Had I been any god of power, I would
Have sunk the sea within the earth, or e'er
It should the good ship so have swallow'd and
The fraughting souls within her.

PROSPERO.　　　　　Be collected:
No more amazement. Tell your piteous heart
There 's no harm done.

MIRANDA.　　　　　O, woe the day!

PROSPERO.　　　　　No harm.
I have done nothing but in care of thee,—
Of thee, my dear one! thee, my daughter!—who
Art ignorant of what thou art, nought knowing
Of whence I am: nor that I am more better
Than Prospero, master of a full poor cell,
And thy no greater father.

MIRANDA. More to know
Did never meddle with my thoughts.
PROSPERO. 'Tis time
I should inform thee further. Lend thy hand,
And pluck my magic garment from me.—So:

Lays down his mantle

Lie there, my art.—Wipe thou thine eyes; have comfort.
The direful spectacle of the wrack, which touch'd
The very virtue of compassion in thee,
I have with such provision in mine art
So safely order'd, that there is no soul—
No, not so much perdition as an hair,
Betid to any creature in the vessel
Which thou heard'st cry, which thou saw'st sink. Sit
down;
For thou must now know further.
MIRANDA. You have often
Begun to tell me what I am, but stopp'd,
And left me to a bootless inquisition,
Concluding, 'Stay; not yet.'
PROSPERO. The hour 's now come,
The very minute bids thee ope thine ear;
Obey and be attentive. Canst thou remember
A time before we came unto this cell?
I do not think thou canst, for then thou wast not
Out three years old
MIRANDA. Certainly, sir, I can.
PROSPERO. By what? by any other house or person?
Of anything the image tell me, that
Hath kept with thy remembrance.
MIRANDA. 'Tis far off;
And rather like a dream than an assurance
That my remembrance warrants. Had I not
Four or five women once that tended me?
PROSPERO. Thou hadst, and more, Miranda. But how is it
That this lives in thy mind? What seest thou else
In the dark backward and abysm of time?
If thou remember'st aught ere thou cam'st here,
How thou cam'st here, thou may'st.
MIRANDA. But that I do not.
PROSPERO. Twelve year since, Miranda, twelve year since,
Thy father was the Duke of Milan and

A prince of power.

MIRANDA.   Sir, are not you my father?

PROSPERO. Thy mother was a piece of virtue, and
She said thou wast my daughter; and thy father
Was Duke of Milan, and his only heir
A princess,—no worse issued.

MIRANDA.   O, the heavens!
What foul play had we that we came from thence?
Or blessed was 't we did?

PROSPERO.   Both, both, my girl:
By foul play, as thou say'st, were we heav'd thence;
But blessedly holp hither.

MIRANDA.   O! my heart bleeds
To think o' the teen that I have turn'd you to,
Which is from my remembrance. Please you, further.

PROSPERO. My brother and thy uncle, call'd Antonio,—
I pray thee, mark me,—that a brother should
Be so perfidious!—he whom next thyself,
Of all the world I lov'd, and to him put
The manage of my state; as at that time
Through all the signiories it was the first,
And Prospero the prime duke; being so reputed
In dignity, and for the liberal arts,
Without a parallel: those being all my study,
The government I cast upon my brother,
And to my state grew stranger, being transported
And rapt in secret studies. Thy false uncle—
Dost thou attend me?

MIRANDA.   Sir, most heedfully.

PROSPERO. Being once perfected how to grant suits,
How to deny them, who t' advance, and who
To trash for over-topping; new created
The creatures that were mine, I say, or chang'd 'em,
Or else new form'd 'em: havin_ both the key
Of officer and office, set all hearts i' the state
To what tune pleas'd his ear; that now he was
The ivy which had hid my princely trunk,
And suck'd my verdure out on't.—Thou attend'st not.

MIRANDA. O, good sir! I do.

PROSPERO.   I pray thee, mark me.
I, thus neglecting worldly ends, all dedicated
To closeness and the bettering of my mind

With that, which, but by being so retir'd,
O'erpriz'd all popular rate, in my false brother
Awak'd an evil nature; and my trust,
Like a good parent, did beget of him
A falsehood in its contrary as great
As my trust was; which had, indeed no limit,
A confidence sans bound. He being thus lorded,
Not only with what my revenue yielded,
But what my power might else exact,—like one,
Who having, into truth, by telling of it,
Made such a sinner of his memory,
To credit his own lie,—he did believe
He was indeed the duke; out o' the substitution,
And executing th' outward face of royalty,
With all prerogative:—Hence his ambition growing,—
Dost thou hear?

MIRANDA.   Your tale, sir, would cure deafness.

PROSPERO. To have no screen between this part he play'd
And him he play'd it for, he needs will be
Absolute Milan. Me, poor man,—my library
Was dukedom large enough: of temporal royalties
He thinks me now incapable; confederates,—
So dry he was for sway,—wi' the king of Naples
To give him annual tribute, do him homage;
Subject his coronet to his crown, and bend
The dukedom, yet unbow'd,—alas, poor Milan!—
To most ignoble stooping.

MIRANDA.   O the heavens!

PROSPERO. Mark his condition and the event; then tell me
If this might be a brother.

MIRANDA.   I should sin
To think but nobly of my grandmother:
Good wombs have borne bad sons.

PROSPERO.   Now the condition.
This King of Naples, being an enemy
To me inveterate, hearkens my brother's suit;
Which was, that he, in lieu o' the premises
Of homage and I know not how much tribute,
Should presently extirpate me and mine
Out of the dukedom, and confer fair Milan,
With all the honours on my brother: whereon,
A treacherous army levied, one midnight

Fated to the purpose did Antonio open
The gates of Milan; and, i' the dead of darkness,
The ministers for the purpose hurried thence
Me and thy crying self.

MIRANDA.   Alack, for pity!
I, not rememb'ring how I cried out then,
Will cry it o'er again: it is a hint,
That wrings mine eyes to 't.

PROSPERO.   Hear a little further,
And then I 'll bring thee to the present business
Which now 's upon us; without the which this story
Were most impertinent.

MIRANDA.   Wherefore did they not
That hour destroy us?

PROSPERO.   Well demanded, wench:
My tale provokes that question. Dear, they durst not,
So dear the love my people bore me, nor set
A mark so bloody on the business; but
With colours fairer painted their foul ends.
In few, they hurried us aboard a bark,
Bore us some leagues to sea; where they prepar'd
A rotten carcass of a boat, not rigg'd,
Nor tackle, sail, nor mast; the very rats
Instinctively have quit it: there they hoist us,
To cry to the sea that roar'd to us; to sigh
To the winds whose pity, sighing back again,
Did us but loving wrong.

MIRANDA.   Alack! what trouble
Was I then to you!

PROSPERO.   O, a cherubin
Thou wast, that did preserve me! Thou didst smile,
Infused with a fortitude from heaven,
When I have deck'd the sea with drops full salt,
Under my burden groan'd; which rais'd in me
An undergoing stomach, to bear up
Against what should ensue.

MIRANDA.   How came we ashore?

PROSPERO. By Providence divine.
Some food we had and some fresh water that
A noble Neapolitan, Gonzalo,
Out of his charity,—who being then appointed
Master of this design,—did give us; with

Rich garments, linens, stuffs, and necessaries,
Which since have steaded much; so, of his gentleness,
Knowing I lov'd my books, he furnish'd me,
From mine own library with volumes that
I prize above my dukedom.

MIRANDA.   Would I might
But ever see that man!

PROSPERO.   Now I arise:—*Resumes his mantle*
Sit still, and hear the last of our sea-sorrow.
Here in this island we arriv'd; and here
Have I, thy schoolmaster, made thee more profit
Than other princes can, that have more time
For vainer hours and tutors not so careful.

MIRANDA. Heavens thank you for 't! And now, I pray you,
    sir,—
For still 'tis beating in my mind,—your reason
For raising this sea-storm?

PROSPERO.   Know thus far forth.
By accident most strange, bountiful Fortune,
Now my dear lady, hath mine enemies
Brought to this shore; and by my prescience
I find my zenith doth depend upon
A most auspicious star, whose influence
If now I court not but omit, my fortunes
Will ever after droop. Here cease more questions;
Thou art inclin'd to sleep; 'tis a good dulness,
And give it way;—I know thou canst not choose.—

                                        Miranda sleeps
Come away, servant, come! I 'm ready now.
Approach, my Ariel; come!

                    Enter Ariel

ARIEL. All hail, great master! Grave sir, hail! I come
To answer thy best pleasure; be 't to fly,
To swim, to dive into the fire, to ride
On the curl'd clouds: to thy strong bidding task
Ariel and all his quality.

PROSPERO.   Hast thou, spirit,
Perform'd to point the tempest that I bade thee?

ARIEL. To every article.
I boarded the king's ship; now on the beak,
Now in the waist, the deck, in every cabin,
I flam'd amazement: sometime I 'd divide

And burn in many places; on the topmast,
The yards, and boresprit, would I flame distinctly,
Then meet, and join: Jove's lightnings, the precursors
O' the dreadful thunder-claps, more momentary
And sight-outrunning were not: the fire and cracks
Of sulphurous roaring the most mighty Neptune
Seem to besiege and make his bold waves tremble,
Yea, his dread trident shake.

PROSPERO.   My brave spirit!
Who was so firm, so constant, that this coil
Would not infect his reason?

ARIEL.   Not a soul
But felt a fever of the mad and play'd
Some tricks of desperation. All but mariners,
Plunged in the foaming brine and quit the vessel,
Then all a-fire with me: the king's son, Ferdinand,
With hair up-staring,—then like reeds, not hair,—
Was the first man that leap'd; cried, 'Hell is empty,
And all the devils are here.'

PROSPERO.   Why, that 's my spirit!
But was not this nigh shore?

ARIEL.   Close by, my master.

PROSPERO. But are they, Ariel, safe?

ARIEL.   Not a hair perish'd;
On their sustaining garments not a blemish,
But fresher than before: and, as thou bad'st me,
In troops I have dispers'd them 'bout the isle.
The king's son have I landed by himself;
Whom I left cooling of the air with sighs
In an odd angle of the isle and sitting,
His arms in this sad knot.

PROSPERO.   Of the king's ship
The mariners, say how thou hast dispos'd,
And all the rest o' the fleet.

ARIEL.   Safely in harbour
Is the king's ship; in the deep nook, where once
Thou call'dst me up at midnight to fetch dew
From the still-vex'd Bermoothes; there she 's hid:
The mariners all under hatches stow'd;
Who, with a charm join'd to their suffer'd labour,
I have left asleep: and for the rest o' the fleet
Which I dispers'd, they all have met again,

And are upon the Mediterranean flote,
Bound sadly home for Naples,
Supposing that they saw the king's ship wrack'd,
And his great person perish.

PROSPERO.   Ariel, thy charge
Exactly is perform'd; but there's more work.
What is the time o' th' day?

ARIEL.   Past the mid season.

PROSPERO. At least two glasses. The time 'twixt six **and**
now
Must by us both be spent most preciously.

ARIEL. Is there more toil? Since thou dost give me pains,
Let me remember thee what thou hast promis'd,
Which is not yet perform'd me.

PROSPERO.   How now! moody?
What is't thou canst demand?

ARIEL.   My liberty.

PROSPERO. Before the time be out! no more!

ARIEL.   I prithee
Remember, I have done thee worthy service;
Told thee no lies, made no mistakings, serv'd
Without or grudge or grumblings: thou didst promise
To bate me a full year.

PROSPERO.   Dost thou forget
From what a torment I did free thee?

ARIEL.   No.

PROSPERO. Thou dost; and think'st it much to tread the
ooze
Of the salt deep,
To run upon the sharp wind of the north,
To do me business in the veins o' th' earth
When it is bak'd with frost.

ARIEL.   I do not, sir.

PROSPERO. Thou liest, malignant thing! Hast thou forgot
The foul witch Sycorax, who with age and envy
Was grown into a hoop? Hast thou forgot her?

ARIEL. No, sir.

PROSPERO.   Thou hast. Where was she born? Speak; tell
me.

ARIEL. Sir, in Argier.

PROSPERO.   O! was she so? I must,
Once in a month, recount what thou hast been,

Which thou forget'st. This damn'd witch, **Sycorax,**
For mischiefs manifold and sorceries terrible
To enter human hearing, from Argier,
Thou know'st, was banish'd: for one thing she did
They would not take her life. Is not this true?

ARIEL.   Ay, sir.

PROSPERO.   This blue-ey'd hag was hither brought with child
And here was left by the sailors. Thou, my slave,
As thou report'st thyself, wast then her servant:
And, for thou wast a spirit too delicate
To act her earthly and abhorr'd commands,
Refusing her grand hests, she did confine thee,
By help of her more potent ministers,
And in her most unmitigable rage,
Into a cloven pine; within which rift
Imprison'd, thou didst painfully remain
A dozen years; within which space she died
And left thee there, where thou didst vent thy groans
As fast as mill-wheels strike. Then was this island,—
Save for the son that she did litter here,
A freckled whelp hag-born,—not honour'd with
A human shape.

ARIEL.   Yes; Caliban her son.

PROSPERO.   Dull thing, I say so; he that Caliban,
Whom now I keep in service. Thou best know'st
What torment I did find thee in; thy groans
Did make wolves howl and penetrate the breasts
Of ever-angry bears; it was a torment
To lay upon the damn'd, which Sycorax
Could not again undo; it was mine art,
When I arriv'd and heard thee, that made gape
The pine, and let thee out.

ARIEL.   I thank thee, master.

PROSPERO.   If thou more murmur'st, I will rend an oak
And peg thee in his knotty entrails till
Thou hast howl'd away twelve winters.

ARIEL.   Pardon, master;
I will be correspondent to command,
And do my spiriting gently.

PROSPERO.   Do so; and after two days
I will discharge thee.

ARIEL.   That 's my noble master!
  What shall I do? say what? what shall I do?
PROSPERO. Go make thyself like a nymph of the sea: be
    subject
  To no sight but thine and mine; invisible
  To every eyeball else. Go, take this shape,
  And hither come in 't: go, hence with diligence!

                                              Exit Ariel

  Awake, dear heart, awake! thou hast slept well;
  Awake!
MIRANDA. (*Waking*) The strangeness of your story put
  Heaviness in me.
PROSPERO.   Shake it off. Come on;
  We 'll visit Caliban my slave, who never
  Yields us kind answer.
MIRANDA.   'Tis a villain, sir,
  I do not love to.look on.
PROSPERO.   But, as 'tis,
  We cannot miss him: he does make our fire,
  Fetch in our wood; and serves in offices
  That profit us.—What ho! slave! Caliban!
  Thou earth, thou! speak.
CALIBAN. (*Within*) There 's wood enough within.
PROSPERO. Come forth, I say; there 's other business for thee:
  Come, thou tortoise! When?
          Re-enter Ariel, like a water-nymph
  Fine apparition! My quaint Ariel,
  Hark in thine ear.
ARIEL.   My lord, it shall be done.   *Exit*
PROSPERO. Thou poisonous slave, got by the devil himself
  Upon thy wicked dam, come forth!
                      Enter Caliban
CALIBAN. As wicked dew as e'er my mother brush'd
  With raven's feather from unwholesome fen
  Drop on you both! A south-west blow on ye,
  And blister you all o'er!
PROSPERO. For this, be sure, to-night thou shalt have cramps,
  Side-stitches that shall pen thy breath up; urchins
  Shall forth at vast of night, that they may work
  All exercise on thee: thou shalt be pinch'd
  As thick as honeycomb, each pinch more stinging
  Than bees that made them.

CALIBAN.   I must eat my dinner.
This island's mine, by Sycorax my mother,
Which thou tak'st from me. When thou camest first,
Thou strok'dst me, and mad'st much of me; wouldst give
    me
Water with berries in 't; and teach me how
To name the bigger light, and how the less,
That burn by day and night: and then I lov'd thee
And show'd thee all the qualities o' th' isle,
The fresh springs, brine-pits, barren place, and fertile.
Cursed be I that did so!—All the charms
Of Sycorax, toads, beetles, bats, light on you!
For I am all the subjects that you have,
Which first was mine own king; and here you sty me
In this hard rock, whiles you do keep from me
The rest o' th' island.

PROSPERO.   Thou most lying slave,
Whom stripes may move, not kindness! I have us'd thee,
Filth as thou art, with human care; and lodg'd thee
In mine own cell, till thou didst seek to violate
The honour of my child.

CALIBAN. Oh ho! Oh ho!—would it had been done!
Thou didst prevent me; I had peopled else
This isle with Calibans.

PROSPERO.   Abhorred slave,
Which any print of goodness will not take,
Being capable of all ill! I pitied thee,
Took pains to make thee speak, taught thee each hour
One thing or other: when thou didst not, savage,
Know thine own meaning, but wouldst gabble like
A thing most brutish, I endow'd thy purposes
With words that made them known: but thy vile race,
Though thou didst learn, had that in 't which good na-
    tures
Could not abide to be with; therefore wast thou
Deservedly confin'd into this rock,
Who hadst deserv'd more than a prison.

CALIBAN. You taught me language; and my profit on 't
Is, I know how to curse: the red plague rid you,
For learning me your language!

PROSPERO.   Hag-seed, hence!
Fetch us in fuel; and be quick, thou 'rt best,

To answer other business. Shrug'st thou, malice?
If thou neglect'st, or dost unwillingly
What I command, I'll rack thee with old cramps,
Fill all thy bones with aches; make thee roar,
That beasts shall tremble at thy din.

CALIBAN.   No, pray thee!—
  (*Aside*) I must obey: his art is of such power,
It would control my dam's god, Setebos,
And make a vassal of him.

PROSPERO.   So, slave; hence! *Exit Caliban*
              Re-enter Ariel, invisible,
          playing and singing; Ferdinand following

ARIEL'S SONG
Come unto these yellow sands,
    And then take hands:
Curtsied when you have, and kiss'd,—
    The wild waves whist,—
Foot it featly here and there;
And, sweet sprites, the burden bear.
    Hark, hark!
                Burden: Bow, wow, *dispersedly*
        The watch-dogs bark:
                Burden: Bow, wow, *dispersedly*
        Hark, hark! I hear
The strain of strutting Chanticleer
                Cry: Cock-a-diddle-dow.

FERDINAND. Where should this music be? I' th' air, or th'
    earth?
It sounds no more;—and sure, it waits upon
Some god o' th' island. Sitting on a bank,
Weeping again the king my father's wrack,
This music crept by me upon the waters,
Allaying both their fury, and my passion,
With its sweet air: thence I have follow'd it,—
Or it hath drawn me rather.—but 'tis gone.
No, it begins again.

ARIEL'S SONG
Full fathom five thy father lies;
    Of his bones are coral made:
Those are pearls that were his eyes:
    Nothing of him that doth fade,

But doth suffer a sea-change
Into something rich and strange.
Sea-nymphs hourly ring his knell:

                              Burden: ding-dong

Hark! now I hear them,—ding-dong, bell.

FERDINAND. The ditty does remember my drown'd father.
This is no mortal business, nor no sound
That the earth owes:—I hear it now above me.

PROSPERO. The fringed curtains of thine eye advance,
And say what thou seest yond.

MIRANDA.   What is 't? a spirit?
Lord, how it looks about! Believe me, sir,
It carries a brave form:—but 'tis a spirit.

PROSPERO. No, wench; it eats and sleeps, and hath such
     senses
As we have, such; this gallant which thou see'st,
Was in the wrack; and, but he 's something stain'd
With grief,—that beauty's canker,—thou might'st call him
A goodly person: he hath lost his fellows
And strays about to find 'em.

MIRANDA.   I might call him
A thing divine; for nothing natural
I ever saw so noble.

PROSPERO.   (*Aside*) It goes on, I see,
As my soul prompts it.—Spirit, fine spirit! I 'll free thee
Within two days for this.

FERDINAND.   Most sure, the goddess
On whom these airs attend!—Vouchsafe, my prayer
May know if you remain upon this island;
And that you will some good instruction give
How I may bear me here: my prime request,
Which I do last pronounce, is,—O you wonder!—
If you be maid or no?

MIRANDA.   No wonder, sir;
But certainly a maid.

FERDINAND.   My language! heavens!—
I am the best of them that speak this speech,
Were I but where 'tis spoken.

PROSPERO.   How! the best?
What wert thou, if the King of Naples heard thee?

FERDINAND. A single thing, as I am now, that wonders
To hear thee speak of Naples. He does hear me;

And, that he does, I weep: myself am Naples,
Who with mine eyes,—ne'er since at ebb,—beheld
The king, my father wrack'd.
MIRANDA.   Alack, for mercy!
FERDINAND. Yes, faith, and all his lords; the Duke of Milan,
And his brave son being twain.
PROSPERO.   (*Aside*) The Duke of Milan,
And his more braver daughter could control thee,
If now 'twere fit to do 't.—At the first sight (*Aside*)
They have changed eyes:—delicate Ariel,
I 'll set thee free for this!—(*To Ferdinand*) A word, good
    sir;
I fear you have done yourself some wrong: a word.
MIRANDA. (*Aside*) Why speaks my father so ungently?
    This
Is the third man that e'er I saw; the first
That e'er I sigh'd for: pity move my father
To be inclin'd my way!
FERDINAND.   (*Aside*) O! if a virgin,
And your affection not gone forth, I 'll make you
The Queen of Naples.
PROSPERO.   Soft, sir: one word more—
    (*Aside*) They are both in either's powers: but this swift
        business
I must uneasy make, lest too light winning
Make the prize light.—(*To Ferdinand*) One word more:
    I charge thee
That thou attend me. Thou dost here usurp
The name thou ow'st not; and hast put thyself
Upon this island as a spy, to win it
From me, the lord on 't.
FERDINAND.   No, as I am a man.
MIRANDA. There 's nothing ill can dwell in such a temple:
If the ill spirit have so fair a house,
Good things will strive to dwell with 't.
PROSPERO.   (*To Ferdinand*) Follow me.—
    (*To Miranda*) Speak not you for him; he 's a traitor.—
    (*To Ferdinand*) Come;
I 'll manacle thy neck and feet together:
Sea-water shalt thou drink; thy food shall be
The fresh-brook mussels, wither'd roots and husks

Wherein the acorn cradled. Follow.

FERDINAND.   No;
I will resist such entertainment till
Mine enemy has more power.
                    He draws, and is charmed from moving

MIRANDA.   O dear father!
Make not too rash a trial of him, for
He 's gentle, and not fearful.

PROSPERO.   What! I say,
My foot my tutor?—Put thy sword up, traitor;
Who mak'st a show, but dar'st not strike, thy conscience
Is so possess'd with guilt: come from thy ward,
For I can here disarm thee with this stick
And make thy weapon drop.

MIRANDA.   Beseech you, father!

PROSPERO. Hence! Hang not on my garments.

MIRANDA.   Sir, have pity:
I 'll be his surety.

PROSPERO.   Silence! One word more
Shall make me chide thee, if not hate thee. What!
An advocate for an imposter? Hush!
Thou think'st there is no more such shapes as he,
Having seen but him and Caliban. Foolish wench!
To the most of men this is a Caliban
And they to him are angels.

MIRANDA.   My affections
Are then most humble; I have no ambition
To see a goodlier man.

PROSPERO. (*To Ferdinand*) Come on; obey:
Thy nerves are in their infancy again,
And have no vigour in them.

FERDINAND.   So they are:
My spirits, as in a dream, are all bound up.
My father's loss, the weakness which I feel,
The wrack of all my friends, or this man's threats,
To whom I am subdued, are but light to me,
Might I but through my prison once a day
Behold this maid: all corners else o' th' earth
Let liberty make use of; space enough
Have I in such a prison.

PROSPERO. (*Aside*) It works.—(*To Ferdinand*) Come on.—

Thou hast done well, fine Ariel!—(*To Ferdinand*) Follow me.—

(*To Ariel*) Hark, what thou else shalt do me.

MIRANDA.   Be of comfort;
My father's of a better nature, sir,
Than he appears by speech: this is unwonted,
Which now came from him.

PROSPERO.   Thou shalt be as free
As mountain winds; but then exactly do
All points of my command.

ARIEL.   To the syllable.

PROSPERO. (*To Ferdinand*) Come, follow.—Speak not for
him.   *Exeunt*

ACT TWO

SCENE ONE

Another Part of the Island.

Enter Alonso, Sebastian, Antonio, Gonzalo, Adrian, Francisco, and others

GONZALO. Beseech you, sir, be merry: you have cause,
So have we all, of joy; for our escape
Is much beyond our loss. Our hint of woe
Is common: every day some sailor's wife,
The masters of some merchant and the merchant,
Have just our theme of woe; but for the miracle,
I mean our preservation, few in millions
Can speak like us: then wisely, good sir, weigh
Our sorrow with our comfort.

ALONSO.   Prithee, peace.

SEBASTIAN. He receives comfort like cold porridge.

ANTONIO. The visitor will not give him o'er so.

SEBASTIAN. Look, he 's winding up the watch of his wit; by
and by it will strike.

GONZALO. Sir,—

SEBASTIAN. One: tell.

GONZALO. When every grief is entertain'd that 's offer'd,
Comes to the entertainer—

SEBASTIAN. A dollar.

GONZALO. Dolour comes to him, indeed: you have spoken
truer than you purposed.

SEBASTIAN. You have taken it wiselier than I meant you
should.

GONZALO. Therefore, my lord,—

ANTONIO. Fie, what a spendthrift is he of his tongue!

ALONSO. I prithee, spare.

GONZALO. Well, I have done: but yet—

SEBASTIAN. He will be talking.

ANTONIO. Which, of he or Adrian, for a good wager, first begins to crow?

SEBASTIAN. The old cock.

ANTONIO. The cockerel.

SEBASTIAN. Done. The wager?

ANTONIO. A laughter.

SEBASTIAN. A match!

ADRIAN. Though this island seem to be desert,—

SEBASTIAN. Ha, ha, ha! So you 're paid.

ADRIAN. Uninhabitable, and almost inaccessible,—

SEBASTIAN. Yet—

ADRIAN. Yet—

ANTONIO. He could not miss it.

ADRIAN. It must needs be of subtle, tender, and delicate temperance.

ANTONIO. Temperance was a delicate wench.

SEBASTIAN. Ay, and a subtle; as he most learnedly delivered.

ADRIAN. The air breathes upon us here most sweetly.

SEBASTIAN. As if it had lungs, and rotten ones.

ANTONIO. Or as 'twere perfumed by a fen.

GONZALO. Here is everything advantageous to life.

ANTONIO. True; save means to live.

SEBASTIAN. Of that there 's none, or little.

GONZALO. How lush and lusty the grass looks! how green!

ANTONIO. The ground indeed is tawny.

SEBASTIAN. With an eye of green in 't.

ANTONIO. He misses not much.

SEBASTIAN. No; he doth but mistake the truth totally.

GONZALO. But the rarity of it is,—which is indeed almost beyond credit,—

SEBASTIAN. As many vouch'd rarities are.

GONZALO. That our garments, being, as they were, drenched in the sea, hold notwithstanding their freshness and glosses; being rather new-dyed than stain'd with salt water.

ANTONIO. If but one of his pockets could speak, would it not say he lies?

SEBASTIAN. Ay, or very falsely pocket up his report.

GONZALO. Methinks, our garments are now as fresh as when we put them on first in Afric, at the marriage of the king's fair daughter Claribel to the King of Tunis.

SEBASTIAN. 'Twas a sweet marriage, and we prosper well
in our return.

ADRIAN. Tunis was never graced before with such a paragon to their queen.

GONZALO. Not since widow Dido's time.

ANTONIO. Widow! a pox o' that! How came that widow in?
Widow Dido!

SEBASTIAN. What if he had said, widower Æneas too?
Good Lord, how you take it!

ADRIAN. Widow Dido, said you? You make me study of
that: she was of Carthage, not of Tunis.

GONZALO. This Tunis, sir, was Carthage.

ADRIAN. Carthage?

GONZALO. I assure you, Carthage.

ANTONIO. His word is more than the miraculous harp.

SEBASTIAN. He hath rais'd the wall, and houses too.

ANTONIO. What impossible matter will he make easy next?

SEBASTIAN. I think he will carry this island home in his
pocket, and give it his son for an apple.

ANTONIO. And, sowing the kernels of it in the sea, bring
forth more islands.

ALONSO. Ay?

ANTONIO. Why, in good time.

GONZALO. (*To Alonso*) Sir, we were talking that our garments seem now as fresh as when we were at Tunis at
the marriage of your daughter, who is now queen.

ANTONIO. And the rarest that e'er came there.

SEBASTIAN. Bate, I beseech you, widow Dido.

ANTONIO. O! widow Dido; ay, widow Dido.

GONZALO. Is not, sir, my doublet as fresh as the first day I
wore it? I mean, in a sort.

ANTONIO. That sort was well fish'd for.

GONZALO. When I wore it at your daughter's marriage?

ALONSO. You cram these words into mine ears, against
The stomach of my sense. Would I had never
Married my daughter there! for, coming thence,
My son is lost; and, in my rate, she too,
Who is so far from Italy remov'd,
I ne'er again shall see her. O thou, mine heir
Of Naples and of Milan! what strange fish
Hath made his meal on thee?

FRANCISCO.   Sir, he may live:

I saw him beat the surges under him,
And ride upon their backs: he trod the water,
Whose enmity he flung aside, and breasted
The surge most swoln that met him: his bold head
'Bove the contentious waves he kept, and oar'd
Himself with his good arms in lusty stroke
To the shore, that o'er his wave-worn basis bow'd,
As stooping to relieve him. I not doubt
He came alive to land.

ALONSO.   No, no; he 's gone.

SEBASTIAN. Sir, you may thank yourself for this great loss,
    That would not bless our Europe with your daughter,
    But rather lose her to an African;
    Where she at least is banish'd from your eye,
    Who hath cause to wet the grief on 't.

ALONSO.   Prithee, peace.

SEBASTIAN. You were kneel'd to and importun'd otherwise
    By all of us; and the fair soul herself
    Weigh'd between loathness and obedience, at
    Which end o' the beam should bow. We have lost your
        son,
    I fear, for ever: Milan and Naples have
    More widows in them of this business' making,
    Than we bring men to comfort them; the fault 's
    Your own.

ALONSO. So is the dearest of the loss.

GONZALO. My lord Sebastian,
    The truth you speak doth lack some gentleness
    And time to speak it in; you rub the sore,
    When you should bring the plaster.

SEBASTIAN.   Very well.

ANTONIO. And most chirurgeonly.

GONZALO. It is foul weather in us all, good sir,
    When you are cloudy.

SEBASTIAN.   Foul weather?

ANTONIO.   Very foul.

GONZALO. Had I plantation of this isle, my lord,—

ANTONIO. He 'd sow 't with nettle-seed.

SEBASTIAN.   Or docks, or mallows.

GONZALO. And were the king on 't, what would I do?

SEBASTIAN. 'Scape being drunk for want of wine.

GONZALO. I' the commonwealth I would by contraries

Execute all things; for no kind of traffic
Would I admit; no name of magistrate;
Letters should not be known; riches, poverty,
And use of service, none; contract, succession,
Bourn, bound of land, tilth, vineyard, none;
No use of metal, corn, or wine, or oil;
No occupation; all men idle, all;
And women too, but innocent and pure;
No sovereignty,—

SEBASTIAN.   Yet he would be king on 't.

ANTONIO. The latter end of his commonwealth forgets the
beginning.

GONZALO. All things in common nature should produce
Without sweat or endeavour: treason, felony,
Sword, pike, knife, gun, or need of any engine,
Would I not have; but nature should bring forth,
Of its own kind, all foison, all abundance,
To feed my innocent people.

SEBASTIAN. No marrying 'mong his subjects?

ANTONIO. None, man; all idle; whores and knaves.

GONZALO. I would with such perfection govern, sir,
To excel the golden age.

SEBASTIAN.   Save his Majesty!

ANTONIO. Long live Gonzalo!

GONZALO.   And,—do you mark me, sir?

ALONSO. Prithee, no more: thou dost talk nothing to me.

GONZALO. I do well believe your Highness; and did it to
minister occasion to these gentlemen, who are of such
sensible and nimble lungs that they always use to laugh
at nothing.

ANTONIO. 'Twas you we laugh'd at.

GONZALO. Who in this kind of merry fooling am nothing to
you; so you may continue and laugh at nothing still.

ANTONIO. What a blow was there given!

SEBASTIAN. An it had not fallen flat-long.

GONZALO. You are gentlemen of brave mettle: you would
lift the moon out of her sphere, if she would continue in
it five weeks without changing.

Enter Ariel, invisible, playing solemn music

SEBASTIAN. We would so, and then go a-bat-fowling.

ANTONIO. Nay, good my lord, be not angry.

GONZALO. No, I warrant you; I will not adventure my dis-

cretion so weakly. Will you laugh me asleep, for I am
very heavy?

ANTONIO. Go sleep, and hear us.

All sleep but Alonso, Sebastian, and Antonio

ALONSO. What! all so soon asleep! I wish mine eyes
Would, with themselves, shut up my thoughts: I find
They are inclin'd to do so.

SEBASTIAN.   Please you, sir,
Do not omit the heavy offer of it:
It seldom visits sorrow; when it doth
It is a comforter.

ANTONIO.   We two, my lord,
Will guard your person while you take your rest,
And watch your safety.

ALONSO.   Thank you. Wondrous heavy.

Alonso sleeps. Exit Ariel

SEBASTIAN. What a strange drowsiness possesses them!

ANTONIO. It is the quality o' the climate.

SEBASTIAN.   Why
Doth it not then our eyelids sink? I find not
Myself dispos'd to sleep.

ANTONIO.   Nor I: my spirits are nimble.
They fell together all, as by consent;
They dropp'd, as by a thunder-stroke. What might,
Worthy Sebastian? O! what might?—No more:—
And yet methinks I see it in thy face,
What thou should'st be. The occasion speaks thee; and
My strong imagination sees a crown
Dropping upon thy head.

SEBASTIAN.   What! art thou waking?

ANTONIO. Do you not hear me speak?

SEBASTIAN.   I do; and surely,
It is a sleepy language, and thou speak'st
Out of thy sleep. What is it thou didst say?
This is a strange repose, to be asleep
With eyes wide open; standing, speaking, moving,
And yet so fast asleep.

ANTONIO.   Noble Sebastian,
Thou let'st thy fortune sleep—die rather; wink'st
Whiles thou art waking.

SEBASTIAN.   Thou dost snore distinctly:
There 's meaning in thy snores.

ANTONIO. I am more serious than my custom: you
    Must be so too, if heed me; which to do
    Trebles thee o'er.
SEBASTIAN.   Well; I am standing water.
ANTONIO. I 'll teach you how to flow.
SEBASTIAN.   Do so: to ebb,
    Hereditary sloth instructs me.
ANTONIO.   O!
    If you but knew how you the purpose cherish
    Whiles thus you mock it! how, in stripping it,
    You more invest it! Ebbing men, indeed,
    Most often do so near the bottom run
    By their own fear or sloth.
SEBASTIAN.   Prithee, say on:
    The setting of thine eye and cheek proclaim
    A matter from thee, and a birth indeed
    Which throes thee much to yield.
ANTONIO.   Thus, sir:
    Although this lord of weak remembrance, this
    Who shall be of as little memory
    When he is earth'd, hath here almost persuaded,—
    For he 's a spirit of persuasion, only
    Professes to persuade,—the king, his son 's alive,
    'Tis as impossible that he 's undrown'd
    As he that sleeps here swims.
SEBASTIAN.   I have no hope
    That he 's undrown'd.
ANTONIO.   O! out of that 'no hope,'
    What great hope have you! no hope that way is
    Another way so high a hope that even
    Ambition cannot pierce a wink beyond,
    But doubts discovery there. Will you grant with me
    That Ferdinand is drown'd?
SEBASTIAN.   He 's gone.
ANTONIO.   Then tell me
    Who 's the next heir of Naples?
SEBASTIAN.   Claribel.
ANTONIO. She that is Queen of Tunis; she that dwells
    Ten leagues beyond man's life; she that from Naples
    Can have no note, unless the sun were post—
    The man i' th' moon 's too slow—till new-born chins
    Be rough and razorable: she that, from whom?

We all were sea-swallow'd, though some cast again,
And by that destiny to perform an act
Whereof what 's past is prologue, what to come
In yours and my discharge.

SEBASTIAN.   What stuff is this!—How say you?
'Tis true my brother's daughter 's Queen of Tunis;
So is she heir of Naples; 'twixt which regions
There is some space.

ANTONIO.   A space whose every cubit
Seems to cry out, 'How shall that Claribel
Measure us back to Naples?—Keep in Tunis,
And let Sebastian wake!'—Say, this were death
That now hath seiz'd them; why, they were no worse
Than now they are. There be that can rule Naples
As well as he that sleeps; lords that can prate
As amply and unnecessarily
As this Gonzalo: I myself could make
A chough of as deep chat. O, that you bore
The mind that I do! what a sleep were this
For your advancement! Do you understand me?

SEBASTIAN. Methinks I do.

ANTONIO.   And how does your content
Tender your own good fortune?

SEBASTIAN.   I remember
You did supplant your brother Prospero.

ANTONIO.   True:
And look how well my garments sit upon me;
Much feater than before; my brother's servants
Were then my fellows; now they are my men.

SEBASTIAN. But, for your conscience,—

ANTONIO. Ay, sir; where lies that? If it were a kibe,
'Twould put me to my slipper: but I feel not
This deity in my bosom: twenty consciences,
That stand 'twixt me and Milan, candied be they,
And melt ere they molest! Here lies your brother,
No better than the earth he lies upon,
If he were that which now he 's like, that 's dead;
Whom I, with this obedient steel,—three inches of it,—
Can lay to bed for ever; whiles you, doing thus,
To the perpetual wink for aye might put
This ancient morsel, this Sir Prudence, who
Should not upbraid our course. For all the rest,

They 'll take suggestion as a cat laps milk;
They 'll tell the clock to any business that
We say befits the hour.

SEBASTIAN.   Thy case, dear friend,
Shall be my precedent: as thou got'st Milan,
I 'll come by Naples. Draw thy sword: one stroke
Shall free thee from the tribute which thou pay'st,
And I the king shall love thee.

ANTONIO.   Draw together;
And when I rear my hand, do you the like,
To fall it on Gonzalo.

SEBASTIAN.   O! but one word.   *They converse apart
Music. Re-enter Ariel, invisible.*

ARIEL. My master through his art foresees the danger
That you, his friend, are in; and sends me forth—
For else his project dies—to keep thee living.

Sings in Gonzalo's ear

While you here do snoring lie,
Open-ey'd Conspiracy
His time doth take.
If of life you keep a care,
Shake off slumber, and beware:
Awake! awake!

ANTONIO. Then let us both be sudden.

GONZALO.   Now, good angels
Preserve the king!   *They wake*

ALONSO. Why, how now! ho, awake! Why are you drawn?
Wherefore this ghastly looking?

GONZALO.   What 's the matter?

SEBASTIAN. Whiles we stood here securing your repose,
Even now, we heard a hollow burst of bellowing
Like bulls, or rather lions; did 't not wake you?
It struck mine ear most terribly.

ALONSO.   I heard nothing.

ANTONIO. O! 'twas a din to fright a monster's ear,
To make an earthquake: sure it was the roar
Of a whole herd of lions.

ALONSO.   Heard you this, Gonzalo?

GONZALO. Upon mine honour, sir, I heard a humming,
And that a strange one too, which did awake me.
I shak'd you, sir, and cried; as mine eyes open'd,
I saw their weapons drawn:—there was a noise,

That 's verily. 'Tis best we stand upon our guard,
Or that we quit this place: let 's draw our weapons.

ALONSO. Lead off this ground, and let 's make further
    search
For my poor son.

GONZALO.   Heavens keep him from these beasts!
For he is, sure, i' the island.

ALONSO.   Lead away.

Exit with the others

ARIEL. Prospero my lord shall know what I have done:
So, king, go safely on to seek thy son.   *Exit*

SCENE TWO

Another Part of the Island.

*Enter Caliban, with
a burden of wood. A noise of thunder heard*

CALIBAN. All the infections that the sun sucks up
    From bogs, fens, flats, on Prosper fall, and make him
    By inch-meal a disease! His spirits hear me,
    And yet I needs must curse. But they 'll nor pinch,
    Fright me with urchin-shows, pitch me i' the mire,
    Nor lead me, like a firebrand, in the dark
    Out of my way, unless he bid 'em; but
    For every trifle are they set upon me:
    Sometime like apes, that mow and chatter at me
    And after bite me; then like hedge-hogs, which
    Lie tumbling in my bare-foot way and mount
    Their pricks at my foot-fall; sometime am I
    All wound with adders, who with cloven tongues
    Do hiss me into madness.—

Enter Trinculo

                    Lo now! lo!
    Here comes a spirit of his, and to torment me
    For bringing wood in slowly: I 'll fall flat;
    Perchance he will not mind me.

TRINCULO. Here 's neither bush nor shrub to bear off any
    weather at all, and another storm brewing; I hear it sing
    i' the wind; yond same black cloud, yond huge one, looks

like a foul bombard that would shed his liquor. If it should thunder as it did before, I know not where to hide my head: yond same cloud cannot choose but fall by pailfuls.—What have we here? a man or a fish? Dead or alive? A fish: he smells like a fish; a very ancient and fish-like smell; a kind of not of the newest Poor-John. A strange fish! Were I in England now,—as once I was,—and had but this fish painted, not a holiday fool there but would give a piece of silver: there would this monster make a man; any strange beast there makes a man. When they will not give a doit to relieve a lame beggar, they will lay out ten to see a dead Indian. Legg'd like a man! and his fins like arms! Warm, o' my troth! I do now let loose my opinion, hold it no longer; this is no fish, but an islander, that hath lately suffered by a thunderbolt. (*Thunder*) Alas, the storm is come again: my best way is to creep under his gaberdine; there is no other shelter hereabout: misery acquaints a man with strange bedfellows. I will here shroud till the dregs of the storm be past.

    Enter Stephano, singing; a bottle in his hand

STEPHANO. I shall no more to sea, to sea,
      Here shall I die a-shore:—
This is a very scurvy tune to sing at a man's funeral:
Well, here 's my comfort.   *Drinks*

    The master, the swabber, the boatswain and I,
      The gunner and his mate,
  Lov'd Mall, Meg, and Marian and Margery,
      But none of us car'd for Kate;
      For she had a tongue with a tang,
      Would cry to a sailor, 'Go hang!'
She lov'd not the savour of tar nor of pitch,
  Yet a tailor might scratch her where-e'er she did itch:
      Then to sea, boys, and let her go hang.
This is a scurvy tune too: but here 's my comfort.
      Drinks

CALIBAN. Do not torment me: O!

STEPHANO. What 's the matter? Have we devils here? Do you put tricks upon us with savages and men of Ind? Ha! I have not 'scaped drowning, to be afeard now of your four legs; for it hath been said, 'As proper a man as ever went on four legs cannot make him give ground': and it shall be said so again while Stephano breathes at 's nostrils.

CALIBAN. The spirit torments me: O!

STEPHANO. This is some monster of the isle with four legs, who hath got, as I take it, an ague. Where the devil should he learn our language? I will give him some relief, if it be but for that: if I can recover him and keep him tame and get to Naples with him, he 's a present for any emperor that ever trod on neat's-leather.

CALIBAN. Do not torment me, prithee; I 'll bring my wood home faster.

STEPHANO. He 's in his fit now and does not talk after the wisest. He shall taste of my bottle: if he have never drunk wine afore it will go near to remove his fit. If I can recover him, and keep him tame, I will not take too much for him: he shall pay for him that hath him, and that soundly.

CALIBAN. Thou dost me yet but little hurt; thou wilt anon, I know it by thy trembling: now Prosper works upon thee.

STEPHANO. Come on your ways: open your mouth; here is that which will give language to you, cat. Open your mouth: this will shake your shaking, I can tell you, and that soundly (*Gives Caliban drink*): you cannot tell who 's your friend: open your chaps again.

TRINCULO. I should know that voice: it should be—but he is drowned; and these are devils. O! defend me.

STEPHANO. Four legs and two voices; a most delicate monster! His forward voice now is to speak well of his friend; his backward voice is to utter foul speeches, and to detract. If all the wine in my bottle will recover him, I will help his ague. Come. Amen! I will pour some in thy other mouth.

TRINCULO. Stephano!

STEPHANO. Doth thy other mouth call me? Mercy! mercy! This is a devil, and no monster: I will leave him; I have no long spoon.

TRINCULO. Stephano!—if thou beest Stephano, touch me, and speak to me; for I am Trinculo:—be not afeard—thy good friend Trinculo.

STEPHANO. If thou beest Trinculo, come forth. I 'll pull thee by the lesser legs: if any be Trinculo's legs, these are

they. Thou art very Trinculo indeed! How cam'st thou to
be the siege of this moon-calf? Can he vent Trinculos?

TRINCULO. I took him to be killed with a thunder-stroke.
But art thou not drowned, Stephano? I hope now thou
art not drowned. Is the storm overblown? I hid me under
the dead moon-calf's gaberdine for fear of the storm. And
art thou living, Stephano? O Stephano! two Neapolitans
'scaped!

STEPHANO. Prithee, do not turn me about: my stomach is
not constant.

CALIBAN. (*Aside*) These be fine things an if they be not
sprites.
That 's a brave god and bears celestial liquor:
I will kneel to him.

STEPHANO. How didst thou 'scape? How cam'st thou
hither? Swear by this bottle, how thou cam'st hither. I
escaped upon a butt of sack, which the sailors heaved
overboard, by this bottle! which I made of the bark of a
tree with mine own hands, since I was cast ashore.

CALIBAN. I 'll swear upon that bottle, to be thy true subject;
for the liquor is not earthly.

STEPHANO. Here: swear then, how thou escapedst.

TRINCULO. Swam ashore, man, like a duck: I can swim like
a duck, I 'll be sworn.

STEPHANO. Here, kiss the book (*Gives Trinculo drink*).
Though thou canst swim like a duck, thou art made like a
goose.

TRINCULO. O Stephano! hast any more of this?

STEPHANO. The whole butt, man: my cellar is in a rock by
the seaside, where my wine is hid. How now, moon-calf!
how does thine ague?

CALIBAN. Hast thou not dropped from heaven?

STEPHANO. Out o' the moon, I do assure thee: I was the
man in the moon, when time was.

CALIBAN. I have seen thee in her, and I do adore thee; my
mistress showed me thee, and thy dog, and thy bush.

STEPHANO. Come, swear to that; kiss the book; I will furnish it anon with new contents; swear.

TRINCULO. By this good light, this is a very shallow monster.—I afeard of him!—a very weak monster.—the man i'
the moon! a most poor credulous monster!—Well drawn,
monster, in good sooth.

CALIBAN. I 'll show thee every fertile inch o' the island;
And I will kiss thy foot. I prithee, be my god.

TRINCULO. By this light, a most perfidious and drunken
monster: when his god 's asleep, he 'll rob his bottle.

CALIBAN. I 'll kiss thy foot: I 'll swear myself thy subject.

STEPHANO. Come on then; down, and swear.

TRINCULO. I shall laugh myself to death at this puppy-
headed monster. A most scurvy monster! I could find in
my heart to beat him,—

STEPHANO. Come, kiss.

TRINCULO. But that the poor monster 's in drink: an abominable monster!

CALIBAN. I 'll shew thee the best springs; I 'll pluck thee
berries;
I 'll fish for thee, and get thee wood enough.
A plague upon the tyrant that I serve!
I 'll bear him no more sticks, but follow thee,
Thou wondrous man.

TRINCULO. A most ridiculous monster, to make a wonder of
a poor drunkard!

CALIBAN. I prithee, let me bring thee where crabs grow;
And I with my long nails will dig thee pig-nuts;
Show thee a jay's nest and instruct thee how
To snare the nimble marmozet; I 'll bring thee
To clust'ring filberts, and sometimes I 'll get thee
Young scamels from the rock. Wilt thou go with me?

STEPHANO. I prithee now, lead the way, without any more
talking.—Trinculo, the king and all our company else being drowned, we will inherit here.—Here; bear my bottle.
—Fellow Trinculo, we 'll fill him by and by again.

CALIBAN. Farewell, master; farewell, farewell!

Sings drunkenly

TRINCULO. A howling monster, a drunken monster.

CALIBAN.   No more dams I 'll make for fish;
            Nor fetch in firing
            At requiring,
         Nor scrape trenchering, nor wash dish;
            'Ban, 'Ban, Ca—Caliban,
            Has a new master—Get a new man.

Freedom, high-day! high-day, freedom! freedom! high-
day, freedom!

STEPHANO. O brave monster! lead the way.   *Exeunt*

ACT THREE

SCENE ONE

Before Prospero's Cell.

Enter Ferdinand, bearing a log

FERDINAND. There be some sports are painful, and their la-
    bour
    Delight in them sets off: some kinds of baseness
    Are nobly undergone, and most poor matters
    Point to rich ends. This my mean task
    Would be as heavy to me as odious; but
    The mistress which I serve quickens what's dead
    And makes my labours pleasures: O! she is
    Ten times more gentle than her father's crabbed.
    And he's compos'd of harshness. I must remove
    Some thousands of these logs and pile them up,
    Upon a sore injunction: my sweet mistress
    Weeps when she sees me work, and says such baseness
    Had never like executor. I forget:
    But these sweet thoughts do even refresh my labours,
    Most busiest when I do it.

            Enter Miranda; and Prospero behind

MIRANDA.   Alas! now pray you,
    Work not so hard: I would the lightning had
    Burnt up those logs that you are enjoin'd to pile!
    Pray, set it down and rest you: when this burns,
    'Twill weep for having wearied you. My father
    Is hard at study; pray now, rest yourself:
    He's safe for these three hours.

FERDINAND.   O most dear mistress,
    The sun will set, before I shall discharge
    What I must strive to do.

MIRANDA.   If you'll sit down,
    I'll bear your logs the while. Pray, give me that;

I 'll carry it to the pile.

FERDINAND.   No, precious creature:
I had rather crack my sinews, break my back,
Than you should such dishonour undergo,
While I sit lazy by.

MIRANDA.   It would become me
As well as it does you: and I should do it
With much more ease; for my good will is to it,
And yours it is against.

PROSPERO. (*Aside*) Poor worm! thou art infected:
This visitation shows it.

MIRANDA.   You look wearily.

FERDINAND. No, noble mistress; 'tis fresh morning with me
When you are by at night. I do beseech you—
Chiefly that I might set it in my prayers—
What is your name?

MIRANDA.   Miranda.—O my father!
I have broke your hest to say so.

FERDINAND.   Admir'd Miranda!
Indeed, the top of admiration; worth
What 's dearest to the world! Full many a lady
I have ey'd with best regard, and many a time
The harmony of their tongues hath into bondage
Brought my too diligent ear: for several virtues
Have I lik'd several women; never any
With so full soul but some defect in her
Did quarrel with the noblest grace she ow'd,
And put it to the foil: but you, O you!
So perfect and so peerless, are created
Of every creature's best.

MIRANDA.   I do not know
One of my sex; no woman's face remember,
Save, from my glass, mine own; nor have I seen
More that I may call men than you, good friend,
And my dear father: how features are abroad,
I am skill-less of; but, by my modesty,—
The jewel in my dower,—I would not wish
Any companion in the world but you;
Nor can imagination form a shape,
Besides yourself, to like of. But I prattle
Something too wildly and my father's precepts
I therein do forget.

FERDINAND.   I am in my condition
A prince, Miranda; I do think, a king;—
I would not so!—and would no more endure
This wooden slavery than to suffer
The flesh-fly blow my mouth.—Hear my soul speak:—
The very instant that I saw you did
My heart fly to your service; there resides,
To make me slave to it; and for your sake
Am I this patient log-man.

MIRANDA.   Do you love me?

FERDINAND. O heaven! O earth! bear witness to this sound,
And crown what I profess with kind event
If I speak true: if hollowly, invert
What best is boded me to mischief! I,
Beyond all limit of what else i' the world,
Do love, prize, honour you.

MIRANDA.   I am a fool
To weep at what I am glad of.

PROSPERO.   (Aside) Fair encounter
Of two most rare affections! Heavens rain grace
On that which breeds between them!

FERDINAND.   Wherefore weep you?

MIRANDA. At mine unworthiness, that dare not offer
What I desire to give; and much less take
What I shall die to want. But this is trifling;
And all the more it seeks to hide itself
The bigger bulk it shows. Hence, bashful cunning!
And prompt me, plain and holy innocence!
I am your wife, if you will marry me;
If not, I 'll die your maid: to be your fellow
You may deny me; but I 'll be your servant
Whether you will or no.

FERDINAND.   My mistress, dearest;
And I thus humble ever.

MIRANDA.   My husband then?

FERDINAND. Ay, with a heart as willing
As bondage e'er of freedom: here 's my hand.

MIRANDA. And mine, with my heart in 't: and now farewell
Till half an hour hence.

FERDINAND.   A thousand thousand!

Exeunt Ferdinand and Miranda severally

PROSPERO. So glad of this as they, I cannot be,

Who are surpris'd withal; but my rejoicing
At nothing can be more. I 'll to my book;
For yet, ere supper time, must I perform
Much business appertaining.　　　　　　　*Exit*

SCENE TWO

Another Part of the Island.

Enter Caliban, with a bottle, Stephano, and Trinculo

STEPHANO. Tell not me:—when the butt is out, we will
drink water; not a drop before: therefore bear up, and
board 'em.—Servant-monster, drink to me.

TRINCULO. Servant-monster! the folly of this island! They
say there 's but five upon this isle: we are three of them;
if th' other two be brained like us, the state totters.

STEPHANO. Drink, servant-monster, when I bid thee: thy
eyes are almost set in thy head.

TRINCULO. Where should they be set else? He were a brave
monster indeed, if they were set in his tail.

STEPHANO. My man-monster hath drowned his tongue in
sack: for my part, the sea cannot drown me; I swam, ere
I could recover the shore, five-and-thirty leagues, off and
on, by this light. Thou shalt be my lieutenant, monster,
or my standard.

TRINCULO. Your lieutenant, if you list; he 's no standard.

STEPHANO. We 'll not run, Monsieur monster.

TRINCULO. Nor go neither: but you 'll lie, like dogs; and yet
say nothing neither.

STEPHANO. Moon-calf, speak once in thy life, if thou beest
a good moon-calf.

CALIBAN. How does thy honour? Let me lick thy shoe. I 'll
not serve him; he is not valiant.

TRINCULO. Thou liest, most ignorant monster: I am in case
to justle a constable. Why, thou deboshed fish thou, was
there ever a man a coward that hath drunk so much sack
as I to-day? Wilt thou tell a monstrous lie, being but half
a fish and half a monster?

CALIBAN. Lo, how he mocks me! wilt thou let him, my
lord?

TRINCULO. 'Lord' quoth he!—that a monster should be such a natural!

CALIBAN. Lo, lo, again! Bite him to death, I prithee.

STEPHANO. Trinculo, keep a good tongue in your head: if you prove a mutineer, the next tree! The poor monster 's my subject, and he shall not suffer indignity.

CALIBAN. I thank my noble lord. Wilt thou be pleas'd
To hearken once again the suit I made thee?

STEPHANO. Marry, will I; kneel, and repeat it: I will stand, and so shall Trinculo.

Enter Ariel, invisible

CALIBAN. As I told thee before, I am subject to a tyrant, a sorcerer, that by his cunning hath cheated me of the island.

ARIEL. Thou liest.

CALIBAN. Thou liest, thou jesting monkey thou;
I would my valiant master would destroy thee;
I do not lie.

STEPHANO. Trinculo, if you trouble him any more in his tale, by this hand, I will supplant some of your teeth.

TRINCULO. Why, I said nothing.

STEPHANO. Mum then and no more.—(*To Caliban*) Proceed.

CALIBAN. I say, by sorcery he got this isle;
From me he got it: if thy greatness will,
Revenge it on him,—for, I know, thou dar 'st;
But this thing dare not,—

STEPHANO. That 's most certain.

CALIBAN. Thou shalt be lord of it and I 'll serve thee.

STEPHANO. How now shall this be compassed? Canst thou bring me to the party?

CALIBAN. Yea, yea, my lord: I 'll yield him thee asleep,
Where thou may'st knock a nail into his head.

ARIEL. Thou liest; thou canst not.

CALIBAN. What a pied ninny's this! Thou scurvy patch!—
I do beseech thy greatness, give him blows,
And take his bottle from him: when that 's gone
He shall drink nought but brine; for I 'll not show him
Where the quick freshes are.

STEPHANO. Trinculo, run into no further danger: interrupt the monster one word further, and, by this hand, I 'll turn my mercy out o' doors and make a stock-fish of thee.

TRINCULO. Why, what did I? I did nothing. I 'll go further off.

STEPHANO. Didst thou not say he lied?

ARIEL. Thou liest.

STEPHANO. Do I so? Take thou that. (*Strikes Trinculo*) As you like this, give me the lie another time.

TRINCULO. I did not give thee the lie:—Out o' your wits and hearing too?—A pox o' your bottle! this can sack and drinking do.—A murrain on your monster, and the devil take your fingers!

CALIBAN. Ha, ha, ha!

STEPHANO. Now, forward with your tale.—Prithee stand further off.

CALIBAN. Beat him enough: after a little time
I 'll beat him too.

STEPHANO.   Stand further.—Come, proceed.

CALIBAN. Why, as I told thee, 'tis a custom with him
I' the afternoon to sleep: there thou may'st brain him,
Having first seiz'd his books; or with a log
Batter his skull, or paunch him with a stake,
Or cut his wezand with thy knife. Remember
First to possess his books; for without them
He 's but a sot, as I am, nor hath not
One spirit to command: they all do hate him
As rootedly as I. Burn but his books;
He has brave utensils,—for so he calls them,—
Which, when he has a house, he 'll deck withal:
And that most deeply to consider is
The beauty of his daughter; he himself
Calls her a nonpareil: I never saw a woman,
But only Sycorax my dam and she;
But she as far surpasseth Sycorax
As great'st does least.

STEPHANO.   Is it so brave a lass?

CALIBAN. Ay, lord; she will become thy bed, I warrant,
And bring thee forth brave brood.

STEPHANO. Monster, I will kill this man; his daughter and
I will be king and queen,—save our graces! and Trinculo
and thyself shall be viceroys. Dost thou like the plot,
Trinculo?

TRINCULO. Excellent.

STEPHANO. Give me thy hand: I am sorry I beat thee; but,

while thou livest, keep a good tongue in thy head.

CALIBAN. Within this half hour will he be asleep;
Wilt thou destroy him then?

STEPHANO.   Ay, on mine honour.

ARIEL. This will I tell my master.

CALIBAN. Thou mak'st me merry: I am full of pleasure.
Let us be jocund: will you troll the catch
You taught me but while-ere?

STEPHANO. At thy request, monster, I will do reason, any
reason: Come on, Trinculo, let us sing.   *Sings*
Flout 'em, and scout 'em; and scout 'em, and flout 'em;
Thought is free.

CALIBAN. That 's not the tune.

                        Ariel plays the tune on a Tabor and Pipe

STEPHANO. What is this same?

TRINCULO. This is the tune of our catch, played by the picture of Nobody.

STEPHANO. If thou beest a man, show thyself in thy likeness: if thou beest a devil, take 't as thou list.

TRINCULO. O, forgive me my sins!

STEPHANO. He that dies pays all debts: I defy thee.—Mercy
upon us!

CALIBAN. Art thou afeard?

STEPHANO. No, monster, not I.

CALIBAN. Be not afeard: the isle is full of noises,
Sounds and sweet airs, that give delight, and hurt not.
Sometimes a thousand twangling instruments
Will hum about mine ears; and sometime voices,
That, if I then had wak'd after long sleep,
Will make me sleep again: and then, in dreaming,
The clouds methought would open and show riches
Ready to drop upon me; that, when I wak'd
I cried to dream again.

STEPHANO. This will prove a brave kingdom to me, where I
shall have my music for nothing.

CALIBAN. When Prospero is destroyed.

STEPHANO. That shall be by and by: I remember the story.

TRINCULO. The sound is going away: let 's follow it, and
after do our work.

STEPHANO. Lead, monster; we 'll follow.—I would I could
see this taborer! he lays it on. Wilt come?

TRINCULO. I 'll follow, Stephano.   *Exeunt*

SCENE THREE

Another Part of the Island.

Enter Alonso, Sebastian, Antonio, Gonzalo, Adrian,
Francisco, and others

GONZALO. By'r lakin, I can go no further, sir;
My old bones ache: here 's a maze trod indeed,
Through forth-rights, and meanders! by your patience,
I needs must rest me.

ALONSO.   Old lord, I cannot blame thee,
Who am myself attach'd with weariness,
To the dulling of my spirits: sit down, and rest.
Even here I will put off my hope, and keep it
No longer for my flatterer: he is drown'd
Whom thus we stray to find; and the sea mocks
Our frustrate search on land. Well, let him go.

ANTONIO. (*Aside to Sebastian*) I am right glad that he 's so
    out of hope.
Do not, for one repulse, forego the purpose
That you resolv'd to effect.

SEBASTIAN. (*Aside to Antonio*) The next advantage
Will we take throughly.

ANTONIO. (*Aside to Sebastian*) Let it be to-night;
For, now they are oppress'd with travel, they
Will not, nor cannot, use such vigilance
As when they are fresh.

SEBASTIAN. (*Aside to Antonio*) I say to-night: no more.
        Solemn and strange music; and Prospero
above, invisible. Enter below several strange Shapes, bring-
ing in a banquet: they dance about it with gentle actions of
salutation; and, inviting the King, &c., to eat, they depart.

ALONSO. What harmony is this? My good friends, hark!

GONZALO. Marvellous sweet music!

ALONSO. Give us kind keepers, heavens! What were these?

SEBASTIAN. A living drollery. Now I will believe
That there are unicorns; that in Arabia
There is one tree, the phœnix' throne; one phœnix

At this hour reigning there.

ANTONIO.   I 'll believe both;
And what does else want credit, come to me,
And I 'll be sworn 'tis true: travellers ne'er did lie,
Though fools at home condemn them.

GONZALO.   If in Naples
I should report this now, would they believe me?
If I should say I saw such islanders,—
For, certes, these are people of the island,—
Who, though they are of monstrous shape, yet, note,
Their manners are more gentle-kind than of
Our human generation you shall find
Many, nay, almost any.

PROSPERO.   (*Aside*) Honest lord,
Thou hast said well; for some of you there present
Are worse than devils.

ALONSO.   I cannot too much muse,
Such shapes, such gesture, and such sound, expressing,—
Although they want the use of tongue,—a kind
Of excellent dumb discourse.

PROSPERO.   (*Aside*) Praise in departing.

FRANCISCO. They vanish'd strangely.

SEBASTIAN.   No matter, since
They have left their viands behind; for we have stom-
achs.—
Will 't please you to taste of what is here?

ALONSO.   Not I.

GONZALO. Faith, sir, you need not fear. When we were boys,
Who would believe that there were mountaineers
Dew-lapp'd like bulls, whose throats had hanging at them
Wallets of flesh? or that there were such men
Whose heads stood in their breasts? which now we find
Each putter-out of five for one will bring us
Good warrant of.

ALONSO.   I will stand to and feed,
Although my last; no matter, since I feel
The best is past.—Brother, my lord the duke,
Stand to and do as we.

            Thunder and lightning.
*Enter Ariel like a harpy; claps his wings upon the table;
    and, with a quaint device, the banquet vanishes.*

ARIEL. You are three men of sin, whom Destiny—

That hath to instrument this lower world
And what is in 't,—the never-surfeited sea
Hath caused to belch up you; and on this island
Where man doth not inhabit; you 'mongst men
Being most unfit to live. I have made you mad;

   Seeing Alonso, Sebastian, &c., draw their swords

And even with such-like valour men hang and drown
Their proper selves. You fools! I and my fellows
Are ministers of fate: the elements
Of whom your swords are temper'd, may as well
Wound the loud winds, or with bemock'd-at stabs
Kill the still-closing waters, as diminish
One dowle that 's in my plume; my fellow-ministers
Are like invulnerable. If you could hurt,
Your swords are now too massy for your strengths,
And will not be uplifted. But, remember,—
For that 's my business to you,—that you three
From Milan did supplant good Prospero;
Expos'd unto the sea, which hath requit it,
Him and his innocent child: for which foul deed
The powers, delaying, not forgetting, have
Incens'd the seas and shores, yea, all the creatures,
Against your peace. Thee of thy son, Alonso,
They have bereft; and do pronounce, by me,
Lingering perdition,—worse than any death
Can be at once,—shall step by step attend
You and your ways; whose wraths to guard you from—
Which here in this most desolate isle, else falls
Upon your heads,—is nothing but heart-sorrow
And a clear life ensuing.

    He vanishes in thunder:
then, to soft music, enter the Shapes again, and dance with
  mocks and mows, and carry out the table

PROSPERO. *(Aside)* Bravely the figure of this harpy hast thou
Perform'd, my Ariel; a grace it had, devouring:
Of my instruction hast thou nothing bated
In what thou hadst to say: so, with good life
And observation strange, my meaner ministers
Their several kinds have done. My high charms work,
And these mine enemies are all knit up
In their distractions: they now are in my power;
And in these fits I leave them, while I visit

Young Ferdinand,—whom they suppose is drown'd,—
And his and mine lov'd darling.   *Exit above*

GONZALO. I' the name of something holy, sir, why stand you
In this strange stare?

ALONSO.   O, it is monstrous! monstrous!
Methought the billows spoke and told me of it;
The winds did sing it to me; and the thunder,
That deep and dreadful organ-pipe, pronounc'd
The name of Prosper: it did bass my trespass.
Therefore my son i' th' ooze is bedded; and
I 'll seek him deeper than e'er plummet sounded,
And with him there lie mudded.   *Exit*

SEBASTIAN.   But one fiend at a time,
I 'll fight their legions o'er.

ANTONIO.   I 'll be thy second.
                    Exeunt Sebastian and Antonio

GONZALO. All three of them are desperate; their great guilt,
Like poison given to work a great time after,
Now 'gins to bite the spirits.—I do beseech you
That are of suppler joints, follow them swiftly
And hinder them from what this ecstasy
May now provoke them to.

ADRIAN.   Follow, I pray you. *Exeunt*

ACT FOUR

SCENE ONE

Before Prospero's Cell.

Enter Prospero, Ferdinand, and Miranda

PROSPERO. If I have too austerely punish'd you,
Your compensation makes amends; for I
Have given you here a third of mine own life,
Or that for which I live; whom once again
I tender to thy hand: all thy vexations
Were but my trials of thy love, and thou
Hast strangely stood the test: here, afore Heaven,
I ratify this my rich gift. O Ferdinand!
Do not smile at me that I boast her off,
For thou shalt find she will outstrip all praise,
And make it halt behind her.

FERDINAND.   I do believe it
Against an oracle.

PROSPERO. Then, as my gift and thine own acquisition
Worthily purchas'd, take my daughter: but
If thou dost break her virgin knot before
All sanctimonious ceremonies may
With full and holy rite be minister'd,
No sweet aspersion shall the heavens let fall
To make this contract grow; but barren hate,
Sour-ey'd disdain and discord shall bestrew
The union of your beds with weeds so loathly
That you shall hate it both: therefore take heed,
As Hymen's lamps shall light you.

FERDINAND.   As I hope
For quiet days, fair issue and long life,
With such love as 'tis now, the murkiest den,
The most opportune place, the strong'st suggestion
Our worser genius can, shall never melt

Mine honour into lust, to take away
The edge of that day's celebration
When I shall think, or Phœbus' steeds are founder'd,
Or Night kept chain'd below.

PROSPERO. Fairly spoke:
Sit then, and talk with her, she is thine own.
What, Ariel! my industrious servant Ariel!

Enter Ariel

ARIEL. What would my potent master? Here I am.

PROSPERO. Thou and thy meaner fellows your last service
Did worthily perform; and I must use you
In such another trick. Go bring the rabble,
O'er whom I give thee·power, here to this place:
Incite them to quick motion; for I must
Bestow upon the eyes of this young couple
Some vanity of mine art: it is my promise,
And they expect it from me.

ARIEL. Presently?

PROSPERO. Ay, with a twink.

ARIEL. Before you can say, 'Come,' and 'Go,'
And breathe twice; and cry, 'so, so,'
Each one, tripping on his toe,
Will be here with mop and mow.
Do you love me, master? no?

PROSPERO. Dearly, my delicate Ariel. Do not approach
Till thou dost hear me call.

ARIEL. Well, I can conceive. *Exit*

PROSPERO. Look thou be true; do not give dalliance
Too much the rein: the strongest oaths are straw
To the fire i' the blood: be more abstemious,
Or else good night your vow!

FERDINAND. I warrant you, sir;
The white-cold virgin snow upon my heart
Abates the ardour of my liver.

PROSPERO. Well.—
Now come, my Ariel! bring a corollary,
Rather than want a spirit: appear, and pertly.
No tongue! all eyes! be silent. *Soft music*

A Masque. Enter Iris.

IRIS. Ceres, most bounteous lady, thy rich leas
Of wheat, rye, barley, vetches, oats, and peas;

Thy turfy mountains, where live nibbling sheep,
And flat meads thatch'd with stover, them to keep;
Thy banks with pioned and twilled brims,
Which spongy April at thy hest betrims,
To make cold nymphs chaste crowns; and thy broom
    groves,
Whose shadow the dismissed bachelor loves,
Being lass-lorn; thy pole-clipt vineyard;
And thy sea-marge, sterile and rocky-hard,
Where thou thyself dost air: the queen o' the sky,
Whose watery arch and messenger am I,
Bids thee leave these; and with her sovereign grace,
Here on this grass-plot, in this very place,
To come and sport; her peacocks fly amain:
Approach, rich Ceres, her to entertain.

Enter Ceres

CERES. Hail, many-colour'd messenger, that ne'er
Dost disobey the wife of Jupiter;
Who with thy saffron wings upon my flowers
Diffusest honey-drops, refreshing showers:
And with each end of thy blue bow dost crown
My bosky acres, and my unshrubb'd down,
Rich scarf to my proud earth; why hath thy queen
Summon'd me hither, to this short-grass'd green?

IRIS. A contract of true love to celebrate,
And some donation freely to estate
On the bless'd lovers.

CERES.   Tell me, heavenly bow,
If Venus or her son, as thou dost know,
Do now attend the queen? since they did plot
The means that dusky Dis my daughter got,
Her and her blind boy's scandal'd company
I have forsworn.

IRIS.   Of her society
Be not afraid; I met her deity
Cutting the clouds towards Paphos and her son
Dove-drawn with her. Here thought they to have done
Some wanton charm upon this man and maid,
Whose vows are, that no bed-rite shall be paid
Till Hymen's torch be lighted; but in vain:
Mars's hot minion is return'd again.

Her waspish-headed son has broke his arrows,
Swears he will shoot no more, but play with sparrows,
And be a boy right out.
CERES.   Highest queen of state,
Great Juno comes; I know her by her gait.
Enter Juno
JUNO. How does my bounteous sister? Go with me
To bless this twain, that they may prosperous be,
And honour'd in their issue.

SONG

JUNO.   Honour, riches, marriage-blessing,
               Long continuance, and increasing,
               Hourly joys be still upon you!
               Juno sings her blessings on you.

CERES.   Earth's increase, foison plenty,
               Barns and garners never empty:
               Vines, with clust'ring bunches growing;
               Plants with goodly burden bowing;
               Spring come to you at the farthest
               In the very end of harvest!
               Scarcity and want shall shun you;
               Ceres' blessing so is on you.

FERDINAND. This is a most majestic vision, and
Harmonious charmingly: May I be bold
To think these spirits?
PROSPERO.   Spirits, which by mine art
I have from their confines call'd to enact
My present fancies.
FERDINAND.   Let me live here ever:
So rare a wonder'd father and a wise,
Makes this place Paradise.
    Juno and Ceres whisper, and send Iris on employment
PROSPERO.   Sweet, now, silence!
Juno and Ceres whisper seriously,
There 's something else to do: hush, and be mute,
Or else our spell is marr'd.
IRIS. You nymphs, call'd Naiades, of the windring brooks,
With your sedg'd crowns, and ever-harmless looks,
Leave your crisp channels, and on this green land
Answer your summons: Juno does command.
Come, temperate nymphs, and help to celebrate
A contract of true love: be not too late.

Enter certain Nymphs

You sun-burn'd sicklemen, of August weary,
Come hither from the furrow, and be merry:
Make holiday: your rye-straw hats put on,
And these fresh nymphs encounter every one
In country footing.

Enter certain Reapers, properly habited:
they join with the Nymphs in a graceful dance; towards
the end whereof Prospero starts suddenly, and speaks; after
which, to a strange, hollow, and confused
noise, they heavily vanish

PROSPERO. (*Aside*) I had forgot that foul conspiracy
Of the beast Caliban, and his confederates
Against my life: the minute of their plot
Is almost come.—(*To the Spirits*) Well done! avoid; no
more!

FERDINAND. This is strange: your father 's in some passion
That works him strongly.

MIRANDA. Never till this day
Saw I him touch'd with anger so distemper'd.

PROSPERO. You do look, my son, in a mov'd sort,
As if you were dismay'd: be cheerful, sir:
Our revels now are ended. These our actors,
As I foretold you, were all spirits and
Are melted into air, into thin air:
And, like the baseless fabric of this vision,
The cloud-capp'd towers, the gorgeous palaces,
The solemn temples, the great globe itself,
Yea, all which it inherit, shall dissolve
And, like this insubstantial pageant faded,
Leave not a rack behind. We are such stuff
As dreams are made on, and our little life
Is rounded with a sleep.—Sir, I am vex'd:
Bear with my weakness; my old brain is troubled.
Be not disturb'd with my infirmity.
If you be pleas'd, retire into my cell
And there repose: a turn or two I 'll walk,
To still my beating mind.

FERDINAND, MIRANDA. We wish your peace. *Exeunt*

PROSPERO. Come with a thought!—(*To them*) I thank thee:
Ariel, come!

Enter Ariel

ARIEL. Thy thoughts I cleave to. What 's thy pleasure?

PROSPERO. Spirit,
We must prepare to meet with Caliban.

ARIEL. Ay, my commander; when I presented Ceres,
I thought to have told thee of it; but I fear'd
Lest I might anger thee.

PROSPERO. Say again, where didst thou leave these varlets?

ARIEL. I told you, sir, they were red-hot with drinking;
So full of valour that they smote the air
For breathing in their faces; beat the ground
For kissing of their feet; yet always bending
Towards their project. Then I beat my tabor;
At which, like unback'd colts, they prick'd their ears,
Advanc'd their eyelids, lifted up their noses
As they smelt music: so I charm'd their ears
That, calf-like, they my lowing follow'd through
Tooth'd briers, sharp furzes, pricking goss and thorns,
Which enter'd their frail shins: at last I left them
I' the filthy-mantled pool beyond your cell,
There dancing up to the chins, that the foul lake
O'erstunk their feet.

PROSPERO. This was well done, my bird.
Thy shape invisible retain thou still:
The trumpery in my house, go bring it hither,
For stale to catch these thieves.

ARIEL. I go, I go. *Exit*

PROSPERO. A devil, a born devil, on whose nature
Nurture can never stick; on whom my pains,
Humanely taken, are all lost, quite lost;
And as with age his body uglier grows,
So his mind cankers. I will plague them all,
Even to roaring.

Re-enter Ariel, loaden with glistering apparel, &c.
Come, hang them on this line.

Prospero and Ariel remain invisible.

Enter Caliban, Stephano, and Trinculo, all wet.

CALIBAN. Pray you, tread softly, that the blind mole may
not
Hear a foot fall: we now are near his cell.

STEPHANO. Monster, your fairy, which you say is a harmless fairy, has done little better than played the Jack with
us.

TRINCULO. Monster, I do smell all horse-piss; at which my
nose is in great indignation.

STEPHANO. So is mine.—Do you hear, monster? If I should
take a displeasure against you, look you,—

TRINCULO. Thou wert but a lost monster.

CALIBAN. Good my lord, give me thy favour still:
Be patient, for the prize I 'll bring thee to
Shall hoodwink this mischance: therefore speak softly;
All 's hush'd as midnight yet.

TRINCULO. Ay, but to lose our bottles in the pool,—

STEPHANO. There is not only disgrace and dishonour in
that, monster, but an infinite loss.

TRINCULO. That 's more to me than my wetting: yet this is
your harmless fairy, monster.

STEPHANO. I will fetch off my bottle, though I be o'er ears
for my labour.

CALIBAN. Prithee, my king, be quiet. Seest thou here,
This is the mouth o' the cell: no noise, and enter.
Do that good mischief, which may make this island
Thine own for ever, and I, thy Caliban,
For aye thy foot-licker.

STEPHANO. Give me thy hand: I do begin to have bloody
thoughts.

TRINCULO. O king Stephano! O peer! O worthy Stephano!
look, what a wardrobe here is for thee!

CALIBAN. Let it alone, thou fool; it is but trash.

TRINCULO. O, ho, monster! we know what belongs to a frip-
pery.—O king Stephano!

STEPHANO. Put off that gown, Trinculo; by this hand, I 'll
have that gown.

TRINCULO. Thy Grace shall have it.

CALIBAN. The dropsy drown this fool! what do you mean
To dote thus on such luggage? Let 's along,
And do the murder first: if he awake,
From toe to crown he 'll fill our skin with pinches;
Make us strange stuff.

STEPHANO. Be you quiet, monster.—Mistress line, is not this
my jerkin? Now is the jerkin under the line: now, jerkin,
you are like to lose your hair and prove a bald jerkin.

TRINCULO. Do, do: we steal by line and level, an 't like
your Grace.

STEPHANO. I thank thee for that jest; here 's a garment for

't: wit shall not go unrewarded while I am king of this
country: 'Steal by line and level,' is an excellent pass of
pate; there's another garment for 't.

TRINCULO. Monster, come, put some lime upon your fingers, and away with the rest.

CALIBAN. I will have none on 't: we shall lose our time,
And all be turn'd to barnacles, or to apes
With foreheads villanous low.

STEPHANO. Monster, lay-to your fingers: help to bear this
away where my hogshead of wine is, or I 'll turn you out
of my kingdom. Go to; carry this.

TRINCULO. And this.

STEPHANO. Ay, and this.

A noise of hunters heard.
Enter divers Spirits, in shape of hounds, and hunt them
about; Prospero and Ariel setting them on.

PROSPERO. Hey, Mountain, hey!

ARIEL. Silver! there it goes, Silver!

PROSPERO. Fury, Fury! there, Tyrant, there! hark, hark!
Caliban, Stephano, and Trinculo are driven out
Go, charge my goblins that they grind their joints
With dry convulsions; shorten up their sinews
With aged cramps, and more pinch-spotted make them
Than pard, or cat o' mountain.

ARIEL.   Hark! they roar.

PROSPERO. Let them be hunted soundly. At this hour
Lie at my mercy all mine enemies:
Shortly shall all my labours end, and thou
Shalt have the air at freedom; for a little,
Follow, and do me service.   *Exeunt*

ACT FIVE

Before the Cell of Prospero.

Enter Prospero in his magic robes; and Ariel

PROSPERO. Now does my project gather to a head:
My charms crack not; my spirits obey, and time
Goes upright with his carriage. How 's the day?
ARIEL. On the sixth hour; at which time, my lord,
You said our work should cease.
PROSPERO.   I did say so
When first I rais'd the tempest. Say, my spirit,
How fares the king and 's followers?
ARIEL.   Confin'd together
In the same fashion as you gave in charge;
Just as you left them: all prisoners, sir,
In the line-grove which weather-fends your cell;
They cannot budge till your release. The king,
His brother, and yours, abide all three distracted,
And the remainder mourning over them,
Brimful of sorrow and dismay; but chiefly
Him, that you term'd sir, 'The good old lord Gonzalo':
His tears run down his beard, like winter's drops
From eaves of reeds; your charm so strongly works them,
That if you now beheld them, your affections
Would become tender.
PROSPERO.   Dost thou think so, spirit?
ARIEL. Mine would, sir, were I human.
PROSPERO.   And mine shall.
Hast thou, which art but air, a touch, a feeling
Of their afflictions, and shall not myself,
One of their kind, that relish all as sharply,
Passion as they, be kindlier mov'd than thou art?
Though with their high wrongs I am struck to the quick,

Yet with my nobler reason 'gainst my fury
Do I take part: the rarer action is
In virtue than in vengeance: they being penitent,
The sole drift of my purpose doth extend
Not a frown further. Go, release them, Ariel.
My charms I 'll break, their senses I 'll restore,
And they shall be themselves.

ARIEL.   I 'll fetch them, sir.   *Exit*

PROSPERO. Ye elves of hills, brooks, standing lakes, and
    groves;
And ye, that on the sands with printless foot
Do chase the ebbing Neptune and do fly him
When he comes back; you demi-puppets, that
By moonshine do the green sour ringlets make
Whereof the ewe not bites; and you, whose pastime)
Is to make midnight mushrooms; that rejoice
To hear the solemn curfew; by whose aid,—
Weak masters though ye be—I have bedimm'd
The noontide sun, call'd forth the mutinous winds,
And 'twixt the green sea and the azur'd vault
Set roaring war: to the dread-rattling thunder
Have I given fire and rifted Jove's stout oak
With his own bolt: the strong-bas'd promontory
Have I made shake; and by the spurs pluck'd up
The pine and cedar: graves at my command
Have wak'd their sleepers, op'd, and let them forth
By my so potent art. But this rough magic
I here abjure; and, when I have requir'd
Some heavenly music,—which even now I do,—
To work mine end upon their senses that
This airy charm is for, I 'll break my staff,
Bury it certain fathoms in the earth,
And, deeper than did ever plummet sound
I 'll drown my book.   *Solemn music*
        Re-enter Ariel: after him, Alonso,
with a frantic gesture, attended by Gonzalo; Sebastian and
Antonio in like manner, attended by Adrian and Francisco.
They all enter the circle which Prospero had made, and
there stand charmed; which Prospero observing, speaks

A solemn air and the best comforter
To an unsettled fancy, cure thy brains,
Now useless, boil'd within thy skull! There stand,

For you are spell-stopp'd.
Holy Gonzalo, honourable man,
Mine eyes, even sociable to the show of thine,
Fall fellowly drops. The charm dissolves apace;
And as the morning steals upon the night,
Melting the darkness, so their rising senses
Begin to chase the ignorant fumes that mantle
Their clearer reason.—O good Gonzalo!
My true preserver, and a loyal sir
To him thou follow'st, I will pay thy graces
Home, both in word and deed.—Most cruelly
Didst thou, Alonso, use me and my daughter:
Thy brother was a furtherer in the act;—
Thou 'rt pinch'd for 't now, Sebastian.—Flesh and blood,
You, brother mine, that entertain'd ambition,
Expell'd remorse and nature; who, with Sebastian,—
Whose inward pinches therefore are most strong,—
Would here have kill'd your king; I do forgive thee,
Unnatural though thou art!—Their understanding
Begins to swell, and the approaching tide
Will shortly fill the reasonable shores
That now lie foul and muddy. Not one of them
That yet looks on me, or would know me.—Ariel,
Fetch me the hat and rapier in my cell:—   *Exit Ariel*
I will discase me, and myself present,
As I was sometime Milan.—Quickly, spirit;
Thou shalt ere long be free.

Ariel re-enters, singing, and helps to attire Prospero

ARIEL.　　Where the bee sucks, there suck I:
　　　　　In a cowslip's bell I lie;
　　　　　There I couch when owls do cry.
　　　　　On the bat's back I do fly
　　　　　After summer merrily:
　　　　　Merrily, merrily shall I live now
　　　　　Under the blossom that hangs on the bough.

PROSPERO. Why, that 's my dainty Ariel! I shall miss thee;
But yet thou shalt have freedom;—so, so, so.—
To the king's ship, invisible as thou art:
There shalt thou find the mariners asleep
Under the hatches; the master and the boatswain
Being awake, enforce them to this place,
And presently, I prithee.

ARIEL. I drink the air before me, and return
  Or e'er your pulse twice beat.   *Exit*

GONZALO. All torment, trouble, wonder, and amazement
  Inhabits here: some heavenly power guide us
  Out of this fearful country!

PROSPERO.   Behold, sir king,
  The wronged Duke of Milan, Prospero.
  For more assurance that a living prince
  Does now speak to thee, I embrace thy body;
  And to thee and thy company I bid
  A hearty welcome.

ALONSO.   Whe'r thou beest he or no,
  Or some enchanted trifle to abuse me,
  As late I have been, I not know: thy pulse
  Beats, as of flesh and blood; and, since I saw thee,
  Th' affliction of my mind amends, with which,
  I fear, a madness held me: this must crave,—
  An if this be at all—a most strange story.
  Thy dukedom I resign, and do entreat
  Thou pardon me my wrongs.—But how should Prospero
  Be living, and be here?

PROSPERO.   First, noble friend,
  Let me embrace thine age, whose honour cannot
  Be measur'd, or confin'd.

GONZALO.   Whether this be,
  Or be not, I 'll not swear.

PROSPERO.   You do yet taste
  Some subtilties o' the isle, that will not let you
  Believe things certain.—Welcome! my friends all:—
  (*Aside to Sebastian and Antonio*) But you, my brace of
  lords, were I so minded,
  I here could pluck his Highness' frown upon you,
  And justify you traitors: at this time
  I will tell no tales.

SEBASTIAN. (*Aside*) The devil speaks in him.

PROSPERO.   No.
  For you, most wicked sir, whom to call brother
  Would even infect my mouth, I do forgive
  Thy rankest fault; all of them; and require
  My dukedom of thee, which, perforce, I know,
  Thou must restore.

ALONSO.   If thou beest Prospero,

Give us particulars of thy preservation;
How thou hast met us here, who three hours since
Were wrack'd upon this shore; where I have lost,—
How sharp the point of this remembrance is!—
My dear son Ferdinand.

PROSPERO.   I am woe for 't, sir.

ALONSO. Irreparable is the loss, and patience
Says it is past her cure.

PROSPERO.   I rather think
You have not sought her help; of whose soft grace,
For the like loss I have her sovereign aid,
And rest myself content.

ALONSO.   You the like loss!

PROSPERO. As great to me, as late; and, supportable
To make the dear loss, have I means much weaker
Than you may call to comfort you, for I
Have lost my daughter.

ALONSO.   A daughter?
O heavens! that they were living both in Naples,
The king and queen there! that they were, I wish
Myself were mudded in that oozy bed
Where my son lies. When did you lose your daughter?

PROSPERO. In this last tempest. I perceive, these lords
At this encounter do so much admire
That they devour their reason, and scarce think
Their eyes do offices of truth, their words
Are natural breath; but, howsoe'er you have
Been justled from your senses, know for certain
That I am Prospero and that very duke
Which was thrust forth of Milan; who most strangely
Upon this shore, where you were wrack'd, was landed,
To be the lord on 't. No more yet of this;
For 'tis a chronicle of day by day,
Not a relation for a breakfast nor
Befitting this first meeting. Welcome, sir;
This cell 's my court: here have I few attendants
And subjects none abroad: pray you, look in.
My dukedom since you have given me again,
I will requite you with as good a thing;
At least bring forth a wonder, to content ye
As much as me my dukedom.

The entrance of the Cell opens,
and discovers Ferdinand and Miranda playing at chess

MIRANDA. Sweet lord, you play me false.

FERDINAND.   No, my dearest love,
I would not for the world.

MIRANDA. Yes, for a score of kingdoms you should wrangle,
And I would call it fair play.

ALONSO.   If this prove
A vision of the island, one dear son
Shall I twice lose.

SEBASTIAN.   A most high miracle!

FERDINAND. Though the seas threaten, they are merciful:
I have curs'd them without cause.   *Kneels to Alonso*

ALONSO.   Now, all the blessings
Of a glad father compass thee about!
Arise, and say how thou cam'st here.

MIRANDA.   O, wonder!
How many goodly creatures are there here!
How beauteous mankind is! O brave new world,
That has such people in 't!

PROSPERO.   'Tis new to thee.

ALONSO. What is this maid, with whom thou wast at play?
Your eld'st acquaintance cannot be three hours:
Is she the goddess that hath sever'd us,
And brought us thus together?

FERDINAND.   Sir, she is mortal;
But by immortal Providence she 's mine;
I chose her when I could not ask my father
For his advice, nor thought I had one. She
Is daughter to this famous Duke of Milan,
Of whom so often I have heard renown,
But never saw before; of whom I have
Receiv'd a second life; and second father
This lady makes him to me.

ALONSO.   I am hers:
But O! how oddly will it sound that I
Must ask my child forgiveness!

PROSPERO.   There, sir, stop:
Let us not burden our remembrances
With a heaviness that 's gone.

GONZALO.   I have inly wept,

Or should have spoke ere this. Look down, you gods,
And on this couple drop a blessed crown;
For it is you that have chalk'd forth the way
Which brought us hither!

ALONZO.   I say, Amen, Gonzalo!

GONZALO. Was Milan thrust from Milan, that his issue
Should become kings of Naples? O, rejoice
Beyond a common joy, and set it down
With gold on lasting pillars. In one voyage
Did Claribel her husband find at Tunis,
And Ferdinand, her brother, found a wife
Where he himself was lost; Prospero his dukedom
In a poor isle; and all of us ourselves,
When no man was his own.

ALONZO. (*To Ferdinand and Miranda*) Give me your hands:
Let grief and sorrow still embrace his heart
That doth not wish you joy!

GONZALO.   Be it so: Amen!

*Re-enter Ariel, with
the Master and Boatswain amazedly following*

O look, sir! look, sir! here are more of us.
I prophesied, if a gallows were on land,
This fellow could not drown.—Now, blasphemy,
That swear'st grace o'erboard, not an oath on shore?
Hast thou no mouth by land? What is the news?

BOATSWAIN. The best news is that we have safely found
Our king and company: the next, our ship,—
Which but three glasses since we gave out split,—
Is tight and yare and bravely rigg'd as when
We first put out to sea.

ARIEL. (*Aside to Prospero*) Sir, all this service
Have I done since I went.

PROSPERO. (*Aside to Ariel*) My tricksy spirit!

ALONZO. These are not natural events; they strengthen
From strange to stranger.—Say, how came you hither?

BOATSWAIN. If I did think, sir, I were well awake,
I 'd strive to tell you. We were dead of sleep,
And,—how we know not,—all clapp'd under hatches,
Where, but even now, with strange and several noises
Of roaring, shrieking, howling, jingling chains,
And mo diversity of sounds, all horrible,
We were awak'd; straightway, at liberty:

Where we, in all her trim, freshly beheld
Our royal, good, and gallant ship; our master
Capering to eye her: on a trice, so please you,
Even in a dream, were we divided from them,
And were brought moping hither.

ARIEL.   (*Aside to Prospero*) Was 't well done?

PROSPERO.   (*Aside to Ariel*) Bravely, my diligence! Thou
shalt be free.

ALONSO. This is as strange a maze as e'er men trod;
And there is in this business more than nature
Was ever conduct of: some oracle
Must rectify our knowledge.

PROSPERO.   Sir, my liege,
Do not infest your mind with beating on
The strangeness of this business: at pick'd leisure
Which shall be shortly, single I 'll resolve you,—
Which to you shall seem probable,—of every
These happen'd accidents; till when, be cheerful,
And think of each thing well.—(*Aside to Ariel*) Come
hither, spirit;
Set Caliban and his companions free;
Untie the spell. (*Exit Ariel*) How fares my gracious sir?
There are yet missing of your company
Some few odd lads that you remember not.

> *Re-enter Ariel, driving in*
Caliban, Stephano, and Trinculo, in their stolen apparel

STEPHANO. Every man shift for all the rest, and let no man
take care for himself, for all is but fortune.—Coragio!
bully-monster, Coragio!

TRINCULO. If these be true spies which I wear in my head,
here 's a goodly sight.

CALIBAN. O Setebos! these be brave spirits, indeed.
How fine my master is! I am afraid
He will chastise me.

SEBASTIAN.   Ha, ha!
What things are these, my lord Antonio?
Will money buy them?

ANTONIO.   Very like; one of them
Is a plain fish, and, no doubt, marketable.

PROSPERO. Mark but the badges of these men, my lords,
Then say, if they be true.—This mis-shapen knave,—
His mother was a witch; and one so strong

That could control the moon, make flows and ebbs,
And deal in her command without her power.
These three have robb'd me; and this demi-devil,—
For he 's a bastard one,—had plotted with them
To take my life: two of these fellows you
Must know and own; this thing of darkness I
Acknowledge mine.

CALIBAN.   I shall be pinch'd to death.

ALONSO. Is not this Stephano, my drunken butler?

SEBASTIAN. He is drunk now: where had he wine?

ALONSO. And Trinculo is reeling-ripe: where should they
Find this grand liquor that hath gilded them?
How cam'st thou in this pickle?

TRINCULO. I have been in such a pickle since I saw you last
that, I fear me, will never out of my bones: I shall not
fear fly-blowing.

SEBASTIAN. Why, how now, Stephano!

STEPHANO. O! touch me not: I am not Stephano, but a
cramp.

PROSPERO. You 'd be king of the isle, sirrah?

STEPHANO. I should have been a sore one then.

ALONSO. This is a strange thing as e'er I look'd on.

Pointing to Caliban

PROSPERO. He is as disproportion'd in his manners
As in his shape.—Go, sirrah, to my cell;
Take with you your companions: as you look
To have my pardon, trim it handsomely.

CALIBAN. Ay, that I will; and I 'll be wise hereafter,
And seek for grace. What a thrice-double ass
Was I, to take this drunkard for a god,
And worship this dull fool!

PROSPERO.   Go to; away!

ALONSO. Hence, and bestow your luggage where you found
it.

SEBASTIAN. Or stole it, rather.

Exeunt Caliban, Stephano, and Trinculo

PROSPERO. Sir, I invite your Highness and your train
To my poor cell, where you shall take your rest
For this one night; which—part of it—I 'll waste
With such discourse as, I not doubt, shall make it
Go quick away; the story of my life
And the particular accidents gone by

Since I came to this isle: and in the morn
I 'll bring you to your ship, and so to Naples,
Where I have hope to see the nuptial
Of these our dear-beloved solemniz'd;
And thence retire me to my Milan, where
Every third thought shall be my grave.

ALONSO.   I long
To hear the story of your life, which must
Take the ear strangely.

PROSPERO.   I 'll deliver all;
And promise you calm seas, auspicious gales
And sail so expeditious that shall catch
Your royal fleet far off.—(*Aside to Ariel*) My Ariel, chick.
That is thy charge: then to the elements
Be free, and fare thou well!—Please you, draw near.

                                                    Exeunt

EPILOGUE

Spoken by Prospero

Now my charms are all o'erthrown,
And what strength I have 's mine own;
Which is most faint: now, 'tis true,
I must be here confin'd by you,
Or sent to Naples. Let me not,
Since I have my dukedom got
And pardon'd the deceiver, dwell
In this bare island by your spell;
But release me from my bands
With the help of your good hands.
Gentle breath of yours my sails
Must fill, or else my project fails,
Which was to please. Now I want
Spirits to enforce, art to enchant;
And my ending is despair,
Unless I be reliev'd by prayer,
Which pierces so that it assaults
Mercy itself and frees all faults.
As you from crimes would pardon'd be,
Let your indulgence set me free.

THE TWO GENTLEMEN
OF VERONA

CAST OF CHARACTERS

DUKE OF MILAN, *Father to Silvia*

VALENTINE }
PROTEUS } *the Two Gentlemen*

ANTONIO, *Father to Proteus*
THURIO, *a foolish rival to Valentine*
EGLAMOUR, *Agent for Silvia, in her escape*
SPEED, *a clownish Servant to Valentine*
LAUNCE, *the like to Proteus*
PANTHINO, *Servant to Antonio*

HOST, *where Julia lodges in Milan*
Outlaws *with Valentine*

JULIA, *beloved of Proteus*
SILVIA, *beloved of Valentine*
LUCETTA, *waiting woman to Julia*

Servants, Musicians

SCENE

Verona; Milan; and the frontiers of Mantua

THE TWO GENTLEMEN OF VERONA

ACT ONE

SCENE ONE

Verona. An open place.

Enter Valentine and Proteus

VALENTINE. Cease to persuade, my loving Proteus:
  Home-keeping youth have ever homely wits.
  Were 't not affection chains thy tender days
  To the sweet glances of thy honour'd love,
  I rather would entreat thy company
  To see the wonders of the world abroad
  Than, living dully sluggardiz'd at home,
  Wear out thy youth with shapeless idleness.
  But since thou lov'st, love still, and thrive therein,
  Even as I would when I to love begin.

PROTEUS. Wilt thou be gone? Sweet Valentine, adieu!
  Think on thy Proteus, when thou haply seest
  Some rare noteworthy object in thy travel:
  Wish me partaker in thy happiness
  When thou dost meet good hap; and in thy danger,
  If ever danger do environ thee,
  Commend thy grievance to my holy prayers,
  For I will be thy beadsman, Valentine.

VALENTINE. And on a love-book pray for my success?

PROTEUS. Upon some book I love I 'll pray for thee.

VALENTINE. That 's on some shallow story of deep love,
  How young Leander cross'd the Hellespont.

PROTEUS. That 's a deep story of a deeper love;
  For he was more than over shoes in love.

VALENTINE. 'Tis true; for you are over boots in love,
  And yet you never swum the Hellespont.
PROTEUS. Over the boots? Nay, give me not the boots.
VALENTINE. No, I will not, for it boots thee not.
PROTEUS.   What?
VALENTINE. To be in love, where scorn is bought with
    groans;
  Coy looks with heart-sore sighs; one fading moment's mirth
  With twenty watchful, weary, tedious nights:
  If haply won, perhaps a hapless gain;
  If lost, why then a grievous labour won:
  However, but a folly bought with wit,
  Or else a wit by folly vanquished.
PROTEUS. So, by your circumstance, you call me fool.
VALENTINE. So, by your circumstance, I fear you 'll prove.
PROTEUS. 'Tis love you cavil at: I am not Love.
VALENTINE. Love is your master, for he masters you;
  And he that is so yoked by a fool,
  Methinks, should not be chronicled for wise.
PROTEUS. Yet writers say, as in the sweetest bud
  The eating canker dwells, so eating love
  Inhabits in the finest wits of all.
VALENTINE. And writers say, as the most forward bud
  Is eaten by the canker ere it blow,
  Even so by love the young and tender wit
  Is turned to folly; blasting in the bud,
  Losing his verdure even in the prime,
  And all the fair effects of future hopes.
  But wherefore waste I time to counsel thee
  That art a votary to fond desire?
  Once more adieu! my father at the road
  Expects my coming, there to see me shipp'd.
PROTEUS. And thither will I bring thee, Valentine.
VALENTINE. Sweet Proteus, no; now let us take our leave.
  To Milan let me hear from thee by letters
  Of thy success in love, and what news else
  Betideth here in absence of thy friend;
  And I likewise will visit thee with mine.
PROTEUS. All happiness bechance to thee in Milan!
VALENTINE. As much to you at home! and so, farewell. *Exit*
PROTEUS. He after honour hunts, I after love:
  He leaves his friends to dignify them more;

I leave myself, my friends and all, for love.
Thou, Julia, thou hast metamorphos'd me;—
Made me neglect my studies, lose my time,
War with good counsel, set the world at nought;
Made wit with musing weak, heart sick with thought.

Enter Speed

SPEED. Sir Proteus, save you! Saw you my master?

PROTEUS. But now he parted hence, to embark for Milan.

SPEED. Twenty to one, then, he is shipp'd already,
And I have play'd the sheep, in losing him.

PROTEUS. Indeed, a sheep doth very often stray,
An if the shepherd be a while away.

SPEED. You conclude that my master is a shepherd, then,
and I a sheep?

PROTEUS. I do.

SPEED. Why then my horns are his horns, whether I wake
or sleep.

PROTEUS. A silly answer, and fitting well a sheep.

SPEED. This proves me still a sheep.

PROTEUS. True, and thy master a shepherd.

SPEED. Nay, that I can deny by a circumstance.

PROTEUS. It shall go hard but I 'll prove it by another.

SPEED. The shepherd seeks the sheep, and not the sheep
the shepherd; but I seek my master, and my master seeks
not me: therefore I am no sheep.

PROTEUS. The sheep for fodder follow the shepherd, the
shepherd for food follows not the sheep; thou for wages
followest thy master, thy master for wages follows not
thee: therefore thou art a sheep.

SPEED. Such another proof will make me cry 'baa.'

PROTEUS. But, dost thou hear? gavest thou my letter to
Julia?

SPEED. Ay, sir: I, a lost mutton, gave your letter to her, a
laced mutton; and she, a laced mutton, gave me, a lost
mutton, nothing for my labour.

PROTEUS. Here 's too small a pasture for such store of mut-
tons.

SPEED. If the ground be overcharged, you were best stick
her.

PROTEUS. Nay, in that you are astray; 'twere best pound you.

SPEED. Nay, sir, less than a pound shall serve me for carrying your letter.

PROTEUS. You mistake: I mean the pound,—a pinfold.

SPEED. From a pound to a pin? fold it over and over,
  'Tis threefold too little for carrying a letter to your lover.

PROTEUS. But what said she? (*Speed nods*) Did she nod?

SPEED. Ay.

PROTEUS. Nod, ay? why, that 's noddy.

SPEED. You mistook, sir: I say she did nod; and you ask me
  if she did nod; and I say, Ay.

PROTEUS. And that set together is—noddy.

SPEED. Now you have taken the pains to set it together,
  take it for your pains.

PROTEUS. No, no; you shall have it for bearing the letter.

SPEED. Well, I perceive I must be fain to bear with you.

PROTEUS. Why, sir, how do you bear with me?

SPEED. Marry, sir, the letter very orderly; having nothing
  but the word 'noddy' for my pains.

PROTEUS. Beshrew me, but you have a quick wit.

SPEED. And yet it cannot overtake your slow purse.

PROTEUS. Come, come; open the matter in brief: what said
  she?

SPEED. Open your purse, that the money and the matter
  may be both at once delivered.

PROTEUS. Well, sir, here is for your pains (*Giving him money*)
  What said she?

SPEED. Truly, sir, I think you'll hardly win her.

PROTEUS. Why? couldst thou perceive so much from her?

SPEED. Sir, I could perceive nothing at all from her; no, not
  so much as a ducat for delivering your letter. And being
  so hard to me that brought your mind, I fear she 'll prove
  as hard to you in telling your mind. Give her no token
  but stones, for she 's as hard as steel.

PROTEUS. What! said she nothing?

SPEED. No, not so much as 'Take this for thy pains.' To tes-
  tify your bounty, I thank you, you have testerned me; in
  requital whereof, henceforth carry your letters yourself.
  And so, sir, I 'll commend you to my master.

PROTEUS. Go, go, be gone, to save your ship from wrack;
  Which cannot perish, having thee aboard,
  Being destin'd to a drier death on shore.—   *Exit Speed*
  I must go send some better messenger:
  I fear my Julia would not deign my lines,
  Receiving them from such a worthless post.   *Exit*

SCENE TWO

Verona. The Garden of Julia's House.

Enter Julia and Lucetta

JULIA. But say, Lucetta, now we are alone,
Wouldst thou then counsel me to fall in love?
LUCETTA. Ay, madam, so you stumble not unheedfully.
JULIA. Of all the fair resort of gentlemen
That every day with parle encounter me,
In thy opinion which is worthiest love?
LUCETTA. Please you repeat their names, I'll show my mind
According to my shallow simple skill.
JULIA. What think'st thou of the fair Sir Eglamour?
LUCETTA. As of a knight well-spoken, neat and fine;
But, were I you, he never should be mine.
JULIA. What think'st thou of the rich Mercatio?
LUCETTA. Well of his wealth; but of himself, so so.
JULIA. What think'st thou of the gentle Proteus?
LUCETTA. Lord, Lord! to see what folly reigns in us!
JULIA. How now! what means this passion at his name?
LUCETTA. Pardon, dear madam; 'tis a passing shame
That I, unworthy body as I am,
Should censure thus on lovely gentlemen.
JULIA. Why not on Proteus, as of all the rest?
LUCETTA. Then thus,—of many good I think him best.
JULIA. Your reason?
LUCETTA. I have no other but a woman's reason:
I think him so because I think him so.
JULIA. And wouldst thou have me cast my love on him?
LUCETTA. Ay, if you thought your love not cast away.
JULIA. Why, he, of all the rest hath never moved me.
LUCETTA. Yet he of all the rest, I think, best loves ye.
JULIA. His little speaking shows his love but small.
LUCETTA. Fire that's closest kept burns most of all.
JULIA. They do not love that do not show their love.
LUCETTA. O! they love least that let men know their love.
JULIA. I would I knew his mind.
LUCETTA.   Peruse this paper, madam.
                                          Gives a letter

JULIA. 'To Julia.'—Say from whom?

LUCETTA.   That the contents will show.

JULIA. Say, say, who gave it thee?

LUCETTA. Sir Valentine's page, and sent, I think, from Pro-
    teus.

He would have given it you, but I, being in the way,
Did in your name receive it; pardon the fault, I pray.

JULIA. Now, by my modesty, a goodly broker!
Dare you presume to harbour wanton lines?
To whisper and conspire against my youth?
Now, trust me, 'tis an office of great worth
And you an officer fit for the place.
There, take the paper: see it be return'd;
Or else return no more into my sight.

LUCETTA. To plead for love deserves more fee than hate.

JULIA. Will ye be gone?

LUCETTA.   That you may ruminate.   *Exit*

JULIA. And yet I would I had o'erlook'd the letter.
It were a shame to call her back again
And pray her to a fault for which I chid her.
What fool is she, that knows I am a maid,
And would not force the letter to my view!
Since maids, in modesty, say 'No' to that
Which they would have the profferer construe 'Ay.'
Fie, fie! how wayward is this foolish love
That, like a testy babe, will scratch the nurse
And presently all humbled kiss the rod!
How churlishly I chid Lucetta hence,
When willingly I would have had her here:
How angerly I taught my brow to frown,
When inward joy enforc'd my heart to smile.
My penance is, to call Lucetta back
And ask remission for my folly past.
What ho! Lucetta!

Re-enter Lucetta

LUCETTA.   What would your ladyship?

JULIA. Is it near dinner-time?

LUCETTA.   I would it were;
That you might kill your stomach on your meat
And not upon your maid.

JULIA. What is 't that you took up so gingerly?

LUCETTA. Nothing.

JULIA. Why didst thou stoop, then?
LUCETTA.   To take a paper up
  That I let fall.
JULIA.   And is that paper nothing?
LUCETTA. Nothing concerning me.
JULIA. Then let it lie for those that it concerns.
LUCETTA. Madam, it will not lie where it concerns,
  Unless it have a false interpreter.
JULIA. Some love of yours hath writ to you in rime.
LUCETTA. That I might sing it, madam, to a tune:
  Give me a note: your ladyship can set.
JULIA. As little by such toys as may be possible;
  Best sing it to the tune of 'Light o' Love.'
LUCETTA. It is too heavy for so light a tune.
JULIA. Heavy! belike it hath some burden, then?
LUCETTA. Ay; and melodious were it, would you sing it.
JULIA. And why not you?
LUCETTA.   I cannot reach so high.
JULIA. Let 's see your song. (*Taking the letter*) How now,
  minion!
LUCETTA. Keep tune there still, so you will sing it out:
  And yet methinks, I do not like this tune.
JULIA. You do not?
LUCETTA.   No, madam; it is too sharp.
JULIA. You, minion, are too saucy.
LUCETTA. Nay, now you are too flat
  And mar the concord with too harsh a descant:
  There wanteth but a mean to fill your song.
JULIA. The mean is drown'd with your unruly bass.
LUCETTA. Indeed, I bid the base for Proteus.
JULIA. This babble shall not henceforth trouble me.
  Here is a coil with protestation!—*Tears the letter*
  Go, get you gone, and let the papers lie:
  You would be fingering them, to anger me.
LUCETTA. She makes it strange; but she would be best
    pleas'd
  To be so anger'd with another letter.   *Exit*
JULIA. Nay, would I were so anger'd with the same!
  O hateful hands, to tear such loving words!
  Injurious wasps, to feed on such sweet honey
  And kill the bees that yield it with your stings!
  I 'll kiss each several paper for amends.

Look, here is writ 'kind Julia': unkind Julia!
As in revenge of thy ingratitude,
I throw thy name against the bruising stones,
Trampling contemptuously on thy disdain.
And here is writ 'love-wounded Proteus':
Poor wounded name! my bosom, as a bed
Shall lodge thee till thy wound be thoroughly heal'd;
And thus I search it with a sovereign kiss.
But twice or thrice was 'Proteus' written down:
Be calm, good wind, blow not a word away
Till I have found each letter in the letter
Except mine own name; that some whirlwind bear
Unto a ragged, fearful-hanging rock,
And throw it thence into the raging sea!
Lo! here in one line is his name twice writ,
'Poor forlorn Proteus, passionate Proteus,
To the sweet Julia':—that I 'll tear away;
And yet I will not, sith so prettily
He couples it to his complaining names:
Thus will I fold them one upon another:
Now kiss, embrace, contend, do what you will.

Re-enter Lucetta

LUCETTA. Madam,
Dinner is ready, and your father stays.
JULIA. Well, let us go.
LUCETTA. What! shall these papers lie like tell-tales here?
JULIA. If you respect them, best to take them up.
LUCETTA. Nay, I was taken up for laying them down;
Yet here they shall not lie, for catching cold.
JULIA. I see you have a month's mind to them.
LUCETTA. Ay, madam, you may say what sights you see;
I see things too, although you judge I wink.
JULIA. Come, come; will 't please you go?   *Exeunt*

SCENE THREE

Verona. A Room in Antonio's House.

Enter Antonio and Panthino

ANTONIO. Tell me, Panthino, what sad talk was that
　Wherewith my brother held you in the cloister?
PANTHINO. 'Twas of his nephew Proteus, your son.
ANTONIO. Why, what of him?
PANTHINO. 　　　　　　　He wonder'd that your lordship
　Would suffer him to spend his youth at home,
　While other men, of slender reputation,
　Put forth their sons to seek preferment out:
　Some to the wars, to try their fortune there;
　Some to discover islands far away;
　Some to the studious universities.
　For any or for all these exercises
　He said that Proteus your son was meet,
　And did request me to importune you
　To let him spend his time no more at home,
　Which would be great impeachment to his age,
　In having known no travel in his youth.
ANTONIO. Nor need'st thou much importune me to that
　Whereon this month I have been hammering.
　I have consider'd well his loss of time,
　And how he cannot be a perfect man,
　Not being tried and tutor'd in the world:
　Experience is by industry achiev'd
　And perfected by the swift course of time.
　Then tell me, whither were I best to send him?
PANTHINO. I think your lordship is not ignorant
　How his companion, youthful Valentine,
　Attends the emperor in his royal court.
ANTONIO. I know it well.
PANTHINO. 'Twere good, I think, your lordship sent him
　　　thither:
　There shall he practise tilts and tournaments,
　Hear sweet discourse, converse with noblemen,
　And be in eye of every exercise
　Worthy his youth and nobleness of birth.

ANTONIO. I like thy counsel; well hast thou advis'd:
  And that thou mayst perceive how well I like it
  The execution of it shall make known.
  Even with the speediest expedition
  I will dispatch him to the emperor's court.
PANTHINO. To-morrow, may it please you, Don Alphonso
  With other gentlemen of good esteem,
  Are journeying to salute the emperor
  And to commend their service to his will.
ANTONIO. Good company; with them shall Proteus go:
  And in good time:—now will we break with him.

Enter Proteus

PROTEUS. Sweet love! sweet lines! sweet life!
  Here is her hand, the agent of her heart;
  Here is her oath for love, her honour's pawn.
  O! that our fathers would applaud our loves,
  To seal our happiness with their consents!
  O heavenly Julia!
ANTONIO. How now! what letter are you reading there?
PROTEUS. May 't please your lordship, 'tis a word or two
  Of commendations sent from Valentine,
  Deliver'd by a friend that came from him.
ANTONIO. Lend me the letter; let me see what news.
PROTEUS. There is no news, my lord; but that he writes
  How happily he lives, how well belov'd
  And daily graced by the emperor;
  Wishing me with him, partner of his fortune.
ANTONIO. And how stand you affected to his wish?
PROTEUS. As one relying on your lordship's will
  And not depending on his friendly wish.
ANTONIO. My will is something sorted with his wish.
  Muse not that I thus suddenly proceed;
  For what I will, I will, and there an end.
  I am resolv'd that thou shalt spend some time
  With Valentinus in the emperor's court:
  What maintenance he from his friends receives,
  Like exhibition thou shalt have from me.
  To-morrow be in readiness to go:
  Excuse it not, for I am peremptory.
PROTEUS. My lord, I cannot be so soon provided:
  Please you, deliberate a day or two.
ANTONIO. Look, what thou want'st shall be sent after thee:

No more of stay; to-morrow thou must go.
Come on, Panthino: you shall be employ'd
To hasten on his expedition.
                                    Exeunt Antonio and Panthino

PROTEUS. Thus have I shunn'd the fire for fear of burning,
And drench'd me in the sea, where I am drown'd.
I fear'd to show my father Julia's letter,
Lest he should take exceptions to my love;
And with the vantage of mine own excuse
Hath he excepted most against my love,
O! how this spring of love resembleth
    The uncertain glory of an April day,
Which now shows all the beauty of the sun,
    And by and by a cloud takes all away!
                            Re-enter Panthino

PANTHINO. Sir Proteus, your father calls for you:
He is in haste; therefore, I pray you, go.

PROTEUS. Why, this it is: my heart accords thereto,
And yet a thousand times it answers, 'no.'   *Exeunt*

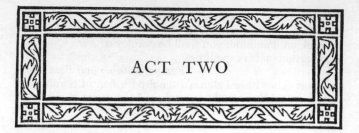

ACT TWO

SCENE ONE

Milan. A Room in the Duke's Palace.

Enter Valentine and Speed

SPEED. Sir, your glove.   *Offering a glove*

VALENTINE.   Not mine; my gloves are on.

SPEED. Why, then this may be yours, for this is but one.

VALENTINE. Ha! let me see: ay, give it me, it 's mine;
  Sweet ornament that decks a thing divine!
  Ah Silvia! Silvia!

SPEED. *(Calling)* Madam Silvia! Madam Silvia!

VALENTINE. How now, sirrah?

SPEED. She is not within hearing, sir.

VALENTINE. Why, sir, who bade you call her?

SPEED. Your worship, sir; or else I mistook.

VALENTINE. Well, you 'll still be too forward.

SPEED. And yet I was last chidden for being too slow.

VALENTINE. Go to, sir. Tell me, do you know Madam Silvia?

SPEED. She that your worship loves?

VALENTINE. Why, how know you that I am in love?

SPEED. Marry, by these special marks: first, you have
learned, like Sir Proteus, to wreathe your arms, like a
malecontent; to relish a love-song, like a robin-redbreast;
to walk alone, like one that had the pestilence; to sigh,
like a schoolboy that had lost his A B C; to weep, like a
young wench that had buried her grandam; to fast, like
one that takes diet; to watch, like one that fears robbing;
to speak puling, like a beggar at Hallowmas. You were
wont, when you laughed, to crow like a cock; when you
walked, to walk like one of the lions; when you fasted, it
was presently after dinner; when you looked sadly, it was
for want of money: and now you are metamorphosed

with a mistress, that, when I look on you, I can hardly
think you my master.

VALENTINE. Are all these things perceived in me?

SPEED. They are all perceived without ye.

VALENTINE. Without me? they cannot.

SPEED. Without you? nay, that 's certain; for, without you
were so simple, none else would: but you are so without
these follies, that these follies are within you and shine
through you like the water in an urinal, that not an eye
that sees you but is a physician to comment on your mal-
ady.

VALENTINE. But tell me, dost thou know my lady Silvia?

SPEED. She that you gaze on so as she sits at supper?

VALENTINE. Hast thou observed that? even she, I mean.

SPEED. Why, sir, I know her not.

VALENTINE. Dost thou know her by my gazing on her, and
yet knowest her not?

SPEED. Is she not hard-favoured, sir?

VALENTINE. Not so fair, boy, as well-favoured.

SPEED. Sir, I know that well enough.

VALENTINE. What dost thou know?

SPEED. That she is not so fair, as, of you, well-favoured.

VALENTINE. I mean that her beauty is exquisite, but her favour infinite.

SPEED. That 's because the one is painted and the other out
of all count.

VALENTINE. How painted? and how out of count?

SPEED. Marry, sir, so painted to make her fair, that no man
counts of her beauty.

VALENTINE. How esteemest thou me? I account of her
beauty.

SPEED. You never saw her since she was deformed.

VALENTINE. How long hath she been deformed?

SPEED. Ever since you loved her.

VALENTINE. I have loved her ever since I saw her, and still
I see her beautiful.

SPEED. If you love her you cannot see her.

VALENTINE. Why?

SPEED. Because Love is blind. O! that you had mine eyes;
or your own eyes had the lights they were wont to have
when you chid at Sir Proteus for going ungartered!

VALENTINE. What should I see then?

SPEED. Your own present folly and her passing deformity:
   for he, being in love, could not see to garter his hose; and
   you, being in love, cannot see to put on your hose.

VALENTINE. Belike, boy, then, you are in love; for last
   morning you could not see to wipe my shoes.

SPEED. True, sir; I was in love with my bed. I thank you,
   you swinged me for my love, which makes me the bolder
   to chide you for yours.

VALENTINE. In conclusion, I stand affected to her.

SPEED. I would you were set, so your affection would cease.

VALENTINE. Last night she enjoined me to write some lines
   to one she loves.

SPEED. And have you.

VALENTINE. I have.

SPEED. Are they not lamely writ?

VALENTINE. No, boy, but as well as I can do them. Peace!
   here she comes.

Enter Silvia

SPEED. (*Aside*) O excellent motion! O exceeding puppet!
   now will he interpret to her.

VALENTINE. Madam and mistress, a thousand good-mor-
   rows.

SPEED. (*Aside*) O! give ye good even: here 's a million of
   manners.

SILVIA. Sir Valentine and servant, to you two thousand.

SPEED. (*Aside*) He should give her interest, and she gives
   it him.

VALENTINE. As you enjoin'd me, I have writ your letter
   Unto the secret nameless friend of yours;
   Which I was much unwilling to proceed in
   But for my duty to your ladyship.   *Gives a letter*

SILVIA. I thank you, gentle servant. 'Tis very clerkly done.

VALENTINE. Now, trust me, madam, it came hardly off;
   For, being ignorant to whom it goes
   I writ at random, very doubtfully.

SILVIA. Perchance you think too much of so much pains?

VALENTINE. No, madam; so it stead you, I will write,
   Please you command, a thousand times as much.
   And yet—

SILVIA. A pretty period! Well, I guess the sequel;
   And yet I will not name it; and yet I care not;
   And yet take this again; and yet I thank you,

Meaning henceforth to trouble you no more.

SPEED. (*Aside*) And yet you will; and yet another yet.

VALENTINE. What means your ladyship? do you not like it?

SILVIA. Yes, yes: the lines are very quaintly writ,
But since unwillingly, take them again:
Nay, take them.   *Gives back the letter*

VALENTINE.   Madam, they are for you.

SILVIA. Ay, ay; you writ them, sir, at my request,
But I will none of them; they are for you.
I would have had them writ more movingly.

VALENTINE. Please you, I 'll write your ladyship another.

SILVIA. And when it 's writ, for my sake read it over:
And if it please you, so; if not, why, so.

VALENTINE. If it please me, madam, what then?

SILVIA. Why, if it please you, take it for your labour:
And so, good-morrow, servant.   *Exit*

SPEED. (*Aside*) O jest unseen, inscrutable, invisible
As a nose on a man's face, or a weathercock on a steeple!
My master sues to her, and she hath taught her suitor,
He being her pupil, to become her tutor.
O excellent device! was there ever heard a better,
That my master, being scribe, to himself should write the
    letter?

VALENTINE. How now, sir! what are you reasoning with
    yourself?

SPEED. Nay, I was riming: 'tis you that have the reason.

VALENTINE. To do what?

SPEED. To be a spokesman from Madam Silvia.

VALENTINE. To whom?

SPEED. To yourself. Why, she wooes you by a figure.

VALENTINE. What figure?

SPEED. By a letter, I should say.

VALENTINE. Why, she hath not writ to me?

SPEED. What need she, when she hath made you write to
    yourself? Why, do you not perceive the jest?

VALENTINE. No, believe me.

SPEED. No believing you, indeed, sir. But did you perceive
    her earnest?

VALENTINE. She gave me none, except an angry word.

SPEED. Why, she hath given you a letter.

VALENTINE. That 's the letter I writ to her friend.

SPEED. And that letter hath she delivered, and there an end.

VALENTINE. I would it were no worse.

SPEED. I 'll warrant you, 'tis as well:

'For often have you writ to her, and she, in modesty,
Or else for want·of idle time, could not again reply;
Or fearing else some messenger that might her mind dis-
cover,
Herself hath taught her love himself to write unto her
lover.'
All this I speak in print, for in print I found it.
Why muse you, sir? 'tis dinner-time.

VALENTINE. I have dined.

SPEED. Ay, but hearken, sir: though the chameleon Love
can feed on the air, I am one that am nourished by my
victuals and would fain have meat. O! be not like your
mistress: be moved, be moved. *Exeunt*

SCENE TWO

Verona. A Room in Julia's House.

Enter Proteus and Julia

PROTEUS. Have patience, gentle Julia.

JULIA. I must, where is no remedy.

PROTEUS. When possibly I can, I will return.

JULIA. If you turn not, you will return the sooner.
Keep this remembrance for thy Julia's sake.

Gives him a ring

PROTEUS. Why, then, we 'll make exchange: here, take you
this. *Gives her another*

JULIA. And seal the bargain with a holy kiss.

PROTEUS. Here is my hand for my true constancy;
And when that hour o'erslips me in the day
Wherein I sigh not, Julia, for thy sake,
The next ensuing hour some foul mischance
Torment me for my love's forgetfulness!
My father stays my coming; answer not.
The tide is now: nay, not thy tide of tears;
That tide will stay me longer than I should.
Julia, farewell. *Exit Julia*
What! gone without a word?

Ay, so true love should do: it cannot speak;
For truth hath better deeds than words to grace it.

Enter Panthino

PANTHINO. Sir Proteus, you are stay'd for.

PROTEUS.   Go; I come, I come.
Alas! this parting strikes poor lovers dumb.   *Exeunt*

SCENE THREE

Verona. A Street.

Enter Launce, leading a dog

LAUNCE. Nay, 'twill be this hour ere I have done weeping:
all the kind of the Launces have this very fault. I have
received my proportion, like the prodigious son, and am
going with Sir Proteus to the imperial's court. I think
Crab my dog be the sourest-natured dog that lives: my
mother weeping, my father wailing, my sister crying, our
maid howling, our cat wringing her hands, and all our
house in a great perplexity, yet did not this cruel-hearted
cur shed one tear. He is a stone, a very pebble stone, and
has no more pity in him than a dog; a Jew would have
wept to have seen our parting: why, my grandam, having no eyes, look you, wept herself blind at my parting.
Nay, I 'll show you the manner of it. This shoe is my
father; no, this left shoe is my father: no, no, this left
shoe is my mother; nay, that cannot be so neither:—yes,
it is so; it is so; it hath the worser sole. This shoe, with
the hole in, is my mother, and this is my father. A vengeance on 't! there 'tis: now, sir, this staff is my sister;
for, look you, she is as white as a lily and as small as a
wand: this hat is Nan, our maid: I am the dog; no, the
dog is himself, and I am the dog,—O! the dog is me, and
I am myself: ay, so, so. Now come I to my father;
'Father, your blessing'; now should not the shoe speak a
word for weeping: now should I kiss my father; well, he
weeps on. Now come I to my mother;—O, that she could
speak now like a wood woman! Well, I kiss her; why,
there 'tis; here 's my mother's breath up and down. Now
come I to my sister; mark the moan she makes: Now the

dog all this while sheds not a tear nor speaks a word; but see how I lay the dust with my tears.

Enter Panthino

PANTHINO. Launce, away, away, aboard! thy master is shipped, and thou art to post after with oars. What 's the matter? why weepest thou, man? Away, ass! you 'll lose the tide if you tarry any longer.

LAUNCE. It is no matter if the tied were lost; for it is the unkindest tied that ever any man tied.

PANTHINO. What 's the unkindest tide?

LAUNCE. Why, he that 's tied here, Crab, my dog.

PANTHINO. Tut, man, I mean thou 'lt lose the flood; and, in losing the flood, lose thy voyage, and, in losing thy voyage, lose thy master; and, in losing thy master, lose thy service; and, in losing thy service—Why dost thou stop my mouth?

LAUNCE. For fear thou shouldst lose thy tongue.

PANTHINO. Where should I lose my tongue?

LAUNCE. In thy tale.

PANTHINO. In thy tail!

LAUNCE. Lose the tide, and the voyage, and the master, and the service, and the tied! Why, man, if the river were dry, I am able to fill it with my tears; if the wind were down, I could drive the boat with my sighs.

PANTHINO. Come, come away, man; I was sent to call thee.

LAUNCE. Sir, call me what thou darest.

PANTHINO. Wilt thou go?

LAUNCE. Well, I will go.   *Exeunt*

SCENE FOUR

Milan. A Room in the Duke's Palace.

Enter Valentine, Silvia, Thurio, and Speed

SILVIA. Servant!

VALENTINE. Mistress?

SPEED. Master, Sir Thurio frowns on you.

VALENTINE. Ay, boy, it 's for love.

SPEED. Not of you.

VALENTINE. Of my mistress, then.

SPEED. 'Twere good you knock'd him.

SILVIA. Servant, you are sad.

VALENTINE. Indeed, madam, I seem so.

THURIO. Seem you that you are not?

VALENTINE. Haply I do.

THURIO. So do counterfeits.

VALENTINE. So do you.

THURIO. What seem I that I am not?

VALENTINE. Wise.

THURIO. What instance of the contrary?

VALENTINE. Your folly.

THURIO. And how quote you my folly?

VALENTINE. I quote it in your jerkin.

THURIO. My jerkin is a doublet.

VALENTINE. Well, then, I 'll double your folly.

THURIO. How?

SILVIA. What, angry, Sir Thurio! do you change colour?

VALENTINE. Give him leave, madam; he is a kind of chameleon.

THURIO. That hath more mind to feed on your blood than live in your air.

VALENTINE. You have said, sir.

THURIO. Ay, sir, and done too, for this time.

VALENTINE. I know it well, sir: you always end ere you begin.

SILVIA. A fine volley of words, gentlemen, and quickly shot off.

VALENTINE. 'Tis indeed, madam; we thank the giver.

SILVIA. Who is that, servant?

VALENTINE. Yourself, sweet lady; for you gave the fire. Sir Thurio borrows his wit from your ladyship's looks, and spends what he borrows kindly in your company.

THURIO. Sir, if you spend word for word with me, I shall make your wit bankrupt.

VALENTINE. I know it well, sir: you have an exchequer of words, and, I think, no other treasure to give your followers; for it appears by their bare liveries that they live by your bare words.

SILVIA. No more, gentlemen, no more. Here comes my father.

Enter Duke

DUKE. Now, daughter Silvia, you are hard beset.
Sir Valentine, your father 's in good health:

What say you to a letter from your friends
Of much good news?

VALENTINE.   My lord, I will be thankful
To any happy messenger from thence.

DUKE. Know ye Don Antonio, your countryman?

VALENTINE. Ay, my good lord; I know the gentleman
To be of worth and worthy estimation,
And not without desert so well reputed.

DUKE. Hath he not a son?

VALENTINE. Ay, my good lord; a son that well deserves
The honour and regard of such a father.

DUKE. You know him well?

VALENTINE. I know him as myself; for from our infancy
We have convers'd and spent our hours together:
And though myself have been an idle truant,
Omitting the sweet benefit of time
To clothe mine age with angel-like perfection,
Yet hath Sir Proteus,—for that 's his name,—
Made use and fair advantage of his days:
His years but young, but his experience old;
His head unmellow'd, but his judgment ripe;
And, in a word,—for far behind his worth
Come all the praises that I now bestow,—
He is complete in feature and in mind
With all good grace to grace a gentleman.

DUKE. Beshrew me, sir, but if he make this good,
He is as worthy for an empress' love
As meet to be an emperor's counsellor.
Well, sir, this gentleman is come to me
With commendation from great potentates;
And here he means to spend his time a while:
I think, 'tis no unwelcome news to you.

VALENTINE. Should I have wish'd a thing, it had been he.

DUKE. Welcome him then according to his worth.
Silvia, I speak to you; and you, Sir Thurio:—
For Valentine, I need not cite him to it.
I 'll send him hither to you presently.   *Exit*

VALENTINE. This is the gentleman I told your ladyship
Had come along with me, but that his mistress
Did hold his eyes lock'd in her crystal looks.

SILVIA. Belike that now she hath enfranchis'd them
Upon some other pawn for fealty.

VALENTINE. Nay, sure, I think she holds them prisoners still.

SILVIA. Nay, then he should be blind; and, being blind,
How could he see his way to seek out you?

VALENTINE. Why, lady, Love hath twenty pairs of eyes.

THURIO. They say that Love hath not an eye at all.

VALENTINE. To see such lovers, Thurio, as yourself:
Upon a homely object Love can wink.

SILVIA. Have done, have done. Here comes the gentleman.

Enter Proteus

VALENTINE. Welcome, dear Proteus! Mistress, I beseech you,
Confirm his welcome with some special favour.

SILVIA. His worth is warrant for his welcome hither,
If this be he you oft have wish'd to hear from.

VALENTINE. Mistress, it is: sweet lady, entertain him
To be my fellow-servant to your ladyship.

SILVIA. Too low a mistress for so high a servant.

PROTEUS. Not so, sweet lady; but too mean a servant
To have a look of such a worthy mistress.

VALENTINE. Leave off discourse of disability:
Sweet lady, entertain him for your servant.

PROTEUS. My duty will I boast of, nothing else.

SILVIA. And duty never yet did want his meed.
Servant, you are welcome to a worthless mistress.

PROTEUS. I 'll die on him that says so but yourself.

SILVIA. That you are welcome?

PROTEUS.   That you are worthless.

Enter a Servant

SERVANT. Madam, my lord your father would speak with you.

SILVIA. I wait upon his pleasure. (*Exit Servant*) Come, Sir Thurio,
Go with me. Once more, new servant, welcome:
I 'll leave you to confer of home-affairs;
When you have done, we look to hear from you.

PROTEUS. We 'll both attend upon your ladyship.

Exeunt Silvia, Thurio, and Speed

VALENTINE. Now, tell me, how do all from whence you came?

PROTEUS. Your friends are well and have them much commended.

VALENTINE. And how do yours?

PROTEUS.   I left them all in health.

VALENTINE. How does your lady and how thrives your
    love?

PROTEUS. My tales of love were wont to weary you;
    I know you joy not in a love-discourse.

VALENTINE. Ay, Proteus, but that life is alter'd now:
    I have done penance for contemning love;
    Whose high imperious thoughts have punish'd me
    With bitter fasts, with penitential groans,
    With nightly tears and daily heart-sore sighs;
    For, in revenge of my contempt of love,
    Love hath chas'd sleep from my enthralled eyes,
    And made them watchers of mine own heart's sorrow.
    O, gentle Proteus! Love 's a mighty lord,
    And hath so humbled me as I confess,
    There is no woe to his correction,
    Nor to his service no such joy on earth.
    Now no discourse, except it be of love;
    Now can I break my fast, dine, sup and sleep,
    Upon the very naked name of love.

PROTEUS. Enough; I read your fortune in your eye.
    Was this the idol that you worship so?

VALENTINE. Even she; and is she not a heavenly saint?

PROTEUS. No; but she is an earthly paragon.

VALENTINE. Call her divine.

PROTEUS.   I will not flatter her.

VALENTINE. O! flatter me, for love delights in praises.

PROTEUS. When I was sick you gave me bitter pills,
    And I must minister the like to you.

VALENTINE. Then speak the truth by her; if not divine,
    Yet let her be a principality,
    Sovereign to all the creatures on the earth.

PROTEUS. Except my mistress.

VALENTINE.   Sweet, except not any,
    Except thou wilt except against my love.

PROTEUS. Have I not reason to prefer mine own?

VALENTINE. And I will help thee to prefer her too:
    She shall be dignified with this high honour,—
    To bear my lady's train, lest the base earth
    Should from her vesture chance to steal a kiss,
    And, of so great a favour growing proud,

Disdain to root the summer-swelling flower,
And make rough winter everlastingly.

PROTEUS. Why, Valentine, what braggardism is this?

VALENTINE. Pardon me, Proteus: all I can is nothing
To her whose worth makes other worthies nothing.
She is alone.

PROTEUS. Then, let her alone.

VALENTINE. Not for the world: why, man, she is mine own,
And I as rich in having such a jewel
As twenty seas, if all their sand were pearl,
The water nectar, and the rocks pure gold.
Forgive me that I do not dream on thee,
Because thou see'st me dote upon my love.
My foolish rival, that her father likes
Only for his possessions are so huge,
Is gone with her along, and I must after,
For love, thou know'st, is full of jealousy.

PROTEUS. But she loves you?

VALENTINE. Ay, and we are betroth'd: nay, more, our mar-
riage-hour,
With all the cunning manner of our flight,
Determin'd of: how I must climb her window,
The ladder made of cords, and all the means
Plotted and 'greed on for my happiness.
Good Proteus, go with me to my chamber,
In these affairs to aid me with thy counsel.

PROTEUS. Go on before; I shall inquire you forth:
I must unto the road, to disembark
Some necessaries that I needs must use,
And then I 'll presently attend you.

VALENTINE. Will you make haste?

PROTEUS. I will.   *Exit Valentine*

Even as one heat another heat expels,
Or as one nail by strength drives out another,
So the remembrance of my former love
Is by a newer object quite forgotten.
Is it mine eye, or Valentinus' praise,
Her true perfection, or my false transgression,
That makes me reasonless to reason thus?
She 's fair; and so is Julia that I love,—
That I did love, for now my love is thaw'd,
Which, like a waxen image 'gainst a fire,

Bears no impression of the thing it was.
Methinks my zeal to Valentine is cold,
And that I love him not as I was wont:
O! but I love his lady too-too much;
And that 's the reason I love him so little.
How shall I dote on her with more advice,
That thus without advice begin to love her?
'Tis but her picture I have yet beheld,
And that hath dazzled my reason's light;
But when I look on her perfections,
There is no reason but I shall be blind.
If I can check my erring love, I will;
If not, to compass her I 'll use my skill.   *Exit*

SCENE FIVE

Milan. A Street.

Enter Speed and Launce

SPEED. Launce! by mine honesty, welcome to Milan!

LAUNCE. Forswear not thyself, sweet youth, for I am not welcome. I reckon this always that a man is never undone till he be hanged; nor never welcome to a place till some certain shot be paid and the hostess say, 'Welcome!'

SPEED. Come on, you madcap, I 'll to the alehouse with you presently; where, for one shot of five pence, thou shalt have five thousand welcomes. But, sirrah, how did thy master part with Madam Julia?

LAUNCE. Marry, after they closed in earnest, they parted very fairly in jest.

SPEED. But shall she marry him?

LAUNCE. No.

SPEED. How then? Shall he marry her?

LAUNCE. No, neither.

SPEED. What, are they broken?

LAUNCE. No, they are both as whole as a fish.

SPEED. Why then, how stands the matter with them?

LAUNCE. Marry, thus; when it stands well with him, it stands well with her.

SPEED. What an ass art thou! I understand thee not.

LAUNCE. What a block art thou, that thou canst not! My staff understands me.

SPEED. What thou sayest?

LAUNCE. Ay, and what I do too: look thee, I 'll but lean, and my staff understands me.

SPEED. It stands under thee, indeed.

LAUNCE. Why, stand-under and under-stand is all one.

SPEED. But tell me true, will 't be a match?

LAUNCE. Ask my dog: if he say ay, it will; if he say no, it will; if he shake his tail and say nothing, it will.

SPEED. The conclusion is, then, that it will.

LAUNCE. Thou shalt never get such a secret from me but by a parable.

SPEED. 'Tis well that I get it so. But, Launce, how sayest thou, that my master is become a notable lover?

LAUNCE. I never knew him otherwise.

SPEED. Than how?

LAUNCE. A notable lubber, as thou reportest him to be.

SPEED. Why, thou whoreson ass, thou mistakest me.

LAUNCE. Why, fool, I meant not thee; I meant thy master.

SPEED. I tell thee, my master is become a hot lover.

LAUNCE. Why, I tell thee, I care not though he burn himself in love. If thou wilt go with me to the alehouse so; if not, thou art a Hebrew, a Jew, and not worth the name of a Christian.

SPEED. Why?

LAUNCE. Because thou hast not so much charity in thee as to go to the ale with a Christian. Wilt thou go?

SPEED. At thy service.   *Exeunt*

SCENE SIX

Milan. A Room in the Duke's Palace.

Enter Proteus

PROTEUS. To leave my Julia, shall I be forsworn;
To love fair Silvia, shall I be forsworn;
To wrong my friend, I shall be much forsworn;
And even that power which gave me first my oath
Provokes me to this threefold perjury:
Love bade me swear, and Love bids me forswear.

O sweet-suggesting Love! if thou hast sinn'd,
Teach me, thy tempted subject, to excuse it.
At first I did adore a twinkling star,
But now I worship a celestial sun.
Unheedful vows may heedfully be broken;
And he wants wit that wants resolved will
To learn his wit to exchange the bad for better.
Fie, fie, unreverend tongue! to call her bad,
Whose sovereignty so oft thou hast preferr'd
With twenty thousand soul-confirming oaths.
I cannot leave to love, and yet I do;
But there I leave to love where I should love.
Julia I lose and Valentine I lose:
If I keep them, I needs must lose myself;
If I lose them, thus find I by their loss,
For Valentine, myself; for Julia, Silvia.
I to myself am dearer than a friend,
For love is still most precious in itself;
And Silvia—witness heaven that made her fair!—
Shows Julia but a swarthy Ethiope.
I will forget that Julia is alive,
Remembering that my love to her is dead;
And Valentine I'll hold an enemy,
Aiming at Silvia as a sweeter friend.
I cannot now prove constant to myself
Without some treachery us'd to Valentine:
This night he meaneth with a corded ladder
To climb celestial Silvia's chamber-window,
Myself in counsel, his competitor.
Now presently, I'll give her father notice
Of their disguising and pretended flight;
Who, all enrag'd, will banish Valentine;
For Thurio, he intends, shall wed his daughter;
But, Valentine being gone, I'll quickly cross,
By some sly trick blunt Thurio's dull proceeding.
Love, lend me wings to make my purpose swift,
As thou hast lent me wit to plot this drift!   *Exit*

SCENE SEVEN

Verona. A Room in Julia's House.

Enter Julia and Lucetta

JULIA. Counsel, Lucetta; gentle girl, assist me:
And e'en in kind love I do conjure thee,
Who art the table wherein all my thoughts
Are visibly character'd and engrav'd,
To lesson me and tell me some good mean
How, with my honour, I may undertake
A journey to my loving Proteus.

LUCETTA. Alas! the way is wearisome and long.

JULIA. A true-devoted pilgrim is not weary
To measure kingdoms with his feeble steps;
Much less shall she that hath Love's wings to fly,
And when the flight is made to one so dear,
Of such divine perfection, as Sir Proteus.

LUCETTA. Better forbear till Proteus make return.

JULIA. O! know'st thou not his looks are my soul's food?
Pity the dearth that I have pined in,
By longing for that food so long a time.
Didst thou but know the inly touch of love,
Thou wouldst as soon go kindle fire with snow
As seek to quench the fire of love with words.

LUCETTA. I do not seek to quench your love's hot fire,
But qualify the fire's extreme rage,
Lest it should burn above the bounds of reason.

JULIA. The more thou damm'st it up, the more it burns.
The current that with gentle murmur glides,
Thou know'st, being stopp'd, impatiently doth rage;
But when his fair course is not hindered,
He makes sweet music with th' enamell'd stones,
Giving a gentle kiss to every sedge
He overtaketh in his pilgrimage;
And so by many winding nooks he strays
With willing sport, to the wild ocean.
Then let me go and hinder not my course:
I 'll be as patient as a gentle stream
And make a pastime of each weary step,

Till the last step have brought me to my love;
And there I 'll rest, as after much turmoil
A blessed soul doth in Elysium.

LUCETTA. But in what habit will you go along?

JULIA. Not like a woman; for I would prevent
The loose encounters of lascivious men.
Gentle Lucetta, fit me with such weeds
As may beseem some well-reputed page.

LUCETTA. Why, then, your ladyship must cut your hair.

JULIA. No, girl; I 'll knit it up in silken strings
With twenty odd-conceited true-love knots:
To be fantastic may become a youth
Of greater time than I shall show to be.

LUCETTA. What fashion, madam, shall I make your
breeches?

JULIA. That fits as well as 'Tell me, good my lord,
What compass will you wear your farthingale?'
Why, even what fashion thou best lik'st, Lucetta.

LUCETTA. You must needs have them with a cod-piece,
madam.

JULIA. Out, out, Lucetta! that will be ill-favour'd.

LUCETTA. A round hose, madam, now 's not worth a pin,
Unless you have a cod-piece to stick pins on.

JULIA. Lucetta, as thou lov'st me, let me have
What thou think'st meet and is most mannerly.
But tell me, wench, how will the world repute me
For undertaking so unstaid a journey?
I fear me, it will make me scandaliz'd.

LUCETTA. If you think so, then stay at home and go not.

JULIA. Nay, that I will not.

LUCETTA. Then never dream on infamy, but go.
If Proteus like your journey when you come,
No matter who 's displeas'd when you are gone.
I fear me, he will scarce be pleas'd withal.

JULIA. That is the least, Lucetta, of my fear:
A thousand oaths, an ocean of his tears,
And instances of infinite of love
Warrant me welcome to my Proteus.

LUCETTA. All these are servants to deceitful men.

JULIA. Base men, that use them to so base effect;
But truer stars did govern Proteus' birth:
His words are bonds, his oaths are oracles,

His love sincere, his thoughts immaculate,
His tears pure messengers sent from his heart,
His heart as far from fraud as heaven from earth.

LUCETTA. Pray heaven he prove so when you come to him!

JULIA. Now, as thou lov'st me, do him not that wrong
To bear a hard opinion of his truth:
Only deserve my love by loving him,
And presently go with me to my chamber,
To take a note of what I stand in need of
To furnish me upon my longing journey.
All that is mine I leave at thy dispose,
My goods, my lands, my reputation;
Only, in lieu thereof, dispatch me hence.
Come, answer not, but to it presently!
I am impatient of my tarriance.   *Exeunt*

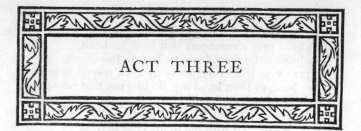

ACT THREE

Milan. An anteroom in the Duke's Palace.

Enter Duke, Thurio, and Proteus

DUKE. Sir Thurio, give us leave, I pray, awhile;
We have some secrets to confer about.   *Exit Thurio*
Now tell me, Proteus, what 's your will with me?

PROTEUS. My gracious lord, that which I would discover
The law of friendship bids me to conceal;
But when I call to mind your gracious favours
Done to me, undeserving as I am,
My duty pricks me on to utter that
Which else no worldly good should draw from me.
Know, worthy prince, Sir Valentine, my friend,
This night intends to steal away your daughter:
Myself am one made privy to the plot.
I know you have determin'd to bestow her
On Thurio, whom your gentle daughter hates;
And should she thus be stol'n away from you
It would be much vexation to your age.
Thus, for my duty's sake, I rather chose
To cross my friend in his intended drift,
Than, by concealing it, heap on your head
A pack of sorrows which would press you down,
Being unprevented, to your timeless grave.

DUKE. Proteus, I thank thee for thine honest care,
Which to requite, command me while I live.
This love of theirs myself have often seen,
Haply, when they have judg'd me fast asleep,
And oftentimes have purpos'd to forbid
Sir Valentine her company and my court;
But fearing lest my jealous aim might err
And so unworthily disgrace the man,—

A rashness that I ever yet have shunn'd,—
I gave him gentle looks, thereby to find
That which thyself hast now disclos'd to me.
And, that thou mayst perceive my fear of this,
Knowing that tender youth is soon suggested,
I nightly lodge her in an upper tower,
The key whereof myself have ever kept;
And thence she cannot be convey'd away.

PROTEUS. Know, noble lord, they have devis'd a mean
How he her chamber-window will ascend
And with a corded ladder fetch her down;
For which the youthful lover now is gone
And this way comes he with it presently;
Where, if it please you, you may intercept him.
But, good my lord, do it so cunningly
That my discovery be not aimed at;
For love of you, not hate unto my friend,
Hath made me publisher of this pretence.

DUKE. Upon mine honour, he shall never know
That I had any light from thee of this.

PROTEUS. Adieu, my lord: Sir Valentine is coming.   *Exit*

Enter Valentine

DUKE. Sir Valentine, whither away so fast?

VALENTINE. Please it your Grace, there is a messenger
That stays to bear my letters to my friends,
And I am going to deliver them.

DUKE. Be they of much import?

VALENTINE. The tenour of them doth but signify
My health and happy being at your court.

DUKE. Nay then, no matter: stay with me awhile;
I am to break with thee of some affairs
That touch me near, wherein thou must be secret.
'Tis not unknown to thee that I have sought
To match my friend Sir Thurio to my daughter.

VALENTINE. I know it well, my lord; and sure, the match
Were rich and honourable; besides, the gentleman
Is full of virtue, bounty, worth, and qualities
Beseeming such a wife as your fair daughter.
Cannot your Grace win her to fancy him?

DUKE. No, trust me: she is peevish, sullen, froward,
Proud, disobedient, stubborn, lacking duty;
Neither regarding that she is my child,

Nor fearing me as if I were her father:
And, may I say to thee, this pride of hers,
Upon advice, hath drawn my love from her;
And, where I thought the remnant of mine age
Should have been cherish'd by her child-like duty,
I now am full resolv'd to take a wife
And turn her out to who will take her in:
Then let her beauty be her wedding-dower;
For me and my possessions she esteems not.

VALENTINE. What would your Grace have me to do in this?

DUKE. There is a lady of Verona here,
Whom I affect; but she is nice and coy
And nought esteems my aged eloquence:
Now therefore, would I have thee to my tutor,
For long agone I have forgot to court;
Besides, the fashion of the time is chang'd,
How and which way I may bestow myself
To be regarded in her sun-bright eye.

VALENTINE. Win her with gifts, if she respect not words:
Dumb jewels often in their silent kind
More than quick words do move a woman's mind.

DUKE. But she did scorn a present that I sent her.

VALENTINE. A woman sometime scorns what best contents
    her.
Send her another; never give her o'er,
For scorn at first makes after-love the more.
If she do frown, 'tis not in hate of you,
But rather to beget more love in you;
If she do chide, 'tis not to have you gone;
For why the fools are mad if left alone.
Take no repulse, whatever she doth say;
For, 'get you gone,' she doth not mean, 'away!'
Flatter and praise, commend, extol their graces;
Though ne'er so black, say they have angels' faces.
That man that hath a tongue, I say, is no man,
If with his tongue he cannot win a woman.

DUKE. But she I mean is promis'd by her friends
Unto a youthful gentleman of worth,
And kept severely from resort of men,
That no man hath access by day to her.

VALENTINE. Why then, I would resort to her by night.

DUKE. Ay, but the doors be lock'd and keys kept safe,

That no man hath recourse to her by night.

VALENTINE. What lets but one may enter at her window?

DUKE. Her chamber is aloft, far from the ground,
    And built so shelving that one cannot climb it
    Without apparent hazard of his life.

VALENTINE. Why then, a ladder quaintly made of cords,
    To cast up, with a pair of anchoring hooks,
    Would serve to scale another Hero's tower,
    So bold Leander would adventure it.

DUKE. Now, as thou art a gentleman of blood,
    Advise me where I may have such a ladder.

VALENTINE. When would you use it? pray, sir, tell me that.

DUKE. This very night; for Love is like a child,
    That longs for every thing that he can come by.

VALENTINE. By seven o'clock I'll get you such a ladder.

DUKE. But hark thee; I will go to her alone:
    How shall I best convey the ladder thither?

VALENTINE. It will be light, my lord, that you may bear it
    Under a cloak that is of any length.

DUKE. A cloak as long as thine will serve the turn?

VALENTINE. Ay, my good lord.

DUKE.   Then let me see thy cloak:
    I'll get me one of such another length.

VALENTINE. Why, any cloak will serve the turn, my lord.

DUKE. How shall I fashion me to wear a cloak?
    I pray thee, let me feel thy cloak upon me.
                            Pulls open Valentine's cloak
    What letter is this same? What's here?—'To Silvia!'
    And here an engine fit for my proceeding!
    I'll be so bold to break the seal for once.   *Reads*
    'My thoughts do harbour with my Silvia nightly;
        And slaves they are to me that send them flying:
    O! could their master come and go as lightly,
        Himself would lodge where senseless they are lying!
    My herald thoughts in thy pure bosom rest them;
        While I, their king, that thither them importune,
    Do curse the grace that with such grace hath bless'd
        them,
        Because myself do want my servants' fortune:
    I curse myself, for they are sent by me,
    That they should harbour where their lord would be.'
    What's here?

'Silvia, this night I will enfranchise thee.'
'Tis so; and here 's the ladder for the purpose.
Why, Phæthon,—for thou art Merops' son,—
Wilt thou aspire to guide the heavenly car
And with thy daring folly burn the world?
Wilt thou reach stars, because they shine on thee?
Go, base intruder! overweening slave!
Bestow thy fawning smiles on equal mates,
And think my patience, more than thy desert,
Is privilege for thy departure hence.
Thank me for this more than for all the favours
Which all too much I have bestow'd on thee.
But if thou linger in my territories
Longer than swiftest expedition
Will give thee time to leave our royal court,
By heaven! my wrath shall far exceed the love
I ever bore my daughter or thyself.
Be gone! I will not hear thy vain excuse;
But, as thou lov'st thy life, make speed from hence.   *Exit*

VALENTINE. And why not death rather than living torment?
To die is to be banish'd from myself;
And Silvia is myself: banish'd from her
Is self from self,—a deadly banishment!
What light is light, if Silvia be not seen?
What joy is joy, if Silvia be not by?
Unless it be to think that she is by
And feed upon the shadow of perfection.
Except I be by Silvia in the night,
There is no music in the nightingale;
Unless I look on Silvia in the day,
There is no day for me to look upon.
She is my essence; and I leave to be,
If I be not by her fair influence
Foster'd, illumin'd, cherish'd, kept alive.
I fly not death, to fly his deadly doom:
Tarry I here, I but attend on death;
But, fly I hence, I fly away from life.

Enter Proteus and Launce

PROTEUS. Run, boy; run, run, and seek him out.
LAUNCE. Soho! soho!
PROTEUS. What seest thou?

LAUNCE. Him we go to find; there 's not a hair on 's head
  but 'tis a Valentine.

PROTEUS. Valentine?

VALENTINE. No.

PROTEUS. Who then? his spirit?

VALENTINE. Neither.

PROTEUS. What then?

VALENTINE. Nothing.

LAUNCE. Can nothing speak? Master, shall I strike?

PROTEUS. Who would'st thou strike?

LAUNCE. Nothing.

PROTEUS. Villain, forbear.

LAUNCE. Why, sir, I 'll strike nothing: I pray you,—

PROTEUS. Sirrah, I say, forbear.—Friend Valentine, a word.

VALENTINE. My ears are stopp'd and cannot hear good news,
  So much of bad already hath possess'd them.

PROTEUS. Then in dumb silence will I bury mine,
  For they are harsh, untuneable and bad.

VALENTINE. Is Silvia dead?

PROTEUS. No, Valentine.

VALENTINE. No Valentine, indeed, for sacred Silvia!
  Hath she forsworn me?

PROTEUS. No, Valentine.

VALENTINE. No Valentine, if Silvia have forsworn me!
  What is your news?

LAUNCE. Sir, there is a proclamation that you are vanished.

PROTEUS. That thou art banished, O, that 's the news,
  From hence, from Silvia, and from me thy friend.

VALENTINE. O, I have fed upon this woe already,
  And now excess of it will make me surfeit.
  Doth Silvia know that I am banished?

PROTEUS. Ay, ay; and she hath offer'd to the doom—
  Which, unrevers'd, stands in effectual force—
  A sea of melting pearl, which some call tears:
  Those at her father's churlish feet she tender'd;
  With them, upon her knees, her humble self;
  Wringing her hands, whose whiteness so became them
  As if but now they waxed pale for woe:
  But neither bended knees, pure hands held up,
  Sad sighs, deep groans, nor silver-shedding tears,
  Could penetrate her uncompassionate sire;

But Valentine, if he be ta'en, must die.
Besides, her intercession chaf'd him so,
When she for thy repeal was suppliant,
That to close prison he commanded her,
With many bitter threats of biding there.

VALENTINE. No more; unless the next word that thou speak'st
Have some malignant power upon my life:
If so, I pray thee, breathe it in mine ear,
As ending anthem of my endless dolour.

PROTEUS. Cease to lament for that thou canst not help,
And study help for that which thou lament'st.
Time is the nurse and breeder of all good.
Here if thou stay, thou canst not see thy love;
Besides, thy staying will abridge thy life.
Hope is a lover's staff; walk hence with that
And manage it against despairing thoughts.
Thy letters may be here, though thou art hence;
Which, being writ to me, shall be deliver'd
Even in the milk-white bosom of thy love.
The time now serves not to expostulate:
Come, I 'll convey thee through the city-gate,
And, ere I part with thee, confer at large
Of all that may concern thy love-affairs.
As thou lov'st Silvia, though not for thyself,
Regard thy danger, and along with me!

VALENTINE. I pray thee, Launce, and if thou seest my boy,
Bid him make haste and meet me at the North-gate.

PROTEUS. Go, sirrah, find him out. Come, Valentine.

VALENTINE. O my dear Silvia! hapless Valentine!

Exeunt Valentine and Proteus

LAUNCE. I am but a fool, look you; and yet I have the wit
to think my master is a kind of a knave: but that 's all
one, if he be but one knave. He lives not now that knows
me to be in love: yet I am in love; but a team of horse
shall not pluck that from me, nor who 'tis I love; and yet
'tis a woman; but what woman, I will not tell myself;
and yet 'tis a milkmaid; yet 'tis not a maid, for she hath
had gossips; yet 'tis a maid, for she is her master's maid,
and serves for wages. She hath more qualities than a
water-spaniel,—which is much in a bare Christian. (*Pulling out a paper*) Here is the catelog of her condition.

'Imprimis, She can fetch and carry.' Why, a horse can do
no more: nay, a horse cannot fetch, but only carry; therefore, is she better than a jade. 'Item, She can milk'; look
you, a sweet virtue in a maid with clean hands.

Enter Speed

SPEED. How now, Signior Launce! what news with your
mastership?

LAUNCE. With my master's ship? why, it is at sea.

SPEED. Well, your old vice still; mistake the word. What
news, then, in your paper?

LAUNCE. The blackest news that ever thou heardest.

SPEED. Why, man, how black?

LAUNCE. Why, as black as ink.

SPEED. Let me read them.

LAUNCE. Fie on thee, jolthead! thou canst not read.

SPEED. Thou liest; I can.

LAUNCE. I will try thee. Tell me this: who begot thee?

SPEED. Marry, the son of my grandfather.

LAUNCE. O, illiterate loiterer! it was the son of thy grandmother. This proves that thou canst not read.

SPEED. Come, fool, come: try me in thy paper.

LAUNCE. There; and Saint Nicholas be thy speed!

SPEED. (*Reads*) 'Imprimis. She can milk.'

LAUNCE. Ay, that she can.

SPEED. 'Item. She brews good ale.'

LAUNCE. And thereof comes the proverb, 'Blessing of your
heart, you brew good ale.'

SPEED. 'Item. She can sew.'

LAUNCE. That's as much as to say, Can she so?

SPEED. 'Item. She can knit.'

LAUNCE. What need a man care for a stock with a wench,
when she can knit him a stock?

SPEED. 'Item. She can wash and scour.'

LAUNCE. A special virtue; for then she need not be washed
and scoured.

SPEED. 'Item. She can spin.'

LAUNCE. Then may I set the world on wheels, when she
can spin for her living.

SPEED. 'Item. She hath many nameless virtues.'

LAUNCE. That's as much as to say, bastard virtues; that, indeed, know not their fathers, and therefore have no
names.

SPEED. 'Here follow her vices.'

LAUNCE. Close at the heels of her virtues.

SPEED. 'Item. She is not to be kissed fasting, in respect of her breath.'

LAUNCE. Well, that fault may be mended with a breakfast. Read on.

SPEED. 'Item. She hath a sweet mouth.'

LAUNCE. That makes amends for her sour breath.

SPEED. 'Item. She doth talk in her sleep.'

LAUNCE. It's no matter for that, so she sleep not in her talk.

SPEED. 'Item. She is slow in words.'

LAUNCE. O villain, that set this down among her vices! To be slow in words is a woman's only virtue: I pray thee, out with 't, and place it for her chief virtue.

SPEED. 'Item. She is proud.'

LAUNCE. Out with that too: it was Eve's legacy, and cannot be ta'en from her.

SPEED. 'Item. She hath no teeth.'

LAUNCE. I care not for that neither, because I love crusts.

SPEED. 'Item. She is curst.'

LAUNCE. Well; the best is, she hath no teeth to bite.

SPEED. 'Item. She will often praise her liquor.'

LAUNCE. If her liquor be good, she shall: if she will not, I will; for good things should be praised.

SPEED. 'Item. She is too liberal.'

LAUNCE. Of her tongue she cannot, for that's writ down she is slow of: of her purse she shall not, for that I'll keep shut: now, of another thing she may, and that cannot I help. Well, proceed.

SPEED. 'Item. She hath more hair than wit, and more faults than hairs, and more wealth than faults.'

LAUNCE. Stop there; I'll have her: she was mine, and not mine, twice or thrice in that last article. Rehearse that once more.

SPEED. 'Item. She hath more hair than wit.'—

LAUNCE. More hair than wit it may be; I'll prove it: the cover of the salt hides the salt, and therefore it is more than the salt; the hair, that covers the wit is more than the wit, for the greater hides the less. What's next?

SPEED. 'And more faults than hairs.'—

LAUNCE. That's monstrous! O, that that were out!

SPEED. 'And more wealth than faults.'

LAUNCE. Why, that word makes the faults gracious. Well,
  I 'll have her; and if it be a match, as nothing is impossible,—

SPEED. What then?

LAUNCE. Why, then will I tell thee,—that thy master stays
  for thee at the North-gate.

SPEED. For me?

LAUNCE. For thee! ay; who art thou? he hath stayed for a
  better man than thee.

SPEED. And must I go to him?

LAUNCE. Thou must run to him, for thou hast stayed so
  long that going will scarce serve the turn.

SPEED. Why didst not tell me sooner? pox of your love-
  letters!   *Exit*

LAUNCE. Now will he be swing'd for reading my letter. An
  unmannerly slave, that will thrust himself into secrets.
  I 'll after, to rejoice in the boy's correction.   *Exit*

SCENE TWO

Milan. A Room in the Duke's Palace.

Enter Duke and Thurio

DUKE. Sir Thurio, fear not but that she will love you,
  Now Valentine is banish'd from her sight.

THURIO. Since his exile she hath despis'd me most,
  Forsworn my company and rail'd at me,
  That I am desperate of obtaining her.

DUKE. This weak impress of love is as a figure
  Trenched in ice, which with an hour's heat
  Dissolves to water and doth lose his form.
  A little time will melt her frozen thoughts,
  And worthless Valentine shall be forgot.

Enter Proteus

  How now, Sir Proteus! Is your countryman
  According to our proclamation gone?

PROTEUS. Gone, my good lord.

DUKE. My daughter takes his going grievously.

PROTEUS. A little time, my lord, will kill that grief.

DUKE. So I believe; but Thurio thinks not so.

Proteus, the good conceit I hold of thee,—
For thou hast shown some sign of good desert,—
Makes me the better to confer with thee.

PROTEUS. Longer than I prove loyal to your Grace
Let me not live to look upon your Grace.

DUKE. Thou know'st how willingly I would effect
The match between Sir Thurio and my daughter.

PROTEUS. I do, my lord.

DUKE. And also, I think, thou art not ignorant
How she opposes her against my will.

PROTEUS. She did, my lord, when Valentine was here.

DUKE. Ay, and perversely she persevers so.
What might we do to make the girl forget
The love of Valentine, and love Sir Thurio?

PROTEUS. The best way is to slander Valentine
With falsehood, cowardice, and poor descent,
Three things that women highly hold in hate.

DUKE. Ay, but she 'll think that it is spoke in hate.

PROTEUS. Ay, if his enemy deliver it:
Therefore it must with circumstance be spoken
By one whom she esteemeth as his friend.

DUKE. Then you must undertake to slander him.

PROTEUS. And that, my lord, I shall be loath to do:
'Tis an ill office for a gentleman,
Especially against his very friend.

DUKE. Where your good word cannot advantage him,
Your slander never can endamage him:
Therefore the office is indifferent,
Being entreated to it by your friend.

PROTEUS. You have prevail'd, my lord. If I can do it,
By aught that I can speak in his dispraise,
She shall not long continue love to him.
But say this weed her love from Valentine,
It follows not that she will love Sir Thurio.

THURIO. Therefore, as you unwind her love from him,
Lest it should ravel and be good to none,
You must provide to bottom it on me;
Which must be done by praising me as much
As you in worth dispraise Sir Valentine.

DUKE. And, Proteus, we dare trust you in this kind,
Because we know, on Valentine's report,
You are already Love's firm votary

And cannot soon revolt and change your mind.
Upon this warrant shall you have access
Where you with Silvia may confer at large;
For she is lumpish, heavy, melancholy,
And, for your friend's sake, will be glad of you;
Where you may temper her, by your persuasion,
To hate young Valentine and love my friend.

PROTEUS. As much as I can do I will effect.
But you, Sir Thurio, are not sharp enough;
You must lay lime to tangle her desires
By wailful sonnets, whose composed rimes
Should be full-fraught with serviceable vows.

DUKE. Ay,
Much is the force of heaven-bred poesy.

PROTEUS. Say that upon the altar of her beauty
You sacrifice your tears, your sighs, your heart.
Write till your ink be dry, and with your tears
Moist it again, and frame some feeling line
That may discover such integrity:
For Orpheus' lute was strung with poets' sinews,
Whose golden touch could soften steel and stones,
Make tigers tame and huge leviathans
Forsake unsounded deeps to dance on sands.
After your dire-lamenting elegies,
Visit by night your lady's chamber-window
With some sweet consort: to their instruments
Tune a deploring dump; the night's dead silence
Will well become such sweet-complaining grievance.
This, or else nothing, will inherit her.

DUKE. This discipline shows thou hast been in love.

THURIO. And thy advice this night I'll put in practice.
Therefore, sweet Proteus, my direction-giver,
Let us into the city presently
To sort some gentlemen well skill'd in music.
I have a sonnet that will serve the turn
To give the onset to thy good advice.

DUKE. About it, gentlemen!

PROTEUS. We'll wait upon your Grace till after-supper,
And afterward determine our proceedings.

DUKE. Even now about it! I will pardon you.   *Exeunt*

ACT FOUR

SCENE ONE

[1-24]

A Forest between Milan and Verona.
Enter certain Outlaws

FIRST OUTLAW. Fellows, stand fast; I see a passenger.

SECOND OUTLAW. If there be ten, shrink not, but down with
'em.

Enter Valentine and Speed

THIRD OUTLAW. Stand, sir, and throw us that you have
about ye;

If not, we 'll make you sit and rifle you.

SPEED. Sir, we are undone: these are the villains

That all the travellers do fear so much.

VALENTINE. My friends,—

FIRST OUTLAW. That's not so, sir; we are your enemies.

SECOND OUTLAW. Peace! we 'll hear him.

THIRD OUTLAW. Ay, by my beard, will we, for he is a
proper man.

VALENTINE. Then know, that I have little wealth to lose.

A man I am cross'd with adversity:

My riches are these poor habiliments,

Of which if you should here disfurnish me,

You take the sum and substance that I have.

SECOND OUTLAW. Whither travel you?

VALENTINE. To Verona.

FIRST OUTLAW. Whence came you?

VALENTINE. From Milan.

THIRD OUTLAW. Have you long sojourn'd there?

VALENTINE. Some sixteen months; and longer might have
stay'd

If crooked fortune had not thwarted me.

SECOND OUTLAW. What! were you banish'd thence?

VALENTINE. I was.

SECOND OUTLAW. For what offence?

VALENTINE. For that which now torments me to rehearse.
I kill'd a man, whose death I much repent;
But yet I slew him manfully, in fight,
Without false vantage or base treachery.

FIRST OUTLAW. Why, ne'er repent it, if it were done so.
But were you banish'd for so small a fault?

VALENTINE. I was, and held me glad of such a doom.

SECOND OUTLAW. Have you the tongues?

VALENTINE. My youthful travel therein made me happy,
Or else I often had been miserable.

THIRD OUTLAW. By the bare scalp of Robin Hood's fat friar,
This fellow were a king for our wild faction!

FIRST OUTLAW. We 'll have him: Sirs, a word.

SPEED. Master, be one of them;
It is an honourable kind of thievery.

VALENTINE. Peace, villain!

SECOND OUTLAW. Tell us this: have you anything to take to?

VALENTINE. Nothing, but my fortune.

THIRD OUTLAW. Know then, that some of us are gentlemen,
Such as the fury of ungovern'd youth
Thrust from the company of awful men:
Myself was from Verona banished
For practising to steal away a lady,
An heir, and near allied unto the duke.

SECOND OUTLAW. And I from Mantua, for a gentleman,
Who, in my mood, I stabb'd unto the heart.

FIRST OUTLAW. And I for such like petty crimes as these.
But to the purpose; for we cite our faults,
That they may hold excus'd our lawless lives;
And, partly, seeing you are beautified
With goodly shape, and by your own report
A linguist, and a man of such perfection
As we do in our quality much want—

SECOND OUTLAW. Indeed, because you are a banish'd man,
Therefore, above the rest, we parley to you.
Are you content to be our general?
To make a virtue of necessity
And live, as we do, in this wilderness?

THIRD OUTLAW. What say'st thou? wilt thou be of our consort?
Say 'ay,' and be the captain of us all:

We 'll do thee homage and be rul'd by thee,
Love thee as our commander and our king.

FIRST OUTLAW. But if thou scorn our courtesy, thou diest.

SECOND OUTLAW. Thou shalt not live to brag what we have offer'd.

VALENTINE. I take your offer and will live with you,
Provided that you do no outrages
On silly women, or poor passengers.

THIRD OUTLAW. No; we detest such vile, base practices.
Come, go with us; we 'll bring thee to our crews,
And show thee all the treasure we have got,
Which, with ourselves, all rest at thy dispose.   *Exeunt*

SCENE TWO

Milan. The Court of the Duke's Palace.

Enter Proteus

PROTEUS. Already have I been false to Valentine,
And now I must be as unjust to Thurio.
Under the colour of commending him,
I have access my own love to prefer:
But Silvia is too fair, too true, too holy,
To be corrupted with my worthless gifts.
When I protest true loyalty to her,
She twits me with my falsehood to my friend;
When to her beauty I commend my vows,
She bids me think how I have been forsworn
In breaking faith with Julia whom I lov'd:
And notwithstanding all her sudden quips,
The least whereof would quell a lover's hope,
Yet, spaniel-like, the more she spurns my love,
The more it grows, and fawneth on her still.
But here comes Thurio: now must we to her window,
And give some evening music to her ear.

Enter Thurio, and Musicians

THURIO. How now, Sir Proteus! are you crept before us?

PROTEUS. Ay, gentle Thurio; for you know that love
Will creep in service where it cannot go.

THURIO. Ay; but I hope, sir, that you love not here.

PROTEUS. Sir, but I do; or else I would be hence.

THURIO. Who? Silvia?

PROTEUS. Ay, Silvia, for your sake.

THURIO. I thank you for your own. Now, gentlemen,
Let 's tune, and to it lustily a while.

Enter Host and Julia behind. Julia in boy's clothes

HOST. Now, my young guest, methinks you 're allycholly: I
pray you, why is it?

JULIA. Marry, mine host, because I cannot be merry.

HOST. Come, we 'll have you merry. I 'll bring you where
you shall hear music and see the gentleman that you
asked for.

JULIA. But shall I hear him speak?

HOST. Ay, that you shall.

JULIA. That will be music.   *Music plays*

HOST. Hark! hark!

JULIA. Is he among these?

HOST. Ay; but peace! let 's hear 'em.

SONG

Who is Silvia? what is she?
  That all our swains commend her?
Holy, fair, and wise is she;
  The heaven such grace did lend her,
That she might admired be.

Is she kind as she is fair?
  For beauty lives with kindness:
Love doth to her eyes repair,
  To help him of his blindness;
And, being help'd, inhabits there.

Then to Silvia let us sing,
  That Silvia is excelling;
She excels each mortal thing
  Upon the dull earth dwelling;
To her let us garlands bring.

HOST. How now! Are you sadder than you were before?
How do you, man? the music likes you not.

JULIA. You mistake; the musician likes me not.

HOST. Why, my pretty youth?

JULIA. He plays false, father.

HOST. How? out of tune on the strings?

JULIA. Not so; but yet so false that he grieves my very
heart-strings.

HOST. You have a quick ear.

JULIA. Ay; I would I were deaf; it makes me have a slow
heart.

HOST. I perceive you delight not in music.

JULIA. Not a whit,—when it jars so.

HOST. Hark! what fine change is in the music!

JULIA. Ay, that change is the spite.

HOST. You would have them always play but one thing?

JULIA. I would always have one play but one thing.
But, host, doth this Sir Proteus that we talk on
Often resort unto this gentlewoman?

HOST. I will tell you what Launce, his man, told me: he
lov'd her out of all nick.

JULIA. Where is Launce?

HOST. Gone to seek his dog; which, to-morrow, by his master's command, he must carry for a present to his lady.

JULIA. Peace! stand aside: the company parts.

PROTEUS. Sir Thurio, fear not you: I will so plead
That you shall say my cunning drift excels.

THURIO. Where meet we?

PROTEUS. At Saint Gregory's well.

THURIO. Farewell.   *Exeunt Thurio and Musicians*
                 Enter Silvia, above, at her window

PROTEUS. Madam, good even to your ladyship.

SILVIA. I thank you for your music, gentlemen.
Who is that that spake?

PROTEUS. One, lady, if you knew his pure heart's truth,
You would quickly learn to know him by his voice.

SILVIA. Sir Proteus, as I take it.

PROTEUS. Sir Proteus, gentle lady, and your servant.

SILVIA. What is your will?

PROTEUS.   That I may compass yours.

SILVIA. You have your wish; my will is even this:
That presently you hie you home to bed.
Thou subtle, perjur'd, false, disloyal man!
Think'st thou I am so shallow, so conceitless,
To be seduced by thy flattery,
That hast deceiv'd so many with thy vows?

Return, return, and make thy love amends.
For me, by this pale queen of night I swear,
I am so far from granting thy request
That I despise thee for thy wrongful suit,
And by and by intend to chide myself
Even for this time I spend in talking to thee.

PROTEUS. I grant, sweet love, that I did love a lady:
But she is dead.

JULIA. (*Aside*) 'Twere false, if I should speak it;
For I am sure she is not buried.

SILVIA. Say that she be; yet Valentine thy friend
Survives; to whom, thyself art witness,
I am betroth'd: and art thou not asham'd
To wrong him with thy importunacy?

PROTEUS. I likewise hear that Valentine is dead.

SILVIA. And so suppose am I; for in his grave,
Assure thyself my love is buried.

PROTEUS. Sweet lady, let me rake it from the earth.

SILVIA. Go to thy lady's grave and call hers thence;
Or, at the least, in hers sepulchre thine.

JULIA. (*Aside*) He heard not that.

PROTEUS. Madam, if your heart be so obdurate,
Vouchsafe me yet your picture for my love,
The picture that is hanging in your chamber:
To that I 'll speak, to that I 'll sigh and weep;
For since the substance of your perfect self
Is else devoted, I am but a shadow,
And to your shadow will I make true love.

JULIA. (*Aside*) If 'twere a substance, you would, sure, deceive it,
And make it but a shadow, as I am.

SILVIA. I am very loath to be your idol, sir;
But, since your falsehood shall become you well
To worship shadows and adore false shapes,
Send to me in the morning and I 'll send it.
And so, good rest.

PROTEUS.   As wretches have o'er night
That wait for execution in the morn.

Exeunt Proteus, and Silvia, above

JULIA. Host, will you go?

HOST. By my halidom, I was fast asleep.

JULIA. Pray you, where lies Sir Proteus?

HOST. Marry, at my house. Trust me, I think
   'tis almost day.

JULIA. Not so; but it hath been the longest night
   That e'er I watch'd and the most heaviest. *Exeunt*

SCENE THREE

The Same.

Enter Eglamour

EGLAMOUR. This is the hour that Madam Silvia
   Entreated me to call, and know her mind:
   There 's some great matter she 'd employ me in.
   Madam, Madam!
         Enter Silvia above, at her window
SILVIA.   Who calls?
EGLAMOUR.   Your servant, and your friend;
   One that attends your ladyship's command.
SILVIA. Sir Eglamour, a thousand times good-morrow.
EGLAMOUR. As many, worthy lady, to yourself.
   According to your ladyship's impose,
   I am thus early come to know what service
   It is your pleasure to command me in.
SILVIA. O Eglamour, thou art a gentleman—
   Think not I flatter, for I swear I do not—
   Valiant, wise, remorseful, well-accomplish'd.
   Thou art not ignorant what dear good will
   I bear unto the banish'd Valentine,
   Nor how my father would enforce me marry
   Vain Thurio, whom my very soul abhors.
   Thyself hast lov'd; and I have heard thee say
   No grief did ever come so near thy heart
   As when thy lady and thy true love died,
   Upon whose grave thou vow'dst pure chastity.
   Sir Eglamour, I would to Valentine,
   To Mantua, where, I hear, he makes abode;
   And, for the ways are dangerous to pass,
   I do desire thy worthy company,
   Upon whose faith and honour I repose.
   Urge not my father's anger, Eglamour,
   But think upon my grief, a lady's grief,
   And on the justice of my flying hence,

To keep me from a most unholy match,
Which heaven and fortune still rewards with plagues.
I do desire thee, even from a heart
As full of sorrows as the sea of sands,
To bear me company and go with me:
If not, to hide what I have said to thee,
That I may venture to depart alone.

EGLAMOUR. Madam, I pity much your grievances;
Which since I know they virtuously are plac'd,
I give consent to go along with you.
Recking as little what betideth me
As much I wish all good befortune you.
When will you go?

SILVIA.   This evening coming.

EGLAMOUR. Where shall I meet you?

SILVIA.   At Friar Patrick's cell,
Where I intend holy confession.

EGLAMOUR. I will not fail your ladyship.
Good-morrow, gentle lady.

SILVIA. Good-morrow, kind Sir Eglamour.   *Exeunt*

SCENE FOUR

The Same.

Enter Launce with his dog

LAUNCE. When a man's servant shall play the cur with him,
look you, it goes hard; one that I brought up of a puppy;
one that I saved from drowning, when three or four of
his blind brothers and sisters went to it. I have taught
him, even as one would say precisely, 'Thus would I
teach a dog.' I was sent to deliver him as a present to
Mistress Silvia from my master, and I came no sooner
into the dining-chamber but he steps me to her trencher
and steals her capon's leg. O! 'tis a foul thing when a cur
cannot keep himself in all companies. I would have, as
one should say, one that takes upon him to be a dog indeed, to be, as it were, a dog at all things. If I had not
had more wit than he, to take a fault upon me that he
did, I think verily he had been hanged for 't: sure as I
live, he had suffered for 't: you shall judge. He thrusts

me himself into the company of three or four gentleman-
like dogs under the duke's table: he had not been there—
bless the mark—a pissing-while, but all the chamber
smelt him. 'Out with the dog!' says one; 'What cur is
that?' says another; 'Whip him out,' says the third;
'Hang him up,' says the duke. I, having been acquainted
with the smell before, knew it was Crab, and goes me to
the fellow that whips the dogs: 'Friend,' quoth I, 'you
mean to whip the dog?' 'Ay, marry, do I,' quoth he. 'You
do him the more wrong,' quoth I; "'twas I did the thing
you wot of.' He makes me no more ado, but whips me
out of the chamber. How many masters would do this for
his servant? Nay, I 'll be sworn, I have sat in the stocks
for puddings he hath stolen, otherwise he had been executed; I have stood on the pillory for geese he hath
killed, otherwise he had suffered for 't; thou thinkest not
of this now. Nay, I remember the trick you served me
when I took my leave of Madam Silvia: did not I bid
thee still mark me and do as I do? When didst thou see
me heave up my leg and make water against a gentlewoman's farthingale? Didst thou ever see me do such a
trick?

Enter Proteus, and Julia in boy's clothes

PROTEUS. Sebastian is thy name? I like thee well
And will employ thee in some service presently.

JULIA. In what you please: I will do what I can.

PROTEUS. I hope thou wilt. (*To Launce*) How now, you
    whoreson peasant!
Where have you been these two days loitering?

LAUNCE. Marry, sir, I carried Mistress Silvia the dog you
    bade me.

PROTEUS. And what says she to my little jewel?

LAUNCE. Marry, she says, your dog was a cur, and tells you,
    currish thanks is good enough for such a present.

PROTEUS. But she received my dog?

LAUNCE. No, indeed, did she not: here have I brought him
    back again.

PROTEUS. What! didst thou offer her this from me?

LAUNCE. Ay, sir: the other squirrel was stolen from me by
    the hangman boys in the market-place; and then I of-
    fered her mine own, who is a dog as big as ten of yours,
    and therefore the gift the greater.

PROTEUS. Go, get thee hence, and find my dog again,
    Or ne'er return again into my sight.
    Away, I say! Stay'st thou to vex me here?
    A slave that still an end turns me to shame. *Exit Launce*
    Sebastian, I have entertained thee
    Partly, that I have need of such a youth,
    That can with some discretion do my business,
    For 't is no trusting to yond foolish lout;
    But chiefly for thy face and thy behaviour,
    Which, if my augury deceive me not,
    Witness good bringing up, fortune, and truth:
    Therefore, know thou, for this I entertain thee.
    Go presently, and take this ring with thee.
    Deliver it to Madam Silvia:
    She lov'd me well deliver'd it to me.
JULIA. It seems, you lov'd not her, to leave her token.
    She 's dead, belike?
PROTEUS.   Not so: I think, she lives.
JULIA. Alas!
PROTEUS. Why dost thou cry 'alas'?
JULIA.   I cannot choose
    But pity her.
PROTEUS. Wherefore should'st thou pity her?
JULIA. Because methinks that she lov'd you as well
    As you do love your lady Silvia.
    She dreams on him that has forgot her love;
    You dote on her, that cares not for your love.
    'Tis pity, love should be so contrary;
    And thinking on it makes me cry, 'alas!'
PROTEUS. Well, well, give her that ring and therewithal
    This letter: that 's her chamber. Tell my lady
    I claim the promise for her heavenly picture.
    Your message done, hie home unto my chamber,
    Where thou shalt find me sad and solitary.   *Exit*
JULIA. How many women would do such a message?
    Alas, poor Proteus! thou hast entertain'd
    A fox to be the shepherd of thy lambs.
    Alas, poor fool! why do I pity him
    That with his very heart despiseth me?
    Because he loves her, he despiseth me;
    Because I love him, I must pity him.
    This ring I gave him when he parted from me,

To bind him to remember my good will;
And now am I—unhappy messenger—
To plead for that which I would not obtain,
To carry that which I would have refus'd,
To praise his faith which I would have disprais'd.
I am my master's true-confirmed love,
But cannot be true servant to my master,
Unless I prove false traitor to myself.
Yet will I woo for him; but yet so coldly
As heaven it knows, I would not have him speed.

Enter Silvia, attended

Gentlewoman, good day! I pray you, be my mean
To bring me where to speak with Madam Silvia.

SILVIA. What would you with her, if that I be she?

JULIA. If you be she, I do entreat your patience
To hear me speak the message I am sent on.

SILVIA. From whom?

JULIA. From my master, Sir Proteus, madam.

SILVIA. O! he sends you for a picture?

JULIA. Ay, madam.

SILVIA. Ursula, bring my picture there. *A picture brought*
Go, give your master this: tell him from me,
One Julia, that his changing thoughts forget,
Would better fit his chamber than this shadow.

JULIA. Madam, please you peruse this letter.—*Gives a letter*
Pardon me, madam, I have unadvis'd
Delivered you a paper that I should not:
This is the letter to your ladyship. *Gives another letter*

SILVIA. I pray thee, let me look on that again.

JULIA. It may not be: good madam, pardon me.

SILVIA. There, hold.
I will not look upon your master's lines:
I know, they are stuff'd with protestations
And full of new-found oaths, which he will break
As easily as I do tear his paper.   *Tears the second letter*

JULIA. Madam, he sends your ladyship this ring.

SILVIA. The more shame for him that he sends it me;
For, I have heard him say a thousand times,
His Julia gave it him at his departure.
Though his false finger have profan'd the ring,
Mine shall not do his Julia so much wrong.

JULIA. She thanks you.

SILVIA. What say'st thou?

JULIA. I thank you, madam, that you tender her.
   Poor gentlewoman! my master wrongs her much.

SILVIA. Dost thou know her?

JULIA. Almost as well as I do know myself:
   To think upon her woes, I do protest
   That I have wept a hundred several times.

SILVIA. Belike she thinks that Proteus hath forsook her.

JULIA. I think she doth, and that 's her cause of sorrow.

SILVIA. Is she not passing fair?

JULIA. She hath been fairer, madam, than she is.
   When she did think my master lov'd her well,
   She, in my judgment, was as fair as you;
   But since she did neglect her looking-glass
   And threw her sun-expelling mask away,
   The air hath starv'd the roses in her cheeks
   And pinch'd the lily-tincture of her face,
   That now she is become as black as I.

SILVIA. How tall was she?

JULIA. About my stature; for, at Pentecost,
   When all our pageants of delight were play'd,
   Our youth got me to play the woman's part,
   And I was trimm'd in Madam Julia's gown,
   Which served me as fit, by all men's judgments,
   As if the garment had been made for me:
   Therefore I know she is about my height.
   And at that time I made her weep agood;
   For I did play a lamentable part.
   Madam, 'twas Ariadne passioning
   For Theseus' perjury and unjust flight;
   Which I so lively acted with my tears
   That my poor mistress, mov'd therewithal
   Wept bitterly, and would I might be dead
   If I in thought felt not her very sorrow!

SILVIA. She is beholding to thee, gentle youth.—
   Alas, poor lady, desolate and left!
   I weep myself to think upon thy words.
   Here, youth, there is my purse: I give thee this
   For thy sweet mistress' sake, because thou lov'st her.
   Farewell.

JULIA. And she shall thank you for 't, if e'er you know
   her.—   *Exit Silvia, with Attendants*

A virtuous gentlewoman, mild and beautiful.
I hope my master's suit will be but cold,
Since she respects my mistress' love so much.
Alas, how love can trifle with itself!
Here is her picture: let me see; I think,
If I had such a tire, this face of mine
Were full as lovely as is this of hers;
And yet the painter flatter'd her a little,
Unless I flatter with myself too much.
Her hair is auburn, mine is perfect yellow:
If that be all the difference in his love
I 'll get me such a colour'd periwig.
Her eyes are grey as glass, and so are mine:
Ay, but her forehead 's low, and mine 's as high.
What should it be that he respects in her
But I can make respective in myself,
If this fond Love were not a blinded god?
Come, shadow, come, and take this shadow up,
For 'tis thy rival. O thou senseless form!
Thou shalt be worshipp'd, kiss'd, lov'd, and ador'd,
And, were there sense in his idolatry,
My substance should be statue in thy stead.
I 'll use thee kindly for thy mistress' sake,
That us'd me so; or else, by Jove I vow,
I should have scratch'd out your unseeing eyes,
To make my master out of love with thee.   *Exit*

ACT FIVE

[1·12; 1·7]   ## SCENE ONE
Milan. An Abbey.

Enter Eglamour

EGLAMOUR. The sun begins to gild the western sky,
   And now it is about the very hour
   That Silvia at Friar Patrick's cell should meet me.
   She will not fail; for lovers break not hours,
   Unless it be to come before their time,
   So much they spur their expedition.
   See, where she comes.

Enter Silvia

                    Lady, a happy evening!
SILVIA. Amen, amen! go on, good Eglamour,
   Out at the postern by the abbey-wall.
   I fear I am attended by some spies.
EGLAMOUR. Fear not: the forest is not three leagues off;
   If we recover that, we 're sure enough.   *Exeunt*

SCENE TWO

Milan. A Room in the Duke's Palace.

Enter Thurio, Proteus, and Julia

THURIO. Sir Proteus, what says Silvia to my suit?
PROTEUS. O, sir, I find her milder than she was;
   And yet she takes exceptions at your person.
THURIO. What! that my leg is too long?
PROTEUS. No, that it is too little.
THURIO. I 'll wear a boot to make it somewhat rounder.
JULIA. (*Aside*) But love will not be spurr'd to what it
      loathes.

THURIO. What says she to my face?

PROTEUS. She says it is a fair one.

THURIO. Nay then, the wanton lies; my face is black.

PROTEUS. But pearls are fair, and the old saying is,
  'Black men are pearls in beauteous ladies' eyes.'

JULIA. (*Aside*) 'Tis true, such pearls as put out ladies'
    eyes;
  For I had rather wink than look on them.

THURIO. How likes she my discourse?

PROTEUS. Ill, when you talk of war.

THURIO. But well, when I discourse of love and peace?

JULIA. (*Aside*) But better, indeed, when you hold your
    peace.

THURIO. What says she to my valour?

PROTEUS. O, sir, she makes no doubt of that.

JULIA. (*Aside*) She needs not, when she knows it coward-
    ice.

THURIO. What says she to my birth?

PROTEUS. That you are well deriv'd.

JULIA. (*Aside*) True; from a gentleman to a fool.

THURIO. Considers she my possessions?

PROTEUS. O, ay; and pities them.

THURIO. Wherefore?

JULIA. (*Aside*) That such an ass should owe them.

PROTEUS. That they are out by lease.

JULIA. Here comes the duke.

Enter Duke

DUKE. How now, Sir Proteus! how now, Thurio!
  Which of you saw Sir Eglamour of late?

THURIO. Not I.

PROTEUS.   Nor I.

DUKE.   Saw you my daughter?

PROTEUS.   Neither.

DUKE. Why then,
  She 's fled unto that peasant Valentine,
  And Eglamour is in her company.
  'Tis true; for Friar Laurence met them both,
  As he in penance wander'd through the forest;
  Him he knew well, and guess'd that it was she,
  But, being mask'd, he was not sure of it;
  Besides, she did intend confession
  At Patrick's cell this even, and there she was not.

These likelihoods confirm her flight from hence.
Therefore, I pray you, stand not to discourse,
But mount you presently and meet with me
Upon the rising of the mountain-foot,
That leads towards Mantua, whither they are fled.
Dispatch, sweet gentlemen, and follow me.   *Exit*

THURIO. Why, this it is to be a peevish girl,
That flies her fortune when it follows her.
I 'll after, more to be reveng'd on Eglamour
Than for the love of reckless Silvia.   *Exit*

PROTEUS. And I will follow, more for Silvia's love
Than hate of Eglamour that goes with her.   *Exit*

JULIA. And I will follow, more to cross that love
Than hate for Silvia that is gone for love.   *Exit*

SCENE THREE

Frontiers of Mantua. The Forest.

Enter Outlaws with Silvia

FIRST OUTLAW. Come, come,
Be patient; we must bring you to our captain.

SILVIA. A thousand more mischances than this one
Have learn'd me how to brook this patiently.

SECOND OUTLAW. Come, bring her away.

FIRST OUTLAW. Where is the gentleman that was with her?

THIRD OUTLAW. Being nimble-footed, he hath outrun us;
But Moyses and Valerius follow him.
Go thou with her to the west end of the wood;
There is our captain. We 'll follow him that 's fled:
The thicket is beset; he cannot 'scape.
            Exeunt all except the First Outlaw and Silvia

FIRST OUTLAW. Come, I must bring you to our captain's
cave.
Fear not; he bears an honourable mind,
And will not use a woman lawlessly.

SILVIA. O Valentine! this I endure for thee.   *Exeunt*

SCENE FOUR

Another Part of the Forest.

Enter Valentine

VALENTINE. How use doth breed a habit in a man!
This shadowy desert, unfrequented woods,
I better brook than flourishing peopled towns.
Here can I sit alone, unseen of any,
And to the nightingale's complaining notes
Tune my distresses and record my woes.
O thou that dost inhabit in my breast,
Leave not the mansion so long tenantless,
Lest, growing ruinous, the building fall
And leave no memory of what it was!
Repair me with thy presence, Silvia!
Thou gentle nymph, cherish thy forlorn swain!

Noise within

What halloing and what stir is this to-day?
These are my mates, that make their wills their law,
Have some unhappy passenger in chase.
They love me well; yet I have much to do
To keep them from uncivil outrages.
Withdraw thee, Valentine: who's this comes here?

Steps aside

Enter Proteus, Silvia, and Julia

PROTEUS. Madam, this service I have done for you—
Though you respect not aught your servant doth—
To hazard life and rescue you from him
That would have forc'd your honour and your love.
Vouchsafe me, for my meed, but one fair look;
A smaller boon than this I cannot beg,
And less than this, I am sure, you cannot give.

VALENTINE. (*Aside*) How like a dream is this I see and hear!
Love, lend me patience to forbear awhile.

SILVIA. O, miserable, unhappy that I am!

PROTEUS. Unhappy were you, madam, ere I came;
But by my coming I have made you happy.

SILVIA. By thy approach thou mak'st me most unhappy.

JULIA. (*Aside*) And me, when he approacheth to your
    presence.
SILVIA. Had I been seized by a hungry lion,
    I would have been a breakfast to the beast,
    Rather than have false Proteus rescue me.
    O! heaven be judge how I love Valentine,
    Whose life 's as tender to me as my soul,
    And full as much—for more there cannot be—
    I do detest false perjur'd Proteus.
    Therefore be gone, solicit me no more.
PROTEUS. What dangerous action, stood it next to death,
    Would I not undergo for one calm look!
    O, 'tis the curse in love, and still approv'd,
    When women cannot love where they 're belov'd!
SILVIA. When Proteus cannot love where he 's belov'd.
    Read over Julia's heart, thy first best love,
    For whose dear sake thou didst then rend thy faith
    Into a thousand oaths; and all those oaths
    Descended into perjury to love me.
    Thou hast no faith left now, unless thou 'dst two,
    And that 's far worse than none: better have none
    Than plural faith which is too much by one.
    Thou counterfeit to thy true friend!
PROTEUS.   In love
    Who respects friend?
SILVIA.   All men but Proteus.
PROTEUS. Nay, if the gentle spirit of moving words
    Can no way change you to a milder form,
    I 'll woo you like a soldier, at arms' end,
    And love you 'gainst the nature of love,—force ye.
SILVIA. O heaven!
PROTEUS.   I 'll force thee yield to my desire.
VALENTINE. (*Coming forward*) Ruffian, let go that rude
    uncivil touch;
    Thou friend of an ill fashion!
PROTEUS.   Valentine!
VALENTINE. Thou common friend, that 's without faith or
    love—
    For such is a friend now—treacherous man!
    Thou hast beguil'd my hopes: nought but mine eye
    Could have persuaded me. Now I dare not say
    I have one friend alive: thou wouldst disprove me.

Who should be trusted now, when one's right hand
Is perjur'd to the bosom? Proteus,
I am sorry I must never trust thee more,
But count the world a stranger for thy sake.
The private wound is deep'st. O time most curst!
'Mongst all foes that a friend should be the worst!

PROTEUS. My shame and guilt confound me.
Forgive me, Valentine. If hearty sorrow
Be a sufficient ransom for offence,
I tender 't here: I do as truly suffer
As e'er I did commit.

VALENTINE.   Then, I am paid;
And once again I do receive thee honest.
Who by repentance is not satisfied
Is nor of heaven, nor earth; for these are pleas'd.
By penitence the Eternal's wrath 's appeas'd:
And, that my love may appear plain and free,
All that was mine in Silvia I give thee.

JULIA. O me unhappy!   *Swoons*

PROTEUS. Look to the boy.

VALENTINE. Why, boy! why, wag! how now! what 's the
    matter?
Look up; speak.

JULIA. O good sir, my master charg'd me
To deliver a ring to Madam Silvia,
Which out of my neglect was never done.

PROTEUS. Where is that ring, boy?

JULIA.   Here 'tis: this is it.   *Gives a ring*

PROTEUS. How! let me see.
Why this is the ring I gave to Julia.

JULIA. O, cry you mercy, sir; I have mistook:
This is the ring you sent to Silvia.   *Shows another ring*

PROTEUS. But how cam'st thou by this ring?
At my depart I gave this unto Julia.

JULIA. And Julia herself did give it me;
And Julia herself hath brought it hither.

PROTEUS. How! Julia!

JULIA. Behold her that gave aim to all thy oaths,
And entertain'd them deeply in her heart:
How oft hast thou with perjury cleft the root!
O Proteus! let this habit make thee blush.
Be thou asham'd that I have took upon me

Such an immodest raiment; if shame live
In a disguise of love.
It is the lesser blot, modesty finds,
Women to change their shapes than men their minds.
PROTEUS. Than men their minds! 'tis true. O heaven! were
    man
But constant, he were perfect: that one error
Fills him with faults; makes him run through all the sins:
Inconstancy falls off ere it begins.
What is in Silvia's face, but I may spy
More fresh in Julia's with a constant eye?
VALENTINE. Come, come, a hand from either.
Let me be blest to make this happy close:
'Twere pity two such friends should be long foes.
PROTEUS. Bear witness, heaven, I have my wish, for ever.
JULIA. And I mine.
       Enter Outlaws with Duke and Thurio
OUTLAW. A prize! a prize! a prize!
VALENTINE. Forbear, forbear, I say; it is my lord the duke.
Your Grace is welcome to a man disgrac'd,
Banished Valentine.
DUKE.   Sir Valentine!
THURIO. Yonder is Silvia; and Silvia 's mine.
VALENTINE. Thurio, give back, or else embrace thy death;
Come not within the measure of my wrath;
Do not name Silvia thine; if once again,
Verona shall not hold thee. Here she stands;
Take but possession of her with a touch;
I dare thee but to breathe upon my love.
THURIO. Sir Valentine, I care not for her, I.
I hold him but a fool that will endanger
His body for a girl that loves him not:
I claim her not, and therefore she is thine.
DUKE. The more degenerate and base art thou,
To make such means for her as thou hast done,
And leave her on such slight conditions.
Now, by the honour of my ancestry,
I do applaud thy spirit, Valentine,
And think thee worthy of an empress' love.
Know then, I here forget all former griefs,
Cancel all grudge, repeal thee home again,
Plead a new state in thy unrivall'd merit,

To which I thus subscribe: Sir Valentine,
Thou art a gentleman and well deriv'd;
Take thou thy Silvia, for thou hast deserv'd her.

VALENTINE. I thank your Grace; the gift hath made me
happy.
I now beseech you, for your daughter's sake,
To grant one boon that I shall ask of you.

DUKE. I grant it, for thine own, whate'er it be.

VALENTINE. These banish'd men, that I have kept withal,
Are men endu'd with worthy qualities:
Forgive them what they have committed here,
And let them be recall'd from their exile.
They are reformed, civil, full of good,
And fit for great employment, worthy lord.

DUKE. Thou hast prevail'd; I pardon them, and thee:
Dispose of them as thou know'st their deserts.
Come, let us go: we will include all jars
With triumphs, mirth, and rare solemnity.

VALENTINE. And as we walk along, I dare be bold
With our discourse to make your Grace to smile.
What think you of this page, my lord?

DUKE. I think the boy hath grace in him: he blushes.

VALENTINE. I warrant you, my lord, more grace than boy.

DUKE. What mean you by that saying?

VALENTINE. Please you, I 'll tell you as we pass along,
That you will wonder what hath fortuned.
Come, Proteus; 'tis your penance, but to hear
The story of your loves discovered:
That done, our day of marriage shall be yours;
One feast, one house, one mutual happiness. *Exeunt*

THE MERRY WIVES OF WINDSOR

CAST OF CHARACTERS

SIR JOHN FALSTAFF
FENTON, *a young Gentleman*
SHALLOW, *a Country Justice*
SLENDER, *Cousin to Shallow*

FORD }
PAGE } *two Gentlemen dwelling at Windsor*

WILLIAM PAGE, *a Boy, Son to Page*
SIR HUGH EVANS, *a Welsh Parson*
DOCTOR CAIUS, *a French Physician*
Host *of the Garter Inn*
BARDOLPH, PISTOL, NYM, *Followers of Falstaff*
ROBIN, *Page to Falstaff*
SIMPLE, *Servant to Slender*
RUGBY, *Servant to Doctor Caius*

MISTRESS FORD
MISTRESS PAGE
ANNE PAGE, *her Daughter, in love with Fenton*
MISTRESS QUICKLY, *Servant to Doctor Caius*
Servants to Page, Ford, &c.

SCENE

Windsor; and the Neighbourhood

THE MERRY WIVES OF WINDSOR

ACT ONE

SCENE ONE

Windsor. Before Page's House.

Enter Justice Shallow, Slender, and Sir Hugh Evans

SHALLOW. Sir Hugh, persuade me not; I will make a Star-chamber matter of it; if he were twenty Sir John Falstaffs he shall not abuse Robert Shallow, esquire.

SLENDER. In the county of Gloster, justice of peace, and 'coram.'

SHALLOW. Ay, cousin Slender, and 'cust-alorum.'

SLENDER. Ay, and 'rato-lorum' too; and a gentleman born, Master Parson; who writes himself 'armigero' in any bill, warrant, quittance, or obligation,—'armigero.'

SHALLOW. Ay, that I do; and have done any time these three hundred years.

SLENDER. All his successors gone before him hath done 't; and all his ancestors that come after him may: they may give the dozen white luces in their coat.

SHALLOW. It is an old coat.

EVANS. The dozen white louses do become an old coat well; it agrees well, passant; it is a familiar beast to man, and signifies love.

SHALLOW. The luce is the fresh fish; the salt fish is an old coat.

SLENDER. I may quarter, coz?

SHALLOW. You may, by marrying.

EVANS. It is marring indeed, if he quarter it.

SHALLOW. Not a whit.

EVANS. Yes, py 'r lady; if he has a quarter of your coat, there is but three skirts for yourself, in my simple conjectures:

but that is all one. If Sir John Falstaff have committed disparagements unto you, I am of the Church, and will be glad to do my benevolence to make atonements and compremises between you.

SHALLOW. The Council shall hear it; it is a riot.

EVANS. It is not meet the Council hear a riot; there is no fear of Got in a riot. The Council, look you, shall desire to hear the fear of Got, and not to hear a riot; take your vizaments in that.

SHALLOW. Ha! o' my life, if I were young again, the sword should end it.

EVANS. It is petter that friends is the sword, and end it; and there is also another device in my prain, which, peradventure, prings goot discretions with it. There is Anne Page, which is daughter to Master Thomas Page, which is pretty virginity.

SLENDER. Mistress Anne Page? She has brown hair, and speaks small like a woman.

EVANS. It is that fery person for all the orld, as just as you will desire; and seven hundred pounds of moneys, and gold and silver, is her grandsire, upon his death's-bed,— Got deliver to a joyful resurrections!—give, when she is able to overtake seventeen years old. It were a goot motion if we leave our pribbles and prabbles, and desire a marriage between Master Abraham and Mistress Anne Page.

SHALLOW. Did her grandsire leave her seven hundred pound?

EVANS. Ay, and her father is make her a petter penny.

SHALLOW. I know the young gentlewoman; she has good gifts.

EVANS. Seven hundred pounds and possibilities is goot gifts.

SHALLOW. Well, let us see honest Master Page. Is Falstaff there?

EVANS. Shall I tell you a lie? I do despise a liar as I do despise one that is false; or as I despise one that is not true. The knight, Sir John, is there; and, I beseech you, be ruled by your well-willers. I will peat the door for Master Page. (*Knocks*) What, hoa! Got pless your house here!

PAGE. (*Within*) Who 's there?

EVANS. Here is Got's plessing, and your friend, and Justice Shallow; and here young Master Slender, that peradventures shall tell you another tale, if matters grow to your likings.

Enter Page

PAGE. I am glad to see your worships well. I thank you for my venison, Master Shallow.

SHALLOW. Master Page, I am glad to see you: much good do it your good heart! I wished your venison better; it was ill killed. How doth good Mistress Page?—And I thank you always with my heart, la! with my heart.

PAGE. Sir, I thank you.

SHALLOW. Sir, I thank you; by yea and no, I do.

PAGE. I am glad to see you, good Master Slender.

SLENDER. How does your fallow greyhound, sir? I heard say he was outrun on Cotsall.

PAGE. It could not be judged, sir.

SLENDER. You'll not confess, you'll not confess.

SHALLOW. That he will not: 'tis your fault, 'tis your fault. 'Tis a good dog.

PAGE. A cur, sir.

SHALLOW. Sir, he's a good dog, and a fair dog; can there be more said? he is good and fair. Is Sir John Falstaff here?

PAGE. Sir, he is within; and I would I could do a good office between you.

EVANS. It is spoke as a Christians ought to speak.

SHALLOW. He hath wronged me, Master Page.

PAGE. Sir, he doth in some sort confess it.

SHALLOW. If it be confessed, it is not redressed: is not that so, Master Page? He hath wronged me; indeed, he hath; —at a word, he hath,—believe me: Robert Shallow, esquire, saith, he is wronged.

PAGE. Here comes Sir John.

Enter Sir John Falstaff, Bardolph, Nym, and Pistol

FALSTAFF. Now, Master Shallow, you'll complain of me to the king?

SHALLOW. Knight, you have beaten my men, killed my deer, and broke open my lodge.

FALSTAFF. But not kissed your keeper's daughter?

SHALLOW. Tut, a pin! This shall be answered.

FALSTAFF. I will answer it straight: I have done all this. That is now answered.

SHALLOW. The Council shall know this.

FALSTAFF. 'Twere better for you if it were known in counsel: you 'll be laughed at.

EVANS. Pauca verba, Sir John; goot worts.

FALSTAFF. Good worts! Good cabbage. Slender, I broke
your head: what matter have you against me?

SLENDER. Marry, sir, I have matter in my head against you;
and against your cony-catching rascals, Bardolph, Nym,
and Pistol. They carried me to the tavern, and made me
drunk, and afterwards picked my pocket.

BARDOLPH. You Banbury cheese!

SLENDER. Ay, it is no matter.

PISTOL. How now, Mephistophilus!

SLENDER. Ay, it is no matter.

NYM. Slice, I say! pauca, pauca; slice! that 's my humour.

SLENDER. Where 's Simple, my man? can you tell, cousin?

EVANS. Peace, I pray you. Now let us understand: there is
three umpires in this matter, as I understand; that is—
Master Page, fidelicet, Master Page; and there is myself,
fidelicet, myself; and the three party is, lastly and finally,
mine host of the Garter.

PAGE. We three, to hear it and end it between them.

EVANS. Fery goot: I will make a prief of it in my note-book;
and we will afterwards ork upon the cause with as great
discreetly as we can.

FALSTAFF. Pistol!

PISTOL. He hears with ears.

EVANS. The tevil and his tam! what phrase is this, 'He hears
with ear'? Why, it is affectations.

FALSTAFF. Pistol, did you pick Master Slender's purse?

SLENDER. Ay, by these gloves, did he,—or I would I might
never come in mine own great chamber again else,—of
seven groats in mill-sixpences, and two Edward shovel-
boards, that cost me two shilling and two pence a-piece
of Yead Miller, by these gloves.

FALSTAFF. Is this true, Pistol?

EVANS. No; it is false, if it is a pick-purse.

PISTOL. Ha, thou mountain foreigner!—Sir John and master
mine,
    I combat challenge of this latten bilbo.
    Word of denial in thy labras here!
    Word of denial: froth and scum, thou liest.

SLENDER. By these gloves, then, 'twas he.

NYM. Be avised, sir, and pass good humours. I will say,
'marry trap,' with you, if you run the nuthook's humour
on me: that is the very note of it.

SLENDER. By this hat, then, he in the red face had it; for
though I cannot remember what I did when you made
me drunk, yet I am not altogether an ass.

FALSTAFF. What say you, Scarlet and John?

BARDOLPH. Why, sir, for my part, I say, the gentleman had
drunk himself out of his five sentences.

EVANS. It is his 'five senses'; fie, what the ignorance is!

BARDOLPH. And being fap, sir, was, as they say, cashier'd;
and so conclusions pass'd the careires.

SLENDER. Ay, you spake in Latin then too; but 'tis no matter. I 'll ne'er be drunk whilst I live again, but in honest,
civil, godly company, for this trick: if I be drunk, I 'll be
drunk with those that have the fear of God, and not with
drunken knaves.

EVANS. So Got udge me, that is a virtuous mind.

FALSTAFF. You hear all these matters denied, gentlemen;
you hear it.

Enter Anne Page,
with wine; Mistress Ford and Mistress Page

PAGE. Nay, daughter, carry the wine in; we 'll drink within.
Exit Anne Page

SLENDER. O heaven! this is Mistress Anne Page.

PAGE. How now, Mistress Ford!

FALSTAFF. Mistress Ford, by my troth, you are very well
met: by your leave, good mistress.   *Kissing her*

PAGE. Wife, bid these gentlemen welcome. Come, we have
a hot venison pasty to dinner: come, gentlemen, I hope
we shall drink down all unkindness.

Exeunt all but Shallow, Slender, and Evans

SLENDER. I had rather than forty shillings I had my Book of
Songs and Sonnets here.

Enter Simple

How now, Simple! Where have you been? I must wait on
myself, must I? You have not the Book of Riddles about
you, have you?

SIMPLE. Book of Riddles! Why, did you not lend it to Alice
Shortcake upon All-Hallowmas last, a fortnight afore
Michaelmas?

SHALLOW. Come, coz; come, coz; we stay for you. A word

with you, coz; marry, this, coz: there is, as 'twere a
tender, a kind of tender, made afar off by Sir Hugh here:
do you understand me?

SLENDER. Ay, sir, you shall find me reasonable: if it be so, I
shall do that that is reason.

SHALLOW. Nay, but understand me.

SLENDER. So I do, sir.

EVANS. Give ear to his motions, Master Slender: I will description the matter to you, if you pe capacity of it.

SLENDER. Nay, I will do as my cousin Shallow says. I pray
you pardon me; he 's a justice of peace in his country,
simple though I stand here.

EVANS. But that is not the question; the question is concerning your marriage.

SHALLOW. Ay, there 's the point, sir.

EVANS. Marry, is it, the very point of it; to Mistress Anne
Page.

SLENDER. Why, if it be so, I will marry her upon any reasonable demands.

EVANS. But can you affection the 'oman? Let us command
to know that of your mouth or of your lips; for divers
philosophers hold that the lips is parcel of the mouth:
therefore, precisely, can you carry your good will to the
maid?

SHALLOW. Cousin Abraham Slender, can you love her?

SLENDER. I hope, sir, I will do as it shall become one that
would do reason.

EVANS. Nay, Got's lords and his ladies! you must speak pos-
sitable, if you can carry her your desires towards her.

SHALLOW. That you must. Will you, upon good dowry,
marry her?

SLENDER. I will do a greater thing than that, upon your request, cousin, in any reason.

SHALLOW. Nay, conceive me, conceive me, sweet coz: what
I do, is to pleasure you, coz. Can you love the maid?

SLENDER. I will marry her, sir, at your request; but if there
be no great love in the beginning, yet heaven may de-
crease it upon better acquaintance, when we are married
and have more occasion to know one another; I hope,
upon familiarity will grow more contempt: but if you
say, 'Marry her,' I will marry her; that I am freely dis-
solved, and dissolutely.

EVANS. It is a fery discretion answer; save, the faul is in the ort 'dissolutely': the ort is, according to our meaning, 'resolutely.' His meaning is goot.

SHALLOW. Ay, I think my cousin meant well.

SLENDER. Ay, or else I would I might be hanged, la!

SHALLOW. Here comes fair Mistress Anne.

Re-enter Anne Page

Would I were young for your sake, Mistress Anne.

ANNE. The dinner is on the table; my father desires your worships' company.

SHALLOW. I will wait on him, fair Mistress Anne.

EVANS. Od's plessed will! I will not be absence at the grace.

Exeunt Shallow and Evans

ANNE. Will 't please your worship to come in, sir?

SLENDER. No, I thank you, forsooth, heartily; I am very well.

ANNE. The dinner attends you, sir.

SLENDER. I am not a-hungry, I thank you forsooth. Go, sir-rah, for all you are my man, go wait upon my cousin Shallow. (*Exit Simple*) A justice of peace sometime may be beholding to his friend for a man. I keep but three men and a boy yet, till my mother be dead; but what though? Yet I live like a poor gentleman born.

ANNE. I may not go in without your worship: they will not sit till you come.

SLENDER. I' faith, I 'll eat nothing; I thank you as much as though I did.

ANNE. I pray you, sir, walk in.

SLENDER. I had rather walk here, I thank you. I bruised my shin th' other day with playing at sword and dagger with a master of fence; three veneys for a dish of stewed prunes;—and, by my troth, I cannot abide the smell of hot meat since. Why do your dogs bark so? Be there bears i' the town?

ANNE. I think there are, sir; I heard them talked of.

SLENDER. I love the sport well; but I shall as soon quarrel at it as any man in England. You are afraid if you see the bear loose, are you not?

ANNE. Ay, indeed, sir.

SLENDER. That 's meat and drink to me, now: I have seen Sackerson loose twenty times, and have taken him by the chain; but, I warrant you, the women have so cried and shrieked at it, that it passed: but women, indeed, cannot abide 'em; they are very ill-favoured rough things.

Re-enter Page

PAGE. Come, gentle Master Slender, come; we stay for you.

SLENDER. I 'll eat nothing, I thank you, sir.

PAGE. By cock and pie, you shall not choose, sir! come, come.

SLENDER. Nay, pray you, lead the way.

PAGE. Come on, sir.

SLENDER. Mistress Anne, yourself shall go first.

ANNE. Not I, sir; pray you, keep on.

SLENDER. Truly, I will not go first: truly, la! I will not do you that wrong.

ANNE. I pray you, sir.

SLENDER. I 'll rather be unmannerly than troublesome. You do yourself wrong, indeed, la!   *Exeunt*

SCENE TWO

The Same.

Enter Sir Hugh Evans and Simple

EVANS. Go your ways, and ask of Doctor Caius' house, which is the way: and there dwells one Mistress Quickly, which is in the manner of his nurse, or his try nurse, or his cook, or his laundry, his washer, and his wringer.

SIMPLE. Well, sir.

EVANS. Nay, it is better yet. Give her this letter; for it is a 'oman that altogether 's acquaintance with Mistress Anne Page: and the letter is, to desire and require her to solicit your master's desires to Mistress Anne Page. I pray you, be gone: I will make an end of my dinner; there 's pippins and seese to come.   *Exeunt*

SCENE THREE

A Room in the Garter Inn.

Enter Falstaff, Host, Bardolph, Nym, Pistol, and Robin

FALSTAFF. Mine host of the Garter!

HOST. What says my bully-rook? Speak scholarly and wisely.

FALSTAFF. Truly, mine host, I must turn away some of my followers.

HOST. Discard, bully Hercules; cashier: let them wag; trot, trot.

FALSTAFF. I sit at ten pounds a week.

HOST. Thou 'rt an emperor, Cæsar, Keisar, and Pheezar. I will entertain Bardolph; he shall draw, he shall tap: said I well, bully Hector?

FALSTAFF. Do so, good mine host.

HOST. I have spoke; let him follow. (*To Bardolph*) Let me see thee froth and lime: I am at a word; follow.

FALSTAFF. Bardolph, follow him. A tapster is a good trade: an old cloak makes a new jerkin; a withered serving-man, a fresh tapster. Go; adieu.

BARDOLPH. It is a life that I have desired. I will thrive.

PISTOL. O base Hungarian wight! wilt thou the splgot wield?   *Exit Bardolph*

NYM. He was gotten in drink; is not the humour conceited?

FALSTAFF. I am glad I am so acquit of this tinderbox; his thefts were too open; his filching was like an unskilful singer; he kept not time.

NYM. The good humour is to steal at a minim's rest.

PISTOL. 'Convey,' the wise it call. 'Steal!' foh! a fico for the phrase!

FALSTAFF. Well, sirs, I am almost out at heels.

PISTOL. Why, then, let kibes ensue.

FALSTAFF. There is no remedy; I must cony-catch, I must shift.

PISTOL. Young ravens must have food.

FALSTAFF. Which of you know Ford of this town?

PISTOL. I ken the wight: he is of substance good.

FALSTAFF. My honest lads, I will tell you what I am about.

PISTOL. Two yards, and more.

FALSTAFF. No quips now, Pistol! Indeed, I am in the waist two yards about; but I am now about no waste; I am about thrift. Briefly, I do mean to make love to Ford's wife: I spy entertainment in her; she discourses, she carves, she gives the leer of invitation: I can construe the action of her familiar style; and the hardest voice of her behaviour, to be Englished rightly, is, 'I am Sir John Falstaff's.'

PISTOL. He hath studied her well, and translated her well, out of honesty into English.

NYM. The anchor is deep: will that humour pass?

FALSTAFF. Now, the report goes she has all the rule of her husband's purse; he hath a legion of angels.

PISTOL. As many devils entertain, and 'To her, boy,' say I.

NYM. The humour rises; it is good: humour me the angels.

FALSTAFF. I have writ me here a letter to her; and here another to Page's wife, who even now gave me good eyes too, examined my parts with most judicious œilliades: sometimes the beam of her view gilded my foot, sometimes my portly belly.

PISTOL. Then did the sun on dunghill shine.

NYM. I thank thee for that humour.

FALSTAFF. O! she did so course o'er my exteriors with such a greedy intention, that the appetite of her eye did seem to scorch me up like a burning-glass. Here's another letter to her: she bears the purse too; she is a region in Guiana, all gold and bounty. I will be 'cheator to them both, and they shall be exchequers to me: they shall be my East and West Indies, and I will trade to them both. (To Pistol) Go bear thou this letter to Mistress Page; (To Nym) and thou this to Mistress Ford. We will thrive, lads, we will thrive.

PISTOL. Shall I Sir Pandarus of Troy become,
And by my side wear steel? Then, Lucifer take all!

NYM. I will run no base humour: here, take the humour-letter. I will keep the haviour of reputation.

FALSTAFF. (To Robin) Hold, sirrah, bear you these letters tightly:
Sail like my pinnace to these golden shores.
Rogues, hence! avaunt! vanish like hailstones, go;
Trudge, plod away o' the hoof; seek shelter, pack!

Falstaff will learn the humour of this age,
French thrift, you rogues: myself and skirted page.

Exeunt Falstaff and Robin

PISTOL. Let vultures gripe thy guts! for gourd and fullam
holds,
And high and low beguile the rich and poor.
Tester I 'll have in pouch when thou shalt lack,
Base Phrygian Turk!

NYM. I have operations in my head, which be humours of
revenge.

PISTOL. Wilt thou revenge?

NYM. By welkin and her star!

PISTOL. With wit or steel?

NYM. With both the humours, I:
I will discuss the humour of this love to Page.

PISTOL.   And I to Ford shall eke unfold
How Falstaff, varlet vile,
His dove will prove, his gold will hold,
And his soft couch defile.

NYM. My humour shall not cool: I will incense Page to deal
with poison; I will possess him with yellowness, for the
revolt of mine is dangerous: that is my true humour.

PISTOL. Thou art the Mars of malcontents: I second thee;
troop on.   *Exeunt*

SCENE FOUR

A Room in Doctor Caius's House.

Enter Mistress Quickly and Simple

QUICKLY. What, John Rugby!—
Enter Rugby
I pray thee, go to the casement, and see if you can see
my master, Master Doctor Caius, coming: if he do, i'
faith, and find anybody in the house, here will be an old
abusing of God's patience and the king's English.

RUGBY. I 'll go watch.

QUICKLY. Go; and we 'll have a posset for 't soon at night, in
faith, at the latter end of a sea-coal fire. (*Exit Rugby*)
An honest, willing, kind fellow, as ever servant shall
come in house withal; and, I warrant you, no tell-tale,

nor no breed-bate: his worst fault is, that he is given to prayer; he is something peevish that way, but nobody but has his fault; but let that pass. Peter Simple you say your name is?

SIMPLE. Ay, for fault of a better.

QUICKLY. And Master Slender 's your master?

SIMPLE. Ay, forsooth.

QUICKLY. Does he not wear a great round beard like a glover's paring-knife?

SIMPLE. No, forsooth: he hath but a little whey-face, with a little yellow beard—a cane-coloured beard.

QUICKLY. A softly-sprighted man, is he not?

SIMPLE. Ay, forsooth; but he is as tall a man of his hands as any is between this and his head: he hath fought with a warrener.

QUICKLY. How say you?—O! I should remember him: does he not hold up his head, as it were, and strut in his gait?

SIMPLE. Yes, indeed, does he.

QUICKLY. Well, heaven send Anne Page no worse fortune! Tell Master Parson Evans I will do what I can for your master: Anne is a good girl, and I wish—

Re-enter Rugby

RUGBY. Out, alas! here comes my master.

QUICKLY. We shall all be shent. Run in here, good young man; go into this closet. (*Shuts Simple in the closet*) He will not stay long. What, John Rugby! John, what, John, I say! Go, John, go inquire for my master; I doubt he be not well, that he comes not home.   *Exit Rugby*

(*Sings*) 'And down, down, adown-a,' &c.

Enter Doctor Caius

CAIUS. Vat is you sing? I do not like dese toys. Pray you, go and vetch me in my closet une boitine verde; a box, a green-a box: do intend vat I speak? a green-a box.

QUICKLY. Ay, forsooth; I 'll fetch it you. (*Aside*) I am glad he went not in himself: if he had found the young man, he would have been horn-mad.

CAIUS. Fe, fe, fe, fe! ma foi, il fait fort chaud. Je m'en vais à la cour,—la grande affaire.

QUICKLY. Is it this, sir?

CAIUS. Oui; mettez le au mon pocket; dépêchez, quickly.— Vere is dat knave Rugby?

QUICKLY. What, John Rugby! John!

Re-enter Rugby

RUGBY. Here, sir.

CAIUS. You are John Rugby, and you are Jack Rugby:
come, take-a your rapier, and come after my heel to de
court.

RUGBY. 'Tis ready, sir, here in the porch.

CAIUS. By my trot, I tarry too long.—Od's me! Qu'ay j'ou-
blié? dere is some simples in my closet, dat I vill not for
de varld I shall leave behind.

QUICKLY. (*Aside*) Ay me! he 'll find the young man there,
and be mad.

CAIUS. O diable! diable! vat is in my closet?—Villain! larron!
(*Pulling Simple out*) Rugby, my rapier!

QUICKLY. Good master, be content.

CAIUS. Verefore shall I be content-a?

QUICKLY. The young man is an honest man.

CAIUS. Vat shall de honest man do in my closet? Dere is no
honest man dat shall come in my closet.

QUICKLY. I beseech you, be not so phlegmatic. Hear the
truth of it: he came of an errand to me from Parson
Hugh.

CAIUS. Vell.

SIMPLE. Ay, forsooth, to desire her to—

QUICKLY. Peace, I pray you.

CAIUS. Peace-a your tongue!—Speak-a your tale.

SIMPLE. To desire this honest gentlewoman, your maid, to
speak a good word to Mistress Anne Page for my master
in the way of marriage.

QUICKLY. This is all, indeed, la! but I 'll ne'er put my finger
in the fire, and need not.

CAIUS. Sir Hugh send-a you?—Rugby, baillez me some
paper: tarry you a little-a while.   *Writes*

QUICKLY. I am glad he is so quiet: if he had been throughly
moved, you should have heard him so loud, and so melancholy. But, notwithstanding, man, I 'll do your master
what good I can; and the very yea and the no is, the
French doctor, my master,—I may call him my master,
look you, for I keep his house; and I wash, wring, brew,
bake, scour, dress meat and drink, make the beds, and do
all myself,—

SIMPLE. 'Tis a great charge to come under one body's hand.

QUICKLY. Are you avis'd o' that? you shall find it a great

charge: and to be up early and down late; but notwithstanding,—to tell you in your ear,—I would have no
words of it,—my master himself is in love with Mistress
Anne Page: but notwithstanding that, I know Anne's
mind, that 's neither here nor there.

CAIUS. You jack'nape, give-a dis letter to Sir Hugh; by gar,
it is a shallenge: I vill cut his troat in de Park; and I vill
teach a scurvy jack-a-nape priest to meddle or make. You
may be gone; it is not good you tarry here: by gar, I vill
cut all his two stones; by gar, he shall not have a stone to
trow at his dog.   *Exit Simple*

QUICKLY. Alas! he speaks but for his friend.

CAIUS. It is no matter-a for dat:—do not you tell-a me dat I
shall have Anne Page for myself? By gar, I vill kill de
Jack priest; and I have appointed mine host of de Jar-
tiere to measure our weapon. By gar, I vill myself have
Anne Page.

QUICKLY. Sir, the maid loves you, and all shall be well. We
must give folks leave to prate: what, the good-jer!

CAIUS. Rugby, come to the court vit me. By gar, if I have
not Anne Page, I shall turn your head out of my door.
Follow my heels, Rugby.   *Exeunt Caius and Rugby*

QUICKLY. You shall have An fool's-head of your own. No, I
know Anne's mind for that: never a woman in Windsor
knows more of Anne's mind than I do; nor can do more
than I do with her, I thank heaven.

FENTON. (*Within*) Who 's within there? ho!

QUICKLY. Who 's there, I trow? Come near the house, I
pray you.

Enter Fenton

FENTON. How now, good woman! how dost thou?

QUICKLY. The better, that it pleases your good worship to
ask.

FENTON. What news? How does pretty Mistress Anne?

QUICKLY. In truth, sir, and she is pretty, and honest, and
gentle; and one that is your friend, I can tell you that by
the way; I praise heaven for it.

FENTON. Shall I do any good, thinkest thou? Shall I not lose
my suit?

QUICKLY. Troth, sir, all is in his hands above; but notwithstanding, Master Fenton, I 'll be sworn on a book, she
loves you. Have not your worship a wart above your eye?

FENTON. Yes, marry have I; what of that?

QUICKLY. Well, thereby hangs a tale. Good faith, it is such another Nan; but, I detest, an honest maid as ever broke bread: we had an hour's talk of that wart. I shall never laugh but in that maid's company;—but, indeed, she is given too much to allicholy and musing. But for you—well, go to.

FENTON. Well, I shall see her to-day. Hold, there 's money for thee; let me have thy voice in my behalf: if thou seest her before me, commend me.

QUICKLY. Will I? i' faith, that we will: and I will tell your worship more of the wart the next time we have confidence; and of other wooers.

FENTON. Well, farewell; I am in great haste now.

QUICKLY. Farewell to your worship.—(*Exit Fenton*) Truly, an honest gentleman: but Anne loves him not; for I know Anne's mind as well as another does. Out upon 't! what have I forgot?   *Exit*

ACT TWO

Before Page's House.
Enter Mistress Page, with a Letter

MRS. PAGE. What! have I 'scaped love-letters in the holiday-
time of my beauty, and am I now a subject for them? Let
me see. (*Reads*)

'Ask me no reason why I love you; for though Love use
Reason for his physician, he admits him not for his counsellor. You are not young, no more am I; go to then,
there 's sympathy; you are merry, so am I; ha! ha! then,
there 's more sympathy; you love sack, and so do I;
would you desire better sympathy? Let it suffice thee,
Mistress Page, at the least, if the love of a soldier can
suffice, that I love thee. I will not say, pity me,—'tis not a
soldier-like phrase; but I say, love me. By me,

> Thine own true knight,
> By day or night,
> Or any kind of light,
> With all his might
> For thee to fight,
>   'John Falstaff.'

What a Herod of Jewry is this! O wicked, wicked world!
one that is well-nigh worn to pieces with age, to show
himself a young gallant. What an unweighed behaviour
hath this Flemish drunkard picked, (with the devil's
name!) out of my conversation, that he dares in this manner assay me? Why, he hath not been thrice in my company! What should I say to him? I was then frugal of my
mirth:—heaven forgive me! Why, I 'll exhibit a bill in the
parliament for the putting down of men. How shall I be
revenged on him? for revenged I will be, as sure as his
guts are made of puddings.

Enter Mistress Ford

MRS. FORD. Mistress Page, trust me, I was going to your house.

MRS. PAGE. And, trust me, I was coming to you. You look very ill.

MRS. FORD. Nay, I 'll ne'er believe that: I have to show to the contrary.

MRS. PAGE. Faith, but you do, in my mind.

MRS. FORD. Well, I do then: yet, I say I could show you to the contrary. O, Mistress Page! give me some counsel.

MRS. PAGE. What 's the matter, woman?

MRS. FORD. O woman, if it were not for one trifling respect, I could come to such honour!

MRS. PAGE. Hang the trifle, woman; take the honour. What is it?—dispense with trifles;—what is it?

MRS. FORD. If I would but go to hell for an eternal moment or so, I could be knighted.

MRS. PAGE. What? thou liest. Sir Alice Ford! These knights will hack; and so thou shouldst not alter the article of thy gentry.

MRS. FORD. We burn daylight: here, read, read; perceive how I might be knighted. I shall think the worse of fat men as long as I have an eye to make difference of men's liking: and yet he would not swear; praised women's modesty; and gave such orderly and well-behaved reproof to all uncomeliness, that I would have sworn his disposition would have gone to the truth of his words; but they do no more adhere and keep place together than the Hundredth Psalm to the tune of 'Green Sleeves.' What tempest, I trow, threw this whale, with so many tuns of oil in his belly, ashore at Windsor? How shall I be revenged on him? I think, the best way were to entertain him with hope, till the wicked fire of lust have melted him in his own grease. Did you ever hear the like?

MRS. PAGE. Letter for letter, but that the name of Page and Ford differs! To thy great comfort in this mystery of ill opinions, here 's the twin brother of thy letter: but let thine inherit first; for, I protest, mine never shall. I warrant, he hath a thousand of these letters, writ with blank space for different names, sure more, and these are of the second edition. He will print them, out of doubt; for he cares not what he puts into the press, when he would put

us two: I had rather be a giantess, and lie under Mount
Pelion. Well, I will find you twenty lascivious turtles ere
one chaste man.

MRS. FORD. Why, this is the very same; the very hand, the
very words. What doth he think of us?

MRS. PAGE. Nay, I know not: it makes me almost ready to
wrangle with mine own honesty. I 'll entertain myself like
one that I am not acquainted withal; for, sure, unless he
know some strain in me, that I know not myself, he
would never have boarded me in this fury.

MRS. FORD. Boarding call you it? I 'll be sure to keep him
above deck.

MRS. PAGE. So will I: if he come under my hatches, I 'll
never to sea again. Let 's be revenged on him: let 's appoint him a meeting; give him a show of comfort in his
suit, and lead him on with a fine-baited delay, till he hath
pawned his horses to mine host of the Garter.

MRS. FORD. Nay, I will consent to act any villany against
him, that may not sully the chariness of our honesty. O,
that my husband saw this letter! it would give eternal
food to his jealousy.

MRS. PAGE. Why, look, where he comes; and my good man
too: he 's as far from jealousy, as I am from giving him
cause; and that, I hope, is an unmeasurable distance.

MRS. FORD. You are the happier woman.

MRS. PAGE. Let 's consult together against this greasy
knight. Come hither.   *They retire*

Enter Ford, Pistol, Page, and Nym

FORD. Well, I hope it be not so.

PISTOL. Hope is a curtal dog in some affairs:
Sir John affects thy wife.

FORD. Why, sir, my wife is not young.

PISTOL. He wooes both high and low, both rich and poor,
Both young and old, one with another, Ford.
He loves the galimaufry: Ford, perpend.

FORD. Love my wife!

PISTOL. With liver burning hot: prevent, or go thou,
Like Sir Actæon he, with Ringwood at thy heels.—
O! odious is the name!

FORD. What name, sir?

PISTOL. The horn, I say. Farewell:
Take heed; have open eye, for thieves do foot by night:

Take heed, ere summer comes or cuckoo-birds do sing.
Away, sir Corporal Nym!
Believe it, Page; he speaks sense. *Exit*

FORD. (*Aside*) I will be patient: I will find out this.

NYM. (*To Page*) And this is true; I like not the humour of
lying. He hath wronged me in some humours: I should
have borne the humoured letter to her, but I have a
sword and it shall bite upon my necessity. He loves your
wife; there 's the short and the long. My name is Corporal Nym; I speak, and I avouch 'tis true: my name is
Nym, and Falstaff loves your wife. Adieu. I love not the
humour of bread and cheese; and there 's the humour of
it. Adieu. *Exit*

PAGE. (*Aside*) 'The humour of it,' quoth 'a! here 's a fellow
frights humour out of his wits.

FORD. I will seek out Falstaff.

PAGE. I never heard such a drawling, affecting rogue.

FORD. If I do find it: well.

PAGE. I will not believe such a Cataian, though the priest o'
the town commended him for a true man.

FORD. 'Twas a good sensible fellow: well.

PAGE. How now, Meg!

MRS. PAGE. Whither go you, George?—Hark you.

MRS. FORD. How now, sweet Frank! why art thou melancholy?

FORD. I melancholy! I am not melancholy. Get you home,
go.

MRS. FORD. Faith, thou hast some crotchets in thy head
now. Will you go, Mistress Page?

MRS. PAGE. Have with you, you 'll come to dinner, George?
(*Aside to Mrs. Ford*) Look, who comes yonder: she shall
be our messenger to this paltry knight.

MRS. FORD. Trust me, I thought on her: she 'll fit it.

Enter Mistress Quickly

MRS. PAGE. You are come to see my daughter Anne?

QUICKLY. Ay, forsooth; and, I pray, how does good Mistress
Anne?

MRS. PAGE. Go in with us, and see: we 'd have an hour's
talk with you. *Exeunt Mistress*
Page, Mistress Ford, and Mistress Quickly

PAGE. How now, Master Ford!

FORD. You heard what this knave told me, did you not?

PAGE. Yes; and you heard what the other told me?

FORD. Do you think there is truth in them?

PAGE. Hang 'em, slaves! I do not think the knight would offer it: but these that accuse him in his intent towards our
wives, are a yoke of his discarded men; very rogues, now
they be out of service.

FORD. Were they his men?

PAGE. Marry, were they.

FORD. I like it never the better for that. Does he lie at the
Garter?

PAGE. Ay, marry, does he. If he should intend this voyage
towards my wife, I would turn her loose to him; and
what he gets more of her than sharp words, let it lie on
my head.

FORD. I do not misdoubt my wife, but I would be loth to
turn them together. A man may be too confident: I
would have nothing 'lie on my head': I cannot be thus
satisfied.

PAGE. Look, where my ranting host of the Garter comes.
There is either liquor in his pate or money in his purse
when he looks so merrily.—

Enter Host and Shallow

How now, mine host!

HOST. How now, bully-rook! thou 'rt a gentleman. Cavaliero-
justice, I say!

SHALLOW. I follow, mine host, I follow. Good even and
twenty, good Master Page! Master Page, will you go with
us? we have sport in hand.

HOST. Tell him, cavaliero-justice; tell him, bully-rook.

SHALLOW. Sir, there is a fray to be fought between Sir
Hugh the Welsh priest and Caius the French doctor.

FORD. Good mine host o' the Garter, a word with you.

HOST. What sayest thou, my bully-rook?   *They go aside*

SHALLOW. (*To Page*) Will you go with us to behold it? My
merry host hath had the measuring of their weapons,
and, I think, hath appointed them contrary places; for,
believe me, I hear the parson is no jester. Hark, I will tell
you what our sport shall be.   *They go aside*

HOST. Hast thou no suit against my knight, my guest-cava-
lier?

FORD. None, I protest: but I 'll give you a pottle of burnt

sack to give me recourse to him and tell him my name is
Brook, only for a jest.

HOST. My hand, bully: thou shalt have egress and regress;
said I well? and thy name shall be Brook. It is a merry
knight. Will you go, mynheers?

SHALLOW. Have with you, mine host.

PAGE. I have heard, the Frenchman hath good skill in his
rapier.

SHALLOW. Tut, sir! I could have told you more. In these
times you stand on distance, your passes, stoccadoes, and
I know not what: 'tis the heart, Master Page; 'tis here, 'tis
here. I have seen the time with my long sword I would
have made you four tall fellows skip like rats.

HOST. Here, boys, here, here! shall we wag?

PAGE. Have with you. I had rather hear them scold than
fight.   *Exeunt Host, Shallow, and Page*

FORD. Though Page be a secure fool, and stands so firmly
on his wife's frailty, yet I cannot put off my opinion so
easily. She was in his company at Page's house, and what
they made there, I know not. Well, I will look further
into 't; and I have a disguise to sound Falstaff. If I find
her honest, I lose not my labour; if she be otherwise, 'tis
labour well bestowed.   *Exit*

SCENE TWO

A Room in the Garter Inn.

Enter Falstaff and Pistol

FALSTAFF. I will not lend thee a penny.

PISTOL. Why, then the world 's mine oyster,
Which I with sword will open.
I will retort the sum in equipage.

FALSTAFF. Not a penny. I have been content, sir, you
should lay my countenance to pawn: I have grated upon
my good friends for three reprieves for you and your
coach-fellow Nym; or else you had looked through the
grate, like a geminy of baboons. I am damned in hell for
swearing to gentlemen my friends, you were good soldiers and tall fellows; and when Mistress Bridget lost the

handle of her fan, I took 't upon mine honour thou hadst it not.

PISTOL. Didst thou not share? Hadst thou not fifteen pence?

FALSTAFF. Reason, you rogue, reason: thinkest thou, I 'll endanger my soul gratis? At a word, hang no more about me; I am no gibbet for you: go: a short knife and a throng!—to your manor of Pichthatch! go. You 'll not bear a letter for me, you rogue!—you stand upon your honour! —Why, thou unconfinable baseness, it is as much as I can do to keep the terms of mine honour precise. I, I, I, myself sometimes, leaving the fear of God on the left hand and hiding mine honour in my necessity, am fain to shuffle, to hedge and to lurch; and yet you, rogue, will ensconce your rags, your cat-a-mountain looks, your red-lattice phrases, and your bold-beating oaths, under the shelter of your honour! You will not do it, you!

PISTOL. I do relent: what wouldst thou more of man?

Enter Robin

ROBIN. Sir, here 's a woman would speak with you.

FALSTAFF. Let her approach.

Enter Mistress Quickly

QUICKLY. Give your worship good-morrow.

FALSTAFF. Good-morrow, good wife.

QUICKLY. Not so, an 't please your worship.

FALSTAFF. Good maid, then.

QUICKLY. I 'll be sworn
As my mother was, the first hour I was born.

FALSTAFF. I do believe the swearer. What with me?

QUICKLY. Shall I vouchsafe your worship a word or two?

FALSTAFF. Two thousand, fair woman; and I 'll vouchsafe thee the hearing.

QUICKLY. There is one Mistress Ford, sir,—I pray, come a little nearer this ways:—I myself dwell with Master Doctor Caius.

FALSTAFF. Well, on: Mistress Ford, you say,—

QUICKLY. Your worship says very true:—I pray your worship, come a little nearer this ways.

FALSTAFF. I warrant thee, nobody hears; mine own people, mine own people.

QUICKLY. Are they so? God bless them, and make them his servants!

FALSTAFF. Well: Mistress Ford; what of her?

QUICKLY. Why, sir, she 's a good creature. Lord, Lord! your worship 's a wanton! Well, heaven forgive you, and all of us, I pray!

FALSTAFF. Mistress Ford; come, Mistress Ford,—

QUICKLY. Marry, this is the short and the long of it. You have brought her into such a canaries as 'tis wonderful: the best courtier of them all, when the court lay at Windsor, could never have brought her to such a canary; yet there has been knights, and lords, and gentlemen, with their coaches, I warrant you, coach after coach, letter after letter, gift after gift; smelling so sweetly—all musk, and so rushling, I warrant you, in silk and gold; and in such alligant terms; and in such wine and sugar of the best and the fairest, that would have won any woman's heart; and, I warrant you, they could never get an eye-wink of her. I had myself twenty angels given me this morning; but I defy all angels, in any such sort, as they say, but in the way of honesty: and, I warrant you, they could never get her so much as sip on a cup with the proudest of them all; and yet there has been earls, nay, which is more, pensioners; but, I warrant you, all is one with her.

FALSTAFF. But what says she to me? Be brief, my good she-Mercury.

QUICKLY. Marry, she hath received your letter; for the which she thanks you a thousand times; and she gives you to notify that her husband will be absence from his house between ten and eleven.

FALSTAFF. Ten and eleven?

QUICKLY. Ay, forsooth; and then you may come and see the picture, she says, that you wot of: Master Ford, her husband, will be from home. Alas! the sweet woman leads an ill life with him; he 's a very jealousy man; she leads a very frampold life with him, good heart.

FALSTAFF. Ten and eleven. Woman, commend me to her; I will not fail her.

QUICKLY. Why, you say well. But I have another messenger to your worship: Mistress Page hath her hearty commendations to you too: and let me tell you in your ear, she 's as fartuous a civil modest wife, and one, I tell you, that will not miss you morning nor evening prayer, as any is in Windsor, whoe'er be the other: and she bade me tell

your worship that her husband is seldom from home;
but, she hopes there will come a time. I never knew a
woman so dote upon a man: surely, I think you have
charms, la; yes, in truth.

FALSTAFF. Not I, I assure thee: setting the attraction of my
good parts aside, I have no other charms.

QUICKLY. Blessing on your heart for 't!

FALSTAFF. But, I pray thee, tell me this: has Ford's wife
and Page's wife acquainted each other how they love
me?

QUICKLY. That were a jest indeed! They have not so little
grace, I hope: that were a trick, indeed! But Mistress
Page would desire you to send her your little page, of all
loves: her husband has a marvellous infection to the little
page; and, truly, Master Page is an honest man. Never a
wife in Windsor leads a better life than she does: do
what she will, say what she will, take all, pay all, go to
bed when she list, rise when she list, all is as she will:
and, truly she deserves it; for if there be a kind woman in
Windsor, she is one. You must send her your page; no
remedy.

FALSTAFF. Why, I will.

QUICKLY. Nay, but do so, then; and, look you, he may come
and go between you both; and in any case have a nay-
word, that you may know one another's mind, and the
boy never need to understand any thing; for 'tis not good
that children should know any wickedness: old folks, you
know, have discretion, as they say, and know the world.

FALSTAFF. Fare thee well: commend me to them both.
There 's my purse; I am yet thy debtor.—Boy, go along
with this woman.—(*Exeunt Mistress Quickly and Robin*)
This news distracts me.

PISTOL. This punk is one of Cupid's carriers.
  Clap on more sails; pursue; up with your fights;
  Give fire! She is my prize, or ocean whelm them all! *Exit*

FALSTAFF. Sayest thou so, old Jack? Go thy ways; I 'll make
more of thy old body than I have done. Will they yet
look after thee? Wilt thou, after the expense of so much
money, be now a gainer? Good body, I thank thee. Let
them say 'tis grossly done; so it be fairly done, no matter.
    Enter Bardolph, with a cup of Sack

BARDOLPH. Sir John, there 's one Master Brook below would

fain speak with you, and be acquainted with you; and hath sent your worship a morning's draught of sack.

FALSTAFF. Brook is his name?

BARDOLPH. Ay, sir.

FALSTAFF. Call him in. (*Exit Bardolph*) Such Brooks are welcome to me, that o'erflow such liquor. Ah, ha! Mistress Ford and Mistress Page, have I encompassed you? Go to; via!

> *Re-enter Bardolph, with Ford disguised*

FORD. Bless you, sir!

FALSTAFF. And you, sir; would you speak with me?

FORD. I make bold to press with so little preparation upon you.

FALSTAFF. You 're welcome. What 's your will?—Give us leave, drawer.   *Exit Bardolph*

FORD. Sir, I am a gentleman that have spent much: my name is Brook.

FALSTAFF. Good Master Brook, I desire more acquaintance of you.

FORD. Good Sir John, I sue for yours: not to charge you; for I must let you understand I think myself in better plight for a lender than you are: the which hath something emboldened me to this unseasoned intrusion; for, they say, if money go before, all ways do lie open.

FALSTAFF. Money is a good soldier, sir, and will on.

FORD. Troth, and I have a bag of money here troubles me: if you will help to bear it, Sir John, take all, or half, for easing me of the carriage.

FALSTAFF. Sir, I know not how I may deserve to be your porter.

FORD. I will tell you, sir, if you will give me the hearing.

FALSTAFF. Speak, good Master Brook; I shall be glad to be your servant.

FORD. Sir, I hear you are a scholar,—I will be brief with you, and you have been a man long known to me, though I had never so good means, as desire, to make myself acquainted with you. I shall discover a thing to you, wherein I must very much lay open mine own imperfection; but, good Sir John, as you have one eye upon my follies, as you hear them unfolded, turn another into the register of your own, that I may pass with a reproof the easier, sith you yourself know how easy it is to be such an offender.

FALSTAFF. Very well, sir; proceed.

FORD. There is a gentlewoman in this town, her husband's name is Ford.

FALSTAFF. Well, sir.

FORD. I have long loved her, and, I protest to you, bestowed much on her; followed her with a doting observance; engrossed opportunities to meet her; fee'd every slight occasion that could but niggardly give me sight of her; not only bought many presents to give her, but have given largely to many to know what she would have given. Briefly, I have pursued her as love hath pursued me; which hath been on the wing of all occasions. But whatsoever I have merited, either in my mind or in my means, meed, I am sure, I have received none; unless experience be a jewel that I have purchased at an infinite rate; and that hath taught me to say this,

Love like a shadow flies when substance love pursues;
Pursuing that that flies, and flying what pursues.

FALSTAFF. Have you received no promise of satisfaction at her hands?

FORD. Never.

FALSTAFF. Have you importuned her to such a purpose?

FORD. Never.

FALSTAFF. Of what quality was your love, then?

FORD. Like a fair house built upon another man's ground; so that I have lost my edifice by mistaking the place where I erected it.

FALSTAFF. To what purpose have you unfolded this to me?

FORD. When I have told you that, I have told you all. Some say, that though she appear honest to me, yet in other places she enlargeth her mirth so far that there is shrewd construction made of her. Now, Sir John, here is the heart of my purpose: you are a gentleman of excellent breeding, admirable discourse, of great admittance, authentic in your place and person, generally allowed for your many war-like, court-like, and learned preparations.

FALSTAFF. O, sir!

FORD. Believe it, for you know it. There is money; spend it, spend it; spend more; spend all I have; only give me so

much of your time in exchange of it, as to lay an amiable
siege to the honesty of this Ford's wife: use your art of
wooing, win her to consent to you; if any man may, you
may as soon as any.

FALSTAFF. Would it apply well to the vehemency of your
affection, that I should win what you would enjoy? Methinks you prescribe to yourself very preposterously.

FORD. O, understand my drift. She dwells so securely on
the excellency of her honour, that the folly of my soul
dares not present itself: she is too bright to be looked
against. Now, could I come to her with any detection in
my hand, my desires had instance and argument to commend themselves: I could drive her then from the ward
of her purity, her reputation, her marriage-vow, and a
thousand other her defences, which now are too-too
strongly embattled against me. What say you to 't, Sir
John?

FALSTAFF. Master Brook, I will first make bold with your
money; next, give me your hand; and last, as I am a
gentleman, you shall, if you will, enjoy Ford's wife.

FORD. O good sir!

FALSTAFF. I say you shall.

FORD. Want no money, Sir John; you shall want none.

FALSTAFF. Want no Mistress Ford, Master Brook; you shall
want none. I shall be with her, I may tell you, by her
own appointment; even as you came in to me, her as-
sistant or go-between parted from me: I say I shall be
with her between ten and eleven; for at that time the
jealous rascally knave her husband will be forth. Come
you to me at night; you shall know how I speed.

FORD. I am blest in your acquaintance. Do you know Ford,
sir?

FALSTAFF. Hang him, poor cuckoldly knave! I know him
not. Yet I wrong him, to call him poor: they say the jealous wittolly knave hath masses of money; for the which
his wife seems to me well-favoured. I will use her as the
key of the cuckoldly rogue's coffer; and there 's my har-
vest-home.

FORD. I would you knew Ford, sir, that you might avoid
him, if you saw him.

FALSTAFF. Hang him, mechanical salt-butter rogue! I will
stare him out of his wits; I will awe him with my cudgel:

it shall hang like a meteor o'er the cuckold's horns. Master Brook, thou shalt know I will predominate over the peasant, and thou shalt lie with his wife. Come to me soon at night. Ford 's a knave, and I will aggravate his style; thou, Master Brook, shalt know him for knave and cuckold. Come to me soon at night. *Exit*

FORD. What a damned Epicurean rascal is this! My heart is ready to crack with impatience. Who says this is improvident jealousy? My wife hath sent to him, the hour is fixed, the match is made. Would any man have thought this? See the hell of having a false woman! My bed shall be abused, my coffers ransacked, my reputation gnawn at; and I shall not only receive this villanous wrong, but stand under the adoption of abominable terms, and by him that does me this wrong. Terms! names! Amaimon sounds well; Lucifer, well; Barbason, well; yet they are devils' additions, the names of fiends: but Cuckold! Wittol!—Cuckold! the devil himself hath not such a name. Page is an ass, a secure ass: he will trust his wife; he will not be jealous. I will rather trust a Fleming with my butter, Parson Hugh the Welshman with my cheese, an Irishman with my aqua-vitæ bottle, or a thief to walk my ambling gelding, than my wife with herself: then she plots, then she ruminates, then she devises; and what they think in their hearts they may effect, they will break their hearts but they will effect. God be praised for my jealousy! Eleven o'clock the hour: I will prevent this, detect my wife, be revenged on Falstaff, and laugh at Page. I will about it; better three hours too soon than a minute too late. Fie, fie, fie! cuckold! cuckold! cuckold!   *Exit*

SCENE THREE

A Field near Windsor.

Enter Caius and Rugby

CAIUS. Jack Rugby!
RUGBY. Sir?
CAIUS. Vat is de clock, Jack?
RUGBY. 'Tis past the hour, sir, that Sir Hugh promised to meet.

CAIUS. By gar, he has save his soul, dat he is no come: he has pray his Pible vell, dat he is no come. By gar, Jack Rugby, he is dead already, if he be come.

RUGBY. He is wise, sir; he knew your worship would kill him, if he came.

CAIUS. By gar, de herring is no dead so as I vill kill him. Take your rapier, Jack; I vill tell you how I vill kill him.

RUGBY. Alas, sir! I cannot fence.

CAIUS. Villany, take your rapier.

RUGBY. Forbear; here 's company.

Enter Host, Shallow, Slender, and Page

HOST. Bless thee, bully doctor!

SHALLOW. Save you, Master Doctor Caius!

PAGE. Now, good Master doctor!

SLENDER. Give you good-morrow, sir.

CAIUS. Vat be all you, one, two, tree, four, come for?

HOST. To see thee fight, to see thee foin, to see thee traverse; to see thee here, to see thee there; to see thee pass thy punto, thy stock, thy reverse, thy distance, thy montant. Is he dead, my Ethiopian? is he dead, my Francisco? ha, bully! What says my Æsculapius? my Galen? my heart of elder? ha! is he dead, bully stale? is he dead?

CAIUS. By gar, he is de coward Jack priest of de vorld; he is not show his face.

HOST. Thou art a Castilian King Urinall Hector of Greece, my boy!

CAIUS. I pray you, bear vitness that me have stay six or seven, two, tree hours for him, and he is no come.

SHALLOW. He is the wiser man, Master doctor: he is a curer of souls, and you a curer of bodies; if you should fight, you go against the hair of your professions. Is it not true, Master Page?

PAGE. Master Shallow, you have yourself been a great fighter, though now a man of peace.

SHALLOW. Bodykins, Master Page, though I now be old and of the peace, if I see a sword out, my finger itches to make one. Though we are justices and doctors and churchmen, Master Page, we have some salt of our youth in us; we are the sons of women, Master Page.

PAGE. 'Tis true, Master Shallow.

SHALLOW. It will be found so, Master Page. Master Doctor Caius, I am come to fetch you home. I am sworn of the peace: you have showed yourself a wise physician, and Sir Hugh hath shown himself a wise and patient churchman. You must go with me, Master doctor.

HOST. Pardon, guest-justice.—A word, Monsieur Mockwater.

CAIUS. Mock-vater! vat is dat?

HOST. Mock-water, in our English tongue, is valour, bully.

CAIUS. By gar, den, I have as mush mock-vater as de Englishman.—Scurvy jack-dog priest! by gar, me vill cut his ears.

HOST. He will clapper-claw thee tightly, bully

CAIUS. Clapper-de-claw! vat is dat?

HOST. That is, he will make thee amends.

CAIUS. By gar, me do look, he shall clapper-de-claw me; for, by gar, me vill have it.

HOST. And I will provoke him to 't, or let him wag.

CAIUS. Me tank you for dat.

HOST. And moreover, bully,—But first, Master guest, and Master Page, and eke Cavaliero Slender, go you through the town to Frogmore.   *Aside to them*

PAGE. Sir Hugh is there, is he?

HOST. He is there: see what humour he is in; and I will bring the doctor about by the fields. Will it do well?

SHALLOW. We will do it.

PAGE, SHALLOW, AND SLENDER. Adieu, good Master doctor.
                        Exeunt Page, Shallow, and Slender

CAIUS. By gar, me vill kill de priest; for he speak for a jack-an-ape to Anne Page.

HOST. Let him die. Sheathe thy impatience; throw cold water on thy choler: go about the fields with me through Frogmore: I will bring thee where Mistress Anne Page is, at a farmhouse a-feasting; and thou shalt woo her. Cried I aim? said I well?

CAIUS. By gar, me tank you for dat: by gar, I love you; and I shall procure-a you de good guest, de earl, de knight, de lords, de gentlemen, my patients.

HOST. For the which I will be thy adversary toward Anne Page: said I well?

CAIUS. By gar, 'tis good; vell said.

HOST. Let us wag, then.

CAIUS. Come at my heels, Jack Rugby.   *Exeunt*

ACT THREE

SCENE ONE

A Field near Frogmore.

Enter Sir Hugh Evans and Simple

EVANS. I pray you now, good Master Slender's serving-man,
and friend Simple by your name, which way have you
looked for Master Caius, that calls himself doctor of
physic?

SIMPLE. Marry, sir, the pittie-ward, the park-ward, every
way; old Windsor way, and every way but the town way.

EVANS. I most fehemently desire you you will also look that
way.

SIMPLE. I will, sir. *Exit*

EVANS. Pless my soul! how full of chollors I am, and trem-
pling of mind! I shall be glad if he have deceived me.
How melancholies I am! I will knog his urinals about his
knave's costard when I have goot opportunities for the
'ork: pless my soul! *Sings*

     To shallow rivers, to whose falls
     Melodious birds sing madrigals;
     There will we make our peds of roses,
     And a thousand fragrant posies.
       To shallow—

Mercy on me! I have a great dispositions to cry. *Sings*

     Melodious birds sing madrigals,—
     When as I sat in Pabylon,—
     And a thousand vagram posies.
       To shallow,—

Re-enter Simple

SIMPLE. Yonder he is coming, this way, Sir Hugh.

EVANS. He 's welcome. *Sings*

     To shallow rivers, to whose falls—

Heaven prosper the right!—what weapons is he?

SIMPLE. No weapons, sir. There comes my master, Master Shallow, and another gentleman, from Frogmore, over the stile, this way.

EVANS. Pray you, give me my gown; or else keep it in your arms.   *Reads in a book*

Enter Page, Shallow, and Slender

SHALLOW. How now, Master Parson! Good-morrow, good Sir Hugh. Keep a gamester from the dice, and a good student from his book, and it is wonderful.

SLENDER. (*Aside*) Ah, sweet Anne Page!

PAGE. Save you, good Sir Hugh!

EVANS. Pless you from His mercy sake, all of you!

SHALLOW. What, the sword and the word! do you study them both, Master Parson?

PAGE. And youthful still in your doublet and hose! this raw rheumatic day?

EVANS. There is reasons and causes for it.

PAGE. We are come to you to do a good office, Master Parson.

EVANS. Fery well: what is it?

PAGE. Yonder is a most reverend gentleman, who, belike having received wrong by some person, is at most odds with his own gravity and patience that ever you saw.

SHALLOW. I have lived fourscore years and upward; I never heard a man of his place, gravity, and learning, so wide of his own respect.

EVANS. What is he?

PAGE. I think you know him; Master Doctor Caius, the renowned French physician.

EVANS. Got's will, and his passion of my heart! I had as lief you would tell me of a mess of porridge.

PAGE. Why?

EVANS. He has no more knowledge in Hibbocrates and Galen,—and he is a knave besides; a cowardly knave as you would desires to be acquainted withal.

PAGE. I warrant you, he 's the man should fight with him.

SLENDER. (*Aside*) O, sweet Anne Page!

SHALLOW. It appears so, by his weapons. Keep them asunder: here comes Doctor Caius.

Enter Host, Caius, and Rugby

PAGE. Nay, good Master parson, keep in your weapon.

SHALLOW. So do you, good Master doctor.

HOST. Disarm them, and let them question: let them keep their limbs whole and hack our English.

CAIUS. I pray you, let-a me speak a word vit your ear: vere-fore vill you not meet-a me?

EVANS. (*Aside to Caius*) Pray you, use your patience: in good time.

CAIUS. By gar, you are de coward, de Jack dog, John ape.

EVANS. (*Aside to Caius*) Pray you, let us not be laughing-stogs to other men's humours; I desire you in friendship, and I will one way or other make you amends: (*Aloud*) I will knog your urinals about your knave's cogscomb for missing your meetings and appointments.

CAIUS. Diable!—Jack Rugby,—mine host de Jarretierre—have I not stay for him to kill him? have I not, at de place I did appoint?

EVANS. As I am a Christians soul, now, look you, this is the place appointed: I 'll be judgment by mine host of the Garter.

HOST. Peace, I say, Gallia and Guallia; French and Welsh, soul-curer and body-curer!

CAIUS. Ay, dat is very good; excellent.

HOST. Peace, I say! hear mine host of the Garter. Am I politic? am I subtle? am I a Machiavel? Shall I lose my doctor? no; he gives me the potions and the motions. Shall I lose my parson, my priest, my Sir Hugh? no; he gives me the proverbs and the no-verbs. Give me thy hand, terres-trial; so;—give me thy hand, celestial; so. Boys of art, I have deceived you both; I have directed you to wrong places: your hearts are mighty, your skins are whole, and let burnt sack be the issue. Come, lay their swords to pawn. Follow me, lads of peace; follow, follow, follow.

SHALLOW. Trust me, a mad host!—Follow, gentlemen, fol-low.

SLENDER. (*Aside*) O, sweet Anne Page!

Exeunt Shallow, Slender, Page, and Host

CAIUS. Ha! do I perceive dat? have you make-a de sot of us, ha, ha?

EVANS. This is well; he has made us his vlouting-stog. I de-sire you that we may be friends and let us knog our prains together to be revenge on this same scall, scurvy, cogging companion, the host of the Garter.

CAIUS. By gar, vit all my heart. He promise to bring me vere is Anne Page: by gar, he deceive me too.

EVANS. Well, I will smite his noddles. Pray you, follow.

Exeunt

SCENE TWO

A Street in Windsor.

Enter Mistress Page and Robin

MRS. PAGE. Nay, keep your way, little gallant: you were wont to be a follower, but now you are a leader. Whether had you rather lead mine eyes, or eye your master's heels?

ROBIN. I had rather, forsooth, go before you like a man than follow him like a dwarf.

MRS. PAGE. O! you are a flattering boy: now I see you 'll be a courtier.

Enter Ford

FORD. Well met, Mistress Page. Whither go you?

MRS. PAGE. Truly, sir, to see your wife. Is she at home?

FORD. Ay; and as idle as she may hang together, for want of company. I think, if your husbands were dead, you two would marry.

MRS. PAGE. Be sure of that,—two other husbands.

FORD. Where had you this pretty weathercock?

MRS. PAGE. I cannot tell what the dickens his name is my husband had him of. What do you call your knight's name, sirrah?

ROBIN. Sir John Falstaff.

FORD. Sir John Falstaff!

MRS. PAGE. He, he; I can never hit on 's name. There is such a league between my good man and he! Is your wife at home indeed?

FORD. Indeed she is.

MRS. PAGE. By your leave, sir: I am sick till I see her.

Exeunt Mistress Page and Robin

FORD. Has Page any brains? Hath he any eyes? Hath he any thinking? Sure, they sleep; he hath no use of them. Why, this boy will carry a letter twenty mile, as easy as a cannon will shoot point-blank twelve score. He pieces out his wife's inclination; he gives her folly motion and advantage: and now she 's going to my wife, and Falstaff's boy with her. A man may hear this shower sing in the wind: and Falstaff's boy with her! Good plots! they are laid; and our revolted wives share damnation together. Well; I will take him, then torture my wife, pluck the borrowed veil of modesty from the so seeming Mistress Page, divulge Page himself for a secure and wilful Actæon; and to these violent proceedings all my neighbours shall cry aim. (*Clock strikes*) The clock gives me my cue, and my assurance bids me search; there I shall find Falstaff. I shall be rather praised for this than mocked; for it is as positive as the earth is firm, that Falstaff is there: I will go.

Enter Page, Shallow,
Slender, Host, Sir Hugh Evans, Caius, and Rugby

PAGE, SHALLOW, &C. Well met, Master Ford.

FORD. Trust me, a good knot. I have good cheer at home; and I pray you all go with me.

SHALLOW. I must excuse myself, Master Ford.

SLENDER. And so must I, sir: we have appointed to dine with Mistress Anne, and I would not break with her for more money than I 'll speak of.

SHALLOW. We have lingered about a match between Anne Page and my cousin Slender, and this day we shall have our answer.

SLENDER. I hope I have your good will, father Page.

PAGE. You have, Master Slender; I stand wholly for you: but my wife, Master doctor, is for you altogether.

CAIUS. Ay, by gar; and de maid is love-a me: my nursh-a Quickly tell me so mush.

HOST. What say you to young Master Fenton? He capers, he dances, he has eyes of youth, he writes verses, he speaks holiday, he smells April and May: he will carry 't, he will carry 't; 'tis in his buttons; he will carry 't.

PAGE. Not by my consent, I promise you. The gentleman is of no having: he kept company with the wild prince and Pointz; he is of too high a region; he knows too much. No, he shall not knit a knot in his fortunes with the finger of my substance: if he take her, let him take her simply; the wealth I have waits on my consent, and my consent goes not that way.

FORD. I beseech you heartily, some of you go home with me to dinner: besides your cheer, you shall have sport; I will show you a monster. Master doctor, you shall go; so shall you, Master Page; and you, Sir Hugh.

SHALLOW. Well, fare you well: we shall have the freer wooing at Master Page's.   *Exeunt Shallow and Slender*

CAIUS. Go home, John Rugby; I come anon.   *Exit Rugby*

HOST. Farewell, my hearts: I will to my honest knight Falstaff, and drink canary with him.   *Exit Host*

FORD. (*Aside*) I think I shall drink in pipe-wine first with him; I 'll make him dance. Will you go, gentles?

ALL. Have with you to see this monster.   *Exeunt*

SCENE THREE

A Room in Ford's House.

Enter Mistress Ford and Mistress Page

MRS. FORD. What, John! what, Robert!

MRS. PAGE. Quickly, quickly:—Is the buck-basket—

MRS. FORD. I warrant. What, Robin, I say!
          Enter Servants with a Basket

MRS. PAGE. Come, come, come.

MRS. FORD. Here, set it down.

MRS. PAGE. Give your men the charge; we must be brief.

MRS. FORD. Marry, as I told you before, John, and Robert, be ready here hard by in the brew-house; and when I suddenly call you, come forth, and without any pause or staggering, take this basket on your shoulders: that done, trudge with it in all haste, and carry it among the whitsters in Datchet-mead, and there empty it in the muddy ditch, close by the Thames side.

MRS. PAGE. You will do it?

MRS. FORD. I have told them over and over; they lack no direction. Be gone, and come when you are called.
          Exeunt Servants

MRS. PAGE. Here comes little Robin.
          Enter Robin

MRS. FORD. How now, my eyas-musket! what news with you?

ROBIN. My master, Sir John, is come in at your back-door, Mistress Ford, and requests your company.

MRS. PAGE. You little Jack-a-Lent, have you been true to us?

ROBIN. Ay, I 'll be sworn. My master knows not of your being here, and hath threatened to put me into everlasting liberty if I tell you of it; for he swears he 'll turn me away.

MRS. PAGE. Thou 'rt a good boy; this secrecy of thine shall be a tailor to thee and shall make thee a new doublet and hose. I 'll go hide me.

MRS. FORD. Do so. Go tell thy master I am alone. (*Exit Robin*) Mistress Page, remember you your cue.

MRS. PAGE. I warrant thee; if I do not act it, hiss me.   *Exit*

MRS. FORD. Go to, then: we 'll use this unwholesome humidity, this gross watery pumpion; we 'll teach him to know turtles from jays.

Enter Falstaff

FALSTAFF. 'Have I caught my heavenly jewel?' Why, now let me die, for I have lived long enough: this is the period of my ambition: O this blessed hour!

MRS. FORD. O, sweet Sir John!

FALSTAFF. Mistress Ford, I cannot cog, I cannot prate, Mistress Ford. Now shall I sin in my wish: I would thy husband were dead. I 'll speak it before the best lord, I would make thee my lady.

MRS. FORD. I your lady, Sir John! Alas, I should be a pitiful lady.

FALSTAFF. Let the court of France show me such another. I see how thine eye would emulate the diamond: thou hast the right arched beauty of the brow that becomes the ship-tire, the tire-valiant, or any tire of Venetian admittance.

MRS. FORD. A plain kerchief, Sir John: my brows become nothing else; nor that well neither.

FALSTAFF. By the Lord, thou art a traitor to say so: thou wouldst make an absolute courtier; and the firm fixture of thy foot would give an excellent motion to thy gait in a semi-circled farthingale. I see what thou wert, if Fortune thy foe were not, Nature thy friend. Come, thou canst not hide it.

MRS. FORD. Believe me, there 's no such thing in me.

FALSTAFF. What made me love thee? let that persuade thee

there's something extraordinary in thee. Come, I cannot
cog and say thou art this and that, like a many of these
lisping hawthorn-buds, that come like women in men's
apparel, and smell like Bucklersbury in simple-time; I
cannot; but I love thee; none but thee; and thou deservest it.

MRS. FORD. Do not betray me, sir. I fear you love Mistress
Page.

FALSTAFF. Thou mightst as well say, I love to walk by the
Counter-gate, which is as hateful to me as the reek of a
lime-kiln.

MRS. FORD. Well, heaven knows how I love you; and you
shall one day find it.

FALSTAFF. Keep in that mind; I'll deserve it.

MRS. FORD. Nay, I must tell you, so you do, or else I could
not be in that mind.

ROBIN. (*Within*) Mistress Ford! Mistress Ford! here's Mistress Page at the door, sweating and blowing and looking
wildly, and would needs speak with you presently.

FALSTAFF. She shall not see me: I will ensconce me behind
the arras.

MRS. FORD. Pray you, do so: she's a very tattling woman
                    Falstaff hides himself
            Re-enter Mistress Page and Robin
What's the matter? how now!

MRS. PAGE. O Mistress Ford! what have you done? You're
shamed, you are overthrown, you're undone for ever!

MRS. FORD. What's the matter, good Mistress Page?

MRS. PAGE. O well-a-day, Mistress Ford! having an honest
man to your husband, to give him such cause of suspicion!

MRS. FORD. What cause of suspicion?

MRS. PAGE. What cause of suspicion! Out upon you! how
am I mistook in you!

MRS. FORD. Why, alas, what's the matter?

MRS. PAGE. Your husband's coming hither, woman, with all
the officers of Windsor, to search for a gentleman that he
says is here now in the house by your consent, to take an
ill advantage of his absence: you are undone.

MRS. FORD. (*Aside*) Speak louder.—'Tis not so, I hope.

MRS. PAGE. Pray heaven it be not so, that you have such a
man here! but 'tis most certain your husband's coming

with half Windsor at his heels, to search for such a one. I
come before to tell you. If you know yourself clear, why,
I am glad of it; but if you have a friend here, convey,
convey him out. Be not amazed; call all your senses to
you: defend your reputation, or bid farewell to your good
life for ever.

MRS. FORD. What shall I do?—There is a gentleman, my
dear friend; and I fear not mine own shame so much as
his peril: I had rather than a thousand pound he were
out of the house.

MRS. PAGE. For shame! never stand 'you had rather' and
'you had rather': your husband 's here at hand; bethink
you of some conveyance: in the house you cannot hide
him. O, how have you deceived me! Look, here is a basket: if he be of any reasonable stature, he may creep in
here; and throw foul linen upon him, as if it were going
to bucking: or—it is whiting-time—send him by your two
men to Datchet-mead.

MRS. FORD. He 's too big to go in there. What shall I do?

FALSTAFF. (*Coming forward*) Let me see 't, let me see 't,
O, let me see 't! I 'll in, I 'll in. Follow your friend's counsel. I 'll in.

MRS. PAGE. What, Sir John Falstaff! Are these your letters,
knight?

FALSTAFF. I love thee, and none but thee; help me away:
let me creep in here. I 'll never—

He gets into the basket; they cover him with foul linen

MRS. PAGE. Help to cover your master, boy. Call your men,
Mistress Ford. You dissembling knight!

MRS. FORD. What, John! Robert! John!   *Exit Robin*
Re-enter Servants

Go, take up these clothes here quickly; where 's the cowl-
staff? look, how you drumble! carry them to the laundress in Datchet-mead; quickly, come.

Enter Ford, Page, Caius, and Sir Hugh Evans

FORD. Pray you, come near: if I suspect without cause, why
then make sport at me; then let me be your jest; I deserve it. How now! what goes here? whither bear you
this?

SERVANTS. To the laundress, forsooth.

MRS. FORD. Why, what have you to do whither they bear
it? You were best meddle with buck-washing.

FORD. Buck! I would I could wash myself of the buck!
Buck, buck, buck! Ay, buck; I warrant you, buck; and of
the season too, it shall appear. (*Exeunt Servants with the
basket*) Gentlemen, I have dreamed to-night; I 'll tell
you my dream. Here, here, here be my keys: ascend my
chambers; search, seek, find out: I 'll warrant we 'll un-
kennel the fox. Let me stop this way first. (*Locking the
door*) So, now uncape.

PAGE. Good Master Ford, be contented: you wrong yourself too much.

FORD. True, Master Page. Up, gentlemen; you shall see
sport anon: follow me, gentlemen.   *Exit*

EVANS. This is fery fantastical humours and jealousies.

CAIUS. By gar, 'tis no de fashion of France; it is not jealous
in France.

PAGE. Nay, follow him, gentlemen; see the issue of his
search.   *Exeunt Page, Caius, and Evans*

MRS. PAGE. Is there not a double excellency in this?

MRS. FORD. I know not which pleases me better; that my
husband is deceived, or Sir John.

MRS. PAGE. What a taking was he in when your husband
asked who was in the basket!

MRS. FORD. I am half afraid he will have need of washing;
so throwing him into the water will do him a benefit.

MRS. PAGE. Hang him, dishonest rascal! I would all of the
same strain were in the same distress.

MRS. FORD. I think my husband hath some special suspicion
of Falstaff's being here; for I never saw him so gross in
his jealousy till now.

MRS. PAGE. I will lay a plot to try that; and we will yet
have more tricks with Falstaff: his dissolute disease will
scarce obey this medicine.

MRS. FORD. Shall we send that foolish carrion Mistress
Quickly to him, and excuse his throwing into the water;
and give him another hope, to betray him to another punishment?

MRS. PAGE. We will do it: let him be sent for to-morrow,
eight o'clock, to have amends.

   Re-enter Ford, Page, Caius, and Sir Hugh Evans

FORD. I cannot find him: may be the knave bragged of that
he could not compass.

MRS. PAGE. (*Aside to Mrs. Ford*) Heard you that?

MRS. FORD. (*Aside to Mrs. Page*) Ay, ay, peace.—You use me well, Master Ford, do you?

FORD. Ay, I do so.

MRS. FORD. Heaven make you better than your thoughts!

FORD. Amen!

MRS. PAGE. You do yourself mighty wrong, Master Ford.

FORD. Ay, ay; I must bear it.

EVANS. If there pe any pody in the house, and in the chambers, and in the coffers, and in the presses, heaven forgive my sins at the day of judgment!

CAIUS. By gar, nor I too, dere is no bodies.

PAGE. Fie, fie, Master Ford: are you not ashamed? What spirit, what devil suggests this imagination? I would not ha' your distemper in this kind for the wealth of Windsor Castle.

FORD. 'Tis my fault, Master Page: I suffer for it.

EVANS. You suffer for a pad conscience: your wife is as honest a 'omans as I will desires among five thousand, and five hundred too.

CAIUS. By gar, I see 'tis an honest woman.

FORD. Well; I promised you a dinner. Come, come, walk in the Park: I pray you, pardon me; I will hereafter make known to you why I have done this. Come, wife; come, Mistress Page. I pray you, pardon me; pray heartily, pardon me.

PAGE. Let 's go in, gentlemen; but, trust me, we 'll mock him. I do invite you to-morrow morning to my house to breakfast; after, we 'll a-birding together: I have a fine hawk for the bush. Shall it be so?

FORD. Any thing.

EVANS. If there is one, I shall make two in the company.

CAIUS. If dere be one or two, I shall make-a de turd.

FORD. Pray you go, Master Page.

EVANS. I pray you now, remembrance to-morrow on the lousy knave, mine host.

CAIUS. Dat is good; by gar, vit all my heart.

EVANS. A lousy knave! to have his gibes and his mockeries!

Exeunt

SCENE FOUR

A Room in Page's House.

Enter Fenton, Anne Page, and Mistress Quickly.
Mistress Quickly stands apart.

FENTON. I see I cannot get thy father's love;
Therefore no more turn me to him, sweet Nan.
ANNE. Alas! how then?
FENTON.   Why, thou must be thyself.
He doth object, I am too great of birth,
And that my state being gall'd with my expense,
I seek to heal it only by his wealth.
Besides these, other bars he lays before me,
My riots past, my wild societies;
And tells me 'tis a thing impossible
I should love thee but as a property.
ANNE. May be he tells you true.
FENTON. No, heaven so speed me in my time to come!
Albeit I will confess thy father's wealth
Was the first motive that I woo'd thee, Anne:
Yet, wooing thee, I found thee of more value
Than stamps in gold or sums in sealed bags;
And 'tis the very riches of thyself
That now I aim at.
ANNE.   Gentle Master Fenton,
Yet seek my father's love; still seek it, sir:
If opportunity and humblest suit
Cannot attain it, why, then,—hark you hither.

                              They converse apart
Enter Shallow and Slender

SHALLOW. Break their talk, Mistress Quickly: my kinsman
shall speak for himself.
SLENDER. I'll make a shaft or a bolt on 't. 'Slid, 'tis but ven-
turing.
SHALLOW. Be not dismayed.
SLENDER. No, she shall not dismay me: I care not for that,
but that I am afeard.
QUICKLY. Hark ye; Master Slender would speak a word
with you.

ANNE. I come to him. (*Aside*) This is my father's choice.
O, what a world of vile ill-favour'd faults
Looks handsome in three hundred pounds a year!

QUICKLY. And how does good Master Fenton? Pray you, a word with you.

SHALLOW. She 's coming; to her, coz. O boy, thou hadst a father!

SLENDER. I had a father, Mistress Anne; my uncle can tell you good jests of him. Pray you, uncle, tell Mistress Anne the jest, how my father stole two geese out of a pen, good uncle.

SHALLOW. Mistress Anne, my cousin loves you.

SLENDER. Ay, that I do; as well as I love any woman in Glostershire.

SHALLOW. He will maintain you like a gentlewoman.

SLENDER. Ay, that I will, come cut and long-tail, under the degree of a squire.

SHALLOW. He will make you a hundred and fifty pounds jointure.

ANNE. Good Master Shallow, let him woo for himself.

SHALLOW. Marry, I thank you for it; I thank you for that good comfort. She calls you, coz: I 'll leave you.

ANNE. Now, Master Slender.

SLENDER. Now, good Mistress Anne.—

ANNE. What is your will?

SLENDER. My will? od 's heartlings! that 's a pretty jest, indeed! I ne'er made my will yet, I thank heaven; I am not such a sickly creature, I give heaven praise.

ANNE. I mean, Master Slender, what would you with me?

SLENDER. Truly, for mine own part, I would little or nothing with you. Your father and my uncle have made motions: if it be my luck, so; if not, happy man be his dole! They can tell you how things go better than I can: you may ask your father; here he comes.

Enter Page and Mistress Page

PAGE. Now, Master Slender: love him, daughter Anne.
Why, how now! what does Master Fenton here?
You wrong me, sir, thus still to haunt my house:
I told you, sir, my daughter is dispos'd of.

FENTON. Nay, Master Page, be not impatient.

MRS. PAGE. Good Master Fenton, come not to my child.

PAGE. She is no match for you.

FENTON. Sir, will you hear me?

PAGE.   No, good Master Fenton.
Come, Master Shallow; come, son Slender, in.
Knowing my mind, you wrong me, Master Fenton.

Exeunt Page, Shallow, and Slender

QUICKLY. Speak to Mistress Page.

FENTON. Good Mistress Page, for that I love your daughter
In such a righteous fashion as I do,
Perforce, against all checks, rebukes and manners,
I must advance the colours of my love
And not retire: let me have your good will.

ANNE. Good mother, do not marry me to yond fool.

MRS. PAGE. I mean it not; I seek you a better husband.

QUICKLY. That 's my master, Master doctor.

ANNE. Alas! I had rather be set quick i' the earth,
And bowl'd to death with turnips.

MRS. PAGE. Come, trouble not yourself. Good Master Fen-
ton,
I will not be your friend, nor enemy:
My daughter will I question how she loves you,
And as I find her, so am I affected.
'Till then, farewell, sir: she must needs go in;
Her father will be angry.

FENTON. Farewell, gentle mistress. Farewell, Nan.

Exeunt Mistress Page and Anne

QUICKLY. This is my doing, now: 'Nay,' said I, 'will you cast
away your child on a fool, and a physician? Look on
Master Fenton.' This is my doing.

FENTON. I thank thee: and I pray thee, once to-night
Give my sweet Nan this ring. There 's for thy pains.

QUICKLY. Now heaven send thee good fortune! (*Exit Fenton*) A kind heart he hath: a woman would run through
fire and water for such a kind heart. But yet I would my
master had Mistress Anne; or I would Master Slender
had her; or, in sooth, I would Master Fenton had her. I
will do what I can for them all three, for so I have promised, and I 'll be as good as my word; but speciously for
Master Fenton. Well, I must of another errand to Sir
John Falstaff from my two mistresses: what a beast am I
to slack it!

SCENE FIVE

A Room in the Garter Inn.

Enter Falstaff and Bardolph

FALSTAFF. Bardolph, I say,—

BARDOLPH. Here, sir.

FALSTAFF. Go fetch me a quart of sack; put a toast in 't.
(*Exit Bardolph*) Have I lived to be carried in a basket,
and to be thrown in the Thames like a barrow of butcher's offal? Well, if I be served such another trick, I 'll have
my brains ta'en out, and buttered, and give them to a dog
for a new year's gift. The rogues slighted me into the
river with as little remorse as they would have drowned
a blind bitch's puppies, fifteen i' the litter; and you may
know by my size that I have a kind of alacrity in sinking:
if the bottom were as deep as hell, I should down. I had
been drowned but that the shore was shelvy and shallow;
a death that I abhor, for the water swells a man, and
what a thing should I have been when I had been
swelled! I should have been a mountain of mummy.

Re-enter Bardolph, with the sack

BARDOLPH. Here 's Mistress Quickly, sir, to speak with you.

FALSTAFF. Come, let me pour in some sack to the Thames
water, for my belly 's as cold as if I had swallowed snow-
balls for pills to cool the reins. Call her in.

BARDOLPH. Come in, woman.

Enter Mistress Quickly

QUICKLY. By your leave. I cry you mercy: give your worship good-morrow.

FALSTAFF. Take away these chalices. Go brew me a pottle
of sack finely.

BARDOLPH. With eggs, sir?

FALSTAFF. Simple of itself; I 'll no pullet-sperm in my brew-
age. (*Exit Bardolph*)—How now!

QUICKLY. Marry, sir, I come to your worship from Mistress
Ford.

FALSTAFF. Mistress Ford! I have had ford enough; I was
thrown into the ford; I have my belly full of ford.

QUICKLY. Alas the day! good heart, that was not her fault;

She does so take on with her men; they mistook their erection.

FALSTAFF. So did I mine, to build upon a foolish woman's promise.

QUICKLY. Well, she laments, sir, for it, that it would yearn your heart to see it. Her husband goes this morning a-birding: she desires you once more to come to her between eight and nine. I must carry her word quickly: she 'll make you amends, I warrant you.

FALSTAFF. Well, I will visit her: tell her so; and bid her think what a man is: let her consider his frailty, and then judge of my merit.

QUICKLY. I will tell her.

FALSTAFF. Do so. Between nine and ten, sayest thou?

QUICKLY. Eight and nine, sir.

FALSTAFF. Well, be gone: I will not miss her.

QUICKLY. Peace be with you, sir.　　　　　　　　　*Exit*

FALSTAFF. I marvel I hear not of Master Brook; he sent me word to stay within. I like his money well. O! here he comes.

Enter Ford, disguised

FORD. Bless you, sir!

FALSTAFF. Now, Master Brook, you come to know what hath passed between me and Ford's wife?

FORD. That, indeed, Sir John, is my business.

FALSTAFF. Master Brook, I will not lie to you: I was at her house the hour she appointed me.

FORD. And how sped you, sir?

FALSTAFF. Very ill-favouredly, Master Brook.

FORD. How so, sir? did she change her determination?

FALSTAFF. No, Master Brook; but the peaking cornuto her husband, Master Brook, dwelling in a continual 'larum of jealousy, comes me in the instant of our encounter, after we had embraced, kissed, protested, and, as it were, spoke the prologue of our comedy; and at his heels a rabble of his companions, thither provoked and instigated by his distemper, and, forsooth, to search his house for his wife's love.

FORD. What! while you were there?

FALSTAFF. While I was there.

FORD. And did he search for you, and could not find you?

FALSTAFF. You shall hear. As good luck would have it,

comes in one Mistress Page; gives intelligence of Ford's
approach; and in her invention, and Ford's wife's dis-
traction, they conveyed me into a buck-basket.

FORD. A buck-basket!

FALSTAFF. By the Lord, a buck-basket! rammed me in with
foul shirts and smocks, socks, foul stockings, greasy nap-
kins; that, Master Brook, there was the rankest compound of villanous smell that ever offended nostril.

FORD. And how long lay you there?

FALSTAFF. Nay, you shall hear, Master Brook, what I have
suffered to bring this woman to evil for your good. Being
thus crammed in the basket, a couple of Ford's knaves,
his hinds, were called forth by their mistress to carry me
in the name of foul clothes to Datchet-lane: they took me
on their shoulders; met the jealous knave their master in
the door, who asked them once or twice what they had in
their basket. I quaked for fear lest the lunatic knave
would have searched it; but Fate, ordaining he should be
a cuckold, held his hand. Well; on went he for a search,
and away went I for foul clothes. But mark the sequel,
Master Brook: I suffered the pangs of three several
deaths: first, an intolerable fright, to be detected with a
jealous rotten bell-wether; next, to be compassed, like a
good bilbo, in the circumference of a peck, hilt to point,
heel to head; and then, to be stopped in, like a strong
distillation, with stinking clothes that fretted in their own
grease: think of that, a man of my kidney, think of that,
that am as subject to heat as butter; a man of continual
dissolution and thaw: it was a miracle to 'scape suffoca-
tion. And in the height of this bath, when I was more
than half stewed in grease, like a Dutch dish, to be
thrown into the Thames, and cooled, glowing hot, in that
surge, like a horse-shoe; think of that, hissing hot, think
of that, Master Brook!

FORD. In good sadness, sir, I am sorry that for my sake you
have suffered all this. My suit then is desperate; you 'll
undertake her no more?

FALSTAFF. Master Brook, I will be thrown into Etna, as I
have been into Thames, ere I will leave her thus. Her
husband is this morning gone a-birding: I have received
from her another embassy of meeting; 'twixt eight and
nine is the hour, Master Brook.

FORD. 'Tis past eight already, sir.

FALSTAFF. Is it? I will then address me to my appointment. Come to me at your convenient leisure, and you shall know how I speed, and the conclusion shall be crowned with your enjoying her: adieu. You shall have her, Master Brook; Master Brook, you shall cuckold Ford.   *Exit*

FORD. Hum! ha! is this a vision? it this a dream? do I sleep? Master Ford, awake! awake, Master Ford! there's a hole made in your best coat, Master Ford. This 'tis to be married: this 'tis to have linen and buck-baskets! Well, I will proclaim myself what I am: I will now take the lecher; he is at my house; he cannot 'scape me; 'tis impossible he should; he cannot creep into a half-penny purse, nor into a pepper-box; but, lest the devil that guides him should aid him, I will search impossible places. Though what I am I cannot avoid, yet to be what I would not, shall not make me tame: if I have horns to make me mad, let the proverb go with me; I'll be horn-mad.   *Exit*

ACT FOUR

SCENE ONE

Windsor. The Street.

Enter Mistress Page, Mistress Quickly, and William

MRS. PAGE. Is he at Master Ford's already, thinkest thou?

QUICKLY. Sure he is by this, or will be presently; but truly, he is very courageous mad about his throwing into the water. Mistress Ford desires you to come suddenly.

MRS. PAGE. I 'll be with her by and by; I 'll but bring my young man here to school. Look, where his master comes; 'tis a playing-day, I see.

Enter Sir Hugh Evans

How now, Sir Hugh! no school to-day?

EVANS. No; Master Slender is get the boys leave to play.

QUICKLY. Blessing of his heart!

MRS. PAGE. Sir Hugh, my husband says my son profits nothing in the world at his book: I pray you, ask him some questions in his accidence.

EVANS. Come hither, William; hold up your head; come.

MRS. PAGE. Come on, sirrah; hold up your head; answer your master, be not afraid.

EVANS. William, how many numbers is in nouns?

WILLIAM. Two.

QUICKLY. Truly, I thought there had been one number more, because they say 'Od's nouns.'

EVANS. Peace your tattlings! What is 'fair,' William?

WILLIAM. Pulcher.

QUICKLY. Polecats! there are fairer things than polecats, sure.

EVANS. You are a very simplicity 'oman: I pray you peace. What is 'lapis,' William?

WILLIAM. A stone.

EVANS. And what is 'a stone,' William?

WILLIAM. A pebble.

EVANS. No, it is 'lapis': I pray you remember in your prain.

WILLIAM. Lapis.

EVANS. That is a good William. What is he, William, that does lend articles?

WILLIAM. Articles are borrowed of the pronoun, and be thus declined, Singulariter, nominativo, hic, hæc, hoc.

EVANS. Nominativo, hig, hag, hog; pray you, mark: genitivo, hujus. Well, what is your accusative case?

WILLIAM. Accusativo, hinc.

EVANS. I pray you, have your remembrance, child; accusativo, hung, hang, hog.

QUICKLY. Hang hog is Latin for bacon, I warrant you.

EVANS. Leave your prabbles, 'oman. What is the focative case, William?

WILLIAM. O vocativo, O.

EVANS. Remember, William; focative is caret.

QUICKLY. And that's a good root.

EVANS. 'Oman, forbear.

MRS. PAGE. Peace!

EVANS. What is your genitive case plural, William?

WILLIAM. Genitive case?

EVANS. Ay.

WILLIAM. Genitive, horum, harum, horum.

QUICKLY. Vengeance of Jenny's case! fie on her! Never name her, child, if she be a whore.

EVANS. For shame, 'oman!

QUICKLY. You do ill to teach the child such words. He teaches him to hick and to hack, which they'll do fast enough of themselves, and to call 'horum': fie upon you!

EVANS. 'Oman, art thou lunatics? hast thou no understandings for thy cases and the numbers and the genders? Thou art as foolish Christian creatures as I would desires.

MRS. PAGE. Prithee, hold thy peace.

EVANS. Show me now, William, some declensions of your pronouns.

WILLIAM. Forsooth, I have forgot.

EVANS. It is qui, quæ, quod; if you forget your 'quis,' your 'quæs,' and your 'quods,' you must be preeches. Go your ways and play; go.

MRS. PAGE. He is a better scholar than I thought he was.

EVANS. He is a good sprag memory. Farewell, Mistress
Page.

MRS. PAGE. Adieu, good Sir Hugh. *Exit Sir Hugh*
Get you home, boy. Come, we stay too long. *Exeunt*

SCENE TWO

A Room in Ford's House.

Enter Falstaff and Mistress Ford

FALSTAFF. Mistress Ford, your sorrow hath eaten up my
sufferance. I see you are obsequious in your love, and I
profess requital to a hair's breadth; not only, Mistress
Ford, in the simple office of love, but in all the accoutre-
ment, complement and ceremony of it. But are you sure
of your husband now?

MRS. FORD. He's a-birding, sweet Sir John.

MRS. PAGE. (*Within*) What ho! gossip Ford! what ho!

MRS. FORD. Step into the chamber, Sir John. *Exit Falstaff*
Enter Mistress Page

MRS. PAGE. How now, sweet heart! who's at home besides
yourself?

MRS. FORD. Why, none but mine own people.

MRS. PAGE. Indeed!

MRS. FORD. No, certainly.—(*Aside to her*) Speak louder.

MRS. PAGE. Truly, I am so glad you have nobody here.

MRS. FORD. Why?

MRS. PAGE. Why, woman, your husband is in his old lunes
again: he so takes on yonder with my husband; so rails
against all married mankind; so curses all Eve's daughters, of what complexion soever; and so buffets himself
on the forehead, crying, 'Peer out, peer out!' that any
madness I ever yet beheld seemed but tameness, civility
and patience, to this his distemper he is in now. I am
glad the fat knight is not here.

MRS. FORD. Why, does he talk of him?

MRS. PAGE. Of none but him; and swears he was carried
out, the last time he searched for him, in a basket: pro-
tests to my husband he is now here, and hath drawn him

and the rest of their company from their sport, to make
another experiment of his suspicion. But I am glad the
knight is not here; now he shall see his own foolery.

MRS. FORD. How near is he, Mistress Page?

MRS. PAGE. Hard by; at street end; he will be here anon.

MRS. FORD. I am undone! the knight is here.

MRS. PAGE. Why then you are utterly shamed, and he 's but
a dead man. What a woman are you! Away with him,
away with him! better shame than murder.

MRS. FORD. Which way should he go? How should I bestow
him? Shall I put him into the basket again?

Re-enter Falstaff

FALSTAFF. No, I 'll come no more i' the basket. May I not go
out ere he come?

MRS. PAGE. Alas! three of Master Ford's brothers watch the
door with pistols, that none shall issue out; otherwise you
might slip away ere he came. But what make you here?

FALSTAFF. What shall I do? I 'll creep up into the chimney.

MRS. FORD. There they always use to discharge their bird-
ing-pieces.

MRS. PAGE. Creep into the kiln-hole.

FALSTAFF. Where is it?

MRS. FORD. He will seek there, on my word. Neither press,
coffer, chest, trunk, well, vault, but he hath an abstract
for the remembrance of such places, and goes to them by
his note: there is no hiding you in the house.

FALSTAFF. I 'll go out, then.

MRS. PAGE. If you go out in your own semblance, you die,
Sir John. Unless you go out disguised,—

MRS. FORD. How might we disguise him?

MRS. PAGE. Alas the day! I know not. There is no woman's
gown big enough for him; otherwise, he might put on a
hat, a muffler, and a kerchief, and so escape.

FALSTAFF. Good hearts, devise something: any extremity
rather than a mischief.

MRS. FORD. My maid's aunt, the fat woman of Brainford,
has a gown above.

MRS. PAGE. On my word, it will serve him; she 's as big as
he is: and there 's her thrummed hat and her muffler too.
Run up, Sir John.

MRS. FORD. Go, go, sweet Sir John: Mistress Page and I
will look some linen for your head.

MRS. PAGE. Quick, quick! we 'll come dress you, straight;
put on the gown the while. *Exit Falstaff*

MRS. FORD. I would my husband would meet him in this
shape: he cannot abide the old woman of Brainford; he
swears she 's a witch; forbade her my house, and hath
threatened to beat her.

MRS. PAGE. Heaven guide him to thy husband's cudgel, and
the devil guide his cudgel afterwards!

MRS. FORD. But is my husband coming?

MRS. PAGE. Ay, in good sadness, is he; and talks of the basket too, howsoever he hath had intelligence.

MRS. FORD. We 'll try that; for I 'll appoint my men to carry
the basket again, to meet him at the door with it, as they
did last time.

MRS. PAGE. Nay, but he 'll be here presently: let 's go dress
him like the witch of Brainford.

MRS. FORD. I 'll first direct my men what they shall do with
the basket. Go up; I 'll bring linen for him straight. *Exit*

MRS. PAGE. Hang him, dishonest varlet! we cannot misuse
him enough.
We 'll leave a proof, by that which we will do,
Wives may be merry, and yet honest too:
We do not act that often jest and laugh;
'Tis old, but true, 'Still swine eats all the draff.' *Exit*
Re-enter Mistress Ford, with two Servants

MRS. FORD. Go, sirs, take the basket again on your shoulders: your master is hard at door; if he bid you set it
down, obey him. Quickly; dispatch. *Exit*

FIRST SERVANT. Come, come, take it up.

SECOND SERVANT. Pray heaven, it be not full of knight
again.

FIRST SERVANT. I hope not; I had as lief bear so much lead.
Enter Ford, Page, Shallow, Caius, and Sir Hugh Evans

FORD. Ay, but if it prove true, Master Page, have you any
way then to unfool me again? Set down the basket, villains. Somebody call my wife. Youth in a basket! O you
panderly rascals! there 's a knot, a ging, a pack, a conspiracy against me: now shall the devil be shamed.
What, wife, I say! Come, come forth! Behold what honest clothes you send forth to bleaching!

PAGE. Why, this passes! Master Ford, you are not to go
loose any longer; you must be pinioned.

EVANS. Why, this is lunatics! this is mad as a mad dog!

SHALLOW. Indeed, Master Ford, this is not well, indeed.

FORD. So say I too, sir.—

Re-enter Mistress Ford

Come hither, Mistress Ford, the honest woman, the modest wife, the virtuous creature, that hath the jealous fool to her husband! I suspect without cause, mistress, do I?

MRS. FORD. Heaven be my witness, you do, if you suspect me in any dishonesty.

FORD. Well said, brazen-face! hold it out. Come forth, sirrah!   *Pulls the clothes out of the basket*

PAGE. This passes!

MRS. FORD. Are you not ashamed? let the clothes alone.

FORD. I shall find you anon.

EVANS. 'Tis unreasonable. Will you take up your wife's clothes? Come away.

FORD. Empty the basket, I say!

MRS. FORD. Why, man, why?

FORD. Master Page, as I am an honest man, there was one conveyed out of my house yesterday in this basket: why may not he be there again? In my house I am sure he is; my intelligence is true; my jealousy is reasonable. Pluck me out all the linen.

MRS. FORD. If you find a man there he shall die a flea's death.

PAGE. Here 's no man.

SHALLOW. By my fidelity, this is not well, Master Ford; this wrongs you.

EVANS. Master Ford, you must pray, and not follow the imaginations of your own heart: this is jealousies.

FORD. Well, he 's not here I seek for.

PAGE. No, nor nowhere else but in your brain.

Servants carry away the basket

FORD. Help to search my house this one time: if I find not what I seek, show no colour for my extremity; let me for ever be your table-sport; let them say of me, 'As jealous as Ford, that searched a hollow walnut for his wife's leman.' Satisfy me once more; once more search with me.

MRS. FORD. What ho, Mistress Page! come you and the old woman down; my husband will come into the chamber.

FORD. Old woman! What old woman 's that?

MRS. FORD. Why, it is my maid's aunt of Brainford.

FORD. A witch, a quean, an old cozening quean! Have I not forbid her my house? She comes of errands, does she? We are simple men; we do not know what 's brought to pass under the profession of fortune-telling. She works by charms, by spells, by the figure, and such daubery as this is, beyond our element: we know nothing. Come down, you witch, you hag, you; come down, I say!

MRS. FORD. Nay, good, sweet husband! good gentlemen, let him not strike the old woman.

Enter Falstaff in women's clothes, led by Mistress Page

MRS. PAGE. Come, Mother Prat; come, give me your hand.

FORD. I 'll 'prat' her.—(*Beats him*) Out of my door, you witch, you rag, you baggage, you polecat, you ronyon! out, out! I 'll conjure you, I 'll fortune-tell you.

Exit Falstaff

MRS. PAGE. Are you not ashamed? I think you have killed the poor woman.

MRS. FORD. Nay, he will do it. 'Tis a goodly credit for you.

FORD. Hang her, witch!

EVANS. By yea and no, I think the 'oman is a witch indeed: I like not when a 'oman has a great peard; I spy a great peard under her muffler.

FORD. Will you follow, gentlemen? I beseech you, follow: see but the issue of my jealousy. If I cry out thus upon no trail, never trust me when I open again.

PAGE. Let 's obey his humour a little further. Come, gentlemen.   *Exeunt Ford, Page, Shallow, Caius, and Evans*

MRS. PAGE. Trust me, he beat him most pitifully.

MRS. FORD. Nay, by the mass, that he did not; he beat him most unpitifully methought.

MRS. PAGE. I 'll have the cudgel hallowed and hung o'er the altar: it hath done meritorious service.

MRS. FORD. What think you? May we, with the warrant of womanhood and the witness of a good conscience, pursue him with any further revenge?

MRS. PAGE. The spirit of wantonness is, sure, scared out of him: if the devil have him not in fee-simple, with fine and recovery, he will never, I think, in the way of waste, attempt us again.

MRS. FORD. Shall we tell our husbands how we have served him?

MRS. PAGE. Yes, by all means; if it be but to scrape the fig-

ures out of your husband's brains. If they can
find in their hearts the poor unvirtuous fat knight shall
be any further afflicted, we two will still be the ministers.

MRS. FORD. I 'll warrant they 'll have him publicly shamed,
and methinks there would be no period to the jest,
should he not be publicly shamed.

MRS. PAGE. Come, to the forge with it then; shape it: I
would not have things cool.   *Exeunt*

SCENE THREE

A Room in the Garter Inn.

Enter Host and Bardolph

BARDOLPH. Sir, the Germans desire to have three of your
horses: the duke himself will be to-morrow at court, and
they are going to meet him.

HOST. What duke should that be comes so secretly? I hear
not of him in the court. Let me speak with the gentlemen; they speak English?

BARDOLPH. Ay, sir; I 'll call them to you.

HOST. They shall have my horses, but I 'll make them pay;
I 'll sauce them: they have had my house a week at command; I have turned away my other guests: they must
come off; I 'll sauce them. Come.   *Exeunt*

SCENE FOUR

A Room in Ford's House.

*Enter Page, Ford, Mistress Page, Mistress Ford,
and Sir Hugh Evans*

EVANS. 'Tis one of the pest discretions of a 'oman as ever I
did look upon.

PAGE. And did he send you both these letters at an instant?

MRS. PAGE. Within a quarter of an hour.

FORD. Pardon me, wife. Henceforth do what thou wilt;
I rather will suspect the sun with cold
Than thee with wantonness: now doth thy honour stand,
In him that was of late an heretic,
As firm as faith.

PAGE.   'Tis well, 'tis well; no more.
  Be not as extreme in submission
  As an offence;
  But let our plot go forward: let our wives
  Yet once again, to make us public sport,
  Appoint a meeting with this old fat fellow,
  Where we may take him and disgrace him for it.

FORD. There is no better way than that they spoke of.

PAGE. How? to send him word they 'll meet him in the park
  at midnight? Fie, fie! he 'll never come.

EVANS. You say he has been thrown into the rivers, and has
  been grievously peaten as an old 'oman: methinks there
  should be terrors in him that he should not come; methinks his flesh is punished, he shall have no desires.

PAGE. So think I too.

MRS. FORD. Devise but how you 'll use him when he comes,
  And let us two devise to bring him thither.

MRS. PAGE. There is an old tale goes that Herne the hunter,
  Sometime a keeper here in Windsor forest,
  Doth all the winter-time, at still midnight,
  Walk round about an oak, with great ragg'd horns;
  And there he blasts the tree, and takes the cattle,
  And makes milch-kine yield blood, and shakes a chain
  In a most hideous and dreadful manner:
  You have heard of such a spirit, and well you know
  The superstitious idle-headed eld
  Receiv'd and did deliver to our age
  This tale of Herne the hunter for a truth.

PAGE. Why, yet there want not many that do fear
  In deep of night to walk by this Herne's oak.
  But what of this?

MRS. FORD.   Marry, this is our device;
  That Falstaff at that oak shall meet with us,
  Disguis'd like Herne with huge horns on his head.

PAGE. Well, let it not be doubted but he 'll come,
  And in this shape when you have brought him thither,
  What shall be done with him? what is your plot?

MRS. PAGE. That likewise have we thought upon, and thus:
  Nan Page my daughter, and my little son,
  And three or four more of their growth, we 'll dress
  Like urchins, ouphs and fairies, green and white,
  With rounds of waxen tapers on their heads,

And rattles in their hands. Upon a sudden,
As Falstaff, she, and I, are newly met,
Let them from forth a sawpit rush at once
With some diffused song: upon their sight,
We two in great amazedness will fly:
Then let them all encircle him about,
And, fairy-like, to pinch the unclean knight;
And ask him why, that hour of fairy revel,
In their so sacred paths he dares to tread
In shape profane.

MRS. FORD.   And till he tell the truth,
Let the supposed fairies pinch him sound
And burn him with their tapers.

MRS. PAGE.   The truth being known,
We 'll all present ourselves, dis-horn the spirit,
And mock him home to Windsor.

FORD.   The children must
Be practis'd well to this, or they 'll ne'er do 't.

EVANS. I will teach the children their behaviours; and I will
be like a jack-an-apes also, to burn the knight with my
taber.

FORD. That will be excellent. I 'll go buy them vizards.

MRS. PAGE. My Nan shall be the queen of all the fairies,
Finely attired in a robe of white.

PAGE. That silk will I go buy:—(Aside) and in that time
Shall Master Slender steal my Nan away,
And marry her at Eton. Go, send to Falstaff straight.

FORD. Nay, I 'll to him again in name of Brook;
He 'll tell me all his purpose. Sure, he 'll come.

MRS. PAGE. Fear not you that. Go, get us properties,
And tricking for our fairies.

EVANS. Let us about it: it is admirable pleasures and fery
honest knaveries.   Exeunt Page, Ford, and Evans

MRS. PAGE. Go, Mistress Ford,   Exit Mistress Ford
Send Quickly to Sir John, to know his mind.
I 'll to the doctor: he hath my good will,
And none but he, to marry with Nan Page.
That Slender, though well landed, is an idiot;
And him my husband best of all affects:
The doctor is well money'd, and his friends
Potent at court: he, none but he, shall have her,
Though twenty thousand worthier come to crave her.
                                        Exit

SCENE FIVE

A Room in the Garter Inn.

Enter Host and Simple

HOST. What wouldst thou have, boor? what, thickskin? speak, breathe, discuss; brief, short, quick, snap.

SIMPLE. Marry, sir, I come to speak with Sir John Falstaff from Master Slender.

HOST. There 's his chamber, his house, his castle, his standing-bed and truckle-bed: 'tis painted about with the story of the Prodigal, fresh and new. Go knock and call: he 'll speak like an Anthropophaginian unto thee: knock, I say.

SIMPLE. There 's an old woman, a fat woman, gone up into his chamber: I 'll be so bold as stay, sir, till she come down; I come to speak with her, indeed.

HOST. Ha! a fat woman! the knight may be robbed: I 'll call. Bully knight! Bully Sir John! speak from thy lungs military: art thou there? it is thine host, thine Ephesian, calls.

FALSTAFF. (Above) How now, mine host!

HOST. Here 's a Bohemian-Tartar tarries the coming down of thy fat woman. Let her descend, bully; let her descend; my chambers are honourable: fie! privacy? fie!

Enter Falstaff

FALSTAFF. There was, mine host, an old fat woman even now with me, but she 's gone.

SIMPLE. Pray you, sir, was 't not the wise woman of Brainford?

FALSTAFF. Ay, marry, was it, muscle-shell: what would you with her?

SIMPLE. My master, sir, Master Slender, sent to her, seeing her go thorough the streets, to know, sir, whether one Nym, sir, that beguiled him of a chain, had the chain or no.

FALSTAFF. I spake with the old woman about it.

SIMPLE. And what says she, I pray, sir?

FALSTAFF. Marry, she says that the very same man that beguiled Master Slender of his chain cozened him of it.

SIMPLE. I would I could have spoken with the woman herself: I had other things to have spoken with her too, from him.

FALSTAFF. What are they? let us know.

HOST. Ay, come; quick.

SIMPLE. I may not conceal them, sir.

HOST. Conceal them, or thou diest.

SIMPLE. Why, sir, they were nothing but about Mistress Anne Page; to know if it were my master's fortune to have her or no.

FALSTAFF. 'Tis, 'tis his fortune.

SIMPLE. What, sir?

FALSTAFF. To have her, or no. Go; say the woman told me so.

SIMPLE. May I be bold to say so, sir?

FALSTAFF. Ay, Sir Tike; who more bold?

SIMPLE. I thank your worship: I shall make my master glad with these tidings.   *Exit*

HOST. Thou art clerkly, thou art clerkly, Sir John. Was there a wise woman with thee?

FALSTAFF. Ay, that there was, mine host; one that hath taught me more wit than ever I learned before in my life: and I paid nothing for it neither, but was paid for my learning.

Enter Bardolph

BARDOLPH. Out, alas, sir! cozenage, mere cozenage!

HOST. Where be my horses? speak well of them, varletto.

BARDOLPH. Run away, with the cozeners; for so soon as I came beyond Eton, they threw me off, from behind one of them, in a slough of mire; and set spurs and away, like three German devils, three Doctor Faustuses.

HOST. They are gone but to meet the duke, villain. Do not say they be fled; Germans are honest men.

Enter Sir Hugh Evans

EVANS. Where is mine host?

HOST. What is the matter, sir?

EVANS. Have a care of your entertainments: there is a friend of mine come to town, tells me, there is three cozen-germans that has cozened all the hosts of Readins, of Maidenhead, of Colebrook, of horses and money. I tell you for good will, look you: you are wise and full of gibes and vlouting-stogs, and 'tis not convenient you should be cozened. Fare you well.   *Exit*

Enter Doctor Caius

CAIUS. Vere is mine host de Jarteer?

HOST. Here, Master doctor, in perplexity and doubtful dilemma.

CAIUS. I cannot tell vat is dat; but it is tell-a me dat you make grand preparation for a duke de Jamany: by my trot, dere is no duke dat de court is know to come. I tell you for good vill: adieu. *Exit*

HOST. Hue and cry, villain! go. Assist me, knight; I am undone. Fly, run, hue and cry, villain! I am undone!

Exeunt Host and Bardolph

FALSTAFF. I would all the world might be cozened, for I have been cozened and beaten too. If it should come to the ear of the court how I have been transformed, and how my transformation hath been washed and cudgelled, they would melt me out of my fat drop by drop, and liquor fishermen's boots with me: I warrant they would whip me with their fine wits till I were as crestfallen as a dried pear. I never prospered since I forswore myself at primero. Well, if my wind were but long enough to say my prayers, I would repent.

Enter Mistress Quickly

Now, whence come you?

QUICKLY. From the two parties, forsooth.

FALSTAFF. The devil take one party and his dam the other! and so they shall be both bestowed. I have suffered more for their sakes, more than the villanous inconstancy of man's disposition is able to bear.

QUICKLY. And have not they suffered? Yes, I warrant; speciously one of them: Mistress Ford, good heart, is beaten black and blue, that you cannot see a white spot about her.

FALSTAFF. What tellest thou me of black and blue? I was beaten myself into all the colours of the rainbow; and I was like to be apprehended for the witch of Brainford: but that my admirable dexterity of wit, my counterfeiting the action of an old woman, delivered me, the knave constable had set me i' the stocks, i' the common stocks, for a witch.

QUICKLY. Sir, let me speak with you in your chamber; you shall hear how things go, and, I warrant, to your content. Here is a letter will say somewhat. Good hearts! what ado here is to bring you together! Sure, one of you does not serve heaven well, that you are so crossed.

FALSTAFF. Come up into my chamber. *Exeunt*

SCENE SIX

Another Room in the Garter Inn.

Enter Fenton and Host

HOST. Master Fenton, talk not to me: my mind is heavy; I
will give over all.

FENTON. Yet hear me speak. Assist me in my purpose,
And, as I am a gentleman, I 'll give thee
A hundred pound in gold more than your loss.

HOST. I will hear you, Master Fenton; and I will, at the
least, keep your counsel.

FENTON. From time to time I have acquainted you
With the dear love I bear to fair Anne Page;
Who, mutually hath answer'd my affection,
So far forth as herself might be her chooser,
Even to my wish. I have a letter from her
Of such contents as you will wonder at;
The mirth whereof so larded with my matter,
That neither singly can be manifested,
Without the show of both; wherein fat Falstaff
Hath a great scare: the image of the jest
I 'll show you here at large. (*Pointing to the Letter*) Hark,
     good mine host:
To-night at Herne's oak, just 'twixt twelve and one,
Must my sweet Nan present the Fairy Queen;
The purpose why, is here: in which disguise,
While other jests are something rank on foot,
Her father hath commanded her to slip
Away with Slender, and with him at Eton
Immediately to marry: she hath consented:
Now, sir,
Her mother, even strong against that match
And firm for Doctor Caius, hath appointed
That he shall likewise shuffle her away,
While other sports are tasking of their minds;
And at the deanery, where a priest attends,
Straight marry her: to this her mother's plot
She, seemingly obedient, likewise hath
Made promise to the doctor. Now, thus it rests:

Her father means she shall be all in white,
And in that habit, when Slender sees his time
To take her by the hand and bid her go,
She shall go with him: her mother hath intended,
The better to denote her to the doctor,—
For they must all be mask'd and vizarded—
That quaint in green she shall be loose enrob'd,
With ribands pendent, flaring 'bout her head;
And when the doctor spies his vantage ripe,
To pinch her by the hand: and on that token
The maid hath given consent to go with him.

HOST. Which means she to deceive, father or mother?

FENTON. Both, my good host, to go along with me:
And here it rests, that you 'll procure the vicar
To stay for me at church 'twixt twelve and one,
And, in the lawful name of marrying,
To give our hearts united ceremony.

HOST. Well, husband your device; I 'll to the vicar.
Bring you the maid, you shall not lack a priest.

FENTON. So shall I evermore be bound to thee;
Besides, I 'll make a present recompense.

ACT FIVE

SCENE ONE

A Room in the Garter Inn.

Enter Falstaff and Mistress Quickly

FALSTAFF. Prithee, no more prattling; go: I 'll hold. This is the third time; I hope good luck lies in odd numbers. Away! go. They say there is divinity in odd numbers, either in nativity, chance or death. Away!

QUICKLY. I 'll provide you a chain, and I 'll do what I can to get you a pair of horns.

FALSTAFF. Away, I say; time wears: hold up your head, and mince. *Exit Mistress Quickly*

Enter Ford, disguised

How now, Master Brook! Master Brook, the matter will be known to-night, or never. Be you in the Park about midnight, at Herne's oak, and you shall see wonders.

FORD. Went you not to her yesterday, sir, as you told me you had appointed?

FALSTAFF. I went to her, Master Brook, as you see, like a poor old man; but I came from her, Master Brook, like a poor old woman. That same knave Ford, her husband, hath the finest mad devil of jealousy in him, Master Brook, that ever governed frenzy. I will tell you: he beat me grievously, in the shape of a woman; for in the shape of a man, Master Brook, I fear not Goliath with a weaver's beam, because I know also life is a shuttle. I am in haste: go along with me; I 'll tell you all, Master Brook. Since I plucked geese, played truant, and whipped top, I knew not what it was to be beaten till lately. Follow me: I 'll tell you strange things of this knave Ford, on whom to-night I will be revenged, and I will deliver his wife into your hand. Follow. Strange things in hand, Master Brook! Follow. *Exeunt*

SCENE TWO

Windsor Park.

Enter Page, Shallow, and Slender

PAGE. Come, come; we 'll couch i' the castle-ditch till we see the light of our fairies. Remember, son Slender, my daughter.

SLENDER. Ay, forsooth; I have spoke with her and we have a nay-word how to know one another. I come to her in white, and cry, 'mum'; she cries, 'budget'; and by that we know one another.

SHALLOW. That 's good too: but what needs either your 'mum', or her 'budget'? the white will decipher her well enough. It hath struck ten o'clock.

PAGE. The night is dark; light and spirits will become it well. Heaven prosper our sport! No man means evil but the devil, and we shall know him by his horns. Let 's away; follow me.   *Exeunt*

SCENE THREE

The Street in Windsor.

Enter Mistress Page, Mistress Ford, and Dr. Caius

MRS. PAGE. Master Doctor, my daughter is in green: when you see your time, take her by the hand, away with her to the deanery, and dispatch it quickly. Go before into the Park: we two must go together.

CAIUS. I know vat I have to do. Adieu.

MRS. PAGE. Fare you well, sir. (*Exit Caius*) My husband will not rejoice so much at the abuse of Falstaff, as he will chafe at the doctor's marrying my daughter: but 'tis no matter; better a little chiding than a great deal of heart break.

MRS. FORD. Where is Nan now and her troop of fairies, and the Welsh devil, Hugh?

MRS. PAGE. They are all couched in a pit hard by Herne's oak, with obscured lights; which, at the very instant of

Falstaff's and our meeting, they will at once display to the night.

MRS. FORD. That cannot choose but amaze him.

MRS. PAGE. If he be not amazed, he will be mocked; if he be amazed, he will every way be mocked.

MRS. FORD. We 'll betray him finely.

MRS. PAGE. Against such lewdsters and their lechery,
Those that betray them do no treachery.

MRS. FORD. The hour draws on: to the oak, to the oak!

Exeunt

SCENE FOUR

Windsor Park.

Enter Sir Hugh Evans, disguised, and others as Fairies

EVANS. Trib, trib, fairies: come; and remember your parts.
Be pold, I pray you; follow me into the pit, and when I give the watch-ords, do as I pid you. Come, come; trib, trib. *Exeunt*

SCENE FIVE

Another part of the Park.
Enter Falstaff disguised as Herne, with a buck's head on

FALSTAFF. The Windsor bell hath struck twelve; the minute draws on. Now, the hot-blooded gods assist me! Remember, Jove, thou wast a bull for thy Europa; love set on thy horns. O powerful love! that, in some respects, makes a beast a man; in some other, a man a beast. You were also, Jupiter, a swan for the love of Leda; O omnipotent love! how near the god drew to the complexion of a goose! A fault done first in the form of a beast; O Jove, a beastly fault! and then another fault in the semblance of a fowl: think on 't, Jove; a foul fault! When gods have hot backs, what shall poor men do? For me, I am here a Windsor stag; and the fattest, I think, i' the forest: send me a cool rut-time, Jove, or who can blame me to piss my tallow? Who comes here? my doe?

Enter Mistress Ford and Mistress Page

MRS. FORD. Sir John! art thou there, my deer? my male deer?

FALSTAFF. My doe with the black scut! Let the sky rain potatoes; let it thunder to the tune of 'Green Sleeves'; hail kissing-comfits and snow eringoes; let there come a tempest of provocation, I will shelter me here.

Embracing her

MRS. FORD. Mistress Page is come with me, sweetheart.

FALSTAFF. Divide me like a brib'd buck, each a haunch: I will keep my sides to myself, my shoulders for the fellow of this walk, and my horns I bequeath your husbands. Am I a woodman, ha? Speak I like Herne the hunter? Why, now is Cupid a child of conscience; he makes restitution. As I am a true spirit, welcome!   *Noise within*

MRS. PAGE. Alas! what noise?

MRS. FORD. Heaven forgive our sins!

FALSTAFF. What should this be?

MRS. FORD. ⎱ Away, away!   *They run off*
MRS. PAGE. ⎰

FALSTAFF. I think the devil will not have me damned, lest the oil that is in me should set hell on fire; he would never else cross me thus.

Enter Sir Hugh Evans, like a Satyr; Pistol as Hobgoblin;
Anne Page, as the Fairy Queen, attended by her Brother
and Others, as Fairies, with waxen tapers on their heads

ANNE. Fairies, black, grey, green, and white,
You moonshine revellers, and shades of night,
You orphan heirs of fixed destiny,
Attend your office and your quality.
Crier Hobgoblin, make the fairy oyes.

PISTOL. Elves, list your names: silence, you airy toys!
Cricket, to Windsor chimneys shalt thou leap:
Where fires thou find'st unrak'd and hearths unswept,
There pinch the maids as blue as bilberry:
Our radiant queen hates sluts and sluttery.

FALSTAFF. They are fairies; he that speaks to them shall die:
I 'll wink and couch: no man their works must eye.

Lies down upon his face

EVANS. Where 's Bede? Go you, and where you find a maid
That, ere she sleep, has thrice her prayers said,

Rein up the organs of her fantasy,
Sleep she as sound as careless infancy;
But those that sleep and think not on their sins,
Pinch them, arms, legs, backs, shoulders, sides, and shins.

ANNE. About, about!
Search Windsor castle, elves, within and out:
Strew good luck, ouphs, on every sacred room,
That it may stand till the perpetual doom,
In state as wholesome as in state 'tis fit,
Worthy the owner, and the owner it.
The several chairs of order look you scour
With juice of balm and every precious flower:
Each fair instalment, coat, and several crest,
With loyal blazon, ever more be blest!
And nightly, meadow-fairies, look you sing,
Like to the Garter's compass, in a ring:
The expressure that it bears, green let it be,
More fertile-fresh than all the field to see;
And, 'Honi soit qui mal y pense' write
In emerald tufts, flowers purple, blue, and white;
Like sapphire, pearl, and rich embroidery,
Buckled below fair knighthood's bending knee:
Fairies use flowers for their charactery.
Away! disperse! But, till 'tis one o'clock,
Our dance of custom round about the oak
Of Herne the hunter, let us not forget.

EVANS. Pray you, lock hand in hand; yourselves in order
    set;
And twenty glow-worms shall our lanthorns be,
To guide our measure round about the tree.
But, stay; I smell a man of middle-earth.

FALSTAFF. Heavens defend me from that Welsh fairy, lest
he transform me to a piece of cheese!

PISTOL. Vile worm, thou wast o'erlook'd even in thy birth.

ANNE. With trial-fire touch me his finger-end:
If he be chaste, the flame will back descend
And turn him to no pain; but if he start,
It is the flesh of a corrupted heart.

PISTOL. A trial! come.

EVANS.   Come, will this wood take fire?
                    They burn him with their tapers

FALSTAFF. Oh, oh, oh!

ANNE. Corrupt, corrupt, and tainted in desire!
   About him, fairies, sing a scornful rime;
   And, as you trip, still pinch him to your time.

SONG

   Fie on sinful fantasy!
   Fie on lust and luxury!
   Lust is but a bloody fire,
   Kindled with unchaste desire,
   Fed in heart, whose flames aspire,
   As thoughts do blow them higher and higher.
   Pinch him, fairies, mutually;
   Pinch him for his villany;
   Pinch him, and burn him, and turn him about,
   Till candles and star-light and moonshine be out.

During this song, the Fairies pinch
Falstaff. Doctor Caius comes one way, and
steals away a Fairy in green; Slender another way,
and takes off a Fairy in white; and Fenton comes, and steals
away Anne Page. A noise of hunting is heard within. The
Fairies run away. Falstaff pulls off his buck's head, and rises

Enter Page, Ford, Mistress
Page and Mistress Ford. They lay hold on Falstaff

PAGE. Nay, do not fly: I think we have watch'd you now:
   Will none but Herne the hunter serve your turn?
MRS. PAGE. I pray you, come, hold up the jest no higher.
   Now, good Sir John, how like you Windsor wives?
   See you these, husband? do not these fair yokes
   Become the forest better than the town?
FORD. Now sir, who's a cuckold now? Master Brook, Fal-
   staff's a knave, a cuckoldly knave; here are his horns,
   Master Brook: and, Master Brook, he hath enjoyed noth-
   ing of Ford's but his buck-basket, his cudgel, and twenty
   pounds of money, which must be paid too, Master Brook;
   his horses are arrested for it, Master Brook.
MRS. FORD. Sir John, we have had ill luck; we could never
   meet. I will never take you for my love again, but I will
   always count you my deer.
FALSTAFF. I do begin to perceive that I am made an ass.
FORD. Ay, and an ox too; both the proofs are extant.
FALSTAFF. And these are not fairies? I was three or four

times in the thought they were not fairies; and yet the
guiltiness of my mind, the sudden surprise of my powers,
drove the grossness of the foppery into a received belief,
in despite of the teeth of all rime and reason, that they
were fairies. See now how wit may be made a Jack-a-
Lent, when 'tis upon ill employment!

EVANS. Sir John Falstaff, serve Got, and leave your desires,
and fairies will not pinse you.

FORD. Well said, fairy Hugh.

EVANS. And leave you your jealousies too, I pray you.

FORD. I will never mistrust my wife again, till thou art able
to woo her in good English.

FALSTAFF. Have I laid my brain in the sun and dried it,
that it wants matter to prevent so gross o'er-reaching as
this? Am I ridden with a Welsh goat too? Shall I have a
coxcomb of frize? 'Tis time I were choked with a piece of
toasted cheese.

EVANS. Seese is not goot to give putter: your pelly is all
putter.

FALSTAFF. 'Seese' and 'putter'! Have I lived to stand at the
taunt of one that makes fritters of English? This is
enough to be the decay of lust and late-walking through
the realm.

MRS. PAGE. Why, Sir John, do you think, though we would
have thrust virtue out of our hearts by the head and
shoulders, and have given ourselves without scruple to
hell, that ever the devil could have made you our delight?

FORD. What, a hodge-pudding? a bag of flax?

MRS. PAGE. A puffed man?

PAGE. Old, cold, withered, and of intolerable entrails?

FORD. And one that is as slanderous as Satan?

PAGE. And as poor as Job?

FORD. And as wicked as his wife?

EVANS. And given to fornications, and to taverns, and sack
and wine and metheglins, and to drinkings and swearings
and starings, pribbles and prabbles?

FALSTAFF. Well, I am your theme: you have the start of
me; I am dejected; I am not able to answer the Welsh
flannel. Ignorance itself is a plummet o'er me: use me as
you will.

FORD. Marry, sir, we'll bring you to Windsor, to one Master

Brook, that you have cozened of money, to whom you should have been a pander: over and above that you have suffered, I think, to repay that money will be a biting affliction.

MRS. FORD. Nay, husband, let that go to make amends; Forgive that sum, and so we 'll all be friends.

FORD. Well, here 's my hand: all is forgiven at last.

PAGE. Yet be cheerful, knight: thou shalt eat a posset tonight at my house; where I will desire thee to laugh at my wife, that now laughs at thee. Tell her, Master Slender hath married her daughter.

MRS. PAGE. (*Aside*) Doctors doubt that: if Anne Page be my daughter, she is, by this, Doctor Caius' wife.

Enter Slender

SLENDER. Whoa, ho! ho! father Page!

PAGE. Son, how now! how now, son! have you dispatched?

SLENDER. Dispatched! I 'll make the best in Glostershire know on 't; would I were hanged, la, else!

PAGE. Of what, son?

SLENDER. I came yonder at Eton to marry Mistress Anne Page, and she 's a great lubberly boy: if it had not been i' the church, I would have swinged him, or he should have swinged me. If I did not think it had been Anne Page, would I might never stir! and 'tis a postmaster's boy.

PAGE. Upon my life, then, you took the wrong.

SLENDER. What need you tell me that? I think so, when I took a boy for a girl. If I had been married to him, for all he was in woman's apparel, I would not have had him.

PAGE. Why, this is your own folly. Did not I tell you how you should know my daughter by her garments?

SLENDER. I went to her in white, and cried, 'mum,' and she cried 'budget,' as Anne and I had appointed; and yet it was not Anne, but a postmaster's boy.

EVANS. Jeshu! Master Slender, cannot you see put marry poys?

PAGE. O I am vexed at heart: what shall I do?

MRS. PAGE. Good George, be not angry: I knew of your purpose; turned my daughter into green; and, indeed, she is now with the doctor at the deanery, and there married.

Enter Doctor Caius

CAIUS. Vere is Mistress Page? By gar, I am cozened: I ha'
married un garçon, a boy; un paysan, by gar, a boy; it is
not Anne Page: by gar, I am cozened.

MRS. PAGE. Why, did you not take her in green?

CAIUS. Ay, by gar, and 'tis a boy: by gar, I 'll raise all Windsor.

FORD. This is strange. Who hath got the right Anne?

PAGE. My heart misgives me: here comes Master Fenton.
Enter Fenton and Anne Page

How now, Master Fenton!

ANNE. Pardon, good father! good my mother, pardon!

PAGE. Now, mistress, how chance you went not with Master Slender?

MRS. PAGE. Why went you not with Master Doctor, maid?

FENTON. You do amaze her: hear the truth of it.
You would have married her most shamefully,
Where there was no proportion held in love.
The truth is, she and I, long since contracted,
Are now so sure that nothing can dissolve us.
The offence is holy that she hath committed,
And this deceit loses the name of craft,
Of disobedience, or unduteous title,
Since therein she doth evitate and shun
A thousand irreligious cursed hours,
Which forced marriage would have brought upon her.

FORD. Stand not amaz'd: here is no remedy:
In love the heavens themselves do guide the state:
Money buys lands, and wives are sold by fate.

FALSTAFF. I am glad, though you have ta'en a special stand
to strike at me, that your arrow hath glanced.

PAGE. Well, what remedy?—Fenton, heaven give thee joy!
What cannot be eschew'd must be embrac'd.

FALSTAFF. When night-dogs run all sorts of deer are chas'd.

MRS. PAGE. Well, I will muse no further. Master Fenton,
Heaven give you many, many merry days!
Good husband, let us every one go home,
And laugh this sport o'er by a country fire;
Sir John and all.

FORD.   Let it be so. Sir John,
To Master Brook you yet shall hold your word;
For he to-night shall lie with Mistress Ford.   *Exeunt*

MEASURE FOR MEASURE

CAST OF CHARACTERS

VINCENT O, *the Duke*
ANGELO, *Lord Deputy in the Duke's absence*
ESCALUS, *an Ancient Lord, joined with Angelo
in the deputation*
CLAUDIO, *a young Gentleman*
LUCIO, *a Fantastic*
Two other like Gentlemen
VARRIUS, *a Gentleman attending on the Duke*
Provost

THOMAS ⎱ *two Friars*
PETER ⎰

A Justice
ELBOW, *a simple Constable*
FROTH, *a foolish Gentleman*
POMPEY, *Tapster to Mistress Overdone*
ABHORSON, *an Executioner*
BARNARDINE, *a dissolute Prisoner*

ISABELLA, *sister to Claudio*
MARIANA, *betrothed to Angelo*
JULIET, *beloved of Claudio*
FRANCISCA, *a Nun*
MISTRESS OVERDONE, *a Bawd*

Lords, Officers, Citizens, Boy, and Attendants

SCENE

Vienna

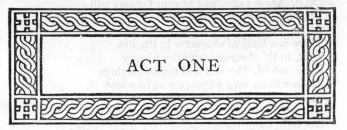

ACT ONE

SCENE ONE

An Apartment in the Duke's Palace.

Enter Duke, Escalus, Lords, and Attendants

DUKE. Escalus.

ESCALUS. My lord?

DUKE. Of government the properties to unfold,
Would seem in me to affect speech and discourse,
Since I am put to know that your own science
Exceeds, in that, the lists of all advice
My strength can give you: then no more remains,
But that, to your sufficiency, as your worth is able,
And let them work. The nature of our people
Our city's institutions, and the terms
For common justice, you're as pregnant in,
As art and practice hath enriched any
That we remember. There is our commission, *Giving it*
From which we would not have you warp. Call hither,
I say, bid come before us Angelo. *Exit an Attendant*
What figure of us think you he will bear?
For you must know, we have with special soul
Elected him our absence to supply,
Lent him our terror, drest him with our love,
And given his deputation all the organs
Of our own power: what think you of it?

ESCALUS. If any in Vienna be of worth
To undergo such ample grace and honour,
It is Lord Angelo.

DUKE.   Look where he comes.
                Enter Angelo

ANGELO. Always obedient to your Grace's will
  I come to know your pleasure.
DUKE.   Angelo,
  There is a kind of character in thy life,
  That, to th' observer doth thy history
  Fully unfold. Thy self and thy belongings
  Are not thine own so proper, as to waste
  Thyself upon thy virtues, they on thee.
  Heaven doth with us as we with torches do,
  Not light them for themselves; for if our virtues
  Did not go forth of us, 'twere all alike
  As if we had them not. Spirits are not finely touch'd
  But to fine issues, nor Nature never lends
  The smallest scruple of her excellence,
  But, like a thrifty goddess, she determines
  Herself the glory of a creditor,
  Both thanks and use. But I do bend my speech
  To one that can my part in him advertise;
  Hold, therefore, Angelo: *Tendering his commission*
  In our remove be thou at full ourself;
  Mortality and mercy in Vienna
  Live in thy tongue and heart. Old Escalus,
  Though first in question, is thy secondary.
  Take thy commission.   *Giving it*
ANGELO.   Now, good my lord,
  Let there be some more test made of my metal,
  Before so noble and so great a figure
  Be stamp'd upon it.
DUKE.   No more evasion:
  We have with a leaven'd and prepared choice
  Proceeded to you; therefore take your honours.
  Our haste from hence is of so quick condition
  That it prefers itself, and leaves unquestion'd
  Matters of needful value. We shall write to you,
  As time and our concernings shall importune,
  How it goes with us: and do look to know
  What doth befall you here. So, fare you well:
  To the hopeful execution do I leave you
  Of your commissions.
ANGELO.   Yet, give leave, my lord,
  That we may bring you something on the way.
DUKE. My haste may not admit it;

Nor need you, on mine honour, have to do
With any scruple: your scope is as mine own,
So to enforce or qualify the laws
As to your soul seems good. Give me your hand;
I 'll privily away: I love the people,
But do not like to stage me to their eyes.
Though it do well, I do not relish well
Their loud applause and Aves vehement,
Nor do I think the man of safe discretion
That does affect it. Once more, fare you well.

ANGELO. The heavens give safety to your purposes!

ESCALUS. Lead forth and bring you back in happiness!

DUKE. I thank you. Fare you well.   *Exit*

ESCALUS. I shall desire you, sir, to give me leave
To have free speech with you; and it concerns me
To look into the bottom of my place:
A power I have, but of what strength and nature
I am not yet instructed.

ANGELO. 'Tis so with me. Let us withdraw together,
And we may soon our satisfaction have
Touching that point.

ESCALUS.   I 'll wait upon your honour.   *Exeunt*

SCENE TWO

A Street.

Enter Lucio and two Gentlemen

LUCIO. If the duke with the other dukes comes not to composition with the King of Hungary, why then, all the
dukes fall upon the king.

FIRST GENTLEMAN. Heaven grant us its peace, but not the
King of Hungary's!

SECOND GENTLEMAN. Amen.

LUCIO. Thou concludest like the sanctimonious pirate, that
went to sea with the Ten Commandments, but scraped
one out of the table.

SECOND GENTLEMAN. 'Thou shalt not steal'?

LUCIO. Ay, that he razed.

FIRST GENTLEMAN. Why, 'twas a commandment to command the captain and all the rest from their functions:

they put forth to steal. There 's not a soldier of us all, that, in the thanksgiving before meat, doth relish the petition well that prays for peace.

SECOND GENTLEMAN. I never heard any soldier dislike it.

LUCIO. I believe thee, for I think thou never wast where grace was said.

SECOND GENTLEMAN. No? a dozen times at least.

FIRST GENTLEMAN. What, in metre?

LUCIO. In any proportion or in any language.

FIRST GENTLEMAN. I think, or in any religion.

LUCIO. Ay; why not? Grace is grace, despite of all controversy: as, for example, thou thyself art a wicked villain, despite of all grace.

FIRST GENTLEMAN. Well, there went but a pair of shears between us.

LUCIO. I grant; as there may between the lists and the velvet: thou art the list.

FIRST GENTLEMAN. And thou the velvet: thou art good velvet; thou art a three-piled piece, I warrant thee. I had as lief be a list of an English kersey as be piled, as thou art piled, for a French velvet. Do I speak feelingly now?

LUCIO. I think thou dost; and, indeed, with most painful feeling of thy speech: I will, out of thine own confession, learn to begin thy health; but, whilst I live, forget to drink after thee.

FIRST GENTLEMAN. I think I have done myself wrong, have I not?

SECOND GENTLEMAN. Yes, that thou hast, whether thou art tainted or free.

LUCIO. Behold, behold, where Madam Mitigation comes! I have purchased as many diseases under her roof as come to—

SECOND GENTLEMAN. To what, I pray?

LUCIO. Judge.

SECOND GENTLEMAN. To three thousand dolours a year.

FIRST GENTLEMAN. Ay, and more.

LUCIO. A French crown more.

FIRST GENTLEMAN. Thou art always figuring diseases in me; but thou art full of error: I am sound.

LUCIO. Nay, not as one would say, healthy; but so sound as things that are hollow: thy bones are hollow; impiety has made a feast of thee.

Enter Mistress Overdone

FIRST GENTLEMAN. How now! which of your hips has the most profound sciatica?

MRS. OVERDONE. Well, well; there 's one yonder arrested and carried to prison was worth five thousand of you all.

SECOND GENTLEMAN. Who 's that, I pray thee?

MRS. OVERDONE. Marry, sir, that 's Claudio, Signior Claudio.

FIRST GENTLEMAN. Claudio to prison! 'Tis not so.

MRS. OVERDONE. Nay, but I know 'tis so. I saw him arrested; saw him carried away; and, which is more, within these three days his head to be chopped off.

LUCIO. But, after all this fooling, I would not have it so. Art thou sure of this?

MRS. OVERDONE. I am too sure of it; and it is for getting Madam Julietta with child.

LUCIO. Believe me, this may be: he promised to meet me two hours since, and he was ever precise in promise-keeping.

SECOND GENTLEMAN. Besides, you know, it draws something near to the speech we had to such a purpose.

FIRST GENTLEMAN. But most of all, agreeing with the proclamation.

LUCIO. Away! let 's go learn the truth of it.

Exeunt Lucio and Gentlemen

MRS. OVERDONE. Thus, what with the war, what with the sweat, what with the gallows and what with poverty, I am custom-shrunk.

Enter Pompey

How now! what 's the news with you?

POMPEY. Yonder man is carried to prison.

MRS. OVERDONE. Well: what has he done?

POMPEY. A woman.

MRS. OVERDONE. But what 's his offence?

POMPEY. Groping for trouts in a peculiar river.

MRS. OVERDONE. What, is there a maid with child by him?

POMPEY. No; but there 's a woman with maid by him. You have not heard of the proclamation, have you?

MRS. OVERDONE. What proclamation, man?

POMPEY. All houses of resort in the suburbs of Vienna must be plucked down.

MRS. OVERDONE. And what shall become of those in the city?

POMPEY. They shall stand for seed: they had gone down too, but that a wise burgher put in for them.

MRS. OVERDONE. But shall all our houses of resort in the suburbs be pulled down?

POMPEY. To the ground, mistress.

MRS. OVERDONE. Why, here 's a change indeed in the commonwealth! What shall become of me?

POMPEY. Come; fear not you: good counsellors lack no clients: though you change your place, you need not change your trade; I 'll be your tapster still. Courage! there will be pity taken on you; you that have worn your eyes almost out in the service, you will be considered.

MRS. OVERDONE. What 's to do here, Thomas tapster? Let 's withdraw.

POMPEY. Here comes Signior Claudio, led by the provost to prison; and there 's Madam Juliet.   *Exeunt*

    Enter Provost, Claudio, Juliet, and Officers

CLAUDIO. Fellow, why dost thou show me thus to the world?
Bear me to prison where I am committed.

PROVOST. I do it not in evil disposition,
But from Lord Angelo by special charge.

CLAUDIO. Thus can the demi-god Authority
Make us pay down for our offence by weight.
The words of heaven; on whom it will, it will;
On whom it will not, so: yet still 'tis just.

    Re-enter Lucio and two Gentlemen

LUCIO. Why, how now, Claudio! whence comes this restraint?

CLAUDIO. From too much liberty, my Lucio, liberty:
As surfeit is the father of much fast,
So every scope by the immoderate use
Turns to restraint. Our natures do pursue—
Like rats that ravin down their proper bane,—
A thirsty evil, and when we drink we die.

LUCIO. If I could speak so wisely under an arrest, I would send for certain of my creditors. And yet, to say the truth, I had as lief have the foppery of freedom as the morality of imprisonment. What 's thy offence, Claudio?

CLAUDIO. What but to speak of would offend again.

LUCIO. What, is 't murder?

CLAUDIO. No.

LUCIO. Lechery?

CLAUDIO. Call it so.

PROVOST. Away, sir! you must go.

CLAUDIO. One word, good friend. Lucio, a word with you.

Takes him aside

LUCIO. A hundred, if they 'll do you any good.
Is lechery so looked after?

CLAUDIO. Thus stands it with me: upon a true contract
I got possession of Julietta's bed:
You know the lady; she is fast my wife,
Save that we do the denunciation lack
Of outward order: this we came not to,
Only for propagation of a dower
Remaining in the coffer of her friends,
From whom we thought it meet to hide our love
Till time had made them for us. But it chances
The stealth of our most mutual entertainment
With character too gross is writ on Juliet.

LUCIO. With child, perhaps?

CLAUDIO.   Unhappily, even so.
And the new deputy now for the duke,—
Whether it be the fault and glimpse of newness,
Or whether that the body public be
A horse whereon the governor doth ride,
Who, newly in the seat, that it may know
He can command, lets it straight feel the spur;
Whether the tyranny be in his place,
Or in his eminence that fills it up,
I stagger in:—but this new governor
Awakes me all the enrolled penalties
Which have, like unscour'd armour, hung by the wall
So long that nineteen zodiacs have gone round,
And none of them been worn; and, for a name,
Now puts the drowsy and neglected act
Freshly on me: 'tis surely for a name.

LUCIO. I warrant it is: and thy head stands so tickle on thy
shoulders that a milkmaid, if she be in love, may sigh it
off. Send after the duke and appeal to him.

CLAUDIO. I have done so, but he 's not to be found.
I prithee, Lucio, do me this kind service.
This day my sister should the cloister enter,

And there receive her approbation:
Acquaint her with the danger of my state;
Implore her, in my voice, that she make friends
To the strict deputy; bid herself assay him:
I have great hope in that; for in her youth
There is a prone and speechless dialect,
Such as move men; beside, she hath prosperous art
When she will play with reason and discourse,
And well she can persuade.

LUCIO. I pray she may: as well for the encouragement of
the like, which else would stand under grievous imposi-
tion, as for the enjoying of thy life, who I would be sorry
should be thus foolishly lost at a game of tick-tack. I 'll to
her.

CLAUDIO. I thank you, good friend Lucio.

LUCIO. Within two hours.

CLAUDIO.   Come, officer, away!   *Exeunt*

SCENE THREE

A Monastery.

Enter Duke and Friar Thomas

DUKE. No, holy father; throw away that thought:
Believe not that the dribbling dart of love
Can pierce a complete bosom. Why I desire thee
To give me secret harbour, hath a purpose
More grave and wrinkled than the aims and ends
Of burning youth.

FRIAR THOMAS.   May your Grace speak of it?

DUKE. My holy sir, none better knows than you
How I have ever lov'd the life remov'd,
And held in idle price to haunt assemblies
Where youth, and cost, and witless bravery keeps.
I have deliver'd to Lord Angelo—
A man of stricture and firm abstinence—
My absolute power and place here in Vienna,
And he supposes me travell'd to Poland;
For so I have strew'd it in the common ear,
And so it is receiv'd. Now, pious sir,
You will demand of me why I do this?

FRIAR THOMAS. Gladly, my lord.

DUKE. We have strict statutes and most biting laws,—
  The needful bits and curbs to headstrong steeds,—
  Which for this fourteen years we have let sleep;
  Even like an o'ergrown lion in a cave,
  That goes not out to prey. Now, as fond fathers,
  Having bound up the threat'ning twigs of birch,
  Only to stick it in their children's sight
  For terror, not to use, in time the rod
  Becomes more mock'd than fear'd; so our decrees,
  Dead to infliction, to themselves are dead,
  And liberty plucks justice by the nose;
  The baby beats the nurse, and quite athwart
  Goes all decorum.

FRIAR THOMAS.   It rested in your Grace
  T' unloose this tied-up justice when you pleas'd;
  And it in you more dreadful would have seem'd
  Than in Lord Angelo.

DUKE.   I do fear, too dreadful:
  Sith 'twas my fault to give the people scope,
  'Twould be my tyranny to strike and gall them
  For what I bid them do: for we bid this be done,
  When evil deeds have their permissive pass
  And not the punishment. Therefore, indeed, my father,
  I have on Angelo impos'd the office,
  Who may, in the ambush of my name, strike home,
  And yet my nature never in the sight
  To do it slander. And to behold his sway,
  I will, as 'twere a brother of your order,
  Visit both prince and people: therefore, I prithee,
  Supply me with the habit, and instruct me
  How I may formally in person bear me
  Like a true friar. Moe reasons for this action
  At our more leisure shall I render you;
  Only, this one: Lord Angelo is precise;
  Stands at a guard with envy; scarce confesses
  That his blood flows, or that his appetite
  Is more to bread than stone: hence shall we see,
  If power change purpose, what our seemers be.   *Exeunt*

SCENE FOUR

A Nunnery.

Enter Isabella and Francisca

ISABELLA. And have you nuns no further privileges?

FRANCISCA. Are not these large enough?

ISABELLA. Yes, truly; I speak not as desiring more,
But rather wishing a more strict restraint
Upon the sisterhood, the votarists of Saint Clare.

LUCIO. (*Within*) Ho! Peace be in this place!

ISABELLA.   Who 's that which calls?

FRANCISCA. It is a man's voice. Gentle Isabella,
Turn you the key, and know his business of him:
You may, I may not; you are yet unsworn.
When you have vow'd, you must not speak with men
But in the presence of the prioress:
Then, if you speak, you must not show your face,
Or, if you show your face, you must not speak.
He calls again; I pray you, answer him.   *Exit*

ISABELLA. Peace and prosperity! Who is 't that calls?

Enter Lucio

LUCIO. Hail, virgin, if you be, as those cheek-roses
Proclaim you are no less! Can you so stead me
As bring me to the sight of Isabella,
A novice of this place, and the fair sister
To her unhappy brother Claudio?

ISABELLA. Why 'her unhappy brother'? let me ask;
The rather for I now must make you know
I am that Isabella and his sister.

LUCIO. Gentle and fair, your brother kindly greets you:
Not to be weary with you, he 's in prison.

ISABELLA. Woe me! for what?

LUCIO. For that which, if myself might be his judge,
He should receive his punishment in thanks:
He hath got his friend with child.

ISABELLA. Sir, make me not your story.

LUCIO.   It is true.
I would not, though 'tis my familiar sin
With maids to seem the lapwing and to jest,

Tongue far from heart, play with all virgins so:
I hold you as a thing ensky'd and sainted;
By your renouncement an immortal spirit,
And to be talk'd with in sincerity,
As with a saint.

ISABELLA. You do blaspheme the good in mocking me.

LUCIO. Do not believe it. Fewness and truth, 'tis thus:
Your brother and his lover have embrac'd:
As those that feed grow full, as blossoming time
That from the seedness the bare fallow brings
To teeming foison, even so her plenteous womb
Expresseth his full tilth and husbandry.

ISABELLA. Some one with child by him? My cousin Juliet?

LUCIO. Is she your cousin?

ISABELLA. Adoptedly; as school-maids change their names
By vain, though apt affection.

LUCIO.   She it is.

ISABELLA. O! let him marry her.

LUCIO.   This is the point.
The duke is very strangely gone from hence;
Bore many gentlemen, myself being one,
In hand and hope of action; but we do learn
By those that know the very nerves of state,
His givings out were of an infinite distance
From his true-meant design. Upon his place,
And with full line of his authority,
Governs Lord Angelo; a man whose blood
Is very snow-broth; one who never feels
The wanton stings and motions of the sense,
But doth rebate and blunt his natural edge
With profits of the mind, study and fast.
He,—to give fear to use and liberty,
Which have for long run by the hideous law,
As mice by lions, hath pick'd out an act,
Under whose heavy sense your brother's life
Falls into forfeit: he arrests him on it,
And follows close the rigour of the statute,
To make him an example. All hope is gone,
Unless you have the grace by your fair prayer
To soften Angelo; and that 's my pith of business
Twixt you and your poor brother.

ISABELLA. Doth he so seek his life?

LUCIO.   He 's censur'd him
Already; and, as I hear, the provost hath
A warrant for his execution.

ISABELLA. Alas! what poor ability 's in me
To do him good?

LUCIO.   Assay the power you have.

ISABELLA. My power? alas! I doubt—

LUCIO.   Our doubts are traitors,
And make us lose the good we oft might win,
By fearing to attempt. Go to Lord Angelo,
And let him learn to know, when maidens sue,
Men give like gods; but when they weep and kneel,
All their petitions are as freely theirs
As they themselves would owe them.

ISABELLA. I 'll see what I can do.

LUCIO.   But speedily.

ISABELLA. I will about it straight;
No longer staying but to give the Mother
Notice of my affair. I humbly thank you:
Commend me to my brother; soon at night
I 'll send him certain word of my success.

LUCIO. I take my leave of you.

ISABELLA.   Good sir, adieu.   *Exeunt*

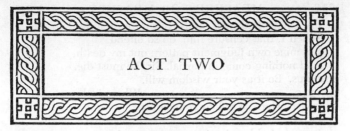

ACT TWO

[1·27]

SCENE ONE

A Hall in Angelo's House.

Enter Angelo, Escalus, a Justice, Provost, Officers,
and other Attendants

ANGELO. We must not make a scarecrow of the law,
　　Setting it up to fear the birds of prey,
　　And let it keep one shape, till custom make it
　　Their perch and not their terror.

ESCALUS. 　　　　　　　　　　　Ay, but yet
　　Let us be keen and rather cut a little,
　　Than fall, and bruise to death. Alas! this gentleman,
　　Whom I would save, had a most noble father.
　　Let but your honour know,—
　　Whom I believe to be most strait in virtue,—
　　That, in the working of your own affections,
　　Had time coher'd with place or place with wishing,
　　Or that the resolute acting of your blood
　　Could have attain'd the effect of your own purpose,
　　Whether you had not, some time in your life,
　　Err'd in this point which now you censure him,
　　And pull'd the law upon you.

ANGELO. 'Tis one thing to be tempted, Escalus,
　　Another thing to fall. I not deny,
　　The jury, passing on the prisoner's life,
　　May in the sworn twelve have a thief or two
　　Guiltier than him they try; what 's open made to justice,
　　That justice seizes: what know the laws
　　That thieves do pass on thieves? 'Tis very pregnant,
　　The jewel that we find, we stoop and take it
　　Because we see it; but what we do not see
　　We tread upon, and never think of it.
　　You may not so extenuate his offence

For I have had such faults; but rather tell me,
When I, that censure him, do so offend,
Let mine own judgment pattern out my death,
And nothing come in partial. Sir, he must die.

ESCALUS. Be it as your wisdom will.

ANGELO.   Where is the provost?

PROVOST. Here, if it like your honour.

ANGELO.   See that Claudio
Be executed by nine to-morrow morning:
Bring him his confessor, let him be prepar'd;
For that 's the utmost of his pilgrimage.   *Exit Provost*

ESCALUS. Well, heaven forgive him, and forgive us all!
Some rise by sin, and some by virtue fall:
Some run from brakes of ice, and answer none,
And some condemned for a fault alone.

Enter Elbow and Officers, with Froth and Pompey

ELBOW. Come, bring them away: if these be good people in
a common-weal that do nothing but use their abuses in
common houses, I know no law: bring them away.

ANGELO. How now, sir! What 's your name, and what 's the
matter?

ELBOW. If it please your honour, I am the poor duke's constable, and my name is Elbow: I do lean upon justice, sir;
and do bring in here before your good honour two notorious benefactors.

ANGELO. Benefactors! Well; what benefactors are they? are
they not malefactors?

ELBOW. If it please your honour, I know not well what they
are; but precise villains they are, that I am sure of, and
void of all profanation in the world that good Christians
ought to have.

ESCALUS. This comes off well: here 's a wise officer.

ANGELO. Go to: what quality are they of? Elbow is your
name? Why dost thou not speak, Elbow?

POMPEY. He cannot, sir: he 's out at elbow.

ANGELO. What are you, sir?

ELBOW. He, sir! a tapster, sir; parcel-bawd; one that serves
a bad woman, whose house, sir, was, as they say, plucked
down in the suburbs; and now she professes a hot-house,
which, I think, is a very ill house too.

ESCALUS. How know you that?

ELBOW. My wife, sir, whom I detest before heaven and your honour,—

ESCALUS. How! thy wife?

ELBOW. Ay, sir; whom, I thank heaven, is an honest woman,—

ESCALUS. Dost thou detest her therefore?

ELBOW. I say, sir, I will detest myself also, as well as she, that this house, if it be not a bawd's house, it is pity of her life, for it is a naughty house.

ESCALUS. How dost thou know that, constable?

ELBOW. Marry, sir, by my wife; who, if she had been a woman cardinally given, might have been accused in fornication, adultery, and all uncleanliness there.

ESCALUS. By the woman's means?

ELBOW. Ay, sir, by Mistress Overdone's means; but as she spit in his face, so she defied him.

POMPEY. Sir, if it please your honour, this is not so.

ELBOW. Prove it before these varlets here, thou honourable man, prove it.

ESCALUS. (*To Angelo*) Do you hear how he misplaces?

POMPEY. Sir, she came in, great with child, and longing,— saving your honour's reverence,—for stewed prunes. Sir, we had but two in the house, which at that very distant time stood, as it were, in a fruit-dish, a dish of some three-pence; your honours have seen such dishes; they are not China dishes, but very good dishes.

ESCALUS. Go to, go to: no matter for the dish, sir.

POMPEY. No, indeed, sir, not of a pin; you are therein in the right: but to the point. As I say, this Mistress Elbow, being, as I say, with child, and being great-bellied, and longing, as I said, for prunes, and having but two in the dish, as I said, Master Froth here, this very man, having eaten the rest, as I said, and, as I say, paying for them very honestly; for, as you know, Master Froth, I could not give you three-pence again.

FROTH. No, indeed.

POMPEY. Very well: you being then, if you be remembered, cracking the stones of the foresaid prunes,—

FROTH. Ay, so I did, indeed.

POMPEY. Why, very well: I telling you then, if you be remembered, that such a one and such a one were past

cure of the thing you wot of, unless they kept very good
diet, as I told you,—

FROTH. All this is true.

POMPEY. Why, very well then.—

ESCALUS. Come, you are a tedious fool: to the purpose.
What was done to Elbow's wife, that he hath cause to
complain of? Come me to what was done to her.

POMPEY. Sir, your honour cannot come to that yet.

ESCALUS. No, sir, nor I mean it not.

POMPEY. Sir, but you shall come to it, by your honour's
leave. And, I beseech you, look into Master Froth here,
sir; a man of fourscore pound a year, whose father died
at Hallowmas. Was 't not at Hallowmas, Master Froth?

FROTH. All-hallownd eve.

POMPEY. Why, very well: I hope here be truths. He, sir,
sitting, as I say, in a lower chair, sir; 'twas in the Bunch
of Grapes, where indeed, you have a delight to sit, have
you not?

FROTH. I have so, because it is an open room and good for
winter.

POMPEY. Why, very well then: I hope here be truths.

ANGELO. This will last out a night in Russia,
When nights are longest there: I 'll take my leave,
And leave you to the hearing of the cause,
Hoping you 'll find good cause to whip them all.

ESCALUS. I think no less. Good-morrow to your lordship.

Exit Angelo

Now, sir, come on: what was done to Elbow's wife, once
more?

POMPEY. Once, sir? there was nothing done to her once.

ELBOW. I beseech you, sir, ask him what this man did to
my wife.

POMPEY. I beseech your honour, ask me.

ESCALUS. Well, sir, what did this gentleman to her?

POMPEY. I beseech you, sir, look in this gentleman's face.
Good Master Froth, look upon his honour; 'tis for a good
purpose. Doth your honour mark his face?

ESCALUS. Ay, sir, very well.

POMPEY. Nay, I beseech you, mark it well.

ESCALUS. Well, I do so.

POMPEY. Doth your honour see any harm in his face?

ESCALUS. Why, no.

POMPEY. I 'll be supposed upon a book, his face is the worst thing about him. Good, then; if his face be the worst thing about him, how could Master Froth do the constable's wife any harm? I would know that of your honour.

ESCALUS. He 's in the right. Constable, what say you to it?

ELBOW. First, an' it like you, the house is a respected house; next, this is a respected fellow, and his mistress is a respected woman.

POMPEY. By this hand, sir, his wife is a more respected person than any of us all.

ELBOW. Varlet, thou liest: thou liest, wicked varlet. The time is yet to come that she was ever respected with man, woman, or child.

POMPEY. Sir, she was respected with him before he married with her.

ESCALUS. Which is the wiser here? Justice, or Iniquity? Is this true?

ELBOW. O thou caitiff! O thou varlet! O thou wicked Hannibal! I respected with her before I was married to her? If ever I was respected with her, or she with me, let not your worship think me the poor duke's officer. Prove this, thou wicked Hannibal, or I 'll have mine action of battery on thee.

ESCALUS. If he took you a box o' th' ear, you might have your action of slander too.

ELBOW. Marry, I thank your good worship for it. What is 't your worship's pleasure I shall do with this wicked caitiff?

ESCALUS. Truly, officer, because he hath some offences in him that thou wouldst discover if thou couldst, let him continue in his courses till thou knowest what they are.

ELBOW. Marry, I thank your worship for it. Thou seest, thou wicked varlet, now, what 's come upon thee: thou art to continue now, thou varlet, thou art to continue.

ESCALUS. Where were you born, friend?

FROTH. Here in Vienna, sir.

ESCALUS. Are you of fourscore pounds a year?

FROTH. Yes, an 't please you, sir.

ESCALUS. So. (*To Pompey*) What trade are you of, sir?

POMPEY. A tapster; a poor widow's tapster.

ESCALUS. Your mistress' name?

POMPEY. Mistress Overdone.

ESCALUS. Hath she had any more than one husband?

POMPEY. Nine, sir; Overdone by the last.

ESCALUS. Nine!—Come hither to me, Master Froth. Master Froth, I would not have you acquainted with tapsters; they will draw you, Master Froth, and you will hang them. Get you gone, and let me hear no more of you.

FROTH. I thank your worship. For mine own part, I never come into any room in a taphouse, but I am drawn in.

ESCALUS. Well: no more of it, Master Froth: farewell. (*Exit Froth*)—Come you hither to me, Master tapster. What 's your name, Master tapster?

POMPEY. Pompey.

ESCALUS. What else?

POMPEY. Bum, sir.

ESCALUS. Troth, and your bum is the greatest thing about you, so that, in the beastliest sense, you are Pompey the Great. Pompey, you are partly a bawd, Pompey, howsoever you colour it in being a tapster, are you not? Come, tell me true; it shall be the better for you.

POMPEY. Truly, sir, I am a poor fellow that would live.

ESCALUS. How would you live, Pompey? by being a bawd? What do you think of the trade, Pompey? is it a lawful trade?

POMPEY. If the law would allow it, sir.

ESCALUS. But the law will not allow it, Pompey; nor it shall not be allowed in Vienna.

POMPEY. Does your worship mean to geld and splay all the youth of the city?

ESCALUS. No, Pompey.

POMPEY. Truly, sir, in my humble opinion, they will to 't then. If your worship will take order for the drabs and the knaves, you need not to fear the bawds.

ESCALUS. There are pretty orders beginning, I can tell you: it is but heading and hanging.

POMPEY. If you head and hang all that offend that way but for ten year together, you 'll be glad to give out a commission for more heads. If this law hold in Vienna ten year, I 'll rent the fairest house in it after threepence a bay. If you live to see this come to pass, say, Pompey told you so.

ESCALUS. Thank you, good Pompey; and, in requital of your prophecy, hark you: I advise you, let me not find

you before me again upon any complaint whatsoever; no,
not for dwelling where you do; if I do, Pompey, I shall
beat you to your tent, and prove a shrewd Cæsar to you.
In plain dealing, Pompey, I shall have you whipt. So, for
this time, Pompey, fare you well.

POMPEY. I thank your worship for your good counsel;—
(*Aside*) but I shall follow it as the flesh and fortune shall
better determine.

Whip me! No, no; let carman whip his jade;
The valiant heart 's not whipt out of his trade.   *Exit*

ESCALUS. Come hither to me, Master Elbow; come hither,
Master constable. How long have you been in this place
of constable?

ELBOW. Seven year and a half, sir.

ESCALUS. I thought, by your readiness in the office, you had
continued in it some time. You say, seven years together?

ELBOW. And a half, sir.

ESCALUS. Alas! it hath been great pains to you! They do you
wrong to put you so oft upon 't. Are there not men in
your ward sufficient to serve it?

ELBOW. Faith, sir, few of any wit in such matters. As they
are chosen, they are glad to choose me for them: I do it
for some piece of money, and go through with all.

ESCALUS. Look you bring me in the names of some six or
seven, the most sufficient of your parish.

ELBOW. To your worship's house, sir?

ESCALUS. To my house. Fare you well.   *Exit Elbow*
What 's o'clock, think you?

JUSTICE. Eleven, sir.

ESCALUS. I pray you home to dinner with me.

JUSTICE. I humbly thank you.

ESCALUS. It grieves me for the death of Claudio;
But there is no remedy.

JUSTICE. Lord Angelo is severe.

ESCALUS.   It is but needful:
Mercy is not itself, that oft looks so;
Pardon is still the nurse of second woe.
But yet, poor Claudio! There 's no remedy.
Come, sir.   *Exeunt*

SCENE TWO

Another Room in the Same.

Enter Provost and a Servant

SERVANT. He 's hearing of a cause: he will come straight:
  I 'll tell him of you.

PROVOST.   Pray you, do. (*Exit Servant*) I 'll know
  His pleasure; may be he will relent. Alas!
  He hath but as offended in a dream:
  All sects, all ages smack of this vice, and he
  To die for it!

                    Enter Angelo

ANGELO.   Now, what 's the matter, provost?

PROVOST. Is it your will Claudio shall die to-morrow?

ANGELO. Did I not tell thee, yea? hadst thou not order?
  Why dost thou ask again?

PROVOST.   Lest I might be too rash.
  Under your good correction, I have seen,
  When, after execution, Judgment hath
  Repented o'er his doom.

ANGELO.   Go to; let that be mine:
  Do you your office, or give up your place,
  And you shall well be spar'd.

PROVOST.   I crave your honour's pardon.
  What shall be done, sir, with the groaning Juliet?
  She 's very near her hour.

ANGELO.   Dispose of her
  To some more fitter place; and that with speed.

                    Re-enter Servant

SERVANT. Here is the sister of the man condemn'd
  Desires access to you.

ANGELO.   Hath he a sister?

PROVOST. Ay, my good lord; a very virtuous maid,
  And to be shortly of a sisterhood,
  If not already.

ANGELO.   Well, let her be admitted.   *Exit Servant*
  See you the fornicatress be remov'd:
  Let her have needful, but not lavish, means;
  There shall be order for 't.

Enter Isabella and Lucio

PROVOST.   God save your honour!

Offering to retire

ANGELO. Stay a little while.—(*To Isabella*) You 're welcome.
  What 's your will?

ISABELLA. I am a woful suitor to your honour,
  Please but your honour hear me.

ANGELO.   Well; what 's your suit?

ISABELLA. There is a vice that most I do abhor,
  And most desire should meet the blow of justice,
  For which I would not plead, but that I must;
  For which I must not plead, but that I am
  At war 'twixt will and will not.

ANGELO.   Well; the matter?

ISABELLA. I have a brother is condemn'd to die:
  I do beseech you, let it be his fault,
  And not my brother.

PROVOST.   (*Aside*) Heaven give thee moving graces!

ANGELO. Condemn the fault, and not the actor of it?
  Why, every fault 's condemn'd ere it be done.
  Mine were the very cipher of a function,
  To fine the faults whose fine stands in record,
  And let go by the actor.

ISABELLA.   O just, but severe law!
  I had a brother, then.—Heaven keep your honour!

Retiring

LUCIO. (*Aside to Isabella*) Give 't not o'er so: to him again,
    entreat him;
  Kneel down before him, hang upon his gown;
  You are too cold; if you should need a pin,
  You could not with more tame a tongue desire it.
  To him, I say!

ISABELLA. Must he needs die?

ANGELO.   Maiden, no remedy.

ISABELLA. Yes; I do think that you might pardon him,
  And neither heaven nor man grieve at the mercy.

ANGELO. I will not do 't.

ISABELLA.   But can you, if you would?

ANGELO. Look, what I will not, that I cannot do.

ISABELLA. But might you do 't, and do the world no wrong,
  If so your heart were touch'd with that remorse
  As mine is to him?

ANGELO.   He 's sentenc'd: 'tis too late.

LUCIO. (*Aside to Isabella*) You are too cold.

ISABELLA. Too late? Why, no; I, that do speak a word,
    May call it back again. Well, believe this,
    No ceremony that to great ones 'longs,
    Not the king's crown, nor the deputed sword,
    The marshal's truncheon, nor the judge's robe,
    Become them with one half so good a grace
    As mercy does.
    If he had been as you, and you as he,
    You would have slipt like him; but he, like you,
    Would not have been so stern.

ANGELO.   Pray you, be gone.

ISABELLA. I would to heaven I had your potency,
    And you were Isabel! Should it then be thus?
    No; I would tell what 'twere to be a judge,
    And what a prisoner.

LUCIO. (*Aside to Isabella*) Ay, touch him; there 's the vein.

ANGELO. Your brother is a forfeit of the law
    And you but waste your words.

ISABELLA.   Alas! alas!
    Why, all the souls that were were forfeit once;
    And He that might the vantage best have took,
    Found out the remedy. How would you be,
    If He, which is the top of judgment, should
    But judge you as you are? O! think on that,
    And mercy then will breathe within your lips,
    Like man new made.

ANGELO.   Be you content, fair maid;
    It is the law, not I, condemn your brother:
    Were he my kinsman, brother, or my son,
    It should be thus with him: he must die to-morrow.

ISABELLA. To-morrow! O! that 's sudden! Spare him, spare
        him!
    He 's not prepar'd for death. Even for our kitchens
    We kill the fowl of season: shall we serve heaven
    With less respect than we do minister
    To our gross selves? Good, good my lord, bethink you:
    Who is it that hath died for this offence?
    There 's many have committed it.

LUCIO.   (*Aside to Isabella*) Ay, well said.

ANGELO. The law hath not been dead, though it hath slept:

Those many had not dar'd to do that evil,
If that the first that did th' edict infringe
Had answer'd for his deed: now 'tis awake,
Takes note of what is done, and, like a prophet,
Looks in a glass, that shows what future evils,
Either new, or by remissness new-conceiv'd,
And so in progress to be hatch'd and born,
Are now to have no successive degrees,
But, ere they live, to end.

ISABELLA.   Yet show some pity.

ANGELO. I show it most of all when I show justice;
For then I pity those I do not know,
Which a dismiss'd offence would after gall,
And do him right, that, answering one foul wrong,
Lives not to act another. Be satisfied:
Your brother dies to-morrow: be content.

ISABELLA. So you must be the first that gives this sentence,
And he that suffers. O! it is excellent
To have a giant's strength, but it is tyrannous
To use it like a giant.

LUCIO. (*Aside to Isabella*) That 's well said.

ISABELLA. Could great men thunder
As Jove himself does, Jove would ne'er be quiet,
For every pelting, petty officer
Would use his heaven for thunder; nothing but thunder,
Merciful heaven!
Thou rather with thy sharp and sulphurous bolt
Split'st the unwedgeable and gnarled oak
Than the soft myrtle; but man, proud man,
Drest in a little brief authority,
Most ignorant of what he 's most assur'd,
His glassy essence, like an angry ape,
Plays such fantastic tricks before high heaven
As make the angels weep; who, with our spleens,
Would all themselves laugh mortal.

LUCIO. (*Aside to Isabella*) O, to him, to him, wench! He
will relent:
He 's coming: I perceive 't.

PROVOST.   (*Aside*) Pray heaven she win him!

ISABELLA. We cannot weigh our brother with ourself:
Great men may jest with saints; 'tis wit in them,
But, in the less foul profanation.

LUCIO. (*Aside to Isabella*) Thou 'rt in the right, girl: more
o' that.

ISABELLA. That in the captain 's but a choleric word,
Which in the soldier is flat blasphemy.

LUCIO. (*Aside to Isabella*) Art advis'd o' that? more on 't.

ANGELO. Why do you put these sayings upon me?

ISABELLA. Because authority, though it err like others,
Hath yet a kind of medicine in itself,
That skins the vice o' the top. Go to your bosom;
Knock there, and ask your heart what it doth know
That 's like my brother's fault: if it confess
A natural guiltiness such as is his,
Let it not sound a thought upon your tongue
Against my brother's life.

ANGELO.   She speaks, and 'tis
Such sense that my sense breeds with it. Fare you well.

ISABELLA. Gentle my lord, turn back.

ANGELO. I will bethink me. Come again to-morrow.

ISABELLA. Hark how I 'll bribe you. Good my lord, turn
back.

ANGELO. How! bribe me?

ISABELLA. Ay, with such gifts that heaven shall share with
you.

LUCIO. (*Aside to Isabella*) You had marr'd all else.

ISABELLA. Not with fond sicles of the tested gold,
Or stones whose rates are either rich or poor
As fancy values them; but with true prayers
That shall be up at heaven and enter there
Ere sun-rise: prayers from preserved souls,
From fasting maids whose minds are dedicate
To nothing temporal.

ANGELO.   Well; come to me to-morrow.

LUCIO. (*Aside to Isabella*) Go to; 'tis well: away!

ISABELLA. Heaven keep your honour safe!

ANGELO.   (*Aside*) Amen:
For I am that way going to temptation,
Where prayers cross.

ISABELLA.   At what hour to-morrow
Shall I attend your lordship?

ANGELO.   At any time 'fore noon.

ISABELLA. Save your honour!

                    Exeunt Isabella, Lucio, and Provost

ANGELO.   From thee; even from thy virtue!
  What 's this? what 's this? Is this her fault or mine?
  The tempter or the tempted, who sins most?
  Ha!
  Not she; nor doth she tempt: but it is I,
  That, lying by the violet in the sun,
  Do as the carrion does, not as the flower,
  Corrupt with virtuous season. Can it be
  That modesty may more betray our sense
  Than woman's lightness? Having waste ground enough,
  Shall we desire to raze the sanctuary,
  And pitch our evils there? O, fie, fie, fie!
  What dost thou, or what art thou, Angelo?
  Dost thou desire her foully for those things
  That make her good? O, let her brother live!
  Thieves for their robbery have authority
  When judges steal themselves. What! do I love her,
  That I desire to hear her speak again,
  And feast upon her eyes? What is 't I dream on?
  O cunning enemy, that, to catch a saint,
  With saints dost bait thy hook! Most dangerous
  Is that temptation that doth goad us on
  To sin in loving virtue: never could the strumpet,
  With all her double vigour, art and nature,
  Once stir my temper; but this virtuous maid
  Subdues me quite. Ever till now,
  When men were fond, I smil'd and wonder'd how.   *Exit*

SCENE THREE

A Room in a Prison.

Enter Duke, disguised as a Friar, and Provost

DUKE. Hail to you, provost! So I think you are.
PROVOST. I am the provost. What 's your will, good friar?
DUKE. Bound by my charity and my bless'd order,
  I come to visit the afflicted spirits
  Here in the prison: do me the common right
  To let me see them and to make me know
  The nature of their crimes, that I may minister
  To them accordingly.

PROVOST. I would do more than that, if more were needful.
Look, here comes one: a gentlewoman of mine,
Who, falling in the flaws of her own youth,
Hath blister'd her report. She is with child,
And he that got it, sentenc'd; a young man
More fit to do another such offence,
Than die for this.

Enter Juliet

DUKE. When must he die?
PROVOST.   As I do think, to-morrow.
   (*To Juliet*) I have provided for you: stay a while,
And you shall be conducted.
DUKE. Repent you, fair one, of the sin you carry?
JULIET. I do, and bear the shame most patiently.
DUKE. I 'll teach you how you shall arraign your conscience,
And try your penitence, if it be sound,
Or hollowly put on.
JULIET.   I 'll gladly learn.
DUKE. Love you the man that wrong'd you?
JULIET. Yes, as I love the woman that wrong'd him.
DUKE. So then it seems your most offenceful act
Was mutually committed?
JULIET.   Mutually.
DUKE. Then was your sin of heavier kind than his.
JULIET. I do confess it, and repent it, father.
DUKE. 'Tis meet so, daughter: but lest you do repent,
As that the sin hath brought you to this shame,
Which sorrow is always toward ourselves, not heaven,
Showing we would not spare heaven as we love it,
But as we stand in fear,—
JULIET. I do repent me, as it is an evil,
And take the shame with joy.
DUKE.   There rest.
Your partner, as I hear, must die to-morrow,
And I am going with instruction to him.
God's grace go with you! Benedicite!   *Exit*
JULIET. Must die to-morrow! O injurious love,
That respites me a life, whose very comfort
Is still a dying horror!
PROVOST.   'Tis pity of him.   *Exeunt*

SCENE FOUR

A Room in Angelo's House.

Enter Angelo

ANGELO. When I would pray and think, I think and pray
　To several subjects: heaven hath my empty words,
　Whilst my invention, hearing not my tongue,
　Anchors on Isabel: heaven in my mouth,
　As if I did but only chew his name,
　And in my heart the strong and swelling evil
　Of my conception. The state, whereon I studied,
　Is like a good thing, being often read,
　Grown fear'd and tedious; yea, my gravity,
　Wherein, let no man hear me, I take pride,
　Could I with boot change for an idle plume,
　Which the air beats for vain. O place! O form!
　How often dost thou with thy case, thy habit,
　Wrench awe from fools, and tie the wiser souls
　To thy false seeming! Blood, thou art blood:
　Let 's write good angel on the devil's horn,
　'Tis not the devil's crest.

Enter a Servant

　How now! who 's there?

SERVANT.　　　　　　One Isabel, a sister,
　Desires access to you.

ANGELO.　　　　　　Teach her the way. *Exit Servant*
　O heavens!
　Why does my blood thus muster to my heart,
　Making both it unable for itself,
　And dispossessing all my other parts
　Of necessary fitness?
　So play the foolish throngs with one that swounds;
　Come all to help him, and so stop the air
　By which he should revive: and even so
　The general, subject to a well-wish'd king,
　Quit their own part, and in obsequious fondness
　Crowd to his presence, where their untaught love
　Must needs appear offence.

Enter Isabella

How now, fair maid!

ISABELLA. I am come to know your pleasure.

ANGELO. That you might know it, would much better please
      me,
   Than to demand what 'tis. Your brother cannot live.

ISABELLA. Even so. Heaven keep your honour!

ANGELO. Yet may he live awhile; and, it may be,
   As long as you or I: yet he must die.

ISABELLA. Under your sentence?

ANGELO. Yea.

ISABELLA. When, I beseech you? that in his reprieve,
   Longer or shorter, he may be so fitted
   That his soul sicken not.

ANGELO. Ha! fie, these filthy vices! It were as good
   To pardon him that hath from nature stolen
   A man already made, as to remit
   Their saucy sweetness that do coin heaven's image
   In stamps that are forbid: 'tis all as easy
   Falsely to take away a life true made,
   As to put metal in restrained means
   To make a false one.

ISABELLA. 'Tis set down so in heaven, but not in earth.

ANGELO. Say you so? Then I shall pose you quickly.
   Which had you rather, that the most just law
   Now took your brother's life; or, to redeem him,
   Give up your body to such sweet uncleanness
   As she that he hath stain'd?

ISABELLA.   Sir, believe this,
   I had rather give my body than my soul.

ANGELO. I talk not of your soul. Our compell'd sins
   Stand more for number than for accompt.

ISABELLA.   How say you?

ANGELO. Nay, I 'll not warrant that; for I can speak
   Against the thing I say. Answer to this:
   I, now the voice of the recorded law,
   Pronounce a sentence on your brother's life:
   Might there not be a charity in sin
   To save this brother's life?

ISABELLA.   Please you to do 't,
   I 'll take it as a peril to my soul;
   It is no sin at all, but charity.

ANGELO. Pleas'd you to do 't, at peril of your soul,

Were equal poise of sin and charity.

ISABELLA. That I do beg his life, if it be sin,
Heaven let me bear it! you granting of my suit,
If that be sin, I 'll make it my morn prayer
To have it added to the faults of mine,
And nothing of your answer.

ANGELO.   Nay, but hear me.
Your sense pursues not mine: either you are ignorant,
Or seem so craftily; and that 's not good.

ISABELLA. Let me be ignorant, and in nothing good,
But graciously to know I am no better.

ANGELO. Thus wisdom wishes to appear most bright
When it doth tax itself; as these black masks
Proclaim an enshield beauty ten times louder
Than beauty could, display'd. But mark me;
To be received plain, I 'll speak more gross:
Your brother is to die.

ISABELLA. So.

ANGELO. And his offence is so, as it appears,
Accountant to the law upon that pain.

ISABELLA. True.

ANGELO. Admit no other way to save his life,—
As I subscribe not that, nor any other,
But in the loss of question,—that you, his sister,
Finding yourself desir'd of such a person,
Whose credit with the judge, or own great place,
Could fetch your brother from the manacles
Of the all-building law; and that there were
No earthly mean to save him, but that either
You must lay down the treasures of your body
To this suppos'd, or else to let him suffer;
What would you do?

ISABELLA. As much for my poor brother as myself:
That is, were I under the terms of death,
Th' impression of keen whips I 'd wear as rubies,
And strip myself to death, as to a bed
That, longing, have been sick for, ere I 'd yield
My body up to shame.

ANGELO.   Then must your brother die.

ISABELLA. And 'twere the cheaper way:
Better it were a brother died at once,
Than that a sister, by redeeming him,

Should die for ever.

ANGELO. Were not you then as cruel as the sentence
That you have slander'd so?

ISABELLA. Ignomy in ransom and free pardon
Are of two houses: lawful mercy
Is nothing kin to foul redemption.

ANGELO. You seem'd of late to make the law a tyrant;
And rather prov'd the sliding of your brother
A merriment than a vice.

ISABELLA. O, pardon me, my lord! it oft falls out,
To have what we would have, we speak not what we
mean.
I something do excuse the thing I hate,
For his advantage that I dearly love.

ANGELO. We are all frail.

ISABELLA.   Else let my brother die,
If not a feodary, but only he
Owe and succeed thy weakness.

ANGELO. Nay, women are frail too.

ISABELLA. Ay, as the glasses where they view themselves,
Which are as easy broke as they make forms.
Women! Help heaven! men their creation mar
In profiting by them. Nay, call us ten times frail,
For we are soft as our complexions are,
And credulous to false prints.

ANGELO.   I think it well:
And from this testimony of your own sex,—
Since I suppose we are made to be no stronger
Than faults may shake our frames,—let me be bold;
I do arrest your words. Be that you are,
That is, a woman; if you be more, you 're none;
If you be one, as you are well express'd
By all external warrants, show it now,
By putting on the destin'd livery.

ISABELLA. I have no tongue but one: gentle my lord,
Let me entreat you speak the former language.

ANGELO. Plainly conceive, I love you.

ISABELLA. My brother did love Juliet; and you tell me
That he shall die for 't.

ANGELO. He shall not, Isabel, if you give me love.

ISABELLA. I know your virtue hath a licence in 't,
Which seems a little fouler than it is,

To pluck on others.

ANGELO.   Believe me, on mine honour,
My words express my purpose.

ISABELLA. Ha! little honour to be much believ'd,
And most pernicious purpose! Seeming, seeming!
I will proclaim thee, Angelo; look for 't:
Sign me a present pardon for my brother,
Or with an outstretch'd throat I 'll tell the world aloud
What man thou art.

ANGELO.   Who will believe thee, Isabel?
My unsoil'd name, the austereness of my life,
My vouch against you, and my place i' the state,
Will so your accusation overweigh,
That you shall stifle in your own report
And smell of calumny. I have begun;
And now I give my sensual race the rein:
Fit thy consent to my sharp appetite;
Lay by all nicety and prolixious blushes,
That banish what they sue for; redeem thy brother
By yielding up thy body to my will,
Or else he must not only die the death,
But thy unkindness shall his death draw out
To lingering sufferance. Answer me to-morrow,
Or, by the affection that now guides me most,
I 'll prove a tyrant to him. As for you,
Say what you can, my false o'erweighs your true.   *Exit*

ISABELLA. To whom should I complain? Did I tell this,
Who would believe me? O perilous mouths!
That bear in them one and the self-same tongue,
Either of condemnation or approof,
Bidding the law make curt'sy to their will;
Hooking both right and wrong to th' appetite,
To follow as it draws. I 'll to my brother:
Though he hath fallen by prompture of the blood,
Yet hath he in him such a mind of honour,
That, had he twenty heads to tender down
On twenty bloody blocks, he 'd yield them up,
Before his sister should her body stoop
To such abhorr'd pollution.
Then, Isabel, live chaste, and, brother, die:
More than our brother is our chastity.
I 'll tell him yet of Angelo's request,
And fit his mind to death, for his soul's rest.   *Exit*

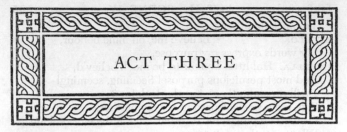

ACT THREE

SCENE ONE

A Room in the Prison.

Enter Duke, as a friar, Claudio, and Provost

DUKE. So then you hope of pardon from Lord Angelo?
CLAUDIO. The miserable have no other medicine
  But only hope:
  I have hope to live, and am prepar'd to die.
DUKE. Be absolute for death; either death or life
  Shall thereby be the sweeter. Reason thus with life:
  If I do lose thee, I do lose a thing
  That none but fools would keep: a breath thou art,
  Servile to all the skyey influences,
  That dost this habitation, where thou keep'st,
  Hourly afflict. Merely, thou art death's fool;
  For him thou labour'st by thy flight to shun,
  And yet run'st toward him still. Thou art not noble:
  For all th' accommodations that thou bear'st
  Are nurs'd by baseness. Thou art by no means valiant;
  For thou dost fear the soft and tender fork
  Of a poor worm. Thy best of rest is sleep,
  And that thou oft provok'st; yet grossly fear'st
  Thy death, which is no more. Thou art not thyself;
  For thou exist'st on many a thousand grains
  That issue out of dust. Happy thou art not;
  For what thou hast not, still thou striv'st to get,
  And what thou hast, forget'st. Thou art not certain;
  For thy complexion shifts to strange effects,
  After the moon. If thou art rich, thou'rt poor;
  For, like an ass whose back with ingots bows,
  Thou bear'st thy heavy riches but a journey,
  And death unloads thee. Friend hast thou none;
  For thine own bowels, which do call thee sire,

The mere effusion of thy proper loins,
Do curse the gout, serpigo, and the rheum,
For ending thee no sooner. Thou hast nor youth nor age;
But, as it were, an after-dinner's sleep,
Dreaming on both; for all thy blessed youth
Becomes as aged, and doth beg the alms
Of palsied eld; and when thou art old and rich,
Thou hast neither heat, affection, limb, nor beauty,
To make thy riches pleasant. What's yet in this
That bears the name of life? Yet in this life
Lie hid moe thousand deaths: yet death we fear,
That makes these odds all even.

CLAUDIO.   I humbly thank you.
To sue to live, I find I seek to die,
And, seeking death, find life: let it come on.

ISABELLA. (*Within*) What ho! Peace here; grace and good
    company!

PROVOST. Who's there? come in: the wish deserves a wel-
    come.

DUKE. Dear sir, ere long I'll visit you again.

CLAUDIO. Most holy sir, I thank you.

                Enter Isabella

ISABELLA. My business is a word or two with Claudio.

PROVOST. And very welcome. Look, signior; here's your
    sister.

DUKE. Provost, a word with you.

PROVOST. As many as you please.

DUKE. Bring me to hear them speak, where I may be con-
    ceal'd.   *Exeunt Duke and Provost*

CLAUDIO. Now, sister, what's the comfort?

ISABELLA. Why, as all comforts are; most good, most good
    indeed.
Lord Angelo, having affairs to heaven,
Intends you for his swift ambassador,
Where you shall be an everlasting leiger:
Therefore, your best appointment make with speed;
To-morrow you set on.

CLAUDIO.   Is there no remedy?

ISABELLA. None, but such remedy, as to save a head
To cleave a heart in twain.

CLAUDIO.   But is there any?

ISABELLA. Yes, brother, you may live:

There is a devilish mercy in the judge,
If you 'll implore it, that will free your life,
But fetter you till death.

CLAUDIO.   Perpetual durance?

ISABELLA. Ay, just; perpetual durance, a restraint,
Though all the world's vastidity you had,
To a determin'd scope.

CLAUDIO.   But in what nature?

ISABELLA. In such a one as, you consenting to 't,
Would bark your honour from that trunk you bear,
And leave you naked.

CLAUDIO.   Let me know the point.

ISABELLA. O, I do fear thee, Claudio; and I quake,
Lest thou a feverous life shouldst entertain,
And six or seven winters more respect
Than a perpetual honour. Dar'st thou die?
The sense of death is most in apprehension,
And the poor beetle, that we tread upon,
In corporal sufferance finds a pang as great
As when a giant dies.

CLAUDIO.   Why give you me this shame?
Think you I can a resolution fetch
From flowery tenderness? If I must die,
I will encounter darkness as a bride,
And hug it in mine arms.

ISABELLA. There spake my brother: there my father's grave
Did utter forth a voice. Yes, thou must die:
Thou art too noble to conserve a life
In base appliances. This outward-sainted deputy,
Whose settled visage and deliberate word
Nips youth i' the head, and follies doth enmew
As falcon doth the fowl, is yet a devil;
His filth within being cast, he would appear
A pond as deep as hell.

CLAUDIO.   The prenzie Angelo?

ISABELLA. O, 'tis the cunning livery of hell,
The damned'st body to invest and cover
In prenzie guards! Dost thou think, Claudio?
If I would yield him my virginity,
Thou mightst be freed.

CLAUDIO.   O heavens! it cannot be.

ISABELLA. Yes, he would give 't thee, from this rank offence,
So to offend him still. This night 's the time
That I should do what I abhor to name,
Or else thou diest to-morrow.
CLAUDIO. Thou shalt not do 't.
ISABELLA. O! were it but my life,
I 'd throw it down for your deliverance
As frankly as a pin.
CLAUDIO. Thanks, dear Isabel.
ISABELLA. Be ready, Claudio, for your death to-morrow.
CLAUDIO. Yes. Has he affections in him,
That thus can make him bite the law by the nose,
When he would force it? Sure, it is no sin;
Or of the deadly seven it is the least.
ISABELLA. Which is the least?
CLAUDIO. If it were damnable, he being so wise,
Why would he for the momentary trick
Be perdurably fin'd? O Isabel!
ISABELLA. What says my brother?
CLAUDIO. Death is a fearful thing.
ISABELLA. And shamed life a hateful.
CLAUDIO. Ay, but to die, and go we know not where;
To lie in cold obstruction and to rot;
This sensible warm motion to become
A kneaded clod; and the delighted spirit
To bathe in fiery floods, or to reside
In thrilling region of thick-ribbed ice;
To be imprison'd in the viewless winds
And blown with restless violence round about
The pendant world; or to be worse than worst
Of those that lawless and incertain thoughts
Imagine howling: 'tis too horrible!
The weariest and most loathed worldly life
That age, ache, penury and imprisonment
Can lay on nature is a paradise
To what we fear of death.
ISABELLA. Alas! alas!
CLAUDIO. Sweet sister, let me live:
What sin you do to save a brother's life,
Nature dispenses with the deed so far
That it becomes a virtue.

ISABELLA.   O you beast!
O faithless coward! O dishonest wretch!
Wilt thou be made a man out of my vice?
Is 't not a kind of incest, to take life
From thine own sister's shame? What should I think?
Heaven shield my mother play'd my father fair;
For such a warped slip of wilderness
Ne'er issu'd from his blood. Take my defiance;
Die, perish! Might but my bending down
Reprieve thee from thy fate, it should proceed.
I 'll pray a thousand prayers for thy death,
No word to save thee.

CLAUDIO. Nay, hear me, Isabel.

ISABELLA.   O, fie, fie, fie!
Thy sin 's not accidental, but a trade.
Mercy to thee would prove itself a bawd:
'Tis best that thou diest quickly.   *Going*

CLAUDIO.   O hear me, Isabella.

                    Re-enter Duke

DUKE. Vouchsafe a word, young sister, but one word.

ISABELLA. What is your will?

DUKE. Might you dispense with your leisure, I would by
    and by have some speech with you: the satisfaction I
    would require is likewise your own benefit.

ISABELLA. I have no superfluous leisure: my stay must be
    stolen out of other affairs; but I will attend you a while.

DUKE. (*Aside to Claudio*) Son, I have overheard what hath
    past between you and your sister. Angelo had never the
    purpose to corrupt her; only he hath made an assay of
    her virtue to practise his judgment with the disposition
    of natures. She, having the truth of honour in her, hath
    made him that gracious denial which he is most glad to
    receive: I am confessor to Angelo, and I know this to be
    true; therefore prepare yourself to death. Do not satisfy
    your resolution with hopes that are fallible: to-morrow
    you must die; go to your knees and make ready.

CLAUDIO. Let me ask my sister pardon. I am so out of love
    with life that I will sue to be rid of it.

DUKE. Hold you there: farewell.   *Exit Claudio*

                    Re-enter Provost

    Provost, a word with you.

PROVOST. What 's your will, father?

DUKE. That now you are come, you will be gone. Leave me awhile with the maid: my mind promises with my habit no loss shall touch her by my company.

PROVOST. In good time.   *Exit*

DUKE. The hand that hath made you fair hath made you good: the goodness that is cheap in beauty makes beauty brief in goodness; but grace, being the soul of your complexion, shall keep the body of it ever fair. The assault that Angelo hath made to you, fortune hath conveyed to my understanding; and, but that frailty hath examples for his falling, I should wonder at Angelo. How would you do to content this substitute, and to save your brother?

ISABELLA. I am now going to resolve him; I had rather my brother die by the law than my son should be unlawfully born. But O, how much is the good duke deceived in Angelo! If ever he return and I can speak to him, I will open my lips in vain, or discover his government.

DUKE. That shall not be much amiss: yet, as the matter now stands, he will avoid your accusation; 'he made trial of you only.' Therefore, fasten your ear on my advisings: to the love I have in doing good a remedy presents itself. I do make myself believe that you may most uprightously do a poor wronged lady a merited benefit, redeem your brother from the angry law, do no stain to your own gracious person, and much please the absent duke, if peradventure he shall ever return to have hearing of this business.

ISABELLA. Let me hear you speak further. I have spirit to do anything that appears not foul in the truth of my spirit.

DUKE. Virtue is bold, and goodness never fearful. Have you not heard speak of Mariana, the sister of Frederick, the great soldier who miscarried at sea?

ISABELLA. I have heard of the lady, and good words went with her name.

DUKE. She should this Angelo have married; was affianced to her by oath, and the nuptial appointed: between which time of the contract, and limit of the solemnity, her brother Frederick was wracked at sea, having in that perished vessel the dowry of his sister. But mark how heavily this befell to the poor gentlewoman: there she lost a noble and renowned brother, in his love toward her ever most kind and natural; with him the portion and sinew of her fortune, her marriage-dowry; with both, her combinate husband, this well-seeming Angelo.

ISABELLA. Can this be so? Did Angelo so leave her?

DUKE. Left her in her tears, and dried not one of them with his comfort; swallowed his vows whole, pretending in her discoveries of dishonour: in few, bestowed her on her own lamentation, which she yet wears for his sake; and he, a marble to her tears, is washed with them, but relents not.

ISABELLA. What a merit were it in death to take this poor maid from the world! What corruption in this life, that it will let this man live! But how out of this can she avail?

DUKE. It is a rupture that you may easily heal; and the cure of it not only saves your brother, but keeps you from dishonour in doing it.

ISABELLA. Show me how, good father.

DUKE. This forenamed maid hath yet in her the continuance of her first affection: his unjust unkindness, that in all reason should have quenched her love, hath, like an impediment in the current, made it more violent and unruly. Go you to Angelo: answer his requiring with a plausible obedience: agree with his demands to the point; only refer yourself to this advantage, first, that your stay with him may not be long, that the time may have all shadow and silence in it, and the place answer to convenience. This being granted in course, and now follows all, we shall advise this wronged maid to stead up your appointment, go in your place; if the encounter acknowledge itself hereafter, it may compel him to her recompense; and here by this is your brother saved, your honour untainted, the poor Mariana advantaged, and the corrupt deputy scaled. The maid will I frame and make fit for his attempt. If you think well to carry this, as you may, the doubleness of the benefit defends the deceit from reproof. What think you of it?

ISABELLA. The image of it gives me content already, and I trust it will grow to a most prosperous perfection.

DUKE. It lies much in your holding up. Haste you speedily to Angelo: if for this night he entreat you to his bed, give him promise of satisfaction. I will presently to St. Luke's;

there, at the moated grange, resides this dejected Mariana: at that place call upon me, and dispatch with Angelo, that it may be quickly.

ISABELLA. I thank you for this comfort. Fare you well, good
father.   *Exeunt*

SCENE TWO

The Street before the Prison.

Enter Duke, as a friar; to him Elbow, Pompey, and Officers

ELBOW. Nay, if there be no remedy for it, but that you will
needs buy and sell men and women like beasts, we shall
have all the world drink brown and white bastard.

DUKE. O heavens! what stuff is here?

POMPEY. 'Twas never merry world, since, of two usuries,
the merriest was put down, and the worser allowed by
order of law a furred gown to keep him warm; and
furred with fox and lamb skins too, to signify that craft,
being richer than innocency, stands for the facing.

ELBOW. Come your way, sir. Bless you, good father friar.

DUKE. And you, good brother father. What offence hath
this man made you, sir?

ELBOW. Marry, sir, he hath offended the law: and, sir, we
take him to be a thief too, sir; for we have found upon
him, sir, a strange picklock, which we have sent to the
deputy.

DUKE. Fie, sirrah: a bawd, a wicked bawd!
The evil that thou causest to be done,
That is thy means to live. Do thou but think
What 'tis to cram a maw or clothe a back
From such a filthy vice: say to thyself,
From their abominable and beastly touches
I drink, I eat, array myself, and live.
Canst thou believe thy living is a life,
So stinkingly depending? Go mend, go mend.

POMPEY. Indeed, it does stink in some sort, sir; but yet, sir,
I would prove—

DUKE. Nay, if the devil have given thee proofs for sin,
Thou wilt prove his. Take him to prison, officer;
Correction and instruction must both work

Ere this rude beast will profit.

ELBOW. He must before the deputy, sir; he has given him
warning. The deputy cannot abide a whoremaster: if he
be a whoremonger, and comes before him, he were as
good go a mile on his errand.

DUKE. That we were all, as some would seem to be,
From our faults, as faults from seeming, free!

ELBOW. His neck will come to your waist,—a cord, sir.

POMPEY. I spy comfort: I cry, bail. Here 's a gentleman
and a friend of mine.

Enter Lucio

LUCIO. How now, noble Pompey! What, at the wheels of
Cæsar? Art thou led in triumph? What, is there none of
Pygmalion's images, newly made woman, to be had now,
for putting the hand in the pocket and extracting it
clutched? What reply? ha? What say'st thou to this tune,
matter and method? Is 't not drowned i' the last rain, ha?
What sayest thou, Trot? Is the world as it was, man?
Which is the way? Is it sad, and few words, or how? The
trick of it?

DUKE. Still thus, and thus, still worse!

LUCIO. How doth my dear morsel, thy mistress? Procures
she still, ha?

POMPEY. Troth, sir, she hath eaten up all her beef, and she
is herself in the tub.

LUCIO. Why, 'tis good; it is the right of it; it must be so:
ever your fresh whore and your powdered bawd: an un-
shunned consequence; it must be so. Art going to prison,
Pompey?

POMPEY. Yes, faith, sir.

LUCIO. Why, 'tis not amiss, Pompey. Farewell. Go, say I
sent thee thither. For debt, Pompey? or how?

ELBOW. For being a bawd, for being a bawd.

LUCIO. Well, then, imprison him. If imprisonment be the
due of a bawd, why, 'tis his right: bawd is he, doubtless,
and of antiquity too; bawd-born. Farewell, good Pompey. Commend me to the prison, Pompey. You will turn
good husband now, Pompey; you will keep the house.

POMPEY. I hope, sir, your good worship will be my bail.

LUCIO. No, indeed will I not, Pompey; it is not the wear. I
will pray, Pompey, to increase your bondage: if you take

it not patiently, why, your mettle is the more. Adieu,
trusty Pompey. Bless you, friar.

DUKE. And you.

LUCIO. Does Bridget paint still, Pompey, ha?

ELBOW. Come your ways, sir; come.

POMPEY. You will not bail me then, sir?

LUCIO. Then, Pompey, nor now. What news abroad, friar?
What news?

ELBOW. Come your ways, sir; come.

LUCIO. Go to kennel, Pompey; go.

Exeunt Elbow, Pompey and Officers

What news, friar, of the duke.

DUKE. I know none. Can you tell me of any?

LUCIO. Some say he is with the Emperor of Russia; other
some, he is in Rome: but where is he, think you?

DUKE. I know not where; but wheresoever, I wish him well.

LUCIO. It was a mad fantastical trick of him to steal from
the state, and usurp the beggary he was never born to.
Lord Angelo dukes it well in his absence; he puts transgression to 't.

DUKE. He does well in 't.

LUCIO. A little more lenity to lechery would do no harm in
him: something too crabbed that way, friar.

DUKE. It is too general a vice, and severity must cure it.

LUCIO. Yes, in good sooth, the vice is of a great kindred; it
is well allied; but it is impossible to extirp it quite, friar,
till eating and drinking be put down. They say this Angelo was not made by man and woman after this downright way of creation: is it true, think you?

DUKE. How should he be made, then?

LUCIO. Some report a sea-maid spawn'd him; some that he
was begot between two stock-fishes. But it is certain that
when he makes water his urine is congealed ice; that I
know to be true; and he is a motion generative; that 's
infallible.

DUKE. You are pleasant, sir, and speak apace.

LUCIO. Why, what a ruthless thing is this in him, for the re-
bellion of a cod-piece to take away the life of a man!
Would the duke that is absent have done this? Ere he
would have hanged a man for the getting a hundred bas-
tards, he would have paid for the nursing a thousand: he

had some feeling of the sport; he knew the service, and
that instructed him to mercy.

DUKE. I never heard the absent duke much detected for
women; he was not inclined that way.

LUCIO. O, sir, you are deceived.

DUKE. 'Tis not possible.

LUCIO. Who? not the duke? yes, your beggar of fifty, and
his use was to put a ducat in her clack-dish; the duke
had crotchets in him. He would be drunk too; that let me
inform you.

DUKE. You do him wrong, surely.

LUCIO. Sir, I was an inward of his. A shy fellow was the
duke; and, I believe I know the cause of his withdraw-
ing.

DUKE. What, I prithee, might be the cause?

LUCIO. No, pardon; 'tis a secret must be locked within the
teeth and the lips; but this I can let you understand, the
greater file of the subject held the duke to be wise.

DUKE. Wise! why, no question but he was.

LUCIO. A very superficial, ignorant, unweighing fellow.

DUKE. Either this is envy in you, folly, or mistaking; the
very stream of his life and the business he hath helmed
must, upon a warranted need, give him a better proclamation. Let him be but testimonied in his own bringings
forth, and he shall appear to the envious a scholar, a
statesman and a soldier. Therefore you speak unskilfully;
or, if your knowledge be more, it is much darkened in
your malice.

LUCIO. Sir, I know him, and I love him.

DUKE. Love talks with better knowledge, and knowledge
with dearer love.

LUCIO. Come, sir, I know what I know.

DUKE. I can hardly believe that, since you know not what
you speak. But, if ever the duke return,—as our prayers
are he may,—let me desire you to make your answer before him: if it be honest you have spoke, you have courage to maintain it. I am bound to call upon you; and, I
pray you, your name?

LUCIO. Sir, my name is Lucio, well known to the duke.

DUKE. He shall know you better, sir, if I may live to report
you.

LUCIO. I fear you not.

DUKE. O! you hope the duke will return no more, or you
imagine me too unhurtful an opposite. But indeed I can
do you little harm; you 'll forswear this again.

LUCIO. I 'll be hanged first: thou art deceived in me, friar.
But no more of this. Canst thou tell if Claudio die to-
morrow or no?

DUKE. Why should he die, sir?

LUCIO. Why? for filling a bottle with a tundish. I would the
duke we talk of were returned again; this ungenitured
agent will unpeople the province with continency; sparrows must not build in his house-eaves, because they are
lecherous. The duke yet would have dark deeds darkly
answered; he would never bring them to light: would he
were returned! Marry, this Claudio is condemned for un-
trussing. Farewell, good friar; I prithee, pray for me. The
duke, I say to thee again, would eat mutton on Fridays.
He 's not past it yet, and I say to thee, he would mouth
with a beggar, though she smelt brown bread and garlic:
say that I said so. Farewell.   *Exit*

DUKE. No might nor greatness in mortality
Can censure 'scape: back-wounding calumny
The whitest virtue strikes. What king so strong
Can tie the gall up in the slanderous tongue?
But who comes here?

Enter Escalus,
Provost, and Officers with Mistress Overdone

ESCALUS. Go; away with her to prison!

MRS. OVERDONE. Good my lord, be good to me; your honour is accounted a merciful man; good my lord.

ESCALUS. Double and treble admonition, and still forfeit in
the same kind? This would make mercy swear, and play
the tyrant.

PROVOST. A bawd of eleven years' continuance, may it
please your honour.

MRS. OVERDONE. My lord, this is one Lucio's information
against me. Mistress Kate Keepdown was with child by
him in the duke's time; he promised her marriage; his
child is a year and a quarter old, come Philip and Jacob:
I have kept it myself, and see how he goes about to
abuse me!

ESCALUS. That fellow is a fellow of much licence: let him
be called before us. Away with her to prison! Go to; no

more words. (*Exeunt Officers with Mistress Overdone*)
Provost, my brother Angelo will not be altered; Claudio
must die to-morrow. Let him be furnished with divines,
and have all charitable preparation: if my brother
wrought by my pity, it should not be so with him.

PROVOST. So please you, this friar hath been with him, and
advised him for the entertainment of death.

ESCALUS. Good even, good father.

DUKE. Bliss and goodness on you!

ESCALUS. Of whence are you?

DUKE. Not of this country, though my chance is now
To use it for my time: I am a brother
Of gracious order, late come from the See,
In special business from his Holiness.

ESCALUS. What news abroad i' the world?

DUKE. None, but there is so great a fever on goodness, that
the dissolution of it must cure it: novelty is only in request; and it is as dangerous to be aged in any kind of
course, as it is virtuous to be constant in any undertaking: there is scarce truth enough alive to make societies
secure, but security enough to make fellowships ac-
cursed. Much upon this riddle runs the wisdom of the
world. This news is old enough, yet it is every day's
news. I pray you, sir, of what disposition was the duke?

ESCALUS. One that, above all other strifes, contended especially to know himself.

DUKE. What pleasure was he given to?

ESCALUS. Rather rejoicing to see another merry, than merry
at anything which professed to make him rejoice: a gentleman of all temperance. But leave we him to his events,
with a prayer they may prove prosperous; and let me desire to know how you find Claudio prepared. I am made
to understand, that you have lent him visitation.

DUKE. He professes to have received no sinister measure
from his judge, but most willingly humbles himself to the
determination of justice; yet had he framed to himself, by
the instruction of his frailty, many deceiving promises of
life, which I, by my good leisure have discredited to him,
and now is he resolved to die.

ESCALUS. You have paid the heavens your function, and the
prisoner the very debt of your calling. I have laboured
for the poor gentleman to the extremest shore of my

modesty; but my brother justice have I found so severe,
that he hath forced me to tell him he is indeed Justice.

DUKE. If his own life answer the straitness of his proceeding, it shall become him well; wherein if he chance to
fail, he hath sentenced himself.

ESCALUS. I am going to visit the prisoner. Fare you well.

DUKE. Peace be with you!   *Exeunt Escalus and Provost*
He, who the sword of heaven will bear
Should be as holy as severe;
Pattern in himself to know,
Grace to stand, and virtue go;
More nor less to others paying
Than by self offences weighing.
Shame to him whose cruel striking
Kills for faults of his own liking!
Twice treble shame on Angelo,
To weed my vice and let his grow!
O, what may man within him hide,
Though angel on the outward side!
How many likeness made in crimes,
Making practice on the times,
To draw with idle spiders' strings
Most pond'rous and substantial things!
Craft against vice I must apply:
With Angelo to-night shall lie
His old betrothed but despis'd:
So disguise shall, by the disguis'd,
Pay with falsehood false exacting,
And perform an old contracting.   *Exit*

ACT FOUR

SCENE ONE [1·27]

The moated Grange at St. Luke's

Enter Mariana and a Boy: Boy sings

Take, O take those lips away,
　　That so sweetly were forsworn;
And those eyes, the break of day,
　　Lights that do mislead the morn:
But my kisses bring again, bring again,
　　Seals of love, but seal'd in vain, seal'd in vain.

MARIANA. Break off thy song, and haste thee quick away:
Here comes a man of comfort, whose advice
Hath often still'd my brawling discontent. *Exit Boy*
　　　　Enter Duke, disguised as before
I cry you mercy, sir; and well could wish
You had not found me here so musical:
Let me excuse me, and believe me so,
My mirth it much displeas'd, but pleas'd my woe.

DUKE. 'Tis good; though music oft hath such a charm
To make bad good, and good provoke to harm.
I pray you tell me, hath anybody inquired for me here
to-day? Much upon this time have I promised here to
meet.

MARIANA. You have not been inquired after: I have sat
here all day.

DUKE. I do constantly believe you. The time is come even
now. I shall crave your forbearance a little; may be I will
call upon you anon, for some advantage to yourself.

MARIANA. I am always bound to you. *Exit*
　　　　Enter Isabella
DUKE. Very well met, and well come.
What is the news from this good deputy?

ISABELLA. He hath a garden circummur'd with brick,

Whose western side is with a vineyard back'd;
And to that vineyard is a planched gate,
That makes his opening with this bigger key;
This other doth command a little door
Which from the vineyard to the garden leads;
There have I made my promise
Upon the heavy middle of the night
To call upon him.

DUKE. But shall you on your knowledge find this way?

ISABELLA. I have ta'en a due and wary note upon't:
With whispering and most guilty diligence,
In action all of precept, he did show me
The way twice o'er.

DUKE.   Are there no other tokens
Between you 'greed concerning her observance?

ISABELLA. No, none, but only a repair i' the dark;
And that I have possess'd him my most stay
Can be but brief; for I have made him know
I have a servant comes with me along,
That stays upon me, whose persuasion is
I come about my brother.

DUKE.   'Tis well borne up.
I have not yet made known to Mariana
A word of this. What ho! within! come forth.

Re-enter Mariana

I pray you, be acquainted with this maid:
She comes to do you good.

ISABELLA.   I do desire the like.

DUKE. Do you persuade yourself that I respect you?

MARIANA. Good friar, I know you do, and oft have found it.

DUKE. Take then this your companion by the hand,
Who hath a story ready for your ear.
I shall attend your leisure: but make haste;
The vaporous night approaches.

MARIANA.   Will 't please you walk aside?

Exeunt Mariana and Isabella

DUKE. O place and greatness! millions of false eyes
Are stuck upon thee: volumes of report
Run with these false and most contrarious quests
Upon thy doings: thousand escapes of wit
Make thee the father of their idle dream,
And rack thee in their fancies!

Re-enter Mariana and Isabella

Welcome! How agreed?

ISABELLA. She 'll take the enterprise upon her, father,
If you advise it.

DUKE.   It is not my consent,
But my entreaty too.

ISABELLA.   Little have you to say
When you depart from him, but, soft and low,
'Remember now my brother.'

MARIANA.   Fear me not.

DUKE. Nor, gentle daughter, fear you not at all.
He is your husband on a pre-contract:
To bring you thus together, 'tis no sin,
Sith that the justice of your title to him
Doth flourish the deceit. Come, let us go:
Our corn 's to reap, for yet our tithe 's to sow.   *Exeunt*

SCENE TWO

A Room in the Prison.

Enter Provost and Pompey

PROVOST. Come hither, sirrah. Can you cut off a man's
head?

POMPEY. If the man be a bachelor, sir, I can; but if he be a
married man, he is his wife's head, and I can never cut
off a woman's head.

PROVOST. Come, sir, leave me your snatches, and yield me
a direct answer. To-morrow morning are to die Claudio
and Barnardine. Here is in our prison a common executioner, who in his office lacks a helper: if you will take it
on you to assist him, it shall redeem you from your gyves;
if not, you shall have your full time of imprisonment, and
your deliverance with an unpitied whipping, for you
have been a notorious bawd.

POMPEY. Sir, I have been an unlawful bawd time out of
mind; but yet I will be content to be a lawful hangman.
I would be glad to receive some instruction from my fellow partner.

PROVOST. What ho, Abhorson! Where 's Abhorson, there?

Enter Abhorson

ABHORSON. Do you call, sir?

PROVOST. Sirrah, here 's a fellow will help you to-morrow
in your execution. If you think it meet, compound with
him by the year, and let him abide here with you; if not,
use him for the present, and dismiss him. He cannot
plead his estimation with you; he hath been a bawd.

ABHORSON. A bawd, sir? Fie upon him! he will discredit our
mystery.

PROVOST. Go to, sir; you weigh equally; a feather will turn
the scale.   *Exit*

POMPEY. Pray, sir, by your good favour—for surely, sir, a
good favour you have, but that you have a hanging look,
—do you call, sir, your occupation a mystery?

ABHORSON. Ay, sir; a mystery.

POMPEY. Painting, sir, I have heard say, is a mystery; and
your whores, sir, being members of my occupation, using
painting, do prove my occupation a mystery: but what
mystery there should be in hanging, if I should be
hanged, I cannot imagine.

ABHORSON. Sir, it is a mystery.

POMPEY. Proof?

ABHORSON. Every true man's apparel fits your thief.

POMPEY. If it be too little for your thief, your true man
thinks it big enough; if it be too big for your thief, your
thief thinks it little enough: so, every true man's apparel
fits your thief.

Re-enter Provost

PROVOST. Are you agreed?

POMPEY. Sir, I will serve him; for I do find that your hangman is a more penitent trade than your bawd, he doth
often ask forgiveness.

PROVOST. You, sirrah, provide your block and your axe to-
morrow four o'clock.

ABHORSON. Come on, bawd; I will instruct thee in my
trade; follow.

POMPEY. I do desire to learn, sir; and, I hope, if you have
occasion to use me for your own turn, you shall find me
yare; for, truly, sir, for your kindness I owe you a good
turn.

PROVOST. Call hither Barnardine and Claudio:
                                  Exeunt Pompey and Abhorson

The one has my pity; not a jot the other,
Being a murderer, though he were my brother.

Enter Claudio

Look, here 's the warrant, Claudio, for thy death:
'Tis now dead midnight, and by eight to-morrow
Thou must be made immortal. Where 's Barnardine?

CLAUDIO. As fast lock'd up in sleep as guiltless labour
When it lies starkly in the traveller's bones;
He will not wake.

PROVOST.   Who can do good on him?
Well, go; prepare yourself. (*Knocking within*) But hark,
    what noise?—
Heaven give your spirits comfort!—(*Exit Claudio*) By and
    by.
I hope it is some pardon or reprieve
For the most gentle Claudio.

Enter Duke, disguised as before
                            Welcome, father.

DUKE. The best and wholesom'st spirits of the night
Envelop you, good provost! Who call'd here of late?

PROVOST. None since the curfew rung.

DUKE. Not Isabel?

PROVOST.   No.

DUKE.   They will, then, ere 't be long.

PROVOST. What comfort is for Claudio?

DUKE. There 's some in hope.

PROVOST.   It is a bitter deputy.

DUKE. Not so, not so: his life is parallel'd
Even with the stroke and line of his great justice:
He doth with holy abstinence subdue
That in himself which he spurs on his power
To qualify in others: were he meal'd with that
Which he corrects, then were he tyrannous;
But this being so, he 's just.—(*Knocking within*) Now
    are they come.   *Exit Provost*
This is a gentle provost: seldom when
The steeled gaoler is the friend of men.   *Knocking*
How now! What noise? That spirit 's possess'd with haste
That wounds the unsisting postern with these strokes.

Re-enter Provost

PROVOST. There he must stay until the officer
Arise to let him in; he is call'd up.

DUKE. Have you no countermand for Claudio yet,
But he must die to-morrow?

PROVOST.   None, sir, none.

DUKE. As near the dawning, provost, as it is,
You shall hear more ere morning.

PROVOST.   Happily
You something know; yet, I believe there comes
No countermand: no such example have we.
Besides, upon the very siege of justice,
Lord Angelo hath to the public ear
Profess'd the contrary.

Enter a Messenger
This is his lordship's man.

DUKE. And here comes Claudio's pardon.

MESSENGER. (*Giving a paper*) My lord hath sent you this
note; and by me this further charge, that you swerve not
from the smallest article of it, neither in time, matter, or
other circumstance. Good-morrow; for, as I take it, it is
almost day.

PROVOST. I shall obey him.   *Exit Messenger*

DUKE. (*Aside*) This is his pardon, purchased by such sin
For which the pardoner himself is in;
Hence hath offence his quick celerity,
When it is borne in high authority.
When vice makes mercy, mercy 's so extended,
That for the fault's love is the offender friended.
Now, sir, what news?

PROVOST. I told you: Lord Angelo, belike thinking me re-
miss in mine office, awakens me with this unwonted putting on; methinks strangely, for he hath not used it before.

DUKE. Pray you, let 's hear.

PROVOST. (*Reads*) 'Whatsoever you may hear to the contrary, let Claudio be executed by four of the clock; and,
in the afternoon, Barnardine. For my better satisfaction,
let me have Claudio's head sent me by five. Let this be
duly performed; with a thought that more depends on it
than we must yet deliver. Thus fail not to do your office,
as you will answer it at your peril.' What say you to this,
sir?

DUKE. What is that Barnardine who is to be executed this
afternoon?

PROVOST. A Bohemian born, but here nursed up and bred; one that is a prisoner nine years old.

DUKE. How came it that the absent duke had not either delivered him to his liberty or executed him? I have heard it was ever his manner to do so.

PROVOST. His friends still wrought reprieves for him; and, indeed, his fact, till now in the government of Lord Angelo, came not to an undoubtful proof.

DUKE. It is now apparent?

PROVOST. Most manifest, and not denied by himself.

DUKE. Hath he borne himself penitently in prison? How seems he to be touched?

PROVOST. A man that apprehends death no more dreadfully but as a drunken sleep; careless, reckless, and fearless of what's past, present, or to come; insensible of mortality, and desperately mortal.

DUKE. He wants advice.

PROVOST. He will hear none. He hath evermore had the liberty of the prison: give him leave to escape hence, he would not: drunk many times a day, if not many days entirely drunk. We have very oft awaked him, as if to carry him to execution, and showed him a seeming warrant for it: it hath not moved him at all.

DUKE. More of him anon. There is written in your brow, provost, honesty and constancy: if I read it not truly, my ancient skill beguiles me; but, in the boldness of my cunning I will lay myself in hazard. Claudio, whom here you have warrant to execute, is no greater forfeit to the law than Angelo who hath sentenced him. To make you understand this in a manifested effect, I crave but four days' respite, for the which you are to do me both a present and a dangerous courtesy.

PROVOST. Pray, sir, in what?

DUKE. In the delaying death.

PROVOST. Alack! how may I do it, having the hour limited, and an express command, under penalty, to deliver his head in the view of Angelo? I may make my case as Claudio's to cross this in the smallest.

DUKE. By the vow of mine order I warrant you, if my instructions may be your guide. Let this Barnardine be this morning executed, and his head borne to Angelo.

PROVOST. Angelo hath seen them both, and will discover the favour.

DUKE. O! death 's a great disguiser, and you may add to it. Shave the head, and tie the beard; and say it was the desire of the penitent to be so bared before his death: you know the course is common. If anything fall to you upon this, more than thanks and good fortune, by the saint whom I profess, I will plead against it with my life.

PROVOST. Pardon me, good father; it is against my oath.

DUKE. Were you sworn to the duke or to the deputy?

PROVOST. To him, and to his substitutes.

DUKE. You will think you have made no offence, if the duke avouch the justice of your dealing?

PROVOST. But what likelihood is in that?

DUKE. Not a resemblance, but a certainty. Yet since I see you fearful, that neither my coat, integrity, nor persuasion can with ease attempt you, I will go further than I meant, to pluck all fears out of you. Look you, sir; here is the hand and seal of the duke: you know the character, I doubt not, and the signet is not strange to you.

PROVOST. I know them both.

DUKE. The contents of this is the return of the duke: you shall anon over-read it at your pleasure, where you shall find within these two days, he will be here. This is a thing that Angelo knows not, for he this very day receives letters of strange tenour; perchance of the duke's death; perchance, his entering into some monastery; but, by chance, nothing of what is writ. Look, the unfolding star calls up the shepherd. Put not yourself into amazement how these things should be: all difficulties are but easy when they are known. Call your executioner, and off with Barnardine's head: I will give him a present shrift and advise him for a better place. Yet you are amaz'd, but this shall absolutely resolve you. Come away; it is almost clear dawn.   *Exeunt*

SCENE THREE

Another Room in the Same.

Enter Pompey

POMPEY. I am as well acquainted here as I was in our
house of profession: one would think it were Mistress
Overdone's own house, for here be many of her old customers. First, here 's young Master Rash; he 's in for a
commodity of brown paper and old ginger, nine-score
and seventeen pounds, of which he made five marks,
ready money: marry, then ginger was not much in request, for the old women were all dead. Then is there
here one Master Caper, at the suit of Master Three-pile
the mercer, for some four suits of peach-colour'd satin,
which now peaches him a beggar. Then have we young
Dizy, and young Master Deep-vow, and Master Copper-
spur, and Master Starve-lackey the rapier and dagger
man, and young Drop-heir that kill'd lusty Pudding, and
Master Forthlight, the tilter, and brave Master Shoe-tie
the great traveller, and wild Half-can that stabbed Pots,
and, I think, forty more; all great doers in our trade, and
are now 'for the Lord's sake.'

Enter Abhorson

ABHORSON. Sirrah, bring Barnardine hither.

POMPEY. Master Barnardine! you must rise and be hanged,
Master Barnardine.

ABHORSON. What ho! Barnardine!

BARNARDINE. (*Within*) A pox o' your throats! Who makes
that noise there? What are you?

POMPEY. Your friends, sir; the hangman. You must be so
good, sir, to rise and be put to death.

BARNARDINE. (*Within*) Away! you rogue, away! I am sleepy.

ABHORSON. Tell him he must awake, and that quickly too.

POMPEY. Pray, Master Barnardine, awake till you are executed, and sleep afterwards.

ABHORSON. Go in to him, and fetch him out.

POMPEY. He is coming, sir, he is coming; I hear his straw
rustle.

ABHORSON. Is the axe upon the block, sirrah?

POMPEY. Very ready, sir.

Enter Barnardine

BARNARDINE. How now, Abhorson! what 's the news with you?

ABHORSON. Truly, sir, I would desire you to clap into your prayers; for, look you, the warrant 's come.

BARNARDINE. You rogue, I have been drinking all night; I am not fitted for 't.

POMPEY. O, the better, sir; for he that drinks all night, and is hang'd betimes in the morning, may sleep the sounder all the next day.

ABHORSON. Look you, sir; here comes your ghostly father: do we jest now, think you?

Enter Duke, disguised as before

DUKE. Sir, induced by my charity, and hearing how hastily you are to depart, I am come to advise you, comfort you, and pray with you.

BARNARDINE. Friar, not I: I have been drinking hard all night, and I will have more time to prepare me, or they shall beat out my brains with billets. I will not consent to die this day, that 's certain.

DUKE. O, sir, you must; and therefore, I beseech you look forward on the journey you shall go.

BARNARDINE. I swear I will not die to-day for any man's persuasion.

DUKE. But hear you.

BARNARDINE. Not a word: if you have anything to say to me, come to my ward; for thence will not I to-day. *Exit*

Enter Provost

DUKE. Unfit to live or die. O, gravel heart!
After him fellows: bring him to the block.

Exeunt Abhorson and Pompey

PROVOST. Now, sir, how do you find the prisoner?

DUKE. A creature unprepar'd, unmeet for death;
And, to transport him in the mind he is
Were damnable.

PROVOST.   Here in the prison, father,
There died this morning of a cruel fever
One Ragozine, a most notorious pirate,
A man of Claudio's years; his beard and head
Just of his colour. What if we do omit
This reprobate till he were well inclin'd,

And satisfy the deputy with the visage
Of Ragozine, more like to Claudio?

DUKE. O, 'tis an accident that heaven provides!
Dispatch it presently: the hour draws on
Prefix'd by Angelo. See this be done,
And sent according to command, whiles I
Persuade this rude wretch willingly to die.

PROVOST. This shall be done, good father, presently.
But Barnardine must die this afternoon:
And how shall we continue Claudio,
To save me from the danger that might come
If he were known alive?

DUKE.   Let this be done:
Put them in secret holds, both Barnardine and Claudio:
Ere twice the sun hath made his journal greeting
To the under generation, you shall find
Your safety manifested.

PROVOST. I am your free dependant.

DUKE. Quick, dispatch,
And send the head to Angelo.   *Exit Provost*
Now will I write letters to Angelo,—
The provost, he shall bear them,—whose contents
Shall witness to him I am near at home,
And that, by great injunctions, I am bound
To enter publicly: him I 'll desire
To meet me at the consecrated fount
A league below the city; and from thence,
By cold gradation and well-balanc'd form,
We shall proceed with Angelo.

Re-enter Provost

PROVOST. Here is the head; I 'll carry it myself.

DUKE. Convenient is it. Make a swift return,
For I would commune with you of such things
That want no ear but yours.

PROVOST.   I 'll make all speed.   *Exit*

ISABELLA. (*Within*) Peace, ho, be here!

DUKE. The tongue of Isabel. She 's come to know
If yet her brother's pardon be come hither;
But I will keep her ignorant of her good,
To make her heavenly comforts of despair,
When it is least expected.

Enter Isabella

ISABELLA.   Ho! by your leave.

DUKE. Good-morning to you, fair and gracious daughter.

ISABELLA. The better, given me by so holy a man.
  Hath yet the deputy sent my brother's pardon?

DUKE. He hath releas'd him, Isabel, from the world:
  His head is off and sent to Angelo.

ISABELLA. Nay, but it is not so.

DUKE. It is no other: show your wisdom, daughter,
  In your close patience.

ISABELLA. O! I will to him and pluck out his eyes!

DUKE. You shall not be admitted to his sight.

ISABELLA. Unhappy Claudio! Wretched Isabel!
  Injurious world! Most damned Angelo!

DUKE. This nor hurts him nor profits you a jot;
  Forbear it therefore; give your cause to heaven.
  Mark what I say, which you shall find
  By every syllable a faithful verity.
  The duke comes home to-morrow; nay, dry your eyes:
  One of our convent, and his confessor,
  Gives me this instance: already he hath carried
  Notice to Escalus and Angelo,
  Who do prepare to meet him at the gates,
  There to give up their power. If you can, pace your wis-
      dom
  In that good path that I would wish it go,
  And you shall have your bosom on this wretch,
  Grace of the duke, revenges to your heart,
  And general honour.

ISABELLA.   I am directed by you.

DUKE. This letter then to Friar Peter give;
  'Tis that he sent me of the duke's return:
  Say, by this token, I desire his company
  At Mariana's house to-night. Her cause and yours,
  I 'll perfect him withal, and he shall bring you
  Before the duke; and to the head of Angelo
  Accuse him home, and home. For my poor self,
  I am combined by a sacred vow
  And shall be absent. Wend you with this letter.
  Command these fretting waters from your eyes
  With a light heart: trust not my holy order,
  If I pervert your course. Who 's here?

Enter Lucio

LUCIO. Good even. Friar, where is the provost?

DUKE. Not within, sir.

LUCIO. O pretty Isabella, I am pale at mine heart to see thine eyes so red: thou must be patient. I am fain to dine and sup with water and bran; I dare not for my head fill my belly; one fruitful meal would set me to 't. But they say the duke will be here to-morrow. By my troth, Isabel, I loved thy brother: if the old fantastical duke of dark corners had been at home, he had lived.   *Exit Isabella*

DUKE. Sir, the duke is marvellous little beholding to your reports; but the best is, he lives not in them.

LUCIO. Friar, thou knowest not the duke so well as I do: he 's a better woodman than thou takest him for.

DUKE. Well, you 'll answer this one day. Fare ye well.

LUCIO. Nay, tarry; I 'll go along with thee: I can tell thee pretty tales of the duke.

DUKE. You have told me too many of him already, sir, if they be true; if not true, none were enough.

LUCIO. I was once before him for getting a wench with child.

DUKE. Did you such a thing?

LUCIO. Yes, marry, did I; but I was fain to forswear it: they would else have married me to the rotten medlar.

DUKE. Sir, your company is fairer than honest. Rest you well.

LUCIO. By my troth, I 'll go with thee to the lane's end. If bawdy talk offend you, we 'll have very little of it. Nay, friar, I am a kind of burr; I shall stick.   *Exeunt*

SCENE FOUR

A Room in Angelo's House.

Enter Angelo and Escalus

ESCALUS. Every letter he hath writ hath disvouched other.

ANGELO. In most uneven and distracted manner. His actions show much like to madness: pray heaven his wisdom be not tainted! And why meet him at the gates, and redeliver our authorities there?

ESCALUS. I guess not.

ANGELO. And why should we proclaim it in an hour before
his entering, that if any crave redress of injustice, they
should exhibit their petitions in the street?

ESCALUS. He shows his reason for that: to have a dispatch
of complaints, and to deliver us from devices hereafter,
which shall then have no power to stand against us.

ANGELO. Well, I beseech you, let it be proclaim'd:
Betimes i' the morn I 'll call you at your house;
Give notice to such men of sort and suit
As are to meet him.

ESCALUS. I shall, sir: fare you well.

ANGELO. Good-night.—   *Exit Escalus*
This deed unshapes me quite, makes me unpregnant
And dull to all proceedings. A deflower'd maid,
And by an eminent body that enforc'd
The law against it! But that her tender shame
Will not proclaim against her maiden loss,
How might she tongue me! Yet reason dares her no:
For my authority bears so credent bulk,
That no particular scandal once can touch:
But it confounds the breather. He should have liv'd,
Save that his riotous youth, with dangerous sense,
Might in the times to come have ta'en revenge,
By so receiving a dishonour'd life
With ransom of such shame. Would yet he had liv'd!
Alack! when once our grace we have forgot,
Nothing goes right: we would, and we would not.   *Exit*

SCENE FIVE

Fields without the Town.

Enter Duke, in his own habit, and Friar Peter

DUKE. These letters at fit time deliver me.   *Giving letters*
The provost knows our purpose and our plot.
The matter being afoot, keep your instruction,
And hold you ever to our special drift,
Though sometimes you do blench from this to that,
As cause doth minister. Go call at Flavius' house,
And tell him where I stay: give the like notice
To Valentinus, Rowland, and to Crassus,

And bid them bring the trumpets to the gate;
But send me Flavius first.

FRIAR PETER.   It shall be speeded well.   *Exit*

Enter Varrius

DUKE. I thank thee, Varrius; thou hast made good haste.
Come, we will walk. There 's other of our friends
Will greet us here anon, my gentle Varrius.   *Exeunt*

SCENE SIX

Street near the City Gate.

Enter Isabella and Mariana

ISABELLA. To speak so indirectly I am loath:
I would say the truth; but to accuse him so,
That is your part: yet I 'm advis'd to do it;
He says, to veil full purpose.

MARIANA.   Be rul'd by him.

ISABELLA. Besides, he tells me that if peradventure
He speak against me on the adverse side,
I should not think it strange; for 'tis a physic
That 's bitter to sweet end.

MARIANA. I would, Friar Peter—

ISABELLA.   O, peace! the friar is come.

Enter Friar Peter

FRIAR PETER. Come; I have found you out a stand most fit,
Where you may have such vantage on the duke,
He shall not pass you. Twice have the trumpets sounded:
The generous and gravest citizens
Have hent the gates, and very near upon
The duke is ent'ring: therefore hence, away!   *Exeunt*

ACT FIVE

[1-23] SCENE ONE

A public Place near the City Gate.

*Mariana, veiled, Isabella, and Friar Peter, at their stand.
Enter Duke, Varrius, Lords, Angelo, Escalus, Lucio,
Provost, Officers, and Citizens at several doors*

DUKE. My very worthy cousin, fairly met!
  Our old and faithful friend, we are glad to see you.

ANGELO. ⎱
ESCALUS. ⎰ Happy return be to your royal Grace!

DUKE. Many and hearty thankings to you both.
  We have made inquiry of you; and we hear
  Such goodness of your justice, that our soul
  Cannot but yield you forth to public thanks,
  Forerunning more requital.

ANGELO.   You make my bonds still greater.

DUKE. O! your desert speaks loud; and I should wrong it,
  To lock it in the wards of covert bosom,
  When it deserves, with characters of brass,
  A forted residence 'gainst the tooth of time
  And razure of oblivion. Give me your hand,
  And let the subject see, to make them know
  That outward courtesies would fain proclaim
  Favours that keep within. Come, Escalus,
  You must walk by us on our other hand;
  And good supporters are you.

        Friar Peter and Isabella come forward

FRIAR PETER. Now is your time: speak loud and kneel before him.

ISABELLA. Justice, O royal duke! Vail your regard
  Upon a wrong'd—I 'd fain have said, a maid!
  O worthy prince! dishonour not your eye
  By throwing it on any other object

Till you have heard me in my true complaint
And given me justice, justice, justice, justice!

DUKE. Relate your wrongs: in what? by whom? be brief;
Here is Lord Angelo shall give you justice:
Reveal yourself to him.

ISABELLA.   O worthy duke!
You bid me seek redemption of the devil.
Hear me yourself; for that which I must speak
Must either punish me, not being believ'd,
Or wring redress from you. Hear me, O, hear me, hear!

ANGELO. My lord, her wits, I fear me, are not firm:
She hath been a suitor to me for her brother
Cut off by course of justice,—

ISABELLA.   By course of justice!

ANGELO. And she will speak most bitterly and strange.

ISABELLA. Most strange, but yet most truly, will I speak.
That Angelo 's forsworn, is it not strange?
That Angelo 's a murderer, is 't not strange?
That Angelo is an adulterous thief,
A hypocrite, a virgin-violator;
Is it not strange, and strange?

DUKE.   Nay, it is ten times strange.

ISABELLA. It is not truer he is Angelo
Than this is all as true as it is strange;
Nay, it is ten times true; for truth is truth
To the end of reckoning.

DUKE.   Away with her! poor soul,
She speaks this in the infirmity of sense.

ISABELLA. O prince, I conjure thee, as thou believ'st
There is another comfort than this world,
That thou neglect me not, with that opinion
That I am touch'd with madness. Make not impossible
That which but seems unlike. 'Tis not impossible
But one, the wicked'st caitiff on the ground,
May seem as shy, as grave, as just, as absolute
As Angelo; even so may Angelo,
In all his dressings, characts, titles, forms,
Be an arch-villain. Believe it, royal prince:
If he be less, he 's nothing; but he 's more,
Had I more name for badness.

DUKE.   By mine honesty,
If she be mad,—as I believe no other,—

Her madness hath the oddest frame of sense,
Such a dependency of thing on thing,
As e'er I heard in madness.

ISABELLA.   O gracious duke!
Harp not on that; nor do not banish reason
For inequality; but let your reason serve
To make the truth appear where it seems hid,
And hide the false seems true.

DUKE.   Many that are not mad
Have, sure, more lack of reason. What would you say?

ISABELLA. I am sister of one Claudio,
Condemn'd upon the act of fornication
To lose his head; condemn'd by Angelo.
I, in probation of a sisterhood,
Was sent to by my brother; one Lucio
As then the messenger,—

LUCIO.   That's I, an't like your Grace:
I came to her from Claudio, and desir'd her
To try her gracious fortune with Lord Angelo
For her poor brother's pardon.

ISABELLA.   That's he indeed.

DUKE. You were not bid to speak.

LUCIO.   No, my good lord,
Nor wish'd to hold my peace.

DUKE.   I wish you now, then;
Pray you, take note of it; and when you have
A business for yourself, pray heaven you then
Be perfect.

LUCIO. I warrant your honour.

DUKE. The warrant's for yourself: take heed to it.

ISABELLA. This gentleman told somewhat of my tale,—

LUCIO. Right.

DUKE. It may be right; but you are in the wrong
To speak before your time. Proceed.

ISABELLA.   I went
To this pernicious caitiff deputy.

DUKE. That's somewhat madly spoken.

ISABELLA.   Pardon it:
The phrase is to the matter.

DUKE. Mended again: the matter; proceed.

ISABELLA. In brief, to set the needless process by,
How I persuaded, how I pray'd, and kneel'd,

How he refell'd me, and how I replied,—
For this was of much length,—the vile conclusion
I now begin with grief and shame to utter.
He would not, but by gift of my chaste body
To his concupiscible intemperate lust,
Release my brother; and, after much debatement,
My sisterly remorse confutes mine honour,
And I did yield to him. But the next morn betimes,
His purpose surfeiting, he sends a warrant
For my poor brother's head.

DUKE.   This is most likely!

ISABELLA. O, that it were as like as it is true!

DUKE. By heaven, fond wretch! thou know'st not what thou
    speak'st,
Or else thou art suborn'd against his honour
In hateful practice. First, his integrity
Stands without blemish; next, it imports no reason
That with such vehemency he should pursue
Faults proper to himself: if he had so offended,
He would have weigh'd thy brother by himself,
And not have cut him off. Some one hath set you on:
Confess the truth, and say by whose advice
Thou cam'st here to complain.

ISABELLA.   And is this all?
Then, O you blessed ministers above,
Keep me in patience; and, with ripen'd time
Unfold the evil which is here wrapt up
In countenance! Heaven shield your Grace from woe,
As I, thus wrong'd, hence unbelieved go!

DUKE. I know you 'd fain be gone. An officer!
To prison with her! Shall we thus permit
A blasting and a scandalous breath to fall
On him so near us? This needs must be a practice.
Who knew of your intent and coming hither?

ISABELLA. One that I would were here, Friar Lodowick.

DUKE. A ghostly father, belike. Who knows that Lodowick?

LUCIO. My lord, I know him; 'tis a meddling friar;
I do not like the man: had he been lay, my lord,
For certain words he spake against your Grace
In your retirement, I had swing'd him soundly.

DUKE. Words against me! This' a good friar, belike!
And to set on this wretched woman here

Against our substitute! Let this friar be found.

LUCIO. But yesternight, my lord, she and that friar,
    I saw them at the prison: a saucy friar,
    A very scurvy fellow.

FRIAR PETER.   Bless'd be your royal Grace!
    I have stood by, my lord, and I have heard
    Your royal ear abus'd. First, hath this woman
    Most wrongfully accus'd your substitute,
    Who is as free from touch or soil with her,
    As she from one ungot.

DUKE.   We did believe no less.
    Know you that Friar Lodowick that she speaks of?

FRIAR PETER. I know him for a man divine and holy;
    Not scurvy, nor a temporary meddler,
    As he 's reported by this gentleman;
    And, on my trust, a man that never yet
    Did, as he vouches, misreport your Grace.

LUCIO. My lord, most villanously; believe it.

FRIAR PETER. Well; he in time may come to clear himself,
    But at this instant he is sick, my lord,
    Of a strange fever. Upon his mere request,
    Being come to knowledge that there was complaint
    Intended 'gainst Lord Angelo, came I hither,
    To speak, as from his mouth, what he doth know
    Is true and false; and what he with his oath
    And all probation will make up full clear,
    Whensoever he 's convented. First, for this woman,
    To justify this worthy nobleman,
    So vulgarly and personally accus'd,
    Her shall you hear disproved to her eyes,
    Till she herself confess it.

DUKE.   Good friar, let 's hear it.
                   Isabella is carried off
           guarded; and Mariana comes forward
    Do you not smile at this, Lord Angelo?—
    O heaven, the vanity of wretched fools!
    Give us some seats. Come, cousin Angelo;
    In this I 'll be impartial; be you judge
    Of your own cause. Is this the witness, friar?
    First, let her show her face, and after speak.

MARIANA. Pardon, my lord; I will not show my face
    Until my husband bid me.

DUKE.   What, are you married?

MARIANA. No, my lord.

DUKE.   Are you a maid?

MARIANA.   No, my lord.

DUKE. A widow, then?

MARIANA.   Neither, my lord.

DUKE.   Why, you
Are nothing, then: neither maid, widow, nor wife?

LUCIO. My lord, she may be a punk; for many of them are
neither maid, widow, nor wife.

DUKE. Silence that fellow: I would he had some cause
To prattle for himself.

LUCIO. Well, my lord.

MARIANA. My lord, I do confess I ne'er was married;
And I confess besides I am no maid:
I have known my husband yet my husband knows not
That ever he knew me.

LUCIO. He was drunk then, my lord: it can be no better.

DUKE. For the benefit of silence, would thou wert so too!

LUCIO. Well, my lord.

DUKE. This is no witness for Lord Angelo.

MARIANA. Now I come to 't, my lord:
She that accuses him of fornication,
In self-same manner doth accuse my husband;
And charges him, my lord, with such a time,
When, I 'll depose, I had him in mine arms,
With all th' effect of love.

ANGELO. Charges she moe than me?

MARIANA.   Not that I know.

DUKE. No? you say your husband.

MARIANA. Why, just, my lord, and that is Angelo,
Who thinks he knows that he ne'er knew my body
But knows he thinks that he knows Isabel's.

ANGELO. This is a strange abuse. Let 's see thy face.

MARIANA. My husband bids me; now I will unmask.
This is that face, thou cruel Angelo,   *Unveiling*
Which once thou swor'st was worth the looking on:
This is the hand which, with a vow'd contract,
Was fast belock'd in thine: this is the body
That took away the match from Isabel,
And did supply thee at thy garden-house
In her imagin'd person.

DUKE.   Know you this woman?

LUCIO. Carnally, she says.

DUKE.   Sirrah, no more!

LUCIO. Enough, my lord.

ANGELO. My lord, I must confess I know this woman;
  And five years since there was some speech of marriage
  Betwixt myself and her, which was broke off,
  Partly for that her promised proportions
  Came short of composition; but, in chief
  For that her reputation was disvalu'd
  In levity: since what time of five years
  I never spake with her, saw her, nor heard from her,
  Upon my faith and honour.

MARIANA.   Noble prince,
  As there comes light from heaven and words from breath,
  As there is sense in truth and truth in virtue,
  I am affianc'd this man's wife as strongly
  As words could make up vows: and, my good lord,
  But Tuesday night last gone in 's garden-house
  He knew me as a wife. As this is true,
  Let me in safety raise me from my knees
  Or else for ever be confixed here,
  A marble monument.

ANGELO.   I did but smile till now:
  Now, good my lord, give me the scope of justice;
  My patience here is touch'd. I do perceive
  These poor informal women are no more
  But instruments of some more mightier member
  That sets them on. Let me have way, my lord,
  To find this practice out.

DUKE.   Ay, with my heart;
  And punish them unto your height of pleasure.
  Thou foolish friar, and thou pernicious woman,
  Compact with her that 's gone, think'st thou thy oaths,
  Though they would swear down each particular saint,
  Were testimonies against his worth and credit
  That 's seal'd in approbation? You, Lord Escalus,
  Sit with my cousin; lend him your kind pains
  To find out this abuse, whence 'tis deriv'd.
  There is another friar that set them on;
  Let him be sent for.

FRIAR PETER. Would he were here, my lord; for he indeed
　　Hath set the women on to this complaint:
　　Your provost knows the place where he abides
　　And he may fetch him.

DUKE.　　　　　　　　　Go do it instantly.   *Exit Provost*
　　And you, my noble and well-warranted cousin,
　　Whom it concerns to hear this matter forth,
　　Do with your injuries as seems you best,
　　In any chastisement: I for awhile will leave you;
　　But stir not you, till you have well determin'd
　　Upon these slanderers.

ESCALUS. My lord, we'll do it throughly.—　　*Exit Duke*
　　Signior Lucio, did not you say you knew that Friar Lodo-
　　wick to be a dishonest person?

LUCIO. Cucullus non facit monachum: honest in nothing,
　　but in his clothes; and one that hath spoke most villanous
　　speeches of the duke.

ESCALUS. We shall entreat you to abide here till he come
　　and enforce them against him. We shall find this friar a
　　notable fellow.

LUCIO. As any in Vienna, on my word.

ESCALUS. Call that same Isabel here once again: I would
　　speak with her. (*Exit an Attendant*) Pray you, my lord,
　　give me leave to question; you shall see how I'll handle
　　her.

LUCIO. Not better than he, by her own report.

ESCALUS. Say you?

LUCIO. Marry, sir, I think, if you handled her privately, she
　　would sooner confess: perchance, publicly, she'll be
　　ashamed.

ESCALUS. I will go darkly to work with her.

LUCIO. That's the way: for women are light at midnight.

　　　　　Re-enter Officers with Isabella

ESCALUS. (*To Isabella*) Come on, mistress: here's a gentle-
　　woman denies all that you have said.

LUCIO. My lord, here comes the rascal I spoke of; here with
　　the provost.

ESCALUS. In very good time: speak not you to him, till we
　　call upon you.

　　　　Enter Duke, disguised as a friar, and Provost

LUCIO. Mum.

ESCALUS. Come, sir. Did you set these women on to slander
  Lord Angelo? They have confessed you did.
DUKE. 'Tis false.
ESCALUS. How! know you where you are?
DUKE. Respect to your great place! and let the devil
  Be sometime honour'd for his burning throne.
  Where is the duke? 'Tis he should hear me speak.
ESCALUS. The duke 's in us, and we will hear you speak:
  Look you speak justly.
DUKE. Boldly, at least. But, O, poor souls!
  Come you to seek the lamb here of the fox?
  Good-night to your redress! Is the duke gone?
  Then is your cause gone too. The duke 's unjust,
  Thus to retort your manifest appeal,
  And put your trial in the villain's mouth
  Which here you come to accuse.
LUCIO. This is the rascal: this is he I spoke of.
ESCALUS. Why, thou unreverend and unhallow'd friar!
  Is 't not enough thou hast suborn'd these women
  To accuse this worthy man, but, in foul mouth,
  And in the witness of his proper ear,
  To call him villain?
  And then to glance from him to the duke himself,
  To tax him with injustice? Take him hence;
  To the rack with him! We 'll touse you joint by joint,
  But we will know his purpose. What! 'unjust'?
DUKE. Be not so hot; the duke
  Dare no more stretch this finger of mine than he
  Dare rack his own: his subject am I not,
  Nor here provincial. My business in this state
  Made me a looker-on here in Vienna,
  Where I have seen corruption boil and bubble
  Till it o'er-run the stew: laws for all faults,
  But faults so countenanc'd, that the strong statutes
  Stand like the forfeits in a barber's shop,
  As much in mock as mark.
ESCALUS. Slander to the state! Away with him to prison!
ANGELO. What can you vouch against him, Signior Lucio?
  Is this the man that you did tell us of?
LUCIO. 'Tis he, my lord. Come hither, goodman bald-pate:
  do you know me?

DUKE. I remember you, sir, by the sound of your voice: I
met you at the prison, in the absence of the duke.

LUCIO. O! did you so? And do you remember what you said
of the duke?

DUKE. Most notedly, sir.

LUCIO. Do you so, sir? And was the duke a flesh-monger, a
fool, and a coward, as you then reported him to be?

DUKE. You must, sir, change persons with me, ere you make
that my report: you, indeed, spoke so of him; and much
more, much worse.

LUCIO. O thou damnable fellow! Did not I pluck thee by
the nose for thy speeches?

DUKE. I protest I love the duke as I love myself.

ANGELO. Hark how the villain would close now, after his
treasonable abuses!

ESCALUS. Such a fellow is not to be talk'd withal.
Away with him to prison! Where is the provost?
Away with him to prison! Lay bolts enough on him, let
him speak no more. Away with those giglots too, and
with the other confederate companion!

                          The Provost lays hands on the Duke

DUKE. Stay, sir; stay awhile.

ANGELO. What! resists he? Help him, Lucio.

LUCIO. Come, sir; come, sir; come, sir; foh! sir. Why, you
bald-pated, lying rascal, you must be hooded, must you?
show your knave's visage, with a pox to you! show your
sheep-biting face, and be hanged an hour! Will 't not off?

                Pulls off the friar's hood, and discovers the Duke

DUKE. Thou art the first knave that e'er made a duke.
First, provost, let me bail these gentle three.
(*To Lucio*) Sneak not away, sir; for the friar and you
Must have a word anon. Lay hold on him.

LUCIO. This may prove worse than hanging.

DUKE. (*To Escalus*) What you have spoke I pardon; sit you
down:
We 'll borrow place of him. (*To Angelo*) Sir, by your
leave.
Hast thou or word, or wit, or impudence,
That yet can do thee office? If thou hast,
Rely upon it till my tale be heard,
And hold no longer out.

ANGELO.   O my dread lord!

I should be guiltier than my guiltiness,
To think I can be undiscernible
When I perceive your Grace, like power divine,
Hath look'd upon my passes. Then, good prince,
No longer session hold upon my shame,
But let my trial be mine own confession:
Immediate sentence then and sequent death
Is all the grace I beg.

DUKE.   Come hither, Mariana.
Say, wast thou e'er contracted to this woman?

ANGELO. I was, my lord.

DUKE. Go take her hence, and marry her instantly.
Do you the office, friar; which consummate,
Return him here again. Go with him, provost.

          Exeunt Angelo, Mariana, Friar Peter, and Provost

ESCALUS. My lord, I am more amaz'd at his dishonour
Than at the strangeness of it.

DUKE.   Come hither, Isabel.
Your friar is now your prince: as I was then
Advertising and holy to your business,
Not changing heart with habit, I am still
Attorney'd at your service.

ISABELLA.   O, give me pardon,
That I, your vassal, have employ'd and pain'd
Your unknown sovereignty!

DUKE.   You are pardon'd, Isabel:
And now, dear maid, be you as free to us.
Your brother's death, I know, sits at your heart;
And you may marvel why I obscur'd myself,
Labouring to save his life, and would not rather
Make rash remonstrance of my hidden power
Than let him so be lost. O most kind maid!
It was the swift celerity of his death,
Which I did think with slower foot came on,
That brain'd my purpose: but, peace be with him!
That life is better life, past fearing death,
Than that which lives to fear: make it your comfort,
So happy is your brother.

ISABELLA.   I do, my lord.

          Re-enter Angelo, Mariana, Friar Peter, and Provost

DUKE. For this new-married man approaching here,
Whose salt imagination yet hath wrong'd

Your well-defended honour, you must pardon
For Mariana's sake. But as he adjudg'd your brother,—
Being criminal, in double violation
Of sacred chastity, and of promise-breach,
Thereon dependent, for your brother's life,—
The very mercy of the law cries out
Most audible, even from his proper tongue,
'An Angelo for Claudio, death for death!'
Haste still pays haste, and leisure answers leisure,
Like doth quit like, and Measure still for Measure.
Then, Angelo, thy fault 's thus manifested,
Which, though thou wouldst deny, denies thee vantage.
We do condemn thee to the very block
Where Claudio stoop'd to death, and with like haste.
Away with him!

MARIANA.   O, my most gracious lord!
I hope you will not mock me with a husband.

DUKE. It is your husband mock'd you with a husband.
Consenting to the safeguard of your honour,
I thought your marriage fit; else imputation,
For that he knew you, might reproach your life
And choke your good to come. For his possessions,
Although by confiscation they are ours,
We do instate and widow you withal,
To buy you a better husband.

MARIANA.   O my dear lord!
I crave no other, nor no better man.

DUKE. Never crave him; we are definitive.

MARIANA. (*Kneeling*) Gentle my liege—

DUKE.   You do but lose your labour.
Away with him to death! (*To Lucio*) Now, sir, to you.

MARIANA. O my good lord! Sweet Isabel, take my part:
Lend me your knees, and, all my life to come,
I 'll lend you all my life to do you service.

DUKE. Against all sense you do importune her:
Should she kneel down in mercy of this fact,
Her brother's ghost his paved bed would break,
And take her hence in horror.

MARIANA.   Isabel,
Sweet Isabel, do yet but kneel by me:
Hold up your hands, say nothing, I 'll speak all.
They say best men are moulded out of faults,

And, for the most, become much more the better
For being a little bad: so may my husband.
O, Isabel! will you not lend a knee?

DUKE. He dies for Claudio's death.

ISABELLA.   (*Kneeling*) Most bounteous sir,
Look, if it please you, on this man condemn'd,
As if my brother liv'd. I partly think
A due sincerity govern'd his deeds,
Till he did look on me: since it is so,
Let him not die. My brother had but justice,
In that he did the thing for which he died:
For Angelo,
His act did not o'ertake his bad intent;
And must be buried but as an intent
That perish'd by the way. Thoughts are no subjects;
Intents but merely thoughts.

MARIANA.   Merely, my lord.

DUKE. Your suit's unprofitable: stand up, I say.
I have bethought me of another fault.
Provost, how came it Claudio was beheaded
At an unusual hour?

PROVOST.   It was commanded so.

DUKE. Had you a special warrant for the deed?

PROVOST. No, my good lord; it was by private message.

DUKE. For which I do discharge you of your office:
Give up your keys.

PROVOST.   Pardon me, noble lord:
I thought it was a fault, but knew it not,
Yet did repent me, after more advice;
For testimony whereof, one in the prison,
That should by private order else have died
I have reserv'd alive.

DUKE.   What's he?

PROVOST.   His name is Barnardine.

DUKE. I would thou hadst done so by Claudio.
Go, fetch him hither: let me look upon him. *Exit Provost*

ESCALUS. I am sorry, one so learned and so wise
As you, Lord Angelo, have still appear'd,
Should slip so grossly, both in the heat of blood,
And lack of temper'd judgment afterward.

ANGELO. I am sorry that such sorrow I procure;
And so deep sticks it in my penitent heart

That I crave death more willingly than mercy:
'Tis my deserving, and I do entreat it.

Re-enter Provost,
with Barnardine, Claudio muffled, and Juliet

DUKE. Which is that Barnardine?

PROVOST.   This, my lord.

DUKE. There was a friar told me of this man.
Sirrah, thou art said to have a stubborn soul,
That apprehends no further than this world,
And squar'st thy life according. Thou 'rt condemn'd:
But, for those earthly faults, I quit them all,
And pray thee take this mercy to provide
For better times to come. Friar, advise him:
I leave him to your hand.—What muffled fellow 's that?

PROVOST. This is another prisoner that I sav'd,
That should have died when Claudio lost his head,
As like almost to Claudio as himself.   *Unmuffles Claudio*

DUKE. (*To Isabella*) If he be like your brother, for his sake
Is he pardon'd; and, for your lovely sake
Give me your hand, and say you will be mine,
He is my brother too. But fitter time for that.
By this, Lord Angelo perceives he 's safe:
Methinks I see a quickening in his eye.
Well, Angelo, your evil quits you well:
Look that you love your wife; her worth worth yours.—
I find an apt remission in myself,
And yet here 's one in place I cannot pardon.—
(*To Lucio*) You, sirrah, that knew me for a fool, a cow-
ard;
One all of luxury, an ass, a madman:
Wherein have I so deserv'd of you,
That you extol me thus?

LUCIO. 'Faith, my lord, I spoke it but according to the trick.
If you will hang me for it, you may; but I had rather it
would please you I might be whipped.

DUKE. Whipp'd first, sir, and hang'd after.
Proclaim it, provost, round about the city,
If any woman 's wrong'd by this lewd fellow,—
As I have heard him swear himself there 's one
Whom he begot with child, let her appear,
And he shall marry her: the nuptial finish'd,
Let him be whipp'd and hang'd.

LUCIO. I beseech your Highness, do not marry me to a
whore. Your Highness said even now, I made you a duke:
good my lord, do not recompense me in making me a
cuckold.

DUKE. Upon mine honour, thou shalt marry her.
Thy slanders I forgive; and therewithal
Remit thy other forfeits. Take him to prison,
And see our pleasure herein executed.

LUCIO. Marrying a punk, my lord, is pressing to death,
whipping, and hanging.

DUKE. Slandering a prince deserves it.
She, Claudio, that you wrong'd, look you restore.
Joy to you, Mariana! love her, Angelo:
I have confess'd her and I know her virtue.
Thanks, good friend Escalus, for thy much goodness:
There 's more behind that is more gratulate.
Thanks, provost, for thy care and secrecy;
We shall employ thee in a worthier place.
Forgive him, Angelo, that brought you home
The head of Ragozine for Claudio's:
The offence pardons itself. Dear Isabel,
I have a motion much imports your good;
Whereto if you 'll a willing ear incline,
What 's mine is yours, and what is yours is mine.
So, bring us to our palace; where we 'll show
What 's yet behind, that 's meet you all should know.

Exeunt

DUKE. Slander'd so? punish I see to it—

THE COMEDY OF ERRORS

SCENE

Ephesus

THE COMEDY OF ERRORS

CAST OF CHARACTERS

Solinus, Duke of Ephesus
Ægeon, a Merchant of Syracuse
Antipholus of Ephesus, Twin Brothers, sons to
Antipholus of Syracuse, Ægeon and Æmilia
Dromio of Ephesus, Twin Brothers, attendants on
Dromio of Syracuse, the two Antipholuses
Balthazar, a Merchant
Angelo, a Goldsmith
Merchant, Friend to Antipholus of Syracuse
A Second Merchant, to whom Angelo is a debtor
Pinch, a Schoolmaster and a Conjurer
Æmilia, Wife to Ægeon, an Abbess at Ephesus
Adriana, Wife to Antipholus of Ephesus
Luciana, her Sister
Luce, Servant to Adriana
A Courtezan
Gaoler, Officers, and other Attendants

THE COMEDY OF ERRORS

SCENE ONE

A Hall in the Duke's Palace.

Enter Duke, Ægeon, Gaoler, Officers, and other Attendants

ÆGEON. Proceed, Solinus, to procure my fall,
    And by the doom of death end woes and all.
DUKE. Merchant of Syracusa, plead no more.
    I am not partial to infringe our laws:
    The enmity and discord which of late
    Sprung from the rancorous outrage of your duke
    To merchants, our well-dealing countrymen,
    Who, wanting guilders to redeem their lives,
    Have seal'd his rigorous statutes with their bloods,
    Excludes all pity from our threat'ning looks.
    For, since the mortal and intestine jars
    'Twixt thy seditious conutrymen and us,
    It hath in solemn synods been decreed,
    Both by the Syracusians and ourselves,
    T' admit no traffic to our adverse towns:
    Nay, more, if any, born at Ephesus
    Be seen at Syracusian marts and fairs;
    Again, if any Syracusian born
    Come to the bay of Ephesus, he dies,
    His goods confiscate to the duke's dispose;
    Unless a thousand marks be levied,
    To quit the penalty and to ransom him.
    Thy substance, valu'd at the highest rate,
    Cannot amount unto a hundred marks;
    Therefore, by law thou art condemn'd to die.
ÆGEON. Yet this my comfort: when your words are done,

My woes end likewise with the evening sun.
DUKE. Well, Syracusian; say, in brief the cause
Why thou departedst from thy native home,
And for what cause thou cam'st to Ephesus.
ÆGEON. A heavier task could not have been impos'd
Than I to speak my griefs unspeakable;
Yet, that the world may witness that my end
Was wrought by nature, not by vile offence,
I 'll utter what my sorrow gives me leave.
In Syracusa was I born, and wed
Unto a woman, happy but for me,
And by me too, had not our hap been bad.
With her I liv'd in joy: our wealth increas'd
By prosperous voyages I often made
To Epidamnum; till my factor's death,
And the great care of goods at random left,
Drew me from kind embracements of my spouse:
From whom my absence was not six months old,
Before herself,—almost at fainting under
The pleasing punishment that women bear,—
Had made provision for her following me,
And soon and safe arrived where I was.
There had she not been long but she became
A joyful mother of two goodly sons;
And, which was strange, the one so like the other,
As could not be distinguish'd but by names.
That very hour, and in the self-same inn,
A meaner woman was delivered
Of such a burden, male twins, both alike.
Those,—for their parents were exceeding poor,—
I bought, and brought up to attend my sons.
My wife, not meanly proud of two such boys,
Made daily motions for our home return:
Unwilling I agreed; alas! too soon
We came aboard.
A league from Epidamnum had we sail'd,
Before the always-wind-obeying deep
Gave any tragic instance of our harm:
But longer did we not retain much hope;
For what obscured light the heavens did grant
Did but convey unto our fearful minds
A doubtful warrant of immediate death;

Which, though myself would gladly have embrac'd,
Yet the incessant weepings of my wife,
Weeping before for what she saw must come,
And piteous plainings of the pretty babes,
That mourn'd for fashion, ignorant what to fear,
Forc'd me to seek delays for them and me.
And this it was, for other means was none:
The sailors sought for safety by our boat,
And left the ship, then sinking-ripe, to us:
My wife, more careful for the latter-born,
Had fasten'd him unto a small spare mast,
Such as seafaring men provide for storms;
To him one of the other twins was bound,
Whilst I had been like heedful of the other.
The children thus dispos'd, my wife and I,
Fixing our eyes on whom our care was fix'd,
Fasten'd ourselves at either end the mast;
And floating straight, obedient to the stream,
Were carried towards Corinth, as we thought.
At length the sun, gazing upon the earth,
Dispers'd those vapours that offended us;
And, by the benefit of his wished light
The seas wax'd calm, and we discovered
Two ships from far making amain to us;
Of Corinth that, of Epidaurus this:
But ere they came,—O! let me say no more;
Gather the sequel by that went before.

DUKE. Nay, forward, old man; do not break off so;
For we may pity, though not pardon thee.

ÆGEON. O! had the gods done so, I had not now
Worthily term'd them merciless to us!
For, ere the ships could meet by twice five leagues,
We were encounter'd by a mighty rock;
Which, being violently borne upon,
Our helpful ship was splitted in the midst;
So that, in this unjust divorce of us
Fortune had left to both of us alike
What to delight in, what to sorrow for.
Her part, poor soul! seeming as burdened
With lesser weight, but not with lesser woe,
Was carried with more speed before the wind,
And in our sight they three were taken up

By fishermen of Corinth, as we thought.
At length, another ship had seized on us,
And, knowing whom it was their hap to save,
Gave healthful welcome to their ship-wrack'd guests;
And would have reft the fishers of their prey,
Had not their bark been very slow of sail;
And therefore homeward did they bend their course.
Thus have you heard me sever'd from my bliss,
That by misfortune was my life prolong'd,
To tell sad stories of my own mishaps.

DUKE. And, for the sake of them thou sorrowest for,
Do me the favour to dilate at full
What hath befall'n of them and thee till now.

ÆGEON. My youngest boy, and yet my eldest care,
At eighteen years became inquisitive
After his brother; and importun'd me
That his attendant—for his case was like,
Reft of his brother, but retain'd his name—
Might bear him company in the quest of him;
Whom whilst I labour'd of a love to see,
I hazarded the loss of whom I lov'd.
Five summers have I spent in furthest Greece,
Roaming clean through the bounds of Asia,
And, coasting homeward, came to Ephesus,
Hopeless to find, yet loath to leave unsought
Or that or any place that harbours men.
But here must end the story of my life;
And happy were I in my timely death,
Could all my travels warrant me they live.

DUKE. Hapless Ægeon, whom the fates have mark'd
To bear the extremity of dire mishap!
Now, trust me, were it not against our laws,
Against my crown, my oath, my dignity,
Which princes, would they, may not disannul,
My soul should sue as advocate for thee.
But though thou art adjudged to the death
And passed sentence may not be recall'd
But to our honour's great disparagement,
Yet will I favour thee in what I can:
Therefore, merchant, I 'll limit thee this day
To seek thy life by beneficial help.
Try all the friends thou hast in Ephesus;

Beg thou, or borrow, to make up the sum,
And live; if no, then thou art doom'd to die.
Gaoler, take him to thy custody

GAOLER. I will, my lord.

ÆGEON. Hopeless and helpless doth Ægeon wend,
But to procrastinate his lifeless end.   *Exeunt*

SCENE TWO

The Mart.

*Enter Antipholus of Syracuse, Dromio of Syracuse,
and a Merchant*

MERCHANT. Therefore, give out you are of Epidamnum,
Lest that your goods too soon be confiscate.
This very day, a Syracusian merchant
Is apprehended for arrival here;
And, not being able to buy out his life,
According to the statute of the town,
Dies ere the weary sun set in the west.
There is your money that I had to keep.

ANTIPHOLUS OF SYRACUSE. Go bear it to the Centaur, where
we host,
And stay there, Dromio, till I come to thee.
Within this hour it will be dinner-time:
Till that, I 'll view the manners of the town,
Peruse the traders, gaze upon the buildings,
And then return and sleep within mine inn,
For with long travel I am stiff and weary.
Get thee away.

DROMIO OF SYRACUSE. Many a man would take you at your
word,
And go indeed, having so good a mean.   *Exit*

ANTIPHOLUS OF SYRACUSE. A trusty villain, sir, that very oft,
When I am dull with care and melancholy,
Lightens my humour with his merry jests.
What, will you walk with me about the town,
And then go to my inn and dine with me?

MERCHANT. I am invited, sir, to certain merchants,
Of whom I hope to make much benefit;
I crave your pardon. Soon at five o'clock,

Please you, I 'll meet with you upon the mart,
And afterward consort you till bed-time:
My present business calls me from you now.

ANTIPHOLUS OF SYRACUSE. Farewell till then: I will go lose
 myself,
And wander up and down to view the city.

MERCHANT. Sir, I commend you to your own content. *Exit*

ANTIPHOLUS OF SYRACUSE. He that commends me to mine
 own content,
Commends me to the thing I cannot get.
I to the world am like a drop of water
That in the ocean seeks another drop;
Who, falling there to find his fellow forth,
Unseen, inquisitive, confounds himself:
So I, to find a mother and a brother,
In quest of them, unhappy, lose myself.

    Enter Dromio of Ephesus

Here comes the almanack of my true date.
What now? How chance thou art return'd so soon?

DROMIO OF EPHESUS. Return'd so soon! rather approach'd
 too late:
The capon burns, the pig falls from the spit,
The clock hath strucken twelve upon the bell;
My mistress made it one upon my cheek:
She is so hot because the meat is cold;
The meat is cold because you come not home;
You come not home because you have no stomach;
You have no stomach, having broke your fast;
But we, that know what 'tis to fast and pray,
Are penitent for your default to-day.

ANTIPHOLUS OF SYRACUSE. Stop in your wind, sir: tell me
 this, I pray:
Where have you left the money that I gave you?

DROMIO OF EPHESUS. O!—sixpence, that I had o' Wednesday
 last
To pay the saddler for my mistress' crupper;
The saddler had it, sir; I kept it not.

ANTIPHOLUS OF SYRACUSE. I am not in a sportive humour
 now.
Tell me, and dally not, where is the money?
We being strangers here, how dar'st thou trust
So great a charge from thine own custody?

DROMIO OF EPHESUS. I pray you, jest, sir, as you sit at
 dinner.
 I from my mistress come to you in post;
 If I return, I shall be post indeed,
 For she will score your fault upon my pate.
 Methinks your maw, like mine, should be your clock
 And strike you home without a messenger.
ANTIPHOLUS OF SYRACUSE. Come, Dromio, come; these jests
 are out of season;
 Reserve them till a merrier hour than this.
 Where is the gold I gave in charge to thee?
DROMIO OF EPHESUS. To me, sir? why, you gave no gold to
 me.
ANTIPHOLUS OF SYRACUSE. Come on, sir knave, have done
 your foolishness,
 And tell me how thou hast dispos'd thy charge.
DROMIO OF EPHESUS. My charge was but to fetch you from
 the mart
 Home to your house, the Phœnix, sir, to dinner:
 My mistress and her sister stays for you.
ANTIPHOLUS OF SYRACUSE. Now, as I am a Christian,
 answer me,
 In what safe place you have bestow'd my money:
 Or I shall break that merry sconce of yours
 That stands on tricks when I am undispos'd.
 Where is the thousand marks thou hadst of me?
DROMIO OF EPHESUS. I have some marks of yours upon my
 pate,
 Some of my mistress' marks upon my shoulders,
 But not a thousand marks between you both.
 If I should pay your worship those again,
 Perchance you will not bear them patiently.
ANTIPHOLUS OF SYRACUSE. Thy mistress' marks! what mis-
 tress, slave, hast thou?
DROMIO OF EPHESUS. Your worship's wife, my mistress at
 the Phœnix;
 She that doth fast till you come home to dinner,
 And prays that you will hie you home to dinner.
ANTIPHOLUS OF SYRACUSE. What! wilt thou flout me thus
 unto my face,
 Being forbid? There, take you that, sir knave. *Strikes him*

DROMIO OF EPHESUS. What mean you, sir? for God's sake,
 hold your hands!
 Nay, an you will not, sir, I 'll take my heels.   *Exit*
ANTIPHOLUS OF SYRACUSE. Upon my life, by some device or
 other
 The villain is o'er-raught of all my money.
 They say this town is full of cozenage;
 As, nimble jugglers that deceive the eye,
 Dark-working sorcerers that change the mind,
 Soul-killing witches that deform the body,
 Disguised cheaters, prating mountebanks,
 And many such-like liberties of sin:
 If it prove so, I will be gone the sooner.
 I 'll to the Centaur, to go seek this slave:
 I greatly fear my money is not safe.   *Exit*

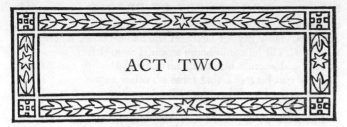

ACT TWO

SCENE ONE

The House of Antipholus of Ephesus.

Enter Adriana and Luciana

ADRIANA. Neither my husband, nor the slave return'd,
  That in such haste I sent to seek his master!
  Sure, Luciana, it is two o'clock.

LUCIANA. Perhaps some merchant hath invited him,
  And from the mart he 's somewhere gone to dinner.
  Good sister, let us dine and never fret:
  A man is master of his liberty:
  Time is their master, and, when they see time,
  They 'll go or come: if so, be patient, sister.

ADRIANA. Why should their liberty than ours be more?

LUCIANA. Because their business still lies out o' door.

ADRIANA. Look, when I serve him so, he takes it ill.

LUCIANA. O! know he is the bridle of your will.

ADRIANA. There 's none but asses will be bridled so.

LUCIANA. Why, headstrong liberty is lash'd with woe.
  There 's nothing situate under heaven's eye
  But hath his bound, in earth, in sea, in sky:
  The beasts, the fishes, and the winged fowls,
  Are their males' subject and at their controls.
  Men, more divine, the masters of all these,
  Lords of the wide world, and wild wat'ry seas,
  Indu'd with intellectual sense and souls,
  Of more pre-eminence than fish and fowls,
  Are masters to their females and their lords:
  Then, let your will attend on their accords.

ADRIANA. This servitude makes you to keep unwed.

LUCIANA. Not this, but troubles of the marriage-bed.

ADRIANA. But, were you wedded, you would bear some
  sway.

LUCIANA. Ere I learn love, I 'll practise to obey.

ADRIANA. How if your husband start some other where?

LUCIANA. Till he come home again, I would forbear.

ADRIANA. Patience unmov'd! no marvel though she pause;
They can be meek that have no other cause.
A wretched soul, bruis'd with adversity,
We bid be quiet when we hear it cry;
But were we burden'd with like weight of pain,
As much, or more, we should ourselves complain:
So thou, that hast no unkind mate to grieve thee,
With urging helpless patience wouldst relieve me:
But if thou live to see like right bereft,
This fool-begged patience in thee will be left.

LUCIANA. Well, I will marry one day, but to try.
Here comes your man: now is your husband nigh.

Enter Dromio of Ephesus

ADRIANA. Say, is your tardy master now at hand?

DROMIO OF EPHESUS. Nay, he 's at two hands with me, and
that my two ears can witness.

ADRIANA. Say, didst thou speak with him? Know'st thou his
mind?

DROMIO OF EPHESUS. Ay, ay, he told his mind upon mine
ear.
Beshrew his hand, I scarce could understand it.

LUCIANA. Spake he so doubtfully, thou couldst not feel his
meaning?

DROMIO OF EPHESUS. Nay, he struck so plainly, I could too
well feel his blows; and withal so doubtfully, that I could
scarce understand them.

ADRIANA. But say, I prithee, is he coming home?
It seems he hath great care to please his wife.

DROMIO OF EPHESUS. Why, mistress, sure my master is
horn-mad.

ADRIANA. Horn-mad, thou villain!

DROMIO OF EPHESUS. I mean not cuckold-mad; but, sure, he
is stark mad.
When I desir'd him to come home to dinner,
He ask'd me for a thousand marks in gold:
' 'Tis dinner time,' quoth I; 'my gold!' quoth he:
'Your meat doth burn,' quoth I; 'my gold!' quoth he:
'Will you come home?' quoth I: 'my gold!' quoth he:
'Where is the thousand marks I gave thee, villain?'

'The pig,' quoth I, 'is burn'd;' 'my gold!' quoth he:
'My mistress, sir,' quoth I: 'hang up thy mistress!
I know not thy mistress: out on thy mistress!'

LUCIANA.   Quoth who?

DROMIO OF EPHESUS.   Quoth my master:
'I know,' quoth he, 'no house, no wife, no mistress.'
So that my errand, due unto my tongue,
I thank him, I bear home upon my shoulders;
For, in conclusion, he did beat me there.

ADRIANA.   Go back again, thou slave, and fetch him home.

DROMIO OF EPHESUS.   Go back again, and be now beaten
    home?
For God's sake, send some other messenger.

ADRIANA.   Back, slave, or I will break thy pate across.

DROMIO OF EPHESUS.   And he will bless that cross with other
    beating:
Between you, I shall have a holy head.

ADRIANA.   Hence, prating peasant! fetch thy master home.

DROMIO OF EPHESUS.   Am I so round with you as you with
    me,
That like a football you do spurn me thus?
You spurn me hence, and he will spurn me hither:
If I last in this service, you must case me in leather. *Exit*

LUCIANA.   Fie, how impatience low'reth in your face!

ADRIANA.   His company must do his minions grace,
Whilst I at home starve for a merry look.
Hath homely age the alluring beauty took
From my poor cheek? then, he hath wasted it:
Are my discourses dull? barren my wit?
If voluble and sharp discourse be marr'd,
Unkindness blunts it more than marble hard:
Do their gay vestments his affections bait?
That 's not my fault; he 's master of my state:
What ruins are in me that can be found
By him not ruin'd? then is he the ground
Of my defeatures. My decayed fair
A sunny look of his would soon repair;
But, too unruly deer, he breaks the pale
And feeds from home: poor I am but his stale.

LUCIANA.   Self-harming jealousy! fie! beat it hence.

ADRIANA.   Unfeeling fools can with such wrongs dispense.
I know his eye doth homage otherwhere,

Or else what lets it but he would be here?
Sister, you know he promis'd me a chain:
Would that alone, alone he would detain,
So he would keep fair quarter with his bed!
I see, the jewel best enamelled
Will lose his beauty; and though gold bides still
That others touch, yet often touching will
Wear gold; and no man that hath a name,
By falsehood and corruption doth it shame.
Since that my beauty cannot please his eye,
I 'll weep what 's left away, and weeping die.

LUCIANA. How many fond fools serve mad jealousy!

Exeunt

SCENE TWO

A public Place.

Enter Antipholus of Syracuse

ANTIPHOLUS OF SYRACUSE. The gold I gave to Dromio is
   laid up
   Safe at the Centaur; and the heedful slave
   Is wander'd forth, in care to seek me out.
   By computation, and mine host's report,
   I could not speak with Dromio since at first
   I sent him from the mart. See, here he comes.

Enter Dromio of Syracuse

   How now, sir! is your merry humour alter'd?
   As you love strokes, so jest with me again.
   You know no Centaur? You receiv'd no gold?
   Your mistress sent to have me home to dinner?
   My house was at the Phœnix? Wast thou mad,
   That thus so madly thou didst answer me?

DROMIO OF SYRACUSE. What answer, sir? when spake I such
   a word?

ANTIPHOLUS OF SYRACUSE. Even now, even here, not half-
   an-hour since.

DROMIO OF SYRACUSE. I did not see you since you sent me
   hence,
   Home to the Centaur, with the gold you gave me.

ANTIPHOLUS OF SYRACUSE. Villain, thou didst deny the
gold's receipt,

And told'st me of a mistress and a dinner;

For which, I hope, thou felt'st I was displeas'd.

DROMIO OF SYRACUSE. I am glad to see you in this merry
vein:

What means this jest? I pray you, master, tell me.

ANTIPHOLUS OF SYRACUSE. Yea, dost thou jeer, and flout
me in the teeth?

Think'st thou I jest? Hold, take thou that, and that.

Beating him

DROMIO OF SYRACUSE. Hold, sir, for God's sake! now your
jest is earnest:

Upon what bargain do you give it me?

ANTIPHOLUS OF SYRACUSE. Because that I familiarly sometimes

Do use you for my fool, and chat with you,

Your sauciness will jest upon my love,

And make a common of my serious hours.

When the sun shines let foolish gnats make sport,

But creep in crannies when he hides his beams.

If you will jest with me, know my aspect,

And fashion your demeanour to my looks,

Or I will beat this method in your sconce.

DROMIO OF SYRACUSE. Sconce, call you it? so you would
leave battering, I had rather have it a head: an you use
these blows long, I must get a sconce for my head and
insconce it too; or else I shall seek my wit in my shoulders. But, I pray, sir, why am I beaten?

ANTIPHOLUS OF SYRACUSE. Dost thou not know?

DROMIO OF SYRACUSE. Nothing, sir, but that I am beaten.

ANTIPHOLUS OF SYRACUSE. Shall I tell you why?

DROMIO OF SYRACUSE. Ay, sir, and wherefore; for they say
every why hath a wherefore.

ANTIPHOLUS OF SYRACUSE. Why, first,—for flouting me; and
then, wherefore,—

For urging it the second time to me.

DROMIO OF SYRACUSE. Was there ever any man thus beaten
out of season,

When, in the why and the wherefore is neither rime nor
reason?

Well, sir, I thank you.

ANTIPHOLUS OF SYRACUSE. Thank me, sir! for what?

DROMIO OF SYRACUSE. Marry, sir, for this something that you gave me for nothing.

ANTIPHOLUS OF SYRACUSE. I 'll make you amends next, to give you nothing for something. But say, sir, is it dinner-time?

DROMIO OF SYRACUSE. No, sir: I think the meat wants that I have.

ANTIPHOLUS OF SYRACUSE. In good time, sir; what 's that?

DROMIO OF SYRACUSE. Basting.

ANTIPHOLUS OF SYRACUSE. Well, sir, then 'twill be dry.

DROMIO OF SYRACUSE. If it be, sir, I pray you eat none of it.

ANTIPHOLUS OF SYRACUSE. Your reason?

DROMIO OF SYRACUSE. Lest it make you choleric, and pur-chase me another dry basting.

ANTIPHOLUS OF SYRACUSE. Well, sir, learn to jest in good time: there 's a time for all things.

DROMIO OF SYRACUSE. I durst have denied that, before you were so choleric.

ANTIPHOLUS OF SYRACUSE. By what rule, sir?

DROMIO OF SYRACUSE. Marry, sir, by a rule as plain as the plain bald pate of Father Time himself.

ANTIPHOLUS OF SYRACUSE. Let 's hear it.

DROMIO OF SYRACUSE. There 's no time for a man to recover his hair that grows bald by nature.

ANTIPHOLUS OF SYRACUSE. May he not do it by fine and re-covery?

DROMIO OF SYRACUSE. Yes, to pay a fine for a periwig and recover the lost hair of another man.

ANTIPHOLUS OF SYRACUSE. Why is Time such a niggard of hair, being, as it is, so plentiful an excrement?

DROMIO OF SYRACUSE. Because it is a blessing that he be-stows on beasts: and what he hath scanted men in hair, he hath given them in wit.

ANTIPHOLUS OF SYRACUSE. Why, but there 's many a man hath more hair than wit.

DROMIO OF SYRACUSE. Not a man of those but he hath the wit to lose his hair.

ANTIPHOLUS OF SYRACUSE. Why, thou didst conclude hairy men plain dealers without wit.

DROMIO OF SYRACUSE. The plainer dealer, the sooner lost: yet he loseth it in a kind of jollity.

ANTIPHOLUS OF SYRACUSE. For what reason?

DROMIO OF SYRACUSE. For two; and sound ones too.

ANTIPHOLUS OF SYRACUSE. Nay, not sound, I pray you.

DROMIO OF SYRACUSE. Sure ones then.

ANTIPHOLUS OF SYRACUSE. Nay, not sure, in a thing falsing.

DROMIO OF SYRACUSE. Certain ones then.

ANTIPHOLUS OF SYRACUSE. Name them.

DROMIO OF SYRACUSE. The one, to save the money that he spends in tiring; the other, that at dinner they should not drop in his porridge.

ANTIPHOLUS OF SYRACUSE. You would all this time have proved there is no time for all things.

DROMIO OF SYRACUSE. Marry, and did, sir; namely, no time to recover hair lost by nature.

ANTIPHOLUS OF SYRACUSE. But your reason was not substantial, why there is no time to recover.

DROMIO OF SYRACUSE. Thus I mend it: Time himself is bald, and therefore to the world's end will have bald followers.

ANTIPHOLUS OF SYRACUSE. I knew 'twould be a bald conclusion. But soft! Who wafts us yonder?

Enter Adriana and Luciana

ADRIANA. Ay, ay, Antipholus, look strange, and frown:
Some other mistress hath thy sweet aspects,
I am not Adriana, nor thy wife.
The time was once when thou unurg'd wouldst vow
That never words were music to thine ear,
That never object pleasing in thine eye,
That never touch well welcome to thy hand,
That never meat sweet-savour'd in thy taste,
Unless I spake, or look'd, or touch'd, or carv'd to thee.
How comes it now, my husband, O! how comes it,
That thou art thus estranged from thyself?
Thyself I call it, being strange to me,
That, undividable, incorporate,
Am better than thy dear self's better part.
Ah! do not tear away thyself from me,
For know, my love, as easy mayst thou fall
A drop of water in the breaking gulf,
And take unmingled thence that drop again,
Without addition or diminishing,
As take from me thyself and not me too.

How dearly would it touch thee to the quick,
Shouldst thou but hear I were licentious,
And that this body, consecrate to thee,
By ruffian lust should be contaminate!
Wouldst thou not spit at me and spurn at me,
And hurl the name of husband in my face,
And tear the stain'd skin off my harlet-brow,
And from my false hand cut the wedding-ring
And break it with a deep-divorcing vow?
I know thou canst; and therefore, see thou do it.
I am possess'd with an adulterate blot;
My blood is mingled with the crime of lust:
For if we two be one and thou play false,
I do digest the poison of thy flesh,
Being strumpeted by thy contagion.
Keep then fair league and truce with thy true bed;
I live unstain'd, thou undishonoured.

ANTIPHOLUS OF SYRACUSE. Plead you to me, fair dame? I
    know you not:
In Ephesus I am but two hours old,
As strange unto your town as to your talk;
Who, every word by all my wit being scann'd,
Want wit in all one word to understand.

LUCIANA. Fie, brother: how the world is chang'd with you!
When were you wont to use my sister thus?
She sent for you by Dromio home to dinner.

ANTIPHOLUS OF SYRACUSE. By Dromio?

DROMIO OF SYRACUSE. By me?

ADRIANA. By thee; and this thou didst return from him,
That he did buffet thee, and in his blows,
Denied my house for his, me for his wife.

ANTIPHOLUS OF SYRACUSE. Did you converse, sir, with this
    gentlewoman?
What is the course and drift of your compact?

DROMIO OF SYRACUSE. I, sir? I never saw her till this time.

ANTIPHOLUS OF SYRACUSE. Villain, thou liest; for even her
    very words
Didst thou deliver to me on the mart.

DROMIO OF SYRACUSE. I never spake with her in all my life.

ANTIPHOLUS OF SYRACUSE. How can she thus then call us by
    our names,
Unless it be by inspiration?

ADRIANA. How ill agrees it with your gravity
   To counterfeit thus grossly with your slave,
   Abetting him to thwart me in my mood!
   Be it my wrong you are from me exempt,
   But wrong not that wrong with a more contempt.
   Come, I will fasten on this sleeve of thine;
   Thou art an elm, my husband, I a vine,
   Whose weakness, married to thy stronger state,
   Makes me with thy strength to communicate:
   If aught possess thee from me, it is dross,
   Usurping ivy, brier, or idle moss;
   Who, all for want of pruning, with intrusion
   Infect thy sap and live on thy confusion.

ANTIPHOLUS OF SYRACUSE. To me she speaks; she moves me
   for her theme!
   What! was I married to her in my dream?
   Or sleep I now and think I hear all this?
   What error drives our eyes and ears amiss?
   Until I know this sure uncertainty,
   I 'll entertain the offer'd fallacy.

LUCIANA. Dromio, go bid the servants spread for dinner.

DROMIO OF SYRACUSE. O, for my beads! I cross me for a
   sinner.
   This is the fairy land: O! spite of spites,
   We talk with goblins, owls, and elvish sprites:
   If we obey them not, this will ensue,
   They 'll suck our breath, or pinch us black and blue.

LUCIANA. Why prat'st thou to thyself and answer'st not?
   Dromio, thou drone, thou snail, thou slug, thou sot!

DROMIO OF SYRACUSE. I am transformed, master, am not I?

ANTIPHOLUS OF SYRACUSE. I think thou art, in mind, and so
   am I.

DROMIO OF SYRACUSE. Nay, master, both in mind and in my
   shape.

ANTIPHOLUS OF SYRACUSE. Thou hast thine own form.

DROMIO OF SYRACUSE.   No, I am an ape.

LUCIANA. If thou art chang'd to aught, 'tis to an ass.

DROMIO OF SYRACUSE. 'Tis true; she rides me and I long for
   grass.
   'Tis so, I am an ass; else it could never be
   But I should know her as well as she knows me.

ADRIANA. Come, come; no longer will I be a fool,

To put the finger in the eye and weep,
Whilst man and master laugh my woes to scorn.
Come, sir, to dinner. Dromio, keep the gate.
Husband, I 'll dine above with you to-day,
And shrive you of a thousand idle pranks.
Sirrah, if any ask you for your master,
Say he dines forth, and let no creature enter.
Come, sister. Dromio, play the porter well.

ANTIPHOLUS OF SYRACUSE. (*Aside*) Am I in earth, in heaven,
        or in hell?
Sleeping or waking? mad or well-advis'd?
Known unto these, and to myself disguis'd!
I 'll say as they say, and persever so,
And in this mist at all adventures go.

DROMIO OF SYRACUSE. Master, shall I be porter at the gate?

ADRIANA. Ay; and let none enter, lest I break your pate.

LUCIANA. Come, come, Antipholus; we dine too late.

Exeunt

ACT THREE

SCENE ONE

Before the House of Antipholus of Ephesus.

Enter Antipholus of Ephesus, Dromio of Ephesus,
Angelo, and Balthazar.

ANTIPHOLUS OF EPHESUS. Good Signior Angelo, you must
  excuse us all;
  My wife is shrewish when I keep not hours;
  Say that I linger'd with you at your shop
  To see the making of her carkanet,
  And that to-morrow you will bring it home.
  But here 's a villain, that would face me down
  He met me on the mart, and that I beat him,
  And charg'd him with a thousand marks in gold,
  And that I did deny my wife and house.
  Thou drunkard, thou, what didst thou mean by this?
DROMIO OF EPHESUS. Say what you will, sir, but I know
  what I know;
  That you beat me at the mart, I have your hand to show:
  If the skin were parchment and the blows you gave were
  ink,
  Your own handwriting would tell you what I think.
ANTIPHOLUS OF EPHESUS. I think thou art an ass.
DROMIO OF EPHESUS.   Marry, so it doth appear
  By the wrongs I suffer and the blows I bear.
  I should kick, being kick'd; and, being at that pass,
  You would keep from my heels and beware of an ass.
ANTIPHOLUS OF EPHESUS. You are sad, Signior Balthazar:
  pray God, our cheer
  May answer my good will and your good welcome here.
BALTHAZAR. I hold your dainties cheap, sir, and your wel-
  come dear.

ANTIPHOLUS OF EPHESUS. O, Signior Balthazar, either at flesh or fish,

A table-full of welcome makes scarce one dainty dish.

BALTHAZAR. Good meat, sir, is common; that every churl affords.

ANTIPHOLUS OF EPHESUS. And welcome more common, for that 's nothing but words.

BALTHAZAR. Small cheer and great welcome makes a merry feast.

ANTIPHOLUS OF EPHESUS. Ay, to a niggardly host and more sparing guest:

But though my cates be mean, take them in good part;

Better cheer may you have, but not with better heart.

But soft! my door is lock'd. Go bid them let us in.

DROMIO OF EPHESUS. Maud, Bridget, Marian, Cicely, Gillian, Ginn!

DROMIO OF SYRACUSE. (*Within*) Mome, malt-horse, capon, coxcomb, idiot, patch!

Either get thee from the door or sit down at the hatch.

Dost thou conjure for wenches, that thou call'st for such store,

When one is one too many? Go, get thee from the door.

DROMIO OF EPHESUS. What patch is made our porter?—My master stays in the street.

DROMIO OF SYRACUSE. (*Within*) Let him walk from whence he came, lest he catch cold on 's feet.

ANTIPHOLUS OF EPHESUS. Who talks within there? ho! open the door.

DROMIO OF SYRACUSE. (*Within*) Right, sir; I 'll tell you when, an you 'll tell me wherefore.

ANTIPHOLUS OF EPHESUS. Wherefore? for my dinner: I have not din'd to-day.

DROMIO OF SYRACUSE. Nor to-day here you must not; come again when you may.

ANTIPHOLUS OF EPHESUS. What art thou that keep'st me out from the house I owe?

DROMIO OF SYRACUSE. (*Within*) The porter for this time, sir, and my name is Dromio.

DROMIO OF EPHESUS. O villain! thou hast stolen both mine office and my name:

The one ne'er got me credit, the other mickle blame.

If thou hadst been Dromio to-day in my place,

    Thou wouldst have chang'd thy face for a name, or thy
       name for an ass.

LUCE. (*Within*) What a coil is there, Dromio! who are those
     at the gate?

DROMIO OF EPHESUS. Let my master in, Luce.

LUCE. (*Within*)   Faith, no; he comes too late;
    And so tell your master.

DROMIO OF EPHESUS.   O Lord! I must laugh.
    Have at you with a proverb: Shall I set in my staff?

LUCE. (*Within*) Have at you with another: that 's—when?
     can you tell?

DROMIO OF SYRACUSE. (*Within*) If thy name be call'd Luce,
    —Luce, thou hast answer'd him well.

ANTIPHOLUS OF EPHESUS. Do you hear, you minion? you 'll
     let us in, I trow?

LUCE. (*Within*) I thought to have ask'd you.

DROMIO OF SYRACUSE. (*Within*)   And you said, no.

DROMIO OF EPHESUS. So come, help: well struck! there was
     blow for blow.

ANTIPHOLUS OF EPHESUS. Thou baggage, let me in.

LUCE. (*Within*) Can you tell for whose sake?

DROMIO OF EPHESUS. Master, knock the door hard.

LUCE. (*Within*) Let him knock till it ache.

ANTIPHOLUS OF EPHESUS. You 'll cry for this, minion, if I beat
     the door down.

LUCE. (*Within*) What needs all that, and a pair of stocks
     in the town?

ADRIANA. (*Within*) Who is that at the door that keeps all
     this noise?

DROMIO OF SYRACUSE. (*Within*) By my troth your town is
     troubled with unruly boys.

ANTIPHOLUS OF EPHESUS. Are you there, wife? you might
     have come before.

ADRIANA. (*Within*) Your wife, sir knave! go, get you from
     the door.

DROMIO OF EPHESUS. If you went in pain, master, this
     'knave' would go sore.

ANGELO. Here is neither cheer, sir, nor welcome: we would
     fain have either.

BALTHAZAR. In debating which was best, we shall part
     with neither.

DROMIO OF EPHESUS. They stand at the door, master: bid
    them welcome hither.

ANTIPHOLUS OF EPHESUS. There is something in the wind,
    that we cannot get in.

DROMIO OF EPHESUS. You would say so, master, if your gar-
    ments were thin.

    Your cake here is warm within; you stand here in the
        cold:

    It would make a man mad as a buck to be so bought and
        sold.

ANTIPHOLUS OF EPHESUS. Go fetch me something: I'll break
    ope the gate.

DROMIO OF SYRACUSE. (*Within*) Break any breaking here,
    and I'll break your knave's pate.

DROMIO OF EPHESUS. A man may break a word with you,
    sir, and words are but wind:

    Ay, and break it in your face, so he break it not behind.

DROMIO OF SYRACUSE. (*Within*) It seems thou wantest break-
    ing: out upon thee, hind!

DROMIO OF EPHESUS. Here's too much 'out upon thee!' I
    pray thee, let me in.

DROMIO OF SYRACUSE. (*Within*) Ay, when fowls have no
    feathers, and fish have no fin.

ANTIPHOLUS OF EPHESUS. Well, I'll break in. Go borrow me
    a crow.

DROMIO OF EPHESUS. A crow without feather? Master,
    mean you so?

    For a fish without a fin, there's a fowl without a feather:

    If a crow help us in, sirrah, we'll pluck a crow together.

ANTIPHOLUS OF EPHESUS. Go get thee gone: fetch me an
    iron crow.

BALTHAZAR. Have patience, sir; O! let it not be so;

    Herein you war against your reputation,

    And draw within the compass of suspect

    The unviolated honour of your wife.

    Once this,—your long experience of her wisdom,

    Her sober virtue, years, and modesty,

    Plead on her part some cause to you unknown;

    And doubt not, sir, but she will well excuse

    Why at this time the doors are made against you.

    Be rul'd by me: depart in patience,

    And let us to the Tiger all to dinner;

And about evening come yourself alone,
To know the reason of this strange restraint.
If by strong hand you offer to break in
Now in the stirring passage of the day,
A vulgar comment will be made of it,
And that supposed by the common rout
Against your yet ungalled estimation,
That may with foul intrusion enter in
And dwell upon your grave when you are dead;
For slander lives upon succession,
For ever housed where it gets possession.

ANTIPHOLUS OF EPHESUS. You have prevail'd: I will depart
    in quiet,
And, in despite of mirth, mean to be merry.
I know a wench of excellent discourse,
Pretty and witty, wild and yet, too, gentle:
There will we dine: this woman that I mean,
My wife,—but, I protest, without desert,—
Hath oftentimes upbraided me withal:
To her will we to dinner. (*To Angelo*) Get you home,
And fetch the chain; by this I know 'tis made:
Bring it, I pray you, to the Porpentine;
For there 's the house: that chain will I bestow,
Be it for nothing but to spite my wife,
Upon mine hostess there. Good sir, make haste.
Since mine own doors refuse to entertain me,
I 'll knock elsewhere, to see if they 'll disdain me.

ANGELO. I 'll meet you at that place some hour hence.

ANTIPHOLUS OF EPHESUS. Do so. This jest shall cost me
    some expense.   *Exeunt*

SCENE TWO

The Same.

Enter Luciana and Antipholus of Syracuse

LUCIANA. And may it be that you have quite forgot
    A husband's office? Shall, Antipholus,
Even in the spring of love, thy love-springs rot?
    Shall love, in building, grow so ruinous?
If you did wed my sister for her wealth,

Then, for her wealth's sake use her with more kind-
ness:
Or, if you like elsewhere, do it by stealth;
Muffle your false love with some show of blindness;
Let not my sister read it in your eye;
Be not thy tongue thy own shame's orator;
Look sweet, speak fair, become disloyalty;
Apparel vice like virtue's harbinger;
Bear a fair presence, though your heart be tainted;
Teach sin the carriage of a holy saint;
Be secret-false: what need she be acquainted?
What simple thief brags of his own attaint?
'Tis double wrong to truant with your bed,
And let her read it in thy looks at board:
Shame hath a bastard fame, well managed;
Ill deeds are doubled with an evil word.
Alas! poor women, make us but believe,
Being compact of credit, that you love us;
Though others have the arm, show us the sleeve;
We in your motion turn, and you may move us.
Then, gentle brother, get you in again;
Comfort my sister, cheer her, call her wife:
'Tis holy sport to be a little vain,
When the sweet breath of flattery conquers strife.
ANTIPHOLUS OF SYRACUSE. Sweet mistress,—what your name
is else, I know not,
Nor by what wonder you do hit of mine,—
Less in your knowledge and your grace you show not
Than our earth's wonder; more than earth divine.
Teach me, dear creature, how to think and speak:
Lay open to my earthy-gross conceit,
Smother'd in errors, feeble, shallow, weak,
The folded meaning of your words' deceit.
Against my soul's pure truth why labour you
To make it wander in an unknown field?
Are you a god? would you create me new?
Transform me then, and to your power I 'll yield.
But if that I am I, then well I know
Your weeping sister is no wife of mine,
Nor to her bed no homage do I owe:
Far more, far more, to you do I decline.
O! train me not, sweet mermaid, with thy note,

To drown me in thy sister flood of tears:
Sing, siren, for thyself, and I will dote:
Spread o'er the silver waves thy golden hairs,
And as a bed I 'll take them and there lie;
And, in that glorious supposition think
He gains by death that hath such means to die:
Let Love, being light, be drowned if she sink!

LUCIANA. What! are you mad, that you do reason so?

ANTIPHOLUS OF SYRACUSE. Not mad, but mated; how, I do not know.

LUCIANA. It is a fault that springeth from your eye.

ANTIPHOLUS OF SYRACUSE. For gazing on your beams, fair sun, being by.

LUCIANA. Gaze where you should, and that will clear your sight.

ANTIPHOLUS OF SYRACUSE. As good to wink, sweet love, as look on night.

LUCIANA. Why call you me love? call my sister so.

ANTIPHOLUS OF SYRACUSE. Thy sister's sister.

LUCIANA. That 's my sister.

ANTIPHOLUS OF SYRACUSE. No;
It is thyself, mine own self's better part;
Mine eye's clear eye, my dear heart's dearer heart;
My food, my fortune, and my sweet hope's aim,
My sole earth's heaven, and my heaven's claim.

LUCIANA. All this my sister is, or else should be.

ANTIPHOLUS OF SYRACUSE. Call thyself sister, sweet, for I aim thee.
Thee will I love and with thee lead my life:
Thou hast no husband yet nor I no wife.
Give me thy hand.

LUCIANA. O! soft, sir; hold you still:
I 'll fetch my sister, to get her good will. *Exit*

Enter Dromio of Syracuse, hastily

ANTIPHOLUS OF SYRACUSE. Why, how now, Dromio!
Where run'st thou so fast?

DROMIO OF SYRACUSE. Do you know me, sir? am I Dromio? am I your man? am I myself?

ANTIPHOLUS OF SYRACUSE. Thou art Dromio, thou art my man, thou art thyself.

DROMIO OF SYRACUSE. I am an ass, I am a woman's man and besides myself.

ANTIPHOLUS OF SYRACUSE. What woman's man? and how besides thyself?

DROMIO OF SYRACUSE. Marry, sir, besides myself, I am due to a woman; one that claims me, one that haunts me, one that will have me.

ANTIPHOLUS OF SYRACUSE. What claim lays she to thee?

DROMIO OF SYRACUSE. Marry, sir, such claim as you would lay to your horse; and she would have me as a beast: not that, I being a beast, she would have me; but that she, being a very beastly creature, lays claim to me.

ANTIPHOLUS OF SYRACUSE. What is she?

DROMIO OF SYRACUSE. A very reverent body; aye, such a one as a man may not speak of, without he say, 'Sir-reverence.' I have but lean luck in the match, and yet is she a wondrous fat marriage.

ANTIPHOLUS OF SYRACUSE. How dost thou mean a fat marriage?

DROMIO OF SYRACUSE. Marry, sir, she 's the kitchen-wench, and all grease; and I know not what use to put her to but to make a lamp of her and run from her by her own light. I warrant her rags and the tallow in them will burn a Poland winter; if she lives till doomsday, she 'll burn a week longer than the whole world.

ANTIPHOLUS OF SYRACUSE. What complexion is she of?

DROMIO OF SYRACUSE. Swart, like my shoe, but her face nothing like so clean kept: for why she sweats; a man may go over shoes in the grime of it.

ANTIPHOLUS OF SYRACUSE. That 's a fault that water will mend.

DROMIO OF SYRACUSE. No, sir, 'tis in grain; Noah's flood could not do it.

ANTIPHOLUS OF SYRACUSE. What 's her name?

DROMIO OF SYRACUSE. Nell, sir; but her name and three quarters,—that is, an ell and three quarters,—will not measure her from hip to hip.

ANTIPHOLUS OF SYRACUSE. Then she bears some breadth?

DROMIO OF SYRACUSE. No longer from head to foot than from hip to hip: she is spherical, like a globe; I could find out countries in her.

ANTIPHOLUS OF SYRACUSE. In what part of her body stands Ireland?

DROMIO OF SYRACUSE. Marry, sir, in her buttocks: I found it
out by the bogs.

ANTIPHOLUS OF SYRACUSE. Where Scotland?

DROMIO OF SYRACUSE. I found it by the barrenness; hard in
the palm of the hand.

ANTIPHOLUS OF SYRACUSE. Where France?

DROMIO OF SYRACUSE. In her forehead; armed and reverted,
making war against her heir.

ANTIPHOLUS OF SYRACUSE. Where England?

DROMIO OF SYRACUSE. I looked for the chalky cliffs, but I
could find no whiteness in them: but I guess it stood in
her chin, by the salt rheum that ran between France and
it.

ANTIPHOLUS OF SYRACUSE. Where Spain?

DROMIO OF SYRACUSE. Faith, I saw not; but I felt it hot in
her breath.

ANTIPHOLUS OF SYRACUSE. Where America, the Indies?

DROMIO OF SYRACUSE. O, sir! upon her nose, all o'er embel-
lished with rubies, carbuncles, sapphires, declining their
rich aspect to the hot breath of Spain, who sent whole ar-
madoes of caracks to be ballast at her nose.

ANTIPHOLUS OF SYRACUSE. Where stood Belgia, the Nether-
lands?

DROMIO OF SYRACUSE. O, sir! I did not look so low. To conclude, this drudge, or diviner, laid claim to me; call'd me
Dromio; swore I was assured to her; told me what privy
marks I had about me, as the mark of my shoulder, the
mole in my neck, the great wart on my left arm, that I,
amazed, ran from her as a witch.

And, I think, if my breast had not been made of faith and
my heart of steel,

She had transform'd me to a curtal dog and made me
turn i' the wheel.

ANTIPHOLUS OF SYRACUSE. Go hie thee presently post to the
road:

An if the wind blow any way from shore,

I will not harbour in this town to-night:

If any bark put forth, come to the mart,

Where I will walk till thou return to me.

If every one knows us and we know none,

'Tis time, I think, to trudge, pack, and be gone.

DROMIO OF SYRACUSE. As from a bear a man would run for
life,
So fly I from her that would be my wife. *Exit*
ANTIPHOLUS OF SYRACUSE. There's none but witches do in-
habit here,
And therefore 'tis high time that I were hence.
She that doth call me husband, even my soul
Doth for a wife abhor; but her fair sister,
Possess'd with such a gentle sovereign grace,
Of such enchanting presence and discourse,
Hath almost made me traitor to myself:
But, lest myself be guilty to self-wrong,
I'll stop mine ears against the mermaid's song.

Enter Angelo, with the chain

ANGELO. Master Antipholus!
ANTIPHOLUS OF SYRACUSE. Ay, that's my name.
ANGELO. I know it well, sir: lo, here is the chain.
I thought to have ta'en you at the Porpentine;
The chain unfinish'd made me stay thus long.
ANTIPHOLUS OF SYRACUSE. What is your will that I shall do
with this?
ANGELO. What please yourself, sir: I have made it for you.
ANTIPHOLUS OF SYRACUSE. Made it for me, sir! I bespoke it
not.
ANGELO. Not once, nor twice, but twenty times you have.
Go home with it, and please your wife withal;
And soon at supper-time I'll visit you,
And then receive my money for the chain.
ANTIPHOLUS OF SYRACUSE. I pray you, sir, receive the money
now,
For fear you ne'er see chain nor money more.
ANGELO. You are a merry man, sir: fare you well.

Exit, leaving the chain

ANTIPHOLUS OF SYRACUSE. What I should think of this, I
cannot tell:
But this I think, there's no man is so vain
That would refuse so fair and offer'd chain.
I see, a man here needs not live by shifts,
When in the streets he meets such golden gifts.
I'll to the mart, and there for Dromio stay:
If any ship put out, then straight away. *Exit*

ACT FOUR

SCENE ONE

A Public Place.

Enter Second Merchant, Angelo, and an Officer

MERCHANT. You know since Pentecost the sum is due,
And since I have not much importun'd you;
Nor now I had not, but that I am bound
To Persia, and want guilders for my voyage:
Therefore make present satisfaction,
Or I 'll attach you by this officer.

ANGELO. Even just the sum that I do owe to you
Is growing to me by Antipholus;
And in the instant that I met with you
He had of me a chain: at five o'clock
I shall receive the money for the same.
Pleaseth you walk with me down to his house,
I will discharge my bond, and thank you too.

*Enter Antipholus of
Ephesus and Dromio of Ephesus from the Courtezan's*

OFFICER. That labour may you save: see where he comes.

ANTIPHOLUS OF EPHESUS. While I go to the goldsmith's
house, go thou
And buy a rope's end, that I will bestow
Among my wife and her confederates,
For locking me out of my doors by day.
But soft! I see the goldsmith. Get thee gone;
Buy thou a rope, and bring it home to me.

DROMIO OF EPHESUS. I buy a thousand pound a year: I buy
a rope!   *Exit*

ANTIPHOLUS OF EPHESUS. A man is well holp up that trusts
to you:
I promised your presence and the chain;
But neither chain nor goldsmith came to me.

Belike you thought our love would last too long,
If it were chain'd together, and therefore came not.

ANGELO. Saving your merry humour, here 's the note
How much your chain weighs to the utmost carat.
The fineness of the gold, and chargeful fashion,
Which doth amount to three odd ducats more
Than I stand debted to this gentleman:
I pray you see him presently discharg'd,
For he is bound to sea and stays but for it.

ANTIPHOLUS OF EPHESUS. I am not furnish'd with the present money;
Besides, I have some business in the town.
Good signior, take the stranger to my house,
And with you take the chain, and bid my wife
Disburse the sum on the receipt thereof:
Perchance I will be there as soon as you.

ANGELO. Then, you will bring the chain to her yourself?

ANTIPHOLUS OF EPHESUS. No; bear it with you, lest I come
not time enough.

ANGELO. Well, sir, I will. Have you the chain about you?

ANTIPHOLUS OF EPHESUS. An if I have not, sir, I hope you
have,
Or else you may return without your money.

ANGELO. Nay, come, I pray you, sir, give me the chain:
Both wind and tide stays for this gentleman,
And I, to blame, have held him here too long.

ANTIPHOLUS OF EPHESUS. Good Lord! you use this dalliance
to excuse
Your breach of promise to the Porpentine.
I should have chid you for not bringing it,
But, like a shrew, you first begin to brawl.

MERCHANT. The hour steals on; I pray you, sir, dispatch.

ANGELO. You hear how he importunes me: the chain!

ANTIPHOLUS OF EPHESUS. Why, give it to my wife and fetch
your money.

ANGELO. Come, come; you know I gave it you even now.
Either send the chain or send by me some token.

ANTIPHOLUS OF EPHESUS. Fie! now you run this humour out
of breath.
Come, where 's the chain? I pray you, let me see it.

MERCHANT. My business cannot brook this dalliance.
Good sir, say whe'r you 'll answer me or no:

If not, I 'll leave him to the officer.

ANTIPHOLUS OF EPHESUS. I answer you! what should I answer you?

ANGELO. The money that you owe me for the chain.

ANTIPHOLUS OF EPHESUS. I owe you none till I receive the chain.

ANGELO. You know I gave it you half an hour since.

ANTIPHOLUS OF EPHESUS. You gave me none: you wrong me much to say so.

ANGELO. You wrong me more, sir, in denying it:
Consider how it stands upon my credit.

MERCHANT. Well, officer, arrest him at my suit.

OFFICER. I do;
And charge you in the duke's name to obey me.

ANGELO. This touches me in reputation.
Either consent to pay this sum for me,
Or I attach you by this officer.

ANTIPHOLUS OF EPHESUS. Consent to pay thee that I never had!
Arrest me, foolish fellow, if thou dar'st.

ANGELO. Here is thy fee: arrest him, officer.
I would not spare my brother in this case,
If he should scorn me so apparently.

OFFICER. I do arrest you, sir: you hear the suit.

ANTIPHOLUS OF EPHESUS. I do obey thee till I give thee bail.
But, sirrah, you shall buy this sport as dear
As all the metal in your shop will answer.

ANGELO. Sir, sir, I shall have law in Ephesus,
To your notorious shame, I doubt it not.

Enter Dromio of Syracuse

DROMIO OF SYRACUSE. Master, there is a bark of Epidamnum
That stays but till her owner comes aboard,
And then she bears away. Our fraughtage, sir,
I have convey'd aboard, and I have bought
The oil, the balsamum, and aqua-vitæ.
The ship is in her trim; the merry wind
Blows fair from land; they stay for nought at all
But for their owner, master, and yourself.

ANTIPHOLUS OF EPHESUS. How now! a madman! Why, thou peevish sheep,
What ship of Epidamnum stays for me?

DROMIO OF SYRACUSE. A ship you sent me to,
　　to hire waftage.
ANTIPHOLUS OF EPHESUS. Thou drunken slave, I sent thee
　　for a rope;
　　And told thee to what purpose, and what end.
DROMIO OF SYRACUSE. You sent me for a rope's end as soon:
　　You sent me to the bay, sir, for a bark.
ANTIPHOLUS OF EPHESUS. I will debate this matter at more
　　leisure,
　　And teach your ears to list me with more heed.
　　To Adriana, villain, hie thee straight;
　　Give her this key, and tell her, in the desk
　　That 's cover'd o'er with Turkish tapestry,
　　There is a purse of ducats: let her send it.
　　Tell her I am arrested in the street,
　　And that shall bail me. Hie thee, slave, be gone!
　　On, officer, to prison till it come.

Exeunt Merchant, Angelo,
Officer, and Antipholus of Ephesus

DROMIO OF SYRACUSE. To Adriana! That is where we din'd,
　　Where Dowsabel did claim me for her husband:
　　She is too big, I hope, for me to compass.
　　Thither I must, although against my will,
　　For servants must their masters' minds fulfil.   *Exit*

SCENE TWO

A Room in the House of Antipholus of Ephesus.

Enter Adriana and Luciana

ADRIANA. Ah! Luciana, did he tempt thee so?
　　Mightst thou perceive austerely in his eye
　　That he did plead in earnest? yea or no?
　　Look'd he or red or pale? or sad or merrily?
　　What observation mad'st thou in this case
　　Of his heart's meteors tilting in his face?
LUCIANA. First he denied you had in him no right.
ADRIANA. He meant he did me none; the more my spite.
LUCIANA. Then swore he that he was a stranger here.
ADRIANA. And true he swore, though yet forsworn he were.
LUCIANA. Then pleaded I for you.

ADRIANA.   And what said he?

LUCIANA. That love I begg'd for you he begg'd of me.

ADRIANA. With what persuasion did he tempt thy love?

LUCIANA. With words that in an honest suit might move.
First, he did praise my beauty, then my speech.

ADRIANA. Didst speak him fair?

LUCIANA.   Have patience, I beseech.

ADRIANA. I cannot, nor I will not hold me still:
My tongue, though not my heart, shall have his will.
He is deformed, crooked, old and sere,
Ill-fac'd, worse bodied, shapeless everywhere;
Vicious, ungentle, foolish, blunt, unkind,
Stigmatical in making, worse in mind.

LUCIANA. Who would be jealous then, of such a one?
No evil lost is wail'd when it is gone.

ADRIANA. Ah! but I think him better than I say,
And yet would herein others' eyes were worse.
Far from her nest the lapwing cries away:
My heart prays for him, though my tongue do curse.

Enter Dromio of Syracuse

DROMIO OF SYRACUSE. Here, go: the desk! the purse! sweet,
now, make haste.

LUCIANA. How hast thou lost thy breath?

DROMIO OF SYRACUSE.   By running fast.

ADRIANA. Where is thy master, Dromio? is he well?

DROMIO OF SYRACUSE. No, he 's in Tartar limbo, worse than
hell.
A devil in an everlasting garment hath him,
One whose hard heart is button'd up with steel;
A fiend, a fairy, pitiless and rough;
A wolf, nay, worse, a fellow all in buff;
A back-friend, a shoulder-clapper, one that counter-
mands
The passages of alleys, creeks and narrow lands;
A hound that runs counter and yet draws dryfoot well;
One that, before the judgment, carries poor souls to hell.

ADRIANA. Why, man, what is the matter?

DROMIO OF SYRACUSE. I do not know the matter: he is
'rested on the case.

ADRIANA. What, is he arrested? tell me at whose suit.

DROMIO OF SYRACUSE. I know not at whose suit he is arrested well;

But he 's in a suit of buff which 'rested him, that can I
tell.

Will you send him, mistress, redemption, the money in
his desk?

ADRIANA. Go fetch it, sister.—(*Exit Luciana*) This I wonder at:

That he, unknown to me, should be in debt:

Tell me, was he arrested on a band?

DROMIO OF SYRACUSE. Not on a band, but on a stronger
thing;

A chain, a chain. Do you not hear it ring?

ADRIANA. What, the chain?

DROMIO OF SYRACUSE. No, no, the bell: 'tis time that I were
gone:

It was two ere I left him, and now the clock strikes one.

ADRIANA. The hours come back! that did I never hear.

DROMIO OF SYRACUSE. O yes; if any hour meet a sergeant, a'
turns back for very fear.

ADRIANA. As if Time were in debt! how fondly dost thou
reason!

DROMIO OF SYRACUSE. Time is a very bankrupt, and owes
more than he 's worth to season.

Nay, he 's a thief too: have you not heard men say,

That Time comes stealing on by night and day?

If Time be in debt and theft, and a sergeant in the way,

Hath he not reason to turn back an hour in a day?

Re-enter Luciana

ADRIANA. Go, Dromio: there 's the money, bear it straight,

And bring thy master home immediately.

Come, sister; I am press'd down with conceit;

Conceit, my comfort and my injury.   *Exeunt*

SCENE THREE

A Public Place.

Enter Antipholus of Syracuse

ANTIPHOLUS OF SYRACUSE. There 's not a man I meet but
doth salute me,

As if I were their well acquainted friend;

And every one doth call me by my name.

Some tender money to me; some invite me;
Some other give me thanks for kindnesses;
Some offer me commodities to buy:
Even now a tailor call'd me in his shop
And show'd me silks that he had bought for me,
And therewithal, took measure of my body.
Sure these are but imaginary wiles,
And Lapland sorcerers inhabit here.

Enter Dromio of Syracuse

DROMIO OF SYRACUSE. Master, here 's the gold you sent me
for.
What! have you got the picture of old Adam new ap-
parelled?

ANTIPHOLUS OF SYRACUSE. What gold is this? What Adam
dost thou mean?

DROMIO OF SYRACUSE. Not that Adam that kept the Paradise, but that Adam that keeps the prison: he that goes
in the calf's skin that was killed for the Prodigal: he that
came behind you, sir, like an evil angel, and bid you forsake your liberty.

ANTIPHOLUS OF SYRACUSE. I understand thee not.

DROMIO OF SYRACUSE. No? why, 'tis a plain case: he that
went, like a base-viol, in a case of leather; the man, sir,
that, when gentlemen are tired, gives them a fob, and
'rests them; he, sir, that takes pity on decayed men and
gives them suits of durance; he that sets up his rest to do
more exploits with his mace than a morris-pike.

ANTIPHOLUS OF SYRACUSE. What, thou meanest an officer?

DROMIO OF SYRACUSE. Ay, sir, the sergeant of the band; he
that brings any man to answer it that breaks his band;
one that thinks a man always going to bed, and says,
'God give you good rest!'

ANTIPHOLUS OF SYRACUSE. Well, sir, there rest in your foolery. Is there any ship puts forth to-night? may we be
gone?

DROMIO OF SYRACUSE. Why, sir, I brought you word an
hour since that the bark Expedition put forth to-night;
and then were you hindered by the sergeant to tarry for
the hoy Delay. Here are the angels that you sent for to
deliver you.

ANTIPHOLUS OF SYRACUSE. The fellow is distract, and so am
I,

And here we wander in illusions:

Some blessed power deliver us from hence!

Enter a Courtezan

COURTEZAN. Well met, well met, Master Antipholus.

I see, sir, you have found the goldsmith now:

Is that the chain you promis'd me to-day?

ANTIPHOLUS OF SYRACUSE. Satan, avoid! I charge thee
tempt me not!

DROMIO OF SYRACUSE. Master, is this Mistress Satan?

ANTIPHOLUS OF SYRACUSE. It is the devil.

DROMIO OF SYRACUSE. Nay, she is worse, she is the devil's
dam, and here she comes in the habit of a light wench:
and thereof comes that the wenches say, 'God damn me';
that 's as much as to say, 'God make me a light wench.' It
is written, they appear to men like angels of light: light is
an effect of fire, and fire will burn; ergo, light wenches
will burn. Come not near her.

COURTEZAN. Your man and you are marvellous merry, sir.
Will you go with me? we 'll mend our dinner here.

DROMIO OF SYRACUSE. Master, if you do, expect spoonmeat,
so bespeak a long spoon.

ANTIPHOLUS OF SYRACUSE. Why, Dromio?

DROMIO OF SYRACUSE. Marry, he must have a long spoon
that must eat with the devil.

ANTIPHOLUS OF SYRACUSE. Avoid thee, fiend! what tell'st
thou me of supping?

Thou art, as you are all, a sorceress:

I conjure thee to leave me and be gone.

COURTEZAN. Give me the ring of mine you had at dinner,

Or, for my diamond, the chain you promis'd,

And I 'll be gone, sir, and not trouble you.

DROMIO OF SYRACUSE. Some devils ask but the parings of
one's nail,

A rush, a hair, a drop of blood, a pin,

A nut, a cherry-stone;

But she, more covetous, would have a chain.

Master, be wise: an if you give it her,

The devil will shake her chain and fright us with it.

COURTEZAN. I pray you, sir, my ring, or else the chain:

I hope you do not mean to cheat me so.

ANTIPHOLUS OF SYRACUSE. Avaunt, thou witch! Come, Dromio, let us go.

DROMIO OF SYRACUSE. 'Fly pride,' says the peacock: mistress, that you know.

Exeunt Antipholus of
Syracuse, and Dromio of Syracuse

COURTEZAN. Now, out of doubt, Antipholus is mad,
Else would he never so demean himself.
A ring he hath of mine worth forty ducats,
And for the same he promis'd me a chain:
Both one and other he denies me now.
The reason that I gather he is mad,
Besides this present instance of his rage,
Is a mad tale he told to-day at dinner,
Of his own doors being shut against his entrance.
Belike his wife, acquainted with his fits,
On purpose shut the doors against his way.
My way is now to hie home to his house,
And tell his wife, that, being lunatic,
He rush'd into my house, and took perforce
My ring away. This course I fittest choose,
For forty ducats is too much to lose.   *Exit*

SCENE FOUR

A Street.

Enter Antipholus of Ephesus and the Officer

ANTIPHOLUS OF EPHESUS. Fear me not, man; I will not
break away:
I 'll give thee, ere I leave thee, so much money,
To warrant thee, as I am 'rested for.
My wife is in a wayward mood to-day,
And will not lightly trust the messenger.
That I should be attach'd in Ephesus,
I tell you, 'twill sound harshly in her ears.

Enter Dromio of Ephesus with a rope's end

Here comes my man: I think he brings the money.
How now, sir! have you that I sent you for?

DROMIO OF EPHESUS. Here 's that, I warrant you, will pay
them all.

ANTIPHOLUS OF EPHESUS. But where 's the money?

DROMIO OF EPHESUS. Why, sir, I gave the money for the rope.

ANTIPHOLUS OF EPHESUS. Five hundred ducats, villain, for a rope?

DROMIO OF EPHESUS. I 'll serve you, sir, five hundred at the rate.

ANTIPHOLUS OF EPHESUS. To what end did I bid thee hie thee home?

DROMIO OF EPHESUS. To a rope's end, sir; and to that end am I return'd.

ANTIPHOLUS OF EPHESUS. And to that end, sir, I will welcome you.   *Beats him*

OFFICER. Good sir, be patient.

DROMIO OF EPHESUS. Nay, 'tis for me to be patient; I am in adversity.

OFFICER. Good now, hold thy tongue.

DROMIO OF EPHESUS. Nay, rather persuade him to hold his hands.

ANTIPHOLUS OF EPHESUS. Thou whoreson, senseless villain!

DROMIO OF EPHESUS. I would I were senseless, sir, that I might not feel your blows.

ANTIPHOLUS OF EPHESUS. Thou art sensible in nothing but blows, and so is an ass.

DROMIO OF EPHESUS. I am an ass indeed: you may prove it by my long ears. I have served him from the hour of my nativity to this instant, and have nothing at his hands for my service but blows. When I am cold, he heats me with beating; when I am warm, he cools me with beating; I am waked with it when I sleep; raised with it when I sit; driven out of doors with it when I go from home; welcomed home with it when I return; nay, I bear it on my shoulders, as a beggar wont her brat; and, I think, when he hath lamed me, I shall beg with it from door to door.

ANTIPHOLUS OF EPHESUS. Come, go along; my wife is coming yonder.

Enter Adriana, Luciana, the Courtezan, and Pinch

DROMIO OF EPHESUS. Mistress, respice finem, respect your end; or rather, to prophesy like the parrot, 'Beware the rope's end.'

ANTIPHOLUS OF EPHESUS. Wilt thou still talk?   *Beats him*

COURTEZAN. How say you now? is not your husband mad?

ADRIANA. His incivility confirms no less.

Good Doctor Pinch, you are a conjurer;
Establish him in his true sense again,
And I will please you what you will demand.

LUCIANA. Alas! how fiery and how sharp he looks.

COURTEZAN. Mark how he trembles in his ecstasy!

PINCH. Give me your hand and let me feel your pulse.

ANTIPHOLUS OF EPHESUS. There is my hand, and let it feel
your ear.   *Strikes him*

PINCH. I charge thee, Satan, hous'd within this man,
To yield possession to my holy prayers,
And to thy state of darkness hie thee straight:
I conjure thee by all the saints in heaven.

ANTIPHOLUS OF EPHESUS. Peace, doting wizard, peace! I am
not mad.

ADRIANA. O! that thou wert not, poor distressed soul!

ANTIPHOLUS OF EPHESUS. You minion, you, are these your
customers?
Did this companion with the saffron face
Revel and feast it at my house to-day,
Whilst upon me the guilty doors were shut
And I denied to enter in my house?

ADRIANA. O husband, God doth know you din'd at home;
Where would you had remain'd until this time,
Free from these slanders and this open shame!

ANTIPHOLUS OF EPHESUS. Din'd at home! Thou villain, what
say'st thou?

DROMIO OF EPHESUS. Sir, sooth to say, you did not dine at
home.

ANTIPHOLUS OF EPHESUS. Were not my doors lock'd up and
I shut out?

DROMIO OF EPHESUS. Perdy, your doors were lock'd and you
shut out.

ANTIPHOLUS OF EPHESUS. And did not she herself revile me
there?

DROMIO OF EPHESUS. Sans fable, she herself revil'd you
there.

ANTIPHOLUS OF EPHESUS. Did not her kitchen-maid rail,
taunt, and scorn me?

DROMIO OF EPHESUS. Certes, she did; the kitchen-vestal
scorn'd you.

ANTIPHOLUS OF EPHESUS. And did not I in rage depart from
thence?

DROMIO OF EPHESUS. In verity you did: my bones bear wit-
ness,
   That since have felt the vigour of his rage.
ADRIANA. Is 't good to soothe him in these contraries?
PINCH. It is no shame: the fellow finds his vein,
   And, yielding to him humours well his frenzy.
ANTIPHOLUS OF EPHESUS. Thou hast suborn'd the goldsmith
   to arrest me.
ADRIANA. Alas! I sent you money to redeem you,
   By Dromio here, who came in haste for it.
DROMIO OF EPHESUS. Money by me! heart and good will
   you might;
   But surely, master, not a rag of money.
ANTIPHOLUS OF EPHESUS. Went'st not thou to her for a
   purse of ducats?
ADRIANA. He came to me, and I deliver'd it.
LUCIANA. And I am witness with her that she did.
DROMIO OF EPHESUS. God and the rope-maker bear me wit-
ness
   That I was sent for nothing but a rope!
PINCH. Mistress, both man and master is possess'd:
   I know it by their pale and deadly looks.
   They must be bound and laid in some dark room.
ANTIPHOLUS OF EPHESUS. Say, wherefore didst thou lock me
   forth to-day?
   And why dost thou deny the bag of gold?
ADRIANA. I did not, gentle husband, lock thee forth.
DROMIO OF EPHESUS. And, gentle master, I receiv'd no gold;
   But I confess, sir, that we were lock'd out.
ADRIANA. Dissembling villain! thou speak'st false in both.
ANTIPHOLUS OF EPHESUS. Dissembling harlot! thou art false
   in all;
   And art confederate with a damned pack
   To make a loathsome abject scorn of me;
   But with these nails I 'll pluck out those false eyes
   That would behold in me this shameful sport.
ADRIANA. O! bind him, bind him, let him not come near me.
PINCH. More company! the fiend is strong within him.
LUCIANA. Ay me! poor man, how pale and wan he looks!
   Enter three or four and bind Antipholus of Ephesus
ANTIPHOLUS OF EPHESUS. What, will you murder me? Thou
   gaoler, thou,

I am thy prisoner: wilt thou suffer them
To make a rescue?

OFFICER.   Masters, let him go:
He is my prisoner, and you shall not have him.

PINCH. Go bind this man, for he is frantic too.

They bind Dromio of Ephesus

ADRIANA. What wilt thou do, thou peevish officer?
Hast thou delight to see a wretched man
Do outrage and displeasure to himself?

OFFICER. He is my prisoner: if I let him go,
The debt he owes will be requir'd of me.

ADRIANA. I will discharge thee ere I go from thee:
Bear me forthwith unto his creditor,
And, knowing how the debt grows, I will pay it.
Good Master doctor, see him safe convey'd
Home to my house. O most unhappy day!

ANTIPHOLUS OF EPHESUS. O most unhappy strumpet!

DROMIO OF EPHESUS. Master, I am here enter'd in bond for
you.

ANTIPHOLUS OF EPHESUS. Out on thee, villain! wherefore
dost thou mad me?

DROMIO OF EPHESUS. Will you be bound for nothing? be
mad, good master; cry, 'the devil!'

LUCIANA. God help, poor souls! how idly do they talk.

ADRIANA. Go bear him hence. Sister, go you with me.—

*Exeunt Pinch and Assistants
with Antipholus of Ephesus and Dromio of Ephesus*

Say now, whose suit is he arrested at?

OFFICER. One Angelo, a goldsmith; do you know him?

ADRIANA. I know the man. What is the sum he owes?

OFFICER. Two hundred ducats.

ADRIANA.   Say, how grows it due?

OFFICER. Due for a chain your husband had of him.

ADRIANA. He did bespeak a chain for me, but had it not.

COURTEZAN. When as your husband all in rage, to-day
Came to my house, and took away my ring,—
The ring I saw upon his finger now,—
Straight after did I meet him with a chain.

ADRIANA. It may be so, but I did never see it.
Come, gaoler, bring me where the goldsmith is:
I long to know the truth hereof at large.

*Enter Antipholus of
Syracuse and Dromio of Syracuse, with rapiers drawn*

LUCIANA. God, for thy mercy! they are loose again.

ADRIANA. And come with naked swords. Let 's call more help

To have them bound again.

OFFICER.   Away! they 'll kill us.

Exeunt Adriana, Luciana, and Officer

ANTIPHOLUS OF SYRACUSE. I see, these witches are afraid of swords.

DROMIO OF SYRACUSE. She that would be your wife now ran from you.

ANTIPHOLUS OF SYRACUSE. Come to the Centaur; fetch our stuff from thence:

I long that we were safe and sound aboard.

DROMIO OF SYRACUSE. Faith, stay here this night, they will surely do us no harm; you saw they speak us fair, give us gold: methinks they are such a gentle nation, that, but for the mountain of mad flesh that claims marriage of me, I could find in my heart to stay here still, and turn witch.

ANTIPHOLUS OF SYRACUSE. I will not stay to-night for all the town;

Therefore away, to get our stuff aboard.   *Exeunt*

ACT FIVE

SCENE ONE

A Street before an Abbey.
Enter Merchant and Angelo

ANGELO. I am sorry, sir, that I have hinder'd you;
But, I protest, he had the chain of me,
Though most dishonestly he doth deny it.
MERCHANT. How is the man esteem'd here in the city?
ANGELO. Of very reverend reputation, sir,
Of credit infinite, highly belov'd,
Second to none that lives here in the city:
His word might bear my wealth at any time.
MERCHANT. Speak softly: yonder, as I think, he walks.
Enter Antipholus of Syracuse and Dromio of Syracuse
ANGELO. 'Tis so; and that self chain about his neck
Which he forswore most monstrously to have.
Good sir, draw near to me, I 'll speak to him.
Signior Antipholus, I wonder much
That you would put me to this shame and trouble;
And not without some scandal to yourself,
With circumstance and oaths so to deny
This chain which now you wear so openly:
Beside the charge, the shame, imprisonment,
You have done wrong to this my honest friend,
Who, but for staying on our controversy,
Had hoisted sail and put to sea to-day.
This chain you had of me; can you deny it?
ANTIPHOLUS OF SYRACUSE. I think I had: I never did deny
it.
MERCHANT. Yes, that you did, sir, and forswore it too.
ANTIPHOLUS OF SYRACUSE. Who heard me to deny it or for-
swear it?

MERCHANT. These ears of mine, thou know'st, did hear
  thee.
  Fie on thee, wretch! 'tis pity that thou liv'st
  To walk where any honest men resort.
ANTIPHOLUS OF SYRACUSE. Thou art a villain to impeach me
  thus:
  I 'll prove mine honour and mine honesty
  Against thee presently, if thou dar'st stand.
MERCHANT. I dare, and do defy thee for a villain.

They draw
Enter Adriana, Luciana, Courtezan, and Others

ADRIANA. Hold! hurt him not, for God's sake! he is mad.
  Some get within him, take his sword away.
  Bind Dromio too, and bear them to my house.
DROMIO OF SYRACUSE. Run, master, run; for God's sake,
  take a house!
  This is some priory: in, or we are spoil'd.

Exeunt Antipholus of
Syracuse and Dromio of Syracuse to the Abbey
Enter the Abbess

ABBESS. Be quiet, people. Wherefore throng you hither?
ADRIANA. To fetch my poor distracted husband hence.
  Let us come in, that we may bind him fast,
  And bear him home for his recovery.
ANGELO. I knew he was not in his perfect wits.
MERCHANT. I am sorry now that I did draw on him.
ABBESS. How long hath this possession held the man?
ADRIANA. This week he hath been heavy, sour, sad,
  And much different from the man he was;
  But, till this afternoon his passion
  Ne'er brake into extremity of rage.
ABBESS. Hath he not lost much wealth by wrack of sea?
  Buried some dear friend? Hath not else his eye
  Stray'd his affection in unlawful love?
  A sin prevailing much in youthful men,
  Who give their eyes the liberty of gazing.
  Which of these sorrows is he subject to?
ADRIANA. To none of these, except it be the last;
  Namely, some love that drew him oft from home.
ABBESS. You should for that have reprehended him.
ADRIANA. Why, so I did.
ABBESS.   Ay, but not rough enough.

ADRIANA. As roughly as my modesty would let me.

ABBESS. Haply, in private.

ADRIANA.   And in assemblies too.

ABBESS. Ay, but not enough.

ADRIANA. It was the copy of our conference:
  In bed, he slept not for my urging it;
  At board, he fed not for my urging it;
  Alone, it was the subject of my theme;
  In company I often glanced it:
  Still did I tell him it was vile and bad.

ABBESS. And thereof came it that the man was mad:
  The venom clamours of a jealous woman
  Poison more deadly than a mad dog's tooth.
  It seems, his sleeps were hinder'd by thy railing,
  And thereof comes it that his head is light.
  Thou say'st his meat was sauc'd with thy upbraidings·
  Unquiet meals make ill digestions;
  Thereof the raging fire of fever bred:
  And what's a fever but a fit of madness?
  Thou say'st his sports were hinder'd by thy brawls:
  Sweet recreation barr'd, what doth ensue
  But moody moping, and dull melancholy,
  Kinsman to grim and comfortless despair,
  And at her heels a huge infectious troop
  Of pale distemperatures and foes to life?
  In food, in sport, and life-preserving rest
  To be disturb'd, would mad or man or beast:
  The consequence is then, thy jealous fits
  Have scar'd thy husband from the use of wits.

LUCIANA. She never reprehended him but mildly
  When he demean'd himself rough, rude, and wildly.
  Why bear you these rebukes and answer not?

ADRIANA. She did betray me to my own reproof.
  Good people, enter, and lay hold on him.

ABBESS. No; not a creature enters in my house.

ADRIANA. Then, let your servants bring my husband forth.

ABBESS. Neither: he took this place for sanctuary,
  And it shall privilege him from your hands
  Till I have brought him to his wits again,
  Or lose my labour in assaying it.

ADRIANA. I will attend my husband, be his nurse,
  Diet his sickness, for it is my office,

And will have no attorney but myself;
And therefore let me have him home with me.

ABBESS. Be patient; for I will not let him stir
Till I have us'd the approved means I have,
With wholesome syrups, drugs, and holy prayers,
To make of him a formal man again.
It is a branch and parcel of mine oath,
A charitable duty of my order;
Therefore depart and leave him here with me.

ADRIANA. I will not hence and leave my husband here;
And ill it doth beseem your holiness
To separate the husband and the wife.

ABBESS. Be quiet, and depart. Thou shalt not have him.

Exit

LUCIANA. Complain unto the duke of this indignity.

ADRIANA. Come, go: I will fall prostrate at his feet,
And never rise until my tears and prayers
Have won his Grace to come in person hither,
And take perforce my husband from the abbess.

SECOND MERCHANT. By this, I think, the dial points at five:
Anon, I 'm sure, the duke himself in person
Comes this way to the melancholy vale,
The place of death and sorry execution,
Behind the ditches of the abbey here.

ANGELO. Upon what cause?

SECOND MERCHANT. To see a reverend Syracusian merchant,
Who put unluckily into this bay
Against the laws and statutes of this town,
Beheaded publicly for his offence.

ANGELO. See where they come: we will behold his death.

LUCIANA. Kneel to the duke before he pass the abbey.

*Enter Duke attended; Ægeon
bare-headed; with the Headsman and other Officers*

DUKE. Yet once again proclaim it publicly,
If any friend will pay the sum for him,
He shall not die; so much we tender him.

ADRIANA. Justice, most sacred duke, against the abbess!

DUKE. She is a virtuous and a reverend lady:
It cannot be that she hath done thee wrong.

ADRIANA. May it please your Grace, Antipholus, my husband,

Whom I made lord of me and all I had,
At your important letters, this ill day
A most outrageous fit of madness took him,
That desperately he hurried through the street,—
With him his bondman, all as mad as he,—
Doing displeasure to the citizens
By rushing in their houses, bearing thence
Rings, jewels, anything his rage did like.
Once did I get him bound and sent him home,
Whilst to take order for the wrongs I went
That here and there his fury had committed.
Anon, I wot not by what strong escape,
He broke from those that had the guard of him,
And with his mad attendant and himself,
Each one with ireful passion, with drawn swords
Met us again, and, madly bent on us
Chas'd us away, till, raising of more aid
We came again to bind them. Then they fled
Into this abbey, whither we pursu'd them;
And here the abbess shuts the gates on us,
And will not suffer us to fetch him out,
Nor send him forth that we may bear him hence.
Therefore, most gracious duke, with thy command
Let him be brought forth, and borne hence for help.
DUKE. Long since thy husband serv'd me in my wars,
And I to thee engag'd a prince's word,
When thou didst make him master of thy bed,
To do him all the grace and good I could.
Go, some of you, knock at the abbey gate
And bid the Lady Abbess come to me.
I will determine this before I stir.

Enter a Servant

SERVANT. O mistress, mistress! shift and save yourself!
My master and his man are both broke loose,
Beaten the maids a-row and bound the doctor,
Whose beard they have sing'd off with brands of fire;
And ever as it blaz'd they threw on him
Great pails of puddled mire to quench the hair.
My master preaches patience to him, and the while
His man with scissors nicks him like a fool;
And sure, unless you send some present help,
Between them they will kill the conjurer.

ADRIANA. Peace, fool! thy master and his man are here,
And that is false thou dost report to us.

SERVANT. Mistress, upon my life, I tell you true;
I have not breath'd almost, since I did see it.
He cries for you and vows, if he can take you,
To scotch your face, and to disfigure you.   *Cry within*
Hark, hark! I hear him, mistress: fly, be gone!

DUKE. Come, stand by me; fear nothing. Guard with hal-
berds!

ADRIANA. Ay me, it is my husband! Witness you,
That he is borne about invisible:
Even now we hous'd him in the abbey here,
And now he 's here, past thought of human reason.

Enter Antipholus of Ephesus and Dromio of Ephesus

ANTIPHOLUS OF EPHESUS. Justice, most gracious duke! O!
grant me justice,
Even for the service that long since I did thee,
When I bestrid thee in the wars and took
Deep scars to save thy life; even for the blood
That then I lost for thee, now grant me justice.

ÆGEON. Unless the fear of death doth make me dote,
I see my son Antipholus and Dromio!

ANTIPHOLUS OF EPHESUS. Justice, sweet prince, against that
woman there!
She whom thou gav'st to me to be my wife,
That hath abused and dishonour'd me,
Even in the strength and height of injury!
Beyond imagination is the wrong
That she this day hath shameless thrown on me.

DUKE. Discover how, and thou shalt find me just.

ANTIPHOLUS OF EPHESUS. This day, great duke, she shut the
doors upon me,
While she with harlots feasted in my house.

DUKE. A grievous fault! Say, woman, didst thou so?

ADRIANA. No, my good lord: myself, he, and my sister
To-day did dine together. So befall my soul
As this is false he burdens me withal!

LUCIANA. Ne'er may I look on day, nor sleep on night,
But she tells to your Highness simple truth!

ANGELO. O perjur'd woman! They are both forsworn:
In this the madman justly chargeth them!

ANTIPHOLUS OF EPHESUS. My liege, I am advised what I say:

Neither disturb'd with the effect of wine,
Nor heady-rash, provok'd with raging ire,
Albeit my wrongs might make one wiser mad.
This woman lock'd me out this day from dinner:
That goldsmith there, were he not pack'd with her,
Could witness it, for he was with me then;
Who parted with me to go fetch a chain,
Promising to bring it to the Porpentine,
Where Balthazar and I did dine together.
Our dinner done, and he not coming thither,
I went to seek him: in the street I met him,
And in his company that gentleman.
There did this perjur'd goldsmith swear me down
That I this day of him receiv'd the chain,
Which, God he knows, I saw not; for the which
He did arrest me with an officer.
I did obey, and sent my peasant home
For certain ducats: he with none return'd.
Then fairly I bespoke the officer
To go in person with me to my house.
By the way we met
My wife, her sister, and a rabble more
Of vile confederates: along with them
They brought one Pinch, a hungry lean-fac'd villain,
A mere anatomy, a mountebank,
A threadbare juggler, and a fortune-teller,
A needy, hollow-ey'd, sharp-looking wretch,
A living-dead man. This pernicious slave,
Forsooth, took on him as a conjurer,
And, gazing in mine eyes, feeling my pulse,
And with no face, as 'twere, out-facing me,
Cries out, I was possess'd. Then, altogether
They fell upon me, bound me, bore me thence,
And in a dark and dankish vault at home
There left me and my man, both bound together;
Till, gnawing with my teeth my bonds in sunder,
I gain'd my freedom, and immediately
Ran hither to your Grace; whom I beseech
To give me ample satisfaction
For these deep shames and great indignities.
ANGELO. My lord, in truth, thus far I witness with him,
That he din'd not at home, but was lock'd out.

DUKE. But had he such a chain of thee, or no?

ANGELO. He had, my lord; and when he ran in here,
These people saw the chain about his neck.

SECOND MERCHANT. Besides, I will be sworn these ears of
mine
Heard you confess you had the chain of him
After you first forswore it on the mart;
And thereupon I drew my sword on you;
And then you fled into this abbey here,
From whence, I think, you are come by miracle.

ANTIPHOLUS OF EPHESUS. I never came within these abbey
walls;
Nor ever didst thou draw thy sword on me;
I never saw the chain, so help me heaven!
And this is false you burden me withal.

DUKE. Why, what an intricate impeach is this!
I think you all have drunk of Circe's cup.
If here you hous'd him, here he would have been;
If he were mad, he would not plead so coldly;
You say he din'd at home; the goldsmith here
Denies that saying. Sirrah, what say you?

DROMIO OF EPHESUS. Sir, he din'd with her there, at the
Porpentine.

COURTEZAN. He did, and from my finger snatch'd that ring.

ANTIPHOLUS OF EPHESUS. 'Tis true, my liege; this ring I had
of her.

DUKE. Saw'st thou him enter at the abbey here?

COURTEZAN. As sure, my liege, as I do see your Grace.

DUKE. Why, this is strange. Go call the abbess hither.

Exit an Attendant

I think you are all mated or stark mad.

ÆGEON. Most mighty duke, vouchsafe me speak a word:
Haply I see a friend will save my life,
And pay the sum that may deliver me.

DUKE. Speak freely, Syracusian, what thou wilt.

ÆGEON. Is not your name, sir, called Antipholus?
And is not that your bondman Dromio?

DROMIO OF EPHESUS. Within this hour I was his bondman,
sir;
But he, I thank him, gnaw'd in two my cords:
Now am I Dromio and his man, unbound.

ÆGEON. I am sure you both of you remember me.

DROMIO OF EPHESUS. Ourselves we do remember, sir, by
>you;
For lately we were bound, as you are now.
You are not Pinch's patient, are you, sir?

ÆGEON. Why look you strange on me? you know me well.

ANTIPHOLUS OF EPHESUS. I never saw you in my life till
>now.

ÆGEON. O! grief hath chang'd me since you saw me last,
And careful hours, with Time's deformed hand,
Have written strange defeatures in my face:
But tell me yet, dost thou not know my voice?

ANTIPHOLUS OF EPHESUS. Neither.

ÆGEON. Dromio, nor thou?

DROMIO OF EPHESUS. No, trust me, sir, not I.

ÆGEON. I am sure thou dost.

DROMIO OF EPHESUS. Ay, sir; but I am sure I do not; and
>whatsoever a man denies, you are now bound to believe
>him.

ÆGEON. Not know my voice! O, time's extremity,
Hast thou so crack'd and splitted my poor tongue
In seven short years, that here my only son
Knows not my feeble key of untun'd cares?
Though now this grained face of mine be hid
In sap-consuming winter's drizzled snow,
And all the conduits of my blood froze up,
Yet hath my night of life some memory,
My wasting lamps some fading glimmer left,
My dull deaf ears a little use to hear:
All these old witnesses, I cannot err,
Tell me thou art my son Antipholus.

ANTIPHOLUS OF EPHESUS. I never saw my father in my life.

ÆGEON. But seven years since, in Syracusa, boy,
Thou know'st we parted: but perhaps, my son,
Thou sham'st to acknowledge me in misery.

ANTIPHOLUS OF EPHESUS. The duke and all that know me in
>the city
Can witness with me that it is not so:
I ne'er saw Syracusa in my life.

DUKE. I tell thee, Syracusian, twenty years
Have I been patron to Antipholus,
During which time he ne'er saw Syracusa.
I see thy age and dangers make thee dote.

Re-enter Abbess, with
Antipholus of Syracuse and Dromio of Syracuse

ABBESS. Most mighty duke, behold a man much wrong'd.
                                        All gather to see him

ADRIANA. I see two husbands, or mine eyes deceive me!

DUKE. One of these men is Genius to the other;
    And so of these: which is the natural man,
    And which the spirit? Who deciphers them?

DROMIO OF SYRACUSE. I, sir, am Dromio: command him
    away.

DROMIO OF EPHESUS. I, sir, am Dromio: pray let me stay.

ANTIPHOLUS OF SYRACUSE. Ægeon art thou not? or else his
    ghost?

DROMIO OF SYRACUSE. O! my old master; who hath bound'
    him here?

ABBESS. Whoever bound him, I will loose his bonds,
    And gain a husband by his liberty.
    Speak, old Ægeon, if thou be'st the man
    That hadst a wife once call'd Æmilia,
    That bore thee at a burden two fair sons.
    O! if thou be'st the same Ægeon, speak,
    And speak unto the same Æmilia!

ÆGEON. If I dream not, thou art Æmilia:
    If thou art she, tell me where is that son
    That floated with thee on the fatal raft?

ABBESS. By men of Epidamnum, he and I,
    And the twin Dromio, all were taken up:
    But by and by rude fishermen of Corinth
    By force took Dromio and my son from them,
    And me they left with those of Epidamnum.
    What then became of them, I cannot tell;
    I to this fortune that you see me in.

DUKE. Why, here begins his morning story right:
    These two Antipholus', these two so like,
    And these two Dromios, one in semblance,
    Besides her urging of her wrack at sea;
    These are the parents to these children,
    Which accidentally are met together.
    Antipholus, thou cam'st from Corinth first?

ANTIPHOLUS OF SYRACUSE. No, sir, not I; I came from Syra-
    cuse.

DUKE. Stay, stand apart; I know not which is which.

ANTIPHOLUS OF EPHESUS. I came from Corinth, my most
    gracious lord,—

DROMIO OF EPHESUS. And I with him.

ANTIPHOLUS OF EPHESUS. Brought to this town by that most
    famous warrior,

  Duke Menaphon, your most renowned uncle.

ADRIANA. Which of you two did dine with me to-day?

ANTIPHOLUS OF SYRACUSE. I, gentle mistress.

ADRIANA. And are not you my husband?

ANTIPHOLUS OF EPHESUS. No; I say nay to that.

ANTIPHOLUS OF SYRACUSE. And so do I; yet did she call me
    so;

  And this fair gentlewoman, her sister here,

  Did call me brother. (*To Luciana*) What I told you then,

  I hope I shall have leisure to make good,

  If this be not a dream I see and hear.

ANGELO. That is the chain, sir, which you had of me.

ANTIPHOLUS OF SYRACUSE. I think it be, sir; I deny it not.

ANTIPHOLUS OF EPHESUS. And you, sir, for this chain ar-
    rested me.

ANGELO. I think I did, sir; I deny it not.

ADRIANA. I sent you money, sir, to be your bail,

  By Dromio; but I think he brought it not.

DROMIO OF EPHESUS. No, none by me.

ANTIPHOLUS OF SYRACUSE. This purse of ducats I receiv'd
    from you,

  And Dromio, my man, did bring them me.

  I see we still did meet each other's man,

  And I was ta'en for him, and he for me,

  And thereupon these errors are arose.

ANTIPHOLUS OF EPHESUS. These ducats pawn I for my
    father here.

DUKE. It shall not need: thy father hath his life.

COURTEZAN. Sir, I must have that diamond from you.

ANTIPHOLUS OF EPHESUS. There, take it; and much thanks
    for my good cheer.

ABBESS. Renowned duke, vouchsafe to take the pains

  To go with us into the abbey here,

  And hear at large discoursed all our fortunes;

  And all that are assembled in this place,

  That by this sympathized one day's error

  Have suffer'd wrong, go keep us company,

And we shall make full satisfaction.
Thirty-three years have I but gone in travail
Of you, my sons; and, till this present hour
My heavy burdens ne'er delivered.
The duke, my husband, and my children both,
And you the calendars of their nativity,
Go to a gossip's feast, and joy with me:
After so long grief such festivity!

DUKE. With all my heart I 'll gossip at this feast.

Exeunt Duke, Abbess,
Ægeon, Courtezan, Merchant, Angelo, and Attendants

DROMIO OF SYRACUSE. Master, shall I fetch your stuff from shipboard?

ANTIPHOLUS OF EPHESUS. Dromio, what stuff of mine hast thou embark'd?

DROMIO OF SYRACUSE. Your goods that lay at host, sir, in the Centaur.

ANTIPHOLUS OF SYRACUSE. He speaks to me. I am your master, Dromio:

Come, go with us; we 'll look to that anon:
Embrace thy brother there; rejoice with him.

Exeunt Antipholus of Syracuse
and Antipholus of Ephesus, Adriana and Luciana

DROMIO OF SYRACUSE. There is a fat friend at your master's house,

That kitchen'd me for you to-day at dinner:
She now shall be my sister, not my wife.

DROMIO OF EPHESUS. Methinks you are my glass, and not my brother:

I see by you I am a sweet-fac'd youth.
Will you walk in to see their gossiping?

DROMIO OF SYRACUSE. Not I, sir; you are my elder.

DROMIO OF EPHESUS. That 's a question: how shall we try it?

DROMIO OF SYRACUSE. We 'll draw cuts for the senior: till then lead thou first.

DROMIO OF EPHESUS. Nay, then, thus:

We came into the world like brother and brother;
And now let 's go hand in hand, not one before another.

Exeunt

MUCH ADO ABOUT NOTHING

CAST OF CHARACTERS

DON PEDRO, *Prince of Arragon*
DON JOHN, *his bastard Brother*
CLAUDIO, *a young Lord of Florence*
BENEDICK, *a young Lord of Padua*
LEONATO, *Governor of Messina*
ANTONIO, *his Brother*
BALTHAZAR, *Servant to Don Pedro*

BORACHIO ⎱ *followers of Don John*
CONRADE ⎰

DOGBERRY, *a Constable*
VERGES, *a Headborough*
FRIAR FRANCIS
A Sexton
A Boy

HERO, *Daughter to Leonato*
BEATRICE, *Niece to Leonato*

MARGARET ⎱ *Waiting-gentlewomen*
URSULA ⎰ *attending on Hero*

Messengers, Watch, Attendants, &c.

SCENE

Messina

ACT ONE

SCENE ONE

Before Leonato's House.

Enter Leonato, Hero, Beatrice and others,
with a Messenger

LEONATO. I learn in this letter that Don Pedro of Arragon comes this night to Messina.

MESSENGER. He is very near by this. He was not three leagues off when I left him.

LEONATO. How many gentlemen have you lost in this action?

MESSENGER. But few of any sort, and none of name.

LEONATO. A victory is twice itself when the achiever brings home full numbers. I find here that Don Pedro hath bestowed much honour on a young Florentine called Claudio.

MESSENGER. Much deserved on his part and equally remembered by Don Pedro. He hath borne himself beyond the promise of his age, doing in the figure of a lamb the feats of a lion: he hath indeed better bettered expectation than you must expect of me to tell you how.

LEONATO. He hath an uncle here in Messina will be very much glad of it.

MESSENGER. I have already delivered him letters, and there appears much joy in him; even so much that joy could not show itself modest enough without a badge of bitterness.

LEONATO. Did he break out into tears?

MESSENGER. In great measure.

LEONATO. A kind overflow of kindness. There are no faces

truer than those that are so washed: how much better is it to weep at joy than to joy at weeping!

BEATRICE. I pray you is Signior Mountanto returned from the wars or no?

MESSENGER. I know none of that name, lady: there was none such in the army of any sort.

LEONATO. What is he that you ask for, niece?

HERO. My cousin means Signior Benedick of Padua.

MESSENGER. O! he is returned, and as pleasant as ever he was.

BEATRICE. He set up his bills here in Messina and challenged Cupid at the flight; and my uncle's fool, reading the challenge, subscribed for Cupid, and challenged him at the bird-bolt. I pray you, how many hath he killed and eaten in these wars? But how many hath he killed? for, indeed, I promised to eat all of his killing.

LEONATO. Faith, niece, you tax Signior Benedick too much; but he 'll be meet with you, I doubt it not.

MESSENGER. He hath done good service, lady, in these wars.

BEATRICE. You had musty victual, and he hath holp to eat it: he is a very valiant trencher-man; he hath an excellent stomach.

MESSENGER. And a good soldier too, lady.

BEATRICE. And a good soldier to a lady; but what is he to a lord?

MESSENGER. A lord to a lord, a man to a man; stuffed with all honourable virtues.

BEATRICE. It is so, indeed; he is no less than a stuffed man; but for the stuffing,—well, we are all mortal.

LEONATO. You must not, sir, mistake my niece. There is a kind of merry war betwixt Signior Benedick and her: they never meet but there 's a skirmish of wit between them.

BEATRICE. Alas! he gets nothing by that. In our last conflict four of his five wits went halting off, and now is the whole man governed with one! so that if he have wit enough to keep himself warm, let him bear it for a difference between himself and his horse; for it is all the wealth that he hath left to be known a reasonable creature. Who is his companion now? He hath every month a new sworn brother.

MESSENGER. Is 't possible?

BEATRICE. Very easily possible: he wears his faith but as the fashion of his hat; it ever changes with the next block.

MESSENGER. I see, lady, the gentleman is not in your books.

BEATRICE. No; an he were, I would burn my study. But, I pray you, who is his companion? Is there no young squarer now that will make a voyage with him to the devil?

MESSENGER. He is most in the company of the right noble Claudio.

BEATRICE. O Lord! he will hang upon him like a disease: he is sooner caught than the pestilence, and the taker runs presently mad. God help the noble Claudio! if he have caught the Benedick, it will cost him a thousand pound ere a' be cured.

MESSENGER. I will hold friends with you, lady.

BEATRICE. Do, good friend.

LEONATO. You will never run mad, niece.

BEATRICE. No, not till a hot January.

MESSENGER. Don Pedro is approached.

Enter Don Pedro, Don John,
Claudio, Benedick, Balthazar, and Others

DON PEDRO. Good Signior Leonato, you are come to meet your trouble: the fashion of the world is to avoid cost, and you encounter it.

LEONATO. Never came trouble to my house in the likeness of your Grace, for trouble being gone, comfort should remain; but when you depart from me, sorrow abides and happiness takes his leave.

DON PEDRO. You embrace your charge too willingly. I think this is your daughter.

LEONATO. Her mo her hath many times told me so.

BENEDICK. Were you in doubt, sir, that you asked her?

LEONATO. Signior Benedick, no; for then you were a child.

DON PEDRO. You have it full, Benedick: we may guess by this what you are, being a man. Truly, the lady fathers herself. Be happy, lady, for you are like an honourable father.

BENEDICK. If Signior Leonato be her father, she would not have his head on her shoulders for all Messina, as like him as she is.

BEATRICE. I wonder that you will still be talking, Signior Benedick: nobody marks you.

BENEDICK. What! my dear Lady Disdain, are you yet living?

BEATRICE. Is it possible Disdain should die while she hath such meet food to feed it as Signior Benedick? Courtesy itself must convert to disdain, if you come in her presence.

BENEDICK. Then is courtesy a turncoat. But it is certain I am loved of all ladies, only you excepted; and I would I could find in my heart that I had not a hard heart; for, truly, I love none.

BEATRICE. A dear happiness to women: they would else have been troubled with a pernicious suitor. I thank God and my cold blood, I am of your humour for that: I had rather hear my dog bark at a crow than a man swear he loves me.

BENEDICK. God keep your ladyship still in that mind; so some gentleman or other shall 'scape a predestinate scratched face.

BEATRICE. Scratching could not make it worse, an 'twere such a face as yours were.

BENEDICK. Well, you are a rare parrot-teacher.

BEATRICE. A bird of my tongue is better than a beast of yours.

BENEDICK. I would my horse had the speed of your tongue, and so good a continuer. But keep your way, i' God's name; I have done.

BEATRICE. You always end with a jade's trick: I know you of old.

DON PEDRO. This is the sum of all, Leonato: Signior Claudio, and Signior Benedick, my dear friend Leonato hath invited you all. I tell him we shall stay here at the least a month, and he heartily prays some occasion may detain us longer: I dare swear he is no hypocrite, but prays from his heart.

LEONATO. If you swear, my lord, you shall not be forsworn. (*To Don John*) Let me bid you welcome, my lord: being reconciled to the prince your brother, I owe you all duty.

DON JOHN. I thank you: I am not of many words, but I thank you.

LEONATO. Please it your Grace lead on?

DON PEDRO. Your hand, Leonato; we will go together.

Exeunt all but Benedick and Claudio

CLAUDIO. Benedick, didst thou note the daughter of Signior Leonato?

BENEDICK. I noted her not; but I looked on her.

CLAUDIO. Is she not a modest young lady?

BENEDICK. Do you question me, as an honest man should do, for my simple true judgment; or would you have me speak after my custom, as being a professed tyrant to their sex?

CLAUDIO. No; I pray thee speak in sober judgment.

BENEDICK. Why, i' faith, methinks she 's too low for a high praise, too brown for a fair praise, and too little for a great praise: only this commendation I can afford her, that were she other than she is, she were unhandsome, and being no other but as she is, I do not like her.

CLAUDIO. Thou thinkest I am in sport: I pray thee tell me truly how thou likest her.

BENEDICK. Would you buy her, that you inquire after her?

CLAUDIO. Can the world buy such a jewel?

BENEDICK. Yea, and a case to put it into. But speak you this with a sad brow, or do you play the flouting Jack, to tell us Cupid is a good hare-finder, and Vulcan a rare carpenter? Come, in what key shall a man take you, to go in the song?

CLAUDIO. In mine eye she is the sweetest lady that ever I looked on.

BENEDICK. I can see yet without spectacles and I see no such matter: there 's her cousin an she were not possessed with a fury, exceeds her as much in beauty as the first of May doth the last of December. But I hope you have no intent to turn husband, have you?

CLAUDIO. I would scarce trust myself, though I had sworn to the contrary, if Hero would be my wife.

BENEDICK. Is 't come to this, i' faith? Hath not the world one man but he will wear his cap with suspicion? Shall I never see a bachelor of threescore again? Go to, i' faith; an thou wilt needs thrust thy neck into a yoke, wear the print of it, and sigh away Sundays. Look! Don Pedro is returned to seek you.

Re-enter Don Pedro

DON PEDRO. What secret hath held you here, that you followed not to Leonato's?

BENEDICK. I would your Grace would constrain me to tell.

DON PEDRO. I charge thee on thy allegiance.

BENEDICK. You hear, Count Claudio: I can be secret as a dumb man; I would have you think so; but on my allegiance, mark you this, on my allegiance: he is in love. With who? Now that is your Grace's part. Mark how short his answer is: with Hero, Leonato's short daughter.

CLAUDIO. If this were so, so were it uttered.

BENEDICK. Like the old tale, my lord: 'it is not so, nor 'twas not so; but, indeed, God forbid it should be so.'

CLAUDIO. If my passion change not shortly, God forbid it should be otherwise.

DON PEDRO. Amen, if you love her; for the lady is very well worthy.

CLAUDIO. You speak this to fetch me in, my lord.

DON PEDRO. By my troth, I speak my thought.

CLAUDIO. And in faith, my lord, I spoke mine.

BENEDICK. And by my two faiths and troths, my lord, I spoke mine.

CLAUDIO. That I love her, I feel.

DON PEDRO. That she is worthy, I know.

BENEDICK. That I neither feel how she should be loved nor know how she should be worthy, is the opinion that fire cannot melt out of me: I will die in it at the stake.

DON PEDRO. Thou wast ever an obstinate heretic in the despite of beauty.

CLAUDIO. And never could maintain his part but in the force of his will.

BENEDICK. That a woman conceived me, I thank her; that she brought me up, I likewise give her most humble thanks: but that I will have a recheat winded in my forehead, or hang my bugle in an invisible baldrick, all women shall pardon me. Because I will not do them the wrong to mistrust any, I will do myself the right to trust none; and the fine is,—for the which I may go the finer,— I will live a bachelor.

DON PEDRO. I shall see thee, ere I die, look pale with love.

BENEDICK. With anger, with sickness, or with hunger, my lord; not with love: prove that ever I lose more blood with love than I will get again with drinking, pick out mine eyes with a ballad-maker's pen, and hang me up at the door of a brothel-house for the sign of blind Cupid.

DON PEDRO. Well, if ever thou dost fall from this faith, thou wilt prove a notable argument.

BENEDICK. If I do, hang me in a bottle like a cat and shoot at me; and he that hits me, let him be clapped on the shoulder, and called Adam.

DON PEDRO. Well, as time shall try:
'In time the savage bull doth bear the yoke.'

BENEDICK. The savage bull may; but if ever the sensible Benedick bear it, pluck off the bull's horns and set them in my forehead; and let me be vilely painted, and in such great letters as they write, 'Here is good horse to hire,' let them signify under my sign 'Here you may see Benedick the married man.'

CLAUDIO. If this should ever happen, thou wouldst be horn-mad.

DON PEDRO. Nay, if Cupid have not spent all his quiver in Venice, thou wilt quake for this shortly.

BENEDICK. I look for an earthquake too then.

DON PEDRO. Well, you will temporize with the hours. In the meantime, good Signior Benedick, repair to Leonato's: commend me to him and tell him I will not fail him at supper; for indeed he hath made great preparation.

BENEDICK. I have almost matter enough in me for such an embassage; and so I commit you—

CLAUDIO. To the tuition of God: from my house, if I had it,—

DON PEDRO. The sixth of July: your loving friend, Benedick.

BENEDICK. Nay, mock not, mock not. The body of your discourse is sometime guarded with fragments, and the guards are but slightly basted on neither: ere you flout old ends any further, examine your conscience: and so I leave you.   *Exit*

CLAUDIO. My liege, your Highness now may do me good.

DON PEDRO. My love is thine to teach: teach it but how,
And thou shalt see how apt it is to learn
Any hard lesson that may do thee good.

CLAUDIO. Hath Leonato any son, my lord?

DON PEDRO. No child but Hero; she 's his only heir.
Dost thou affect her, Claudio?

CLAUDIO.   O! my lord,
When you went onward on this ended action,
I looked upon her with a soldier's eye,

That lik'd, but had a rougher task in hand
Than to drive liking to the name of love;
But now I am return'd, and that war-thoughts
Have left their places vacant, in their rooms
Come thronging soft and delicate desires,
All prompting me how fair young Hero is,
Saying, I lik'd her ere I went to wars.

DON PEDRO. Thou wilt be like a lover presently,
And tire the hearer with a book of words.
If thou dost love fair Hero, cherish it,
And I will break with her, and with her father,
And thou shalt have her. Was't not to this end
That thou began'st to twist so fine a story?

CLAUDIO. How sweetly do you minister to love,
That know love's grief by his complexion!
But lest my liking might too sudden seem,
I would have salv'd it with a longer treatise.

DON PEDRO. What need the bridge much broader than the
flood?
The fairest grant is the necessity.
Look, what will serve is fit: 'tis once, thou lov'st,
And I will fit thee with the remedy.
I know we shall have revelling to-night:
I will assume thy part in some disguise,
And tell fair Hero I am Claudio;
And in her bosom I'll unclasp my heart,
And take her hearing prisoner with the force
And strong encounter of my amorous tale:
Then, after to her father will I break;
And the conclusion is, she shall be thine.
In practice let us put it presently.   *Exeunt*

SCENE TWO

A Room in Leonato's House.

Enter Leonato and Antonio, meeting

LEONATO. How now, brother! Where is my cousin, your
son? Hath he provided this music?

ANTONIO. He is very busy about it. But, brother, I can tell
you strange news that you yet dreamt not of.

LEONATO. Are they good?

ANTONIO. As the event stamps them: but they have a good cover; they show well outward. The prince and Count Claudio, walking in a thick-pleached alley in my orchard, were thus much overheard by a man of mine: the prince discovered to Claudio that he loved my niece your daughter, and meant to acknowledge it this night in a dance; and, if he found her accordant, he meant to take the present time by the top and instantly break with you of it.

LEONATO. Hath the fellow any wit that told you this?

ANTONIO. A good sharp fellow: I will send for him; and question him yourself.

LEONATO. No, no; we will hold it as a dream till it appear itself: but I will acquaint my daughter withal, that she may be the better prepared for an answer, if peradventure this be true. Go you, and tell her of it. (*Several persons cross the stage*) Cousins, you know what you ave to do. O! I cry you mercy, friend; go you with me, and I will use your skill. Good cousin, have a care this busy time.   *Exeunt*

SCENE THREE

Another Room in Leonato's House.

Enter Don John and Conrade

CONRADE. What the good-year, my lord! why are you thus out of measure sad?

DON JOHN. There is no measure in the occasion that breeds; therefore the sadness is without limit.

CONRADE. You should hear reason.

DON JOHN. And when I have heard it, what blessing brings it?

CONRADE. If not a present remedy, at least a patient sufferance.

DON JOHN. I wonder that thou, being,—as thou say'st thou art,—born under Saturn, goest about to apply a moral medicine to a mortifying mischief. I cannot hide what I am: I must be sad when I have cause, and smile at no man's jests; eat when I have stomach, and wait for no man's leisure; sleep when I am drowsy, and tend on no man's business; laugh when I am merry, and claw no man in his humour.

CONRADE. Yea; but you must not make the full show of this till you may do it without controlment. You have of late stood out against your brother, and he hath ta'en you newly into his grace; where it is impossible you should take true root but by the fair weather that you make yourself: it is needful that you frame the season for your own harvest.

DON JOHN. I had rather be a canker in a hedge than a rose in his grace; and it better fits my blood to be disdained of all than to fashion a carriage to rob love from any: in this, though I cannot be said to be a flattering honest man, it must not be denied but I am a plain-dealing villain. I am trusted with a muzzle and enfranchised with a clog; therefore I have decreed not to sing in my cage. If I had my mouth, I would bite; if I had my liberty, I would do my liking: in the meantime, let me be that I am, and seek not to alter me.

CONRADE. Can you make no use of your discontent?

DON JOHN. I make all use of it, for I use it only. Who comes here?

Enter Borachio

What news, Borachio?

BORACHIO. I came yonder from a great supper: the prince, your brother, is royally entertained by Leonato; and I can give you intelligence of an intended marriage.

DON JOHN. Will it serve for any model to build mischief on? What is he for a fool that betroths himself to unquietness?

BORACHIO. Marry, it is your brother's right hand.

DON JOHN. Who? the most exquisite Claudio?

BORACHIO. Even he.

DON JOHN. A proper squire! And who, and who? which way looks he?

BORACHIO. Marry, on Hero, the daughter and heir of Leonato.

DON JOHN. A very forward March-chick! How came you to this?

BORACHIO. Being entertained for a perfumer, as I was smoking a musty room, comes me the prince and Claudio, hand in hand, in sad conference: I whipt me behind the arras, and there heard it agreed upon that the prince should woo Hero for himself, and having obtained her, give her to Count Claudio.

DON JOHN. Come, come; let us thither: this may prove food to my displeasure. That young start-up hath all the glory of my overthrow: if I can cross him any way, I bless myself every way. You are both sure, and will assist me?

CONRADE. } To the death, my lord.
BORACHIO. }

DON JOHN. Let us to the great supper: their cheer is the greater that I am subdued. Would the cook were of my mind! Shall we go to prove what 's to be done?

BORACHIO. We 'll wait upon your lordship.   *Exeunt*

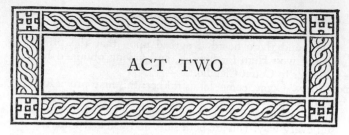

ACT TWO

A Hall in Leonato's House.

Enter Leonato, Antonio, Hero, Beatrice, and Others

LEONATO. Was not Count John here at supper?

ANTONIO. I saw him not.

BEATRICE. How tartly that gentleman looks! I never can see him but I am heart-burned an hour after.

HERO. He is of a very melancholy disposition.

BEATRICE. He were an excellent man that were made just in the mid-way between him and Benedick: the one is too like an image, and says nothing; and the other too like my lady's eldest son, evermore tattling.

LEONATO. Then half Signior Benedick's tongue in Count John's mouth, and half Count John's melancholy in Signior Benedick's face,—

BEATRICE. With a good leg and a good foot, uncle, and money enough in his purse, such a man would win any woman in the world, if a' could get her good will.

LEONATO. By my troth, niece, thou wilt never get thee a husband, if thou be so shrewd of thy tongue.

ANTONIO. In faith, she 's too curst.

BEATRICE. Too curst is more than curst: I shall lessen God's sending that way; for it is said, 'God sends a curst cow short horns'; but to a cow too curst he sends none.

LEONATO. So, by being too curst, God will send you no horns?

BEATRICE. Just, if he send me no husband; for the which blessing I am at him upon my knees every morning and evening. Lord! I could not endure a husband with a beard on his face: I had rather lie in the woollen.

LEONATO. You may light on a husband that hath no beard.

BEATRICE. What should I do with him? dress him in my ap-

parel and make him my waiting-gentlewoman? He that
hath a beard is more than a youth, and he that hath no
beard is less than a man; and he that is more than a
youth is not for me; and he that is less than a man, I am
not for him: therefore I will even take sixpence in earnest
of the bear-ward, and lead his apes into hell.

LEONATO. Well then, go you into hell?

BEATRICE. No; but to the gate; and there will the devil
meet me, like an old cuckold, with horns on his head, and
say, 'Get you to heaven, Beatrice, get you to heaven;
here 's no place for you maids': so deliver I up my apes,
and away to Saint Peter for the heavens; he shows me
where the bachelors sit, and there live we as merry as the
day is long.

ANTONIO. (*To Hero*) Well, niece, I trust you will be ruled
by your father.

BEATRICE. Yes, faith; it is my cousin's duty to make curtsy,
and say, 'Father, as it please you':—but yet for all that,
cousin, let him be a handsome fellow, or else make another curtsy, and say, 'Father, as it please me.'

LEONATO. Well, niece, I hope to see you one day fitted with
a husband.

BEATRICE. Not till God make men of some other metal than
earth. Would it not grieve a woman to be over-mastered
with a piece of valiant dust? to make an account of her
life to a clod of wayward marl? No, uncle, I 'll none:
Adam's sons are my brethren; and truly, I hold it a sin to
match in my kindred.

LEONATO. Daughter, remember what I told you: if the
prince do solicit you in that kind, you know your answer.

BEATRICE. The fault will be in the music, cousin, if you be
not wooed in good time: if the prince be too important,
tell him there is measure in everything, and so dance out
the answer. For, hear me, Hero: wooing, wedding, and
repenting, is as a Scotch jig, a measure, and a cinque-
pace: the first suit is hot and hasty, like a Scotch jig, and
full as fantastical; the wedding, mannerly-modest, as a
measure, full of state and ancientry; and then comes Repentance, and, with his bad legs, falls into the cinque-
pace faster and faster, till he sink into his grave.

LEONATO. Cousin, you apprehend passing shrewdly.

BEATRICE. I have a good eye, uncle: I can see a church by daylight.

LEONATO. The revellers are entering, brother: make good room.

Enter Don Pedro, Claudio, Benedick, Balthazar, Don John, Borachio, Margaret, Ursula, and Others, masked

DON PEDRO. Lady, will you walk about with your friend?

HERO. So you walk softly and look sweetly and say nothing, I am yours for the walk; and especially when I walk away.

DON PEDRO. With me in your company?

HERO. I may say so, when I please.

DON PEDRO. And when please you to say so?

HERO. When I like your favour; for God defend the lute should be like the case!

DON PEDRO. My visor is Philemon's roof; within the house is Jove.

HERO. Why, then, your visor should be thatch'd.

DON PEDRO. Speak low, if you speak love. *Takes her aside*

BALTHAZAR. Well, I would you did like me.

MARGARET. So would not I, for your own sake; for I have many ill qualities.

BALTHAZAR. Which is one?

MARGARET. I say my prayers aloud.

BALTHAZAR. I love you the better; the hearers may cry Amen.

MARGARET. God match me with a good dancer!

BALTHAZAR. Amen.

MARGARET. And God keep him out of my sight when the dance is done! Answer, clerk.

BALTHAZAR. No more words: the clerk is answered.

URSULA. I know you well enough: you are Signior Antonio.

ANTONIO. At a word, I am not.

URSULA. I know you by the waggling of your head.

ANTONIO. To tell you true, I counterfeit him.

URSULA. You could never do him so ill-well, unless you were the very man. Here 's his dry hand up and down: you are he, you are he.

ANTONIO. At a word, I am not.

URSULA. Come, come; do you think I do not know you by your excellent wit? Can virtue hide itself? Go to, mum, you are he: graces will appear, and there 's an end.

BEATRICE. Will you not tell me who told you so?

BENEDICK. No, you shall pardon me.

BEATRICE. Nor will you not tell me who you are?

BENEDICK. Not now.

BEATRICE. That I was disdainful, and that I had my good wit out of the 'Hundred Merry Tales.' Well, this was Signior Benedick that said so.

BENEDICK. What's he?

BEATRICE. I am sure you know him well enough.

BENEDICK. Not I, believe me.

BEATRICE. Did he never make you laugh?

BENEDICK. I pray you, what is he?

BEATRICE. Why, he is the prince's jester: a very dull fool; only his gift is in devising impossible slanders: none but libertines delight in him; and the commendation is not in his wit, but in his villany; for he both pleases men and angers them, and then they laugh at him and beat him. I am sure he is in the fleet: I would he had boarded me!

BENEDICK. When I know the gentleman, I'll tell him what you say.

BEATRICE. Do, do: he'll but break a comparison or two on me; which, peradventure not marked or not laughed at, strikes him into melancholy; and then there's a partridge wing saved, for the fool will eat no supper that night. (*Music within*) We must follow the leaders.

BENEDICK. In every good thing.

BEATRICE. Nay, if they lead to any ill, I will leave them at the next turning.

*Dance. Then exeunt all
but Don John, Borachio, and Claudio*

DON JOHN. Sure my brother is amorous on Hero, and hath withdrawn her father to break with him about it. The ladies follow her and but one visor remains.

BORACHIO. And that is Claudio: I know him by his bearing.

DON JOHN. Are not you Signior Benedick?

CLAUDIO. You know me well; I am he.

DON JOHN. Signior, you are very near my brother in his love: he is enamoured on Hero; I pray you, dissuade him from her; she is no equal for his birth: you may do the part of an honest man in it.

CLAUDIO. How know you he loves her?

DON JOHN. I heard him swear his affection.

BORACHIO. So did I too; and he swore he would marry her to-night.

DON JOHN. Come, let us to the banquet.

Exeunt Don John and Borachio

CLAUDIO. Thus answer I in name of Benedick,
But hear these ill news with the ears of Claudio.
'Tis certain so; the prince woos for himself.
Friendship is constant in all other things
Save in the office and affairs of love:
Therefore all hearts in love use their own tongues;
Let every eye negotiate for itself
And trust no agent; for beauty is a witch
Against whose charms faith melteth into blood.
This is an accident of hourly proof,
Which I mistrusted not. Farewell, therefore, Hero!

Re-enter Benedick

BENEDICK. Count Claudio?

CLAUDIO. Yea, the same.

BENEDICK. Come, will you go with me?

CLAUDIO. Whither?

BENEDICK. Even to the next willow, about your own business, count. What fashion will you wear the garland of? About your neck, like a usurer's chain? or under your arm, like a lieutenant's scarf? You must wear it one way, for the prince hath got your Hero.

CLAUDIO. I wish him joy of her.

BENEDICK. Why, that 's spoken like an honest drovier: so they sell bullocks. But did you think the prince would have served you thus?

CLAUDIO. I pray you, leave me.

BENEDICK. Ho! now you strike like the blind man: 'twas the boy that stole your meat, and you 'll beat the post.

CLAUDIO. If it will not be, I 'll leave you.   *Exit*

BENEDICK. Alas! poor hurt fowl. Now will he creep into sedges. But, that my lady Beatrice should know me, and not know me! The prince's fool! Ha! it may be I go under that title because I am merry. Yea, but so I am apt to do myself wrong; I am not so reputed: it is the base though bitter disposition of Beatrice that puts the world into her person, and so gives me out. Well, I 'll be revenged as I may.

Re-enter Don Pedro

DON PEDRO. Now, signior, where 's the count? Did you see him?

BENEDICK. Troth, my lord, I have played the part of Lady Fame. I found him here as melancholy as a lodge in a warren. I told him, and I think I told him true, that your Grace had got the good will of this young lady; and I offered him my company to a willow tree, either to make him a garland, as being forsaken, or to bind him up a rod, as being worthy to be whipped.

DON PEDRO. To be whipped! What 's his fault?

BENEDICK. The flat transgression of a school-boy, who, being overjoy'd with finding a bird's nest, shows it his companion, and he steals it.

DON PEDRO. Wilt thou make a trust a transgression? The transgression is in the stealer.

BENEDICK. Yet it had not been amiss the rod had been made, and the garland too; for the garland he might have worn himself, and the rod he might have bestowed on you, who, as I take it, have stolen his bird's nest.

DON PEDRO. I will but teach them to sing, and restore them to the owner.

BENEDICK. If their singing answer your saying, by my faith, you say honestly.

DON PEDRO. The Lady Beatrice hath a quarrel to you: the gentleman that danced with her told her she is much wronged by you.

BENEDICK. O! she misused me past the endurance of a block: an oak but with one green leaf on it, would have answered her: my very visor began to assume life and scold with her. She told me, not thinking I had been myself, that I was the prince's jester; that I was duller than a great thaw; huddling jest upon jest with such impossible conveyance upon me, that I stood like a man at a mark, with a whole army shooting at me. She speaks poniards, and every word stabs: if her breath were as terrible as her terminations, there were no living near her; she would infect to the north star. I would not marry her, though she were endowed with all that Adam had left him before he transgressed: she would have made Hercules have turned spit, yea, and have cleft his club to make the fire too. Come, talk not of her; you shall find her the infernal Ate in good apparel. I would to God some scholar would

conjure her, for certainly, while she is here, a man may
live as quiet in hell as in a sanctuary; and people sin
upon purpose because they would go thither; so, indeed,
all disquiet, horror and perturbation follow her.

Re-enter Claudio, Beatrice, Hero, and Leonato

DON PEDRO. Look! here she comes.

BENEDICK. Will your Grace command me any service to the
world's end? I will go on the slightest errand now to the
Antipodes that you can devise to send me on; I will fetch
you a toothpicker now from the furthest inch of Asia;
bring you the length of Prester John's foot; fetch you a
hair off the Great Cham's beard; do you any embassage
to the Pigmies, rather than hold three words' conference
with this harpy. You have no employment for me?

DON PEDRO. None, but to desire your good company.

BENEDICK. O God, sir, here 's a dish I love not: I cannot endure my Lady Tongue.   *Exit*

DON PEDRO. Come, lady, come; you have lost the heart of
Signior Benedick.

BEATRICE. Indeed, my lord, he lent it me awhile; and I gave
him use for it, a double heart for a single one: marry,
once before he won it of me with false dice, therefore
your Grace may well say I have lost it.

DON PEDRO. You have put him down, lady, you have put
him down.

BEATRICE. So I would not he should do me, my lord, lest I
should prove the mother of fools. I have brought Count
Claudio, whom you sent me to seek.

DON PEDRO. Why, how now, count! wherefore are you sad?

CLAUDIO. Not sad, my lord.

DON PEDRO. How then? Sick?

CLAUDIO. Neither, my lord.

BEATRICE. The count is neither sad, nor sick, nor merry,
nor well; but civil count, civil as an orange, and something of that jealous complexion.

DON PEDRO. I' faith, lady, I think your blazon to be true;
though, I 'll be sworn, if he be so, his conceit is false.
Here, Claudio, I have wooed in thy name, and fair Hero
is won; I have broke with her father, and, his good will
obtained; name the day of marriage, and God give thee
joy!

LEONATO. Count, take of me my daughter, and with her my

fortunes: his Grace hath made the match, and all grace
say Amen to it!

BEATRICE. Speak, count, 'tis your cue.

CLAUDIO. Silence is the perfectest herald of joy: I were but
little happy, if I could say how much. Lady, as you are
mine, I am yours: I give away myself for you and dote
upon the exchange.

BEATRICE. Speak, cousin; or, if you cannot, stop his mouth
with a kiss, and let not him speak neither.

DON PEDRO. In faith, lady, you have a merry heart.

BEATRICE. Yea, my lord; I thank it, poor fool, it keeps on
the windy side of care. My cousin tells him in his ear that
he is in her heart.

CLAUDIO. And so she doth, cousin.

BEATRICE. Good Lord, for alliance! Thus goes every one to
the world but I, and I am sunburnt. I may sit in a corner
and cry heigh-ho for a husband!

DON PEDRO. Lady Beatrice, I will get you one.

BEATRICE. I would rather have one of your father's getting.
Hath your Grace ne'er a brother like you? Your father got
excellent husbands, if a maid could come by them.

DON PEDRO. Will you have me, lady?

BEATRICE. No, my lord, unless I might have another for
working days: your Grace is too costly to wear every day.
But, I beseech your Grace, pardon me; I was born to
speak all mirth and no matter.

DON PEDRO. Your silence most offends me, and to be merry
best becomes you; for, out of question, you were born in
a merry hour.

BEATRICE. No, sure, my lord, my mother cried; but then
there was a star danced, and under that was I born. Cousins, God give you joy!

LEONATO. Niece, will you look to those things I told you of?

BEATRICE. I cry you mercy, uncle. By your Grace's pardon.

Exit

DON PEDRO. By my troth, a pleasant spirited lady.

LEONATO. There 's little of the melancholy element in her,
my lord: she is never sad but when she sleeps; and not
ever sad then, for I have heard my daughter say, she hath
often dreamed of unhappiness and waked herself with
laughing.

DON PEDRO. She cannot endure to hear tell of a husband.

LEONATO. O! by no means: she mocks all her wooers out of suit.

DON PEDRO. She were an excellent wife for Benedick.

LEONATO. O Lord! my lord, if they were but a week married, they would talk themselves mad.

DON PEDRO. Count Claudio, when mean you to go to church?

CLAUDIO. To-morrow, my lord. Time goes on crutches till love have all his rites.

LEONATO. Not till Monday, my dear son, which is hence a just seven-night; and a time too brief too, to have all things answer my mind.

DON PEDRO. Come, you shake the head at so long a breathing; but, I warrant thee, Claudio, the time shall not go dully by us. I will in the interim undertake one of Hercules' labours, which is, to bring Signior Benedick and the Lady Beatrice into a mountain of affection the one with the other. I would fain have it a match; and I doubt not but to fashion it, if you three will but minister such assistance as I shall give you direction.

LEONATO. My lord, I am for you, though it cost me ten nights' watchings.

CLAUDIO. And I, my lord.

DON PEDRO. And you too, gentle Hero?

HERO. I will do any modest office, my lord, to help my cousin to a good husband.

DON PEDRO. And Benedick is not the unhopefullest husband that I know. Thus far can I praise him; he is of a noble strain, of approved valour, and confirmed honesty. I will teach you how to humour your cousin, that she shall fall in love with Benedick; and I, with your two helps, will so practise on Benedick that, in despite of his quick wit and his queasy stomach, he shall fall in love with Beatrice. If we can do this, Cupid is no longer an archer: his glory shall be ours, for we are the only love-gods. Go in with me, and I will tell you my drift.   *Exeunt*

SCENE TWO

Another Room in Leonato's House.

Enter Don John and Borachio

DON JOHN. It is so; the Count Claudio shall marry the daughter of Leonato.

BORACHIO. Yea, my lord; but I can cross it.

DON JOHN. Any bar, any cross, any impediment will be medicinable to me: I am sick in displeasure to him, and whatsoever comes athwart his affection ranges evenly with mine. How canst thou cross this marriage?

BORACHIO. Not honestly, my lord; but so covertly that no dishonesty shall appear in me.

DON JOHN. Show me briefly how.

BORACHIO. I think I told your lordship, a year since, how much I am in the favour of Margaret, the waiting-gentle-woman to Hero.

DON JOHN. I remember.

BORACHIO. I can, at any unseasonable instant of the night, appoint her to look out at her lady's chamber-window.

DON JOHN. What life is in that, to be the death of this marriage?

BORACHIO. The poison of that lies in you to temper. Go you to the prince your brother; spare not to tell him, that he hath wronged his honour in marrying the renowned Claudio,—whose estimation do you mightily hold up,—to a contaminated stale, such a one as Hero.

DON JOHN. What proof shall I make of that?

BORACHIO. Proof enough to misuse the prince, to vex Claudio, to undo Hero, and kill Leonato. Look you for any other issue?

DON JOHN. Only to despite them, I will endeavour any thing.

BORACHIO. Go, then; find me a meet hour to draw Don Pedro and the Count Claudio alone: tell them that you know that Hero loves me; intend a kind of zeal both to the prince and Claudio, as—in love of your brother's honour, who hath made this match, and his friend's reputation, who is thus like to be cozened with the semblance of a maid,—that you have discovered thus. They will scarcely believe this without trial: offer them instances, which shall bear no less likelihood than to see me at her chamber-window, hear me call Margaret Hero; hear Margaret term me Claudio; and bring them to see this the very night before the intended wedding: for in the meantime I will so fashion the matter that Hero shall be absent; and there shall appear such seeming truth of Hero's disloyalty, that jealousy shall be called assurance, and all the preparation overthrown.

DON JOHN. Grow this to what adverse issue it can, I will put it in practice. Be cunning in the working this, and thy fee is a thousand ducats.

BORACHIO. Be you constant in the accusation, and my cunning shall not shame me.

DON JOHN. I will presently go learn their day of marriage.

Exeunt

SCENE THREE

Leonato's Garden.

Enter Benedick

BENEDICK. Boy!

Enter a Boy

BOY. Signior?

BENEDICK. In my chamber-window lies a book; bring it hither to me in the orchard.

BOY. I am here already, sir.

BENEDICK. I know that; but I would have thee hence, and here again. (*Exit Boy*) I do much wonder that one man, seeing how much another man is a fool when he dedicates his behaviours to love, will, after he hath laughed at such shallow follies in others, become the argument of his own scorn by falling in love: and such a man is Claudio. I have known, when there was no music with him but the drum and the fife; and now had he rather hear the tabor and the pipe: I have known, when he would have walked ten mile afoot to see a good armour; and now will he lie ten nights awake, carving the fashion of a new doublet. He was wont to speak plain and to the purpose, like an hon-

est man and a soldier; and now is he turned orthogra-
pher; his words are a very fantastical banquet, just so
many strange dishes. May I be so converted, and see with
these eyes? I cannot tell; I think not: I will not be sworn
but love may transform me to an oyster; but I 'll take my
oath on it, till he have made an oyster of me, he shall
never make me such a fool. One woman is fair, yet I am
well; another is wise, yet I am well; another virtuous, yet
I am well; but till all graces be in one woman, one woman
shall not come in my grace. Rich she shall be, that 's certain; wise, or I 'll none; virtuous, or I 'll never cheapen her;
fair, or I 'll never look on her; mild, or come not near me;
noble, or not I for an angel; of good discourse, an excellent musician, and her hair shall be of what colour it
please God. Ha! the prince and Monsieur Love! I will
hide me in the arbour.   *Withdraws*

Enter Don Pedro, Leonato,
and Claudio, followed by Balthazar and Musicians

DON PEDRO. Come, shall we hear this music?

CLAUDIO. Yea, my good lord. How still the evening is,
As hush'd on purpose to grace harmony!

DON PEDRO. See you where Benedick hath hid himself?

CLAUDIO. O! very well, my lord: the music ended,
We 'll fit the kid-fox with a penny-worth.

DON PEDRO. Come, Balthazar, we 'll hear that song again.

BALTHAZAR. O! good my lord, tax not so bad a voice
To slander music any more than once.

DON PEDRO. It is the witness still of excellency,
To put a strange face on his own perfection.
I pray thee, sing, and let me woo no more.

BALTHAZAR. Because you talk of wooing, I will sing;
Since many a wooer doth commence his suit
To her he thinks not worthy; yet he wooes;
Yet will he swear he loves.

DON PEDRO.   Nay, pray thee, come;
Or if thou wilt hold longer argument,
Do it in notes.

BALTHAZAR.   Note this before my notes;
There 's not a note of mine that 's worth the noting.

DON PEDRO. Why these are very crotchets that he speaks;
Notes, notes, forsooth, and nothing!   *Music*

BENEDICK. Now, divine air! now is his soul ravished! Is it

not strange that sheeps' guts should hale souls out of
men's bodies? Well, a horn for my money, when all 's
done.

BALTHAZAR'S SONG

Sigh no more, ladies, sigh no more,
 Men were deceivers ever;
One foot in sea, and one on shore,
 To one thing constant never.
  Then sigh not so,
  But let them go,
 And be you blithe and bonny,
Converting all your sounds of woe
 Into Hey nonny, nonny.
Sing no more ditties, sing no mo
 Of dumps so dull and heavy;
The fraud of men was ever so,
 Since summer first was leavy.
  Then sigh not so,
  But let them go,
 And be you blithe and bonny,
Converting all your sounds of woe
 Into Hey nonny, nonny.

DON PEDRO. By my troth, a good song.

BALTHAZAR. And an ill singer, my lord.

DON PEDRO. Ha, no, no, faith; thou singest well enough for
a shift.

BENEDICK. (*Aside*) An he had been a dog that should have
howled thus, they would have hanged him; and I pray
God his bad voice bode no mischief. I had as lief have
heard the night-raven, come what plague could have
come after it.

DON PEDRO. Yea, marry; dost thou hear, Balthazar? I pray
thee, get us some excellent music, for to-morrow night we
would have it at the Lady Hero's chamber-window.

BALTHAZAR. The best I can, my lord.

DON PEDRO. Do so: farewell. (*Exeunt Balthazar and Musicians*) Come hither, Leonato: what was it you told me
of to-day, that your niece Beatrice was in love with Signior Benedick?

CLAUDIO. O! ay:—(*Aside to Don Pedro*) Stalk on, stalk on;
the fowl sits. I did never think that lady would have loved
any man.

LEONATO. No, nor I neither; but most wonderful that she should so dote on Signior Benedick, whom she hath in all outward behaviours seemed ever to abhor.

BENEDICK. (*Aside*) Is 't possible? Sits the wind in that corner?

LEONATO. By my troth, my lord, I cannot tell what to think of it but that she loves him with an enraged affection: it is past the infinite of thought.

DON PEDRO. May be she doth but counterfeit.

CLAUDIO. Faith, like enough.

LEONATO. O God! counterfeit! There was never counterfeit of passion came so near the life of passion as she discovers it.

DON PEDRO. Why, what effects of passion shows she?

CLAUDIO. (*Aside*) Bait the hook well: this fish will bite.

LEONATO. What effects, my lord? She will sit you; (*To Claudio*) You heard my daughter tell you how.

CLAUDIO. She did, indeed.

DON PEDRO. How, how, I pray you? You amaze me: I would have thought her spirit had been invincible against all assaults of affection.

LEONATO. I would have sworn it had, my lord; especially against Benedick.

BENEDICK. (*Aside*) I should think this a gull, but that the white-bearded fellow speaks it: knavery cannot, sure, hide itself in such reverence.

CLAUDIO. (*Aside*) He hath ta'en the infection: hold it up.

DON PEDRO. Hath she made her affection known to Benedick?

LEONATO. No; and swears she never will: that 's her torment.

CLAUDIO. 'Tis true, indeed; so your daughter says: 'Shall I,' says she, 'that have so oft encountered him with scorn, write to him that I love him?'

LEONATO. This says she now when she is beginning to write to him; for she 'll be up twenty times a night, and there will she sit in her smock till she have writ a sheet of paper: my daughter tells us all.

CLAUDIO. Now you talk of a sheet of paper, I remember a pretty jest your daughter told us of.

LEONATO. O! when she had writ it, and was reading it over, she found Benedick and Beatrice between the sheet?

CLAUDIO. That.

LEONATO. O! she tore the letter into a thousand halfpence; railed at herself, that she should be so immodest to write to one that she knew would flout her: 'I measure him,' says she, 'by my own spirit; for I should flout him, if he writ to me; yea, though I love him, I should.'

CLAUDIO. Then down upon her knees she falls, weeps, sobs, beats her heart, tears her hair, prays, curses; 'O sweet Benedick! God give me patience!'

LEONATO. She doth indeed; my daughter says so; and the ecstasy hath so much overborne her, that my daughter is sometimes afeard she will do a desperate outrage to herself. It is very true.

DON PEDRO. It were good that Benedick knew of it by some other, if she will not discover it.

CLAUDIO. To what end? He would but make a sport of it and torment the poor lady worse.

DON PEDRO. An he should, it were an alms to hang him. She 's an excellent sweet lady, and, out of all suspicion, she is virtuous.

CLAUDIO. And she is exceeding wise.

DON PEDRO. In everything but in loving Benedick.

LEONATO. O! my lord, wisdom and blood combating in so tender a body, we have ten proofs to one that blood hath the victory. I am sorry for her, as I have just cause, being her uncle and her guardian.

DON PEDRO. I would she had bestowed this dotage on me; I would have daffed all other respects and made her half myself. I pray you, tell Benedick of it, and hear what a' will say.

LEONATO. Were it good, think you?

CLAUDIO. Hero thinks surely she will die; for she says she will die if he love her not, and she will die ere she make her love known, and she will die if he woo her, rather than she will bate one breath of her accustomed crossness.

DON PEDRO. She doth well: if she should make tender of her love, 'tis very possible he 'll scorn it; for the man,—as you know all,—hath a contemptible spirit.

CLAUDIO. He is a very proper man.

DON PEDRO. He hath indeed a good outward happiness.

CLAUDIO. 'Fore God, and in my mind, very wise.

DON PEDRO. He doth indeed show some sparks that are like wit.

LEONATO. And I take him to be valiant.

DON PEDRO. As Hector, I assure you: and in the managing of quarrels you may say he is wise; for either he avoids them with great discretion, or undertakes them with a most Christian-like fear.

LEONATO. If he do fear God, a' must necessarily keep peace: if he break the peace, he ought to enter into a quarrel with fear and trembling.

DON PEDRO. And so will he do; for the man doth fear God, howsoever it seems not in him by some large jests he will make. Well, I am sorry for your niece. Shall we go seek Benedick, and tell him of her love?

CLAUDIO. Never tell him, my lord: let her wear it out with good counsel.

LEONATO. Nay, that 's impossible: she may wear her heart out first.

DON PEDRO. Well, we will hear further of it by your daughter: let it cool the while. I love Benedick well, and I could wish he would modestly examine himself, to see how much he is unworthy to have so good a lady.

LEONATO. My lord, will you walk? Dinner is ready.

CLAUDIO. (*Aside*) If he do not dote on her upon this, I will never trust my expectation.

DON PEDRO. (*Aside*) Let there be the same net spread for her; and that must your daughter and her gentlewoman carry. The sport will be, when they hold one an opinion of another's dotage, and no such matter: that 's the scene that I would see, which will be merely a dumb-show. Let us send her to call him in to dinner.

   Exeunt Don Pedro, Claudio, and Leonato

BENEDICK. (*Advancing from the arbour*) This can be no trick: the conference was sadly borne. They have the truth of this from Hero. They seem to pity the lady: it seems, her affections have their full bent. Love me! why, it must be requited. I hear how I am censured: they say I will bear myself proudly, if I perceive the love come from her; they say too that she will rather die than give any sign of affection. I did never think to marry: I must not seem proud: happy are they that hear their detractions, and can put them to mending. They say the lady is fair:

'tis a truth, I can bear them witness; and virtuous: 'tis so, I cannot reprove it; and wise, but for loving me: by my troth, it is no addition to her wit, nor no great argument of her folly, for I will be horribly in love with her. I may chance have some odd quirks and remnants of wit broken on me, because I have railed so long against marriage; but doth not the appetite alter? A man loves the meat in his youth that he cannot endure in his age. Shall quips and sentences and these paper bullets of the brain awe a man from the career of his humour? No; the world must be peopled. When I said I would die a bachelor, I did not think I should live till I were married. Here comes Beatrice. By this day! she 's a fair lady: I do spy some marks of love in her.

Enter Beatrice

BEATRICE. Against my will I am sent to bid you come in to dinner.

BENEDICK. Fair Beatrice, I thank you for your pains.

BEATRICE. I took no more pains for those thanks than you take pains to thank me: if it had been painful, I would not have come.

BENEDICK. You take pleasure then in the message?

BEATRICE. Yea, just so much as you may take upon a knife's point, and choke a daw withal. You have no stomach, signior: fare you well.   *Exit*

BENEDICK. Ha! 'Against my will I am sent to bid you come in to dinner,' there 's a double meaning in that. 'I took no more pains for those thanks than you took pains to thank me,' that 's as much as to say, Any pains that I take for you is as easy as thanks. If I do not take pity of her, I am a villain; if I do not love her, I am a Jew. I will go get her picture.   *Exit*

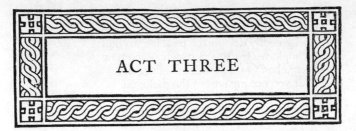

ACT THREE

SCENE ONE
Leonato's Garden.

Enter Hero, Margaret, and Ursula

HERO. Good Margaret, run thee to the parlour;
   There shalt thou find my cousin Beatrice
   Proposing with the prince and Claudio:
   Whisper her ear, and tell her, I and Ursula
   Walk in the orchard, and our whole discourse
   Is all of her; say that thou overheard'st us,
   And bid her steal into the pleached bower,
   Where honey-suckles, ripen'd by the sun,
   Forbid the sun to enter; like favourites,
   Made proud by princes, that advance their pride
   Against that power that bred it. There will she hide her,
   To listen our propose. This is thy office;
   Bear thee well in it and leave us alone.

MARGARET. I 'll make her come, I warrant you, presently.
                                          Exit

HERO. Now, Ursula, when Beatrice doth come,
   As we do trace this alley up and down,
   Our talk must only be of Benedick:
   When I do name him, let it be thy part
   To praise him more than ever man did merit.
   My talk to thee must be how Benedick
   Is sick in love with Beatrice: of this matter
   Is little Cupid's crafty arrow made,
   That only wounds by hearsay.
                Enter Beatrice, behind
                          Now begin;
   For look where Beatrice, like a lapwing, runs
   Close by the ground, to hear our conference.

URSULA. The pleasant'st angling is to see the fish

Cut with her golden oars the silver stream,
And greedily devour the treacherous bait:
So angle we for Beatrice; who even now
Is couched in the woodbine coverture.
Fear you not my part of the dialogue.

HERO. Then go we near her, that her ear lose nothing
Of the false sweet bait that we lay for it.

They advance to the bower

No, truly, Ursula, she is too disdainful;
I know her spirits are as coy and wild
As haggerds of the rock.

URSULA.   But are you sure
That Benedick loves Beatrice so entirely?

HERO. So says the prince, and my new-trothed lord.

URSULA. And did they bid you tell her of it, madam?

HERO. They did entreat me to acquaint her of it;
But I persuaded them, if they lov'd Benedick,
To wish him wrestle with affection,
And never to let Beatrice know of it.

URSULA. Why did you so? Doth not the gentleman
Deserve as full as fortunate a bed
As ever Beatrice shall couch upon?

HERO. O god of love! I know he doth deserve
As much as may be yielded to a man;
But nature never fram'd a woman's heart
Of prouder stuff than that of Beatrice;
Disdain and scorn ride sparkling in her eyes,
Misprising what they look on, and her wit
Values itself so highly, that to her
All matter else seems weak. She cannot love,
Nor take no shape nor project of affection,
She is so self-endear'd.

URSULA.   Sure, I think so;
And therefore certainly it were not good
She knew his love, lest she make sport at it.

HERO. Why, you speak truth. I never yet saw man,
How wise, how noble, young, how rarely featur'd,
But she would spell him backward: if fair-fac'd,
She would swear the gentleman should be her sister;
If black, why, Nature, drawing of an antick,
Made a foul blot; if tall, a lance ill-headed;
If low, an agate very vilely cut;

If speaking, why, a vane blown with all winds;
If silent, why, a block moved with none.
So turns she every man the wrong side out,
And never gives to truth and virtue that
Which simpleness and merit purchaseth.

URSULA. Sure, sure, such carping is not commendable.

HERO. No; not to be so odd and from all fashions
As Beatrice is, cannot be commendable.
But who dare tell her so? If I should speak,
She would mock me into air: O! she would laugh me
Out of myself, press me to death with wit.
Therefore let Benedick, like cover'd fire,
Consume away in sighs, waste inwardly:
It were a better death than die with mocks,
Which is as bad as die with tickling.

URSULA. Yet tell her of it: hear what she will say.

HERO. No; rather I will go to Benedick,
And counsel him to fight against his passion.
And, truly, I'll devise some honest slanders
To stain my cousin with. One doth not know
How much an ill word may empoison liking.

URSULA. O! do not do your cousin such a wrong.
She cannot be so much without true judgment,—
Having so swift and excellent a wit
As she is priz'd to have,—as to refuse
So rare a gentleman as Signior Benedick.

HERO. He is the only man of Italy,
Always excepted my dear Claudio.

URSULA. I pray you, be not angry with me, madam,
Speaking my fancy; Signior Benedick,
For shape, for bearing, argument and valour,
Goes foremost in report through Italy.

HERO. Indeed, he hath an excellent good name.

URSULA. His excellence did earn it, ere he had it.
When are you married, madam?

HERO. Why, every day, to-morrow. Come, go in:
I'll show thee some attires, and have thy counsel
Which is the best to furnish me to-morrow.

URSULA. She's lim'd, I warrant you: we have caught her,
madam.

HERO. If it prove so, then loving goes by haps:
Some Cupid kills with arrows, some with traps.

Exeunt Hero and Ursula

BEATRICE. (*Advancing*) What fire is in mine ears? Can this
    be true?
    Stand I condemn'd for pride and scorn so much?
Contempt, farewell! and maiden pride, adieu!
    No glory lives behind the back of such.
And, Benedick, love on; I will requite thee,
    Taming my wild heart to thy loving hand:
If thou dost love, my kindness shall incite thee
    To bind our loves up in a holy band;
For others say thou dost deserve, and I
Believe it better than reportingly.   *Exit*

SCENE TWO

A Room in Leonato's House.

Enter Don Pedro, Claudio, Benedick, and Leonato

DON PEDRO. I do but stay till your marriage be consummate,
and then go I toward Arragon.

CLAUDIO. I 'll bring you thither, my lord, if you 'll vouchsafe
me.

DON PEDRO. Nay, that would be as great a soil in the new
gloss of your marriage, as to show a child his new coat and
forbid him to wear it. I will only be bold with Benedick
for his company; for, from the crown of his head to the
sole of his foot, he is all mirth; he hath twice or thrice cut
Cupid's bow-string, and the little hangman dare not shoot
at him. He hath a heart as sound as a bell, and his tongue
is the clapper; for what his heart thinks his tongue speaks.

BENEDICK. Gallants, I am not as I have been.

LEONATO. So say I: methinks you are sadder.

CLAUDIO. I hope he be in love.

DON PEDRO. Hang him, truant! there 's no true drop of blood
in him, to be truly touched with love. If he be sad, he
wants money.

BENEDICK. I have the tooth-ache.

DON PEDRO. Draw it.

BENEDICK. Hang it.

CLAUDIO. You must hang it first, and draw it afterwards.

DON PEDRO. What! sigh for the tooth-ache?

LEONATO. Where is but a humour or a worm?

BENEDICK. Well, every one can master a grief but he that has it.

CLAUDIO. Yet say I, he is in love.

DON PEDRO. There is no appearance of fancy in him, unless it be a fancy that he hath to strange disguises; as, to be a Dutchman to-day, a Frenchman to-morrow, or in the shape of two countries at once, as a German from the waist downward, all slops, and a Spaniard from the hip upward, no doublet. Unless he have a fancy to this foolery, as it appears he hath, he is no fool for fancy, as you would have it appear he is.

CLAUDIO. If he be not in love with some woman, there is no believing old signs: a' brushes his hat a mornings; what should that bode?

DON PEDRO. Hath any man seen him at the barber's?

CLAUDIO. No, but the barber's man hath been seen with him; and the old ornament of his cheek hath already stuffed tennis-balls.

LEONATO. Indeed he looks younger than he did, by the loss of a beard.

DON PEDRO. Nay, a' rubs himself with civet: can you smell him out by that?

CLAUDIO. That's as much as to say the sweet youth's in love.

DON PEDRO. The greatest note of it is his melancholy.

CLAUDIO. And when was he wont to wash his face?

DON PEDRO. Yea, or to paint himself? for the which, I hear what they say of him.

CLAUDIO. Nay, but his jesting spirit; which is now crept into a lute-string, and new-governed by stops.

DON PEDRO. Indeed, that tells a heavy tale for him. Conclude, conclude he is in love.

CLAUDIO. Nay, but I know who loves him.

DON PEDRO. That would I know too: I warrant, one that knows him not.

CLAUDIO. Yes, and his ill conditions; and in despite of all, dies for him.

DON PEDRO. She shall be buried with her face upwards.

BENEDICK. Yet is this no charm for the tooth-ache. Old signior, walk aside with me: I have studied eight or nine wise words to speak to you, which these hobby-horses must not hear.   *Exeunt Benedick and Leonato*

DON PEDRO. For my life, to break with him about Beatrice.

CLAUDIO. 'Tis even so. Hero and Margaret have by this played their parts with Beatrice, and then the two bears will not bite one another when they meet.

Enter Don John

DON JOHN. My lord and brother, God save you!

DON PEDRO. Good den, brother.

DON JOHN. If your leisure served, I would speak with you.

DON PEDRO. In private?

DON JOHN. If it please you; yet Count Claudio may hear, for what I would speak of concerns him.

DON PEDRO. What 's the matter?

DON JOHN. (*To Claudio*) Means your lordship to be married to-morrow?

DON PEDRO. You know he does.

DON JOHN. I know not that, when he knows what I know.

CLAUDIO. If there be any impediment, I pray you discover it.

DON JOHN. You may think I love you not: let that appear hereafter, and aim better at me by that I now will manifest. For my brother, I think he holds you well, and in dearness of heart hath holp to effect your ensuing marriage; surely suit ill-spent, and labour ill bestowed!

DON PEDRO. Why, what 's the matter?

DON JOHN. I came hither to tell you; and circumstances shortened,—for she hath been too long a talking of,—the lady is disloyal.

CLAUDIO. Who, Hero?

DON JOHN. Even she: Leonato's Hero, your Hero, every man's Hero.

CLAUDIO. Disloyal?

DON JOHN. The word 's too good to paint out her wickedness; I could say, she were worse: think you of a worse title, and I will fit her to it. Wonder not till further warrant: go but with me to-night, you shall see her chamber-window entered, even the night before her wedding-day: if you love her then, to-morrow wed her; but it would better fit your honour to change your mind.

CLAUDIO. May this be so?

DON PEDRO. I will not think it.

DON JOHN. If you dare not trust that you see, confess not that you know. If you will follow me, I will show you

enough; and when you have seen more and heard more,
proceed accordingly.

CLAUDIO. If I see any thing to-night why I should not marry
her to-morrow, in the congregation, where I should wed,
there will I shame her.

DON PEDRO. And, as I wooed for thee to obtain her, I will
join with thee to disgrace her.

DON JOHN. I will disparage her no further till you are my
witnesses: bear it coldly but till midnight, and let the issue
show itself.

DON PEDRO. O day untowardly turned!

CLAUDIO. O mischief strangely thwarting!

DON JOHN. O plague right well prevented! So will you say
when you have seen the sequel.   *Exeunt*

SCENE THREE

A Street.

Enter Dogberry and Verges, with the Watch

DOGBERRY. Are you good men and true?

VERGES. Yea, or else it were pity but they should suffer sal-
vation, body and soul.

DOGBERRY. Nay, that were a punishment too good for them,
if they should have any allegiance in them, being chosen
for the prince's watch.

VERGES. Well, give them their charge, neighbour Dogberry.

DOGBERRY. First, who think you the most desartless man to
be constable?

FIRST WATCH. Hugh Oatcake, sir, or George Seacoal; for
they can write and read.

DOGBERRY. Come hither, neighbour Seacoal. God hath
blessed you with a good name: to be a well-favoured man
is the gift of fortune; but to write and read comes by nature.

SECOND WATCH. Both which, Master constable,--

DOGBERRY. You have: I knew it would be your answer. Well,
for your favour, sir, why, give God thanks, and make no
boast of it; and for your writing and reading, let that appear when there is no need of such vanity. You are
thought here to be the most senseless and fit man for the

constable of the watch; therefore bear you the lanthorn.
This is your charge: you shall comprehend all vagrom
men; you are to bid any man stand, in the prince's name.

WATCH. How, if a' will not stand?

DOGBERRY. Why, then, take no note of him, but let him go;
and presently call the rest of the watch together, and
thank God you are rid of a knave.

VERGES. If he will not stand when he is bidden, he is none of
the prince's subjects.

DOGBERRY. True, and they are to meddle with none but the
prince's subjects. You shall also make no noise in the
streets: for, for the watch to babble and to talk is most
tolerable and not to be endured.

SECOND WATCH. We will rather sleep than talk: we know
what belongs to a watch.

DOGBERRY. Why, you speak like an ancient and most quiet
watchman, for I cannot see how sleeping should offend;
only have a care that your bills be not stolen. Well, you
are to call at all the alehouses, and bid those that are
drunk get them to bed.

WATCH. How if they will not?

DOGBERRY. Why then, let them alone till they are sober: if
they make you not then the better answer, you may say
they are not the men you took them for.

WATCH. Well, sir.

DOGBERRY. If you meet a thief, you may suspect him, by virtue of your office, to be no true man; and, for such kind of
men, the less you meddle or make with them, why, the
more is for your honesty.

SECOND WATCH. If we know him to be a thief, shall we not
lay hands on him?

DOGBERRY. Truly, by your office, you may; but I think they
that touch pitch will be defiled. The most peaceable way
for you, if you do take a thief, is, to let him show himself
what he is and steal out of your company.

VERGES. You have been always called a merciful man, partner.

DOGBERRY. Truly, I would not hang a dog by my will, much
more a man who hath any honesty in him.

VERGES. If you hear a child cry in the night, you must call to
the nurse and bid her still it.

SECOND WATCH. How if the nurse be asleep and will not hear us?

DOGBERRY. Why, then, depart in peace, and let the child wake her with crying; for the ewe that will not hear her lamb when it baes, will never answer a calf when he bleats.

VERGES. 'Tis very true.

DOGBERRY. This is the end of the charge. You constable, are to present the prince's own person: if you meet the prince in the night, you may stay him.

VERGES. Nay, by 'r lady, that I think, a' cannot.

DOGBERRY. Five shillings to one on 't, with any man that knows the statues, he may stay him: marry, not without the prince be willing; for, indeed, the watch ought to offend no man, and it is an offence to stay a man against his will.

VERGES. By 'r lady, I think it be so.

DOGBERRY. Ha, ah, ha! Well, masters, good-night: an there be any matter of weight chances, call up me: keep your fellows' counsels and your own, and good-night. Come, neighbour.

SECOND WATCH. Well, masters, we hear our charge: let us go sit here upon the church-bench till two, and then all go to bed.

DOGBERRY. One word more, honest neighbours. I pray you, watch about Signior Leonato's door; for the wedding being there to-morrow, there is a great coil to-night. Adieu; be vigitant, I beseech you.   *Exeunt Dogberry and Verges*
                        Enter Borachio and Conrade

BORACHIO. What, Conrade!

WATCH. (*Aside*) Peace! stir not.

BORACHIO. Conrade, I say!

CONRADE. Here, man, I am at thy elbow.

BORACHIO. Mass, and my elbow itched; I thought there would a scab follow.

CONRADE. I will owe thee an answer for that; and now forward with thy tale.

BORACHIO. Stand thee close then under this pent-house, for it drizzles rain, and I will, like a true drunkard, utter all to thee.

WATCH. (*Aside*) Some treason, masters; yet stand close.

BORACHIO. Therefore know, I have earned of Don John a thousand ducats.

CONRADE. Is it possible that any villany should be so dear?

BORACHIO. Thou shouldst rather ask if it were possible any villany should be so rich; for when rich villains have need of poor ones, poor ones may make what price they will.

CONRADE. I wonder at it.

BORACHIO. That shows thou art unconfirmed. Thou knowest that the fashion of a doublet, or a hat, or a cloak, is nothing to a man.

CONRADE. Yes, it is apparel.

BORACHIO. I mean, the fashion.

CONRADE. Yes, the fashion is the fashion.

BORACHIO. Tush! I may as well say the fool 's the fool. But seest thou not what a deformed thief this fashion is?

WATCH. (Aside) I know that Deformed; a' has been a vile thief this seven years; a' goes up and down like a gentleman: I remember his name.

BORACHIO. Didst thou not hear somebody?

CONRADE. No: 'twas the vane on the house.

BORACHIO. Seest thou not, I say, what a deformed thief this fashion is? how giddily he turns about all the hot bloods between fourteen and five-and-thirty? sometime fashioning them like Pharaoh's soldiers in the reechy painting; sometime like god Bel's priests in the old church-window; sometime like the shaven Hercules in the smirched wormeaten tapestry, where his cod-piece seems as massy as his club?

CONRADE. All this I see, and I see that the fashion wears out more apparel than the man. But art not thou thyself giddy with the fashion too, that thou hast shifted out of thy tale into telling me of the fashion?

BORACHIO. Not so, neither; but know, that I have to-night wooed Margaret, the Lady Hero's gentlewoman, by the name of Hero: she leans me out at her mistress' chamberwindow, bids me a thousand times good-night,—I tell this tale vilely:—I should first tell thee how the prince, Claudio, and my master, planted and placed and possessed by my master Don John, saw afar off in the orchard this amiable encounter.

CONRADE. And thought they Margaret was Hero?

BORACHIO. Two of them did, the prince and Claudio; but

the devil my master, knew she was Margaret; and partly by his oaths, which first possessed them, partly by the dark night, which did deceive them, but chiefly by my villany, which did confirm any slander that Don John had made, away went Claudio enraged; swore he would meet her, as he was appointed, next morning at the temple, and there, before the whole congregation, shame her with what he saw o'er night, and send her home again without a husband.

FIRST WATCH. We charge you in the prince's name, stand!

SECOND WATCH. Call up the right Master constable. We have here recovered the most dangerous piece of lechery that ever was known in the commonwealth.

FIRST WATCH. And one Deformed is one of them: I know him, a' wears a lock.

CONRADE. Masters, masters!

SECOND WATCH. You 'll be made bring Deformed forth, I warrant you.

CONRADE. Masters,—

FIRST WATCH. Never speak: we charge you let us obey you to go with us.

BORACHIO. We are like to prove a goodly commodity, being taken up of these men's bills.

CONRADE. A commodity in question, I warrant you. Come, we 'll obey you. *Exeunt*

SCENE FOUR

A Room in Leonato's House.

Enter Hero, Margaret, and Ursula

HERO. Good Ursula, wake my cousin Beatrice, and desire her to rise.

URSULA. I will, lady.

HERO. And bid her come hither.

URSULA. Well. *Exit*

MARGARET. Troth, I think your other rabato were better.

HERO. No, pray thee, good Meg, I 'll wear this.

MARGARET. By my troth 's not so good; and I warrant your cousin will say so.

HERO. My cousin 's a fool, and thou art another: I 'll wear none but this.

MARGARET. I like the new tire within excellently, if the hair were a thought browner; and your gown 's a most rare fashion, i' faith. I saw the Duchess of Milan's gown that they praise so.

HERO. O! that exceeds, they say.

MARGARET. By my troth 's but a night-gown in respect of yours: cloth o' gold, and cuts, and laced with silver, set with pearls, down sleeves, side sleeves, and skirts round, underborne with a bluish tinsel; but for a fine, quaint, graceful, and excellent fashion, yours is worth ten on 't.

HERO. God give me joy to wear it! for my heart is exceeding heavy.

MARGARET. 'Twill be heavier soon by the weight of a man.

HERO. Fie upon thee! art not ashamed?

MARGARET. Of what, lady? of speaking honourably? is not marriage honourable in a beggar? Is not your lord honourable without marriage? I think you would have me say, 'saving your reverence, a husband': an bad thinking do not wrest true speaking, I 'll offend nobody. Is there any harm in 'the heavier for a husband'? None, I think, an it be the right husband and the right wife; otherwise 'tis light, and not heavy: ask my Lady Beatrice else; here she comes.

Enter Beatrice

HERO. Good-morrow, coz.

BEATRICE. Good-morrow, sweet Hero.

HERO. Why, how now! do you speak in the sick tune?

BEATRICE. I am out of all other tune, methinks.

MARGARET. Clap 's into 'Light o' love'; that goes without a burden: do you sing it, and I 'll dance it.

BEATRICE. Ye light o' love with your heels! Then, if your husband have stables enough, you 'll see he shall lack no barns.

MARGARET. O illegitimate construction! I scorn that with my heels.

BEATRICE. 'Tis almost five o'clock, cousin; 'tis time you were ready. By my troth, I am exceeding ill. Heigh-ho!

MARGARET. For a hawk, a horse, or a husband?

BEATRICE. For the letter that begins them all, H.

MARGARET. Well, an you be not turned Turk, there's no
more sailing by the star.

BEATRICE. What means the fool, trow?

MARGARET. Nothing I; but God send every one their heart's
desire!

HERO. These gloves the count sent me; they are an excellent
perfume.

BEATRICE. I am stuffed, cousin, I cannot smell.

MARGARET. A maid, and stuffed! there's goodly catching of
cold.

BEATRICE. O, God help me! God help me! how long have
you professed apprehension?

MARGARET. Ever since you left it. Doth not my wit become
me rarely!

BEATRICE. It is not seen enough, you should wear it in your
cap. By my troth, I am sick.

MARGARET. Get you some of this distilled Carduus Benedictus, and lay it to your heart: it is the only thing for a
qualm.

HERO. There thou prick'st her with a thistle.

BEATRICE. Benedictus! why Benedictus? You have some
moral in this Benedictus.

MARGARET. Moral! no, by my troth, I have no moral meaning; I meant, plain holy-thistle. You may think, perchance,
that I think you are in love: nay, by 'r lady, I am not such a
fool to think what I list; nor I list not to think what I can;
nor, indeed, I cannot think, if I would think my heart out
of thinking, that you are in love, or that you will be in love,
or that you can be in love. Yet Benedick was such another, and now is he become a man: he swore he would
never marry; and yet now, in despite of his heart, he eats
his meat without grudging: and how you may be converted, I know not; but methinks you look with your eyes
as other women do.

BEATRICE. What pace is this that thy tongue keeps?

MARGARET. Not a false gallop.

Re-enter Ursula

URSULA. Madam, withdraw: the prince, the count, Signior
Benedick, Don John, and all the gallants of the town, are
come to fetch you to church.

HERO. Help to dress me, good coz, good Meg, good Ursula.

Exeunt

SCENE FIVE

Another Room in Leonato's House.

Enter Leonato with Dogberry and Verges

LEONATO. What would you with me, honest neighbour?

DOGBERRY. Marry, sir, I would have some confidence with you, that decerns you nearly.

LEONATO. Brief, I pray you; for you see it is a busy time with me.

DOGBERRY. Marry, this it is, sir.

VERGES. Yes, in truth it is, sir.

LEONATO. What is it, my good friends?

DOGBERRY. Goodman Verges, sir, speaks a little off the matter: an old man, sir, and his wits are not so blunt, as, God help, I would desire they were; but, in faith, honest as the skin between his brows.

VERGES. Yes, I thank God, I am as honest as any man living, that is an old man and no honester than I.

DOGBERRY. Comparisons are odorous: palabras, neighbour Verges.

LEONATO. Neighbours, you are tedious.

DOGBERRY. It pleases your worship to say so, but we are the poor duke's officers; but truly, for mine own part, if I were as tedious as a king, I could find in my heart to bestow it all of your worship.

LEONATO. All thy tediousness on me! ha?

DOGBERRY. Yea, an 't were a thousand pound more than 'tis; for I hear as good exclamation on your worship, as of any man in the city, and though I be but a poor man, I am glad to hear it.

VERGES. And so am I.

LEONATO. I would fain know what you have to say.

VERGES. Marry, sir, our watch to-night, excepting your worship's presence, ha' ta'en a couple of as arrant knaves as any in Messina.

DOGBERRY. A good old man, sir; he will be talking; as they say, 'when the age is in, the wit is out.' God help us! it is a world to see! Well said, i' faith, neighbour Verges: well, God 's a good man; an two men ride of a horse, one must

ride behind. An honest soul, i' faith, sir; by my troth he is,
as ever broke bread: but God is to be worshipped: all men
are not alike; alas! good neighbour.

LEONATO. Indeed, neighbour, he comes too short of you.

DOGBERRY. Gifts that God gives.

LEONATO. I must leave you.

DOGBERRY. One word, sir: our watch, sir, hath indeed com-
prehended two aspicious persons, and we would have
them this morning examined before your worship.

LEONATO. Take their examination yourself, and bring it me:
I am now in great haste, as may appear unto you.

DOGBERRY. It shall be suffigance.

LEONATO. Drink some wine ere you go: fare you well.

Enter a Messenger

MESSENGER. My lord, they stay for you to give your daughter to her husband.

LEONATO. I 'll wait upon them: I am ready.

Exeunt Leonato and Messenger

DOGBERRY. Go, good partner, go, get you to Francis Seacoal;
bid him bring his pen and inkhorn to the gaol: we are
now to examination these men.

VERGES. And we must do it wisely.

DOGBERRY. We will spare for no wit, I warrant you; here 's
that shall drive some of them to a *non-come*: only get the
learned writer to set down our excommunication, and
meet me at the gaol. *Exeunt*

ACT FOUR

The Inside of a Church.

Enter Don Pedro, Don John, Leonato, Friar Francis, Claudio, Benedick, Hero, Beatrice, &c.

LEONATO. Come, Friar Francis, be brief: only to the plain form of marriage, and you shall recount their particular duties afterwards.

FRIAR. You come hither, my lord, to marry this lady?

CLAUDIO. No.

LEONATO. To be married to her, friar; you come to marry her.

FRIAR. Lady, you come hither to be married to this count?

HERO. I do.

FRIAR. If either of you know any inward impediment, why you should not be conjoined, I charge you, on your souls, to utter it.

CLAUDIO. Know you any, Hero?

HERO. None, my lord.

FRIAR. Know you any, count?

LEONATO. I dare make his answer; none.

CLAUDIO. O! what men dare do! what men may do! what men daily do, not knowing what they do!

BENEDICK. How now! Interjections? Why then, some be of laughing, as ah! ha! he!

CLAUDIO. Stand thee by, friar. Father, by your leave:
Will you with free and unconstrained soul
Give me this maid, your daughter?

LEONATO. As freely, son, as God did give her me.

CLAUDIO. And what have I to give you back whose worth
May counterpoise this rich and precious gift?

DON PEDRO. Nothing, unless you render her again.

CLAUDIO. Sweet prince, you learn me noble thankfulness.

    There, Leonato, take her back again:
    Give not this rotten orange to your friend;
    She 's but the sign and semblance of her honour.
    Behold! how like a maid she blushes here.
    O! what authority and show of truth
    Can cunning sin cover itself withal.
    Comes not that blood as modest evidence
    To witness simple virtue? Would you not swear,
    All you that see her, that she were a maid,
    By these exterior shows? But she is none:
    She knows the heat of a luxurious bed;
    Her blush is guiltiness, not modesty.

LEONATO. What do you mean, my lord?

CLAUDIO.   Not to be married,
    Not to knit my soul to an approved wanton.

LEONATO. Dear my lord, if you, in your own proof,
    Have vanquish'd the resistance of her youth,
    And made defeat of her virginity,—

CLAUDIO. I know what you would say: if I have known her,
    You 'll say she did embrace me as a husband,
    And so extenuate the 'forehand sin:
    No, Leonato,
    I never tempted her with word too large;
    But, as a brother to his sister, show'd
    Bashful sincerity and comely love.

HERO. And seem'd I ever otherwise to you?

CLAUDIO. Out on thee! Seeming! I will write against it:
    You seem to me as Dian in her orb,
    As chaste as is the bud ere it be blown;
    But you are more intemperate in your blood
    Than Venus, or those pamper'd animals
    That rage in savage sensuality.

HERO. Is my lord well, that he doth speak so wide?

LEONATO. Sweet prince, why speak not you?

DON PEDRO.   What should I speak?
    I stand dishonour'd, that have gone about
    To link my dear friend to a common stale.

LEONATO. Are these things spoken, or do I but dream?

DON JOHN. Sir, they are spoken, and these things are true.

BENEDICK. This looks not like a nuptial.

HERO.   True! O God!

CLAUDIO. Leonato, stand I here?

Is this the prince? Is this the prince's brother?
Is this face Hero's? Are our eyes our own?

LEONATO. All this is so; but what of this, my lord?

CLAUDIO. Let me but move one question to your daughter;
And by that fatherly and kindly power
That you have in her, bid her answer truly.

LEONATO. I charge thee do so, as thou art my child.

HERO. O, God defend me! how am I beset!
What kind of catechizing call you this?

CLAUDIO. To make you answer truly to your name.

HERO. Is it not Hero? Who can blot that name
With any just reproach?

CLAUDIO.   Marry, that can Hero:
Hero itself can blot out Hero's virtue.
What man was he talk'd with you yesternight
Out at your window, betwixt twelve and one?
Now, if you are a maid, answer to this.

HERO. I talk'd with no man at that hour, my lord.

DON PEDRO. Why, then are you no maiden. Leonato,
I am sorry you must hear: upon mine honour,
Myself, my brother, and this grieved count,
Did see her, hear her, at that hour last night,
Talk with a ruffian at her chamber-window;
Who hath indeed, most like a liberal villain,
Confess'd the vile encounters they have had
A thousand times in secret.

DON JOHN. Fie, fie! they are not to be nam'd, my lord,
Not to be spoke of;
There is not chastity enough in language
Without offence to utter them. Thus, pretty lady,
I am sorry for thy much misgovernment.

CLAUDIO. O Hero! what a Hero hadst thou been,
If half thy outward graces had been plac'd
About thy thoughts and counsels of thy heart!
But fare thee well, most foul, most fair! Farewell,
Thou pure impiety, and impious purity!
For thee I'll lock up all the gates of love,
And on my eyelids shall conjecture hang,
To turn all beauty into thoughts of harm,
And never shall it more be gracious.

LEONATO. Hath no man's dagger here a point for me?

Hero swoons

BEATRICE. Why, how now, cousin! wherefore sink you
 down?

DON JOHN. Come, let us go. These things, come thus to light,
 Smother her spirits up.

> *Exeunt Don Pedro, Don John and Claudio*

BENEDICK. How doth the lady?

BEATRICE.   Dead, I think! help, uncle!
 Hero! why, Hero! Uncle! Signior Benedick!
 Friar!

LEONATO. O Fate! take not away thy heavy hand:
 Death is the fairest cover for her shame
 That may be wish'd for.

BEATRICE.   How now, cousin Hero!

FRIAR. Have comfort, lady,

LEONATO. Dost thou look up?

FRIAR.   Yea; wherefore should she not?

LEONATO. Wherefore! Why, doth not every earthly thing
 Cry shame upon her? Could she here deny
 The story that is printed in her blood?
 Do not live, Hero; do not ope thine eyes;
 For, did I think thou wouldst not quickly die,
 Thought I thy spirits were stronger than thy shames,
 Myself would, on the rearward of reproaches,
 Strike at thy life. Griev'd I, I had but one?
 Chid I for that at frugal nature's frame?
 O! one too much by thee. Why had I one?
 Why ever wast thou lovely in mine eyes?
 Why had I not with charitable hand
 Took up a beggar's issue at my gates,
 Who smirched thus, and mir'd with infamy,
 I might have said, 'No part of it is mine;
 This shame derives itself from unknown loins'?
 But mine, and mine I lov'd, and mine I prais'd,
 And mine that I was proud on, mine so much
 That I myself was to myself not mine,
 Valuing of her; why, she—O! she is fallen
 Into a pit of ink, that the wide sea
 Hath drops too few to wash her clean again,
 And salt too little which may season give
 To her foul-tainted flesh.

BENEDICK.   Sir, sir, be patient.
 For my part, I am so attir'd in wonder,

I know not what to say.

BEATRICE. O! on my soul, my cousin is belied!

BENEDICK. Lady, were you her bedfellow last night?

BEATRICE. No, truly, not; although, until last night
I have this twelvemonth been her bedfellow.

LEONATO. Confirm'd, confirm'd! O! that is stronger made,
Which was before barr'd up with ribs of iron.
Would the two princes lie? and Claudio lie,
Who lov'd her so, that, speaking of her foulness,
Wash'd it with tears? Hence from her! let her die.

FRIAR. Hear me a little;
For I have only been silent so long,
And given way unto this course of fortune,
By noting of the lady: I have mark'd
A thousand blushing apparitions
To start into her face; a thousand innocent shames
In angel whiteness bear away those blushes;
And in her eye there hath appear'd a fire,
To burn the errors that these princes hold
Against her maiden truth. Call me a fool;
Trust not my reading nor my observations,
Which with experimental seal doth warrant
The tenour of my book; trust not my age,
My reverence, calling, nor my divinity,
If this sweet lady lie not guiltless here
Under some biting error.

LEONATO.   Friar, it cannot be.
Thou seest that all the grace that she hath left
Is, that she will not add to her damnation
A sin of perjury: she not denies it.
Why seek'st thou then to cover with excuse
That which appears in proper nakedness?

FRIAR. Lady, what man is he you are accus'd of?

HERO. They know that do accuse me, I know none;
If I know more of any man alive
Than that which maiden modesty doth warrant,
Let all my sins lack mercy! O, my father!
Prove you that any man with me convers'd
At hours unmeet, or that I yesternight
Maintain'd the change of words with any creature,
Refuse me, hate me, torture me to death.

FRIAR. There is some strange misprision in the princes.

BENEDICK. Two of them have the very bent of honour;
And if their wisdoms be misled in this,
The practice of it lives in John the bastard,
Whose spirits toil in frame of villanies.

LEONATO. I know not. If they speak but truth of her,
These hands shall tear her; if they wrong her honour,
The proudest of them shall well hear of it.
Time hath not yet so dried this blood of mine,
Nor age so eat up my invention,
Nor fortune made such havoc of my means,
Nor my bad life reft me so much of friends,
But they shall find, awak'd in such a kind,
Both strength of limb and policy of mind,
Ability in means and choice of friends,
To quit me of them throughly.

FRIAR.   Pause awhile,
And let my counsel sway you in this case.
Your daughter here the princes left for dead;
Let her awhile be secretly kept in,
And publish it that she is dead indeed:
Maintain a mourning ostentation;
And on your family's old monument
Hang mournful epitaphs and do all rites
That appertain unto a burial.

LEONATO. What shall become of this? What will this do?

FRIAR. Marry, this well carried shall on her behalf
Change slander to remorse; that is some good
But not for that dream I on this strange course,
But on this travail look for greater birth.
She dying, as it must be so maintain'd,
Upon the instant that she was accus'd,
Shall be lamented, pitied and excus'd
Of every hearer; for it so falls out
That what we have we prize not to the worth
Whiles we enjoy it, but being lack'd and lost,
Why, then we rack the value, then we find
The virtue that possession would not show us
Whiles it was ours. So will it fare with Claudio:
When he shall hear she died upon his words,
The idea of her life shall sweetly creep
Into his study of imagination,
And every lovely organ of her life

Shall come apparell'd in more precious habit,
More moving-delicate, and full of life
Into the eye and prospect of his soul,
Than when she liv'd indeed: then shall he mourn,—
If ever love had interest in his liver,—
And wish he had not so accused her,
No, though he thought his accusation true.
Let this be so, and doubt not but success
Will fashion the event in better shape
Than I can lay it down in likelihood.
But if all aim but this be levell'd false,
The supposition of the lady's death
Will quench the wonder of her infamy:
And if it sort not well, you may conceal her,—
As best befits her wounded reputation,—
In some reclusive and religious life,
Out of all eyes, tongues, minds, and injuries.

BENEDICK. Signior Leonato, let the friar advise you:
And though you know my inwardness and love
Is very much unto the prince and Claudio,
Yet, by mine honour, I will deal in this
As secretly and justly as your soul
Should with your body.

LEONATO.   Being that I flow in grief,
The smallest twine may lead me.

FRIAR. 'Tis well consented: presently away;
For to strange sores strangely they strain the cure.
Come, lady, die to live: this wedding day
Perhaps is but prolong'd: have patience and endure.

Exeunt Friar, Hero, and Leonato

BENEDICK. Lady Beatrice, have you wept all this while?

BEATRICE. Yea, and I will weep a while longer.

BENEDICK. I will not desire that.

BEATRICE. You have no reason; I do it freely.

BENEDICK. Surely I do believe your fair cousin is wronged.

BEATRICE. Ah! how much might the man deserve of me that
would right her.

BENEDICK. Is there any way to show such friendship?

BEATRICE. A very even way, but no such friend.

BENEDICK. May a man do it?

BEATRICE. It is a man's office, but not yours.

BENEDICK. I do love nothing in the world so well as you: is not that strange?

BEATRICE. As strange as the thing I know not. It were as possible for me to say I loved nothing so well as you; but believe me not, and yet I lie not; I confess nothing, nor I deny nothing. I am sorry for my cousin.

BENEDICK. By my sword, Beatrice, thou lovest me.

BEATRICE. Do not swear by it, and eat it.

BENEDICK. I will swear by it that you love me; and I will make him eat it that says I love not you.

BEATRICE. Will you not eat your word?

BENEDICK. With no sauce that can be devised to it. I protest I love thee.

BEATRICE. Why then, God forgive me!

BENEDICK. What offence, sweet Beatrice?

BEATRICE. You have stayed me in a happy hour: I was about to protest I loved you.

BENEDICK. And do it with all thy heart.

BEATRICE. I love you with so much of my heart that none is left to protest.

BENEDICK. Come, bid me do anything for thee.

BEATRICE. Kill Claudio.

BENEDICK. Ha! not for the wide world.

BEATRICE. You kill me to deny it. Farewell.

BENEDICK. Tarry, sweet Beatrice.

BEATRICE. I am gone, though I am here: there is no love in you: nay, I pray you, let me go.

BENEDICK. Beatrice,—

BEATRICE. In faith, I will go.

BENEDICK. We 'll be friends first.

BEATRICE. You dare easier be friends with me than fight with mine enemy.

BENEDICK. Is Claudio thine enemy?

BEATRICE. Is he not approved in the height a villain, that hath slandered, scorned, dishonoured my kinswoman? O! that I were a man. What! bear her in hand until they come to take hands, and then, with public accusation, uncovered slander, unmitigated rancour,—O God, that I were a man! I would eat his heart in the market-place.

BENEDICK. Hear me, Beatrice,—

BEATRICE. Talk with a man out at a window! a proper saying!

BENEDICK. Nay, but Beatrice,—

BEATRICE. Sweet Hero! she is wronged, she is slandered, she is undone.

BENEDICK. Beat——

BEATRICE. Princes and counties! Surely, a princely testimony, a goodly Count Comfect; a sweet gallant, surely! O! that I were a man for his sake, or that I had any friend would be a man for my sake! But manhood is melted into curtsies, valour into compliment, and men are only turned into tongue, and trim ones too: he is now as valiant as Hercules, that only tells a lie and swears it. I cannot be a man with wishing, therefore I will die a woman with grieving.

BENEDICK. Tarry, good Beatrice. By this hand, I love thee.

BEATRICE. Use it for my love some other way than swearing by it.

BENEDICK. Think you in your soul the Count Claudio hath wronged Hero?

BEATRICE. Yea, as sure as I have a thought or a soul.

BENEDICK. Enough! I am engaged, I will challenge him. I will kiss your hand, and so leave you. By this hand, Claudio shall render me a dear account. As you hear of me, so think of me. Go, comfort your cousin: I must say she is dead; and so, farewell.   *Exeunt*

SCENE TWO

A Prison.

Enter Dogberry, Verges, and Sexton, in gowns; and the Watch, with Conrade and Borachio

DOGBERRY. Is our whole dissembly appeared?

VERGES. O! a stool and a cushion for the sexton.

SEXTON. Which be the malefactors?

DOGBERRY. Marry, that am I and my partner.

VERGES. Nay, that 's certain: we have the exhibition to examine.

SEXTON. But which are the offenders that are to be examined? Let them come before Master constable.

DOGBERRY. Yea, marry, let them come before me. What is your name, friend?

BORACHIO. Borachio.

DOGBERRY. Pray write down Borachio. Yours, sirrah?

CONRADE. I am a gentleman, sir, and my name is Conrade.

DOGBERRY. Write down Master Gentleman Conrade. Masters, do you serve God?

CONRADE.   } Yea, sir, we hope.
BORACHIO.   }

DOGBERRY. Write down that they hope they serve God: and write God first; for God defend but God should go before such villains! Masters, it is proved already that you are little better than false knaves, and it will go near to be thought so shortly. How answer you for yourselves?

CONRADE. Marry, sir, we say we are none.

DOGBERRY. A marvellous witty fellow, I assure you; but I will go about with him. Come you hither, sirrah; a word in your ear: sir, I say to you, it is thought you are false knaves.

BORACHIO. Sir, I say to you we are none.

DOGBERRY. Well, stand aside. 'Fore God, they are both in a tale. Have you writ down, that they are none?

SEXTON. Master constable, you go not the way to examine: you must call forth the watch that are their accusers.

DOGBERRY. Yea, marry, that's the eftest way. Let the watch come forth. Masters, I charge you, in the prince's name, accuse these men.

FIRST WATCH. This man said, sir, that Don John, the prince's brother, was a villain.

DOGBERRY. Write down Prince John a villain. Why, that is flat perjury, to call a prince's brother villain.

BORACHIO. Master constable,—

DOGBERRY. Pray thee, fellow, peace: I do not like thy look, I promise thee.

SEXTON. What heard you him say else?

SECOND WATCH. Marry, that he had received a thousand ducats of Don John for accusing the Lady Hero wrongfully.

DOGBERRY. Flat burglary as ever was committed.

VERGES. Yea, by the mass, that it is.

SEXTON. What else, fellow?

FIRST WATCH. And that Count Claudio did mean, upon his words, to disgrace Hero before the whole assembly, and not marry her.

DOGBERRY. O villain! thou wilt be condemned into everlasting redemption for this.

SEXTON. What else?

SECOND WATCH. This is all.

SEXTON. And this is more, masters, than you can deny. Prince John is this morning secretly stolen away: Hero was in this manner accused, in this very manner refused, and, upon the grief of this, suddenly died. Master Constable, let these men be bound, and brought to Leonato's: I will go before and show him their examination.   *Exit*

DOGBERRY. Come, let them be opinioned.

VERGES. Let them be in the hands—

CONRADE. Off, coxcomb!

DOGBERRY. God's my life! where's the sexton? let him write down the prince's officer coxcomb. Come, bind them. Thou naughty varlet!

CONRADE. Away! you are an ass; you are an ass.

DOGBERRY. Dost thou not suspect my place? Dost thou not suspect my years? O that he were here to write me down an ass! but, masters, remember that I am an ass; though it be not written down, yet forget not that I am an ass. No, thou villain, thou art full of piety, as shall be proved upon thee by good witness. I am a wise fellow; and, which is more, an officer; and, which is more, a householder; and, which is more, as pretty a piece of flesh as any in Messina; and one that knows the law, go to; and a rich fellow enough, go to; and a fellow that hath had losses; and one that hath two gowns, and everything handsome about him. Bring him away. O that I had been writ down an ass!   *Exeunt*

ACT FIVE

SCENE ONE

Before Leonato's House.

Enter Leonato and Antonio

ANTONIO. If you go on thus, you will kill yourself
  And 'tis not wisdom thus to second grief
  Against yourself.
LEONATO.   I pray thee, cease thy counsel,
  Which falls into mine ears as profitless
  As water in a sieve: give not me counsel;
  Nor let no comforter delight mine ear
  But such a one whose wrongs do suit with mine:
  Bring me a father that so lov'd his child,
  Whose joy of her is overwhelm'd like mine,
  And bid him speak of patience;
  Measure his woe the length and breadth of mine,
  And let it answer every strain for strain,
  As thus for thus and such a grief for such,
  In every lineament, branch, shape, and form:
  If such a one will smile, and stroke his beard;
  Bid sorrow wag, cry 'hem' when he should groan,
  Patch grief with proverbs; make misfortune drunk
  With candle-wasters; bring him yet to me,
  And I of him will gather patience.
  But there is no such man; for, brother, men
  Can counsel and speak comfort to that grief
  Which they themselves not feel; but, tasting it,
  Their counsel turns to passion, which before
  Would give preceptial medicine to rage,
  Fetter strong madness in a silken thread,
  Charm ache with air and agony with words.
  No, no; 'tis all men's office to speak patience
  To those that wring under the load of sorrow,

But no man's virtue nor sufficiency
To be so moral when he shall endure
The like himself. Therefore give me no counsel:
My griefs cry louder than advertisement.

ANTONIO. Therein do men from children nothing differ.

LEONATO. I pray thee, peace! I will be flesh and blood;
For there was never yet philosopher
That could endure the toothache patiently,
However they have writ the style of gods
And made a push at chance and sufferance.

ANTONIO. Yet bend not all the harm upon yourself;
Make those that do offend you suffer too.

LEONATO. There thou speak'st reason: nay, I will do so.
My soul doth tell me Hero is belied;
And that shall Claudio know; so shall the prince,
And all of them that thus dishonour her.

ANTONIO. Here come the prince and Claudio hastily.

Enter Don Pedro and Claudio

DON PEDRO. Good den, good den.

CLAUDIO.   Good-day to both of you.

LEONATO. Hear you, my lords,—

DON PEDRO.   We have some haste, Leonato.

LEONATO. Some haste, my lord! well, fare you well, my lord:
Are you so hasty now?—well, all is one.

DON PEDRO. Nay, do not quarrel with us, good old man.

ANTONIO. If he could right himself with quarrelling,
Some of us would lie low.

CLAUDIO.   Who wrongs him?

LEONATO. Marry, thou dost wrong me; thou dissembler,
thou.
Nay, never lay thy hand upon thy sword;
I fear thee not.

CLAUDIO.   Marry, beshrew my hand,
If it should give your age such cause of fear.
In faith, my hand meant nothing to my sword.

LEONATO. Tush, tush, man! never fleer and jest at me:
I speak not like a dotard nor a fool,
As, under privilege of age, to brag
What I have done being young, or what would do,
Were I not old. Know, Claudio, to thy head,
Thou hast so wrong'd mine innocent child and me
That I am forc'd to lay my reverence by,

And, with grey hairs and bruise of many days,
Do challenge thee to trial of a man.
I say thou hast belied mine innocent child:
Thy slander hath gone through and through her heart,
And she lies buried with her ancestors;
O! in a tomb where never scandal slept,
Save this of hers, fram'd by thy villany!

CLAUDIO. My villany?

LEONATO.   Thine, Claudio; thine, I say.

DON PEDRO. You say not right, old man.

LEONATO.   My lord, my lord,
I 'll prove it on his body, if he dare,
Despite his nice fence and his active practice,
His May of youth and bloom of lustihood.

CLAUDIO. Away! I will not have to do with you.

LEONATO. Canst thou so daff me? Thou hast kill'd my child;
If thou kill'st me, boy, thou shalt kill a man.

ANTONIO. He shall kill two of us, and men indeed:
But that 's no matter; let him kill one first:
Win me and wear me; let him answer me.
Come, follow me, boy; come, sir boy, come, follow me.
Sir boy, I 'll whip you from your foining fence;
Nay, as I am a gentleman, I will.

LEONATO. Brother,—

ANTONIO. Content yourself. God knows I lov'd my niece;
And she is dead, slander'd to death by villains,
That dare as well answer a man indeed
As I dare take a serpent by the tongue.
Boys, apes, braggarts, Jacks, milksops!

LEONATO.   Brother Antony,—

ANTONIO. Hold your content. What, man! I know them, yea,
And what they weigh, even to the utmost scruple,
Scambling, out-facing, fashion-monging boys,
That lie and cog and flout, deprave and slander,
Go antickly, show outward hideousness,
And speak off half a dozen dangerous words,
How they might hurt their enemies, if they durst;
And this is all!

LEONATO. But, brother Antony,—

ANTONIO.   Come, 'tis no matter:
Do not you meddle, let me deal in this.

DON PEDRO. Gentlemen both, we will not wake your pa-
tience.
My heart is sorry for your daughter's death;
But, on my honour, she was charg'd with nothing
But what was true and very full of proof.

LEONATO. My lord, my lord—

DON PEDRO.   I will not hear you.

LEONATO.   No?
Come, brother, away. I will be heard.—

ANTONIO. And shall, or some of us will smart for it.

                          Exeunt Leonato and Antonio
                          Enter Benedick

DON PEDRO. See, see; here comes the man we went to seek.

CLAUDIO. Now, signior, what news?

BENEDICK. Good-day, my lord.

DON PEDRO. Welcome, signior: you are almost come to part
almost a fray.

CLAUDIO. We had like to have had our two noses snapped
off with two old men without teeth.

DON PEDRO. Leonato and his brother. What thinkest thou?
Had we fought, I doubt we should have been too young
for them.

BENEDICK. In a false quarrel there is no true valour. I came
to seek you both.

CLAUDIO. We have been up and down to seek thee; for we
are high-proof melancholy, and would fain have it beaten
away. Wilt thou use thy wit?

BENEDICK. It is in my scabbard; shall I draw it?

DON PEDRO. Dost thou wear thy wit by thy side?

CLAUDIO. Never any did so, though very many have been
beside their wit. I will bid thee draw, as we do the minstrels; draw, to pleasure us.

DON PEDRO. As I am an honest man, he looks pale. Art thou
sick, or angry?

CLAUDIO. What, courage, man! What though care killed a
cat, thou hast mettle enough in thee to kill care.

BENEDICK. Sir, I shall meet your wit in the career, an you
charge it against me. I pray you choose another subject.

CLAUDIO. Nay then, give him another staff: this last was
broke cross.

DON PEDRO. By this light, he changes more and more: I
think he be angry indeed.

CLAUDIO. If he be, he knows how to turn his girdle.

BENEDICK. Shall I speak a word in your ear?

CLAUDIO. God bless me from a challenge!

BENEDICK. (*Aside to Claudio*) You are a villain, I jest not: I will make it good how you dare, with what you dare, and when you dare. Do me right, or I will protest your cowardice. You have killed a sweet lady, and her death shall fall heavy on you. Let me hear from you.

CLAUDIO. Well I will meet you, so I may have good cheer.

DON PEDRO. What, a feast, a feast?

CLAUDIO. I' faith, I thank him; he hath bid me to a calf's-head and a capon, the which if I do not carve most curiously, say my knife 's naught. Shall I not find a woodcock too?

BENEDICK. Sir, your wit ambles well; it goes easily.

DON PEDRO. I 'll tell thee how Beatrice praised thy wit the other day. I said, thou hadst a fine wit. 'True,' says she, 'a fine little one.' 'No,' said I, 'a great wit.' 'Right,' said she, 'a great gross one.' 'Nay,' said I, 'a good wit.' 'Just,' said she, 'it hurts nobody.' 'Nay,' said I, 'the gentleman is wise.' 'Certain,' said she, 'a wise gentleman.' 'Nay,' said I, 'he hath the tongues.' 'That I believe,' said she, 'for he swore a thing to me on Monday night, which he forswore on Tuesday morning: there 's a double tongue; there 's two tongues.' Thus did she, an hour together, trans-shape thy particular virtues; yet at last she concluded with a sigh, thou wast the properest man in Italy.

CLAUDIO. For the which she wept heartily and said she cared not.

DON PEDRO. Yea, that she did; but yet, for all that, an if she did not hate him deadly, she would love him dearly. The old man's daughter told us all.

CLAUDIO. All, all; and moreover, God saw him when he was hid in the garden.

DON PEDRO. But when shall we set the savage bull's horns on the sensible Benedick's head?

CLAUDIO. Yea, and text underneath, 'Here dwells Benedick the married man!'

BENEDICK. Fare you well, boy: you know my mind. I will leave you now to your gossip-like humour: you break jests as braggarts do their blades, which, God be thanked, hurt not. My lord, for your many courtesies I thank thee: I must discontinue your company. Your brother the bastard is fled from Messina: you have, among you, killed a sweet and innocent lady. For my Lord Lack-beard there, he and I shall meet; and till then, peace be with him.

DON PEDRO. He is in earnest.

CLAUDIO. In most profound earnest; and, I 'll warrant you, for the love of Beatrice.

DON PEDRO. And hath challenged thee?

CLAUDIO. Most sincerely.

DON PEDRO. What a pretty thing man is when he goes in his doublet and hose and leaves off his wit!

CLAUDIO. He is then a giant to an ape; but then is an ape a doctor to such a man.

DON PEDRO. But, soft you; let me be: pluck up, my heart, and be sad! Did he not say my brother was fled?

Enter Dogberry, Verges,
and the Watch, with Conrade and Borachio

DOGBERRY. Come, you sir: if justice cannot tame you, she shall ne'er weigh more reasons in her balance. Nay, an you be a cursing hypocrite once, you must be looked to.

DON PEDRO. How now! two of my brother's men bound! Borachio, one!

CLAUDIO. Hearken after their offence, my lord.

DON PEDRO. Officers, what offence have these men done?

DOGBERRY. Marry, sir, they have committed false report; moreover, they have spoken untruths; secondarily, they are slanders; sixth and lastly, they have belied a lady; thirdly, they have verified unjust things; and to conclude, they are lying knaves.

DON PEDRO. First, I ask thee what they have done; thirdly, I ask thee what 's their offence; sixth and lastly, why they are committed; and, to conclude, what you lay to their charge?

CLAUDIO. Rightly reasoned, and in his own division; and, by my troth, there 's one meaning well suited.

DON PEDRO. Who have you offended, masters, that you are thus bound to your answer? This learned constable is too cunning to be understood. What 's your offence?

BORACHIO. Sweet prince, let me go no further to mine answer: do you hear me, and let this count kill me. I have deceived even your very eyes: what your wisdoms could not discover, these shallow fools have brought to light;

who, in the night overheard me confessing to this man
how Don John your brother incensed me to slander the
Lady Hero; how you were brought into the orchard and
saw me court Margaret in Hero's garments; how you dis-
graced her, when you should marry her. My villany they
have upon record; which I had rather seal with my death
than repeat over to my shame. The lady is dead upon
mine and my master's false accusation; and, briefly, I desire nothing but the reward of a villain.

DON PEDRO. Runs not this speech like iron through your
    blood?

CLAUDIO. I have drunk poison whiles he utter'd it.

DON PEDRO. But did my brother set thee on to this?

BORACHIO. Yea; and paid me richly for the practice of it.

DON PEDRO. He is compos'd and fram'd of treachery:
    And fled he is upon this villany.

CLAUDIO. Sweet Hero! now thy image doth appear
    In the rare semblance that I lov'd it first.

DOGBERRY. Come, bring away the plaintiffs: by this time
our sexton hath reformed Signior Leonato of the matter.
And masters, do not forget to specify, when time and
place shall serve, that I am an ass.

VERGES. Here, here comes Master Signior Leonato, and the
sexton too.

    Re-enter Leonato, Antonio, and the Sexton

LEONATO. Which is the villain? Let me see his eyes,
    That, when I note another man like him,
    I may avoid him. Which of these is he?

BORACHIO. If you would know your wronger, look on me.

LEONATO. Art thou the slave that with thy breath hast kill'd
    Mine innocent child?

BORACHIO.   Yea, even I alone.

LEONATO. No, not so, villain; thou beliest thyself:
    Here stand a pair of honourable men;
    A third is fled, that had a hand in it.
    I thank you, princes, for my daughter's death:
    Record it with your high and worthy deeds.
    'Twas bravely done, if you bethink you of it.

CLAUDIO. I know not how to pray your patience;
    Yet I must speak. Choose your revenge yourself;
    Impose me to what penance your invention
    Can lay upon my sin: yet sinn'd I not

But in mistaking.

DON PEDRO.   By my soul, nor I:
And yet, to satisfy this good old man,
I would bend under any heavy weight
That he 'll enjoin me to.

LEONATO. I cannot bid you bid my daughter live;
That were impossible: but, I pray you both,
Possess the people in Messina here
How innocent she died; and if your love
Can labour aught in sad invention,
Hang her an epitaph upon her tomb,
And sing it to her bones: sing it to-night.
To-morrow morning come you to my house,
And since you could not be my son-in-law,
Be yet my nephew. My brother hath a daughter,
Almost the copy of my child that 's dead,
And she alone is heir to both of us:
Give her the right you should have given her cousin,
And so dies my revenge.

CLAUDIO.   O noble sir,
Your over-kindness doth wring tears from me!
I do embrace your offer; and dispose
For henceforth of poor Claudio.

LEONATO. To-morrow then I will expect your coming;
To-night I take my leave. This naughty man
Shall face to face be brought to Margaret,
Who, I believe, was pack'd in all this wrong,
Hir'd to it by your brother.

BORACHIO.   No, by my soul she was not;
Nor knew not what she did when she spoke to me;
But always hath been just and virtuous
In anything that I do know by her.

DOGBERRY. Moreover, sir,—which, indeed, is not under
white and black,—this plaintiff here, the offender, did call
me ass: I beseech you, let it be remembered in his punishment. And also, the watch heard them talk of one Deformed: they say he wears a key in his ear and a lock
hanging by it, and borrows money in God's name, the
which he hath used so long and never paid, that now men
grow hard-hearted, and will lend nothing for God's sake.
Pray you, examine him upon that point.

LEONATO. I thank thee for thy care and honest pains.

DOGBERRY. Your worship speaks like a most thankful and reverend youth, and I praise God for you.

LEONATO. There 's for thy pains.

DOGBERRY. God save the foundation!

LEONATO. Go, I discharge thee of thy prisoner, and I thank thee.

DOGBERRY. I leave an arrant knave with your worship; which I beseech your worship to correct yourself, for the example of others. God keep your worship! I wish your worship well; God restore you to health! I humbly give you leave to depart, and if a merry meeting may be wished, God prohibit it! Come, neighbour.

Exeunt Dogberry and Verges

LEONATO. Until to-morrow morning, lords, farewell.

ANTONIO. Farewell, my lords: we look for you to-morrow.

DON PEDRO. We will not fail.

CLAUDIO.   To-night I 'll mourn with Hero.

Exeunt Don Pedro and Claudio

LEONATO. (*To the Watch*) Bring you these fellows on. We 'll talk with Margaret,

How her acquaintance grew with this lewd fellow.

Exeunt

SCENE TWO

Leonato's Garden.

Enter Benedick and Margaret, meeting

BENEDICK. Pray thee, sweet Mistress Margaret, deserve well at my hands by helping me to the speech of Beatrice.

MARGARET. Will you then write me a sonnet in praise of my beauty?

BENEDICK. In so high a style, Margaret, that no man living shall come over it; for, in most comely truth, thou deservest it.

MARGARET. To have no man come over me! why, shall I always keep below stairs?

BENEDICK. Thy wit is as quick as the greyhound's mouth; it catches.

MARGARET. And yours as blunt as the fencer's foils, which hit, but hurt not.

BENEDICK. A most manly wit, Margaret; it will not hurt a woman: and so, I pray thee, call Beatrice. I give thee the bucklers.

MARGARET. Give us the swords, we have bucklers of our own.

BENEDICK. If you use them, Margaret, you must put in the pikes with a vice; and they are dangerous weapons for maids.

MARGARET. Well, I will call Beatrice to you, who I think hath legs.

BENEDICK. And therefore will come.   *Exit Margaret*

> The god of love,
> That sits above,
> And knows me, and knows me,
> How pitiful I deserve,—

I mean, in singing; but in loving, Leander the good swimmer, Troilus the first employer of pandars, and a whole book full of these quondam carpet-mongers, whose names yet run smoothly in the even road of a blank verse, why, they were never so truly turned over and over as my poor self, in love. Marry, I cannot show it in rime; I have tried: I can find out no rime to 'lady' but 'baby,' an innocent rime; for 'scorn,' 'horn,' a hard rime; for 'school,' 'fool,' a babbling rime; very ominous endings: no, I was not born under a riming planet, nor I cannot woo in festival terms.

Enter Beatrice

Sweet Beatrice, wouldst thou come when I called thee?

BEATRICE. Yea, signior; and depart when you bid me.

BENEDICK. O stay but till then!

BEATRICE. 'Then' is spoken; fare you well now: and yet, ere I go, let me go with that I came for; which is, with knowing what hath passed between you and Claudio.

BENEDICK. Only foul words; and thereupon I will kiss thee.

BEATRICE. Foul words is but foul wind, and foul wind is but foul breath, and foul breath is noisome; therefore I will depart unkissed.

BENEDICK. Thou hast frighted the word out of his right sense, so forcible is thy wit. But I must tell thee plainly, Claudio undergoes my challenge, and either I must

shortly hear from him, or I will subscribe him a coward.
And, I pray thee now, tell me, for which of my bad parts
didst thou first fall in love with me?

BEATRICE. For them all together; which maintained so politic a state of evil that they will not admit any good part
to intermingle with them. But for which of my good parts
did you first suffer love for me?

BENEDICK. 'Suffer love,' a good epithet! I do suffer love indeed, for I love thee against my will.

BEATRICE. In spite of your heart, I think. Alas, poor heart!
If you spite it for my sake, I will spite it for yours; for I
will never love that which my friend hates.

BENEDICK. Thou and I are too wise to woo peaceably.

BEATRICE. It appears not in this confession: there's not one
wise man among twenty that will praise himself.

BENEDICK. An old, an old instance, Beatrice, that lived in
the time of good neighbours. If a man do not erect in this
age his own tomb ere he dies, he shall live no longer in
monument than the bell rings and the widow weeps.

BEATRICE. And how long is that think you?

BENEDICK. Question: why, an hour in clamour and a quarter in rheum: therefore it is most expedient for the wise,
—if Don Worm, his conscience, find no impediment to the
contrary,—to be the trumpet of his own virtues, as I am to
myself. So much for praising myself, who, I myself will
bear witness, is praiseworthy. And now tell me, how doth
your cousin?

BEATRICE. Very ill.

BENEDICK. And how do you?

BEATRICE. Very ill too.

BENEDICK. Serve God, love me, and mend. There will I
leave you too, for here comes one in haste.

Enter Ursula

URSULA. Madam, you must come to your uncle. Yonder's
old coil at home: it is proved, my Lady Hero hath been
falsely accused, the prince and Claudio mightily abused;
and Don John is the author of all, who is fled and gone.
Will you come presently?

BEATRICE. Will you go hear this news, signior?

BENEDICK. I will live in thy heart, die in thy lap, and be
buried in thy eyes; and moreover I will go with thee to
thy uncle's.   *Exeunt*

SCENE THREE

The Inside of a Church.

Enter Don Pedro, Claudio, and Attendants, with music and tapers

CLAUDIO. Is this the monument of Leonato?
A LORD. It is, my lord.
CLAUDIO. (*Reads from a scroll*)

> Done to death by slanderous tongues
>   Was the Hero that here lies:
> Death, in guerdon of her wrongs,
>   Gives her fame which never dies.
> So the life that died with shame
> Lives in death with glorious fame.

> Hang thou there upon the tomb,
> Praising her when I am dumb.

Now, music, sound, and sing your solemn hymn.

SONG

> Pardon, goddess of the night,
> Those that slew thy virgin knight;
> For the which, with songs of woe,
> Round about her tomb they go.
>   Midnight, assist our moan;
>   Help us to sigh and groan,
>   Heavily, heavily:
>   Graves, yawn and yield your dead,
>   Till death be uttered,
>   Heavily, heavily.

CLAUDIO. Now, unto thy bones good-night!
    Yearly will I do this rite.
DON PEDRO. Good-morrow, masters: put your torches out.
    The wolves have prey'd; and look, the gentle day,
Before the wheels of Phœbus, round about
    Dapples the drowsy east with spots of grey.
Thanks to you all, and leave us: fare you well.
CLAUDIO. Good-morrow, masters: each his several way.

DON PEDRO. Come, let us hence, and put on other weeds;
    And then to Leonato's we will go.
CLAUDIO. And Hymen now with luckier issue speed 's,
    Than this for whom we render'd up this woe!   *Exeunt*

SCENE FOUR

A Room in Leonato's House.

*Enter Leonato, Antonio, Benedick, Beatrice, Margaret,
Ursula, Friar Francis, and Hero*

FRIAR. Did I not tell you she was innocent?
LEONATO. So are the prince and Claudio, who accus'd her
    Upon the error that you heard debated:
    But Margaret was in some fault for this,
    Although against her will, as it appears
    In the true course of all the question.
ANTONIO. Well, I am glad that all things sort so well.
BENEDICK. And so am I, being else by faith enforc'd
    To call young Claudio to a reckoning for it.
LEONATO. Well, daughter, and you gentlewomen all,
    Withdraw into a chamber by yourselves,
    And when I send for you, come hither mask'd:
    The prince and Claudio promis'd by this hour
    To visit me.   *Exeunt ladies*
            You know your office, brother;
    You must be father to your brother's daughter,
    And give her to young Claudio.
ANTONIO. Which I will do with confirm'd countenance.
BENEDICK. Friar, I must entreat your pains, I think.
FRIAR. To do what, signior?
BENEDICK. To bind me, or undo me; one of them.
    Signior Leonato, truth it is, good signior,
    Your niece regards me with an eye of favour.
LEONATO. That eye my daughter lent her: 'tis most true.
BENEDICK. And I do with an eye of love requite her.
LEONATO. The sight whereof I think, you had from me,
    From Claudio, and the prince. But what 's your will?
BENEDICK. Your answer, sir, is enigmatical:
    But, for my will, my will is your good will
    May stand with ours, this day to be conjoin'd

In the state of honourable marriage:

In which, good friar, I shall desire your help.

LEONATO. My heart is with your liking.

FRIAR.   And my help.

Here come the prince and Claudio.

    Enter Don Pedro and Claudio, with Attendants

DON PEDRO. Good-morrow to this fair assembly.

LEONATO. Good-morrow, prince; good-morrow, Claudio:

We here attend you. Are you yet determin'd

To-day to marry with my brother's daughter?

CLAUDIO. I 'll hold my mind, were she an Ethiop.

LEONATO. Call her forth, brother: here 's the friar ready.

                                       Exit Antonio

DON PEDRO. Good-morrow, Benedick. Why what 's the matter,

That you have such a February face,

So full of frost, of storm and cloudiness?

CLAUDIO. I think he thinks upon the savage bull.

Tush! fear not, man, we 'll tip thy horns with gold,

And all Europa shall rejoice at thee,

As once Europa did at lusty Jove,

When he would play the noble beast in love.

BENEDICK. Bull Jove, sir, had an amiable low:

And some such strange bull leap'd your father's cow,

And got a calf in that same noble feat,

Much like to you, for you have just his bleat.

CLAUDIO. For this I owe you: here come other reckonings.

    Re-enter Antonio, with the ladies masked

Which is the lady I must seize upon?

ANTONIO. This same is she, and I do give you her.

CLAUDIO. Why, then she 's mine. Sweet, let me see your

face.

LEONATO. No, that you shall not, till you take her hand

Before this friar, and swear to marry her.

CLAUDIO. Give me your hand: before this holy friar,

I am your husband, if you like of me.

HERO. And when I liv'd, I was your other wife: *Unmasking*

And when you lov'd, you were my other husband.

CLAUDIO. Another Hero!

HERO.   Nothing certainer:

One Hero died defil'd, but I do live,

And surely as I live, I am a maid.

DON PEDRO. The former Hero! Hero that is dead!

LEONATO. She died, my lord, but whiles her slander liv'd.

FRIAR. All this amazement can I qualify:
  When after that the holy rites are ended,
  I 'll tell you largely of fair Hero's death:
  Meantime, let wonder seem familiar,
  And to the chapel let us presently.

BENEDICK. Soft and fair, friar. Which is Beatrice?

BEATRICE. (*Unmasking*) I answer to that name. What is
  your will?

BENEDICK. Do not you love me?

BEATRICE.   Why, no; no more than reason.

BENEDICK. Why, then, your uncle and the prince and Claudio
  Have been deceived; for they swore you did.

BEATRICE. Do not you love me?

BENEDICK.   Troth, no; no more than reason.

BEATRICE. Why, then, my cousin, Margaret, and Ursula,
  Are much deceiv'd; for they did swear you did.

BENEDICK. They swore that you were almost sick for me.

BEATRICE. They swore that you were well-nigh dead for
  me.

BENEDICK. 'Tis no such matter. Then, you do not love me?

BEATRICE. No, truly, but in friendly recompense.

LEONATO. Come, cousin, I am sure you love the gentleman.

CLAUDIO. And I 'll be sworn upon 't that he loves her;
  For here 's a paper written in his hand,
  A halting sonnet of his own pure brain,
  Fashion'd to Beatrice.

HERO.   And here 's another,
  Writ in my cousin's hand, stolen from her pocket,
  Containing her affection unto Benedick.

BENEDICK. A miracle! here 's our own hands against our
  hearts. Come, I will have thee; but, by this light, I take
  thee for pity.

BEATRICE. I would not deny you; but, by this good day, I
  yield upon great persuasion, and partly to save your life,
  for I was told you were in a consumption.

BENEDICK. Peace! I will stop your mouth.   *Kisses her*

DON PEDRO. How dost thou, Benedick, the married man?

BENEDICK. I 'll tell thee what, prince; a college of witcrack-
  ers cannot flout me out of my humour. Dost thou think I

care for a satire or an epigram? No; if a man will be beaten with brains, a' shall wear nothing handsome about him. In brief, since I do purpose to marry, I will think nothing to any purpose that the world can say against it; and therefore never flout at me for what I have said against it, for man is a giddy thing, and this is my conclusion. For thy part, Claudio, I did think to have beaten thee; but, in that thou art like to be my kinsman, live unbruised, and love my cousin.

CLAUDIO. I had well hoped thou wouldst have denied Beatrice, that I might have cudgelled thee out of thy single life, to make thee a double-dealer; which, out of question, thou wilt be, if my cousin do not look exceeding narrowly to thee.

BENEDICK. Come, come, we are friends. Let 's have a dance ere we are married, that we may lighten our own hearts and our wives' heels.

LEONATO. We 'll have dancing afterward.

BENEDICK. First, of my word; therefore play, music! Prince, thou art sad; get thee a wife, get thee a wife: there is no staff more reverend than one tipped with horn.

Enter a Messenger

MESSENGER. My lord, your brother John is ta'en in flight, And brought with armed men back to Messina.

BENEDICK. Think not on him till to-morrow: I 'll devise thee brave punishments for him. Strike up, pipers!

Dance. Exeunt

LOVE'S LABOUR'S LOST

CAST OF CHARACTERS

FERDINAND, *King of Navarre*

BEROWNE
LONGAVILLE } *Lords, attending on the King*
DUMAINE

BOYET } *Lords, attending on the Princess of*
MARCADE } *France*

DON ADRIANO DE ARMADO, *a fantastical Spaniard*

SIR NATHANIEL, *a Curate*

HOLOFERNES, *a Schoolmaster*

DULL, *a Constable*

COSTARD, *a Clown*

MOTH, *Page to Armado*

A Forester

The PRINCESS of France

ROSALINE
MARIA } *Ladies, attending on the Princess*
KATHARINE

JAQUENETTA, *a country Wench*

Officers and Others, Attendants on the King and
Princess

SCENE

Navarre

LOVE'S LABOUR'S LOST

ACT ONE

SCENE ONE

The King of Navarre's Park.

Enter the King, Berowne, Longaville, and Dumaine

KING. Let fame, that all hunt after in their lives,
Live register'd upon our brazen tombs,
And then grace us in the disgrace of death;
When, spite of cormorant devouring Time,
The endeavour of this present breath may buy
That honour which shall bate his scythe's keen edge,
And make us heirs of all eternity.
Therefore, brave conquerors,—for so you are,
That war against your own affections
And the huge army of the world's desires,—
Our late edict shall strongly stand in force:
Navarre shall be the wonder of the world;
Our court shall be a little academe,
Still and contemplative in living art.
You three, Berowne, Dumaine, and Longaville,
Have sworn for three years' term to live with me,
My fellow-scholars, and to keep those statutes
That are recorded in this schedule here:
Your oaths are pass'd; and now subscribe your names,
That his own hand may strike his honour down
That violates the smallest branch herein.
If you are arm'd to do, as sworn to do,
Subscribe to your deep oaths, and keep it too.
LONGAVILLE. I am resolv'd; 'tis but a three years' fast:
The mind shall banquet, though the body pine:
Fat paunches have lean pates, and dainty bits

Make rich the ribs, but bankrupt quite the wits.

DUMAINE. My loving lord, Dumaine is mortified:
The grosser manner of these world's delights
He throws upon the gross world's baser slaves:
To love, to wealth, to pomp, I pine and die;
With all these living in philosophy.

BEROWNE. I can but say their protestation over;
So much, dear liege, I have already sworn,
That is, to live and study here three years.
But there are other strict observances;
As, not to see a woman in that term,
Which I hope well is not enrolled there:
And one day in a week to touch no food,
And but one meal on every day beside;
The which I hope is not enrolled there:
And then, to sleep but three hours in the night,
And not be seen to wink of all the day,—
When I was wont to think no harm all night
And make a dark night too of half the day,—
Which I hope well is not enrolled there.
O! these are barren tasks, too hard to keep,
Not to see ladies, study, fast, not sleep.

KING. Your oath is pass'd to pass away from these.

BEROWNE. Let me say no, my liege, an if you please.
I only swore to study with your Grace,
And stay here in your court for three years' space.

LONGAVILLE. You swore to that, Berowne, and to the rest.

BEROWNE. By yea and nay, sir, then I swore in jest.
What is the end of study? Let me know.

KING. Why, that to know which else we should not know.

BEROWNE. Things hid and barr'd, you mean, from common
    sense?

KING. Ay, that is study's god-like recompense.

BEROWNE. Come on then; I will swear to study so,
To know the thing I am forbid to know;
As thus: to study where I well may dine,
    When I to feast expressly am forbid;
Or study where to meet some mistress fine,
    When mistresses from common sense are hid;
Or, having sworn too hard-a-keeping oath,
Study to break it, and not break my troth.
If study's gain be thus, and this be so,

Study knows that which yet it doth not know.
Swear me to this, and I will ne'er say no.

KING. These be the stops that hinder study quite,
And train our intellects to vain delight.

BEROWNE. Why, all delights are vain; but that most vain
Which, with pain purchas'd doth inherit pain:
As, painfully to pore upon a book,
  To seek the light of truth; while truth the while
Doth falsely blind the eyesight of his look:
  Light seeking light doth light of light beguile:
So, ere you find where light in darkness lies,
Your light grows dark by losing of your eyes.
Study me how to please the eye indeed,
  By fixing it upon a fairer eye,
Who dazzling so, that eye shall be his heed,
  And give him light that it was blinded by.
Study is like the heaven's glorious sun,
  That will not be deep-search'd with saucy looks;
Small have continual plodders ever won,
  Save base authority from others' books.
These earthly godfathers of heaven's lights
  That give a name to every fixed star,
Have no more profit of their shining nights
  Than those that walk and wot not what they are.
Too much to know is to know nought but fame;
And every godfather can give a name.

KING. How well he 's read, to reason against reading!

DUMAINE. Proceeded well, to stop all good proceeding!

LONGAVILLE. He weeds the corn, and still lets grow the
weeding.

BEROWNE. The spring is near, when green geese are
a-breeding.

DUMAINE. How follows that?

BEROWNE.   Fit in his place and time.

DUMAINE. In reason nothing.

BEROWNE.   Something then, in rime.

KING. Berowne is like an envious sneaping frost
  That bites the first-born infants of the spring.

BEROWNE. Well, say I am: why should proud summer boast
  Before the birds have any cause to sing?
Why should I joy in an abortive birth?
  At Christmas I no more desire a rose

Than wish a snow in May's new-fangled mirth;
    But like of each thing that in season grows.
So you, to study now it is too late,
Climb o'er the house to unlock the little gate.

KING. Well, sit you out: go home, Berowne: adieu!

BEROWNE. No, my good lord; I have sworn to stay with
    you:
And though I have for barbarism spoke more
    Than for that angel knowledge you can say,
Yet confident I 'll keep to what I swore,
    And bide the penance of each three years' day.
Give me the paper; let me read the same;
    And to the strict'st decrees I 'll write my name.

KING. How well this yielding rescues thee from shame!

BEROWNE. Item, 'That no woman shall come within a mile
of my court.' Hath this been proclaimed?

LONGAVILLE. Four days ago.

BEROWNE. Let 's see the penalty. 'On pain of losing her
tongue.' Who devised this penalty?

LONGAVILLE. Marry, that did I.

BEROWNE.   Sweet lord, and why?

LONGAVILLE. To fright them hence with that dread penalty.

BEROWNE. A dangerous law against gentility!
    Item. 'If any man be seen to talk with a woman within
the term of three years, he shall endure such public shame
as the rest of the court can possibly devise.'
This article, my liege, yourself must break;
    For well you know here comes in embassy
The French king's daughter with yourself to speak—
    A maid of grace and complete majesty—
About surrender up of Aquitaine
    To her decrepit, sick, and bed-rid father:
Therefore this article is made in vain,
    Or vainly comes th' admired princess hither.

KING. What say you, lords? why, this was quite forgot.

BEROWNE. So study evermore is overshot:
    While it doth study to have what it would,
It doth forget to do the thing it should;
    And when it hath the thing it hunteth most,
'Tis won as towns with fire; so won, so lost.

KING. We must of force dispense with this decree;
    She must lie here on mere necessity.

BEROWNE. Necessity will make us all forsworn
 Three thousand times within this three years' space;
For every man with his affects is born,
 Not by night master'd, but by special grace.
If I break faith this word shall speak for me,
I am forsworn 'on mere necessity.'
So to the laws at large I write my name: *Subscribes*
 And he that breaks them in the least degree
Stands in attainder of eternal shame:
 Suggestions are to others as to me;
But I believe, although I seem so loath,
I am the last that will last keep his oath.
But is there no quick recreation granted?

KING. Ay, that there is. Our court, you know, is haunted
 With a refined traveller of Spain;
A man in all the world's new fashion planted,
 That hath a mint of phrases in his brain;
One whom the music of his own vain tongue
 Doth ravish like enchanting harmony;
A man of complements, whom right and wrong
 Have chose as umpire of their mutiny:
This child of fancy, that Armado hight,
 For interim to our studies shall relate
In high-born words the worth of many a knight
 From tawny Spain lost in the world's debate.
How you delight, my lords, I know not, I;
But, I protest, I love to hear him lie,
And I will use him for my minstrelsy.

BEROWNE. Armado is a most illustrious wight,
A man of fire-new words, fashion's own knight.

LONGAVILLE. Costard the swain and he shall be our sport;
And, so to study, three years is but short.

   Enter Dull, with a letter, and Costard

DULL. Which is the duke's own person?

BEROWNE. This, fellow. What wouldst?

DULL. I myself reprehend his own person, for I am his
 Grace's tharborough: but I would see his own person in
 flesh and blood.

BEROWNE. This is he.

DULL. Signior Arm—Arm—commends you. There 's villany
 abroad: this letter will tell you more.

COSTARD. Sir, the contempts thereof are as touching me.

KING. A letter from the magnificent Armado.

BEROWNE. How long soever the matter, I hope in God for high words.

LONGAVILLE. A high hope for a low heaven: God grant us patience!

BEROWNE. To hear, or forbear laughing?

LONGAVILLE. To hear meekly, sir, and to laugh moderately; or to forbear both.

BEROWNE. Well, sir, be it as the style shall give us cause to climb in the merriness.

COSTARD. The matter is to me, sir, as concerning Jaquenetta. The manner of it is, I was taken with the manner.

BEROWNE. In what manner?

COSTARD. In manner and form following, sir; all those three: I was seen with her in the manor-house, sitting with her upon the form, and taken following her into the park; which, put together, is, in manner and form following. Now, sir, for the manner,—it is the manner of a man to speak to a woman, for the form,—in some form.

BEROWNE. For the following, sir?

COSTARD. As it shall follow in my correction; and God defend the right!

KING. Will you hear this letter with attention?

BEROWNE. As we would hear an oracle.

COSTARD. Such is the simplicity of man to hearken after the flesh.

KING. 'Great deputy, the welkin's vicegerent, and sole dominator of Navarre, my soul's earth's God, and body's fostering patron,'

COSTARD. Not a word of Costard yet.

KING. 'So it is,'—

COSTARD. It may be so; but if he say it is so, he is, in telling true, but so.—

KING. Peace!

COSTARD. Be to me and every man that dares not fight.

KING. No words!

COSTARD. Of other men's secrets, I beseech you.

KING. 'So it is, besieged with sable-coloured melancholy, I did commend the black-oppressing humour to the most wholesome physic of thy health-giving air; and, as I am a gentleman, betook myself to walk. The time when? About the sixth hour; when beasts most graze, birds best peck,

and men sit down to that nourishment which is called
supper: so much for the time when. Now for the ground
which; which, I mean, I walked upon; it is ycleped thy
park. Then for the place where; where, I mean, I did encounter that most obscene and preposterous event, that
draweth from my snow-white pen the ebon-coloured ink,
which here thou viewest, beholdest, surveyest, or seest.
But to the place where, it standeth north-north-east and
by east from the west corner of thy curious-knotted garden: there did I see that low-spirited swain, that base
minnow of thy mirth,'—

COSTARD. Me.

KING. 'that unlettered small-knowing soul,'—

COSTARD. Me.

KING. 'that shallow vessel,'—

COSTARD. Still me.

KING. 'which, as I remember, hight Costard,'—

COSTARD. O me.

KING. 'sorted and consorted, contrary to thy established proclaimed edict and continent canon, with—with,—O! with
but with this I passion to say wherewith,'—

COSTARD. With a wench.

KING. 'with a child of our grandmother Eve, a female; or,
for thy more sweet understanding, a woman. Him, I,—as
my ever-esteemed duty pricks me on,—have sent to thee,
to receive the meed of punishment, by thy sweet Grace's
officer, Antony Dull; a man of good repute, carriage,
bearing, and estimation.'

DULL. Me, an 't please you; I am Antony Dull.

KING. 'For Jaquenetta,—so is the weaker vessel called which
I apprehended with the aforesaid swain,—I keep her as a
vessel of thy law's fury; and shall, at the least of thy sweet
notice, bring her to trial. Thine, in all compliments of devoted and heart-burning heat of duty,

'Don Adriano de Armado.'

BEROWNE. This is not so well as I looked for, but the best
that ever I heard.

KING. Ay, the best for the worst. But, sirrah, what say you
to this?

COSTARD. Sir, I confess the wench.

KING. Did you hear the proclamation?

COSTARD. I do confess much of the hearing it, but little of
the marking of it.

KING. It was proclaimed a year's imprisonment to be taken with a wench.

COSTARD. I was taken with none, sir: I was taken with a damosel.

KING. Well, it was proclaimed 'damosel.'

COSTARD. This was no damosel neither, sir: she was a virgin.

KING. It is so varied too; for it was proclaimed 'virgin.'

COSTARD. If it were, I deny her virginity: I was taken with a maid.

KING. This maid will not serve your turn, sir.

COSTARD. This maid will serve my turn, sir.

KING. Sir, I will pronounce your sentence: you shall fast a week with bran and water.

COSTARD. I had rather pray a month with mutton and porridge.

KING. And Don Armado shall be your keeper.
My Lord Berowne, see him deliver'd o'er:
And go we, lords, to put in practice that
   Which each to other hath so strongly sworn.
            Exeunt King, Longaville, and Dumaine

BEROWNE. I 'll lay my head to any good man's hat,
   These oaths and laws will prove an idle scorn.
Sirrah, come on.

COSTARD. I suffer for the truth, sir: for true it is I was taken with Jaquenetta, and Jaquenetta is a true girl; and therefore welcome the sour cup of prosperity! Affliction may one day smile again; and till then, sit thee down, sorrow!
                    Exeunt

SCENE TWO

The Same.

Enter Armado and Moth

ARMADO. Boy, what sign is it when a man of great spirit grows melancholy?

MOTH. A great sign, sir, that he will look sad.

ARMADO. Why, sadness is one and the self-same thing, dear imp.

MOTH. No, no; O Lord, sir, no.

ARMADO. How canst thou part sadness and melancholy, my

tender juvenal?

MOTH. By a familiar demonstration of the working, my tough senior.

ARMADO. Why tough senior? Why tough senior?

MOTH. Why tender juvenal? Why tender juvenal?

ARMADO. I spoke it, tender juvenal, as a congruent epithe-ton appertaining to thy young days, which we may nomi-nate tender.

MOTH. And I, tough senior, as an appertinent title to your old time, which we may name tough.

ARMADO. Pretty, and apt.

MOTH. How mean you, sir? I pretty, and my saying apt? or I apt, and my saying pretty?

ARMADO. Thou pretty, because little.

MOTH. Little pretty, because little. Wherefore apt?

ARMADO. And therefore apt, because quick.

MOTH. Speak you this in my praise, master?

ARMADO. In thy condign praise.

MOTH. I will praise an eel with the same praise.

ARMADO. What! that an eel is ingenious?

MOTH. That an eel is quick.

ARMADO. I do say thou art quick in answers: thou heatest my blood.

MOTH. I am answered, sir.

ARMADO. I love not to be crossed.

MOTH. (*Aside*) He speaks the mere contrary: crosses love not him.

ARMADO. I have promised to study three years with the duke.

MOTH. You may do it in an hour, sir.

ARMADO. Impossible.

MOTH. How many is one thrice told?

ARMADO. I am ill at reckoning; it fitteth the spirit of a tap-ster.

MOTH. You are a gentleman and a gamester, sir.

ARMADO. I confess both: they are both the varnish of a com-plete man.

MOTH. Then, I am sure you know how much the gross sum of deuce-ace amounts to.

ARMADO. It doth amount to one more than two.

MOTH. Which the base vulgar do call three.

ARMADO. True,

MOTH. Why, sir, is this such a piece of study? Now, here 's three studied, ere you 'll thrice wink; and how easy it is to put 'years' to the word 'three,' and study three years in two words, the dancing horse will tell you.

ARMADO. A most fine figure!

MOTH. To prove you a cipher.

ARMADO. I will hereupon confess I am in love; and as it is base for a soldier to love, so am I in love with a base wench. If drawing my sword against the humour of affection would deliver me from the reprobate thought of it, I would take Desire prisoner, and ransom him to any French courtier for a new devised curtsy. I think scorn to sigh: methinks I should outswear Cupid. Comfort me, boy: what great men have been in love?

MOTH. Hercules, master.

ARMADO. Most sweet Hercules! More authority, dear boy, name more; and, sweet my child, let them be men of good repute and carriage.

MOTH. Samson, master: he was a man of good carriage, great carriage, for he carried the town-gates on his back like a porter; and he was in love.

ARMADO. O well-knit Samson! strong-jointed Samson! I do excel thee in my rapier as much as thou didst me in carrying gates. I am in love too. Who was Samson's love, my dear Moth?

MOTH. A woman, master.

ARMADO. Of what complexion?

MOTH. Of all the four, or the three, or the two, or one of the four.

ARMADO. Tell me precisely of what complexion.

MOTH. Of the sea-water green, sir.

ARMADO. Is that one of the four complexions?

MOTH. As I have read, sir; and the best of them too.

ARMADO. Green indeed is the colour of lovers; but to have a love of that colour, methinks Samson had small reason for it. He surely affected her for her wit.

MOTH. It was so, sir, for she had a green wit.

ARMADO. My love is most immaculate white and red.

MOTH. Most maculate thoughts, master, are masked under such colours.

ARMADO. Define, define, well-educated infant.

MOTH. My father's wit, and my mother's tongue, assist me!

ARMADO. Sweet invocation of a child; most pretty and pathetical!

MOTH. If she be made of white and red,
  Her faults will ne'er be known,
 For blushing cheeks by faults are bred,
  And fears by pale white shown:
 Then if she fear, or be to blame,
  By this you shall not know,
 For still her cheeks possess the same
  Which native she doth owe.

A dangerous rime, master, against the reason of white and red.

ARMADO. Is there not a ballad, boy, of the King and the Beggar?

MOTH. The world was very guilty of such a ballad some three ages since; but I think now 'tis not to be found; or, if it were, it would neither serve for the writing nor the tune.

ARMADO. I will have that subject newly writ o'er, that I may example my digression by some mighty precedent. Boy, I do love that country girl that I took in the park with the rational hind Costard: she deserves well.

MOTH. (*Aside*) To be whipped; and yet a better love than my master.

ARMADO. Sing, boy: my spirit grows heavy in love.

MOTH. And that 's great marvel, loving a light wench.

ARMADO. I say, sing.

MOTH. Forbear till this company be past.

   Enter Dull, Costard, and Jaquenetta

DULL. Sir, the duke's pleasure is, that you keep Costard safe: and you must let him take no delight nor no penance, but a' must fast three days a week. For this damsel, I must keep her at the park; she is allowed for the day-woman. Fare you well.

ARMADO. I do betray myself with blushing. Maid!

JAQUENETTA. Man?

ARMADO. I will visit thee at the lodge.

JAQUENETTA. That 's hereby.

ARMADO. I know where it is situate.

JAQUENETTA. Lord, how wise you are!

ARMADO. I will tell thee wonders.

JAQUENETTA. With that face?

ARMADO. I love thee.

JAQUENETTA. So I heard you say.

ARMADO. And so farewell.

JAQUENETTA. Fair weather after you!

DULL. Come, Jaquenetta, away!

Exeunt Dull and Jaquenetta

ARMADO. Villain, thou shalt fast for thy offences ere thou be pardoned.

COSTARD. Well, sir, I hope, when I do it, I shall do it on a full stomach.

ARMADO. Thou shalt be heavily punished.

COSTARD. I am more bound to you than your fellows, for they are but lightly rewarded.

ARMADO. Take away this villain: shut him up.

MOTH. Come, you transgressing slave: away!

COSTARD. Let me not be pent up, sir: I will fast, being loose.

MOTH. No, sir; that were fast and loose: thou shalt to prison.

COSTARD. Well, if ever I do see the merry days of desolation that I have seen, some shall see—

MOTH. What shall some see?

COSTARD. Nay, nothing, Master Moth, but what they look upon. It is not for prisoners to be too silent in their words; and therefore I will say nothing: I thank God I have as little patience as another man, and therefore I can be quiet. *Exeunt Moth and Costard*

ARMADO. I do affect the very ground, which is base, where her shoe, which is baser, guided by her foot, which is basest, doth tread. I shall be forsworn,—which is a great argument of falsehood,—if I love. And how can that be true love which is falsely attempted? Love is a familiar; Love is a devil: there is no evil angel but Love. Yet was Samson so tempted, and he had an excellent strength; yet was Solomon so seduced, and he had a very good wit. Cupid's butt-shaft is too hard for Hercules' club, and therefore too much odds for a Spaniard's rapier. The first and second clause will not serve my turn; the passado he respects not, the duello he regards not: his disgrace is to be called boy, but his glory is, to subdue men. Adieu, valour! rust, rapier! be still, drum! for your manager is in love; yea, he loveth. Assist me some extemporal god of rime, for I am sure I shall turn sonneter. Devise, wit; write, pen; for I am for whole volumes in folio. *Exit*

ACT TWO

SCENE ONE

*The King of Navarre's Park. A Pavilion and Tents
at a distance.*

*. Enter the Princess of France, Rosaline, Maria, Katharine,
Boyet, Lords, and other Attendants*

BOYET. Now, madam, summon up your dearest spirits:
    Consider whom the king your father sends,
    To whom he sends, and what 's his embassy:
    Yourself, held precious in the world's esteem,
    To parley with the sole inheritor
    Of all perfections that a man may owe,
    Matchless Navarre; the plea of no less weight
    Than Aquitaine, a dowry for a queen.
    Be now as prodigal of all dear grace
    As Nature was in making graces dear
    When she did starve the general world beside,
    And prodigally gave them all to you.
PRINCESS. Good Lord Boyet, my beauty, though but mean,
    Needs not the painted flourish of your praise:
    Beauty is bought by judgment of the eye,
    Not utter'd by base sale of chapmen's tongues.
    I am less proud to hear you tell my worth
    Than you much willing to be counted wise
    In spending your wit in the praise of mine.
    But now to task the tasker: good Boyet,
    You are not ignorant, all-telling fame
    Doth noise abroad, Navarre hath made a vow,
    Till painful study shall out-wear three years,
    No woman may approach his silent court:
    Therefore to us seemth it a needful course,
    Before we enter his forbidden gates,
    To know his pleasure; and in that behalf,

Bold of your worthiness, we single you
As our best-moving fair solicitor.
Tell him, the daughter of the King of France,
On serious business, craving quick dispatch,
Importunes personal conference with his Grace.
Haste, signify so much; while we attend,
Like humble-visag'd suitors, his high will.

BOYET. Proud of employment, willingly I go.

PRINCESS. All pride is willing pride, and yours is so.

Exit Boyet

Who are the votaries, my loving lords,
That are vow-fellows with this virtuous duke?

FIRST LORD. Lord Longaville is one.

PRINCESS.   Know you the man?

MARIA. I know him, madam: at a marriage feast,
Between Lord Perigort and the beauteous heir
Of Jacques Falconbridge, solemnized
In Normandy, saw I this Longaville.
A man of sovereign parts he is esteem'd,
Well fitted in the arts, glorious in arms:
Nothing becomes him ill that he would well.
The only soil of his fair virtue's gloss,—
If virtue's gloss will stain with any soil,—
Is a sharp wit match'd with too blunt a will;
Whose edge hath power to cut, whose will still wills
It should none spare that come within his power.

PRINCESS. Some merry mocking lord, belike; is't so?

MARIA. They say so most that most his humours know.

PRINCESS. Such short-liv'd wits do wither as they grow.
Who are the rest?

KATHARINE. The young Dumaine, a well-accomplish'd youth,
Of all that virtue love for virtue lov'd:
Most power to do most harm, least knowing ill,
For he hath wit to make an ill shape good,
And shape to win grace though he had no wit.
I saw him at the Duke Alençon's once;
And much too little of that good I saw
Is my report to his great worthiness.

ROSALINE. Another of these students at that time
Was there with him, if I have heard a truth:
Berowne they call him; but a merrier man,
Within the limit of becoming mirth,

I never spent an hour's talk withal.
His eye begets occasion for his wit;
For every object that the one doth catch
The other turns to a mirth-moving jest,
Which his fair tongue, conceit's expositor,
Delivers in such apt and gracious words,
That aged ears play truant at his tales,
And younger hearings are quite ravished;
So sweet and voluble is his discourse.

PRINCESS. God bless my ladies! are they all in love,
That every one her own hath garnished
With such bedecking ornaments of praise?

FIRST LORD. Here comes Boyet.

Re-enter Boyet

PRINCESS.   Now, what admittance, lord?

BOYET. Navarre had notice of your fair approach;
And he and his competitors in oath
Were all address'd to meet you, gentle lady,
Before I came. Marry, thus much I have learnt;
He rather means to lodge you in the field,
Like one that comes here to besiege his court,
Than seek a dispensation for his oath,
To let you enter his unpeeled house.
Here comes Navarre.   *The Ladies mask*

Enter King, Longaville, Dumaine, Berowne, and Attendants

KING. Fair princess, welcome to the court of Navarre.

PRINCESS. 'Fair,' I give you back again; and 'welcome' I
have not yet: the roof of this court is too high to be yours,
and welcome to the wide fields too base to be mine.

KING. You shall be welcome, madam, to my court.

PRINCESS. I will be welcome, then: conduct me thither.

KING. Hear me, dear lady; I have sworn an oath.

PRINCESS. Our Lady help my lord! he 'll be forsworn.

KING. Not for the world, fair madam, by my will.

PRINCESS. Why, will shall break it; will, and nothing else.

KING. Your ladyship is ignorant what it is.

PRINCESS. Were my lord so, his ignorance were wise,
Where now his knowledge must prove ignorance.
I hear your Grace hath sworn out house-keeping:
'Tis deadly sin to keep that oath, my lord,
And sin to break it.
But pardon me, I am too sudden-bold:

To teach a teacher ill beseemeth me.
Vouchsafe to read the purpose of my coming,
And suddenly resolve me in my suit.   *Gives a paper*

KING. Madam, I will, if suddenly I may.

PRINCESS. You will the sooner that I were away,
For you 'll prove perjur'd if you make me stay.

BEROWNE. Did not I dance with you in Brabant once?

ROSALINE. Did not I dance with you in Brabant once?

BEROWNE. I know you did.

ROSALINE.   How needless was it then
To ask the question!

BEROWNE.   You must not be so quick.

ROSALINE. 'Tis 'long of you that spur me with such questions.

BEROWNE. Your wit 's too hot, it speeds too fast, 'twill tire.

ROSALINE. Not till it leave the rider in the mire.

BEROWNE. What time o' day?

ROSALINE. The hour that fools should ask.

BEROWNE. Now fair befall your mask!

ROSALINE. Fair fall the face it covers!

BEROWNE. And send you many lovers!

ROSALINE. Amen, so you be none.

BEROWNE. Nay, then I will be gone.

KING. Madam, your father here doth intimate
The payment of a hundred thousand crowns;
Being but the one half of an entire sum
Disbursed by my father in his wars.
But say that he, or we,—as neither have,—
Receiv'd that sum, yet there remains unpaid
A hundred thousand more; in surety of the which,
One part of Aquitaine is bound to us,
Although not valued to the money's worth.
If then the king your father will restore
But that one half which is unsatisfied,
We will give up our right in Aquitaine,
And hold fair friendship with his Majesty.
But that it seems, he little purposeth,
For here he doth demand to have repaid
A hundred thousand crowns; and not demands,
On payment of a hundred thousand crowns,
To have his title live in Aquitaine;
Which we much rather had depart withal,

And have the money by our father lent,
Than Aquitaine, so gelded as it is.
Dear princess, were not his requests so far
From reason's yielding, your fair self should make
A yielding 'gainst some reason in my breast,
And go well satisfied to France again.

PRINCESS. You do the king my father too much wrong
And wrong the reputation of your name,
In so unseeming to confess receipt
Of that which hath so faithfully been paid.

KING. I do protest I never heard of it;
And if you prove it, I 'll repay it back
Or yield up Aquitaine.

PRINCESS.   We arrest your word.
Boyet, you can produce acquittances
For such a sum from special officers
Of Charles his father.

KING.   Satisfy me so.

BOYET. So please your Grace, the packet is not come
Where that and other specialties are bound:
To-morrow you shall have a sight of them.

KING. It shall suffice me: at which interview
All liberal reason I will yield unto.
Meantime, receive such welcome at my hand
As honour, without breach of honour, may
Make tender of to thy true worthiness.
You may not come, fair princess, in my gates;
But here without you shall be so receiv'd,
As you shall deem yourself lodg'd in my heart,
Though so denied fair harbour in my house.
Your own good thoughts excuse me, and farewell:
To-morrow shall we visit you again.

PRINCESS. Sweet health and fair desires consort your Grace!

KING. Thy own wish wish I thee in every place!

                    Exeunt King and his Train

BEROWNE. Lady, I will commend you to mine own heart.

ROSALINE. Pray you, do my commendations; I would be glad
     to see it.

BEROWNE. I would you heard it groan.

ROSALINE. Is the fool sick?

BEROWNE. Sick at the heart.

ROSALINE. Alack! let it blood.

BEROWNE. Would that do it good?

ROSALINE. My physic says, 'ay.'

BEROWNE. Will you prick 't with your eye?

ROSALINE. No point, with my knife.

BEROWNE. Now, God save thy life!

ROSALINE. And yours from long living!

BEROWNE. I cannot stay thanksgiving.   *Retiring*

DUMAINE. Sir, I pray you, a word: what lady is that same?

BOYET. The heir of Alençon, Katharine her name.

DUMAINE. A gallant lady. Monsieur, fare you well.   *Exit*

LONGAVILLE. I beseech you a word: what is she in the white?

BOYET. A woman sometimes, an you saw her in the light.

LONGAVILLE. Perchance light in the light. I desire her name.

BOYET. She hath but one for herself; to desire that, were a shame.

LONGAVILLE. Pray you, sir, whose daughter?

BOYET. Her mother's, I have heard.

LONGAVILLE. God's blessing on your beard!

BOYET. Good sir, be not offended.
  She is an heir of Falconbridge.

LONGAVILLE. Nay, my choler is ended.
  She is a most sweet lady.

BOYET. Not unlike, sir; that may be.   *Exit Longaville*

BEROWNE. What's her name, in the cap?

BOYET. Rosaline, by good hap.

BEROWNE. Is she wedded or no?

BOYET. To her will, sir, or so.

BEROWNE. You are welcome, sir. Adieu.

BOYET. Farewell to me, sir, and welcome to you.

> *Exit Berowne.—Ladies unmask*

MARIA. That last is Berowne, the merry madcap lord:
  Not a word with him but a jest.

BOYET.   And every jest but a word.

PRINCESS. It was well done of you to take him at his word.

BOYET. I was as willing to grapple, as he was to board.

MARIA. Two hot sheeps, marry!

BOYET.   And wherefore not ships?
  No sheep, sweet lamb, unless we feed on your lips.

MARIA. You sheep, and I pasture: shall that finish the jest?

BOYET. So you grant pasture for me.   *Offering to kiss her*

MARIA.   Not so, gentle beast.
  My lips are no common, though several they be.

BOYET. Belonging to whom?

MARIA.   To my fortunes and me.

PRINCESS. Good wits will be jangling; but, gentles, agree.
This civil war of wits were much better us'd
On Navarre and his book-men, for here 'tis abus'd.

BOYET. If my observation,—which very seldom lies,
By the heart's still rhetoric disclosed with eye,
Deceive me not now, Navarre is infected.

PRINCESS. With what?

BOYET. With that which we lovers entitle affected.

PRINCESS. Your reason.

BOYET. Why, all his behaviours did make their retire
To the court of his eye, peeping thorough desire;
His heart, like an agate, with your print impress'd,
Proud with his form, in his eye pride express'd:
His tongue, all impatient to speak and not see,
Did stumble with haste in his eyesight to be;
All senses to that sense did make their repair,
To feel only looking on fairest of fair,
Methought all his senses were lock'd in his eye,
As jewels in crystal for some prince to buy;
Who, tend'ring their own worth from where they were
    glass'd,
Did point you to buy them, along as you pass'd.
His face's own margent did quote such amazes,
That all eyes saw his eyes enchanted with gazes.
I 'll give you Aquitaine, and all that is his,
An' you give him for my sake but one loving kiss.

PRINCESS. Come to our pavilion: Boyet is dispos'd.

BOYET. But to speak that in words which his eye hath dis-
    clos'd.
I only have made a mouth of his eye,
By adding a tongue which I know will not lie.

ROSALINE. Thou art an old love-monger, and speak'st skil-
    fully.

MARIA. He is Cupid's grandfather and learns news of him.

ROSALINE. Then was Venus like her mother, for her father is
    but grim.

BOYET. Do you hear, my mad wenches?

MARIA.   No.

BOYET.   What, then, do you see?

ROSALINE. Ay, our way to be gone.

BOYET.   You are too hard for me.
                                            Exeunt

ACT THREE

The King of Navarre's Park.

Enter Armado and Moth

ARMADO. Warble, child; make passionate my sense of hearing.

MOTH. (*Singing*) Concolinel,—

ARMADO. Sweet air! Go, tenderness of years; take this key, give enlargement to the swain, bring him festinately hither; I must employ him in a letter to my love.

MOTH. Master, will you win your love with a French brawl?

ARMADO. How meanest thou? brawling in French?

MOTH. No, my complete master; but to jig off a tune at the tongue's end, canary to it with your feet, humour it with turning up your eyelids, sigh a note and sing a note, sometime through the throat, as if you swallowed love by singing love, sometime through the nose, as if you snuffed up love by smelling love; with your hat penthouse-like o'er the shop of your eyes; with your arms crossed on your thin belly-doublet like a rabbit on a spit; or your hands in your pocket like a man after the old painting; and keep not too long in one tune, but a snip and away. These are complements, these are humours, these betray nice wenches, that would be betrayed without these; and make them men of note,—do you note me?—that most are affected to these.

ARMADO. How hast thou purchased this experience?

MOTH. By my penny of observation.

ARMADO. But O—but O,—

MOTH. 'The hobby-horse is forgot.'

ARMADO. Callest thou my love 'hobby-horse'?

MOTH. No, master; the hobby-horse is but a colt, and your love perhaps, a hackney. But have you forgot your love?

ARMADO. Almost I had.

MOTH. Negligent student! learn her by heart.

ARMADO. By heart, and in heart, boy.

MOTH. And out of heart, master: all those three I will prove.

ARMADO. What wilt thou prove?

MOTH. A man, if I live; and this, by, in, and without, upon
the instant: by heart you love her, because your heart cannot come by her; in heart you love her, because your heart
is in love with her; and out of heart you love her, being
out of heart that you cannot enjoy her.

ARMADO. I am all these three.

MOTH. And three times as much more, and yet nothing at
all.

ARMADO. Fetch hither the swain: he must carry me a letter.

MOTH. A message well sympathized; a horse to be ambassador for an ass.

ARMADO. Ha, ha! what sayest thou?

MOTH. Marry, sir, you must send the ass upon the horse, for
he is very slow-gaited. But I go.

ARMADO. The way is but short: away!

MOTH. As swift as lead, sir.

ARMADO. Thy meaning, pretty ingenious?
Is not lead a metal heavy, dull, and slow?

MOTH. Minime, honest master; or rather, master, no.

ARMADO. I say, lead is slow.

MOTH.   You are too swift, sir, to say so:
Is that lead slow which is fir'd from a gun?

ARMADO. Sweet smoke of rhetoric!
He reputes me a cannon; and the bullet, that's he:
I shoot thee at the swain.

MOTH.   Thump then, and I flee.   *Exit*

ARMADO. A most acute juvenal; volable and free of grace!
By thy favour, sweet welkin, I must sigh in thy face:
Most rude melancholy, valour gives thee place.
My herald is return'd.

Re-enter Moth with Costard

MOTH. A wonder, master! here's a costard broken in a shin.

ARMADO. Some enigma, some riddle: come, thy l'envoy; begin.

COSTARD. No egma, no riddle, no l'envoy; no salve in the
mail, sir. O! sir, plantain, a plain plantain: no l'envoy, no
l'envoy: no salve, sir, but a plantain.

ARMADO. By virtue, thou enforcest laughter; thy silly

thought, my spleen; the heaving of my lungs provokes me
to ridiculous smiling: O! pardon me, my stars. Doth the
inconsiderate take salve for l'envoy, and the word l'envoy
for a salve?

MOTH. Do the wise think them other? Is not l'envoy a salve?

ARMADO. No, page: it is an epilogue or discourse, to make
plain
Some obscure precedence that hath tofore been sain.
I will example it:
> The fox, the ape, and the humble-bee
> Were still at odds, being but three.

There's the moral. Now the l'envoy.

MOTH. I will add the l'envoy. Say the moral again.

ARMADO. The fox, the ape, and the humble-bee
Were still at odds, being but three.

MOTH.   Until the goose came out of door,
And stay'd the odds by adding four.

Now will I begin your moral, and do you follow with my
l'envoy.
> The fox, the ape, and the humble-bee,
> Were still at odds, being but three.

ARMADO. Until the goose came out of door,
Staying the odds by adding four.

MOTH. A good l'envoy, ending in the goose.
Would you desire more?

COSTARD. The boy hath sold him a bargain, a goose, that's
flat.
Sir, your pennyworth is good an your goose be fat.
To sell a bargain well is as cunning as fast and loose:
Let me see; a fat l'envoy; ay, that's a fat goose.

ARMADO. Come hither, come hither. How did this argument
begin?

MOTH. By saying that a costard was broken in a shin. Then
call'd you for the l'envoy.

COSTARD. True, and I for a plantain: thus came your argu-
ment in;
Then the boy's fat l'envoy, the goose that you bought;
And he ended the market.

ARMADO. But tell me; how was there a costard broken in a
shin?

MOTH. I will tell you sensibly.

COSTARD. Thou hast no feeling of it, Moth: I will speak that
l'envoy:

> I, Costard, running out, that was safely within,
> Fell over the threshold and broke my shin.

ARMADO. We will talk no more of this matter.

COSTARD. Till there be more matter in the shin.

ARMADO. Sirrah Costard, I will enfranchise thee.

COSTARD. O! marry me to one Frances: I smell some l'envoy,
some goose, in this.

ARMADO. By my sweet soul, I mean setting thee at liberty,
enfreedoming thy person: thou wert immured, restrained,
captivated bound.

COSTARD. True, true, and now you will be my purgation and
let me loose.

ARMADO. I give thee thy liberty, set thee from durance; and
in lieu thereof, impose upon thee nothing but this:—(*Giving a letter*) Bear this significant to the country maid
Jaquenetta. (*Giving money*) There is remuneration; for
the best ward of mine honour is rewarding my depend-
ents. Moth, follow.   *Exit*

MOTH. Like the sequel, I. Signior Costard, adieu.

COSTARD. My sweet ounce of man's flesh! my incony Jew!
                                                  Exit Moth

Now will I look to his remuneration. Remuneration! O!
that 's the Latin word for three farthings: three farthings,
remuneration. 'What 's the price of this inkle?' 'One
penny.' 'No, I 'll give you a remuneration': why, it carries
it. Remuneration! why, it is a fairer name than French
crown. I will never buy and sell out of this word.

Enter Berowne

BEROWNE. O! my good knave Costard, exceedingly well
met.

COSTARD. Pray you, sir, how much carnation riband may a
man buy for a remuneration?

BEROWNE. What is a remuneration?

COSTARD. Marry, sir, halfpenny farthing.

BEROWNE. Why then, three-farthing-worth of silk.

COSTARD. I thank your worship. God be wi' you!

BEROWNE. Stay, slave; I must employ thee:

> As thou wilt win my favour, good my knave,
> Do one thing for me that I shall entreat.

COSTARD. When would you have it done, sir?

BEROWNE. O, this afternoon.

COSTARD. Well, I will do it, sir! fare you well.

BEROWNE. O, thou knowest not what it is.

COSTARD. I shall know, sir, when I have done it.

BEROWNE. Why, villain, thou must know first.

COSTARD. I will come to your worship to-morrow morning.

BEROWNE. It must be done this afternoon. Hark, slave, it is
but this:
The princess comes to hunt here in the park,
And in her train there is a gentle lady;
When tongues speak sweetly, then they name her name,
And Rosaline they call her: ask for her
And to her white hand see thou do commend
This seal'd-up counsel. (*Gives him a shilling*) There 's
thy guerdon: go.

COSTARD. Gardon, O sweet gardon! better than remuneration; a 'leven-pence farthing better. Most sweet gardon;
I will do it, sir, in print. Gardon! remuneration!   *Exit*

BEROWNE. And I,—
Forsooth, in love! I, that have been love's whip;
A very beadle to a humorous sigh;
A critic, nay, a night-watch constable,
A domineering pedant o'er the boy,
Than whom no mortal so magnificent!
This wimpled, whining, purblind, wayward boy,
This senior-junior, giant-dwarf, Dan Cupid;
Regent of love-rimes, lord of folded arms,
The anointed sovereign of sighs and groans,
Liege of all loiterers and malecontents,
Dread prince of plackets, king of codpieces,
Sole imperator and great general
Of trotting 'paritors: O my little heart!
And I to be a corporal of his field,
And wear his colours like a tumbler's hoop!
What I! I love! I sue! I seek a wife!
A woman that is like a German clock,
Still a-repairing, ever out of frame,
And never going aright, being a watch,
But being watch'd that it may still go right!
Nay, to be perjur'd, which is worst of all;
And, among three, to love the worst of all;

A wightly wanton with a velvet brow,
With two pitch balls stuck in her face for eyes;
Ay, and, by heaven, one that will do the deed
Though Argus were her eunuch and her guard:
And I to sigh for her! to watch for her!
To pray for her! Go to; it is a plague
That Cupid will impose for my neglect
Of his almighty dreadful little might.
Well, I will love, write, sigh, pray, sue, and groan:
Some men must love my lady, and some Joan.   *Exit*

ACT FOUR

SCENE ONE

The King of Navarre's Park.

*Enter the Princess, Rosaline, Maria, Katharine,
Boyet, Lords, Attendants, and a Forester*

PRINCESS. Was that the king, that spurr'd his horse so hard
　Against the steep uprising of the hill?
BOYET. I know not; but I think it was not he.
PRINCESS. Whoe'er a' was, a' show'd a mounting mind.
　Well, lords, to-day we shall have our dispatch;
　On Saturday we will return to France.
　Then, forester, my friend, where is the bush
　That we must stand and play the murderer in?
FORESTER. Hereby, upon the edge of yonder coppice;
　A stand where you may make the fairest shoot.
PRINCESS. I thank my beauty, I am fair that shoot,
　And thereupon thou speak'st the fairest shoot.
FORESTER. Pardon me, madam, for I meant not so.
PRINCESS. What, what? first praise me, and again say no?
　O short-liv'd pride! Not fair? alack for woe!
FORESTER. Yes, madam, fair.
PRINCESS. 　　　　　　　　Nay, never paint me now:
　Where fair is not, praise cannot mend the brow.
　Here, good my glass (*Gives money*):—Take this for tell-
　　ing true:
　Fair payment for foul words is more than due.
FORESTER. Nothing but fair is that which you inherit.
PRINCESS. See, see! my beauty will be sav'd by merit.
　O heresy in fair, fit for these days!
　A giving hand, though foul, shall have fair praise.
　But come, the bow: now mercy goes to kill,
　And shooting well is then accounted ill.
　Thus will I save my credit in the shoot:
　Not wounding, pity would not let me do 't;

If wounding, then it was to show my skill,
That more for praise than purpose meant to kill.
And out of question so it is sometimes,
Glory grows guilty of detested crimes,
When, for fame's sake, for praise, an outward part,
We bend to that the working of the heart;
As I for praise alone now seek to spill
The poor deer's blood, that my heart means no ill.

BOYET. Do not curst wives hold that self-sovereignty
Only for praise' sake, when they strive to be
Lords o'er their lords?

PRINCESS. Only for praise; and praise we may afford
To any lady that subdues a lord.

Enter Costard

BOYET. Here comes a member of the commonwealth.

COSTARD. God dig-you-den all! Pray you, which is the head
lady?

PRINCESS. Thou shalt know her, fellow, by the rest that have
no heads.

COSTARD. Which is the greatest lady, the highest?

PRINCESS. The thickest, and the tallest.

COSTARD. The thickest, and the tallest! it is so; truth is truth.
An your waist, mistress, were as slender as my wit,
One o' these maids' girdles for your waist should be fit.
Are not you the chief woman? You are the thickest here.

PRINCESS. What 's your will, sir? What 's your will?

COSTARD. I have a letter from Monsieur Berowne to one
Lady Rosaline.

PRINCESS. O! thy letter, thy letter; he 's a good friend of
mine.
Stand aside, good bearer. Boyet, you can carve;
Break up this capon.

BOYET.   I am bound to serve.
This letter is mistook; it importeth none here;
It is writ to Jaquenetta.

PRINCESS.   We will read it, I swear.
Break the neck of the wax, and every one give ear.

BOYET. 'By heaven, that thou art fair, is most infallible; true,
that thou art beauteous; truth itself, that thou art lovely.
More fairer than fair, beautiful than beauteous, truer than
truth itself, have commiseration on thy heroical vassall
The magnanimous and most illustrate king Cophetua set

eye upon the pernicious and indubitate beggar Zenelophon, and he it was that might rightly say veni, vidi, vici; which to anatomize in the vulgar—O base and obscure vulgar!—videlicet, he came, saw, and overcame: he came, one; saw, two; overcame, three. Who came? the king: Why did he come? to see: Why did he see? to overcome: To whom came he? to the beggar: What saw he? the beggar. Whom overcame he? the beggar. The conclusion is victory: on whose side? the king's; the captive is enriched: on whose side? the beggar's. The catastrophe is a nuptial: on whose side? the king's, no, on both in one, or one in both. I am the king, for so stands the comparison; thou the beggar, for so witnesseth thy lowliness. Shall I command thy love? I may: Shall I enforce thy love? I could: Shall I entreat thy love? I will. What shalt thou exchange for rags? robes; for tittles? titles; for thyself? me. Thus, expecting thy reply, I profane my lips on thy foot, my eyes on thy picture, and my heart on thy every part.

> Thine, in the dearest design of Industry,
>
> > Don Adriano de Armado.

'Thus dost thou hear the Nemean lion roar
'Gainst thee, thou lamb, that standest as his prey:
Submissive fall his princely feet before,
  And he from forage will incline to play.
But if thou strive, poor soul, what art thou then?
Food for his rage, repasture for his den.'

PRINCESS. What plume of feathers is he that indited this letter?

What vane? what weathercock? did you ever hear better?

BOYET. I am much deceiv'd but I remember the style.

PRINCESS. Else your memory is bad, going o'er it erewhile.

BOYET. This Armado is a Spaniard, that keeps here in court;
A phantasime, a Monarcho, and one that makes sport
To the prince and his book-mates.

PRINCESS.   Thou, fellow, a word.
Who gave thee this letter?

COSTARD.   I told you; my lord.

PRINCESS. To whom shouldst thou give it?

COSTARD.   From my lord to my lady.

PRINCESS. From which lord, to which lady?

COSTARD. From my lord Berowne, a good master of mine,
To a lady of France, that he call'd Rosaline.

PRINCESS. Thou hast mistaken his letter. Come, lords, away.
Here, sweet, put up this: 'twill be thine another day.

Exeunt Princess and Train

BOYET. Who is the suitor? who is the suitor?

ROSALINE.   Shall I teach you to know?

BOYET. Ay, my continent of beauty.

ROSALINE.   Why, she that bears the bow.
Finely put off!

BOYET. My lady goes to kill horns; but, if thou marry,
Hang me by the neck if horns that year miscarry.
Finely put on!

ROSALINE. Well then, I am the shooter.

BOYET.   And who is your deer?

ROSALINE. If we choose by the horns, yourself: come not
near.
Finely put on, indeed!

MARIA. You still wrangle with her, Boyet, and she strikes at
the brow.

BOYET. But she herself is hit lower: have I hit her now?

ROSALINE. Shall I come upon thee with an old saying, that
was a man when King Pepin of France was a little boy, as
touching the hit it?

BOYET. So may I answer thee with one as old, that was a
woman when Queen Guinever of Britain was a little
wench, as touching the hit it.

ROSALINE. Thou canst not hit it, hit it, hit it,
Thou canst not hit it, my good man.

BOYET.   An I cannot, cannot, cannot,
An I cannot, another can.

Exeunt Rosaline and Katharine

COSTARD. By my troth, most pleasant: how both did fit it!

MARIA. A mark marvellous well shot, for they both did hit it!

BOYET. A mark! O! mark but that mark; a mark, says my
lady!
Let the mark have a prick in 't, to mete at, if it may be.

MARIA. Wide o' the bow hand! i' faith your hand is out.

COSTARD. Indeed a' must shoot nearer, or he 'll ne'er hit the
clout.

BOYET. An' if my hand be out, then belike your hand is in.

COSTARD. Then will she get the upshoot by cleaving the pin.

MARIA. Come, come, you talk greasily; your lips grow foul.

COSTARD. She 's too hard for you at pricks, sir: challenge her
to bowl.

BOYET. I fear too much rubbing. Good night, my good owl.

Exeunt Boyet and Maria

COSTARD. By my soul, a swain! a most simple clown!
Lord, lord how the ladies and I have put him down!
O' my troth, most sweet jests! most incony vulgar wit!
When it comes so smoothly off, so obscenely, as it were, so
fit,
Armado, o' the one side, O! a most dainty man.
To see him walk before a lady, and to bear her fan!
To see him kiss his hand! and how most sweetly a' will
swear!
And his page o' t'other side, that handful of wit!
Ah! heavens, it is a most pathetical nit.
(*Shouting within*) Sola, sola!   *Exit running*

SCENE TWO

The Same.

Enter Holofernes, Sir Nathaniel, and Dull

NATHANIEL. Very reverend sport, truly: and done in the
testimony of a good conscience.

HOLOFERNES. The deer was, as you know, sanguis, in blood;
ripe as a pomewater, who now hangeth like a jewel in the
ear of cælo, the sky, the welkin, the heaven; and anon
falleth like a crab on the face of terra, the soil, the land,
the earth.

NATHANIEL. Truly, Master Holofernes, the epithets are
sweetly varied, like a scholar at the least: but, sir, I assure
ye, it was a buck of the first head.

HOLOFERNES. Sir Nathaniel, haud credo.

DULL. 'Twas not a haud credo; 'twas a pricket.

HOLOFERNES. Most barbarous intimation! yet a kind of in-
sinuation, as it were, in via, in way, of explication; facere,
as it were, replication, or, rather, ostentare, to show, as it
were, his inclination,—after his undressed, unpolished, un-
educated, unpruned, untrained, or, rather, unlettered, or,
ratherest, unconfirmed fashion,—to insert again my haud
credo for a deer.

DULL. I said the deer was not a haud credo; 'twas a pricket.

HOLOFERNES. Twice sod simplicity, bis coctus!

O! thou monster Ignorance, how deformed dost thou look!

NATHANIEL. Sir, he hath not fed of the dainties that are bred
of a book;

he hath not eat paper, as it were; he hath not drunk ink:
his intellect is not replenished; he is only an animal, only
sensible in the duller parts:

And such barren plants are set before us, that we thankful
should be,

Which we of taste and feeling are, for those parts that do
fructify in us more than he;

For as it would ill become me to be vain, indiscreet, or a
fool:

So, were there a patch set on learning, to see him in a
school:

But, omne bene, say I; being of an old Father's mind,

Many can brook the weather that love not the wind.

DULL. You two are book-men: can you tell by your wit,

What was a month old at Cain's birth, that 's not five
weeks old as yet?

HOLOFERNES. Dictynna, goodman Dull: Dictynna, goodman
Dull.

DULL. What is Dictynna?

NATHANIEL. A title to Phœbe, to Luna, to the moon.

HOLOFERNES. The moon was a month old when Adam was
no more;

And raught not to five weeks when he came to five-score.
The allusion holds in the exchange.

DULL. 'Tis true indeed: the collusion holds in the exchange.

HOLOFERNES. God comfort thy capacity! I say, the allusion
holds in the exchange.

DULL. And I say the pollusion holds in the exchange, for the
moon is never but a month old; and I say beside that 'twas
a pricket that the princess killed.

HOLOFERNES. Sir Nathaniel, will you hear an extemporal
epitaph on the death of the deer? and, to humour the ignorant, I have call'd the deer the princess killed, a pricket.

NATHANIEL. Perge, good Master Holofernes, perge; so it
shall please you to abrogate scurrility.

HOLOFERNES. I will something affect the letter; for it argues
facility.

The preyful princess pierc'd and prick'd a pretty pleasing
  pricket;
    Some say a sore; but not a sore, till now made sore with
      shooting.
The dogs did yell; put L to sore, then sorel jumps from
  thicket;
    Or pricket, sore, or else sorel; the people fall a hooting.
If sore be sore, then L to sore makes fifty sores one sorel!
Of one sore I a hundred make, by adding but one more L.

NATHANIEL. A rare talent!

DULL. (*Aside*) If a talent be a claw, look how he claws him
  with a talent.

HOLOFERNES. This is a gift that I have, simple, simple; a
  foolish extravagant spirit, full of forms, figures, shapes,
  objects, ideas, apprehensions, motions, revolutions: these
  are begot in the ventricle of memory, nourished in the
  womb of pia mater, and delivered upon the mellowing of
  occasion. But the gift is good in those in whom it is acute,
  and I am thankful for it.

NATHANIEL. Sir, I praise the Lord for you, and so may my
  parishioners; for their sons are well tutored by you, and
  their daughters profit very greatly under you: you are a
  good member of the commonwealth.

HOLOFERNES. Mehercle! if their sons be ingenuous, they
  shall want no instruction; if their daughters be capable, I
  will put it to them. But, vir sapit qui pauca loquitur. A
  soul feminine saluteth us.

Enter Jaquenetta and Costard

JAQUENETTA. God give you good-morrow, Master parson.

HOLOFERNES. Master parson, quasi pers-on. An if one should
  be pierced, which is the one?

COSTARD. Marry, Master schoolmaster, he that is likest to a
  hogshead.

HOLOFERNES. Piercing a hogshead! a good lustre or conceit
  in a turf of earth; fire enough for a flint, pearl enough for a
  swine: 'tis pretty; it is well.

JAQUENETTA. Good Master parson (*giving a letter to Nathaniel*), be so good as read me this letter: it was given me
  by Costard, and sent me from Don Armado: I beseech
  you, read it.

HOLOFERNES. 'Fauste, precor gelida quando pecus omne sub
  umbra Ruminat,' and so forth. Ah! good old Mantuan. I

may speak of thee as the traveller doth of Venice:
   —Venetia, Venetia,
    Chi non te vede, non te pretia.
Old Mantuan! old Mantuan! Who understandeth thee not,
loves thee not. Ut, re, sol, la, mi, fa. Under pardon, sir,
what are the contents? or, rather, as Horace says in his—
What, my soul, verses?

NATHANIEL. Ay, sir, and very learned.

HOLOFERNES. Let me hear a staff, a stanze, a verse: lege,
domine.

NATHANIEL. (*Reads*) 'If love make me forsworn, how shall
  I swear to love?
 Ah! never faith could hold, if not to beauty vow'd;
Though to myself forsworn, to thee I 'll faithful prove;
 Those thoughts to me were oaks, to thee like osiers
  bow'd.
Study his bias leaves and makes his book thine eyes,
 Where all those pleasures live that art would compre-
  hend:
If knowledge be the mark, to know thee shall suffice.
 Well learned is that tongue that well can thee com-
  mend;
All ignorant that soul that sees thee without wonder;
 Which is to me some praise that I thy parts admire.
Thy eye Jove's lightning bears, thy voice his dreadful
  thunder,
 Which, not to anger bent, is music and sweet fire.
Celestial as thou art, O! pardon love this wrong,
That sings heaven's praise with such an earthly tongue!'

HOLOFERNES. You find not the apostrophas, and so miss the
accent: let me supervise the canzonet. Here are only numbers ratified; but, for the elegancy, facility, and golden
cadence of poesy, caret. Ovidious Naso was the man: and
why, indeed, Naso, but for smelling out the odoriferous
flowers of fancy, the jerks of invention? Imitari is nothing;
so doth the hound his master, the ape his keeper, the
'tired horse his rider. But, damosella virgin, was this directed to you?

JAQUENETTA. Ay, sir; from one Monsieur Berowne, one of
the strange queen's lords.

HOLOFERNES. I will overglance the superscript. To the
snow-white hand of the most beauteous Lady Rosaline.'

I will look again on the intellect of the letter, for the nomination of the party writing to the person written unto: 'Your ladyship's, in all desired employment, Berowne.'— Sir Nathaniel, this Berowne is one of the votaries with the king; and here he hath framed a letter to a sequent of the stranger queen's, which, accidentally, or by the way of progression, hath miscarried. Trip and go, my sweet; deliver this paper into the royal hand of the king; it may concern much. Stay not thy compliment; I forgive thy duty: adieu.

JAQUENETTA. Good Costard, go with me. Sir, God save your life!

COSTARD. Have with thee, my girl.

Exeunt Costard and Jaquenetta

NATHANIEL. Sir, you have done this in the fear of God, very religiously; and, as a certain Father saith—

HOLOFERNES. Sir, tell not me of the Father; I do fear colourable colours. But to return to the verses: did they please you, Sir Nathaniel?

NATHANIEL. Marvellous well for the pen.

HOLOFERNES. I do dine to-day at the father's of a certain pupil of mine; where, if before repast it shall please you to gratify the table with a grace, I will, on my privilege I have with the parents of the foresaid child or pupil, undertake your ben venuto; where I will prove those verses to be very unlearned, neither savouring of poetry, wit, nor invention. I beseech your society.

NATHANIEL. And thank you too; for society—saith the text—is the happiness of life.

HOLOFERNES. And, certes, the text most infallibly concludes it.—(*To Dull*) Sir, I do invite you too: you shall not say me nay: pauca verba. Away! the gentles are at their game, and we will to our recreation. *Exeunt*

SCENE THREE

The Same.

Enter Berowne, with a paper

BEROWNE. The king he is hunting the deer; I am coursing myself: they have pitched a toil; I am toiling in a pitch,—pitch that defiles: defile! a foul word! Well, sit thee down, sorrow! for so they say the fool said, and so say I, and I the fool: well proved, wit! By the Lord, this love is as mad as Ajax: it kills sheep: it kills me, I a sheep: well proved again o' my side! I will not love; if I do, hang me; i' faith, I will not. O! but her eye,—by this light, but for her eye, I would not love her; yes, for her two eyes. Well, I do nothing in the world but lie, and lie in my throat. By heaven, I do love, and it hath taught me to rime, and to be melancholy; and here is part of my rime, and here my melancholy. Well, she hath one o' my sonnets already: the clown bore it, the fool sent it, and the lady hath it: sweet clown, sweeter fool, sweetest lady! By the world, I would not care a pin if the other three were in. Here comes one with a paper: God give him grace to groan!   *Gets up into a tree*

Enter the King, with a paper

KING. Ah me!

BEROWNE. (*Aside*) Shot, by heaven! Proceed, sweet Cupid: thou hast thumped him with thy bird-bolt under the left pap. In faith, secrets!

KING. (*Reads*) 'So sweet a kiss the golden sun gives not
    To those fresh morning drops upon the rose,
As thy eye-beams, when their fresh rays have smote
    The night of dew that on my cheeks down flows;
Nor shines the silver moon one half so bright
    Through the transparent bosom of the deep,
As doth thy face through tears of mine give light;
    Thou shin'st in every tear that I do weep:
No drop but as a coach doth carry thee;
    So ridest thou triumphing in my woe.
Do but behold the tears that swell in me,
    And they thy glory through my grief will show:
But do not love thyself; then thou wilt keep

My tears for glasses, and still make me weep.
O queen of queens! how far thou dost excel,
No thought can think, nor tongue of mortal tell.'

How shall she know my griefs? I 'll drop the paper:
Sweet leaves, shade folly. Who is he comes here?

Steps aside

What, Longaville! and reading! listen, ear.

Enter Longaville, with a paper

BEROWNE. Now, in thy likeness, one more fool appear!
LONGAVILLE. Ay me! I am forsworn.
BEROWNE. Why, he comes in like a perjure, wearing papers.
KING. In love, I hope: sweet fellowship in shame!
BEROWNE. One drunkard loves another of the name.
LONGAVILLE. Am I the first that have been perjur'd so?
BEROWNE. I could put thee in comfort: not by two that I
know:
Thou mak'st the triumviry, the corner-cap of society,
The shape of love's Tyburn, that hangs up simplicity.
LONGAVILLE. I fear these stubborn lines lack power to move.
O sweet Maria, empress of my love!
These numbers will I tear, and write in prose.
BEROWNE. O! rimes are guards on wanton Cupid's hose:
Disfigure not his slop.
LONGAVILLE.   This same shall go. (*Reads*)
'Did not the heavenly rhetoric of thine eye,
    'Gainst whom the world cannot hold argument,
Persuade my heart to this false perjury?
    Vows for thee broke deserve not punishment.
A woman I forswore; but I will prove,
    Thou being a goddess, I forswore not thee:
My vow was earthly, thou a heavenly love;
    Thy grace, being gain'd, cures all disgrace in me.
Vows are but breath, and breath a vapour is:
    Then thou, fair sun, which on my earth dost shine,
Exhal'st this vapour-vow; in thee it is:
    If broken, then, it is no fault of mine:
If by me broke, what fool is not so wise
To lose an oath to win a paradise!'
BEROWNE. This is the liver-vein, which makes flesh a deity;
A green goose a goddess; pure, pure idolatry.
God amend us, God amend! we are much out o' the way.

LONGAVILLE. By whom shall I send this?—Company! stay.

Steps aside

BEROWNE. All hid, all hid; an old infant play.
Like a demi-god here sit I in the sky,
And wretched fools' secrets heedfully o'er-eye.
More sacks to the mill! O heavens! I have my wish.

Enter Dumaine, with a paper

Dumaine transform'd: four woodcocks in a dish!

DUMAINE. O most divine Kate!

BEROWNE. O most profane coxcomb!

DUMAINE. By heaven, the wonder of a mortal eye!

BEROWNE. By earth, she is but corporal; there you lie.

DUMAINE. Her amber hairs for foul have amber quoted.

BEROWNE. An amber-colour'd raven was well noted.

DUMAINE. As upright as the cedar.

BEROWNE.   Stoop, I say;
Her shoulder is with child.

DUMAINE.   As fair as day.

BEROWNE. Ay, as some days; but then no sun must shine.

DUMAINE. O! that I had my wish.

LONGAVILLE.   And I had mine!

KING. And I mine too, good Lord!

BEROWNE. Amen, so I had mine. Is not that a good word?

DUMAINE. I would forget her; but a fever she
Reigns in my blood, and will remember'd be.

BEROWNE. A fever in your blood! why, then incision
Would let her out in saucers: sweet misprision!

DUMAINE. Once more I 'll read the ode that I have writ.

BEROWNE. Once more I 'll mark how love can vary wit.

DUMAINE. (*Reads*) 'On a day, alack the day!
Love, whose month is ever May,
Spied a blossom passing fair
Playing in the wanton air:
Through the velvet leaves the wind,
All unseen, 'gan passage find;
That the lover, sick to death,
Wish'd himself the heaven's breath.
Air, quoth he, thy cheeks may blow
Air, would I might triumph so!
But alack! my hand is sworn
Ne'er to pluck thee from thy thorn:
Vow, alack! for youth unmeet,

Youth so apt to pluck a sweet.
Do not call it sin in me,
That I am forsworn for thee;
Thou for whom e'en Jove would swear
Juno but an Ethiop were;
And deny himself for Jove,
Turning mortal for thy love.'

This will I send, and something else more plain,
That shall express my true love's fasting pain.
O! would the King, Berowne, and Longaville
Were lovers too. Ill, to example ill,
Would from my forehead wipe a perjur'd note;
For none offend where all alike do dote.

LONGAVILLE. (*Advancing*) Dumaine, thy love is far from charity,
That in love's grief desir'st society:
You may look pale, but I should blush, I know,
To be o'erheard and taken napping so.

KING. (*Advancing*) Come, sir, you blush: as his your case is such;
You chide at him, offending twice as much:
You do not love Maria; Longaville
Did never sonnet for her sake compile,
Nor never lay his wreathed arms athwart
His loving bosom to keep down his heart.
I have been closely shrouded in this bush,
And mark'd you both, and for you both did blush.
I heard your guilty rimes, observ'd your fashion,
Saw sighs reek from you, noted well your passion:
Ay me! says one; O Jove! the other cries;
One, her hairs were gold, crystal the other's eyes:
(*To Longaville*) You would for paradise break faith and troth;
(*To Dumaine*) And Jove, for your love, would infringe an oath.
What will Berowne say, when that he shall hear
A faith infringed, which such zeal did swear?
How will he scorn! how will he spend his wit!
How will he triumph, leap and laugh at it!
For all the wealth that ever I did see,
I would not have him know so much by me.

BEROWNE. Now step I forth to whip hypocrisy. *Descends*

Ah! good my liege, I pray thee, pardon me:
Good heart! what grace hast thou, thus to reprove
These worms for loving, that art most in love?
Your eyes do make no coaches; in your tears
There is no certain princess that appears:
You 'll not be perjur'd, 'tis a hateful thing:
Tush! none but minstrels like of sonneting.
But are you not asham'd? nay, are you not,
All three of you, to be thus much o'ershot?
You found his mote; the king your mote did see;
But I a beam do find in each of three.
O! what a scene of foolery have I seen.
Of sighs, of groans, of sorrow, and of teen;
O me! with what strict patience have I sat,
To see a king transformed to a gnat;
To see great Hercules whipping a gig,
And profound Solomon to tune a jig,
And Nestor play at push-pin with the boys,
And critic Timon laugh at idle toys!
Where lies thy grief? O! tell me, good Dumaine,
And, gentle Longaville, where lies thy pain?
And where my liege's? all about the breast:
A caudle, ho!

KING.   Too bitter is thy jest.
Are we betray'd thus to thy over-view?

BEROWNE. Not you to me, but I betray'd by you:
I, that am honest; I, that hold it sin
To break the vow I am engaged in;
I am betray'd, by keeping company
With men like men, men of inconstancy.
When shall you see me write a thing in rime?
Or groan for Joan? or spend a minute's time
In pruning me? When shall you hear that I
Will praise a hand, a foot, a face, an eye,
A gait, a state, a brow, a breast, a waist,
A leg, a limb?—

KING.   Soft! Whither away so fast?
A true man or a thief that gallops so?

BEROWNE. I post from love; good lover, let me go.
          Enter Jaquenetta and Costard

JAQUENETTA. God bless the king!

KING.   What present hast thou there?

COSTARD. Some certain treason.

KING.   What makes treason here?

COSTARD. Nay, it makes nothing, sir.

KING.   If it mar nothing neither,
The treason and you go in peace away together.

JAQUENETTA. I beseech your Grace, let this letter be read:
Our parson misdoubts it; 'twas treason, he said.

KING. Berowne, read it over—   *Giving the letter to him*
Where hadst thou it?

JAQUENETTA. Of Costard.

KING. Where hadst thou it?

COSTARD. Of Dun Adramadio, Dun Adramadio.

                      Berowne tears the letter

KING. How now! what is in you? why dost thou tear it?

BEROWNE. A toy, my liege, a toy: your Grace needs not fear
    it.

LONGAVILLE. It did move him to passion, and therefore let's
    hear it.

DUMAINE. (*Picking up the pieces*) It is Berowne's writing,
    and here is his name.

BEROWNE. (*To Costard*) Ah, you whoreson loggerhead, you
    were born to do me shame.

    Guilty, my lord, guilty; I confess, I confess.

KING. What?

BEROWNE. That you three fools lack'd me fool to make up
    the mess;

    He, he, and you, and you my liege, and I,

    Are pick-purses in love, and we deserve to die.

    O! dismiss this audience, and I shall tell you more.

DUMAINE. Now the number is even.

BEROWNE.   True, true; we are four.
Will these turtles be gone?

KING.   Hence, sirs; away!

COSTARD. Walk aside the true folk, and let the traitors stay.

                Exeunt Costard and Jaquenetta

BEROWNE. Sweet lords, sweet lovers, O! let us embrace.

    As true we are as flesh and blood can be:

    The sea will ebb and flow, heaven show his face;

        Young blood doth not obey an old decree:

    We cannot cross the cause why we were born;

    Therefore, of all hands must we be forsworn.

KING. What! did these rent lines show some love of thine?
BEROWNE. 'Did they,' quoth you? Who sees the heavenly
      Rosaline,
  That, like a rude and savage man of Inde,
    At the first opening of the gorgeous east,
  Bows not his vassal head, and, strucken blind,
    Kisses the base ground with obedient breast?
  What peremptory eagle-sighted eye
    Dares look upon the heaven of her brow,
  That is not blinded by her majesty?
KING. What zeal, what fury hath inspir'd thee now?
  My love, her mistress, is a gracious moon;
    She, an attending star, scarce seen a light.
BEROWNE. My eyes are then no eyes, nor I Berowne:
    O! but for my love, day would turn to night.
  Of all complexions the cull'd sovereignty
    Do meet, as at a fair, in her fair cheek;
  Where several worthies make one dignity,
    Where nothing wants that want itself doth seek.
  Lend me the flourish of all gentle tongues,—
    Fie, painted rhetoric! O! she needs it not:
  To things of sale a seller's praise belongs;
    She passes praise; then praise too short doth blot.
  A wither'd hermit, five-score winters worn,
    Might shake off fifty, looking in her eye:
  Beauty doth varnish age, as if new-born,
    And gives the crutch the cradle's infancy.
  O! 'tis the sun that maketh all things shine.
KING. By heaven, thy love is black as ebony.
BEROWNE. Is ebony like her? O wood divine!
  A wife of such wood were felicity.
  O! who can give an oath? where is a book?
    That I may swear beauty doth beauty lack,
  If that she learn not of her eye to look:
    No face is fair that is not full so black.
KING. O paradox! Black is the badge of hell,
    The hue of dungeons and the scowl of night;
  And beauty's crest becomes the heavens well.
BEROWNE. Devils soonest tempt, resembling spirit of light.
  O! if in black my lady's brows be deck'd,
    It mourns that painting and usurping hair
  Should ravish doters with a false aspect;

And therefore is she born to make black fair.
Her favour turns the fashion of the days,
   For native blood is counted painting now;
And therefore red, that would avoid dispraise,
   Paints itself black, to imitate her brow.

DUMAINE. To look like her are chimney-sweepers black.

LONGAVILLE. And since her time are colliers counted bright.

KING. And Ethiops of their sweet complexion crack.

DUMAINE. Dark needs no candles now, for dark is light.

BEROWNE. Your mistresses dare never come in rain,
   For fear their colours should be wash'd away.

KING. 'Twere good yours did; for, sir, to tell you plain,
   I 'll find a fairer face not wash'd to-day.

BEROWNE. I 'll prove her fair, or talk till doomsday here.

KING. No devil will fright thee then so much as she.

DUMAINE. I never knew man hold vile stuff so dear.

LONGAVILLE. Look, here 's thy love: (*Showing his shoe*) my
   foot and her face see.

BEROWNE. O! if the streets were paved with thine eyes,
   Her feet were much too dainty for such tread.

DUMAINE. O vile! then, as she goes, what upward lies
   The street should see as she walk'd over head.

KING. But what of this? Are we not all in love?

BEROWNE. Nothing so sure; and thereby all forsworn.

KING. Then leave this chat; and good Berowne, now prove
   Our loving lawful, and our faith not torn.

DUMAINE. Ay, marry, there; some flattery for this evil.

LONGAVILLE. O! some authority how to proceed;
   Some tricks, some quillets, how to cheat the devil.

DUMAINE. Some salve for perjury.

BEROWNE.   O, 'tis more than need.
Have at you, then, affection's men-at-arms:
Consider what you first did swear unto,
To fast, to study, and to see no woman;
Flat treason 'gainst the kingly state of youth.
Say, can you fast? your stomachs are too young,
And abstinence engenders maladies.
And where that you have vow'd to study, lords,
In that each of you hath forsworn his book,
Can you still dream and pore and thereon look?
For when would you, my lord, or you, or you,
Have found the ground of study's excellence
Without the beauty of a woman's face?

From women's eyes this doctrine I derive:
They are the ground, the books, the academes,
From whence doth spring the true Promethean fire.
Why, universal plodding poisons up
The nimble spirits in the arteries,
As motion and long-during action tires
The sinewy vigour of the traveller.
Now, for not looking on a woman's face,
You have in that forsworn the use of eyes,
And study too, the causer of your vow;
For where is any author in the world
Teaches such beauty as a woman's eye?
Learning is but an adjunct to ourself,
And where we are our learning likewise is:
Then when ourselves we see in ladies' eyes,
Do we not likewise see our learning there?
O! we have made a vow to study, lords,
And in that vow we have forsworn our books:
For when would you, my liege, or you, or you,
In leaden contemplation have found out
Such fiery numbers as the prompting eyes
Of beauty's tutors have enrich'd you with?
Other slow arts entirely keep the brain,
And therefore, finding barren practisers,
Scarce show a harvest of their heavy toil;
But love, first learned in a lady's eyes,
Lives not alone immured in the brain,
But, with the motion of all elements,
Courses as swift as thought in every power,
And gives to every power a double power,
Above their functions and their offices.
It adds a precious seeing to the eye;
A lover's eyes will gaze an eagle blind;
A lover's ear will hear the lowest sound,
When the suspicious head of theft is stopp'd:
Love's feeling is more soft and sensible
Than are the tender horns of cockled snails:
Love's tongue proves dainty Bacchus gross in taste.
For valour, is not Love a Hercules,
Still climbing trees in the Hesperides?
Subtle as Sphinx; as sweet and musical
As bright Apollo's lute, strung with his hair;
And when Love speaks, the voice of all the gods

Makes heaven drowsy with the harmony.
Never durst poet touch a pen to write
Until his ink were temper'd with Love's sighs;
O! then his lines would ravish savage ears,
And plant in tyrants mild humility.
From women's eyes this doctrine I derive:
They sparkle still the right Promethean fire;
They are the books, the arts, the academes,
That show, contain, and nourish all the world;
Else none at all in aught proves excellent.
Then fools you were these women to forswear,
Or, keeping what is sworn, you will prove fools.
For wisdom's sake, a word that all men love,
Or for love's sake, a word that loves all men,
Or for men's sake, the authors of these women;
Or women's sake, by whom we men are men,
Let us once lose our oaths to find ourselves,
Or else we lose ourselves to keep our oaths.
It is religion to be thus forsworn;
For charity itself fulfils the law;
And who can sever love from charity?

KING. Saint Cupid, then! and, soldiers, to the field!

BEROWNE. Advance your standards, and upon them, lords!
Pell-mell, down with them! but be first advis'd,
In conflict that you get the sun of them.

LONGAVILLE. Now to plain-dealing; lay these glozes by;
Shall we resolve to woo these girls of France?

KING. And win them too: therefore let us devise
Some entertainment for them in their tents.

BEROWNE. First, from the park let us conduct them thither;
Then homeward every man attach the hand
Of his fair mistress: in the afternoon
We will with some strange pastime solace them,
Such as the shortness of the time can shape;
For revels, dances, masks, and merry hours,
Forerun fair Love, strewing her way with flowers.

KING. Away, away! no time shall be omitted,
That will betime, and may by us be fitted.

BEROWNE. Allons! allons! Sow'd cockle reap'd no corn;
And justice always whirls in equal measure:
Light wenches may prove plagues to men forsworn;
If so, our copper buys no better treasure.   *Exeunt*

ACT FIVE

SCENE ONE

The King of Navarre's Park.

Enter Holofernes, Sir Nathaniel, and Dull

HOLOFERNES. Satis quod sufficit.

NATHANIEL. I praise God for you, sir: your reasons at dinner have been sharp and sententious; pleasant without scurrility, witty without affection, audacious without impudency, learned without opinion, and strange without heresy. I did converse this quondam day with a companion of the king's, who is intituled, nominated, or called, Don Adriano de Armado.

HOLOFERNES. Novi hominem tanquam te: his humour is lofty, his discourse peremptory, his tongue filed, his eye ambitious, his gait majestical, and his general behaviour vain, ridiculous, and thrasonical. He is too picked, too spruce, too affected, too odd, as it were, too peregrinate, as I may call it.

NATHANIEL. A most singular and choice epithet.

Draws out his table-book

HOLOFERNES. He draweth out the thread of his verbosity finer than the staple of his argument. I abhor such fanatical phantasimes, such insociable and point-devise companions; such rackers of orthography, as to speak dout, fine, when he should say, doubt; det, when he should pronounce, debt,—d, e, b, t, not d, e, t: he clepeth a calf, cauf; half, hauf; neighbour vocatur nebour, neigh abbreviated ne. This is abhominable, which he would call abominable,—it insinuateth me of insanie: ne intelligis, domine? To make frantic, lunatic.

NATHANIEL. Laus Deo bone intelligo.

HOLOFERNES. Bone? bone, for bene: Priscian a little scratched; 'twill serve.

Enter Armado, Moth, and Costard

NATHANIEL. Videsne quis venit?

HOLOFERNES. Video, et gaudeo.

ARMADO. (*To Moth*) Chirrah!

HOLOFERNES. Quare Chirrah, not sirrah?

ARMADO. Men of peace, well encountered.

HOLOFERNES. Most military sir, salutation.

MOTH. (*Aside to Costard*) They have been at a great feast of languages, and stolen the scraps.

COSTARD. O! they have lived long on the almsbasket of words. I marvel thy master hath not eaten thee for a word; for thou art not so long by the head as honorificabilitudinitatibus: thou art easier swallowed than a flapdragon.

MOTH. Peace! the peal begins.

ARMADO. (*To Holofernes*) Monsieur, are you not lettered?

MOTH. Yes, yes; he teaches boys the hornbook. What is a, b, spelt backward, with the horn on his head?

HOLOFERNES. Ba, pueritia, with a horn added.

MOTH. Ba! most silly sheep with a horn. You hear his learning.

HOLOFERNES. Quis, quis, thou consonant?

MOTH. The third of the five vowels, if you repeat them; or the fifth, if I.

HOLOFERNES. I will repeat them,—a, e, i,—

MOTH. The sheep; the other two concludes it,—o, u.

ARMADO. Now, by the salt wave of the Mediterraneum, a sweet touch, a quick venew of wit! snip, snap, quick and home! it rejoiceth my intellect: true wit!

MOTH. Offered by a child to an old man; which is wit-old.

HOLOFERNES. What is the figure? what is the figure?

MOTH. Horns.

HOLOFERNES. Thou disputest like an infant; go, whip thy gig.

MOTH. Lend me your horn to make one, and I will whip about your infamy circum circa. A gig of a cuckold's horn.

COSTARD. An I had but one penny in the world, thou shouldst have it to buy gingerbread. Hold, there is the very remuneration I had of thy master, thou half-penny purse of wit, thou pigeon-egg of discretion. O! an the heavens were so pleased that thou wert but my bastard,

what a joyful father wouldst thou make me. Go to; thou
hast it ad dunghill, at the fingers' ends, as they say.

HOLOFERNES. O! I smell false Latin; dunghill for unguem.

ARMADO. Arts-man, præambula: we will be singled from
the barbarous. Do you not educate youth at the charge-
house on the top of the mountain?

HOLOFERNES. Or mons, the hill.

ARMADO. At your sweet pleasure, for the mountain.

HOLOFERNES. I do, sans question.

ARMADO. Sir, it is the king's most sweet pleasure and affection to congratulate the princess at her pavilion in the
posteriors of this day, which the rude multitude call the
afternoon.

HOLOFERNES. The posterior of the day, most generous sir, is
liable, congruent, and measurable for the afternoon: the
word is well culled, chose, sweet and apt, I do assure you,
sir; I do assure.

ARMADO. Sir, the king is a noble gentleman, and my familiar, I do assure ye, very good friend. For what is inward
between us, let it pass: I do beseech thee, remember thy
curtsy; I beseech thee, apparel thy head: and among
other importunate and most serious designs, and of great
import indeed, too, but let that pass: for I must tell thee,
it will please his Grace, by the world, sometime to lean
upon my poor shoulder, and with his royal finger, thus
dally with my excrement, with my mustachio: but, sweet
heart, let that pass. By the world, I recount no fable:
some certain special honours it pleaseth his greatness to
impart to Armado, a soldier, a man of travel, that hath
seen the world: but let that pass. The very all of all is,
but, sweet heart, I do implore secrecy, that the king
would have me present the princess, sweet chuck, with
some delightful ostentation, or show, or pageant, or antick, or firework. Now, understanding that the curate and
your sweet self are good at such eruptions and sudden
breaking out of mirth, as it were, I have acquainted you
withal, to the end to crave your assistance.

HOLOFERNES. Sir, you shall present before her the Nine
Worthies. Sir Nathaniel, as concerning some entertainment of time, some show in the posterior of this day, to
be rendered by our assistance, at the king's command,
and this most gallant, illustrate, and learned gentleman,

before the princess; I say, none so fit as to present the
Nine Worthies.

NATHANIEL. Where will you find men worthy enough to
present them?

HOLOFERNES. Joshua, yourself; myself, or this gallant gentleman, Judas Maccabæus; this swain, because of his
great limb, or joint, shall pass Pompey the Great; the
page, Hercules,—

ARMADO. Pardon, sir, error: he is not quantity enough for
that Worthy's thumb: he is not so big as the end of his
club.

HOLOFERNES. Shall I have audience? He shall present Hercules in minority: his enter and exit shall be strangling a
snake; and I will have an apology for that purpose.

MOTH. An excellent device! so, if any of the audience hiss,
you may cry, 'Well done, Hercules! now thou crushest
the snake!' that is the way to make an offence gracious,
though few have the grace to do it.

ARMADO. For the rest of the Worthies?—

HOLOFERNES. I will play three myself.

MOTH. Thrice-worthy gentleman!

ARMADO. Shall I tell you a thing?

HOLOFERNES. We attend.

ARMADO. We will have, if this fadge not, an antick. I beseech you, follow.

HOLOFERNES. Via, goodman Dull! thou hast spoken no
word all this while.

DULL. Nor understood none neither, sir.

HOLOFERNES. Allons! we will employ thee.

DULL. I 'll make one in a dance, or so; or I will play the
tabor to the Worthies, and let them dance the hay.

HOLOFERNES. Most dull, honest Dull, to our sport, away!

Exeunt

SCENE TWO

The Same. Before the Princess's Pavilion.

Enter the Princess, Katharine, Rosaline, and Maria

PRINCESS. Sweet hearts, we shall be rich ere we depart,
   If fairings come thus plentifully in:
   A lady wall'd about with diamonds!
   Look you what I have from the loving king.
ROSALINE. Madam, came nothing else along with that?
PRINCESS. Nothing but this! yes, as much love in rime
   As would be cramm'd up in a sheet of paper,
   Writ o' both sides the leaf, margent and all,
   That he was fain to seal on Cupid's name.
ROSALINE. That was the way to make his godhead wax;
   For he hath been five thousand years a boy.
KATHARINE. Ay, and a shrewd unhappy gallows too.
ROSALINE. You 'll ne'er be friends with him: a' kill'd your
   sister.
KATHARINE. He made her melancholy, sad, and heavy;
   And so she died: had she been light, like you,
   Of such a merry, nimble, stirring spirit,
   She might ha' been a grandam ere she died;
   And so may you, for a light heart lives long.
ROSALINE. What 's your dark meaning, mouse, of this light
   word?
KATHARINE. A light condition in a beauty dark.
ROSALINE. We need more light to find your meaning out.
KATHARINE. You 'll mar the light by taking it in snuff;
   Therefore, I 'll darkly end the argument.
ROSALINE. Look, what you do, you do it still i' the dark.
KATHARINE. So do not you, for you are a light wench.
ROSALINE. Indeed I weigh not you, and therefore light.
KATHARINE. You weigh me not. O! that 's you care not for
   me.
ROSALINE. Great reason; for, 'past cure is still past care.'
PRINCESS. Well bandied both; a set of wit well play'd.
   But Rosaline, you have a favour too:
   Who sent it? and what is it?
ROSALINE.   I would you knew:

An if my face were but as fair as yours,
My favour were as great; be witness this.
Nay, I have verses too, I thank Berowne:
The numbers true; and, were the numbering too,
I were the fairest goddess on the ground:
I am compared to twenty thousand fairs.
O! he hath drawn my picture in his letter.

PRINCESS. Anything like?

ROSALINE. Much in the letters, nothing in the praise.

PRINCESS. Beauteous as ink; a good conclusion.

KATHARINE. Fair as a text B in a copy-book.

ROSALINE. 'Ware pencils! how? Let me not die your debtor,
My red dominical, my golden letter:
O, that your face were not so full of O's!

KATHARINE. A pox of that jest! and beshrew all shrows!

PRINCESS. But what was sent to you from fair Dumaine?

KATHARINE. Madam, this glove.

PRINCESS.   Did he not send you twain?

KATHARINE. Yes, madam; and moreover,
Some thousand verses of a faithful lover:
A huge translation of hypocrisy,
Vilely compil'd, profound simplicity.

MARIA. This, and these pearls to me sent Longaville:
The letter is too long by half a mile.

PRINCESS. I think no less. Dost thou not wish in heart
The chain were longer and the letter short?

MARIA. Ay, or I would these hands might never part.

PRINCESS. We are wise girls to mock our lovers so.

ROSALINE. They are worse fools to purchase mocking so.
That same Berowne I 'll torture ere I go.
O that I knew he were but in by the week!
How I would make him fawn, and beg, and seek,
And wait the season, and observe the times,
And spend his prodigal wits in bootless rimes,
And shape his service wholly to my hests,
And make him proud to make me proud that jests!
So perttaunt-like would I o'ersway his state
That he should be my fool, and I his fate.

PRINCESS. None are so surely caught, when they are
catch'd,
As wit turn'd fool: folly, in wisdom hatch'd,
Hath wisdom's warrant and the help of school

And wit's own grace to grace a learned fool.

ROSALINE. The blood of youth burns not with such excess
As gravity's revolt to wantonness.

MARIA. Folly in fools bears not so strong a note
As foolery in the wise, when wit doth dote;
Since all the power thereof it doth apply
To prove, by wit, worth in simplicity.

Enter Boyet

PRINCESS. Here comes Boyet, and mirth is in his face.

BOYET. O! I am stabb'd with laughter. Where 's her Grace?

PRINCESS. Thy news, Boyet?

BOYET.   Prepare, madam, prepare!—
Arm, wenches, arm! encounters mounted are
Against your peace: Love doth approach disguis'd,
Armed in arguments; you 'll be surpris'd:
Muster your wits; stand in your own defence
Or hide your heads like cowards, and fly hence.

PRINCESS. Saint Denis to Saint Cupid! What are they
That charge their breath against us? Say, scout, say.

BOYET. Under the cool shade of a sycamore
I thought to close mine eyes some half an hour,
When, lo! to interrupt my purpos'd rest,
Toward that shade I might behold addrest
The king and his companions: warily
I stole into a neighbour thicket by,
And overheard what you shall overhear;
That, by and by, disguis'd they will be here.
Their herald is a pretty knavish page,
That well by heart hath conn'd his embassage:
Action and accent did they teach him there;
'Thus must thou speak, and thus thy body bear.'
And ever and anon they made a doubt
Presence majestical would put him out;
'For,' quoth the king, 'an angel shalt thou see;
Yet fear not thou, but speak audaciously.'
The boy replied, 'An angel is not evil;
I should have fear'd her had she been a devil.'
With that all laugh'd and clapp'd him on the shoulder,
Making the bold wag by their praises bolder.
One rubb'd his elbow thus, and fleer'd, and swore
A better speech was never spoke before;
Another, with his finger and his thumb,

Cry'd 'Via! we will do 't, come what will come';
The third he caper'd and cried, 'All goes well';
The fourth turn'd on the toe, and down he fell.
With that, they all did tumble on the ground,
With such a zealous laughter, so profound,
That in this spleen ridiculous appears,
To check their folly, passion's solemn tears.

PRINCESS. But what, but what, come they to visit us?

BOYET. They do, they do; and are apparell'd thus,
Like Muscovites or Russians, as I guess.
Their purpose is to parle, to court and dance;
And every one his love-feat will advance
Unto his several mistress, which they 'll know
By favours several which they did bestow.

PRINCESS. And will they so? The gallants shall be task'd:
For, ladies, we will every one be mask'd,
And not a man of them shall have the grace,
Despite of suit, to see a lady's face.
Hold, Rosaline, this favour thou shalt wear,
And then the king will court thee for his dear:
Hold, take thou this, my sweet, and give me thine,
So shall Berowne take me for Rosaline,
And change you favours too; so shall your loves
Woo contrary, deceiv'd by these removes.

ROSALINE. Come on, then; wear the favours most in sight.

KATHARINE. But in this changing what is your intent?

PRINCESS. The effect of my intent is, to cross theirs:
They do it but in mocking merriment;
And mock for mock is only my intent.
Their several counsels they unbosom shall
To loves mistook and so be mock'd withal
Upon the next occasion that we meet,
With visages display'd, to talk and greet.

ROSALINE. But shall we dance, if they desire us to 't?

PRINCESS. No, to the death, we will not move a foot:
Nor to their penn'd speech render we no grace;
But while 'tis spoke each turn away her face.

BOYET. Why, that contempt will kill the speaker's heart,
And quite divorce his memory from his part.

PRINCESS. Therefore I do it; and I make no doubt,
The rest will ne'er come in, if he be out.
There 's no such sport as sport by sport o'erthrown,

To make theirs ours and ours none but our own:
So shall we stay, mocking intended game,
And they, well mock'd, depart away with shame.
                              Trumpets sound within
BOYET. The trumpet sounds: be mask'd; the maskers come.
                              The Ladies mask

Enter Blackamoors with music;
Moth; the King, Berowne, Longaville, and Dumaine
in Russian habits, and masked

MOTH. 'All hail, the richest beauties on the earth!'
BOYET. Beauties no richer than rich taffeta.
MOTH. 'A holy parcel of the fairest dames,
                    The Ladies turn their backs to him
That ever turn'd their—backs—to mortal views!'
BEROWNE. 'Their eyes,' villain, 'their eyes.'
MOTH. 'That ever turn'd their eyes to mortal views! Out'—
BOYET. True; 'out,' indeed.
MOTH. 'Out of your favours, heavenly spirits, vouchsafe
    Not to behold'—
BEROWNE. 'Once to behold,' rogue.
MOTH. 'Once to behold with your sun-beamed eyes,
    —with your sun-beamed eyes'—
BOYET. They will not answer to that epithet;
    You were best call it 'daughter-beamed eyes.'
MOTH. They do not mark me, and that brings me out.
BEROWNE. Is this your perfectness? be gone, you rogue!
                              Exit Moth
ROSALINE. What would these strangers? Know their minds,
        Boyet:
    If they do speak our language, 'tis our will
    That some plain man recount their purposes:
    Know what they would.
BOYET. What would you with the princess?
BEROWNE. Nothing but peace and gentle visitation.
ROSALINE. What would they, say they?
BOYET. Nothing but peace and gentle visitation.
ROSALINE. Why, that they have; and bid them so be gone.
BOYET. She says, you have it, and you may be gone.
KING. Say to her, we have measur'd many miles,
    To tread a measure with her on this grass.
BOYET. They say, that they have measur'd many a mile,
    To tread a measure with you on this grass.

ROSALINE. It is not so. Ask them how many inches
Is in one mile: if they have measur'd many,
The measure then of one is easily told.

BOYET. If to come hither you have measur'd miles,
And many miles, the princess bids you tell
How many inches do fill up one mile?

BEROWNE. Tell her we measure them by weary steps.

BOYET. She hears herself.

ROSALINE.   How many weary steps,
Of many weary miles you have o'ergone,
Are number'd in the travel of one mile?

BEROWNE. We number nothing that we spend for you:
Our duty is so rich, so infinite,
That we may do it still without accompt.
Vouchsafe to show the sunshine of your face,
That we, like savages, may worship it.

ROSALINE. My face is but a moon, and clouded too.

KING. Blessed are clouds, to do as such clouds do!
Vouchsafe, bright moon, and these thy stars, to shine,
Those clouds remov'd, upon our watery eyne.

ROSALINE. O vain petitioner! beg a greater matter;
Thou now request'st but moonshine in the water.

KING. Then, in our measure but vouchsafe one change.
Thou bid'st me beg; this begging is not strange.

ROSALINE. Play, music, then! Nay, you must do it soon.
                                        Music plays
Not yet! no dance! thus change I like the moon.

KING. Will you not dance? How come you thus estrang'd?

ROSALINE. You took the moon at full, but now she 's chang'd.

KING. Yet still she is the moon, and I the man.
The music plays; vouchsafe some motion to it.

ROSALINE. Our ears vouchsafe it.

KING.   But your legs should do it.

ROSALINE. Since you are strangers, and come here by chance,
We 'll not be nice: take hands: we will not dance.

KING. Why take we hands then?

ROSALINE.   Only to part friends.
Curtsy, sweet hearts; and so the measure ends.

KING. More measure of this measure: be not nice.

ROSALINE. We can afford no more at such a price.

KING. Prize you yourselves? what buys your company?

ROSALINE. Your absence only.

KING.   That can never be.

ROSALINE. Then cannot we be bought: and so, adieu;
   Twice to your visor, and half once to you!

KING. If you deny to dance, let 's hold more chat.

ROSALINE. In private, then.

KING.   I am best pleas'd with that.

                                They converse apart

BEROWNE. White-handed mistress, one sweet word with
   thee.

PRINCESS. Honey, and milk, and sugar; there are three.

BEROWNE. Nay then, two treys, an if you grow so nice,
   Metheglin, wort, and malmsey: well run, dice!
   There 's half a dozen sweets.

PRINCESS.   Seventh sweet, adieu:
   Since you can cog, I 'll play no more with you.

BEROWNE. One word in secret.

PRINCESS.   Let it not be sweet.

BEROWNE. Thou griev'st my gall.

PRINCESS.   Gall! bitter.

BEROWNE.   Therefore meet.

                                They converse apart

DUMAINE. Will you vouchsafe with me to change a word?

MARIA. Name it.

DUMAINE.   Fair lady,—

MARIA.   Say you so? Fair lord,
   Take that for your fair lady.

DUMAINE.   Please it you,
   As much in private, and I 'll bid adieu.

                                They converse apart

KATHARINE. What! was your visor made without a tongue?

LONGAVILLE. I know the reason, lady, why you ask.

KATHARINE. O! for your reason; quickly, sir; I long.

LONGAVILLE. You have a double tongue within your mask,
   And would afford my speechless visor half.

KATHARINE. 'Veal,' quoth the Dutchman. Is not 'veal' a calf?

LONGAVILLE. A calf, fair lady!

KATHARINE.   No, a fair lord calf.

LONGAVILLE. Let 's part the word.

KATHARINE.   No, I 'll not be your half:
   Take all, and wean it: it may prove an ox.

LONGAVILLE. Look, how you butt yourself in these sharp
    mocks.

  Will you give horns, chaste lady? do not so.

KATHARINE. Then die a calf, before your horns do grow.

LONGAVILLE. One word in private with you, ere I die.

KATHARINE. Bleat softly then; the butcher hears you cry.

                              They converse apart

BOYET. The tongues of mocking wenches are as keen
    As is the razor's edge invisible,

  Cutting a smaller hair than may be seen,
    Above the sense of sense; so sensible

  Seemeth their conference; their conceits have wings

  Fleeter than arrows, bullets, wind, thought, swifter things.

ROSALINE. Not one word more, my maids: break off, break
    off.

BEROWNE. By heaven, all dry-beaten with pure scoff!

KING. Farewell, mad wenches: you have simple wits.

PRINCESS. Twenty adieus, my frozen Muscovits.

           Exeunt King, Lords, Music, and Attendants

  Are these the breed of wits so wonder'd at?

BOYET. Tapers they are, with your sweet breaths puff'd out.

ROSALINE. Well-liking wits they have; gross, gross; fat, fat.

PRINCESS. O poverty in wit, kingly-poor flout!

  Will they not, think you, hang themselves to-night?
    Or ever, but in visors, show their faces?

  This pert Berowne was out of countenance quite.

ROSALINE. O! they were all in lamentable cases.

  The king was weeping-ripe for a good word.

PRINCESS. Berowne did swear himself out of all suit.

MARIA. Dumaine was at my service, and his sword:

  'No point,' quoth I: my servant straight was mute.

KATHARINE. Lord Longaville said, I came o'er his heart;
    And trow you what he call'd me?

PRINCESS.   Qualm, perhaps.

KATHARINE. Yes, in good faith.

PRINCESS.   Go, sickness as thou art!

ROSALINE. Well, better wits have worn plain statute-caps.

  But will you hear? The king is my love sworn.

PRINCESS. And quick Berowne hath plighted faith to me.

KATHARINE. And Longaville was for my service born.

MARIA. Dumaine is mine, as sure as bark on tree.

BOYET. Madam, and pretty mistresses, give ear:
 Immediately they will again be here
 In their own shapes; for it can never be
 They will digest this harsh indignity.
PRINCESS. Will they return?
BOYET.   They will, they will, God knows;
 And leap for joy, though they are lame with blows:
 Therefore change favours; and, when they repair,
 Blow like sweet roses in this summer air.
PRINCESS. How blow? how blow? speak to be understood.
BOYET. Fair ladies mask'd, are roses in their bud:
 Dismask'd, their damask sweet commixture shown,
 Are angels vailing clouds, or roses blown.
PRINCESS. Avaunt perplexity! What shall we do
 If they return in their own shapes to woo?
ROSALINE. Good madam, if by me you 'll be advis'd,
 Let 's mock them still, as well known as disguis'd.
 Let us complain to them what fools were here,
 Disguis'd like Muscovites, in shapeless gear;
 And wonder what they were, and to what end
 Their shallow shows and prologue vilely penn'd,
 And their rough carriage so ridiculous,
 Should be presented at our tent to us.
BOYET. Ladies, withdraw: the gallants are at hand.
PRINCESS. Whip to our tents, as roes run over land.
    Exeunt Princess, Rosaline, Katharine, and Maria
    Enter the King, Berowne,
  Longaville, and Dumaine in their proper habits
KING. Fair sir, God save you! Where is the princess?
BOYET. Gone to her tent. Please it your Majesty,
 Command me any service to her thither?
KING. That she vouchsafe me audience for one word.
BOYET. I will; and so will she, I know, my lord.   *Exit*
BEROWNE. This fellow pecks up wit, as pigeons pease,
 And utters it again when God doth please:
 He is wit's pedlar, and retails his wares
 At wakes and wassails, meetings, markets, fairs;
 And we that sell by gross, the Lord doth know,
 Have not the grace to grace it with such show.
 This gallant pins the wenches on his sleeve;
 Had he been Adam, he had tempted Eve:
 He can carve too, and lisp: why, this is he

That kiss'd his hand away in courtesy;
This is the ape of form, monsieur the nice,
That, when he plays at tables, chides the dice
In honourable terms: nay, he can sing
A mean most meanly, and in ushering
Mend him who can: the ladies call him, sweet;
The stairs, as he treads on them, kiss his feet.
This is the flower that smiles on every one,
To show his teeth as white as whales-bone;
And consciences, that will not die in debt,
Pay him the due of honey tongu'd Boyet.

KING. A blister on his sweet tongue, with my heart,
That put Armado's page out of his part!

Re-enter the Princess, ushered
by Boyet; Rosaline, Maria, Katharine, and Attendants

BEROWNE. See where it comes! Behaviour, what wert thou,
Till this man show'd thee? and what art thou now?

KING. All hail, sweet madam, and fair time of day!

PRINCESS. 'Fair,' in 'all hail,' is foul, as I conceive.

KING. Construe my speeches better, if you may.

PRINCESS. Then wish me better: I will give you leave.

KING. We came to visit you, and purpose now
   To lead you to our court: vouchsafe it then.

PRINCESS. This field shall hold me, and so hold your vow:
   Nor God, nor I, delights in perjur'd men.

KING. Rebuke me not for that which you provoke:
   The virtue of your eye must break my oath.

PRINCESS. Your nick-name virtue; vice you should have spoke;
   For virtue's office never breaks men's troth.
Now, by my maiden honour, yet as pure
   As the unsullied lily, I protest,
A world of torments though I should endure,
   I would not yield to be your house's guest;
So much I hate a breaking cause to be
Of heavenly oaths, vow'd with integrity.

KING. O! you have liv'd in desolation here,
   Unseen, unvisited, much to our shame.

PRINCESS. Not so, my lord; it is not so, I swear;
   We have had pastime here and pleasant game.
A mess of Russians left us but of late.

KING. How, madam! Russians?

PRINCESS.   Ay, in truth, my lord;
  Trim gallants, full of courtship and of state.
ROSALINE. Madam, speak true. It is not so, my lord:
  My lady, to the manner of the days,
  In courtesy gives undeserving praise.
  We four, indeed, confronted were with four
  In Russian habit: here they stay'd an hour,
  And talk'd apace; and in that hour, my lord,
  They did not bless us with one happy word.
  I dare not call them fools; but this I think,
  When they are thirsty, fools would fain have drink.
BEROWNE. This jest is dry to me. Fair gentle sweet,
  Your wit makes wise things foolish: when we greet,
  With eyes best seeing, heaven's fiery eye,
  By light we lose light: your capacity
  Is of that nature that to your huge store
  Wise things seem foolish and rich things but poor.
ROSALINE. This proves you wise and rich, for in my eye—
BEROWNE. I am a fool, and full of poverty.
ROSALINE. But that you take what doth to you belong,
  It were a fault to snatch words from my tongue.
BEROWNE. O! I am yours, and all that I possess.
ROSALINE. All the fool mine?
BEROWNE.   I cannot give you less.
ROSALINE. Which of the visors was it that you wore?
BEROWNE. Where? when? what visor? why demand you
    this?
ROSALINE. There, then, that visor; that superfluous case
  That hid the worse, and show'd the better face.
KING. We are descried: they 'll mock us now downright.
DUMAINE. Let us confess, and turn it to a jest.
PRINCESS. Amaz'd, my lord? Why looks your Highness sad?
ROSALINE. Help! hold his brows! he 'll swound. Why look
    you pale?
  Sea-sick, I think, coming from Muscovy.
BEROWNE. Thus pour the stars down plagues for perjury.
    Can any face of brass hold longer out?—
  Here stand I, lady; dart thy skill at me;
    Bruise me with scorn, confound me with a flout;
  Thrust thy sharp wit quite through my ignorance;
    Cut me to pieces with thy keen conceit;
  And I will wish thee never more to dance,

Nor never more in Russian habit wait.
O! never will I trust to speeches penn'd,
   Nor to the motion of a school-boy's tongue,
Nor never come in visor to my friend,
   Nor woo in rime, like a blind harper's song,
Taffeta phrases, silken terms precise,
   Three-pil'd hyperboles, spruce affectation,
Figures pedantical; these summer flies
   Have blown me full of maggot ostentation:
I do forswear them; and I here protest,
   By this white glove,—how white the hand, God knows,—
Henceforth my wooing mind shall be express'd
   In russet yeas and honest kersey noes:
And, to begin, wench,—so God help me, la!—
My love to thee is sound, sans crack or flaw.

ROSALINE. Sans 'sans,' I pray you.

BEROWNE.   Yet I have a trick
Of the old rage: bear with me, I am sick;
I 'll leave it by degrees. Soft! let us see:
Write, 'Lord have mercy on us' on those three;
They are infected, in their hearts it lies;
They have the plague, and caught it of your eyes:
These lords are visited; you are not free,
For the Lord's tokens on you do I see.

PRINCESS. No, they are free that gave these tokens to us.

BEROWNE. Our states are forfeit: seek not to undo us.

ROSALINE. It is not so. For how can this be true,
That you stand forfeit, being those that sue?

BEROWNE. Peace! for I will not have to do with you.

ROSALINE. Nor shall not, if I do as I intend.

BEROWNE. Speak for yourselves: my wit is at an end.

KING. Teach us, sweet madam, for our rude transgression
Some fair excuse.

PRINCESS.   The fairest is confession.
Were you not here, but even now, disguis'd?

KING. Madam, I was.

PRINCESS.   And were you well advis'd?

KING. I was, fair madam.

PRINCESS.   When you then were here,
What did you whisper in your lady's ear?

KING. That more than all the world I did respect her.

PRINCESS. When she shall challenge this, you will reject her.

KING. Upon mine honour, no.

PRINCESS.   Peace! peace! forbear;
  Your oath once broke, you force not to forswear.

KING. Despise me, when I break this oath of mine.

PRINCESS. I will; and therefore keep it. Rosaline,
  What did the Russian whisper in your ear?

ROSALINE. Madam, he swore that he did hold me dear
  As precious eyesight, and did value me
  Above this world; adding thereto, moreover,
  That he would wed me, or else die my lover.

PRINCESS. God give thee joy of him! the noble lord
  Most honourably doth uphold his word.

KING. What mean you, madam? by my life, my troth,
  I never swore this lady such an oath.

ROSALINE. By heaven you did; and to confirm it plain,
  You gave me this: but take it, sir, again.

KING. My faith and this the princess I did give:
  I knew her by this jewel on her sleeve.

PRINCESS. Pardon me, sir, this jewel did she wear;
  And Lord Berowne, I thank him, is my dear.
  What, will you have me, or your pearl again?

BEROWNE. Neither of either; I remit both twain.
  I see the trick on 't: here was a consent,
  Knowing aforehand of our merriment,
  To dash it like a Christmas comedy.
  Some carry-tale, some please-man, some slight zany,
  Some mumble-news, some trencher-knight, some Dick,
  That smiles his cheek in years, and knows the trick
  To make my lady laugh when she 's dispos'd,
  Told our intents before; which once disclos'd,
  The ladies did change favours, and then we,
  Following the signs, woo'd but the sign of she.
  Now, to our perjury to add more terror,
  We are again forsworn, in will and error.
  Much upon this it is: (*To Boyet*) and might not you
  Forestall our sport, to make us thus untrue?
  Do not you know my lady's foot by the squire,
      And laugh upon the apple of her eye?
  And stand between her back, sir, and the fire,
      Holding a trencher, jesting merrily?
  You put our page out: go, you are allow'd;

Die when you will, a smock shall be your shroud.
You leer upon me, do you? There 's an eye
Wounds like a leaden sword.

BOYET.   Full merrily
Hath this brave manage, this career, been run.

BEROWNE. Lo! he is tilting straight. Peace! I have done.

Enter Costard

Welcome, pure wit! thou partest a fair fray.

COSTARD. O Lord, sir, they would know
Whether the three Worthies shall come in or no.

BEROWNE. What, are there but three?

COSTARD.   No, sir; but it is vara fine,
For every one pursents three.

BEROWNE.   And three times thrice is nine.

COSTARD. Not so, sir; under correction, sir, I hope, it is not
so.
You cannot beg us, sir, I can assure you, sir; we know
what we know:
I hope, sir, three times thrice, sir,—

BEROWNE.   Is not nine.

COSTARD. Under correction, sir, we know whereuntil it doth
amount.

BEROWNE. By Jove, I always took three threes for nine.

COSTARD. O Lord, sir! it were pity you should get your living by reckoning, sir.

BEROWNE. How much is it?

COSTARD. O Lord, sir! the parties themselves, the actors, sir,
will show whereuntil it doth amount: for mine own part,
I am, as they say, but to parfect one man in one poor man,
Pompion the Great, sir.

BEROWNE. Art thou one of the Worthies?

COSTARD. It pleased them to think me worthy of Pompion
the Great: for mine own part, I know not the degree of
the Worthy, but I am to stand for him.

BEROWNE. Go, bid them prepare.

COSTARD. We will turn it finely off, sir; we will take some
care.   *Exit*

KING. Berowne, they will shame us; let them not approach.

BEROWNE. We are shame-proof, my lord; and 'tis some policy
To have one show worse than the king's and his company.

KING. I say they shall not come.

PRINCESS. Nay, my good lord, let me o'errule you now.
That sport best pleases that doth least know how:
Where zeal strives to content, and the contents
Die in the zeal of those which it presents;
Their form confounded makes most form in mirth,
When great things labouring perish in their birth.

BEROWNE. A right description of our sport, my lord.

Enter Armado

ARMADO. Anointed, I implore so much expense of thy royal
sweet breath as will utter a brace of words.

*Armado converses with
the King, and delivers a paper to him*

PRINCESS. Doth this man serve God?

BEROWNE. Why ask you?

PRINCESS. He speaks not like a man of God's making.

ARMADO. That's all one, my fair, sweet, honey monarch;
for, I protest, the schoolmaster is exceeding fantastical;
too-too vain; too-too vain: but we will put it, as they say,
to fortuna de la guerra. I wish you the peace of mind,
most royal couplement! *Exit*

KING. Here is like to be a good presence of Worthies. He
presents Hector of Troy; the swain, Pompey the Great;
the parish curate, Alexander; Armado's page, Hercules;
the pedant, Judas Maccabæus:
And if these four Worthies in their first show thrive,
These four will change habits and present the other five.

BEROWNE. There is five in the first show.

KING. You are deceived, 'tis not so.

BEROWNE. The pedant, the braggart, the hedge-priest, the
fool, and the boy:—
Abate throw at novum, and the whole world again
Cannot pick out five such, take each one in his vein.

KING. The ship is under sail, and here she comes amain.

Enter Costard armed, for Pompey

COSTARD. 'I Pompey am,'—

BOYET. You lie, you are not he.

COSTARD. 'I Pompey am,'—

BOYET. With libbard's head on knee.

BEROWNE. Well said, old mocker: I must needs be friends
with thee.

COSTARD. 'I Pompey am, Pompey surnam'd the Big,'—

DUMAINE. 'The Great.'

COSTARD. It is 'Great,' sir; 'Pompey surnam'd the Great;
    That oft in field, with targe and shield, did make my foe
      to sweat:
    And travelling along this coast, I here am come by
      chance,
    And lay my arms before the legs of this sweet lass of
      France.'
  If your ladyship would say, 'Thanks, Pompey,' I had done.
PRINCESS. Great thanks, great Pompey.
COSTARD. 'Tis not so much worth; but I hope I was perfect. I
  made a little fault in 'Great.'
BEROWNE. My hat to a halfpenny, Pompey proves the best
  Worthy.

      Enter Sir Nathaniel armed, for Alexander

NATHANIEL. 'When in the world I liv'd, I was the world's
  commander;
  By east, west, north, and south, I spread my conquering
    might:
  My scutcheon plain declares that I am Alisander,'—
BOYET. Your nose says, no, you are not; for it stands too
  right.
BEROWNE. Your nose smells 'no,' in this, most tender-smell-
  ing knight.
PRINCESS. The conqueror is dismay'd. Proceed, good Alex-
  ander.
NATHANIEL. 'When in the world I liv'd, I was the world's
  commander';—
BOYET. Most true; 'tis right: you were so, Alisander.
BEROWNE. Pompey the Great,—
COSTARD. Your servant, and Costard.
BEROWNE. Take away the conqueror, take away Alisander.
COSTARD. (*To Nathaniel*) O! sir, you have overthrown Alisander the conqueror! You will be scraped out of the
  painted cloth for this: your lion, that holds his poll-axe
  sitting on a close-stool, will be given to Ajax: he will be the
  ninth Worthy. A conqueror, and afeard to speak! run
  away for shame, Alisander! (*Nathaniel retires*) There, an
  't shall please you: a foolish mild man; an honest man,
  look you, and soon dashed! He is a marvellous good neighbour, faith, and a very good bowler; but, for Alisander,—
  alas, you see how 'tis,—a little o'erparted. But there are

Worthies a-coming will speak their mind in some other sort.

PRINCESS. Stand aside, good Pompey.

Enter Holofernes armed,
for Judas; and Moth armed, for Hercules

HOLOFERNES. 'Great Hercules is presented by this imp,
 Whose club kill'd Cerberus, that three-headed canis;
And, when he was a babe, a child, a shrimp,
 Thus did he strangle serpents in his manus.
Quoniam, he seemeth in minority,
Ergo, I come with this apology.'
Keep some state in thy exit, and vanish.—   *Moth retires*
'Judas I am.'—

DUMAINE. A Judas!

HOLOFERNES. Not Iscariot, sir.

'Judas I am, ycleped Maccabæus.'

DUMAINE. Judas Maccabæus clipt is plain Judas.

BEROWNE. A kissing traitor. How art thou prov'd Judas?

HOLOFERNES. 'Judas I am.'—

DUMAINE. The more shame for you, Judas.

HOLOFERNES. What mean you, sir?

BOYET. To make Judas hang himself.

HOLOFERNES. Begin, sir; you are my elder.

BEROWNE. Well follow'd: Judas was hanged on an elder.

HOLOFERNES. I will not be put out of countenance.

BEROWNE. Because thou hast no face.

HOLOFERNES. What is this?

BOYET. A cittern-head.

DUMAINE. The head of a bodkin.

BEROWNE. A death's face in a ring.

LONGAVILLE. The face of an old Roman coin, scarce seen.

BOYET. The pommel of Cæsar's falchion.

DUMAINE. The carved-bone face on a flask.

BEROWNE. Saint George's half-cheek in a brooch.

DUMAINE. Ay, and in a brooch of lead.

BEROWNE. Ay, and worn in the cap of a tooth-drawer.
And now forward; for we have put thee in countenance.

HOLOFERNES. You have put me out of countenance.

BEROWNE. False: we have given thee faces.

HOLOFERNES. But you have outfaced them all.

BEROWNE. An thou wert a lion, we would do so.

BOYET. Therefore, as he is an ass, let him go.

And so adieu, sweet Jude! nay, why dost thou stay?

DUMAINE. For the latter end of his name.

BEROWNE. For the ass to the Jude? give it him:—Judas, away!

HOLOFERNES. This is not generous, not gentle, not humble.

BOYET. A light for Monsieur Judas! it grows dark, he may stumble.

PRINCESS. Alas! poor Maccabæus, how hath he been baited.

Enter Armado armed, for Hector

BEROWNE. Hide thy head, Achilles: here comes Hector in arms.

DUMAINE. Though my mocks come home by me, I will now be merry.

KING. Hector was but a Troyan in respect of this.

BOYET. But is this Hector?

KING. I think Hector was not so clean-timbered.

LONGAVILLE. His calf is too big for Hector.

DUMAINE. More calf, certain.

BOYET. No; he is best indued in the small.

BEROWNE. This cannot be Hector.

DUMAINE. He's a god or a painter; for he makes faces.

ARMADO. 'The armipotent Mars, of lances the almighty,
    Gave Hector a gift,'—

DUMAINE. A gilt nutmeg.

BEROWNE. A lemon.

LONGAVILLE. Stuck with cloves.

DUMAINE. No, cloven.

ARMADO. Peace!

'The armipotent Mars, of lances the almighty,
    Gave Hector a gift, the heir of Ilion;
A man so breath'd, that certain he would fight ye
    From morn till night, out of his pavilion.
I am that flower,'—

DUMAINE.   That mint.

LONGAVILLE.   That columbine.

ARMADO. Sweet Lord Longaville, rein thy tongue.

LONGAVILLE. I must rather give it the rein, for it runs against Hector.

DUMAINE. Ay, and Hector's a greyhound.

ARMADO. The sweet war-man is dead and rotten; sweet chucks, beat not the bones of the buried; when he breathed, he was a man. But I will forward with my device. (*To the Princess*) Sweet royalty, bestow on me the sense of hearing.

PRINCESS. Speak, brave Hector; we are much delighted.

ARMADO. I do adore thy sweet Grace's slipper.

BOYET. (*Aside to Dumaine*) Loves her by the foot.

DUMAINE. (*Aside to Boyet*) He may not by the yard.

ARMADO. 'This Hector far surmounted Hannibal,'—

COSTARD. The party is gone; fellow Hector, she is gone; she is two months on her way.

ARMADO. What meanest thou?

COSTARD. Faith, unless you play the honest Troyan, the poor wench is cast away: she 's quick; the child brags in her belly already: 'tis yours.

ARMADO. Dost thou infamonize me among potentates? Thou shalt die.

COSTARD. Then shall Hector be whipped for Jaquenetta that is quick by him, and hanged for Pompey that is dead by him.

DUMAINE. Most rare Pompey!

BOYET. Renowned Pompey!

BEROWNE. Greater than great, great, great, great Pompey! Pompey the Huge!

DUMAINE. Hector trembles.

BEROWNE. Pompey is moved. More Ates, more Ates! stir them on! stir them on!

DUMAINE. Hector will challenge him.

BEROWNE. Ay, if a' have no more man's blood in 's belly than will sup a flea.

ARMADO. By the north pole, I do challenge thee.

COSTARD. I will not fight with a pole, like a northern man: I 'll slash; I 'll do it by the sword. I bepray you, let me borrow my arms again.

DUMAINE. Room for the incensed Worthies!

COSTARD. I 'll do it in my shirt.

DUMAINE. Most resolute Pompey!

MOTH. Master, let me take you a button-hole lower. Do you not see Pompey is uncasing for the combat? What mean you? you will lose your reputation.

ARMADO. Gentlemen and soldiers, pardon me; I will not combat in my shirt.

DUMAINE. You may not deny it; Pompey hath made the challenge.

ARMADO. Sweet bloods, I both may and will.

BEROWNE. What reason have you for 't?

ARMADO. The naked truth of it is, I have no shirt. I go wool-
ward for penance.

BOYET. True, and it was enjoined him in Rome for want of
linen; since when, I 'll be sworn, he wore none but a dish-
clout of Jaquenetta's, and that a' wears next his heart for
a favour.

Enter Monsieur Marcade, a Messenger

MARCADE. God save you, madam!

PRINCESS. Welcome, Marcade;
But that thou interrupt'st our merriment.

MARCADE. I am sorry, madam; for the news I bring
Is heavy in my tongue. The king your father—

PRINCESS. Dead, for my life!

MARCADE. Even so: my tale is told.

BEROWNE. Worthies, away! The scene begins to cloud.

ARMADO. For my own part, I breathe free breath. I have
seen the day of wrong through the little hole of discretion,
and I will right myself like a soldier.   *Exeunt Worthies*

KING. How fares your Majesty?

PRINCESS. Boyet, prepare: I will away to-night.

KING. Madam, not so: I do beseech you, stay.

PRINCESS. Prepare, I say. I thank you, gracious lords,
For all your fair endeavours; and entreat,
Out of a new-sad soul, that you vouchsafe
In your rich wisdom to excuse or hide
The liberal opposition of our spirits,
If over-boldly we have borne ourselves
In the converse of breath; your gentleness
Was guilty of it. Farewell, worthy lord!
A heavy heart bears not a nimble tongue,
Excuse me so, coming so short of thanks
For my great suit so easily obtain'd.

KING. The extreme part of time extremely forms
All causes to the purpose of his speed,
And often, at his very loose, decides
That which long process could not arbitrate:
And though the mourning brow of progeny
Forbid the smiling courtesy of love
The holy suit which fain it would convince;
Yet, since love's argument was first on foot,

Let not the cloud of sorrow justle it
From what it purpos'd; since, to wail friends lost
Is not by much so wholesome-profitable
As to rejoice at friends but newly found.

PRINCESS. I understand you not: my griefs are double.

BEROWNE. Honest plain words best pierce the ear of grief:
And by these badges understand the king.
For your fair sakes have we neglected time,
Play'd foul play with our oaths. Your beauty, ladies,
Hath much deform'd us, fashioning our humours
Even to the opposed end of our intents;
And what in us hath seem'd ridiculous,—
As love is full of unbefitting strains;
All wanton as a child, skipping and vain;
Form'd by the eye, and, therefore, like the eye,
Full of stray shapes, of habits and of forms,
Varying in subjects, as the eye doth roll
To every varied object in his glance:
Which parti-coated presence of loose love
Put on by us, if, in your heavenly eyes,
Have misbecome our oaths and gravities,
Those heavenly eyes, that look into these faults,
Suggested us to make. Therefore, ladies,
Our love being yours, the error that love makes
Is likewise yours: we to ourselves prove false,
By being once false for ever to be true
To those that make us both,—fair ladies, you:
And even that falsehood, in itself a sin,
Thus purifies itself and turns to grace.

PRINCESS. We have receiv'd your letters full of love;
Your favours, the embassadors of love;
And, in our maiden council, rated them
At courtship, pleasant jest, and courtesy,
As bombast and as lining to the time.
But more devout than this in our respects
Have we not been; and therefore met your loves
In their own fashion, like a merriment.

DUMAINE. Our letters, madam, show'd much more than jest.

LONGAVILLE. So did our looks.

ROSALINE.   We did not quote them so.

KING. Now, at the latest minute of the hour.
Grant us your loves.

PRINCESS.   A time, methinks, too short
To make a world-without-end bargain in.
No, no, my lord, your Grace is perjur'd much,
Full of dear guiltiness; and therefore this:
If for my love,—as there is no such cause,—
You will do aught, this shall you do for me:
Your oath I will not trust; but go with speed
To some forlorn and naked hermitage,
Remote from all the pleasures of the world;
There stay, until the twelve celestial signs
Have brought about their annual reckoning.
If this austere insociable life
Change not your offer made in heat of blood;
If frosts and fasts, hard lodging and thin weeds,
Nip not the gaudy blossoms of your love,
But that it bear this trial and last love;
Then, at the expiration of the year,
Come challenge me, challenge me by these deserts,
And, by this virgin palm now kissing thine,
I will be thine; and, till that instant, shut
My woful self up in a mourning house,
Raining the tears of lamentation
For the remembrance of my father's death.
If this thou do deny, let our hands part;
Neither intitled in the other's heart.

KING. If this, or more than this, I would deny,
    To flatter up these powers of mine with rest,
The sudden hand of death close up mine eye!
    Hence ever then my heart is in thy breast.

BEROWNE. And what to me, my love? and what to me?

ROSALINE. You must be purged too, your sins are rack'd:
You are attaint with faults and perjury;
Therefore, if you my favour mean to get,
A twelvemonth shall you spend, and never rest,
But seek the weary beds of people sick.

DUMAINE. But what to me, my love? but what to me?

KATHARINE. A wife! A beard, fair health, and honesty;
    With three-fold love I wish you all these three.

DUMAINE. O! shall I say, I thank you, gentle wife?

KATHARINE. Not so, my lord. A twelvemonth and a day
    I 'll mark no words that smooth-fac'd wooers say:
Come when the king doth to my lady come;

Then, if I have much love, I 'll give you some.

DUMAINE. I 'll serve thee true and faithfully till then.

KATHARINE. Yet swear not, lest you be forsworn again.

LONGAVILLE. What says Maria?

MARIA.   At the twelvemonth's end
I 'll change my black gown for a faithful friend.

LONGAVILLE. I 'll stay with patience; but the time is long.

MARIA. The liker you; few taller are so young.

BEROWNE. Studies my lady? mistress, look on me.
Behold the window of my heart, mine eye,
What humble suit attends thy answer there;
Impose some service on me for thy love.

ROSALINE. Oft have I heard of you, my Lord Berowne,
Before I saw you, and the world's large tongue
Proclaims you for a man replete with mocks;
Full of comparisons and wounding flouts,
Which you on all estates will execute
That lie within the mercy of your wit:
To weed this wormwood from your fruitful brain,
And therewithal to win me, if you please,—
Without the which I am not to be won,—
You shall this twelvemonth term, from day to day,
Visit the speechless sick, and still converse
With groaning wretches; and your task shall be,
With all the fierce endeavour of your wit
To enforce the pained impotent to smile.

BEROWNE. To move wild laughter in the throat of death?
It cannot be; it is impossible:
Mirth cannot move a soul in agony.

ROSALINE. Why, that 's the way to choke a gibing spirit,
Whose influence is begot of that loose grace
Which shallow laughing hearers give to fools.
A jest's prosperity lies in the ear
Of him that hears it, never in the tongue
Of him that makes it: then, if sickly ears,
Deaf'd with the clamours of their own dear groans,
Will hear your idle scorns, continue them,
And I will have you and that fault withal;
But if they will not, throw away that spirit,
And I shall find you empty of that fault,
Right joyful of your reformation.

BEROWNE. A twelvemonth! well, befall what will befall,

I 'll jest a twelvemonth in a hospital.

PRINCESS. (*To the King*) Ay, sweet my lord; and so I take
   my leave.

KING. No, madam; we will bring you on your way.

BEROWNE. Our wooing doth not end like an old play;
   Jack hath not Jill; these ladies' courtesy
   Might well have made our sport a comedy.

KING. Come, sir, it wants a twelvemonth and a day,
   And then 'twill end.

BEROWNE.   That 's too long for a play.

Enter Armado

ARMADO. Sweet Majesty, vouchsafe me,—

PRINCESS. Was not that Hector?

DUMAINE. The worthy knight of Troy.

ARMADO. I will kiss thy royal finger, and take leave. I am a
   votary; I have vowed to Jaquenetta to hold the plough for
   her sweet love three years. But, most esteemed greatness,
   will you hear the dialogue that the two learned men have
   compiled in praise of the owl and the cuckoo? it should
   have followed in the end of our show.

KING. Call them forth quickly; we will do so.

ARMADO. Holla! approach.

*Re-enter Holofernes,
Nathaniel, Moth, Costard, and others*

This side is Hiems, Winter; this Ver, the Spring; the one
maintained by the owl, the other by the cuckoo. Ver, begin.

SPRING

I

When daisies pied and violets blue
   And lady-smocks all silver-white
And cuckoo-buds of yellow hue
   Do paint the meadows with delight,
The cuckoo then, on every tree,
Mocks married men; for thus sings he,
             Cuckoo;
Cuckoo, cuckoo: O, word of fear,
Unpleasing to a married ear!

II

When shepherds pipe on oaten straws,
　　And merry larks are ploughmen's clocks,
When turtles tread, and rooks, and daws,
　　And maidens bleach their summer smocks,
The cuckoo then, on every tree,
Mocks married men; for thus sings he,
　　　　　　　Cuckoo;
Cuckoo, cuckoo: O, word of fear,
Unpleasing to a married ear!

WINTER

III

When icicles hang by the wall,
　　And Dick the shepherd blows his nail
And Tom bears logs into the hall,
　　And milk comes frozen home in pail,
When blood is nipp'd, and ways be foul,
Then nightly sings the staring owl,
　　　　　　　Tu-who;
Tu-whit, tu-who—a merry note,
While greasy Joan doth keel the pot.

IV

When all aloud the wind doth blow,
　　And coughing drowns the parson's saw,
And birds sit brooding in the snow,
　　And Marian's nose looks red and raw,
When roasted crabs hiss in the bowl,
Then nightly sings the staring owl,
　　　　　　　Tu-who;
Tu-whit, tu-who—a merry note,
While greasy Joan doth keel the pot.

ARMADO. The words of Mercury are harsh after the songs of
Apollo. You, that way: we, this way.   *Exeunt*

A MIDSUMMER-NIGHT'S DREAM

CAST OF CHARACTERS

THESEUS, *Duke of Athens*
EGEUS, *Father to Hermia*
LYSANDER }
DEMETRIUS } *in love with Hermia*
PHILOSTRATE, *Master of the Revels of Theseus*
QUINCE, *a Carpenter*
SNUG, *a Joiner*
BOTTOM, *a Weaver*
FLUTE, *a Bellows-mender*
SNOUT, *a Tinker*
STARVELING, *a Tailor*
HIPPOLYTA, *Queen of the Amazons, betrothed to Theseus*
HERMIA, *Daughter to Egeus, in love with Lysander*
HELENA, *in love with Demetrius*
OBERON, *King of the Fairies*
TITANIA, *Queen of the Fairies*
PUCK, *or Robin Goodfellow*
PEASE-BLOSSOM
COBWEB } *Fairies*
MOTH
MUSTARD-SEED
Other Fairies attending their King and Queen
Attendants on Theseus and Hippolyta

SCENE

Athens, and a Wood near it

A MIDSUMMER-NIGHT'S DREAM

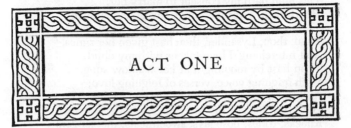

ACT ONE

SCENE ONE

Athens. The Palace of Theseus.

Enter Theseus, Hippolyta, Philostrate, and Attendants

THESEUS. Now, fair Hippolyta, our nuptial hour
    Draws on apace: four happy days bring in
    Another moon; but O! methinks how slow
    This old moon wanes; she lingers my desires,
    Like to a step-dame, or a dowager
    Long withering out a young man's revenue.

HIPPOLYTA. Four days will quickly steep themselves in
    night;
    Four nights will quickly dream away the time;
    And then the moon, like to a silver bow
    New-bent in heaven, shall behold the night
    Of our solemnities.

THESEUS.   Go, Philostrate,
    Stir up the Athenian youth to merriments;
    Awake the pert and nimble spirit of mirth;
    Turn melancholy forth to funerals;
    The pale companion is not for our pomp. *Exit Philostrate*
    Hippolyta, I woo'd thee with my sword,
    And won thy love doing thee injuries;
    But I will wed thee in another key,
    With pomp, with triumph, and with revelling.
      Enter Egeus, Hermia, Lysander, and Demetrius

EGEUS. Happy be Theseus, our renowned duke!

THESEUS. Thanks, good Egeus: what 's the news with thee?

EGEUS. Full of vexation come I, with complaint

Against my child, my daughter Hermia.
Stand forth, Demetrius. My noble lord,
This man hath my consent to marry her.
Stand forth, Lysander: and, my gracious duke,
This man hath bewitch'd the bosom of my child:
Thou, thou, Lysander, thou hast given her rimes,
And interchang'd love-tokens with my child;
Thou hast by moonlight at her window sung,
With feigning voice, verses of feigning love;
And stol'n the impression of her fantasy
With bracelets of thy hair, rings, gawds, conceits,
Knacks, trifles, nosegays, sweetmeats, messengers
Of strong prevailment in unharden'd youth;
With cunning hast thou filch'd my daughter's heart;
Turn'd her obedience, which is due to me,
To stubborn harshness. And, my gracious duke,
Be it so she will not here before your Grace
Consent to marry with Demetrius,
I beg the ancient privilege of Athens,
As she is mine, I may dispose of her;
Which shall be either to this gentleman,
Or to her death, according to our law
Immediately provided in that case.

THESEUS. What say you, Hermia? Be advis'd, fair maid.
To you, your father should be as a god;
One that compos'd your beauties, yea, and one
To whom you are but as a form in wax
By him imprinted, and within his power
To leave the figure or disfigure it.
Demetrius is a worthy gentleman.

HERMIA. So is Lysander.

THESEUS. In himself he is;
But, in this kind, wanting your father's voice,
The other must be held the worthier.

HERMIA. I would my father look'd but with my eyes.

THESEUS. Rather your eyes must with his judgment look.

HERMIA. I do entreat your Grace to pardon me.
I know not by what power I am made bold,
Nor how it may concern my modesty
In such a presence here to plead my thoughts;
But I beseech your Grace, that I may know
The worst that may befall me in this case,

If I refuse to wed Demetrius.

THESEUS. Either to die the death, or to abjure
Forever the society of men.
Therefore, fair Hermia, question your desires;
Know of your youth, examine well your blood,
Whether, if you yield not to your father's choice,
You can endure the livery of a nun,
For aye to be in shady cloister mew'd,
To live a barren sister all your life,
Chanting faint hymns to the cold fruitless moon.
Thrice blessed they that master so their blood,
To undergo such maiden pilgrimage;
But earthlier happy is the rose distill'd,
Than that which withering on the virgin thorn
Grows, lives, and dies, in single blessedness.

HERMIA. So will I grow, so live, so die, my lord,
Ere I will yield my virgin patent up
Unto his lordship, whose unwished yoke
My soul consents not to give sovereignty.

THESEUS. Take time to pause; and, by the next new moon,—
The sealing-day betwixt my love and me
For everlasting bond of fellowship,—
Upon that day either prepare to die
For disobedience to your father's will,
Or else to wed Demetrius, as he would;
Or on Diana's altar to protest
For aye austerity and single life.

DEMETRIUS. Relent, sweet Hermia; and, Lysander, yield
Thy crazed title to my certain right.

LYSANDER. You have her father's love, Demetrius;
Let me have Hermia's: do you marry him.

EGEUS. Scornful Lysander! true, he hath my love,
And what is mine my love shall render him;
And she is mine, and all my right of her
I do estate unto Demetrius.

LYSANDER. I am, my lord, as well deriv'd as he,
As well possess'd; my love is more than his;
My fortunes every way as fairly rank'd
If not with vantage, as Demetrius';
And, which is more than all these boasts can be,
I am belov'd of beauteous Hermia.
Why should not I then prosecute my right?

Demetrius, I 'll avouch it to his head,
Made love to Nedar's daughter, Helena,
And won her soul; and she, sweet lady, dotes,
Devoutly dotes, dotes in idolatry,
Upon this spotted and inconstant man.

THESEUS. I must confess that I have heard so much,
And with Demetrius thought to have spoke thereof;
But, being over-full of self-affairs,
My mind did lose it. But, Demetrius, come;
And come, Egeus; you shall go with me,
I have some private schooling for you both.
For you, fair Hermia, look you arm yourself
To fit your fancies to your father's will,
Or else the law of Athens yields you up,
Which by no means we may extenuate,
To death, or to a vow of single life.
Come, my Hippolyta: what cheer, my love?
Demetrius and Egeus, go along:
I must employ you in some business
Against our nuptial, and confer with you
Of something nearly that concerns yourselves.

EGEUS. With duty and desire we follow you.

Exeunt Theseus,
Hippolyta, Egeus, Demetrius, and Train

LYSANDER. How now, my love! Why is your cheek so pale?
How chance the roses there do fade so fast?

HERMIA. Belike for want of rain, which I could well
Beteem them from the tempest of mine eyes.

LYSANDER. Ay me! for aught that ever I could read,
Could ever hear by tale or history,
The course of true love never did run smooth;
But, either it was different in blood,—

HERMIA. O cross! too high to be enthrall'd to low.

LYSANDER. Or else misgraffed in respect of years,—

HERMIA. O spite! too old to be engag'd to young.

LYSANDER. Or else it stood upon the choice of friends,—

HERMIA. O hell! to choose love by another's eye.

LYSANDER. Or, if there were a sympathy in choice,
War, death, or sickness did lay siege to it,
Making it momentany as a sound,
Swift as a shadow, short as any dream,
Brief as the lightning in the collied night,

That, in a spleen, unfolds both heaven and earth,
And ere a man hath power to say, 'Behold!'
The jaws of darkness do devour it up:
So quick bright things come to confusion.

HERMIA. If then true lovers have been ever cross'd,
It stands as an edict in destiny:
Then let us teach our trial patience,
Because it is a customary cross,
As due to love as thoughts and dreams and sighs,
Wishes and tears, poor fancy's followers.

LYSANDER. A good persuasion: therefore, hear me, Hermia.
I have a widow aunt, a dowager
Of great revenue, and she hath no child:
From Athens is her house remote seven leagues;
And she respects me as her only son.
There, gentle Hermia, may I marry thee,
And to that place the sharp Athenian law
Cannot pursue us. If thou lov'st me then,
Steal forth thy father's house to-morrow night,
And in the wood, a league without the town,
Where I did meet thee once with Helena,
To do observance to a morn of May,
There will I stay for thee.

HERMIA.   My good Lysander!
I swear to thee by Cupid's strongest bow,
By his best arrow with the golden head,
By the simplicity of Venus' doves,
By that which knitteth souls and prospers loves,
And by that fire which burn'd the Carthage queen,
When the false Troyan under sail was seen,
By all the vows that ever men have broke,—
In number more than ever women spoke,—
In that same place thou hast appointed me,
To-morrow truly will I meet with thee.

LYSANDER. Keep promise, love. Look, here comes Helena.

Enter Helena

HERMIA. God speed fair Helena! Whither away?

HELENA. Call you me fair? That fair again unsay.
Demetrius loves your fair: O happy fair!
Your eyes are lode-stars! and your tongue's sweet air
More tuneable than lark to shepherd's ear,
When wheat is green, when hawthorn buds appear.

    Sickness is catching: O! were favour so,
Yours would I catch, fair Hermia, ere I go;
My ear should catch your voice, my eye your eye,
My tongue should catch your tongue's sweet melody.
Were the world mine, Demetrius being bated,
The rest I'd give to be to you translated.
O! teach me how you look, and with what art
You sway the motion of Demetrius' heart.

HERMIA. I frown upon him, yet he loves me still.

HELENA. O! that your frowns would teach my smiles such skill.

HERMIA. I give him curses, yet he gives me love.

HELENA. O! that my prayers could such affection move.

HERMIA. The more I hate, the more he follows me.

HELENA. The more I love, the more he hateth me.

HERMIA. His folly, Helena, is no fault of mine.

HELENA. None, but your beauty: would that fault were mine!

HERMIA. Take comfort: he no more shall see my face;
Lysander and myself will fly this place.
Before the time I did Lysander see,
Seem'd Athens as a paradise to me:
O! then, what graces in my love do dwell,
That he hath turn'd a heaven unto a hell.

LYSANDER. Helen, to you our minds we will unfold.
To-morrow night, when Phœbe doth behold
Her silver visage in the watery glass,
Decking with liquid pearl the bladed grass,—
A time that lovers' flights doth still conceal,—
Through Athens' gates have we devis'd to steal.

HERMIA. And in the wood, where often you and I
Upon faint primrose-beds were wont to lie,
Emptying our bosoms of their counsel sweet,
There my Lysander and myself shall meet;
And thence from Athens turn away our eyes,
To seek new friends and stranger companies.
Farewell, sweet playfellow: pray thou for us;
And good luck grant thee thy Demetrius!
Keep word, Lysander: we must starve our sight
From lovers' food till morrow deep midnight.

LYSANDER. I will, my Hermia.—(*Exit Hermia*) Helena, adieu:

As you on him, Demetrius dote on you!   *Exit*

HELENA. How happy some o'er other some can be!
    Through Athens I am thought as fair as she;
    But what of that? Demetrius thinks not so;
    He will not know what all but he do know;
    And as he errs, doting on Hermia's eyes,
    So I, admiring of his qualities.
    Things base and vile, holding no quantity,
    Love can transpose to form and dignity.
    Love looks not with the eyes, but with the mind,
    And therefore is wing'd Cupid painted blind.
    Nor hath Love's mind of any judgment taste;
    Wings and no eyes figure unheedy haste:
    And therefore is Love said to be a child,
    Because in choice he is so oft beguil'd.
    As waggish boys in game themselves forswear,
    So the boy Love is perjur'd every where;
    For ere Demetrius look'd on Hermia's eyne,
    He hail'd down oaths that he was only mine;
    And when this hail some heat from Hermia felt,
    So he dissolv'd, and showers of oaths did melt.
    I will go tell him of fair Hermia's flight:
    Then to the wood will he to-morrow night
    Pursue her; and for this intelligence
    If I have thanks, it is a dear expense:
    But herein mean I to enrich my pain,
    To have his sight thither and back again.   *Exit*

SCENE TWO

The Same. A Room in Quince's House.

*Enter Quince, Snug, Bottom, Flute, Snout,
and Starveling*

QUINCE. Is all our company here?

BOTTOM. You were best to call them generally, man by man,
    according to the scrip.

QUINCE. Here is the scroll of every man's name, which is
    thought fit, through all Athens, to play in our interlude be-
    fore the duke and the duchess on his wedding-day at
    night.

BOTTOM. First, good Peter Quince, say what the play treats
on; then read the names of the actors, and so grow to a
point.

QUINCE. Marry, our play is, The most lamentable comedy,
and most cruel death of Pyramus and Thisby.

BOTTOM. A very good piece of work, I assure you, and a
merry. Now, good Peter Quince, call forth your actors by
the scroll. Masters, spread yourselves.

QUINCE. Answer as I call you. Nick Bottom, the weaver.

BOTTOM. Ready. Name what part I am for, and proceed.

QUINCE. You, Nick Bottom, are set down by Pyramus.

BOTTOM. What is Pyramus? a lover, or a tyrant?

QUINCE. A lover, that kills himself most gallantly for love.

BOTTOM. That will ask some tears in the true performing of
it: if I do it, let the audience look to their eyes; I will move
storms, I will condole in some measure. To the rest: yet
my chief humour is for a tyrant. I could play Ercles rarely,
or a part to tear a cat in, to make all split.

> The raging rocks
> And shivering shocks
> Shall break the locks
>   Of prison gates:
> And Phibbus' car
> Shall shine from far
> And make and mar
>   The foolish Fates.

This was lofty! Now name the rest of the players. This is
Ercles' vein, a tyrant's vein; a lover is more condoling.

QUINCE. Francis Flute, the bellows-mender.

FLUTE. Here, Peter Quince.

QUINCE. You must take Thisby on you.

FLUTE. What is Thisby? a wandering knight?

QUINCE. It is the lady that Pyramus must love.

FLUTE. Nay, faith, let not me play a woman; I have a beard
coming.

QUINCE. That 's all one: you shall play it in a mask, and you
may speak as small as you will.

BOTTOM. An I may hide my face, let me play Thisby too. I 'll
speak in a monstrous little voice, 'Thisne, Thisne!' 'Ah,
Pyramus, my lover dear; thy Thisby dear, and lady dear!'

QUINCE. No, no; you must play Pyramus; and Flute, you
Thisby.

BOTTOM. Well, proceed.

QUINCE. Robin Starveling, the tailor.

STARVELING. Here, Peter Quince.

QUINCE. Robin Starveling, you must play Thisby's mother. Tom Snout, the tinker.

SNOUT. Here, Peter Quince.

QUINCE. You, Pyramus's father; myself, Thisby's father; Snug, the joiner, you the lion's part: and, I hope, here is a play fitted.

SNUG. Have you the lion's part written? pray you, if it be, give it me, for I am slow of study.

QUINCE. You may do it extempore, for it is nothing but roaring.

BOTTOM. Let me play the lion too. I will roar, that I will do any man's heart good to hear me; I will roar, that I will make the duke say, 'Let him roar again, let him roar again.'

QUINCE. An you should do it too terribly, you would fright the duchess and the ladies, that they would shriek; and that were enough to hang us all.

ALL. That would hang us, every mother's son.

BOTTOM. I grant you, friends, if that you should fright the ladies out of their wits, they would have no more discretion but to hang us; but I will aggravate my voice so that I will roar you as gently as any sucking dove; I will roar you as 'twere any nightingale.

QUINCE. You can play no part but Pyramus; for Pyramus is a sweet-faced man; a proper man, as one shall see in a summer's day; a most lovely, gentleman-like man; therefore, you must needs play Pyramus.

BOTTOM. Well, I will undertake it. What beard were I best to play it in?

QUINCE. Why, what you will.

BOTTOM. I will discharge it in either your straw-colour beard, your orange-tawny beard, your purple-ingrain beard, or your French-crown colour beard, your perfect yellow.

QUINCE. Some of your French crowns have no hair at all, and then you will play bare-faced. But masters, here are your parts; and I am to entreat you, request you, and desire you, to con them by to-morrow night, and meet me in the palace wood, a mile without the town, by moonlight:

there will we rehearse; for if we meet in the city, we shall
be dogged with company, and our devices known. In the
meantime I will draw a bill of properties, such as our play
wants. I pray you, fail me not.

BOTTOM. We will meet; and there we may rehearse more
obscenely and courageously. Take pains; be perfect;
adieu.

QUINCE. At the duke's oak we meet.

BOTTOM. Enough; hold, or cut bow-strings.   *Exeunt*

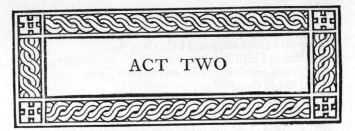

ACT TWO

SCENE ONE

A Wood near Athens.

Enter a Fairy on one side, and Puck on the other

PUCK. How now, spirit! whither wander you?

FAIRY. Over hill, over dale,
  Thorough bush, thorough brier,
 Over park, over pale,
  Thorough flood, thorough fire,
I do wander every where,
Swifter than the moone's sphere;
And I serve the fairy queen,
To dew her orbs upon the green:
The cowslips tall her pensioners be;
In their gold coats spots you see;
Those be rubies, fairy favours,
In those freckles live their savours:
I must go seek some dew-drops here,
And hang a pearl in every cowslip's ear.
Farewell, thou lob of spirits: I 'll be gone;
Our queen and all her elves come here anon.

PUCK. The king doth keep his revels here to-night:
Take heed the queen come not within his sight;
For Oberon is passing fell and wrath,
Because that she as her attendant hath
A lovely boy, stol'n from an Indian king;
She never had so sweet a changeling;
And jealous Oberon would have the child
Knight of his train, to trace the forests wild;
But she, perforce, withholds the loved boy,
Crowns him with flowers, and makes him all her joy.
And now they never meet in grove, or green,
By fountain clear, or spangled starlight sheen,

　　But they do square; that all their elves, for fear,
　　Creep into acorn-cups and hide them there.
FAIRY.　Either I mistake your shape and making quite,
　　Or else you are that shrewd and knavish sprite
　　Call'd Robin Goodfellow: are you not he
　　That frights the maidens of the villagery;
　　Skim milk, and sometimes labour in the quern,
　　And bootless make the breathless housewife churn;
　　And sometime make the drink to bear no barm;
　　Mislead night-wanderers, laughing at their harm?
　　Those that Hobgoblin call you and sweet Puck,
　　You do their work, and they shall have good luck:
　　Are you not he?
PUCK.　　　　　　　　Fairy, thou speak'st aright;
　　I am that merry wanderer of the night.
　　I jest to Oberon, and make him smile
　　When I a fat and bean-fed horse beguile,
　　Neighing in likeness of a filly foal:
　　And sometime lurk I in a gossip's bowl,
　　In very likeness of a roasted crab;
　　And, when she drinks, against her lips I bob
　　And on her wither'd dewlap pour the ale.
　　The wisest aunt, telling the saddest tale,
　　Sometime for three-foot stool mistaketh me;
　　Then slip I from her bum, down topples she,
　　And 'tailor' cries, and falls into a cough;
　　And then the whole quire hold their hips and loff;
　　And waxen in their mirth, and neeze, and swear
　　A merrier hour was never wasted there.
　　But, room, fairy! here comes Oberon.
FAIRY.　And here my mistress. Would that he were gone!
　　　　　　　Enter Oberon from one side,
　　with his Train; and Titania from the other, with hers
OBERON.　Ill met by moonlight, proud Titania.
TITANIA.　What! jealous Oberon. Fairies, skip hence:
　　I have forsworn his bed and company.
OBERON.　Tarry, rash wanton! am not I thy lord?
TITANIA.　Then, I must be thy lady; but I know
　　When thou hast stol'n away from fairy land,
　　And in the shape of Corin sat all day,
　　Playing on pipes of corn, and versing love
　　To amorous Phillida. Why art thou here,

Come from the furthest steppe of India?
But that, forsooth, the bouncing Amazon,
Your buskin'd mistress and your warrior love,
To Theseus must be wedded, and you come
To give their bed joy and prosperity.

OBERON. How canst thou thus for shame, Titania,
Glance at my credit with Hippolyta,
Knowing I know thy love to Theseus?
Didst thou not lead him through the glimmering night
From Perigouna, whom he ravished?
And make him with fair Ægle break his faith,
With Ariadne, and Antiopa?

TITANIA. These are the forgeries of jealousy:
And never, since the middle summer's spring,
Met we on hill, in dale, forest, or mead,
By paved fountain, or by rushy brook,
Or in the beached margent of the sea,
To dance our ringlets to the whistling wind,
But with thy brawls thou hast disturb'd our sport.
Therefore the winds, piping to us in vain,
As in revenge, have suck'd up from the sea
Contagious fogs; which, falling in the land,
Have every pelting river made so proud
That they have overborne their continents:
The ox hath therefore stretch'd his yoke in vain,
The ploughman lost his sweat, and the green corn
Hath rotted ere his youth attain'd a beard:
The fold stands empty in the drowned field,
And crows are fatted with the murrion flock;
The nine men's morris is fill'd up with mud,
And the quaint mazes in the wanton green
For lack of tread are undistinguishable:
The human mortals want their winter here:
No night is now with hymn or carol blest:
Therefore the moon, the governess of floods,
Pale in her anger, washes all the air,
That rheumatic diseases do abound:
And thorough this distemperature we see
The seasons alter: hoary-headed frosts
Fall in the fresh lap of the crimson rose,
And on old Hiems' thin and icy crown
An odorous chaplet of sweet summer buds

Is, as in mockery, set. The spring, the summer,
The childing autumn, angry winter, change
Their wonted liveries, and the mazed world,
By their increase, now knows not which is which.
And this same progeny of evil comes
From our debate, from our dissension:
We are their parents and original.

OBERON. Do you amend it then; it lies in you.
Why should Titania cross her Oberon?
I do but beg a little changeling boy,
To be my henchman.

TITANIA.   Set your heart at rest;
The fairy land buys not the child of me.
His mother was a votaress of my order:
And, in the spiced Indian air, by night,
Full often hath she gossip'd by my side,
And sat with me on Neptune's yellow sands,
Marking the embarked traders on the flood;
When we have laugh'd to see the sails conceive
And grow big-bellied with the wanton wind;
Which she, with pretty and with swimming gait
Following,—her womb then rich with my young squire,—
Would imitate, and sail upon the land,
To fetch me trifles, and return again,
As from a voyage, rich with merchandise.
But she, being mortal, of that boy did die;
And for her sake I do rear up her boy,
And for her sake I will not part with him.

OBERON. How long within this wood intend you stay?

TITANIA. Perchance, till after Theseus' wedding-day.
If you will patiently dance in our round,
And see our moonlight revels, go with us;
If not, shun me, and I will spare your haunts.

OBERON. Give me that boy, and I will go with thee.

TITANIA. Not for thy fairy kingdom. Fairies, away!
We shall chide downright, if I longer stay.

                    Exit Titania with her Train

OBERON. Well, go thy way: thou shalt not from this grove
Till I torment thee for this injury.
My gentle Puck, come hither. Thou remember'st
Since once I sat upon a promontory,
And heard a mermaid on a dolphin's back

Uttering such dulcet and harmonious breath,
That the rude sea grew civil at her song,
And certain stars shot madly from their spheres
To hear the sea-maid's music.

PUCK.   I remember.

OBERON. That very time I saw, but thou couldst not,
Flying between the cold moon and the earth,
Cupid all arm'd: a certain aim he took
At a fair vestal throned by the west,
And loos'd his love-shaft smartly from his bow,
As it should pierce a hundred thousand hearts;
But I might see young Cupid's fiery shaft
Quench'd in the chaste beams of the watery moon,
And the imperial votaress passed on,
In maiden-meditation, fancy-free.
Yet mark'd I where the bolt of Cupid fell:
It fell upon a little western flower,
Before milk-white, now purple with love's wound,
And maidens call it, Love-in-idleness.
Fetch me that flower; the herb I show'd thee once
The juice of it on sleeping eyelids laid
Will make or man or woman madly dote
Upon the next live creature that it sees.
Fetch me this herb; and be thou here again
Ere the leviathan can swim a league.

PUCK. I 'll put a girdle round about the earth
In forty minutes.   *Exit*

OBERON.   Having once this juice
I 'll watch Titania when she is asleep,
And drop the liquor of it in her eyes:
The next thing then she waking looks upon,
Be it on lion, bear, or wolf, or bull,
On meddling monkey, or on busy ape,
She shall pursue it with the soul of love:
And ere I take this charm off from her sight,
As I can take it with another herb,
I 'll make her render up her page to me.
But who comes here? I am invisible,
And I will overhear their conference.

            Enter Demetrius, Helena following him

DEMETRIUS. I love thee not, therefore pursue me not.
Where is Lysander and fair Hermia?

The one I 'll slay, the other slayeth me.
Thou told'st me they were stol'n into this wood;
And here am I, and wood within this wood,
Because I cannot meet my Hermia.
Hence! get thee gone, and follow me no more.

HELENA. You draw me, you hard-hearted adamant:
But yet you draw not iron, for my heart
Is true as steel: leave you your power to draw,
And I shall have no power to follow you.

DEMETRIUS. Do I entice you? Do I speak you fair?
Or, rather, do I not in plainest truth
Tell you I do not nor I cannot love you?

HELENA. And even for that do I love you the more.
I am your spaniel; and, Demetrius,
The more you beat me, I will fawn on you:
Use me but as your spaniel, spurn me, strike me,
Neglect me, lose me; only give me leave,
Unworthy as I am, to follow you.
What worser place can I beg in your love,
And yet a place of high respect with me,
Than to be used as you use your dog?

DEMETRIUS. Tempt not too much the hatred of my spirit,
For I am sick when I do look on you.

HELENA. And I am sick when I look not on you.

DEMETRIUS. You do impeach your modesty too much,
To leave the city, and commit yourself
Into the hands of one that loves you not;
To trust the opportunity of night
And the ill counsel of a desert place
With the rich worth of your virginity.

HELENA. Your virtue is my privilege: for that
It is not night when I do see your face,
Therefore I think I am not in the night;
Nor doth this wood lack worlds of company,
For you in my respect are all the world:
Then how can it be said I am alone,
When all the world is here to look on me?

DEMETRIUS. I 'll run from thee and hide me in the brakes,
And leave thee to the mercy of wild beasts.

HELENA. The wildest hath not such a heart as you.
Run when you will, the story shall be chang'd;
Apollo flies, and Daphne holds the chase;

The dove pursues the griffin; the mild hind
Makes speed to catch the tiger: bootless speed,
When cowardice pursues and valour flies.

DEMETRIUS. I will not stay thy questions: let me go;
Or, if thou follow me, do not believe
But I shall do thee mischief in the wood.

HELENA. Ay, in the temple, in the town, the field,
You do me mischief. Fie, Demetrius!
Your wrongs do set a scandal on my sex.
We cannot fight for love, as men may do;
We should be woo'd and were not made to woo.

Exit Demetrius

I 'll follow thee and make a heaven of hell,
To die upon the hand I love so well.   *Exit*

OBERON. Fare thee well, nymph: ere he do leave this grove,
Thou shalt fly him, and he shall seek thy love.

Re-enter Puck

Hast thou the flower there? Welcome, wanderer.

PUCK. Ay, there it is.

OBERON.   I pray thee, give it me.
I know a bank whereon the wild thyme blows,
Where oxlips and the nodding violet grows
Quite over-canopied with luscious woodbine,
With sweet musk-roses, and with eglantine:
There sleeps Titania some time of the night,
Lull'd in these flowers with dances and delight;
And there the snake throws her enamell'd skin,
Weed wide enough to wrap a fairy in:
And with the juice of this I 'll streak her eyes,
And make her full of hateful fantasies.
Take thou some of it, and seek through this grove:
A sweet Athenian lady is in love
With a disdainful youth: anoint his eyes;
But do it when the next thing he espies
May be the lady. Thou shalt know the man
By the Athenian garments he hath on.
Effect it with some care, that he may prove
More fond on her than she upon her love.
And look thou meet me ere the first cock crow.

PUCK. Fear not, my lord, your servant shall do so.   *Exeunt*

SCENE TWO

Another Part of the Wood.

Enter Titania, with her Train

TITANIA. Come, now a roundel and a fairy song;
Then, for the third part of a minute, hence;
Some to kill cankers in the musk-rose buds,
Some war with rere-mice for their leathern wings,
To make my small elves coats, and some keep back
The clamorous owl, that nightly hoots, and wonders
At our quaint spirits. Sing me now asleep;
Then to your offices, and let me rest.

The Fairies sing

I.

You spotted snakes with double tongue,
  Thorny hedge-hogs, be not seen;
Newts, and blind-worms, do no wrong;
  Come not near our fairy queen.
    Philomel, with melody,
    Sing in our sweet lullaby;
Lulla, lulla, lullaby; lulla, lulla, lullaby:
    Never harm,
    Nor spell, nor charm,
  Come our lovely lady nigh;
So, good night, with lullaby.

II.

Weaving spiders come not here;
  Hence, you long-legg'd spinners, hence!
Beetles, black, approach not near;
  Worm nor snail, do no offence.

Philomel, with melody, &c.

FAIRY. Hence, away! now all is well.
One aloof stand sentinel.

Exeunt Fairies. Titania sleeps
Enter Oberon, and squeezes the flower on Titania's eyelids

OBERON. What thou seest when thou dost wake
 Do it for thy true-love take;
 Love and languish for his sake:
 Be it ounce, or cat, or bear,
 Pard, or boar with bristled hair,
 In thy eye that shall appear
 When thou wak'st, it is thy dear.
 Wake when some vile thing is near.   *Exit*

    Enter Lysander and Hermia

LYSANDER. Fair love, you faint with wandering in the wood;
 And to speak troth, I have forgot our way:
 We 'll rest us, Hermia, if you think it good,
 And tarry for the comfort of the day.
HERMIA. Be it so, Lysander: find you out a bed,
 For I upon this bank will rest my head.
LYSANDER. One turf shall serve as pillow for us both;
 One heart, one bed, two bosoms, and one troth.
HERMIA. Nay, good Lysander; for my sake, my dear,
 Lie further off yet, do not lie so near.
LYSANDER. O! take the sense, sweet, of my innocence,
 Love takes the meaning in love's conference.
 I mean that my heart unto yours is knit,
 So that but one heart we can make of it;
 Two bosoms interchained with an oath;
 So then two bosoms and a single troth.
 Then by your side no bed-room me deny,
 For, lying so, Hermia, I do not lie.
HERMIA. Lysander riddles very prettily:
 Now much beshrew my manners and my pride,
 If Hermia meant to say Lysander lied.
 But, gentle friend, for love and courtesy
 Lie further off; in human modesty,
 Such separation as may well be said
 Becomes a virtuous bachelor and a maid,
 So far be distant; and, good-night, sweet friend.
 Thy love ne'er alter till thy sweet life end!
LYSANDER. Amen, amen, to that fair prayer, say I;
 And then end life when I end loyalty!
       Retires a little distance
 Here is my bed: sleep give thee all his rest!
HERMIA. With half that wish the wisher's eyes be press'd!
          They sleep

Enter Puck

PUCK. Through the forest have I gone,
But Athenian found I none,
On whose eyes I might approve
This flower's force in stirring love.
Night and silence! who is here?
Weeds of Athens he doth wear:
This is he, my master said,
Despised the Athenian maid;
And here the maiden, sleeping sound,
On the dank and dirty ground.
Pretty soul! she durst not lie
Near this lack-love, this kill-courtesy.
     Squeezes the flower on Lysander's eyelids
Churl, upon thy eyes I throw
All the power this charm doth owe.
When thou wak'st, let love forbid
Sleep his seat on thy eyelid:
So awake when I am gone;
For I must now to Oberon.   *Exit*
     Enter Demetrius and Helena, running
HELENA. Stay, though thou kill me, sweet Demetrius.
DEMETRIUS. I charge thee, hence, and do not haunt me thus.
HELENA. O! wilt thou darkling leave me? do not so.
DEMETRIUS. Stay, on thy peril: I alone will go.
                          Exit Demetrius
HELENA. O! I am out of breath in this fond chase.
The more my prayer, the lesser is my grace.
Happy is Hermia, wheresoe'er she lies;
For she hath blessed and attractive eyes.
How came her eyes so bright? Not with salt tears:
If so, my eyes are oftener wash'd than hers.
No, no, I am as ugly as a bear;
For beasts that meet me run away for fear;
Therefore no marvel though Demetrius
Do, as a monster, fly my presence thus.
What wicked and dissembling glass of mine
Made me compare with Hermia's sphery eyne?
But who is here? Lysander! on the ground!
Dead? or asleep? I see no blood, no wound.
Lysander, if you live, good sir, awake.
LYSANDER. (*Awaking*) And run through fire I will for thy
     sweet sake.

Transparent Helena! Nature shows art,
That through thy bosom makes me see thy heart.
Where is Demetrius? O! how fit a word
Is that vile name to perish on my sword.

HELENA. Do not say so, Lysander; say not so.
What though he love your Hermia? Lord! what though?
Yet Hermia still loves you: then be content.

LYSANDER. Content with Hermia! No: I do repent
The tedious minutes I with her have spent.
Not Hermia, but Helena I love:
Who will not change a raven for a dove?
The will of man is by his reason sway'd,
And reason says you are the worthier maid.
Things growing are not ripe until their season;
So I, being young, till now ripe not to reason;
And touching now the point of human skill,
Reason becomes the marshal to my will,
And leads me to your eyes; where I o'erlook
Love's stories written in love's richest book.

HELENA. Wherefore was I to this keen mockery born?
When at your hands did I deserve this scorn?
Is 't not enough, is 't not enough, young man,
That I did never, no, nor never can,
Deserve a sweet look from Demetrius' eye,
But you must flout my insufficiency?
Good troth, you do me wrong, good sooth, you do,
In such disdainful manner me to woo.
But fare you well: perforce I must confess
I thought you lord of more true gentleness.
O! that a lady of one man refus'd,
Should of another therefore be abus'd.   *Exit*

LYSANDER. She sees not Hermia. Hermia, sleep thou there;
And never mayst thou come Lysander near.
For, as a surfeit of the sweetest things
The deepest loathing to the stomach brings;
Or, as the heresies that men do leave
Are hated most of those they did deceive:
So thou, my surfeit and my heresy,
Of all be hated, but the most of me!
And, all my powers, address your love and might
To honour Helen, and to be her knight.   *Exit*

HERMIA. (*Awaking*) Help me, Lysander, help me! do thy
best

To pluck this crawling serpent from my breast.
Ay me, for pity! what a dream was here!
Lysander, look how I do quake with fear:
Methought a serpent eat my heart away,
And you sat smiling at his cruel prey.
Lysander! what! remov'd?—Lysander! lord!
What! out of hearing? gone? no sound, no word?
Alack! where are you? speak, an if you hear;
Speak, of all loves! I swound almost with fear.
No! then I well perceive you are not nigh:
Either death or you I 'll find immediately.   *Exit*

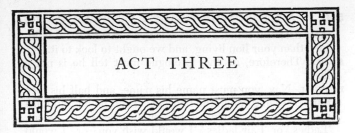

ACT THREE

[1·28]

SCENE ONE

A Wood. Titania lying asleep.

Enter Quince, Snug, Bottom, Flute, Snout, and Starveling

BOTTOM. Are we all met?

QUINCE. Pat, pat; and here 's a marvellous convenient place for our rehearsal. This green plot shall be our stage, this hawthorn-brake our tiring-house; and we will do it in action as we will do it before the duke.

BOTTOM. Peter Quince,—

QUINCE. What say'st thou, bully Bottom?

BOTTOM. There are things in this comedy of Pyramus and Thisby that will never please. First, Pyramus must draw a sword to kill himself, which the ladies cannot abide. How answer you that?

SNOUT. By 'r lakin, a parlous fear.

STARVELING. I believe we must leave the killing out, when all is done.

BOTTOM. Not a whit: I have a device to make all well. Write me a prologue; and let the prologue seem to say, we will do no harm with our swords, and that Pyramus is not killed indeed; and, for the more better assurance, tell them that I, Pyramus, am not Pyramus, but Bottom the weaver: this will put them out of fear.

QUINCE. Well, we will have such a prologue, and it shall be written in eight and six.

BOTTOM. No, make it two more: let it be written in eight and eight.

SNOUT. Will not the ladies be afeard of the lion?

STARVELING. I fear it, I promise you.

BOTTOM. Masters, you ought to consider with yourselves: to bring in,—God shield us!—a lion among ladies, is a

most dreadful thing; for there is not a more fearful wild-
fowl than your lion living, and we ought to look to it.

SNOUT. Therefore, another prologue must tell he is not a
lion.

BOTTOM. Nay, you must name his name, and half his face
must be seen through the lion's neck; and he himself must
speak through, saying thus, or to the same defect,
'Ladies,' or 'Fair ladies,' 'I would wish you,' or, 'I would
request you,' or, 'I would entreat you, not to fear, not to
tremble: my life for yours. If you think I come hither as a
lion, it were pity of my life: no, I am no such thing: I am
a man as other men are': and there indeed let him name
his name, and tell them plainly he is Snug the joiner.

QUINCE. Well, it shall be so. But there is two hard things,
that is, to bring the moonlight into a chamber; for, you
know, Pyramus and Thisby meet by moonlight.

SNUG. Doth the moon shine that night we play our play?

BOTTOM. A calendar, a calendar! look in the almanack; find
out moonshine, find out moonshine.

QUINCE. Yes, it doth shine that night.

BOTTOM. Why, then may you leave a casement of the great
chamber-window, where we play, open; and the moon
may shine in at the casement.

QUINCE. Ay; or else one must come in with a bush of thorns
and a lanthorn, and say he comes to disfigure, or to present, the person of Moonshine. Then, there is another
thing: we must have a wall in the great chamber; for
Pyramus and Thisby, says the story, did talk through the
chink of a wall.

SNUG. You can never bring in a wall. What say you, Bottom?

BOTTOM. Some man or other must present Wall; and let him
have some plaster, or some loam, or some rough-cast about
him, to signify wall; and let him hold his fingers thus, and
through that cranny shall Pyramus and Thisby whisper.

QUINCE. If that may be, then all is well. Come, sit down,
every mother's son, and rehearse your parts. Pyramus,
you begin: when you have spoken your speech, enter
into that brake; and so every one according to his cue.

Enter Puck behind

PUCK. What hempen homespuns have we swaggering here,
So near the cradle of the fairy queen?
What! a play toward; I'll be an auditor;
An actor too perhaps, if I see cause.

QUINCE. Speak, Pyramus.—Thisby, stand forth.

BOTTOM. 'Thisby, the flowers have odious savours sweet'—

QUINCE. Odorous, odorous.

BOTTOM.—'odours savours sweet:

   So hath thy breath, my dearest Thisby dear.

  But hark, a voice! stay thou but here awhile,

    And by and by I will to thee appear.'   *Exit*

PUCK. A stranger Pyramus than e'er play'd here!   *Exit*

FLUTE. Must I speak now?

QUINCE. Ay, marry, must you; for you must understand, he goes but to see a noise that he heard, and is to come again.

FLUTE. 'Most radiant Pyramus, most lily-white of hue,

  Of colour like the red rose on triumphant brier,

  Most brisky juvenal, and eke most lovely Jew,

  As true as truest horse that yet would never tire,

  I 'll meet thee, Pyramus, at Ninny's tomb.'

QUINCE. 'Ninus' tomb,' man. Why, you must not speak that yet; that you answer to Pyramus: you speak all your part at once, cues and all. Pyramus, enter: your cue is past; it is 'never tire.'

FLUTE. O!—'As true as truest horse, that yet would never tire.'

    Re-enter Puck, and Bottom with an ass's head

BOTTOM. 'If I were fair, Thisby, I were only thine.'

QUINCE. O monstrous! O strange! we are haunted.

   Pray, masters! fly, masters!—Help!   *Exeunt Clowns*

PUCK. I 'll follow you, I 'll lead you about a round,

  Through bog, through bush, through brake, through brier:

  Sometimes a horse I 'll be, sometime a hound,

   A hog, a headless bear, sometime a fire;

  And neigh, and bark, and grunt, and roar, and burn.

  Like horse, hound, hog, bear, fire, at every turn.   *Exit*

BOTTOM. Why do they run away? this is a knavery of them to make me afeard.

        Re-enter Snout

SNOUT. O Bottom, thou art changed! what do I see on thee?

BOTTOM. What do you see? you see an ass-head of your own, do you?   *Exit Snout*

        Re-enter Quince

QUINCE. Bless thee, Bottom! bless thee! thou art translated.

                          Exit

BOTTOM. I see their knavery: this is to make an ass of me;
to fright me, if they could. But I will not stir from this
place, do what they can: I will walk up and down here,
and I will sing, that they shall hear I am not afraid.
(*Sings*)

> The ousel-cock, so black of hue,
>   With orange-tawny bill,
> The throstle with his note so true,
>   The wren with little quill.

TITANIA. (*Awaking.*) What angel wakes me from my flowery bed?

BOTTOM. (*Sings*) The finch, the sparrow, and the lark,
>   The plain-song cuckoo gray,
> Whose note full many a man doth mark,
>   And dares not answer, nay.

For indeed, who would set his wit to so foolish a bird?
Who would give a bird the lie, though he cry 'cuckoo'
never so?

TITANIA. I pray thee, gentle mortal, sing again:
Mine ear is much enamour'd of thy note;
So is mine eye enthralled to thy shape;
And thy fair virtue's force, perforce, doth move me,
On the first view, to say, to swear, I love thee.

BOTTOM. Methinks, mistress, you should have little reason
for that: and yet, to say the truth, reason and love keep
little company together now-a-days. The more the pity,
that some honest neighbours will not make them friends.
Nay, I can gleek upon occasion.

TITANIA. Thou art as wise as thou art beautiful.

BOTTOM. Not so, neither; but if I had wit enough to get out
of this wood, I have enough to serve mine own turn.

TITANIA. Out of this wood do not desire to go:
Thou shalt remain here, whe'r thou wilt or no.
I am a spirit of no common rate;
The summer still doth tend upon my state;
And I do love thee: therefore, go with me;
I 'll give thee fairies to attend on thee,
And they shall fetch thee jewels from the deep,
And sing, while thou on pressed flowers dost sleep:
And I will purge thy mortal grossness so
That thou shalt like an airy spirit go.
Pease-blossom! Cobweb! Moth! and Mustard-seed!

Enter Four Fairies

PEASE-BLOSSOM. Ready.

COBWEB.   And I.

MUSTARD-SEED.   And I.

ALL FOUR.   Where shall we go?

TITANIA. Be kind and courteous to this gentleman;
Hop in his walks, and gambol in his eyes;
Feed him with apricocks and dewberries,
With purple grapes, green figs, and mulberries.
The honey-bags steal from the humble-bees,
And for night-tapers crop their waxen thighs,
And light them at the fiery glow-worm's eyes,
To have my love to bed, and to arise;
And pluck the wings from painted butterflies
To fan the moonbeams from his sleeping eyes:
Nod to him, elves, and do him courtesies.

PEASE-BLOSSOM. Hail, mortal!

COBWEB. Hail!

MOTH. Hail!

MUSTARD-SEED. Hail!

BOTTOM. I cry your worships mercy, heartily: I beseech
your worship's name.

COBWEB. Cobweb.

BOTTOM. I shall desire you of more acquaintance, good
Master Cobweb: if I cut my finger, I shall make bold
with you. Your name, honest gentleman?

PEASE-BLOSSOM. Pease-blossom.

BOTTOM. I pray you, commend me to Mistress Squash, your
mother, and to Master Peascod, your father. Good Master Pease-blossom, I shall desire you of more acquaintance too. Your name, I beseech you, sir?

MUSTARD-SEED. Mustard-seed.

BOTTOM. Good Master Mustard-seed, I know your patience
well: that same cowardly, giant-like ox-beef hath de-
voured many a gentleman of your house. I promise you,
your kindred hath made my eyes water ere now. I desire
you of more acquaintance, good Master Mustard-seed.

TITANIA. Come, wait upon him: lead him to my bower.
The moon methinks, looks with a watery eye;
And when she weeps, weeps every little flower,
Lamenting some enforced chastity.
Tie up my love's tongue, bring him silently.   *Exeunt*

SCENE TWO

Another Part of the Wood.

Enter Oberon

OBERON. I wonder if Titania be awak'd;
Then, what it was that next came in her eye,
Which she must dote on in extremity.
Here comes my messenger.

Enter Puck

How now, mad spirit!
What night-rule now about this haunted grove?
PUCK. My mistress with a monster is in love.
Near to her close and consecrated bower,
While she was in her dull and sleeping hour,
A crew of patches, rude mechanicals,
That work for bread upon Athenian stalls,
Were met together to rehearse a play
Intended for great Theseus' nuptial day.
The shallowest thick-skin of that barren sort,
Who Pyramus presented in their sport
Forsook his scene, and enter'd in a brake,
When I did him at this advantage take;
An ass's nowl I fixed on his head:
Anon his Thisby must be answered,
And forth my mimick comes. When they him spy,
As wild geese that the creeping fowler eye,
Or russet-pated choughs, many in sort,
Rising and cawing at the gun's report,
Sever themselves, and madly sweep the sky;
So, at his sight, away his fellows fly,
And, at our stamp, here o'er and o'er one falls;
He murder cries, and help from Athens calls.
Their sense thus weak, lost with their fears thus strong,
Made senseless things begin to do them wrong;
For briers and thorns at their apparel snatch;
Some sleeves, some hats, from yielders all things catch.
I led them on in this distracted fear,
And left sweet Pyramus translated there;

When in that moment, so it came to pass,
Titania wak'd and straightway lov'd an ass.

OBERON. This falls out better than I could devise.
But hast thou yet latch'd the Athenian's eyes
With the love-juice, as I did bid thee do?

PUCK. I took him sleeping,—that is finish'd too,—
And the Athenian woman by his side;
That, when he wak'd, of force she must be ey'd.

Enter Demetrius and Hermia

OBERON. Stand close: this is the same Athenian.

PUCK. This is the woman; but not this the man.

DEMETRIUS. O! why rebuke you him that loves you so?
Lay breath so bitter on your bitter foe.

HERMIA. Now I but chide; but I should use thee worse,
For thou, I fear, hast given me cause to curse.
If thou hast slain Lysander in his sleep,
Being o'er shoes in blood, plunge in knee deep,
And kill me too.
The sun was not so true unto the day
As he to me. Would he have stol'n away
From sleeping Hermia? I 'll believe as soon
This whole earth may be bor'd, and that the moon
May through the centre creep, and so displease
Her brother's noontide with the Antipodes.
It cannot be but thou hast murder'd him;
So should a murderer look, so dead, so grim.

DEMETRIUS. So should the murder'd look, and so should I,
Pierc'd through the heart with your stern cruelty;
Yet you, the murderer, look as bright, as clear,
As yonder Venus in her glimmering sphere.

HERMIA. What 's this to my Lysander? where is he?
Ah! good Demetrius, wilt thou give him me?

DEMETRIUS. I had rather give his carcass to my hounds.

HERMIA. Out, dog! out, cur! thou driv'st me past the bounds
Of maiden's patience. Hast thou slain him then?
Henceforth be never number'd among men!
O! once tell true, tell true, e'en for my sake;
Durst thou have look'd upon him being awake,
And hast thou kill'd him sleeping? O brave touch!
Could not a worm, an adder, do so much?
An adder did it; for with doubler tongue

Than thine, thou serpent, never adder stung.

DEMETRIUS. You spend your passion on a mispris'd mood:
I am not guilty of Lysander's blood,
Nor is he dead, for aught that I can tell.

HERMIA. I pray thee, tell me then that he is well.

DEMETRIUS. An if I could, what should I get therefore?

HERMIA. A privilege never to see me more.
And from thy hated presence part I so;
See me no more, whe'r he be dead or no.   *Exit*

DEMETRIUS. There is no following her in this fierce vein:
Here therefore for awhile I will remain.
So sorrow's heaviness doth heavier grow
For debt that bankrupt sleep doth sorrow owe
Which now in some slight measure it will pay,
If for his tender here I make some stay.

                                    Lies down and sleeps

OBERON. What has thou done? thou hast mistaken quite,
And laid the love-juice on some true-love's sight:
Of thy misprision must perforce ensue
Some true-love turn'd, and not a false turn'd true.

PUCK. Then fate o'er-rules, that, one man holding troth,
A million fail, confounding oath on oath.

OBERON. About the wood go swifter than the wind,
And Helena of Athens look thou find:
All fancy-sick she is, and pale of cheer
With sighs of love, that cost the fresh blood dear.
By some illusion see thou bring her here:
I'll charm his eyes against she do appear.

PUCK. I go, I go; look how I go;
Swifter than arrow from the Tartar's bow.   *Exit*

OBERON.   Flower of this purple dye,
             Hit with Cupid's archery,
             Sink in apple of his eye.
             When his love he doth espy,
             Let her shine as gloriously
             As the Venus of the sky.
             When thou wak'st, if she be by,
             Beg of her for remedy.

                        Re-enter Puck

PUCK.   Captain of our fairy band,
             Helena is here at hand,
             And the youth, mistook by me,

       Pleading for a lover's fee.
       Shall we their fond pageant see?
       Lord, what fools these mortals be!

OBERON. Stand aside: the noise they make
       Will cause Demetrius to awake.

PUCK. Then will two at once woo one;
       That must needs be sport alone;
       And those things do best please me
       That befall preposterously.

       Enter Lysander and Helena

LYSANDER. Why should you think that I should woo in
    scorn?
    Scorn and derision never come in tears:
  Look, when I vow, I weep; and vows so born,
    In their nativity all truth appears.
  How can these things in me seem scorn to you,
  Bearing the badge of faith to prove them true?

HELENA. You do advance your cunning more and more.
    When truth kills truth, O devilish-holy fray!
  These vows are Hermia's: will you give her o'er?
    Weigh oath with oath, and you will nothing weigh:
  Your vows, to her and me, put in two scales,
  Will even weigh, and both as light as tales.

LYSANDER. I had no judgment when to her I swore.

HELENA. Nor none, in my mind, now you give her o'er.

LYSANDER. Demetrius loves her, and he loves not you.

DEMETRIUS. (*Awaking*) O Helen! goddess, nymph, perfect,
    divine!
  To what, my love, shall I compare thine eyne?
  Crystal is muddy. O! how ripe in show
  Thy lips, those kissing cherries, tempting grow;
  This pure congealed white, high Taurus' snow,
  Fann'd with the eastern wind, turns to a crow
  When thou hold'st up thy hand. O! let me kiss
  That princess of pure white, this seal of bliss.

HELENA. O spite! O hell! I see you all are bent
  To set against me for your merriment:
  If you were civil and knew courtesy,
  You would not do me thus much injury.
  Can you not hate me, as I know you do,
  But you must join in souls to mock me too?
  If you were men, as men you are in show,

You would not use a gentle lady so;
To vow, and swear, and superpraise my parts,
When I am sure you hate me with your hearts.
You both are rivals, and love Hermia,
And now both rivals, to mock Helena:
A trim exploit, a manly enterprise,
To conjure tears up in a poor maid's eyes
With your derision! none of noble sort
Would so offend a virgin, and extort
A poor soul's patience all to make you sport.

LYSANDER. You are unkind, Demetrius; be not so;
For you love Hermia; this you know I know:
And here, with all good will, with all my heart,
In Hermia's love I yield you up my part;
And yours of Helena to me bequeath,
Whom I do love, and will do to my death.

HELENA. Never did mockers waste more idle breath.

DEMETRIUS. Lysander, keep thy Hermia; I will none:
If e'er I lov'd her, all that love is gone.
My heart with her but as guest-wise sojourn'd,
And now to Helen it is home return'd,
There to remain.

LYSANDER.   Helen, it is not so.

DEMETRIUS. Disparage not the faith thou dost not know,
Lest to thy peril thou aby it dear.
Look! where thy love comes: yonder is thy dear.

Re-enter Hermia

HERMIA. Dark night, that from the eye his function takes,
The ear more quick of apprehension makes;
Wherein it doth impair the seeing sense,
It pays the hearing double recompense.
Thou art not by mine eye, Lysander, found;
Mine ear, I thank it, brought me to thy sound.
But why unkindly didst thou leave me so?

LYSANDER. Why should he stay, whom love doth press to go?

HERMIA. What love could press Lysander from my side?

LYSANDER. Lysander's love, that would not let him bide,
Fair Helena, who more engilds the night
Than all yon fiery oes and eyes of light.
Why seek'st thou me? Could not this make thee know,
The hate I bear thee made me leave thee so?

HERMIA. You speak not as you think: it cannot be.

HELENA. Lo! she is one of this confederacy.
  Now I perceive they have conjoin'd all three
  To fashion this false sport in spite of me.
  Injurious Hermia! most ungrateful maid!
  Have you conspir'd, have you with these contriv'd
  To bait me with this foul derision?
  Is all the counsel that we two have shar'd,
  The sister-vows, the hours that we have spent,
  When we have chid the hasty-footed time
  For parting us, O! is it all forgot?
  All school-days' friendship, childhood innocence?
  We, Hermia, like two artificial gods,
  Have with our neelds created both one flower,
  Both on one sampler, sitting on one cushion,
  Both warbling of one song, both in one key,
  As if our hands, our sides, voices, and minds,
  Had been incorporate. So we grew together,
  Like to a double cherry, seeming parted,
  But yet an union in partition;
  Two lovely berries moulded on one stem;
  So, with two seeming bodies, but one heart;
  Two of the first, like coats in heraldry,
  Due but to one, and crowned with one crest.
  And will you rent our ancient love asunder,
  To join with men in scorning your poor friend?
  It is not friendly, 'tis not maidenly:
  Our sex, as well as I, may chide you for it,
  Though I alone do feel the injury.
HERMIA. I am amazed at your passionate words.
  I scorn you not: it seems that you scorn me.
HELENA. Have you not set Lysander, as in scorn,
  To follow me and praise my eyes and face,
  And made your other love, Demetrius,—
  Who even but now did spurn me with his foot,—
  To call me goddess, nymph, divine and rare,
  Precious, celestial? Wherefore speaks he this
  To her he hates? and wherefore doth Lysander
  Deny your love, so rich within his soul,
  And tender me, forsooth, affection,
  But by your setting on, by your consent?
  What though I be not so in grace as you,
  So hung upon with love, so fortunate,

But miserable most to love unlov'd?
This you should pity rather than despise.

HERMIA. I understand not what you mean by this.

HELENA. Ay, do, persever, counterfeit sad looks,
Make mouths upon me when I turn my back;
Wink each at other; hold the sweet jest up:
This sport, well carried, shall be chronicled.
If you have any pity, grace, or manners,
You would not make me such an argument.
But, fare ye well: 'tis partly mine own fault,
Which death or absence soon shall remedy.

LYSANDER. Stay, gentle Helena! hear my excuse:
My love, my life, my soul, fair Helena!

HELENA. O excellent!

HERMIA.   Sweet, do not scorn her so.

DEMETRIUS. If she cannot entreat, I can compel.

LYSANDER. Thou canst compel no more than she entreat:
Thy threats have no more strength than her weak prayers.
Helen, I love thee; by my life, I do:
I swear by that which I will lose for thee,
To prove him false that says I love thee not.

DEMETRIUS. I say I love thee more than he can do.

LYSANDER. If thou say so, withdraw, and prove it too.

DEMETRIUS. Quick, come!

HERMIA.   Lysander, whereto tends all this?

LYSANDER. Away, you Ethiop!

DEMETRIUS.   No, no, sir! You
Seem to break loose; take on, as you would follow,
But yet come not: you are a tame man, go!

LYSANDER. (To Hermia) Hang off, thou cat, thou burr! vile
thing, let loose,
Or I will shake thee from me like a serpent.

HERMIA. Why are you grown so rude? what change is this,
Sweet love,—

LYSANDER. Thy love! out, tawny Tartar, out!
Out, loathed medicine! hated poison, hence!

HERMIA. Do you not jest?

HELENA.   Yes, sooth; and so do you.

LYSANDER. Demetrius, I will keep my word with thee.

DEMETRIUS. I would I had your bond, for I perceive
A weak bond holds you: I'll not trust your word.

LYSANDER. What! should I hurt her, strike her, kill her dead?

Although I hate her, I 'll not harm her so.

HERMIA. What! can you do me greater harm than hate?
Hate me! wherefore? O me! what news, my love?
Am not I Hermia? Are not you Lysander?
I am as fair now as I was erewhile.
Since night you lov'd me; yet, since night you left me:
Why, then you left me,—O, the gods forbid!—
In earnest, shall I say?

LYSANDER.   Ay, by my life;
And never did desire to see thee more.
Therefore be out of hope, of question, doubt;
Be certain, nothing truer: 'tis no jest,
That I do hate thee and love Helena.

HERMIA. O me! you juggler! you canker-blossom!
You thief of love! what! have you come by night
And stol'n my love's heart from him?

HELENA.   Fine, i' faith!
Have you no modesty, no maiden shame,
No touch of bashfulness? What! will you tear
Impatient answers from my gentle tongue?
Fie, fie! you counterfeit, you puppet you!

HERMIA. Puppet! why, so: ay, that way goes the game.
Now I perceive that she hath made compare
Between our statures: she hath urg'd her height,
And with her personage, her tall personage,
Her height, forsooth, she hath prevail'd with him.
And are you grown so high in his esteem,
Because I am so dwarfish and so low?
How low am I, thou painted maypole? speak;
How low am I? I am not yet so low
But that my nails can reach unto thine eyes.

HELENA. I pray you, though you mock me, gentlemen,
Let her not hurt me: I was never curst;
I have no gift at all in shrewishness;
I am a right maid for my cowardice:
Let her not strike me. You perhaps may think,
Because she is something lower than myself,
That I can match her.

HERMIA.   Lower! hark, again.

HELENA. Good Hermia, do not be so bitter with me.
I evermore did love you, Hermia,
Did ever keep your counsels, never wrong'd you;

Save that, in love unto Demetrius,
I told him of your stealth unto this wood.
He follow'd you; for love I follow'd him;
But he hath chid me hence, and threaten'd me
To strike me, spurn me, nay, to kill me too:
And now, so you will let me quiet go,
To Athens will I bear my folly back,
And follow you no further: let me go:
You see how simple and how fond I am.

HERMIA. Why, get you gone. Who is 't that hinders you?

HELENA. A foolish heart, that I leave here behind.

HERMIA. What! with Lysander?

HELENA.   With Demetrius.

LYSANDER. Be not afraid: she shall not harm thee, Helena.

DEMETRIUS. No, sir; she shall not, though you take her part.

HELENA. O! when she 's angry, she is keen and shrewd.
She was a vixen when she went to school:
And though she be but little, she is fierce.

HERMIA. 'Little' again! nothing but 'low' and 'little'!
Why will you suffer her to flout me thus?
Let me come to her.

LYSANDER.   Get you gone, you dwarf;
You minimus, of hindering knot-grass made;
You bead, you acorn!

DEMETRIUS.   You are too officious
In her behalf that scorns your services.
Let her alone; speak not of Helena;
Take not her part, for, if thou dost intend
Never so little show of love to her,
Thou shalt aby it.

LYSANDER.   Now she holds me not;
Now follow, if thou dar'st, to try whose right,
Or thine or mine, is most in Helena.

DEMETRIUS. Follow! nay, I 'll go with thee, cheek by jowl.
                    Exeunt Lysander and Demetrius

HERMIA. You, mistress, all this coil is 'long of you:
Nay, go not back.

HELENA.   I will not trust you, I,
Nor longer stay in your curst company.
Your hands than mine are quicker for a fray,
My legs are longer though, to run away.   *Exit*

HERMIA. I am amaz'd, and know not what to say.   *Exit*

OBERON. This is thy negligence: still thou mistak'st,
    Or else commit'st thy knaveries wilfully.
PUCK. Believe me, king of shadows, I mistook.
    Did not you tell me I should know the man
    By the Athenian garments he had on?
    And so far blameless proves my enterprise,
    That I have 'nointed an Athenian's eyes;
    And so far am I glad it so did sort,
    As this their jangling I esteem a sport.
OBERON. Thou see'st these lovers seek a place to fight:
    Hie therefore, Robin, overcast the night;
    The starry welkin cover thou anon
    With drooping fog as black as Acheron;
    And lead these testy rivals so astray,
    As one come not within another's way.
    Like to Lysander sometime frame thy tongue,
    Then stir Demetrius up with bitter wrong;
    And sometime rail thou like Demetrius;
    And from each other look thou lead them thus,
    Till o'er their brows death-counterfeiting sleep
    With leaden legs and batty wings doth creep:
    Then crush this herb into Lysander's eye;
    Whose liquor hath this virtuous property,
    To take from thence all error with his might,
    And make his eyeballs roll with wonted sight.
    When they next wake, all this derision
    Shall seem a dream and fruitless vision;
    And back to Athens shall the lovers wend,
    With league whose date till death shall never end
    Whiles I in this affair do thee employ,
    I'll to my queen and beg her Indian boy;
    And then I will her charmed eye release
    From monster's view, and all things shall be peace.
PUCK. My fairy lord, this must be done with haste,
    For night's swift dragons cut the clouds full fast,
    And yonder shines Aurora's harbinger;
    At whose approach, ghosts, wandering here and there,
    Troop home to churchyards: damned spirits all,
    That in cross-ways and floods have burial,
    Already to their wormy beds are gone;
    For fear lest day should look their shames upon,
    They wilfully themselves exile from light,

And must for aye consort with black-brow'd night.   420]

OBERON. But we are spirits of another sort.
I with the morning's love have oft made sport;
And, like a forester, the groves may tread,
Even till the eastern gate, all fiery-red,
Opening on Neptune with fair blessed beams,
Turns into yellow gold his salt green streams.
But, notwithstanding, haste; make no delay:
We may effect this business yet ere day.   *Exit Oberon*

PUCK.   Up and down, up and down;
I will lead them up and down:
I am fear'd in field and town;
Goblin, lead them up and down.
Here comes one.

Re-enter Lysander

LYSANDER. Where art thou, proud Demetrius? speak thou
now.

PUCK. Here, villain! drawn and ready. Where art thou?

LYSANDER. I will be with thee straight.

PUCK.   Follow me, then,
To plainer ground. *Exit Lysander, as following the voice*
Re-enter Demetrius

DEMETRIUS.   Lysander! speak again.
Thou runaway, thou coward, art thou fled?
Speak! In some bush? Where dost thou hide thy head?

PUCK. Thou coward! art thou bragging to the stars,
Telling the bushes that thou look'st for wars,
And wilt not come? Come, recreant; come, thou child;
I 'll whip thee with a rod: he is defil'd
That draws a sword on thee.

DEMETRIUS.   Yea, art thou there?

PUCK. Follow my voice: we 'll try no manhood here. *Exeunt*
Re-enter Lysander

LYSANDER. He goes before me and still dares me on:
When I come where he calls, then he is gone.
The villain is much lighter-heel'd than I:
I follow'd fast, but faster he did fly;
That fallen am I in dark uneven way,
And here will rest me. (*Lies down*) Come, thou gentle
day!
For if but once thou show me thy grey light,
I 'll find Demetrius and revenge this spite.   *Sleeps*

Re-enter Puck and Demetrius

PUCK. Ho! ho! ho! Coward, why com'st thou not?

DEMETRIUS. Abide me, if thou dar'st; for well I wot
  Thou runn'st before me, shifting every place,
  And dar'st not stand, nor look me in the face.
  Where art thou now?

PUCK.   Come hither: I am here.

DEMETRIUS. Nay then, thou mock'st me. Thou shalt buy
  this dear,
  If ever I thy face by daylight see:
  Now, go thy way. Faintness constraineth me
  To measure out my length on this cold bed:
  By day's approach look to be visited.

                            Lies down and sleeps

Re-enter Helena

HELENA. O weary night! O long and tedious night,
  Abate thy hours! shine, comforts, from the east!
  That I may back to Athens by daylight,
  From these that my poor company detest:
  And sleep, that sometimes shuts up sorrow's eye,
  Steal me awhile from mine own company.

                            Lies down and sleeps

PUCK.   Yet but three? Come one more;
        Two of both kinds make up four.
        Here she comes, curst and sad:
        Cupid is a knavish lad,
        Thus to make poor females mad.

Re-enter Hermia

HERMIA. Never so weary, never so in woe,
  Bedabbled with the dew and torn with briers,
  I can no further crawl, no further go;
  My legs can keep no pace with my desires.
  Here will I rest me till the break of day.
  Heavens shield Lysander, if they mean a fray!

                            Lies down and sleeps

PUCK.   On the ground
Sleep sound:
I 'll apply
To your eye,
Gentle lover, remedy.

Squeezing the juice on Lysander's eyes

When thou wak'st,
Thou tak'st
True delight
In the sight
Of thy former lady's eye:
And the country proverb known,
That every man should take his own,
In your waking shall be shown:

Jack shall have Jill;
Nought shall go ill;
The man shall have his mare again,
And all shall be well.   *Exit*

ACT FOUR

SCENE ONE

A Wood. Lysander,
Demetrius, Helena, and Hermia lying asleep.
Enter Titania and Bottom, Fairies attending;
Oberon behind unseen

TITANIA. Come, sit thee down upon this flowery bed,
  While I thy amiable cheeks do coy,
And stick musk-roses in thy sleek smooth head,
  And kiss thy fair large ears, my gentle joy.

BOTTOM. Where 's Pease-blossom?

PEASE-BLOSSOM. Ready.

BOTTOM. Scratch my head, Pease-blossom. Where 's Mounsieur Cobweb?

COBWEB. Ready.

BOTTOM. Mounsieur Cobweb, good mounsieur, get your weapons in your hand, and kill me a red-hipped humble-bee on the top of a thistle; and, good mounsieur, bring me the honey-bag. Do not fret yourself too much in the action, mounsieur; and, good mounsieur, have a care the honey-bag break not; I would be loath to have you overflown with a honey-bag, signior. Where's Mounsieur Mustard-seed?

MUSTARD-SEED. Ready.

BOTTOM. Give me your neaf, Mounsieur Mustard-seed. Pray you, leave your curtsy, good mounsieur.

MUSTARD-SEED. What 's your will?

BOTTOM. Nothing, good mounsieur, but to help Cavalery Cobweb to scratch. I must to the barber's, mounsieur, for methinks I am marvellous hairy about the face; and I am such a tender ass, if my hair do but tickle me, I must scratch.

TITANIA. What, wilt thou hear some music, my sweet love?

BOTTOM. I have a reasonable good ear in music: let us have the tongs and the bones.

TITANIA. Or say, sweet love, what thou desir'st to eat.

BOTTOM. Truly, a peck of provender: I could munch your good dry oats. Methinks I have a great desire to a bottle of hay: good hay, sweet hay, hath no fellow.

TITANIA. I have a venturous fairy that shall seek
The squirrel's hoard, and fetch thee thence new nuts.

BOTTOM. I had rather have a handful or two of dried pease. But, I pray you, let none of your people stir me: I have an exposition of sleep come upon me.

TITANIA. Sleep thou, and I will wind thee in my arms.
Fairies, be gone, and be all ways away.   *Exeunt Fairies*
So doth the woodbine the sweet honeysuckle
Gently entwist; the female ivy so
Enrings the barky fingers of the elm.
O! how I love thee; how I dote on thee!   *They sleep*
                          Enter Puck

OBERON. (*Advancing*) Welcome, good Robin. See'st thou
this sweet sight?
Her dotage now I do begin to pity:
For, meeting her of late behind the wood,
Seeking sweet favours for this hateful fool,
I did upbraid her and fall out with her;
For she his hairy temples then had rounded
With coronet of fresh and fragrant flowers;
And that same dew, which sometime on the buds
Was wont to swell like round and orient pearls,
Stood now within the pretty flowerets' eyes
Like tears that did their own disgrace bewail.
When I had at my pleasure taunted her,
And she in mild terms begg'd my patience,
I then did ask of her her changeling child;
Which straight she gave me, and her fairy sent
To bear him to my bower in fairy land.
And now I have the boy, I will undo
This hateful imperfection of her eyes:
And, gentle Puck, take this transformed scalp
From off the head of this Athenian swain,
That he, awaking when the other do,
May all to Athens back again repair,
And think no more of this night's accidents
But as the fierce vexation of a dream.
But first I will release the fairy queen.
                 Touching her eyes with an herb

Be as thou wast wont to be;
See as thou wast wont to see:
Dian's bud o'er Cupid's flower
Hath such force and blessed power.
Now, my Titania; wake you, my sweet queen.

TITANIA. My Oberon! what visions have I seen!
Methought I was enamour'd of an ass.

OBERON. There lies your love.

TITANIA.   How came these things to pass?
O! how mine eyes do loathe his visage now.

OBERON. Silence, awhile. Robin, take off this head.
Titania, music call; and strike more dead
Than common sleep of all these five the sense.

TITANIA. Music, ho! music! such as charmeth sleep.   *Music*

PUCK. When thou wak'st, with thine own fool's eyes peep.

OBERON. Sound, music! (*Still, music*) Come, my queen,
    take hands with me,
And rock the ground whereon these sleepers be.   *Dance*
Now thou and I are new in amity,
And will to-morrow midnight solemnly
Dance in Duke Theseus' house triumphantly,
And bless it to all fair prosperity.
There shall the pairs of faithful lovers be
Wedded, with Theseus, all in jollity.

PUCK. Fairy king, attend, and mark:
I do hear the morning lark.

OBERON. Then, my queen, in silence sad,
Trip we after the night's shade;
We the globe can compass soon,
Swifter than the wandering moon.

TITANIA. Come, my lord; and in our flight
Tell me how it came this night
That I sleeping here was found
With these mortals on the ground.
                    Exeunt. Horns winded within
Enter Theseus, Hippolyta, Egeus, and Train

THESEUS. Go, one of you, find out the forester;
For now our observation is perform'd;
And since we have the vaward of the day,
My love shall hear the music of my hounds.
Uncouple in the western valley; let them go:
Dispatch, I say, and find the forester.
We will, fair queen, up to the mountain's top,

And mark the musical confusion
Of hounds and echo in conjunction.

HIPPOLYTA. I was with Hercules and Cadmus once,
When in a wood of Crete they bay'd the bear
With hounds of Sparta: never did I hear
Such gallant chiding; for, besides the groves,
The skies, the fountains, every region near
Seem'd all one mutual cry. I never heard
So musical a discord, such sweet thunder.

THESEUS. My hounds are bred out of the Spartan kind,
So flew'd, so sanded; and their heads are hung
With ears that sweep away the morning dew;
Crook-knee'd, and dew-lapp'd like Thessalian bulls;
Slow in pursuit, but match'd in mouth like bells,
Each under each. A cry more tuneable
Was never holla'd to, nor cheer'd with horn,
In Crete, in Sparta, nor in Thessaly:
Judge, when you hear. But, soft! what nymphs are these?

EGEUS. My lord, this is my daughter here asleep;
And this, Lysander; this Demetrius is;
This Helena, old Nedar's Helena:
I wonder of their being here together.

THESEUS. No doubt they rose up early to observe
The rite of May, and, hearing our intent,
Came here in grace of our solemnity.
But speak, Egeus, is not this the day
That Hermia should give answer of her choice?

EGEUS. It is, my lord.

THESEUS. Go, bid the huntsmen wake them with their horns.

*Horns and shout within. Lysander,
Demetrius, Hermia, and Helena, wake and start up*

Good-morrow, friends. Saint Valentine is past:
Begin these wood-birds but to couple now?

LYSANDER. Pardon, my lord.   *He and the rest kneel*

THESEUS.   I pray you all, stand up.
I know you two are rival enemies:
How comes this gentle concord in the world,
That hatred is so far from jealousy,
To sleep by hate, and fear no enmity?

LYSANDER. My lord, I shall reply amazedly,
Half sleep, half waking: but as yet, I swear,
I cannot truly say how I came here;
But, as I think,—for truly would I speak,

And now I do bethink me, so it is,—
I came with Hermia hither: our intent
Was to be gone from Athens, where we might,
Without the peril of the Athenian law—

EGEUS. Enough, enough, my lord! you have enough:
I beg the law, the law, upon his head.
They would have stol'n away; they would, Demetrius,
Thereby to have defeated you and me;
You of your wife, and me of my consent,
Of my consent that she should be your wife.

DEMETRIUS. My lord, fair Helen told me of their stealth,
Of this their purpose hither, to this wood;
And I in fury hither follow'd them,
Fair Helena in fancy following me.
But, my good lord, I wot not by what power,—
But by some power it is,—my love to Hermia,
Melted as doth the snow, seems to me now
As the remembrance of an idle gaud
Which in my childhood I did dote upon;
And all the faith, the virtue of my heart,
The object and the pleasure of mine eye,
Is only Helena. To her, my lord,
Was I betroth'd ere I saw Hermia:
But, like in sickness, did I loathe this food;
But, as in health, come to my natural taste,
Now do I wish it, love it, long for it,
And will for evermore be true to it.

THESEUS. Fair lovers, you are fortunately met:
Of this discourse we more will hear anon.
Egeus, I will overbear your will,
For in the temple, by and by, with us,
These couples shall eternally be knit:
And, for the morning now is something worn,
Our purpos'd hunting shall be set aside.
Away with us, to Athens: three and three,
We 'll hold a feast in great solemnity.
Come, Hippolyta.

> *Exeunt Theseus, Hippolyta, Egeus, and Train*

DEMETRIUS. These things seem small and undistinguishable,
Like far-off mountains turned into clouds.

HERMIA. Methinks I see these things with parted eye,
When everything seems double.

HELENA.   So methinks:

And I have found Demetrius, like a jewel,
Mine own, and not mine own.

DEMETRIUS.   Are you sure
That we are awake? It seems to me
That yet we sleep, we dream. Do you not think
The duke was here, and bid us follow him?

HERMIA. Yea; and my father.

HELENA.   And Hippolyta.

LYSANDER. And he did bid us follow to the temple.

DEMETRIUS. Why then, we are awake. Let 's follow him;
And by the way let us recount our dreams.   *Exeunt*

BOTTOM. (*Awaking*) When my cue comes, call me, and I
will answer: my next is, 'Most fair Pyramus.' Heigh-ho!
Peter Quince! Flute, the bellows-mender! Snout, the
tinker! Starveling! God 's my life! Stolen hence, and left
me asleep! I have had a most rare vision. I have had a
dream, past the wit of man to say what dream it was: man
is but an ass, if he go about to expound this dream. Methought I was—there is no man can tell what. Methought I
was,—and methought I had,—but man is but a patched
fool, if he will offer to say what methought I had. The eye
of man hath not heard, the ear of man hath not seen, man's
hand is not able to taste, his tongue to conceive, nor his
heart to report, what my dream was. I will get Peter
Quince to write a ballad of this dream; it shall be called
Bottom's Dream, because it hath no bottom; and I will
sing it in the latter end of a play, before the duke: peradventure, to make it the more gracious, I shall sing it at her
death.   *Exit*

SCENE TWO

Athens. A Room in Quince's House.

Enter Quince, Flute, Snout, and Starveling

QUINCE. Have you sent to Bottom's house? is he come home
yet?

STARVELING. He cannot be heard of. Out of doubt he is
transported.

FLUTE. If he come not, then the play is marred: it goes not
forward, doth it?

QUINCE. It is not possible: you have not a man in all Athens able to discharge Pyramus but he.

FLUTE. No; he hath simply the best wit of any handicraft man in Athens.

QUINCE. Yea, and the best person too; and he is a very paramour for a sweet voice.

FLUTE. You must say, 'paragon': a paramour is, God bless us! a thing of naught.

Enter Snug

SNUG. Masters, the duke is coming from the temple, and there is two or three lords and ladies more married: if our sport had gone forward, we had all been made men.

FLUTE. O sweet bully Bottom! Thus hath he lost sixpence a day during his life; he could not have 'scaped sixpence a day: an the duke had not given him sixpence a day for playing Pyramus, I 'll be hanged; he would have deserved it: sixpence a day in Pyramus, or nothing.

Enter Bottom

BOTTOM. Where are these lads? where are these hearts?

QUINCE. Bottom! O most courageous day! O most happy hour!

BOTTOM. Masters, I am to discourse wonders: but ask me not what; for if I tell you, I am no true Athenian. I will tell you everything, right as it fell out.

QUINCE. Let us hear, sweet Bottom.

BOTTOM. Not a word of me. All that I will tell you is, that the duke hath dined. Get your apparel together, good strings to your beards, new ribbons to your pumps; meet presently at the palace; every man look o'er his part; for the short and the long is, our play is preferred. In any case, let Thisby have clean linen; and let not him that plays the lion pare his nails, for they shall hang out for the lion's claws. And, most dear actors, eat no onions nor garlic, for we are to utter sweet breath, and I do not doubt but to hear them say, it is a sweet comedy. No more words: away! go; away.　　　　　　　　　　　　　　*Exeunt*

ACT FIVE

Athens. An Apartment in the Palace of Theseus.

*Enter Theseus, Hippolyta, Philostrate, Lords,
and Attendants*

HIPPOLYTA. 'Tis strange, my Theseus, that these lovers
    speak of.
THESEUS. More strange than true. I never may believe
    These antique fables, nor these fairy toys.
    Lovers and madmen have such seething brains,
    Such shaping fantasies, that apprehend
    More than cool reason ever comprehends.
    The lunatic, the lover, and the poet,
    Are of imagination all compact:
    One sees more devils than vast hell can hold,
    That is, the madman; the lover, all as frantic,
    Sees Helen's beauty in a brow of Egypt:
    The poet's eye, in a fine frenzy rolling,
    Doth glance from heaven to earth, from earth to heaven;
    And, as imagination bodies forth
    The forms of things unknown, the poet's pen
    Turns them to shapes, and gives to airy nothing
    A local habitation and a name.
    Such tricks hath strong imagination,
    That, if it would but apprehend some joy,
    It comprehends some bringer of that joy;
    Or in the night, imagining some fear,
    How easy is a bush suppos'd a bear!
HIPPOLYTA. But all the story of the night told over,
    And all their minds transfigur'd so together,
    More witnesseth than fancy's images,
    And grows to something of great constancy,
    But, howsoever, strange and admirable.

THESEUS. Here come the lovers, full of joy and mirth.
　　Enter Lysander, Demetrius, Hermia, and Helena
　　Joy, gentle friends! joy, and fresh days of love
　　Accompany your hearts!
LYSANDER.　　　　　　　　More than to us
　　Wait in your royal walks, your board, your bed!
THESEUS. Come now; what masques, what dances shall we
　　　　have,
　　To wear away this long age of three hours
　　Between our after-supper and bed-time?
　　Where is our usual manager of mirth?
　　What revels are in hand? Is there no play,
　　To ease the anguish of a torturing hour?
　　Call Philostrate.
PHILOSTRATE.　　　　　Here, mighty Theseus.
THESEUS. Say, what abridgment have you for this evening?
　　What masque? what music? How shall we beguile
　　The lazy time, if not with some delight?
PHILOSTRATE. There is a brief how many sports are ripe;
　　Make choice of which your Highness will see first.
　　　　　　　　　　　　　　　　　Gives a paper
THESEUS. 'The battle with the Centaurs, to be sung
　　By an Athenian eunuch to the harp.'
　　We 'll none of that: that have I told my love,
　　In glory of my kinsman Hercules.
　　'The riot of the tipsy Bacchanals,
　　Tearing the Thracian singer in their rage.'
　　That is an old device; and it was play'd
　　When I from Thebes came last a conqueror.
　　'The thrice three Muses mourning for the death
　　Of Learning, late deceas'd in beggary.'
　　That is some satire keen and critical,
　　Not sorting with a nuptial ceremony.
　　'A tedious brief scene of young Pyramus
　　And his love Thisby; very tragical mirth.
　　Merry and tragical! tedious and brief!
　　That is, hot ice and wonderous strange snow.
　　How shall we find the concord of this discord?
PHILOSTRATE. A play there is, my lord, some ten words long,
　　Which is as brief as I have known a play;
　　But by ten words, my lord, it is too long,
　　Which makes it tedious; for in all the play

There is not one word apt, one player fitted.
And tragical, my noble lord, it is;
For Pyramus therein doth kill himself.
Which when I saw rehears'd, I must confess,
Made mine eyes water; but more merry tears
The passion of loud laughter never shed.

THESEUS. What are they that do play it?

PHILOSTRATE. Hard-handed men, that work in Athens here,
Which never labour'd in their minds till now,
And now have toil'd their unbreath'd memories
With this same play, against your nuptial.

THESEUS. And we will hear it.

PHILOSTRATE.   No, my noble lord;
It is not for you: I have heard it over,
And it is nothing, nothing in the world;
Unless you can find sport in their intents,
Extremely stretch'd and conn'd with cruel pain,
To do you service.

THESEUS.   I will hear that play;
For never anything can be amiss,
When simpleness and duty tender it.
Go, bring them in: and take your places, ladies.

                                         Exit Philostrate

HIPPOLYTA. I love not to see wretchedness o'ercharg'd,
And duty in his service perishing.

THESEUS. Why, gentle sweet, you shall see no such thing.

HIPPOLYTA. He says they can do nothing in this kind.

THESEUS. The kinder we, to give them thanks for nothing.
Our sport shall be to take what they mistake:
And what poor duty cannot do, noble respect
Takes it in might, not merit.
Where I have come, great clerks have purposed
To greet me with premeditated welcomes;
Where I have seen them shiver and look pale,
Make periods in the midst of sentences,
Throttle their practis'd accent in their fears,
And, in conclusion, dumbly have broke off,
Not paying me a welcome. Trust me, sweet,
Out of this silence yet I pick'd a welcome;
And in the modesty of fearful duty
I read as much as from the rattling tongue
Of saucy and audacious eloquence.

Love, therefore, and tongue-tied simplicity
In least speak most, to my capacity.
Re-enter Philostrate
PHILOSTRATE. So please your Grace, the Prologue is
address'd.
THESEUS. Let him approach.   *Flourish of trumpets*
Enter Quince for the Prologue
PROLOGUE. If we offend, it is with our good will.
That you should think, we come not to offend,
But with good will. To show our simple skill,
That is the true beginning of our end.
Consider then we come but in despite.
We do not come as minding to content you,
Our true intent is. All for your delight,
We are not here. That you should here repent you,
The actors are at hand; and, by their show,
You shall know all that you are like to know.
THESEUS. This fellow doth not stand upon points.
LYSANDER. He hath rid his prologue like a rough colt; he
knows not the stop. A good moral, my lord: it is not
enough to speak, but to speak true.
HIPPOLYTA. Indeed he hath played on his prologue like a
child on a recorder; a sound, but not in government.
THESEUS. His speech was like a tangled chain; nothing im-
paired, but all disordered. Who is next?
Enter Pyramus and Thisby,
Wall, Moonshine, and Lion, as in dumb show
PROLOGUE. Gentles, perchance you wonder at this show;
But wonder on, till truth make all things plain.
This man is Pyramus, if you would know;
This beauteous lady Thisby is, certain.
This man, with lime and rough-cast, doth present
Wall, that vile Wall which did these lovers sunder;
And through Wall's chink, poor souls, they are content
To whisper, at the which let no man wonder.
This man, with lanthorn, dog, and bush of thorn,
Presenteth Moonshine; for, if you will know,
By moonshine did these lovers think no scorn
To meet at Ninus' tomb, there, there to woo.
This grisly beast, which Lion hight by name,
The trusty Thisby, coming first by night,
Did scare away, or rather did affright;

And, as she fled, her mantle she did fall,
Which Lion vile with bloody mouth did stain.
Anon comes Pyramus, sweet youth and tall,
And finds his trusty Thisby's mantle slain:
Whereat, with blade, with bloody blameful blade,
He bravely broach'd his boiling bloody breast;
And Thisby, tarrying in mulberry shade,
His dagger drew, and died. For all the rest,
Let Lion, Moonshine, Wall, and lovers twain,
At large discourse, while here they do remain.

Exeunt Prologue, Pyramus, Thisby, Lion, and Moonshine

THESEUS. I wonder, if the lion be to speak.

DEMETRIUS. No wonder, my lord: one lion may, when many asses do.

WALL. In this same interlude it doth befall
That I, one Snout by name, present a wall;
And such a wall, as I would have you think,
That had in it a crannied hole or chink,
Through which the lovers, Pyramus and Thisby,
Did whisper often very secretly.
This loam, this rough-cast, and this stone doth show
That I am that same wall; the truth is so;
And this the cranny is, right and sinister,
Through which the fearful lovers are to whisper.

THESEUS. Would you desire lime and hair to speak better?

DEMETRIUS. It is the wittiest partition that ever I heard discourse, my lord.

THESEUS. Pyramus draws near the wall: silence!

Re-enter Pyramus

PYRAMUS. O grim-look'd night! O night with hue so black!
O night, which ever art when day is not!
O night! O night! alack, alack, alack!
I fear my Thisby's promise is forgot.
And thou, O wall! O sweet, O lovely wall!
That stand'st between her father's ground and mine;
Thou wall, O wall! O sweet, and lovely wall!
Show me thy chink to blink through with mine eyne.

Wall holds up his fingers

Thanks, courteous wall: Jove shield thee well for this!
But what see I? No Thisby do I see.
O wicked wall! through whom I see no bliss;
Curs'd be thy stones for thus deceiving me!

THESEUS. The wall, methinks, being sensible, should curse again.

PYRAMUS. No, in truth, sir, he should not. 'Deceiving me,' is Thisby's cue: she is to enter now, and I am to spy her through the wall. You shall see, it will fall pat as I told you. Yonder she comes.

Re-enter Thisby

THISBY. O wall! full often hast thou heard my moans,
    For parting my fair Pyramus and me:
  My cherry lips have often kiss'd thy stones,
    Thy stones with lime and hair knit up in thee.

PYRAMUS. I see a voice: now will I to the chink,
  To spy an I can hear my Thisby's face.
  Thisby!

THISBY. My love! thou art my love, I think.

PYRAMUS. Think what thou wilt, I am thy lover's grace;
  And, like Limander, am I trusty still.

THISBY. And I like Helen, till the Fates me kill.

PYRAMUS. Not Shafalus to Procrus was so true.

THISBY. As Shafalus to Procrus, I to you.

PYRAMUS. O! kiss me through the hole of this vile wall.

THISBY. I kiss the wall's hole, not your lips at all.

PYRAMUS. Wilt thou at Ninny's tomb meet me straightway?

THISBY. 'Tide life, 'tide death, I come without delay.

                    Exeunt Pyramus and Thisby

WALL. Thus have I, Wall, my part discharged so;
  And, being done, thus Wall away doth go.   *Exit*

THESEUS. Now is the mural down between the two neighbours.

DEMETRIUS. No remedy, my lord, when walls are so wilful to hear without warning.

HIPPOLYTA. This is the silliest stuff that ever I heard.

THESEUS. The best in this kind are but shadows, and the worst are no worse, if imagination amend them.

HIPPOLYTA. It must be your imagination then, and not theirs.

THESEUS. If we imagine no worse of them than they of themselves, they may pass for excellent men. Here come two noble beasts in, a man and a lion.

Re-enter Lion and Moonshine

LION. You, ladies, you, whose gentle hearts do fear
    The smallest monstrous mouse that creeps on floor,

May now perchance both quake and tremble here,
 When lion rough in wildest rage doth roar.
Then know that I, one Snug the joiner, am
A lion-fell, nor else no lion's dam:
For, if I should as lion come in strife
Into this place, 'twere pity on my life.

THESEUS. A very gentle beast, and of a good conscience.

DEMETRIUS. The very best at a beast, my lord, that e'er I saw.

LYSANDER. This lion is a very fox for his valour.

THESEUS. True; and a goose for his discretion.

DEMETRIUS. Not so, my lord; for his valour cannot carry his discretion, and the fox carries the goose.

THESEUS. His discretion, I am sure, cannot carry his valour, for the goose carries not the fox. It is well: leave it to his discretion, and let us listen to the moon.

MOON. This lanthorn doth the horned moon present;—

DEMETRIUS. He should have worn the horns on his head.

THESEUS. He is no crescent, and his horns are invisible within the circumference.

MOON. This lanthorn doth the horned moon present;
 Myself the man i' the moon do seem to be.

THESEUS. This is the greatest error of all the rest. The man should be put into the lanthorn: how is it else the man i' the moon?

DEMETRIUS. He dares not come there for the candle; for, you see, it is already in snuff.

HIPPOLYTA. I am aweary of this moon: would he would change!

THESEUS. It appears, by his small light of discretion, that he is in the wane; but yet, in courtesy, in all reason, we must stay the time.

LYSANDER. Proceed, Moon.

MOON. All that I have to say, is, to tell you that the lanthorn is the moon; I, the man in the moon; this thorn-bush, my thorn-bush; and this dog, my dog.

DEMETRIUS. Why, all these should be in the lanthorn; for all these are in the moon. But, silence! here comes Thisby.

Re-enter Thisby

THISBY. This is old Ninny's tomb. Where is my love?

LION. (*Roaring*) Oh—.   *Thisby runs off*

DEMETRIUS. Well roared, Lion.

THESEUS. Well run, Thisby.

HIPPOLYTA. Well shone, Moon. Truly, the moon shines with
a good grace.

The Lion tears Thisby's mantle, and exit

THESEUS. Well moused, Lion.

DEMETRIUS. And then came Pyramus.

LYSANDER. And so the lion vanished.

Re-enter Pyramus

PYRAMUS. Sweet moon, I thank thee for thy sunny beams;
　　I thank thee, moon, for shining now so bright,
For, by thy gracious, golden, glittering streams,
　　I trust to taste of truest Thisby's sight.
　　　　　　　But stay, O spite!
　　　　　　　But mark, poor knight,
　　　　　What dreadful dole is here!
　　　　　Eyes, do you see?
　　　　　How can it be?
　　　　O dainty duck! O dear!
　　　　　Thy Mantle good,
　　　　　What! stain'd with blood!
　　　　Approach, ye Furies fell!
　　　　　　O Fates, come, come,
　　　　　　Cut thread and thrum;
　　　　Quail, crush, conclude, and quell!

THESEUS. This passion, and the death of a dear friend, would
go near to make a man look sad.

HIPPOLYTA. Beshrew my heart, but I pity the man.

PYRAMUS. O! wherefore, Nature, didst thou lions frame?
　　Since lion vile hath here deflower'd my dear?
Which is—no, no—which was the fairest dame
　　That liv'd, that lov'd, that lik'd, that look'd with cheer.
　　　　　　Come tears, confound;
　　　　　　Out, sword, and wound
　　　　　The pap of Pyramus:
　　　　　　Ay, that left pap,
　　　　　　Where heart doth hop:
　　　　Thus die I, thus, thus, thus.　　*Stabs himself*
　　　　　　Now am I dead,
　　　　　　Now am I fled;
　　　　My soul is in the sky:
　　　　　　Tongue, lose thy light!
　　　　　　Moon, take thy flight!　　*Exit Moonshine*
　　　　Now die, die, die, die, die.　　　　*Dies*

DEMETRIUS. No die, but an ace, for him; for he is
but one.

LYSANDER. Less than an ace, man, for he is dead; he is nothing.

THESEUS. With the help of a surgeon, he might yet recover,
and prove an ass.

HIPPOLYTA. How chance Moonshine is gone before Thisby
comes back and finds her lover?

THESEUS. She will find him by starlight. Here she comes;
and her passion ends the play.

Re-enter Thisby

HIPPOLYTA. Methinks she should not use a long one for such
a Pyramus: I hope she will be brief.

DEMETRIUS. A mote will turn the balance, which Pyramus,
which Thisby, is the better: he for a man, God warrant
us; she for a woman, God bless us.

LYSANDER. She hath spied him already with those sweet eyes.

DEMETRIUS. And thus she moans, videlicet:—

THISBY.   Asleep, my love?
                What, dead, my dove?
            O Pyramus, arise!
                Speak, speak! Quite dumb?
                Dead, dead! A tomb
            Must cover thy sweet eyes.
                These lily lips,
                This cherry nose,
            These yellow cowslip cheeks,
                Are gone, are gone:
                Lovers, make moan!
            His eyes were green as leeks.
                O, Sisters Three,
                Come, come to me,
            With hands as pale as milk;
                Lay them in gore,
                Since you have shore
            With shears his thread of silk.
                Tongue, not a word:
                Come, trusty sword:
            Come, blade, my breast imbrue: *Stabs herself*
                And farewell, friends;
                Thus Thisby ends:
            Adieu, adieu, adieu.   *Dies*

THESEUS. Moonshine and Lion are left to bury the dead.

DEMETRIUS. Ay, and Wall too.

BOTTOM. No, I assure you; the wall is down that parted their fathers. Will it please you to see the epilogue, or to hear a Bergomask dance between two of our company?

THESEUS. No epilogue, I pray you; for your play needs no excuse. Never excuse; for when the players are all dead, there need none to be blamed. Marry, if he that writ it had played Pyramus, and hanged himself in Thisby's garter, it would have been a fine tragedy: and so it is, truly, and very notably discharged. But come, your Bergomask: let your epilogue alone.   *A dance*

The iron tongue of midnight hath told twelve;
Lovers, to bed; 'tis almost fairy time.
I fear we shall out-sleep the coming morn,
As much as we this night have overwatch'd,
This palpable-gross play hath well beguil'd
The heavy gait of night. Sweet friends, to bed.
A fortnight hold we this solemnity,
In nightly revels, and new jollity.   *Exeunt*

SCENE TWO

Enter Puck

PUCK.   Now the hungry lion roars,
            And the wolf behowls the moon;
        Whilst the heavy ploughman snores,
            All with weary task fordone.
        Now the wasted brands do glow,
            Whilst the screech-owl, screeching loud,
        Puts the wretch that lies in woe
            In remembrance of a shroud.
        Now it is the time of night
            That the graves, all gaping wide,
        Every one lets forth his sprite,
            In the church-way paths to glide:
        And we fairies, that do run
            By the triple Hecate's team,
        From the presence of the sun,
            Following darkness like a dream,
        Now are frolic; not a mouse
        Shall disturb this hallow'd house:
        I am sent with broom before,
        To sweep the dust behind the door.

Enter Oberon and Titania, with their Train

OBERON.   Through the house give glimmering light
            By the dead and drowsy fire;
        Every elf and fairy sprite
            Hop as light as bird from brier
        And this ditty after me
        Sing and dance it trippingly.

TITANIA.   First, rehearse your song by rote,
        To each word a warbling note:
        Hand in hand, with fairy grace,
        Will we sing, and bless this place.

                                    Song and dance

OBERON.   Now, until the break of day,
        Through this house each fairy stray.
        To the best bride-bed will we,
        Which by us shall blessed be;
        And the issue there create

Ever shall be fortunate.
So shall all the couples three
Ever true in loving be;
And the blots of Nature's hand
Shall not in their issue stand:
Never mole, hare-lip, nor scar,
Nor mark prodigious, such as are
Despised in nativity,
Shall upon their children be.
With this field-dew consecrate,
Every fairy take his gait,
And each several chamber bless,
Through this palace, with sweet peace;
Ever shall in safety rest,
And the owner of it blest.
  Trip away;
  Make no stay;
Meet me all by break of day.
    Exeunt Oberon, Titania, and Train

PUCK. If we shadows have offended,
Think but this, and all is mended,
That you have but slumber'd here
While these visions did appear.
And this weak and idle theme,
No more yielding but a dream,
Gentles, do not reprehend:
If you pardon, we will mend.
And, as I 'm an honest Puck,
If we have unearned luck
Now to 'scape the serpent's tongue,
We will make amends ere long;
Else the Puck a liar call:
So, good-night unto you all.
Give me your hands, if we be friends,
And Robin shall restore amends.   *Exit*

The Best of the World's Best Books
COMPLETE LIST OF TITLES IN
THE MODERN LIBRARY

76 ADAMS, HENRY: *The Education of Henry Adams*
310 AESCHYLUS: *The Complete Greek Tragedies,* Vol. I
311 AESCHYLUS: *The Complete Greek Tragedies,* Vol. II
101 AIKEN, CONRAD (Editor): *A Comprehensive Anthology of American Poetry*
127 AIKEN, CONRAD (Editor): *20th-Century American Poetry*
145 ALEICHEM, SHOLOM: *Selected Stories*
104 ANDERSON, SHERWOOD: *Winesburg, Ohio*
259 AQUINAS, ST. THOMAS: *Introduction to St. Thomas Aquinas*
248 ARISTOTLE: *Introduction to Aristotle*
228 ARISTOTLE: *Politics*
246 ARISTOTLE: *Rhetoric and Poetics*
160 AUDEN, W. H.: *Selected Poetry*
263 AUGUSTINE, ST.: *Confessions*
264 AUSTEN, JANE: *Pride and Prejudice* and *Sense and Sensibility*
256 BACON, FRANCIS: *Selected Writings*
299 BALZAC: *Cousin Bette*
193 BALZAC: *Droll Stories*
245 BALZAC: *Père Goriot* and *Eugénie Grandet*
116 BEERBOHM, MAX: *Zuleika Dobson*
22 BELLAMY, EDWARD: *Looking Backward*
184 BENNETT, ARNOLD: *The Old Wives' Tale*
231 BERGSON, HENRI: *Creative Evolution*
285 BLAKE, WILLIAM: *Selected Poetry and Prose*
71 BOCCACCIO: *The Decameron*
282 BOSWELL, JAMES: *The Life of Samuel Johnson*
64 BRONTË, CHARLOTTE: *Jane Eyre*
106 BRONTË, EMILY: *Wuthering Heights*
198 BROWNING, ROBERT: *Selected Poetry*
15 BUCK, PEARL: *The Good Earth*
32 BURCKHARDT, JACOB: *The Civilization of the Renaissance in Italy*
241 BURK, JOHN N.: *The Life and Works of Beethoven*
289 BURKE, EDMUND: *Selected Writings*
136 BUTLER, SAMUEL: *Erewhon* and *Erewhon Revisited*
13 BUTLER, SAMUEL: *The Way of All Flesh*
195 BYRON, LORD: *Selected Poetry*
24 BYRON, LORD: *Don Juan*
295 CAESAR, JULIUS: *The Gallic War and Other Writings*
51 CALDWELL, ERSKINE: *God's Little Acre*
249 CALDWELL, ERSKINE: *Tobacco Road*
109 CAMUS, ALBERT: *The Plague*
79 CARROLL, LEWIS: *Alice in Wonderland, etc.*
165 CASANOVA, JACQUES: *Memoirs of Casanova*
150 CELLINI, BENVENUTO: *Autobiography of Cellini*
174 CERVANTES: *Don Quixote*
161 CHAUCER: *The Canterbury Tales*
171 CHEKHOV, ANTON: *Best Plays*
50 CHEKHOV, ANTON: *Short Stories*
272 CICERO: *Basic Works*
279 COLERIDGE: *Selected Poetry and Prose*
251 COLETTE: *Six Novels*

235 COMMAGER, HENRY STEELE & NEVINS, ALLAN: *A Short History of the United States*
306 CONFUCIUS: *The Wisdom of Confucius*
186 CONRAD, JOSEPH: *Lord Jim*
275 CONRAD, JOSEPH: *Nostromo*
34 CONRAD, JOSEPH: *Victory*
105 COOPER, JAMES FENIMORE: *The Pathfinder*
194 CORNEILLE & RACINE: *Six Plays by Corneille and Racine*
130 CRANE, STEPHEN: *The Red Badge of Courage*
214 CUMMINGS, E. E.: *The Enormous Room*
236 DANA, RICHARD HENRY: *Two Years Before the Mast*
208 DANTE: *The Divine Comedy*
122 DEFOE, DANIEL: *Moll Flanders*
92 DEFOE, DANIEL: *Robinson Crusoe* and *A Journal of the Plague Year*
43 DESCARTES, RENÉ: *Philosophical Writings*
173 DEWEY, JOHN: *Human Nature and Conduct*
110 DICKENS, CHARLES: *David Copperfield*
204 DICKENS, CHARLES: *Pickwick Papers*
308 DICKENS, CHARLES: *Our Mutual Friend*
189 DICKENS, CHARLES: *A Tale of Two Cities*
25 DICKINSON, EMILY: *Selected Poems*
23 DINESEN, ISAK: *Out of Africa*
54 DINESEN, ISAK: *Seven Gothic Tales*
12 DONNE, JOHN: *Complete Poetry and Selected Prose*
205 DOS PASSOS, JOHN: *Three Soldiers*
293 DOSTOYEVSKY, FYODOR: *Best Short Stories*
151 DOSTOYEVSKY, FYODOR: *The Brothers Karamazov*
199 DOSTOYEVSKY, FYODOR: *Crime and Punishment*
55 DOSTOYEVSKY, FYODOR: *The Possessed*
5 DOUGLAS, NORMAN: *South Wind*
206 DOYLE, SIR ARTHUR CONAN: *The Adventures and Memoirs of Sherlock Holmes*
8 DREISER, THEODORE: *Sister Carrie*
69 DUMAS, ALEXANDRE: *Camille*
143 DUMAS, ALEXANDRE: *The Three Musketeers*
227 DU MAURIER, DAPHNE: *Rebecca*
192 EMERSON, RALPH WALDO: *The Journals*
91 EMERSON, RALPH WALDO: *Essays and Other Writings*
331 ERASMUS, DESIDERIUS: *The Praise of Folly*
314 EURIPIDES: *The Complete Greek Tragedies*, Vol. V
271 FAULKNER, WILLIAM: *Absalom, Absalom!*
175 FAULKNER, WILLIAM: *Go Down, Moses*
88 FAULKNER, WILLIAM: *Light in August*
61 FAULKNER, WILLIAM: *Sanctuary*
187 FAULKNER, WILLIAM: *The Sound and the Fury* and *As I Lay Dying*
324 FAULKNER, WILLIAM: *Selected Short Stories*
117 FIELDING, HENRY: *Joseph Andrews*
185 FIELDING, HENRY: *Tom Jones*
28 FLAUBERT, GUSTAVE: *Madame Bovary*
102 FORESTER, C. S.: *The African Queen*
210 FRANCE, ANATOLE: *Penguin Island*
298 FRANK, ANNE: *Diary of a Young Girl*
39 FRANKLIN, BENJAMIN: *Autobiograph*, etc.
96 FREUD, SIGMUND: *The Interpretation of Dreams*
242 FROST, ROBERT: *Poems of Robert Frost*
36 GEORGE, HENRY: *Progress and Poverty*
327 GIDE, ANDRÉ: *The Counterfeiters*
177 GOETHE: *Faust*

40 GOGOL, NIKOLAI: *Dead Souls*   [*Writings*
291 GOLDSMITH, OLIVER: *The Vicar of Wakefield and Other*
20 GRAVES, ROBERT: *I, Claudius*
286 GUNTHER, JOHN: *Death Be Not Proud*
265 HACKETT, FRANCIS: *The Personal History of Henry the Eighth*
163 HAGGARD, H. RIDER: *She and King Solomon's Mines*
320 HAMILTON, EDITH: *The Greek Way*
135 HARDY, THOMAS: *Jude the Obscure*
17 HARDY, THOMAS: *The Mayor of Casterbridge*
121 HARDY, THOMAS: *The Return of the Native*
72 HARDY, THOMAS: *Tess of the D'Urbervilles*
233 HART & KAUFMAN: *Six Plays*
329 HART, MOSS: *Act One*
250 HARTE, BRET: *Best Stories*
93 HAWTHORNE, NATHANIEL: *The Scarlet Letter*
239 HEGEL: *The Philosophy of Hegel*
223 HELLMAN, LILLIAN: *Six Plays*
26 HENRY, O.: *Best Short Stories*
255 HERODOTUS: *The Persian Wars*
328 HERSEY, JOHN: *Hiroshima*
166 HOMER: *The Iliad*
167 HOMER: *The Odyssey*
141 HORACE: *Complete Works*
302 HOWARD, JOHN TASKER: *World's Great Operas*
277 HOWELLS, WILLIAM DEAN: *The Rise of Silas Lapham*
89 HUDSON, W. H.: *Green Mansions*
35 HUGO, VICTOR: *The Hunchback of Notre Dame*
209 HUXLEY, ALDOUS: *Antic Hay*
48 HUXLEY, ALDOUS: *Brave New World*
180 HUXLEY, ALDOUS: *Point Counter Point*
305 IBSEN, HENRIK: *Six Plays*
307 IBSEN, HENRIK: *The Wild Duck and Other Plays*
240 IRVING, WASHINGTON: *Selected Writings*
16 JAMES, HENRY: *The Bostonians*
107 JAMES, HENRY: *The Portrait of a Lady*
169 JAMES, HENRY: *The Turn of the Screw*
269 JAMES, HENRY: *Washington Square*
244 JAMES, HENRY: *The Wings of the Dove*
114 JAMES, WILLIAM: *The Philosophy of William James*
70 JAMES, WILLIAM: *The Varieties of Religious Experience*
234 JEFFERSON, THOMAS: *The Life and Selected Writings*
124 JOYCE, JAMES: *Dubliners*
300 JUNG, C. G.: *Basic Writings*
318 KAFKA, FRANZ: *The Trial*
283 KAFKA, FRANZ: *Selected Stories*
297 KANT: *Critique of Pure Reason*
266 KANT: *The Philosophy of Kant*
233 KAUFMAN & HART: *Six Plays*
273 KEATS: *Complete Poetry and Selected Prose*
303 KIERKEGAARD, SØREN: *A Kierkegaard Anthology*
99 KIPLING, RUDYARD: *Kim*
74 KOESTLER, ARTHUR: *Darkness at Noon*
262 LAOTSE: *The Wisdom of Laotse*
148 LAWRENCE, D. H.: *Lady Chatterley's Lover*
128 LAWRENCE, D. H.: *The Rainbow*
333 LAWRENCE, D. H.: *Sons and Lovers*
68 LAWRENCE, D. H.: *Women in Love*
252 LEWIS, SINCLAIR: *Dodsworth*
221 LEWIS, SINCLAIR: *Cass Timberlane*

325   LIVY: *A History of Rome*
56   LONGFELLOW, HENRY W.: *Poems*
77   LOUŸS, PIERRE: *Aphrodite*
95   LUDWIG, EMIL: *Napoleon*
65   MACHIAVELLI: *The Prince* and *The Discourses*
321   MAILER, NORMAN: *The Naked and the Dead*
33   MALRAUX, ANDRÉ: *Man's Fate*
309   MALTHUS, THOMAS ROBERT: *On Population*
182   MARQUAND, JOHN P.: *The Late George Apley*
202   MARX, KARL: *Capital and Other Writings*
14   MAUGHAM, W. SOMERSET: *Best Short Stories*
270   MAUGHAM, W. SOMERSET: *Cakes and Ale*
27   MAUGHAM, W. SOMERSET: *The Moon and Sixpence*
176   MAUGHAM, W. SOMERSET: *Of Human Bondage*
98   MAUPASSANT, GUY DE: *Best Short Stories*
46   MAUROIS, ANDRÉ: *Disraeli*
119   MELVILLE, HERMAN: *Moby Dick*
253   MEREDITH, GEORGE: *The Egoist*
134   MEREDITH, GEORGE: *The Ordeal of Richard Feverel*
138   MEREJKOWSKI, DMITRI: *The Romance of Leonardo da Vinci*
296   MICHENER, JAMES A.: *Selected Writings*
322   MILL, JOHN STUART: *Selections*
132   MILTON, JOHN: *Complete Poetry and Selected Prose*
78   MOLIERE: *Eight Plays*
218   MONTAIGNE: *Selected Essays*
191   NASH, OGDEN: *Selected Verse*   [tory of the United States
235   NEVINS, ALLAN & COMMAGER, HENRY STEELE: *A Short His-*
113   NEWMAN, CARDINAL JOHN H.: *Apologia Pro Vita Sua*
9   NIETZSCHE, FRIEDRICH: *Thus Spake Zarathustra*
81   NOSTRADAMUS: *Oracles*
67   ODETS, CLIFFORD: *Six Plays*
42   O'HARA, JOHN: *Appointment in Samarra*
211   O'HARA, JOHN: *Selected Short Stories*
323   O'HARA, JOHN: *Butterfield 8*
146   O'NEILL, EUGENE: *The Emperor Jones, Anna Christie* and *The Hairy Ape*   [the Sea
111   O'NEILL, EUGENE: *The Long Voyage Home: Seven Plays of*
232   PALGRAVE, FRANCIS (Editor): *The Golden Treasury*
123   PARKER, DOROTHY: *Collected Short Stories*
237   PARKER, DOROTHY: *Collected Poetry*
267   PARKMAN, FRANCIS: *The Oregon Trail*
164   PASCAL, BLAISE: *Penseés and The Provincial Letters*
86   PATER, WALTER: *The Renaissance*
103   PEPYS, SAMUEL: *Passages from the Diary*
247   PERELMAN, S. J.: *The Best of S. J. Perelman*
153   PLATO: *The Republic*
181   PLATO: *The Works of Plato*
82   POE, EDGAR ALLAN: *Selected Poetry and Prose*
196   POLO, MARCO: *The Travels of Marco Polo*
257   POPE, ALEXANDER: *Selected Works*
284   PORTER, KATHERINE ANNE: *Flowering Judas*
45   PORTER, KATHERINE ANNE: *Pale Horse, Pale Rider*
120   PROUST, MARCEL: *The Captive*
220   PROUST, MARCEL: *Cities of the Plain*
213   PROUST, MARCEL: *The Guermantes Way*
278   PROUST, MARCEL: *The Past Recaptured*
59   PROUST, MARCEL: *Swann's Way*
260   PROUST, MARCEL: *The Sweet Cheat Gone*
172   PROUST, MARCEL: *Within a Budding Grove*

194 RACINE & CORNEILLE: *Six Plays by Corneille and Racine*
62 READE, CHARLES: *The Cloister and the Hearth*
215 REED, JOHN: *Ten Days That Shook the World*
140 RENAN, ERNEST: *The Life of Jesus*
10 RICHARDSON, SAMUEL: *Clarissa*
200 RODGERS & HAMMERSTEIN: *Six Plays*
154 ROSTAND, EDMOND: *Cyrano de Bergerac*
243 ROUSSEAU, JEAN JACQUES: *The Confessions*
53 RUNYON, DAMON: *Famous Stories*
137 RUSSELL, BERTRAND: *Selected Papers of Bertrand Russell*
280 SAKI: *Short Stories*
301 SALINGER, J. D.: *Nine Stories*
90 SALINGER, J. D.: *The Catcher in the Rye*
292 SANTAYANA, GEORGE: *The Sense of Beauty*
52 SCHOPENHAUER: *The Philosophy of Schopenhauer*
281 SCHULBERG, BUDD: *What Makes Sammy Run?*
2,3 SHAKESPEARE, WILLIAM: *Tragedies*—complete, 2 vols.
4,5 SHAKESPEARE, WILLIAM: *Comedies*—complete, 2 vols.
6 SHAKESPEARE, WILLIAM: *Histories* } complete, 2 vols.
7 SHAKESPEARE, WILLIAM: *Histories, Poems* } complete, 2 vols.
19 SHAW, BERNARD: *Four Plays*   [*and the Lion*
294 SHAW, BERNARD: *Saint Joan, Major Barbara,* and *Androcles*
112 SHAW, IRWIN: *The Young Lions*
319 SHAW, IRWIN: *Selected Short Stories*
274 SHELLEY: *Selected Poetry and Prose*
159 SMOLLETT, TOBIAS: *Humphry Clinker*
312 SOPHOCLES I: *Complete Greek Tragedies,* Vol. III
313 SOPHOCLES II: *Complete Greek Tragedies,* Vol. IV
60 SPINOZA: *The Philosophy of Spinoza*
332 STEIN, GERTRUDE: *Selected Writings*
115 STEINBECK, JOHN: *In Dubious Battle*
29 STEINBECK, JOHN: *Of Mice and Men*
216 STEINBECK, JOHN: *Tortilla Flat*
157 STENDHAL: *The Red and the Black*
147 STERNE, LAURENCE: *Tristram Shandy*
254 STEWART, GEORGE R.: *Storm*
31 STOKER, BRAM: *Dracula*
11 STONE, IRVING: *Lust for Life*
261 STOWE, HARRIET BEECHER: *Uncle Tom's Cabin*
212 STRACHEY, LYTTON: *Eminent Victorians*
188 SUETONIUS: *Lives of the Twelve Caesars*
100 SWIFT, JONATHAN: *Gulliver's Travels and Other Writings*
49 SYMONDS, JOHN A.: *The Life of Michelangelo*
222 TACITUS: *Complete Works*
230 TENNYSON: *Selected Poetry*
80 THACKERAY, WILLIAM: *Henry Esmond*
131 THACKERAY, WILLIAM: *Vanity Fair*
38 THOMPSON, FRANCIS: *Complete Poems*
155 THOREAU, HENRY DAVID: *Walden and Other Writings*
58 THUCYDIDES: *Complete Writings*
85 THURBER, JAMES: *The Thurber Carnival*
37 TOLSTOY, LEO: *Anna Karenina*
41 TROLLOPE, ANTHONY: *Barchester Towers* and *The Warden*
21 TURGENEV, IVAN: *Fathers and Sons*
162 TWAIN, MARK: *A Connecticut Yankee in King Arthur's Court*
190 VASARI, GIORGIO: *Lives of the Most Eminent Painters, Sculptors and Architects*
63 VEBLEN, THORSTEIN: *The Theory of the Leisure Class*
156 VINCI, LEONARDO DA: *The Notebooks*
75 VIRGIL: *The Aeneid, Eclogues* and *Georgics*

47   VOLTAIRE: *Candide and Other Writings*
178 WALPOLE, HUGH: *Fortitude*
170 WARREN, ROBERT PENN: *All The King's Men*
219 WEBB, MARY: *Precious Bane*
225 WEIDMAN, JEROME: *I Can Get It for You Wholesale*
197 WELLS, H. G.: *Tono Bungay*
290 WELTY, EUDORA: *Selected Stories*
299 WHARTON, EDITH: *The Age of Innocence*
97   WHITMAN, WALT: *Leaves of Grass*
125 WILDE, OSCAR: *Dorian Gray* and *De Profundis*
83   WILDE, OSCAR: *The Plays of Oscar Wilde*
84   WILDE, OSCAR: *Poems* and *Fairy Tales*
126 WODEHOUSE, P. J.: *Selected Stories*
268 WORDSWORTH: *Selected Poetry*
44   YEATS, W. B. (Editor): *Irish Fairy and Folk Tales*
179 YOUNG, G. F.: *The Medici*
207 ZIMMERN, ALFRED: *The Greek Commonwealth*
142 ZOLA, ÉMILE: *Nana*

MISCELLANEOUS

288 *An Anthology of Irish Literature*
330 *Anthology of Medieval Lyrics*
326 *The Apocrypha*
201 *The Arabian Nights' Entertainments*
87   *Best American Humorous Short Stories*
18   *Best Russian Short Stories*
129 *Best Spanish Stories*
     Complete Greek Tragedies
310 Volume I (Aeschylus I)
311 Volume II (Aeschylus II)
312 Volume III (Sophocles I)
313 Volume IV (Sophocles II)
314 Volume V (Euripedes I)
101 *A Comprehensive Anthology of American Poetry*
226 *The Consolation of Philosophy*
94   *Eight Famous Elizabethan Plays*
224 *Eighteenth-Century Plays*
73   *Famous Ghost Stories*
139 *The Federalist*
30   *Five Great Modern Irish Plays*
144 *Fourteen Great Detective Stories*
108 *Great German Short Novels and Stories*
168 *Great Modern Short Stories*
238 *Great Tales of the American West*
203 *The Greek Poets*
118 *Stories of Modern Italy*
217 *The Latin Poets*
149 *The Making of Man: An Outline of Anthropology*
183 *Making of Society*
133 *Medieval Romances*
1   *The Modern Library Dictionary*
258 *New Voices in the American Theatre*
152 *Outline of Abnormal Psychology*
66   *Outline of Psychoanalysis*
287 *Restoration Plays*
158 *Seven Famous Greek Plays*
57   *The Short Bible*
276 *Six Modern American Plays*
38   *Six American Plays for Today*
127 *Twentieth-Century American Poetry*

MODERN LIBRARY GIANTS

*A series of sturdily bound and handsomely printed,
full-sized library editions of books formerly available
only in expensive sets. These volumes contain from
600 to 1,400 pages each.*

THE MODERN LIBRARY GIANTS REPRESENT A
SELECTION OF THE WORLD'S GREATEST BOOKS

G76 ANDERSEN & GRIMM: *Tales*
G74 AUGUSTINE, ST.: *The City of God*
G58 AUSTEN, JANE: *Complete Novels*
G70 BLAKE, WILLIAM & DONNE, JOHN: *Complete Poetry*
G2 BOSWELL, JAMES: *Life of Samuel Johnson*
G17 BROWNING, ROBERT: *Poems and Plays*
G14 BULFINCH: *Mythology* (Illustrated)
G35 BURY, J. B.: *A History of Greece*
G13 CARLYLE, THOMAS: *The French Revolution*
G28 CARROLL, LEWIS: *Complete Works*
G15 CERVANTES: *Don Quixote* (Illustrated)
G33 COLLINS, WILKIE: *The Moonstone* and *The Woman in White*
G27 DARWIN, CHARLES: *Origin of Species* and *The Descent of Man*
G43 DEWEY, JOHN: *Intelligence in the Modern World: John Dewey's Philosophy*
G70 DONNE, JOHN & BLAKE, WILLIAM: *Complete Poetry*
G36 DOSTOYEVSKY, FYODOR: *The Brothers Karamazov*
G60 DOSTOYEVSKY, FYODOR: *The Idiot*
G51 ELIOT, GEORGE: *Best-Known Novels*
G41 FARRELL, JAMES T.: *Studs Lonigan*
G82 FAULKNER, WILLIAM: *The Faulkner Reader*
G39 FREUD, SIGMUND: *The Basic Writings*
G6
G7 } GIBBON, EDWARD: *The Decline and Fall of the Roman Empire*
G8   (Complete in three volumes)
G25 GILBERT & SULLIVAN: *Complete Plays*
G76 GRIMM & ANDERSEN: *Tales*
G37 HAWTHORNE, NATHANIEL: *Complete Novels and Selected Tales*
G78 HOLMES, OLIVER WENDELL: *The Mind and Faith of Justice Holmes*
G19 HOMER: *Complete Works*
G3 HUGO, VICTOR: *Les Miserables*
G18 IBSEN, HENRIK: *Eleven Plays*
G11 JAMES, HENRY: *Short Stories*
G52 JOYCE, JAMES: *Ulysses*
G24 LAMB, CHARLES: *The Complete Works and Letters*
G4 KEATS & SHELLEY: *Complete Poems*
G20 LINCOLN, ABRAHAM: *The Life and Writings of Abraham Lincoln*
G84 MANN, THOMAS: *Stories of Three Decades*
G26 MARX, KARL: *Capital*

G57   MELVILLE, HERMAN: *Selected Writings*
G38   MURASAKA, LADY: *The Tale of Genji*
G30   MYERS, GUSTAVUS: *History of the Great American Fortunes*
G34   NIETZSCHE, FRIEDRICH: *The Philosophy of Nietzsche*
G55   O'NEILL, EUGENE: *Nine Plays*
G68   PAINE, TOM: *Selected Work*
G86   PASTERNAK, BORIS: *Doctor Zhivago*
G5   PLUTARCH: *Lives* (The Dryden Translation)
G40   POE, EDGAR ALLAN: *Complete Tales and Poems*
G29   PRESCOTT, WILLIAM H.: *The Conquest of Mexico* and *The
          Conquest of Peru*
G62   PUSHKIN: *Poems, Prose and Plays*
G65   RABELAIS: *Complete Works*
G12   SCOTT, SIR WALTER: *The Most Popular Novels* (Quentin
          Durward, Ivanhoe & Kenilworth)
G4   SHELLEY & KEATS: *Complete Poems*
G32   SMITH, ADAM: *The Wealth of Nations*
G61   SPAETH, SIGMUND: *A Guide to Great Orchestral Music*
G75   STEVENSON, ROBERT LOUIS: *Selected Writings*
G53   SUE, EUGENE: *The Wandering Jew*
G42   TENNYSON: *The Poems and Plays*
G23   TOLSTOY, LEO: *Anna Karenina*
G1   TOLSTOY, LEO: *War and Peace*
G49   TWAIN, MARK: *Tom Sawyer* and *Huckleberry Finn*
G50   WHITMAN, WALT: *Leaves of Grass*
G83   WILSON, EDMUND: *The Shock of Recognition*

MISCELLANEOUS

G77   *An Anthology of Famous American Stories*
G54   *An Anthology of Famous British Stories*
G67   *Anthology of Famous English and American Poetry*
G81   *An Encyclopedia of Modern American Humor*
G47   *The English Philosophers from Bacon to Mill*
G16   *The European Philosophers from Descartes to Nietzsche*
G31   *Famous Science-Fiction Stories: Adventures in Time and
          Space*
G85   *Great Ages and Ideas of the Jewish People*
G72   *Great Tales of Terror and the Supernatural*
G9   *Great Voices of the Reformation*
G48   *The Metropolitan Opera Guide*
G46   *A New Anthology of Modern Poetry*
G69   *One Hundred and One Years' Entertainment*
G21   *Sixteen Famous American Plays*
G63   *Sixteen Famous British Plays*
G71   *Sixteen Famous European Plays*
G45   *Stoic and Epicurean Philosophers*
G22   *Thirty Famous One-Act Plays*
G66   *Three Famous Murder Novels*
          Before the Fact, Francis Iles
          Trent's Last Case, E. C. Bentley
          The House of the Arrow, A. E. W. Mason
G10   *Twelve Famous Plays of the Restoration and Eighteenth
          Century* (1660–1820)
          (Congreve, Wycherley, Gay, Goldsmith, Sheridan, etc.)
G56   *The Wisdom of Catholicism*
G59   *The Wisdom of China and India*
G79   *The Wisdom of Israel*